Test 1 = 60/60

Test 2 = 67 %

Test 3 = 81 %

Test 4 = $\frac{98}{50}$

Math Exam
Thurs 8 30

Test 1 - $\frac{72}{100}$

Test 2 = 88 %

$$4 \overline{\smash{)}300}$$
75
$\frac{38}{20}$

52
100
67
$\frac{81}{300}$

NELDA W. ROUECHE

Business Mathematics

A COLLEGIATE APPROACH

THIRD EDITION

PRENTICE-HALL, INC., ENGLEWOOD CLIFFS, N.J. 07632

Library of Congress Cataloging in Publication Data

Roueche, Nelda W
   Business mathematics, a collegiate approach.

   Includes index.
   1. Business mathematics. I.   Title.
HF5691.R68 1978   513′.93   78-16746
ISBN 0-13-105007-9

Printed in the United States of America

10 9 8 7 6 5 4

PRENTICE-HALL INTERNATIONAL, INC., *London*
PRENTICE-HALL OF AUSTRALIA PTY. LIMITED *Sydney*
PRENTICE-HALL OF CANADA, LTD., *Toronto*
PRENTICE-HALL OF INDIA PRIVATE LIMITED, *New Delhi*
PRENTICE-HALL OF JAPAN, INC., *Tokyo*
PRENTICE-HALL OF SOUTHEAST ASIA PTE. LTD., *Singapore*
WHITEHALL BOOKS LIMITED, *Wellington, New Zealand*

CONTENTS ✓

iv

PREFACE

The previous editions of *Business Mathematics: A Collegiate Approach* have been consistently accepted across the nation. The success of the book confirms that it has accomplished its primary objective, which is to familiarize students with a wide range of business procedures that require the use of mathematics. The text sharpens the mathematical skills of students preparing to enter business employment as it simultaneously provides an introduction to accounting, finance, insurance, and other more advanced math-related business subjects. The scope of this course should provide a valuable experience for all students anticipating a career in business.

The third edition of *Business Mathematics* has retained the many student oriented features that won earlier acclaim. At the same time, the new edition has introduced several improvements that will make it even easier for the student to use. Along with these improvements, the material has been updated to include recent trends in business procedure and the most current business information and rates. Prior to publication, the book was thoroughly reviewed. It was praised by one of its reviewers as being " . . . extremely well-balanced, utilizing as many illustrative examples as might be needed to achieve total clarity."

The use of *Business Mathematics* has not been limited to one type of student or one type of course. While the book is most often used for a one-term course, it contains enough material to be the textbook for a longer course that goes into greater detail. The book has also been frequently used for courses that combine the study of business math and business machines.

The original manuscript was designed for use in community and junior college business programs, being intended to meet the special needs of students who lacked extensive math preparation. However, its approach has proved to be effective with all types of students. As a result, *Business Mathematics* has been accepted in the lower-level business programs of other colleges and universities. The book offers several advantages to the student:

- A business-oriented review of arithmetic, equations, and per cent is included. This essential review is comprehensive but is also brief enough so that the majority of class time can be devoted to topics of a distinct business nature.

- The discussion of each topic begins with an introduction that describes its terminology and its business applications. I have attempted to keep these explanations as brief as possible, without sacrificing content, and have made a special effort to make this material precise and easy to read.

- A large number of examples are given, including an example for every type of problem that the student might be assigned. Examples are explained in detail and all steps are included to ensure that the student understands the entire solution.

- The text contains over 1,000 problems. These appear at the end of each section and are arranged in order of increasing difficulty. The problems are paired so that one can be used in class, while a similar problem can be given as homework. Each section contains two *types* of problems: There are computation problems, designed for quick mastery of technique, as well as written problems, which ensure that the student completely understands the principle that has been discussed. My objective is to teach mathematical procedures used in business rather than to provide tedious exercises in arithmetic. Thus, all problems contain numbers that are as compatible as possible—they cancel each other and/or work out to relatively whole-numbered answers.

- Student learning objectives introduce each chapter and describe the specific skills to be developed. The instructor of an individualized class can use the objectives to identify course or grading requirements. In either an individualized or traditional setting, students can use the objectives as a guide for study.

- Elementary algebra (equation solving) is used where it is logical and natural to do so. Experience has shown that (1) students inevitably make many mistakes when they attempt to memorize several variations of a single formula, whereas (2) they can easily learn simple equation-solving techniques (as reviewed in Chapter 2). Since the same basic techniques apply in numerous topics, the student will be much more successful learning each formula only once and using equations to solve for the different variables.

- The text concentrates on retail topics because the majority of business math students will eventually seek employment in the retail field. The coverage of finance is less extensive but there is enough material for the student to become familiar with both investment and credit.

- All tables required to solve problems are conveniently grouped in Appendix C. Since the tables are at the back of the book, students can refer to them during an exam without having their text open to the main body of material.

Among the many new features of the third edition are the following highlights:

- Fresh assignment selections have been provided for instructors since more than one-half of the problems in this edition are new. All discussions and examples are extensively revised and updated. The text includes current insurance and interest rates, as well as the most recent rates and forms for social security and federal income tax withholding.

- The first text reference to a key term is made conspicuous by the use of **boldface**. Key terms are defined in the glossaries that appear at the end of every chapter.

- The learning objectives have become more valuable through the addition of cross references. After each objective there is a list of the section, examples, and problems that should be studied in order to accomplish that objective.

- In response to user requests, I have added new sections on the normal curve and standard deviation, the metric system, interest-adjusted net cost of life insurance, inventory evaluation (by weighted average, FIFO, and LIFO), proportion, and additional sales terms. I have also expanded the coverage of existing topics by including discussions of open accounts and CD's, medical payment and no-fault insurance, and markup and markdown diagrams.

An Instructor's Manual is available upon adoption and contains, for the instructor's convenience, solutions to all problems in the text. It also includes suggestions for organizing the course and teaching suggestions related to each chapter, as well as sample quizzes and a final examination.

Over the years, I have received brief notes or long letters from many users of the text. I am always delighted to receive suggestions, as your experiences provide an invaluable aid in pinpointing ways to communicate more effectively with the students. In preparing the third edition, I am especially indebted to the following people:

- Julian Bernard of Bronx Community College, Patricia H. Eyer of Northern Virginia Community College at Annandale, and Dennis P. Gallon and Edward L. Grieger III, both of Florida Junior College at Jacksonville, who graciously submitted many specific suggestions for the pending revision. Professors Bernard and Eyer later reviewed the revised manuscript and offered additional ideas for its refinement. Special thanks go to Professor Bernard, whose contributions during both phases are by far the most extensive in my experience as an author.

- Judy F. Frieling, who not only typed the entire manuscript revision and the Instructor's Manual but also assisted with the organization and proofreading of the materials.

- At Prentice-Hall, Judith L. Rothman, Editor of Quantitative Analysis for Business-Marketing and especially Ken Cashman who did all in his power to accommodate an author who "only wants everything to be perfect."

This third edition is dedicated to my children, Michelle and Jay, whose positive and enthusiastic attitudes toward life are a constant inspiration to their mother.

NELDA W. ROUECHE

Austin, Texas

TO THE STUDENT

This author has not forgotten what it is like to be a student. I clearly remember wishing that a book had more examples, or trying to determine what happened in the steps that were left out, or wondering what some vague explanation was supposed to mean. So when I began *Business Mathematics: A Collegiate Approach*, it was designed not for the instructor, but especially for you, the student.

The author is also aware that, unfortunately, many people cringe whenever the word "math" is mentioned. Please don't! You need not be a genius to learn business math. Successful completion of business math requires only two things—time and effort. If you are willing to supply these, you can be assured that your efforts will be rewarded. And you will find it is well worth the effort required, for business math is a very practical course. It will acquaint you with a large number of business procedures where math is required. Regardless of what business position you may later accept, almost any mathematics required by that job will have been introduced in business math. (The text will serve as a good on-the-job reference book after you graduate.)

Some math books are used only as a source of assignment problems. That is not the case with this text; it is intended to be read. Read it carefully and thoroughly. The explanations will familiarize you with the business applications of each topic and the special terminology associated with it. The examples include *every* type of problem which you will be required to solve; so study them carefully. If you are not sure whether you could work out a similar problem, take out a pencil and paper and try working the example itself (without looking at the calculation in the text). Make a practice of reading each section before it is discussed in class; this will enable you to better understand the instructor's discussion and examples. Certainly, never try to complete the problems until you have first read the lesson. If something seems unclear when you first read it, read it again.

Of course, you will want to keep a notebook for taking notes in class. Try to take very complete notes on both the instructor's lecture and examples. Also use the notebook to record your own helpful hints, such as a way you have discovered for recognizing a problem, a mistake you have made and need to be alert for, the best method for solving a certain type of problem, some important point you need to remember, and so on. Things which you understand clearly at one point have a way of becoming hazy later on unless you have made notes as a reminder.

When working out the assigned problems, use a dark *pencil* (everybody makes a few careless mistakes) and don't skip steps, unless you are quite adept at math. If a set of problems requires a formula, write it with each problem. Always start by listing the information which is given and indicating what must be found. Allow plenty of space for each problem; many mistakes are made because the problem becomes so crowded that the student cannot read his/her numbers or determine what the sequence of steps has been. Always complete the entire assignment, referring back to the examples when necessary. If you absolutely cannot solve a problem, ask for assistance from your instructor; (s)he is there to help you learn and will be happy to answer your questions.

Never hesitate to ask questions in class—especially not for fear of what other students may think. If you go on to the next section with a question still in mind, you may find yourself unable to understand the topic discussed there. (Besides, when one student has a question, others usually have the same question. But everyone can't wait for someone else to speak up!)

The first step in preparing for an hour quiz is to keep all the problems that you have worked out organized so that you can study them. Sometimes things you thought you knew may be hard to reproduce; so practice writing all the formulas that may be included on the quiz. Test yourself on the problems: Read the problems and briefly write down the steps or formulas that would be required, or simply set up the problem. Then check what you have written against a similar problem that you have worked previously. (It is seldom necessary to work a review problem completely; if you can set it up correctly, you can almost certainly solve it.) Review the learning objectives as well as the Glossary.

During a quiz, work as quickly as possible without being careless. When quizzes are returned to you, correct your errors and save the quiz papers as study material for the final exam.

As indicated above, this study plan will require substantial time and effort, but you will also learn much useful information in the process. Best wishes for success in business math, and good luck in the business world.

NELDA W. ROUECHE

PART

I

Review

CHAPTER 1

Review of Operations

CHAPTER 1 OBJECTIVES

Upon completion of Chapter 1, the student will be able to:

1. Define and use correctly the terminology associated with each topic.

2. Multiply efficiently using
   a. Numbers containing zeros (example: $307 \times 1,400$)
      (*Examples 1, 2; Problems 1, 2*);
   b. Decimal numbers with fractions (example: $15 \times 3.5\frac{1}{4}$) (*Example 3*);
   c. Numbers with exponents (example: 3^4) (*Example 4*).

3. Simplify fractions containing
   a. Decimal parts $\left(\text{example: } \dfrac{6}{1.5}\right)$;

   b. Fractional parts $\left(\text{example: } \dfrac{6}{1\frac{1}{2}}\right)$.

      (*Example 5; Problems 3, 4*)

4. Find negative differences (losses) (*Example 6; Problems 3, 4*).

5. Simplify expressions containing parentheses of the type $(1 - dt)$ **or** $S(1 + rt)$.
   (*Examples 7–9; Problems 5, 6*)

6. Round off numbers to a specified decimal place.
   (*Example 10; Problems 7, 8*)

7. Round a multiplication product to an accurate number of digits, based on
   the digits of the original numbers (*Example 11; Problems 9–12*).

The normal, day-to-day operations of most businesses require frequent computations with numbers. Many of these computations are done in modern business by machines. Some computations, however, are still performed manually. And even those processes whose final calculations will be done automatically must first be set up correctly, so that the proper numbers will be fed into the machines and the proper operation performed.

The following topics are presented in order to eliminate some of the weaknesses which many students often have in working with specific types of numbers. A more comprehensive review is included as Appendix A, "Arithmetic," for those students who need further practice.

Multiplication   Whenever a number is to be multiplied by some *number ending in zeros*, the zeros should be written to the right of the actual problem; the zeros are then brought down and affixed to the right of the product without actually entering into the **operation.** If either number contains a decimal, this also does not affect the problem until the operation has been completed.

Example One

(a) 125×40.

```
   125
 × 4|0
 ──────
 5,00|0
```

(b) $2.13 \times 1,500$.

```
   2.13
 × 15|00
 ──────
 1,065
 2 13
 ──────
 3,195.|00
```

(c) $13,000 \times 18$.

```
     18
 × 13,|000
 ──────
   54
   18
 ──────
 234,|000
```

When multiplying by a *number containing inner zeros*, students often write whole rows of zeros unnecessarily in order to assure themselves that the other digits will be correctly aligned. These useless zeros can be eliminated if one will remember the following rule: On each line of multiplication, the first digit written down goes directly underneath the digit that was used for multiplying.

Example Two   (a) $2,145 \times 307$.

	RIGHT			INEFFICIENT

$$
\begin{array}{r}
2,145 \\
\times \quad 307 \\
\hline
15\ 015 \\
643\ 5 \quad\ \ \\
\hline
658,515
\end{array}
$$

$$
\begin{array}{r}
2,145 \\
\times \quad 307 \\
\hline
15\ 015 \\
00\ 00 \\
643\ 5 \quad\ \ \\
\hline
658,515
\end{array}
$$

(b) 1005×7208.

$$
\begin{array}{r}
7,208 \\
\times 1,005 \\
\hline
36\ 040 \\
7\ 208 \quad\ \ \\
\hline
7,244,040
\end{array}
$$

When multiplying a **whole number** by a **mixed number** (a mixed number is a whole number plus a fraction), one should first multiply by the fraction and then multiply the other numbers in the usual manner. If a decimal is involved, the decimal point is marked off in the usual way—the fraction does not increase the number of decimal places.

Example Three   (a) $24 \times 15\frac{3}{4}$.

$$
\begin{array}{r}
24 \\
\times 15\frac{3}{4} \\
\hline
18 \\
120 \quad \\
24 \quad\ \ \\
\hline
378
\end{array}
$$
  $(\frac{3}{4} \times 24 = 18)$

(b) $35 \times 1.3\frac{3}{7}$.

$$
\begin{array}{r}
3\ 5 \\
\times 1.3\frac{3}{7} \\
\hline
1\ 5 \\
10\ 5 \quad \\
35 \quad\ \ \\
\hline
47.0
\end{array}
$$

There are several different ways to indicate that multiplication is required. The common symbols are the "times" sign ("$\times$") and the raised dot ("$\cdot$"). Many formulas contain letters (called **variables**) which are written together; this indicates that the numbers which these variables represent are to be multiplied. A number written beside a variable indicates multiplication of the number and variable. Numbers or letters within parentheses written together should also be multiplied. A number or variable written adjoining parentheses should be multiplied by the expression within the parentheses. Thus,

$$3 \cdot 5 = 3 \times 5$$

$$Prt = P \times r \times t$$

$$4k = 4 \times k$$

$$(2.5)(4)(6.8) = 2.5 \times 4 \times 6.8$$

$$7(12) = 7 \times 12$$

Some few problems require the use of exponents. An **exponent** is merely a number which, when written as a superscript to the right of another number, called the **base,** indicates how many times the base is to be written in repeated multiplication times itself.

Example Four

(a) $x^2 = x \cdot x$

(b) $5^3 = 5 \cdot 5 \cdot 5 = 125$

(c) $2^4 = 2 \cdot 2 \cdot 2 \cdot 2 = 16$

(d) $(1.02)^3 = (1.02)(1.02)(1.02)$
$$= 1.061208$$

Division   Recall that a fraction indicates division—the numerator of the fraction (above the line) is to be divided by the denominator (below the line). Thus, if the denominator contains a fraction, it must be inverted and multiplied by the numerator *of the entire fraction.* If the denominator contains a decimal, it must be moved to the end of the number and the decimal in the numerator moved a corresponding number of places.

Example Five

(a) $\dfrac{3}{\frac{3}{4}} = \dfrac{3}{1} \div \dfrac{3}{4} = \dfrac{3}{1} \times \dfrac{4}{3} = \dfrac{4}{1} = 4$

(b) $\dfrac{6}{1\frac{1}{2}} = \dfrac{6}{\frac{3}{2}} = \dfrac{6}{1} \div \dfrac{3}{2} = \dfrac{\overset{2}{6}}{1} \times \dfrac{2}{3} = \dfrac{4}{1} = 4$

(c) $\dfrac{4}{.5} = \dfrac{4.0}{.5} = \dfrac{40}{5} = 8$

(d) $\dfrac{5.2}{.13} = \dfrac{5.20}{.13} = \dfrac{520}{13} = 40$

(e) $\dfrac{2.31}{.3} = \dfrac{2.31}{.3} = \dfrac{23.1}{3} = 7.7$

Subtraction

Unfortunately, business expenses sometimes exceed the funds budgeted for them. In this case, the **deficit** is called a **negative difference.** (It is also common to say that the account is "in the red.") A negative difference is found by taking the numerical difference between the larger and smaller numbers. The result is indicated as being a deficit either by placing a minus sign before the number or by placing the result in parentheses (the method used on most financial statements).

Example Six

(a)
Bank balance	$598.00
Checks written	− 650.00
Deficit	−$ 52.00

(b)
Profit earned	$3,500.00
Salary owed	− 4,700.00
Negative difference	($1,200.00)

Parentheses

Several formulas used in finding simple interest and simple discount contain parentheses. The student should be familiar with the correct procedure to follow in working with parentheses: If a parentheses contains both multiplication and addition or multiplication and subtraction, the multiplication should be performed first and the addition or subtraction last. (This procedure simply follows the standard rule for order of operations: Multiplication and division should always be performed before addition and subtraction. Thus, $3 \times 4 - 8 = 12 - 8 = 4$; and $9 + 16 \div 8 = 9 + 2 = 11$.)

Example Seven

(a) $(1 + rt) = (1 + \frac{\overset{3}{\cancel{6}}}{100} \cdot \frac{1}{\cancel{2}})$ (where $r = \frac{6}{100}$ and $t = \frac{1}{2}$)

$\qquad = (1 + \frac{3}{100})$

$\qquad = (\frac{100}{100} + \frac{3}{100})$

$\qquad = (\frac{103}{100})$

(b) $(1 - dt) = (1 - \frac{\overset{2}{\cancel{8}}}{100} \cdot \frac{1}{\cancel{4}})$ (where $d = \frac{8}{100}$ and $t = \frac{1}{4}$)

$\qquad = (1 - \frac{2}{100})$

$\qquad = (\frac{100}{100} - \frac{2}{100})$

$\qquad = (\frac{98}{100})$

(c) $(1 + rt) = (1 + \frac{\overset{2}{\cancel{8}}}{100} \cdot \frac{7}{\underset{3}{\cancel{12}}})$ (where $r = \frac{8}{100}$ and $t = \frac{7}{12}$)

$\qquad = (1 + \frac{14}{300})$

$\qquad = (\frac{300}{300} + \frac{14}{300})$

$\qquad = (\frac{314}{300})$

If a parenthesis is preceded by a number, that number is to be multiplied times the whole expression within the parentheses. That is, the terms within the parentheses should be consolidated into a single number or fraction, if possible, *before* multiplying. Consider the formula $P(1 + rt)$ when $P = \$600$, $r = \frac{5}{100}$, and $t = \frac{1}{3}$:

Example Eight

RIGHT	*WRONG*
$P(1 + rt) = \$600(1 + \frac{5}{100} \cdot \frac{1}{3})$	$P(1 + rt) = \$600(1 + \frac{5}{100} \cdot \frac{1}{3})$
$\qquad = 600(1 + \frac{5}{300})$	$\qquad = \$600(1 + \frac{5}{300})$
$\qquad = 600(\frac{300}{300} + \frac{5}{300})$	$\qquad = \overset{2}{\cancel{600}}(1 + \frac{5}{\cancel{300}})$
$\qquad = \overset{2}{\cancel{600}}(\frac{305}{\cancel{300}})$	$\qquad = 2(6)$
$\qquad = \$610$	$\qquad = \$12$

If it is impossible to consolidate the terms within the parentheses into a single number or fraction, then the number in front of the parentheses must be multiplied times *each* separate term within the parentheses. (Separate terms may be identified by the fact that plus or minus signs always appear between them.)

Example Nine

(a) $\overset{\frown}{P(1+rt)} = P \cdot 1 + P \cdot rt = P + Prt$

(b) $\overset{\frown}{S(1-dt)} = S \cdot 1 - S \cdot dt = S - Sdt$

(c) $S(1-dt)$ with $S = \$400$ and $d = \frac{6}{100}$ becomes

$$S(1-dt) = \$\overset{\frown}{400(1} - \frac{6}{100}t)$$

$$= 400 \cdot 1 - \overset{4}{\cancel{400}} \cdot \frac{6}{\cancel{100}}t$$

$$= 400 - 24t$$

Rounding off Decimals

The general rule for rounding off decimals is as follows:

If the last decimal place that one wishes to include is followed by any digit from 0 through 4, the figure in question remains unchanged. If followed by any digit from 5 through 9, the digit in question is increased by one.

Example Ten

(a) Rounding off to tenths (to one decimal place):
14.3)274=14.3

(b) Rounding off to hundredths (to two decimal places):
5.37)812=5.38

(c) Rounding off to thousandths (to three decimal places):
0.032)569=0.033

(d) Rounding off 24.14759:
to tenths: 24.1
to hundredths: 24.15
to thousandths: 24.148

NOTE: A special case sometimes arises when the last digit that one wishes to use is followed by a single 5 (with no other succeeding digits). In this case, particularly when the numbers in question should total 100 per cent, one may use the following rule:

If the last digit to be included is an odd number, round it off to the next higher number; if the digit in question is even, leave it unchanged.

The following example illustrates this case:

(e) Round to the nearest per cent:

$$\begin{array}{r} 62.5\% = 62\% \\ +37.5\% = 38\% \\ \hline 100.0\% = 100\% \end{array}$$

**Accuracy of
Computation**

Business, engineering, manufacturing, and the like all demand careful accuracy in their calculations, processes, and products. Computational accuracy is dependent on the number of significant digits used. **Significant digits** are digits obtained by precise measurement rather than by rough approximation. For example, 4,283' has four significant digits; 4,300' has only two significant digits if it was measured only to the nearest hundred feet. Similarly, 8.75 has three significant digits; 9 has one significant digit. There are two significant digits in 9.0 if a measurement made to the nearest tenth falls between 8.95 and 9.05.

The concept of significant digits requires that the following rule be observed: The result obtained from a mathematical calculation can never be more accurate than the least accurate figure used in making the calculation. Specifically, additional accuracy (more significant digits) cannot be created artificially by the simple use of a mathematical operation (such as multiplication).

This rule requires an initial calculation to be rounded off in many instances. The answer must at least be rounded off so as to contain no more than the number of decimal places contained in the original figure which had the *least number of decimal places*. To be more exact, the answer should contain no more significant digits than the original number which had the *fewest significant digits*.

**Example
Eleven**

(a) Find the area of a room 17.27 feet in length and 13.6 feet in width.

$A = lw$

$ = 17.27 \times 13.6$

$ = 234.872$

$ = 234.9$ square feet   (since 13.6 had only one decimal place)

or

$ = 235$ square feet   (since 13.6 had three significant digits)

This rule is of particular importance in computing amounts invested at compound interest, since tables containing many decimal places are used. Students will want to minimize work by using no more of these decimal places than are necessary—but at the same time, obtain an answer that is correct to the nearest cent.

To do this, one should first estimate the answer to determine the number of digits it will contain (including the cent's place). This number plus one more (to ensure absolute accuracy) will determine the number of digits one needs to copy from the table.

It should be noted that any known exact amount (such as $350) is considered accurate for any number of decimal places desired.

(b) Suppose an interest problem requires that $200 be multiplied by the table value 1.48594740. We wish to use only enough digits from the table to ensure that our answer is correct to the nearest cent.

First, estimate the value of the tabular number: it is approximately 1.5. Therefore, the answer we obtain will be approximately $200 × 1.5 = $300.

The number $300.00 contains 5 digits; thus we must copy 5 + 1 = 6 digits from the table. (The sixth digit from the table will be rounded off using the previously discussed rules for rounding off decimals.) The number 1.48594740, rounded to six digits, equals 1.48595.

Thus, $200 × 1.48595 = $297.19000 = $297.19 is the solution correct to the nearest cent.

(c) Find $1,500 times 1.86102237 correct to the nearest cent, using no more digits than necessary.

1.86102237 approximately equals 2.
2 × $1,500 = $3,000, which contains 6 digits
(including the cent's digits).
6 + 1 = 7 digits are required from the table.
$1,500 × 1.861022 = $2,791.533000 = $2,791.53,
correct to cents.

(d) Find $800 × 0.50752126 correct to cents, using no more digits than necessary.

0.50752126 approximately equals .5.
$800 × .5 = $400, which has 5 digits (to the nearest cent).
5 + 1 = 6 digits are required from the table.
$800 × 0.507521 = $406.016800 = $406.02.

NOTE: The zero before the decimal in the number 0.50752126 does not qualify as a significant digit (that is, as a digit which should be counted), because the zero could have been omitted without changing the value of the number.

Another suggestion that minimizes work is to substitute fractional equivalents for per cents (such as $\frac{1}{3}$ for $33\frac{1}{3}\%$, or $\frac{3}{7}$ for $42\frac{6}{7}\%$) in computations. Such equivalents usually simplify calculations done manually and often provide more accurate results than the more tedious computations performed with rounded decimal equivalents. For this reason, even students using machines are often advised to use fractional equivalents (a two-step process). Thus, all students should familiarize themselves with the per cents having convenient fractional equivalents. A table of these equivalents appears on page 58, as part of a topic on the use of fractional equivalents to speed multiplication.

Problem Solving Students often read a problem, decide that they do not know how to solve it, and simply "give up" without writing anything at all. By attacking problems in an organized manner, however, you can succeed with many problems for which the solution process was not at all obvious on first reading:

1. Make a list of all information that was given. Name the term that each given amount represents and/or associate each with a letter that can be used in an equation or formula. (For instance, overhead = $3,000 or $r = 5\%$.)

2. Based on the question asked in the problem, indicate what needs to be found. (For example, markup = ?% of selling price; or $P = ?\$$.)

3. Ask yourself how this unknown quantity could logically be found. (A formula, such as $I = Prt$? An algebraic equation based on the question in the problem? Some process, such as using a table to determine annual percentage rate for monthly payments?)

4. After deciding on a logical method above, reexamine your list of given information. Do you already have everything required in order to use this method? If not, could your given information be used to compute the additional information required by this method?

5. Attempt some calculations using the method you selected. Examine your result to decide whether it really answers the question that was asked and whether that answer is reasonable. (If necessary, go back to step 3 and consider another method. For instance, the unknown quantity may be included in several different formulas and could perhaps be found using a different formula than was first tried.)

The foregoing approach may not be foolproof, of course, but it certainly increases your chances for success. You have no doubt heard the expression, "If all else fails, read the directions." In this case, the "directions" are the examples in the text, and the author assumes that they will be read before any problems are attempted!

CHAPTER 1 *Problems*

Find the product.

1. (a) 15×60 (b) 20×312 (c) 400×37
(d) $27 \times 1,200$ (e) $2,500 \times 114$ (f) $1,425 \times 504$
(g) 208×729 (h) $1,006 \times 24,304$ (i) $2,050 \times 354$
(j) $28 \times 2.3\frac{1}{4}$ (k) $1.75 \times 14\frac{2}{5}$ (l) $15\frac{3}{8} \times 0.24$
(m) $3.6 \times 14\frac{2}{9}$ (n) $2.7 \times 1.2\frac{1}{3}$ (o) 2^4
(p) 3^5 (q) 6^3 (r) 1.04^2

2. (a) 68×30 (b) 50×271 (c) 143×400
(d) $1,600 \times 72$ (e) $3,700 \times 194$ (f) $1,536 \times 402$
(g) 108×625 (h) $2,004 \times 18,308$ (i) $1,060 \times 524$
(j) $24 \times 3.4\frac{1}{2}$ (k) $3.6 \times 18\frac{4}{9}$ (l) $1.25 \times 5.1\frac{3}{5}$
(m) $4.8\frac{3}{8} \times 0.64$ (n) $3.5 \times 7.5\frac{2}{7}$ (o) 4^3
(p) 2^5 (q) 5^4 (r) 1.06^2

Divide or subtract, as indicated.

3. (a) $\dfrac{9}{\frac{3}{5}}$ (b) $\dfrac{14}{2\frac{1}{3}}$

   (c) $\dfrac{21}{0.3}$ (d) $\dfrac{9.8}{0.14}$

   (e) $\dfrac{2.34}{0.6}$ (f) Bank balance $\$870$
                        Checks written -925

(g) Value of stock $ 950
    Cost of stock   − 1,200

(h) Advertising budget $107
    Advertising expense   − 135

(i) Gross profit $3,115
    Expenses   − 3,789

4. (a) $\dfrac{25}{\frac{5}{7}}$

(b) $\dfrac{18}{4\frac{1}{2}}$

(c) $\dfrac{20}{0.4}$

(d) $\dfrac{7.5}{0.15}$

(e) $\dfrac{2.56}{0.8}$

(f) Gross profit $15,200
    Expenses   − 18,500

(g) Utilities budget $2,400
    Utilities cost   − 2,900

(h) Escrow for taxes $1,750
    Taxes assessed   − 2,100

(i) Insurance coverage $1,575
    Hospital charges   − 1,850

Find the value of each expression.

5. (a) $(1 + \frac{4}{100} \cdot \frac{1}{2})$ (b) $(1 + \frac{7}{100} \cdot \frac{1}{4})$ (c) $(1 - \frac{8}{100} \cdot \frac{1}{4})$

(d) $(1 - \frac{5}{100} \cdot \frac{1}{2})$ (e) $(1 + \frac{4}{100} \times \frac{5}{12})$ (f) $(1 - \frac{6}{100} \cdot \frac{1}{4})$

(g) $300(1 + \frac{6}{100} \cdot \frac{1}{3})$ (h) $200(1 - \frac{7}{100} \cdot \frac{1}{2})$ (i) $400(1 + \frac{5}{100}t)$

(j) $540(1 - r \cdot \frac{1}{3})$ (k) $a(1 - bc)$

6. (a) $(1 + \frac{10}{100} \times \frac{1}{2})$ (b) $(1 - \frac{5}{100} \cdot \frac{1}{3})$ (c) $(1 - \frac{7}{100} \times \frac{1}{6})$

(d) $(1 + \frac{7}{100} \cdot \frac{1}{2})$ (e) $(1 + \frac{8}{100} \cdot \frac{1}{6})$ (f) $(1 - \frac{6}{100} \cdot \frac{7}{12})$

(g) $500(1 + \frac{9}{100} \cdot \frac{1}{3})$ (h) $800(1 - \frac{5}{100} \cdot \frac{1}{2})$ (i) $600(1 + \frac{6}{100}t)$

(j) $480(1 - r \cdot \frac{1}{4})$ (k) $a(1 + bc)$

Round off each number as indicated.

7. (a) to tenths:
5.14
319.392
26.83

(b) to hundredths:
7.9348
14.697
121.345

(c) to thousandths:
59.9997
0.4035
6.2119

(d) to tenths, hundredths, and thousandths:
8.8479
3.2595

8. (a) to tenths:
   14.279
   5.348
   127.85

   (c) to thousandths:
   196.5084
   4.0395
   32.6227

(b) to hundredths:
   8.915
   13.068
   0.6646

(d) to tenths, hundredths, and
   thousandths:
   6.4875
   29.9608

Compute each product. Round first according to the least accurate decimal, and then round according to the least number of significant digits.

9. (a) 8.61×13.5
   (c) 3.45×7.002

(b) 1.5×4.03
(d) $50.6 \times .32$

10. (a) 16.5×4.25
   (c) 15.8×0.94

(b) 7.12×3.6
(d) 6.34×2.002

Compute each product, correct to the nearest cent. Use no more digits than are necessary.

11. (a) 600×1.50252492
   (c) $2,000 \times 0.40324726$

(b) 900×2.00159734
(d) 40×16.09689554

12. (a) 400×1.8982985583
   (c) $3,000 \times 0.3624462196$

(b) 500×2.3186582759
(d) 20×44.8651767837

CHAPTER 1 *Glossary*

Base. A number that is to be used in multiplication times itself.

Deficit. The result when a larger number is subtracted from a smaller number.

Exponent. A superscript that indicates how many times a base is to be written in repeated multiplication times itself. (Example: The exponent 3 denotes that $5^3 = 5 \cdot 5 \cdot 5 = 125$.)

Mixed number. A number that combines a whole number and a fraction. (Example: $12\frac{1}{2}$.)

Negative difference. (See "Deficit.")

Operation. Any of the arithmetic processes of addition, subtraction, multiplication, or division.

Significant digits. Digits obtained by precise measurement rather than by rough approximation (or artificially by computation).

Variable. A letter or symbol used to represent a number.

Whole number. A number from the set $\{0, 1, 2, 3, \ldots\}$, which has no decimal or fractional part.

CHAPTER 2

Review of

Equations

CHAPTER 2 OBJECTIVES

Upon completion of Chapter 2, the student will be able to:

1. Define and use correctly the terminology associated with each topic.

2. Solve basic equations that require only
   a. Combining the similar terms of the equation; and/or
   b. Using the operations of addition, subtraction, multiplication, and division.
   c. Examples:

$$x - 12 = 16, \quad 5y - 4 = 6 - 3y \quad \text{or} \quad \frac{3x}{4} + 5 = 23$$

   (*Section 1; Examples 1–11; Problems 1–36*)

3. Express any written problem in a concise sentence which provides the structure for the equation that solves the problem.
   (*Section 2; Examples 1–8; Problems 1–36*)

4. a. Express numbers in ratios
      (*Section 3; Example 1; Problems 1, 2, 5–8*);
   b. Use proportions to find numerical amounts.
      (*Examples 2–4; Problems 3, 4, 9–24*).

5. Convert repeating decimals (such as 0.7777 . . . or 0.345345345 . . .) to their equivalent fractions (*Section 4; Examples 1–4; Problems 1, 2*).

2

The procedure required to solve many problems in business mathematics is much more obvious when one has a basic knowledge of equation-solving techniques. The equations we will consider, such as $x - 7 = 5$ or $\frac{2}{3}y + 5 = y + 2$, are **first-degree equations in one variable**. "First-degree" means that the variable, or letter, in each equation has an exponent of 1 (although this exponent is not usually written; that is, x means x^1). Notice that the "one variable" (letter) may appear more than one time, but there will only be one distinct variable in any given equation. Before starting to solve any actual equations, a discussion of some of the characteristics of equations may prove helpful.

SECTION 1
Basic Equations

An **equation** may be compared to an old-fashioned balancing scale. The "equals" sign is the center post of the scale and the two sides of the equation balance each other as do the pans of the scale.

We know that one can either add weights or remove them from the pans of a scale; but as long as one makes the same changes in both pans, the scales remain in balance. The same is true of equations: In solving an equation, one may perform any operation (addition, subtraction, multiplication, or division); and as long as the same operation is performed with the same numbers on both sides of the equation, the balance of the equation will not be upset.

The object in solving any equation with unknowns in it is to determine what value of the unknown quantity (the *variable*) will make the equation a true statement. Basically, this is accomplished by isolating the variable **term** or terms on one side of the equation and the ordinary numbers on the other side, as follows:

$$\text{Variables} = \text{Numbers}$$

or

$$\text{Numbers} = \text{Variables}$$

For instance, given $5p - 3 = 2p + 15$, we isolate the variable terms on one side and the numbers on the other to obtain $5p - 2p = 15 + 3$. The **similar terms** are isolated by performing exactly the same operation on both sides of the equation, as demonstrated in Example One.

There are only four basic equation forms—those whose solution requires a single operation of either addition, subtraction, multiplication, or division. All other equations are variations or combinations of these four forms. We shall now consider several elementary equations, beginning with the four basic forms.

In the basic equation forms to follow, there will be only one number associated with the unknown (variable) on the same side of the equation. The student should first determine which operation is involved with this number. The solution of the equation will then require that the *opposite* operation be performed on both sides of the equation.

Example One Solve for x in the equation: $\qquad x + 9 = 24$

In order to isolate the variable x on the left side of the equation, we need to remove the 9. In the original equation, the 9 is added to x; therefore, we must perform the opposite of addition, or *subtract* 9 from both sides.

$$x + 9 = 24$$

(Subtract 9 from both sides) $\qquad x + 9 - 9 = 24 - 9$

$(9 - 9 = 0;$ and $x + 0 = x)$ $\qquad x + 9 - 9 = 24 - 9$

$$x = 15$$

NOTE: Numbers or variables in a given equation may be added or subtracted only if they are on the *same side* of the equation; thus, in Example 1, equation-solving techniques were used to get 24 and 9 on the same side of the equation before the numbers could be combined. Also, students who have had little experience in solving equations should develop the following habit: On each succeeding line of the problem, first copy the adjusted equation resulting from the previous step; then perform the next step.

Example Two
Solve for r: $\qquad r - 26 = 47$

The 26 is subtracted from r; therefore, we must *add* 26 to both sides of the equation.

$$r - 26 = 47$$

(Add 26 to both sides) $\qquad r - 26 + 26 = 47 + 26$

$(-26 + 26 = 0)$ $\qquad \underbrace{r - 26 + 26}_{} = \underbrace{47 + 26}_{}$

$$r = 73$$

Example Three
Solve for y: $\qquad 4y = 72$

The expression $4y$ means "4 times y" (or $4 \times y$). Any number that multiplies a variable is called a **coefficient**; in this equation, 4 is the coefficient of y.

Since 4 multiplies y, we must perform the opposite of multiplication, or *divide* 4 into both sides of the equation.

$$4y = 72$$

(Divide both sides by 4) $\qquad \dfrac{4y}{4} = \dfrac{72}{4}$

$(\frac{4}{4} = 1;\ 1y = y)$ $\qquad \dfrac{^1\!\!\not4 y}{\not4} = \dfrac{72}{4}$

$$y = 18$$

Example Four
Solve for k: $\qquad \dfrac{k}{3} = 17$

Example Four (cont.)   Since k is divided by 3, we must *multiply* both sides of the equation by 3.

$$\frac{k}{3} = 17$$

(Multiply both sides by 3) $$\frac{3}{1} \cdot \frac{k}{3} = 17 \cdot 3$$

$$\frac{{}^1\!\!\not{3}}{1} \cdot \frac{k}{\not{3}} = 17 \cdot 3$$

$$k = 51$$

Now let us consider some variations and combinations of the basic equation forms.

Example Five   Solve for t: $$\frac{2t}{3} = 36$$

Just as $\dfrac{2 \times 12}{3}$ gives the same result as $\frac{2}{3} \times 12$, so $\dfrac{2t}{3}$ is the same as $\frac{2}{3}t$. In order to solve the equation for t, we need to remove the coefficient $\frac{2}{3}$ and obtain a coefficient of 1. This can be accomplished easily by multiplying by the reciprocal of $\frac{2}{3}$. The **reciprocal** of any number is the result obtained when the number is inverted (that is, the numerator and denominator are interchanged.) Thus, the reciprocal of $\frac{2}{3}$ is $\frac{3}{2}$.

$$\frac{2t}{3} = 36$$

(Multiply by $\frac{3}{2}$, the reciprocal of $\frac{2}{3}$) $$\frac{{}^1\!\not{3}}{\not{2}} \cdot \frac{{}^1\!\not{2}}{\not{3}}t = \not{36} \cdot \frac{3}{\not{2}}^{\,18}$$

$(\frac{3}{2} \cdot \frac{2}{3} = 1; \; 1t = t)$ $t \;\; = \;\; 54$

Example Six   Solve for p: $6p + p - 3p = 48$

We must first combine the three p terms into a single p term. This is done by adding and/or subtracting the coefficients, whichever the

Example Six (cont.)   signs indicate. (Recall that $p = 1p$.)

$$6p + p - 3p = 48$$

(Combine the coefficients:
$6 + 1 - 3 = 4$)

$$4p = 48$$

(Divide both sides by 4)

$$\frac{\cancel{4}p}{\cancel{4}} = \frac{48}{4}$$

$$p = 12$$

Example Seven   Solve for m: $4m + 5 = 33$

When one side of an equation contains both a variable term and a number term, it is customary to work with the number term first, in order to obtain an altered equation of the type

Variable term = Numbers

$$4m + 5 = 33$$

(Subtract 5 from both sides) $4m + \cancel{5} \, \cancel{-5} = 33 - 5$

$$4m = 28$$

(Divide by 4)

$$\frac{4m}{4} = \frac{28}{4}$$

$$m = 7$$

Example Eight   Solve for n: $6 = \dfrac{n}{7} - 3$

We must first isolate the variable term so that

Numbers = Variable term

$$6 = \frac{n}{7} - 3$$

(Add 3 to both sides) $6 + 3 = \dfrac{n}{7} - \cancel{3} \, \cancel{+3}$

$$9 = \frac{n}{7}$$

(Multiply by 7) $7 \cdot 9 = \dfrac{n}{\cancel{7}} \cdot \cancel{7}$

$$63 = n$$

Example Nine Solve for s: $\dfrac{3s}{5} - 4 = 14$

$$\dfrac{3s}{5} - 4 = 14$$

(Add 4) $\dfrac{3s}{5} - \cancel{4 + 4} = 14 + 4$

$$\dfrac{3s}{5} = 18$$

(Multiply by $\frac{5}{3}$) $\dfrac{\overset{1}{\cancel{5}}}{\cancel{3}} \cdot \dfrac{\cancel{3}s}{\cancel{5}} = \overset{6}{\cancel{18}} \cdot \dfrac{5}{\cancel{3}}$

$$s = 30$$

Example Ten Solve for z: $9(z - 3) = 45$

Recall that the coefficient 9 must multiply times each term within the parentheses.

$$9(z - 3) = 45$$

$$9z - 27 = 45$$

(Add 27 to both sides) $9z - \cancel{27 + 27} = 45 + 27$

$$9z = 72$$

(Divide by 9) $\dfrac{9z}{9} = \dfrac{72}{9}$

$$z = 8$$

Example Eleven Solve for d: $7d + 4 = 5d + 14$

Remember that variable terms or number terms can be added and/or subtracted only when they appear on the same side of the equation. Therefore, the first steps will involve getting all the variable terms on one side of the equation and all the number terms on the other. When the solution of an equation requires that both of these steps be done, it is customary—though not essential—to work with the variable terms first.

$$7d + 4 = 5d + 14$$

(Subtract $5d$ from both sides) $7d - 5d + 4 = \cancel{5d - 5d} + 14$

$$2d + 4 = 14$$

(Subtract 4 from both sides) $2d + \cancel{4 - 4} = 14 - 4$

$$2d = 10$$

Example Eleven (cont.) (Divide by 2)

$$1x + 12 = 27 \qquad \frac{2d}{2} = \frac{10}{2}$$
$$x = 15 \qquad d = 5$$

SECTION 1 *Problems*

Solve the following equations.

1. $1x + 12 = 27$ 2. $x + 24 = 42$ 3. $y - 5 = 38$

4. $t - 12 = 19$ 5. $5x = 45$ 6. $6y = 54$

7. $\dfrac{t}{18} = 3$ 8. $\dfrac{r}{12} = 5$ 9. $7c + 4 = 25$

10. $8k + 6 = 46$ 11. $2x - 8 = 16$ 12. $3s - 7 = 29$

13. $3y + 6y - y = 48$ 14. $4p - p + 7p = 80$ 15. $7x = 50 - 3x$

16. $9d = 96 - 3d$ 17. $7v = 2v + 10$ 18. $14q = 8q + 42$

19. $3(2k - 5) = 6$ 20. $4(3g - 2) = 52$ 21. $9m - 12 = 5m - 7$

22. $13x - 14 = 9x - 8$ 23. $2x + 8 = 11 - 3x$ 24. $5t + 4 = 25 - 4t$

25. $4n - 7 = 8 - n$ 26. $13z - 6 = 8 - 5z$ 27. $12x - 11 = 2(x - 3)$

28. $7(p - 2) = 2p - 9$ 29. $\dfrac{y}{6} + 8 = 11$ 30. $\dfrac{c}{9} + 12 = 15$

31. $\dfrac{q}{5} - 4 = 5$ 32. $\dfrac{k}{4} - 7 = 1$ 33. $\dfrac{4y}{7} + 9 = 17$

34. $\dfrac{2d}{5} + 7 = 13$ 35. $7 = \dfrac{3n}{8} - 5$ 36. $16 = \dfrac{3s}{4} - 11$

SECTION 2
Written Problems

Many business problems of a mathematical nature can have no predetermined formula applied to them. In these cases, it is necessary that the business person be able to set the facts of the situation into an original equation to obtain the solution.

An equation is simply a mathematical sentence (a statement of equality). If one can express the facts of a mathematical problem in a clear, concise, English sentence, the mathematical sentence (equation) will follow in exactly the same pattern. (By the same token, it might also be said that a student who cannot express the facts in a clear, English sentence probably does not understand the situation well enough to be able to obtain a mathematical solution.)

One fact that helps immensely in converting English sentences into mathematical sentences is that the *verb* of the English sentences corresponds to the *equals sign* of the equations. The mathematical equivalents of several other words will be pointed out in the following examples.

Example One

What number increased by 25 gives 83?

$$n \quad + \quad 25 \quad = \quad 83$$

Thus,

$$n + 25 = 83$$

$$n + 25 - 25 = 83 - 25$$

$$n = 58$$

Example Two

Advertising expense last month was $80 less than utilities expense. If $475 was spent for advertising, how much were utilities?

$$a = u \quad - \quad \$80$$
$$\$475 = u \quad - \quad \$80$$
$$\$475 + 80 = u \quad - \quad \$80 + 80$$
$$\$555 = u$$

Example Three

About $\frac{1}{5}$ of a family's net (after tax) monthly income is budgeted for food. What is their net monthly income, if food bills average $58 per week? (Assume that 4 weeks equal 1 month.)

One-fifth of net income is food expense

$$\frac{1}{5} \quad \times \quad I \quad = \quad (4 \times \$58)$$

$$\frac{I}{5} = \$232$$

$$\cancel{5} \times \frac{I}{\cancel{5}} = 232 \times 5$$

$$I = \$1,160$$

475 _ 80

Example Four

A training workshop held by Field Sales Corp. cost the firm $1,800. If 75 salespeople attended the workshop, what was the cost per participant?

Number of participants	times	cost per participant	equals	total
75	×	c	=	$1,800

$$75c = 1,800$$

$$\frac{\cancel{75}c}{\cancel{75}} = \frac{1,800}{75}$$

$$c = \$24$$

Example Five

The state welfare department pays $\frac{2}{3}$ of the cost of daycare for indigent children. The remaining balance is financed by Whitworth County. If the state paid $1,400 for daycare, what was the total cost of the daycare project?

Two-thirds	of	total cost	was	state's share
$\frac{2}{3}$	×	c	=	$1,400

$$\frac{2c}{3} = 1,400$$

$$\frac{3}{2} \cdot \frac{2c}{3} = \cancel{1,400} \times \frac{3}{\cancel{2}} \quad^{700}$$

$$c = \$2,100$$

Example Six

The number of color televisions sold at Entertainment Associates was four times the combined total of stereos and radios. If their sales included 52 TVs and 4 radios, how many stereos were sold?

TVs	were	four	times	stereos and radios combined
t	=	4	×	$(s+r)$
52	=	4	×	$(s+4)$

$$52 = 4(s+4)$$

$$52 = 4s+16$$

$$52-16 = 4s+16-16$$

$$\frac{36}{4} = \frac{4s}{4}$$

$$9 = s \quad \text{(stereos)}$$

**Example
Seven**

Harris and Smith together sold 36 new insurance policies. If Harris sold three times as many policies as Smith, how many sales did each make?

NOTE: When a problem involves two amounts, it is usually easier to let the variable of your equation represent the smaller quantity.

Since Harris sold three times as many policies as Smith, then Smith is the smaller quantity:

$$\underline{\text{Harris}}\ \ \underline{\text{sold}}\ \ \underline{\text{three}}\ \ \underline{\text{times}}\ \ \underline{\text{Smith}}$$
$$H\ \ \ =\ \ \ \ \ 3\ \ \ \ \times\ \ \ \ S$$

Now,

$$\underline{\text{Harris}}\ \underline{\text{and}}\ \underline{\text{Smith}}\ \underline{\text{together}}\ \underline{\text{sold}}\ \underline{\text{36}}\ \underline{\text{policies}}$$

$$H + S = 36$$
$$\downarrow$$
$$3S + S = 36$$
$$\frac{4S}{4} = \frac{36}{4}$$

(Smith's sales) $\quad S = 9$ policies

(Harris' sales) $\quad H = 3S$
$$= 3 \times 9$$
$$= 27 \text{ policies}$$

**Example
Eight**

C and W Catering charges $3 for a barbeque dinner and $5 for a steak dinner. A recent dinner for 250 people totaled $950. How many of each type of dinner were served?

Solution

We know that a total of 250 dinners were served. Suppose we knew there were 50 barbeque dinners; how would we find the number of steak dinners? (Steak $= 250 - 50$.) Regardless of the actual number of each type of dinner,

$$\text{Barbeque} + \text{Steak} = 250$$
$$b + s = 250$$
$$b = 250 - s$$

**Example
Eight
(cont.)**   Now,

Cost of Bar-B-Q	plus	cost of steak	totals	$950
$3 \times b$	+	$5 \times s$	=	$950
$3(250 - s)$	+	$5s$	=	950
$750 - 3s$	+	$5s$	=	950
750	+	$2s$	=	950
~~750 - 750~~	+	$2s$	=	$950 - 750$
		$\dfrac{2s}{2}$	=	$\dfrac{200}{2}$
(Steak dinners)		s	=	100 dinners
(Barbeque dinners)		b	=	$250 - s$
			=	$250 - 100$
			=	150 dinners

SECTION 2 *Problems*

"Translate" the following **expressions** *into algebraic symbols.*

1.
(a) 8 times n
(b) $\frac{3}{5}$ of r
(c) A number increased by 5
(d) $15 less than p
(e) a, b, and c together
(f) x is 5 times y
(g) Twice the sum of s and t
(h) The cost of m matinee tickets at $4 per ticket
(i) j sold 4 more than k
(j) d totals 2.5 times y and z combined
(k) v equals 8 less than half w
(l) q cost $\frac{3}{4}$ as much as r

2.
(a) 4 times g
(b) $\frac{2}{3}$ of k
(c) 6 more than c
(d) An amount decreased by $12

(e) p and g together
(f) d is $5 less than e
(g) Four times the sum of b and c
(h) The cost of j cases of juice at $6 per case
(i) m is 3 times n
(j) c sold twice d and f combined
(k) $\frac{2}{5}$ of p amounted to $500
(l) v totaled $\frac{3}{8}$ as much as w

Express each of the following as both an English equation and a math equation, and solve.

3. What number when increased by 27 gives 85?

4. What number when decreased by 27 gives 85?

5. The regular price of an electronic calculator, decreased by $15, gives a sale price of $19. What was the regular price?

6. The list price of a tape recorder, increased by $7, gives a new list price of $54. What was the previous price?

7. Chandler's Appliances charge $15 more than the Thrifty Wholesale Company for a vacuum cleaner. If Chandler's price is $69, what would the cleaner cost at Thrifty Company?

8. The Mod Shop charges $12 less than The Coat Rack for a winter jacket. If the Mod Shop's price is $45, how much does The Coat Rack charge?

9. One-sixth of a company's employees are women. What is the total number of employees, if there are 15 women?

10. One-third of Karol Motor Co.'s customers are "repeat" buyers. How many total customers have purchased cars, if 32 people had previously bought cars there?

11. Approximately $\frac{2}{7}$ of the employees of a plant took no sick leave during December. If there were 120 employees without an absence, how many people does the firm employ?

12. Ware Manufacturing finds that $\frac{4}{5}$ of its employees buy the group insurance offered at the firm. If 144 employees are covered by the insurance plan, how many people does Ware employ?

13. The Toy Box found that 7 less than $\frac{3}{10}$ of its sales were layaways. If there were 53 packages in layaway, how many sales were made?

14. Some 15 more than $\frac{2}{3}$ of the orders at Central Chemical Co. were telephone orders. How many orders were received altogether, if 75 orders were placed by phone?

15. According to the state policy, $1,000 more than $\frac{3}{5}$ the cost of a new school for Lincoln County will be paid by the state; the county will finance the remaining portion. If the state pays $361,000, what will be the total cost of the school?

16. Some $500 more than $\frac{5}{8}$ of the United Way budget has been pledged during the first week of the campaign. If $60,500 has been pledged, what is the total budget?

17. A sales representative made 85 sales during his 5-day work week. How many sales did he average each day?

18. Mary Scott paid $1,200 in car expenses during the year. If she drove 8,000 miles, what was her cost per mile?

19. Depreciation of $1,500 was claimed on a knitting machine. If 3,000 bolts of cloth were manufactured on the machine, what was the depreciation per unit (per bolt)?

20. Pedro Garcia received a stock dividend check of $640. If he owns 400 shares of stock, how much was the dividend per share?

21. The weaving department of a factory occupies 3.5 times as much floor space as the shipping department. The weaving department occupies 4,200 square feet. How large is the shipping department?

22. The sales department employs 4.8 times as many people as the accounting department. How many people work in accounting, if the sales staff includes 24 people?

23. The number of lawn mowers sold at Barton Hardware is twice the number of edgers and tillers combined. Sales included 26 lawn mowers and 3 tillers. How many edgers were sold?

24. The number of apartments for lease is five times the combined total of houses and duplexes. If a realtor lists 75 apartments and 9 duplexes, how many houses are available?

25. Television commercials cost Highland Furniture three times as much as their radio and newspaper ads together. What was spent for newspaper ads if TV commercials ran $210 and radio spots cost $20?

26. Brand X camera sells four times as many cameras as brands Y and Z together. Find the number of brand Z sold, if 64 brand X and 4 brand Y were sold.

27. Garland and White together sold 135 tickets to a civic club supper. If White sold twice as many tickets as Garland, how many tickets did each man sell?

28. The plumbing and electrical contracts on a new home totaled $9,600. If the plumbing cost three times as much as the electrical contract, how much was each contract?

29. A chair company has been producing about 1,540 chairs per day, working two shifts. The second shift has produced about 1.2 times as many chairs as the first shift. How many chairs have been produced by each shift?

30. Sales of dresses and pantsuits together totaled 68 outfits. The pantsuit sales were 2.4 times the sales of dresses. How many of each were sold?

31. A home buyer pays $300 per month for the mortgage, taxes, and home insurance combined. The mortgage payment is 24 times the insurance, and the taxes are five times the insurance. How much of the payment is spent for each item?

32. A student budgets $180 for food, clothing, and transportation expenses combined. Her food costs twice as much as transportation, and clothing costs 1.5 times transportation. How much was each expenditure?

33. One style of shoes costs $8 wholesale in patent leather and $10 in cowhide. An invoice for $390 accompanies an order of 45 pairs of shoes. How many pairs of each style were bought?

34. An order for 35 records and tapes cost The Disc Shop $120. The wholesale cost of records is $3 and the tapes is $4. How many of each were included?

35. The Cinema sold 120 tickets for a total of $280. If children's tickets are $1 and adult tickets are $3, how many of each ticket were sold?

36. History books cost $9 each and English texts are $12 each. The bookstore's order for 27 books totaled $279. How many of each book were purchased?

SECTION 3

Ratio and Proportion

A **ratio** is a way of comparing numbers. When two numbers are being compared, the ratio may be written in any of three ways: for example, (1) 3 to 5, (2) 3:5, or (3) $\frac{3}{5}$. Method 3 indicates that common fractions (which are **rational numbers**) are also ratios. (Notice that "rational" and "ratio" are variations of the same word.) If more than two numbers are being compared, the ratio is written in either of the first two ways: as 3 to 2 to 4 or $3:2:4$.

Ratios are often used instead of per cent in order to compare items of expense, particularly when the per cent would have exceeded 100 per cent. In this case, it is customary to reduce the ratio to a comparison to 1; as 1.3 to 1 or $\frac{2.47}{1}$. (A ratio is "reduced" by expressing it as a common fraction and reducing the fraction. A ratio is reduced to "a comparison to 1" by dividing the denominator into the numerator.) Ratios may also be used as a basis for dividing expenses among several categories, which we will consider when apportioning overhead in a later chapter.

Example One

Determine the following ratios:

(a) There are 20 doctors and 48 registered nurses on the staff of Neuman County Hospital. What is the ratio of doctors to nurses?

$$\text{Doctors to registered nurses} = \frac{\text{Doctors}}{\text{Nurses}} = \frac{20}{48} = \frac{5}{12}$$

The ratio of doctors to registered nurses is 5 to 12, or $5:12$, or $\frac{5}{12}$.

(b) Net sales of Warner Corp. were $105,000 this year, as compared to $84,000 last year. What is the ratio of this year's sales to last year's?

$$\text{Current sales to previous} = \frac{\text{Current sales}}{\text{Previous sales}} = \frac{\$105,000}{\$84,000}$$

$$= \frac{5}{4} = 1.25 \quad \text{or} \quad \frac{1.25}{1}$$

The ratio may be given correctly in any of the following forms: 5 to 4 or 1.25 to 1; 5:4 or 1.25:1; $\frac{5}{4}$ or $\frac{1.25}{1}$. Since most actual business figures would not reduce to a common fraction like $\frac{5}{4}$, business ratios are usually computed by ordinary division, without attempting to reduce the fraction. Thus,

$$\frac{\$105,000}{\$84,000} = 1.25 = \frac{1.25}{1} \quad \text{or} \quad 1.25 \text{ to } 1$$

The term "proportion" is frequently used in connection with ratio. A **proportion** is simply a mathematical statement that two ratios are equal. Thus, $\frac{6}{10} = \frac{3}{5}$ is a proportion. The same proportion could also be indicated $6:10::3:5$, which is read "six is to ten as three is to five."

A proportion may be used to find an unknown amount if we first know the ratio that exists between this unknown and another, known amount. This method is particularly useful when relationships (ratios) are given as per cent. Such proportions are then solved like ordinary equations.

Example Two   The net profit of Gaines Wholesalers was 5% of its net sales. What was the net profit if the firm had $60,000 in net sales?

Solution   Since 5% = $\frac{5}{100}$, then

$$\frac{\text{Profit}}{\text{Net sales}} = \frac{5}{100}$$

$$\frac{P}{\$60{,}000} = \frac{5}{100}$$

$$(60{,}000)\frac{P}{60{,}000} = \frac{5}{100}(60{,}000)$$

$$P = \$3{,}000$$

For any given proportion, the **cross products** are always equal. Given $\frac{6}{10} = \frac{3}{5}$, the cross products are computed

$$\frac{6}{10} \diagup\!\!\!\!\diagdown \frac{3}{5}$$

$$6 \cdot 5 = 3 \cdot 10$$

$$30 = 30$$

Cross products* are useful in solving any proportion where the unknown appears in the denominator, as follows.

Example Three   Hartman and Post, who are sales representatives for Shields & Co., received orders last week in the ratio of $\frac{2}{3}$. How many orders did Post

---

* Cross products are a shortcut which produces the same result that is obtained when both sides of an equation are multiplied by the product of the two given denominators. Given $\frac{6}{10} = \frac{3}{5}$, then $50(\frac{6}{10}) = 50(\frac{3}{5})$, which gives $30 = 30$, as before.

Example Three (cont.) sell, if Hartman sold 26 orders?

$$\frac{\text{Hartman}}{\text{Post}} = \frac{2}{3}$$

$$\frac{26}{P} = \frac{2}{3}$$

$$3 \cdot 26 = 2P$$

$$\frac{78}{2} = \frac{2P}{2}$$

$$39 = P$$

Example Four Citizens of San Rio paid $29 for 700 kilowatt-hours (kWh) of electricity. What was the bill for a family that used 1,400 kWh?

$$\frac{\text{Cost}}{\text{kWh}} = \frac{\$29}{700}$$

$$\frac{c}{1,400} = \frac{\$29}{700}$$

$$(1,400)\frac{c}{1,400} = \frac{29}{700}(1,400)$$

$$c = \$58$$

SECTION 3 *Problems*

Reduce the following ratios and express in each of the three ratio forms.

1. (a) 9 to 15
   (b) $600 to $24,000
   (c) 720 to 1,200
   (d) 65 to 20
   (e) $22,000 to $5,000

2. (a) 35 to 56
   (b) 150 to 450
   (c) $1,000 to $2,500
   (d) 72 to 48
   (e) $36,000 to $16,000

Find the missing element in each proportion in Problems 3 and 4.

3. (a) $\dfrac{x}{18} = \dfrac{5}{6}$

   (b) $\dfrac{r}{12} = \dfrac{7}{4}$

   (c) $\dfrac{8}{b} = \dfrac{2}{5}$

   (d) $\dfrac{9}{y} = \dfrac{3}{2}$

4. (a) $\dfrac{c}{24} = \dfrac{3}{8}$

(b) $\dfrac{s}{15} = \dfrac{9}{5}$

(c) $\dfrac{12}{v} = \dfrac{4}{11}$

(d) $\dfrac{35}{n} = \dfrac{7}{6}$

5. Jacobs Parts Division employs 45 people in office and administrative positions and 600 people in the assembly plant. What is the ratio of white collar to blue collar workers?

6. The Guilford National Bank has 60 part-time and 96 full-time employees. What is the ratio of part- to full-time employees?

7. Randolph & Cline employ 50 persons, of whom 36 have had at least some college training. What is the ratio of college-trained employees to non-college-trained personnel?

8. Of the 80 persons employed at Butterflavor Bakery, 56 have joined the company's insurance program. What is the ratio of insured to noninsured employees?

9. The Major Automobile Co. spent $6,440,000 for advertising in magazines and newspapers, and $2,800,000 for television commercials. What was the ratio of printed ad costs to TV advertising costs?

10. Mesa City issued June building permits for $810,000 in commercial construction and $450,000 in residential construction. What was the ratio of commercial to residential building costs?

11. The average high school graduate earns only 75% as much as the average college graduate. What does the average high school graduate earn, if college graduates average $16,000?

12. The operating expenses of Catawba Textiles were 28% of their net sales last month. Find the operating expenses if net sales were $75,000.

13. The cost of goods purchased by Allworth Hardware was 62% of their net sales. If $3,100 was spent for merchandise, how much were their net sales?

14. A new model food freezer requires only 85% as much electricity as the previous model. How much did the old model require if the new model requires 680 watts?

15. The ratio of coups to sedans sold at Georgetown Motors was $\frac{5}{6}$. Find the number of coups sold if there were 24 sedans purchased.

16. August and September sales at Dilman Department Store were in the ratio $\frac{11}{8}$. If September sales totaled $320,000, what was the August sales volume?

17. The ratio of fiction to nonfiction books sold at The Book Shelf is $\frac{10}{7}$. How many nonfiction books were sold during a day when 150 fiction titles sold?

18. The net profit earned at The Stitchery Shop is distributed to owners A and B in the ratio 3:5. If A receives $2,400, how much does B get?

19. An automatic check processor can process 1,200 checks in 30 minutes. How many checks can the machine process in 3 hours?

20. A nurse counted 18 heartbeats in 15 seconds. At this rate, how many times will the heart beat in 1 minute?

21. Natural gas costs Gulf Lighting and Power $1.50 per 1,000 cubic feet. What does it cost to fuel a generator which uses 360,000 cubic feet of gas?

22. After 5 hours a truck driver had covered a distance of 260 miles. At this rate, how long will it take to complete his 1,300-mile trip?

23. A microwave oven uses 15 kilowatt-hours of electricity during an average 30-day period. How many days can the microwave be operated while using 60 kWh?

24. Electricity in Jackson County costs $18 for 700 kilowatt-hours. If an optometrist receives a $90 electrical bill, how many kilowatt-hours were used?

SECTION 4

Repeating Decimals

Fractions are often easier to work with than decimals, especially if no calculating machine is available. It is desirable, then, that students be capable of changing decimal numbers to their fractional equivalents.

Decimal numbers which terminate (or end) are easy to change to an exact fractional equivalent. You are probably already familiar with the procedure—which is to pronounce the decimal value of the number and convert it to the fractional form. For example,

$$0.625 = 625 \text{ thousandths} = \frac{625}{1,000} = \frac{5}{8}$$

Decimal numbers which neither terminate nor repeat themselves do not have an exact fractional equivalent. The only way to approximate the fractional value of such a number is to round it off at some digit and then treat it as though it had terminated. Thus,

$$0.624973 \ldots = \text{approx. } 0.625$$
$$= \text{approx. } 625 \text{ thousandths}$$
$$= \text{approx. } \frac{625}{1,000}$$
$$= \text{approx. } \frac{5}{8}$$

For any decimal number which does not terminate but which contains a *repeating* digit or series of digits, however, there exists a fraction that is exactly equal to the decimal number. The procedure for converting such a nonterminating, **repeating decimal** to its fractional equivalent employs some of the techniques of equation solving:

1. Let N equal the nonterminating, repeating decimal number. Multiply each side of the equation by 10, 100, 1,000, or by some multiple of

10—until the decimal point has passed to the right of *one complete repetition* of the repeating digits.

2. Subtract some number from the number obtained in step 1, so that the difference is a *whole number*. Usually one need only subtract N from the number obtained in step 1. However, it is sometimes necessary to multiply again by 10 or 100, so that the digits in the decimal portions of both numbers will repeat in the same order and the difference will be a whole number.

3. Solve the difference of the two equations for N, thereby obtaining the fractional equivalent of the original decimal number.

Example One

Convert $0.5555\ldots$ to its fractional equivalent.

Step

Let $N = 0.5555\ldots$

(1)
(2)

$$10N = 5.5555\ldots$$
$$\underline{-\ N = -.5555\ldots}$$
$$9N = 5.0000\ldots$$

(3)

$$9N = 5$$

$$\frac{9N}{9} = \frac{5}{9}$$

$$N = \tfrac{5}{9}$$

Example Two

What fraction is equivalent to $0.484848\ldots$?

Step

Let $N = 0.484848\ldots$

(1)
(2)

$$100N = 48.484848\ldots$$
$$\underline{-\ N = -\ .484848\ldots}$$
$$99N = 48.000000\ldots$$

(3)

$$99N = 48$$

$$\frac{99N}{99} = \frac{48}{99}$$

$$N = \tfrac{16}{33}$$

Example Three   Find the fraction equal to $0.16666\ldots$.

Step   Let $N = 0.16666\ldots$

(1) $100N = 16.6666\ldots$
(2) $-\ 10N = -\ 1.6666\ldots$
                           $\overline{90N = 15.0000\ldots}$

(3) $90N = 15$

$$\frac{90N}{90} = \frac{15}{90}$$

$$N = \tfrac{1}{6}$$

Example Four   Convert $0.625625625\ldots$ to a fraction.
Step
(1) $1{,}000N = 625.625625625\ldots$
(2) $-\quad N = -\quad .625625625\ldots$
                     $\overline{999N = 625.000000000\ldots}$

(3) $999N = 625$

$$\frac{999N}{999} = \frac{625}{999}$$

$$N = \tfrac{625}{999}$$

NOTE: In order for a number to be classified as a repeating decimal, the *same digits* must repeat indefinitely *in the same order*. Thus $0.31313131\ldots$ is a repeating decimal; $0.31311311131111\ldots$ is not a repeating decimal.

SECTION 4 *Problems*

Convert each decimal to its fractional equivalent.

1. (a) $0.33333\ldots$
   (b) $0.181818\ldots$
   (c) $0.234234234\ldots$
   (d) $0.38888\ldots$
   (e) $0.71333\ldots$
   (f) $0.616161\ldots$

2. (a) $0.22222\ldots$
   (b) $0.363636\ldots$
   (c) $0.465465465\ldots$
   (d) $0.83333\ldots$
   (e) $0.87333\ldots$
   (f) $0.595959\ldots$

Coefficient. A number that multiplies a variable or a quantity in a set of parentheses. [Example: 3 is a coefficient in $3x$ or in $3(x+z)$.]

Cross products. The equal products obtained when each numerator of a proportion is multiplied by the opposite denominator. (Given $\frac{3}{4} = \frac{9}{12}$, the cross products $3 \cdot 12$ and $4 \cdot 9$ both equal 36.)

Equation. A mathematical statement that two expressions (or an expression and a number) are equal.

Expression. Any indicated mathematical operation(s) written without an equals sign.
$$\left[\text{Example: } 2x+3 \quad \text{or} \quad \frac{3t}{5}-1.\right]$$

First-degree equation in one variable. An equation with one distinct variable whose highest exponent (degree) is 1. [Example: $2x+7 = x+12$.]

Proportion. A mathematical statement that two ratios are equal ($\frac{3}{4} = \frac{9}{12}$).

Ratio. A comparison of two (or more) numbers, frequently indicated by a common fraction. [Examples: 4 to 7; $4:7$; $\frac{4}{7}$.]

Rational number. A number that can be expressed as a common fraction (the quotient of two integers.)

Reciprocal. The result obtained when a number is inverted by interchanging the numerator and the denominator. [Example: The reciprocal of $\frac{3}{4}$ is $\frac{4}{3}$.]

Repeating decimal. A decimal number that repeats the same digit(s) in the same order. [Examples: $0.8333\ldots$; $0.234234234\ldots$.]

Similar terms. Terms that include the same variable. [Example: The expression $5x + x - 2x$ contains three similar terms.]

Terms. The products, quotients, or numbers in a mathematical expression that are separated by plus or minus signs. [Example: The expression $4x - \dfrac{3x}{5} + 7$ contains three terms.]

CHAPTER 3

Review of

Per Cent

CHAPTER 3 OBJECTIVES

Upon completion of Chapter 3, the student will be able to:

1. Define and use correctly the terminology associated with each topic.

2. a. Change a per cent to its equivalent decimal or fraction (*Section 1; Examples 1, 2; Problems 1–32*); or
   b. Change a decimal or fraction to its equivalent per cent. (*Examples 3, 4; Problems 1–32*).

3. Use an equation to find the missing element in a percentage relationship. (Example: What per cent of 30 is 25?; or, 60 is 120% of what number?) (*Section 2; Example 1; Problems 1–36*).

4. Use the basic equation form "___% of Original = Change?" to find the per cent of change (increase or decrease). (Example: $33 is what per cent more than $27?) (*Section 2; Example 2; Problems 37–48*).

5. Given a word problem containing per cents, express the problem in a concise sentence which translates into an equation that solves the problem *(Section 3; Examples 1–5; Problems 1–48)*.

6. Use aliquot parts of $1 and 100 in order to multiply efficiently. (*Section 4; Examples 1, 2; Problems 1–30*)

3

Per cent is a fundamental topic with which everyone has some familiarity. We know that per cent can be used to compare numbers that appear to be quite different. For instance, whereas the relative sizes of $\frac{7}{15}$ and $\frac{17}{35}$ would be difficult to determine from the fractions themselves, we know that per cent provides a much better basis of comparison. Specifically, per cent uses a common denominator of 100 and compares the number of parts out of 100 to which each fraction is equivalent. In this respect, per cent is another application of ratio, which we studied previously.

Although the use of per cent is taught in grade schools, it is an elusive topic which many adults have not mastered adequately. However, per cent is one of the most frequently applied mathematical concepts in all areas of business. It is thus extremely important that anyone entering business be capable of accurate per cent calculations.

SECTION 1
Basics

The use of per cent will be easier if the student remembers that **per cent** means **hundredths**. That is, the expression "46%" may just as correctly be read "46 hundredths." The word "hundredths" denotes either a common fraction with 100 as denominator or a decimal fraction of two decimal places. Thus,

$$46\% = 46 \text{ hundredths} = \tfrac{46}{100} \quad \text{or} \quad 0.46$$

Per cents must first be changed to either a fractional or decimal form before a per cent of any number can be found. These conversions are simplified by applying the fact that "per cent" means "hundredths."

A. *Changing a Per Cent to a Decimal*

When people think of per cent, they normally think of the most common per cents, those between 1% and 99%. These are the per cents that occupy the first two places in the decimal representation of a per cent. (For example, 99% = 99 hundredths = 0.99 and 1% = 1 hundredth = 0.01.)

43

A.1. When converting per cents to decimals, write the whole per cents between 1% and 99% in the first two decimal places.

When this rule is followed, the other digits will then naturally fall into their correct places, as demonstrated below.

Example One

% to Decimal

Express each of the following per cents as a decimal.

(a) $5\% = 5$ hundredths $= 0.05$

(b) $86\% = 86$ hundredths $= 0.86$

(c) $16.3\% = 0.163$ (since $16\% = 0.16$)

(d) $131\% = 1.31$ (since $31\% = 0.31$)

(e) $122.75\% = 1.2275$ (since $22\% = 0.22$)

(f) $6.09\% = 0.0609$ (since $6\% = 0.06$)

(g) $0.4\% = 0.004$ (since $0\% = 0.00$)

(h) $0.03\% = 0.0003$ (since $0\% = 0.00$)

Some per cents are written using common fractions. To change a fraction to a decimal, one must divide the numerator by the denominator.

$$\frac{n}{d}\overline{)}\qquad \text{or} \qquad d\overline{)n}$$

A.2. When a fractional per cent is to be changed to a decimal, one may first convert the fractional per cent to a decimal per cent and then convert the decimal per cent to an ordinary decimal.

(Machine calculations of the decimal per cent may be rounded to the third decimal place.)

Fractional % to Decimal

(i) $\frac{7}{8}\%$: Recall that $\frac{7}{8}$ means $8\overline{)7.000}^{\,.875} = 0.875$

      And since $\frac{7}{8} = 0.875$,

      then $\frac{7}{8}\% = 0.875\% = 0.00875$

(j) $\frac{4}{7}\%$: First, $\frac{4}{7}$ means $7\overline{)4.00}^{\,.57\frac{1}{7}} = 0.57\frac{1}{7}$ (or 0.571)

      Then $\frac{4}{7} = 0.57\frac{1}{7}$

      implies that $\frac{4}{7}\% = 0.57\frac{1}{7}\% = 0.0057\frac{1}{7}$ (or 0.00571)

A fractional per cent always indicates a per cent less than 1% (or, we may say it indicates that fractional part of 1%). Thus, $\frac{1}{4}\% = \frac{1}{4}$ of 1%; $\frac{3}{5}\% = \frac{3}{5}$ of 1%.

When the given fraction is a common one for which the decimal equivalent is known, the process of *converting a fractional per cent to a decimal* may be shortened:

A.3. Write two zeros to the right of the decimal point (0.00) to indicate the per cent is less than 1%, and then write the digits normally used to denote the decimal equivalent of the fraction:

> (k) $\frac{1}{4}\%$: $(\frac{1}{4}\% = \frac{1}{4}$ of 1%)
>
> To show that the per cent is less than 1%, write: 0.00
> To indicate $\frac{1}{4}$, affix the digits "25"
> ($\frac{1}{4} = 25$ hundredths):   0.0025
>
> Thus, $\frac{1}{4}\% = 0.0025$. (This may be easily verified, since $4 \times 0.0025 = 0.0100 = 1\%$.)

> (l) $\frac{2}{3}\%$: $(\frac{2}{3}\% = \frac{2}{3}$ of 1%)
>
> Indicate a per cent less than 1%:   0.00
> Affix the digits $66\frac{2}{3}$: $0.0066\frac{2}{3}$

B. *Changing a Per Cent to a Fraction*   The procedure for changing a per cent to a fraction is summarized in Rule B.1.

B.1. After an ordinary per cent has been changed to hundredths (by dropping the per cent sign and placing the number over a denominator of 100), the resulting fraction should be reduced to lowest terms.

(An improper fraction—one in which the numerator is greater than the denominator—is considered to be in lowest terms provided that it cannot be further reduced.)

Example Two

% to Fraction

Convert each per cent to its fractional equivalent in lowest terms:

(a) $45\% = 45$ hundredths $= \frac{45}{100} = \frac{9}{20}$

(b) $8\% = 8$ hundredths $= \frac{8}{100} = \frac{4}{25}$

(c) $175\% = 175$ hundredths $= \frac{175}{100} = \frac{7}{4}$

Per cents containing fractions may be converted to their ordinary fractional equivalents by altering the above procedure slightly. The fact that "per cent" means "hundredths" may also be shown as

$$\% = \text{hundredth} = \tfrac{1}{100}$$

B.2. Per cents containing fractions are changed to ordinary fractions by substituting $\tfrac{1}{100}$ for the % sign and multiplying.

Now let us apply this fact to change some fractional per cents to common fractions:

*% with
Fraction to
Fraction*

(d) $12\tfrac{1}{2}\% = 12\tfrac{1}{2} \times \tfrac{1}{100} = \tfrac{25}{2} \times \tfrac{1}{100} = \tfrac{25}{200} = \tfrac{1}{8}$

(e) $55\tfrac{5}{9}\% = 55\tfrac{5}{9} \times \tfrac{1}{100} = \tfrac{500}{9} \times \tfrac{1}{100} = \tfrac{500}{900} = \tfrac{5}{9}$

(f) $\tfrac{1}{3}\% = \tfrac{1}{3} \times \tfrac{1}{100} = \tfrac{1}{300}$

B.3. Decimal per cents may be converted to fractions by applying the following procedure:
1. Change the per cent to its decimal equivalent.
2. Pronounce the value of the decimal; then write this number as a fraction and reduce it.

*Decimal
% to
Fraction*

(g) 22.5%:
1. Since $22\% = 0.22$, then $22.5\% = 0.225$
2. $0.225 = 225$ thousandths $= \tfrac{225}{1,000} = \tfrac{9}{40}$

(h) 0.56%:
Since $0\% = 0.00$, then $0.56\% = 0.0056$

$$= 56 \text{ ten-thousandths}$$

$$= \tfrac{56}{10,000}$$

$$= \tfrac{7}{1,250}$$

(i) 0.6%:

$$0.6\% = 0.006$$

$$= 6 \text{ thousandths}$$

$$= \tfrac{6}{1,000}$$

$$= \tfrac{3}{500}$$

C. *Changing a
Decimal to
a Per Cent*

Just as "per cent" means "hundredths," so is the opposite also true—that is, *hundredths = per cent.* Rule C states an important concept that should be remembered when working with decimals and per cents.

C. When a decimal number is to be changed to a per cent, the hundredths places of the decimal indicate the whole "per cents" between 1% and 99% (0.01 = 1%, and 0.99 = 99%).

By first isolating the whole per cents between 1% and 99%, the student will have no difficulty in placing the other digits correctly.

   If there is to be a decimal point in the per cent, it will come after the hundredth's place of the decimal number. (This is why it is sometimes said, "to change a decimal to a per cent, move the decimal point two places to the right and add a per cent sign.")

Example Three

Express each of these decimals as a per cent.

Decimal to %

(a) $0.67 = 67$ hundredths $= 67\%$

(b) $0.82\frac{1}{2} = 82\frac{1}{2}$ hundredths $= 82\frac{1}{2}\%$

(c) $0.08 = 8$ hundredths $= 8\%$

(d) 0.721 (Since $0.72 = 72\%$, then $0.721 = 72.1\%$.)

It may prove helpful to circle the first two decimal places, as an aid in identifying the per cents between 1% and 99%.

(e) 1.459   Given 1.459, the .45 indicates 45%.

Thus, $1.459 = 145.9\%$.

(f) 0.9   Given 0.9, the .9 or .90 denotes 90%.

So $0.9 = 90\%$.

(g) 0.0026   Given 0.0026, the 0.00 represents 0%.

Hence, $0.0026 = 0.26\%$.

D. *Changing a Fraction to Per Cent* The procedure for changing a fraction to a per cent is summarized in Rule D.

D. To change a fraction to a per cent, apply the following steps.

1. Convert the fraction to its decimal equivalent by dividing the numerator by the denominator:

$$\frac{n}{d} \quad \text{or} \quad d\overline{)n}.$$

   (Machine calculations may be rounded to the third decimal place.)
2. Then change the decimal to a per cent, as illustrated in the preceding example.

Example Four

Fraction to %

Change each fraction to its equivalent per cent.

(a) $\frac{5}{8} = \dfrac{.625}{8)\overline{5.000}} = 0.625 = 62.5\%$

(b) $\frac{7}{18} = \dfrac{.38\frac{16}{18}}{18)\overline{7.00}} = 0.38\frac{8}{9} = 38\frac{8}{9}\%$ (or 38.9%)

(c) $\frac{5}{4} = \dfrac{1.25}{4)\overline{5.00}} = 1.25 = 125\%$

(d) $1\frac{4}{5}$ (since $\frac{4}{5} = \dfrac{.80}{5)\overline{4.00}} = 0.80$) $= 1.80 = 180\%$

or

$1\frac{4}{5} = \frac{9}{5} = \dfrac{1.80}{5)\overline{9.00}} = 1.80 = 180\%$

(e) $2\frac{3}{4}$ (since $\frac{3}{4} = 0.75$) $= 2.75 = 275\%$

or

$2\frac{3}{4} = \frac{11}{4} = 2.75 = 275\%$

SECTION 1 *Problems*

Express each per cent as (1) *a decimal, and* (2) *a fraction in its lowest terms.*

all divisible by 3

1. 35%
2. 18%
3. 6%
4. 4%

5. 53%
6. 47%
7. 26.5%
8. 35.8%

9. 4.15%
10. 8.64%
11. 41.75%
12. 57.25%

13. 145%
14. 105%
15. 1.45%
16. 1.05%

17. 0.2%
18. 0.8%
19. 0.28%
20. 0.56%

21. 112.5%
22. 137.5%
23. $\frac{3}{4}\%$
24. $\frac{1}{4}\%$

25. $\frac{3}{8}\%$
26. $\frac{2}{5}\%$
27. $22\frac{2}{9}\%$
28. $28\frac{4}{7}\%$

29. $83\frac{1}{3}\%$
30. $45\frac{5}{11}\%$
31. $7\frac{1}{2}\%$
32. $8\frac{1}{3}\%$

Express each of the following as a per cent.

33. 0.73
34. 0.64
35. 0.07
36. 0.09

37. 0.395
38. 0.844
39. 0.028
40. 0.056

41. 2.35   **42.** 1.19   **43.** 1.745   **44.** 1.321

45. 0.025   **46.** 0.047   **47.** 0.625   **48.** 0.196

49. 0.001   **50.** 0.004   **51.** 0.0038   **52.** 0.0057

53. 4.6   **54.** 2.1   **55.** 0.7   **56.** 0.5

57. $\frac{3}{7}$ **58.** $\frac{7}{8}$ **59.** $\frac{5}{12}$ **60.** $\frac{2}{13}$

61. $1\frac{3}{4}$ **62.** $2\frac{2}{5}$ **63.** $2\frac{5}{13}$ **64.** $1\frac{3}{11}$

(handwritten: .0475% = .00475   .00365 = .365%)

SECTION 2
Per Cent
Equation Forms

All problems that involve the use of per cent are some variation of the basic per cent form: "Some per cent of one number equals another number." This basic **per cent equation form** may be abbreviated as indicated below:

$$\underline{}\% \text{ of } \underline{} = \underline{} \qquad \text{or} \qquad x\% \text{ of } y = z$$

(handwritten: $\frac{3}{8}\% = \frac{3}{800}$)

Given in reverse order, the equation form is

$$\underline{} = \underline{}\% \text{ of } \underline{} \qquad \text{or} \qquad z = x\% \text{ of } y$$

(handwritten: $\frac{3}{7} = \frac{300}{7}\% = 43\frac{6}{7}\%$)

Since there can be only one unknown in an elementary equation, there are only three variations of the basic equation form: The unknown can be either (1) the per cent (or **rate**), (2) the first number (often called the **base**), or (3) the second number (often called the **percentage**).

Equation-solving procedures which were studied earlier will be applied to solve percentage problems. Recall that before a per cent of any number can be computed, the per cent must first be changed to either a fraction or a decimal. Conversely, if the unknown represents a per cent, the solution to the equation will be a decimal or fraction which must then be converted to the per cent.

Example One

(a) 70% of 52 is what number?

$$0.7 \times 52 = n$$

$$36.4 = n$$

Observe that 70% is the rate and 52 is the base (the number which the per cent multiplies). The percentage is 36.4. (This is somewhat

Example One (cont.)

confusing since the percentage is not a per cent; the rate is the per cent. However, this confusion is avoided by using the per cent equation form above.)

(b) What per cent of 9 is 4?

$$r \times 9 = 4$$

or

$$9r = 4$$

$$\frac{9r}{9} = \frac{4}{9}$$

$$r = \frac{4}{9}$$

$$r = 44\frac{4}{9}\%$$

(c) $66\frac{2}{3}\%$ of what number is 12?

$$\frac{2}{3} \times n = 12$$

or

$$\frac{2n}{3} = 12$$

$$\frac{3}{2} \times \frac{2n}{3} = \frac{3}{2} \times 12$$

$$n = 18$$

Many of the formulas used to solve mathematical problems in business are nothing more than the basic per cent equation form with different words (or variables) substituted for the per cent and the first and second numbers. The methods used to solve the formulas are identical to those of Example 1 above.

One such formula is used to find **per cent of change** (that is, per cent of increase or decrease). In words, the formula can be stated, "What per cent of the original number is the change?" In more abbreviated form it is

_____% of Original = Change?

Example Two

(a) What per cent more than 24 is 33?

1. *Original Number.* To have "more than 24" implies that we originally had 24; thus, 24 is the original number. In general, it can be said that the "original number" is the number that follows the words "more than" or "less than" in the stated problem.

2. *Change.* The "change" is the amount of increase or decrease that occurred. That is, the change is the numerical difference

**Example
Two
(cont.)**
between the two numbers in the problem. (The fact that it may be a negative difference is not important to this formula.) Thus, the change in this example is $33 - 24 = 9$.

$$\text{\_\_\_\_}\% \text{ of Original} = \text{Change}$$
$$\text{\_\_\_\_}\% \text{ of} \qquad 24 = 9$$
$$24x = 9$$
$$\frac{24x}{24} = \frac{9}{24}$$
$$x = \tfrac{3}{8}$$
$$x = 37\tfrac{1}{2}\%$$

Thus, 24, increased by $37\tfrac{1}{2}\%$ of itself, gives 33.

(b) 22 is what per cent less than 40?

Original $= 40$

Change $= 40 - 22$

$\qquad = 18$

$\text{\_\_\_\_}\%$ of Original $=$ Change

$40r = 18$

$\dfrac{40r}{40} = \dfrac{18}{40}$

$r = \tfrac{9}{20}$

$r = 45\%$

Thus, 40 decreased by 45% of itself is 22.

This formula is often applied to changes in the prices of merchandise or stocks and to changes in volume of business from one year to the next. Other applications include increase in cost of living or unemployment and decrease in expenses or net profit.

SECTION 2 *Problems*

Use equations to obtain the following solutions. Express per cent remainders either as fractions or rounded to tenths. (Example: $42\tfrac{6}{7}\%$ or 42.9%.)

1. 13% of 120 is what number?

2. 5% of 180 is what number?

3. $7\tfrac{1}{2}\%$ of 60 is what amount?

4. $4\tfrac{1}{2}\%$ of 80 is what amount?

$$14 \quad N\% \times 60 = \frac{45}{60}$$
$$\frac{60}{60} \quad N\% = .75$$
$$N = 79\%$$

5. 78% of 20 is how much?

6. 42% of 75 is how much?

7. How much is $\frac{1}{4}$% of 240?

8. How much is $\frac{3}{4}$% of 360?

9. What is $33\frac{1}{3}$% of 45?

10. What is $87\frac{1}{2}$% of 56?

11. 0.35% of 200 is what number?

12. 0.6% of 150 is what number?

13. What per cent of 48 is 32?

14. What per cent of 60 is 45?

15. What per cent of 32 is 48?

16. What per cent of 45 is 60?

17. What per cent of 150 is 93?

18. What per cent of 80 is 28?

19. 12 is what per cent of 27?

20. 20 is what per cent of 32?

21. 5.4 is what per cent of 180?

22. 6.6 is what per cent of 165?

23. 40 is what per cent of 32?

24. 72 is what per cent of 48?

25. 44% of what number is 33?

26. 84% of what number is 105?

27. 3% of what amount is 4.5?

28. 7% of what number is 16.8?

29. $42\frac{6}{7}$% of what number is 9?

30. $37\frac{1}{2}$% of what amount is 18?

31. 9 is $2\frac{1}{4}$% of what amount?

32. 21 is $3\frac{1}{2}$% of what number?

33. 27 is 135% of what number?

34. 78 is 195% of what amount?

35. 5.4 is 0.9% of what amount?

36. 4.5 is 0.6% of what number?

37. What per cent more than 24 is 36?

38. What per cent more than 60 is 75?

39. What per cent less than 36 is 24?

40. What per cent less than 75 is 60?

41. 63 is what per cent more than 45?

42. 46 is what per cent more than 40?

43. 32 is what per cent less than 50?

44. 36 is what per cent less than 75?

45. $54 is what per cent more than $42?

46. $55 is what per cent more than $40?

47. What per cent less than $600 is $597?

48. What per cent less than $750 is $747?

SECTION 3
Word Problems
Using Per Cents

Three primary types of per cent applications are illustrated by the following five examples. These types are:

1. The basic per cent equation form: ____% of ____ = ____ (Examples 1 and 2).

2. Finding *per cent* of change (increase or decrease), using ____% of Original = Change (Example 3).

(handwritten top margin)

(30.) $\dfrac{.375 \times n = 18}{.375} \quad \dfrac{}{.375}$

$n = 48$

3. Finding an *amount* that has been increased or decreased by a per cent of itself (Examples 4 and 5).

Example One

A direct-mail campaign by a magazine produced $16,000 in renewals and new subscriptions. If renewals totaled $10,000, what per cent of the subscriptions were renewals?

What per cent of subscriptions were renewals?

| ___% | × | $16,000 | = | $10,000 |

$16,000r \quad = \quad 10,000$

$\dfrac{16,000r}{16,000} = \dfrac{10,000}{16,000}$

$r \quad = \quad 0.625$

$\quad = \quad 62.5\%$

(handwritten)

$\dfrac{N \times 45 = 60}{45} \quad \dfrac{45}{4}$

$N = \dfrac{4}{3} 1.333$

$N = 133.33\%$

Example Two

Thirty-five per cent of a payment made to a partnership land purchase was tax deductible. If a partner receives a notice that he qualifies for a $700 tax deduction, how much was his total payment?

(handwritten) (30)

35% of payment was tax deduction

| 35% | × | p | = | $700 |

$0.35p \quad = \quad 700$

$\dfrac{0.35p}{0.35} = \dfrac{700.00}{0.35}$

$p \quad = \quad \$2,000$

(handwritten)

$\dfrac{N \times 80 = 28}{80} \quad \dfrac{}{80}$

$N = \dfrac{14}{40}$

$N = .35$

35%

$\dfrac{1}{8} = .125$

Example Three

Last year's sales were $45,000; sales for this year totaled $48,600. What was the per cent of increase in sales?

Original = $45,000   ___% of Original = Change?

Change = $48,600 − $45,000   ___% of $45,000 = $3,600

= $3,600 $45,000r = 3,600$

$\dfrac{45,000r}{45,000} = \dfrac{3,600}{45,000}$

$r = 0.08$

$r = 8\%$

(handwritten)

$\dfrac{6.6}{165} = \dfrac{N \times 165}{165}$

$.04 = N$

$4\% = N$

Example Four

What number decreased by 12% of itself gives 66?

What number	decreased by	(12% of itself)	gives	66?
n	—	$(0.12 \times n)$	=	66
n^*	—	$0.12n$	=	66
		$0.88n$	=	66
		$\dfrac{\cancel{0.88}n}{\cancel{0.88}}$	=	$\dfrac{66.00}{0.88}$
		n	=	75

Example Five

Labor expenses (wages) at a construction project increased by 10% this month. If wages totaled \$13,200 this month, how much were last month's wages?

Old wages	increased by	10% (of itself)	equals	new wages
w	+	$(10\% \times w)$	=	\$13,200
w	+	$0.1w$	=	13,200
		$\dfrac{1.1w}{1.1}$	=	$\dfrac{13,200.0}{1.1}$
		w	=	\$12,000

NOTE: Per cents are never used just by themselves. In an equation, any per cent that is included must be a per cent *of* ("times") some other number or variable.

For convenience, the following problems are divided into two parts, each of which covers all of the given examples. Part I covers the three types of problems in the same order as presented in the examples: (1) Examples 1 and 2, see Problems 1–14; (2) Example 3, see Problems 15–20; (3) Examples 4 and 5, see Problems 21–32. For those who need additional practice, Part II also covers each example, but with the order scrambled somewhat in order to provide practice in identifying each type.

*Recall that $n = 1n$; thus,

$$n - 0.12n = 1n - 0.12n$$
$$= 1.00n - 0.12n$$
$$= 0.88n$$

PART ONE

1. An agent charges $510 to sell a house. If the sale price was $17,000, what per cent of the total purchase price is the realtor's fee?

2. A stock that sold for $47.25 paid a dividend of $3.78. What per cent return did the stock pay?

3. A family with a monthly spendable income of $750 averages $135 monthly for automobile expenses (car payment, insurance, gasoline, repairs, etc.). What per cent of their income is spent for car expenses?

4. A printing firm with average monthly sales income of $15,000 budgets $1,800 for materials (paper and ink). What per cent of their sales is budgeted for materials?

5. A worker whose gross (before tax) wages were $600 finds that $30 was deducted for medical insurance. What per cent of the gross wages was the insurance premium?

6. Of the 75 drivers employed for at least 10 years by National Freight Express, there are 69 drivers who have never had an accident of any kind. What per cent of these experienced drivers have perfect safety records?

7. A construction company placed a bid of $750,000 for a college building. If they expected $8\frac{1}{3}$% of the bid to be net profit, how much net profit does the construction company hope to make on the building?

8. Self-employed people paid 7.9% of their income for Social Security. How much was the Social Security payment on an income of $12,000?

9. Twenty per cent of graduates at a high school went to college the fall following graduation. If 55 people entered college, how many graduates were there?

10. The fee charged by a professional collection agency is $33\frac{1}{3}$% of the payments collected. If the agency's earnings are $5,200, how much has the firm collected?

11. The gross profit made on a pair of men's shoes was 15% of the cost. What had the shoes cost, if the gross profit was $3.30?

12. Inventory represents 65% of a discount store's total assets. What are the total assets of the firm, if the inventory is valued at $195,000?

13. A homeowner pays 1.45% of the assessed value of his home for property taxes. If his taxes were $174, what is the assessed value of his home?

14. A stock purchase includes $35 for the broker's fee, which is computed at 2.5% of the stocks' value. What was the value of the stocks?

15. During a clearance sale, the price of a dress was dropped from $36 to $27. What per cent reduction can the store advertise?

16. A house that cost $56,000 several years ago is now appraised at $70,000. By what per cent has the house appreciated (increased in value)?

17. Construction costs have risen so that a building which could have been built for $64,000 two years ago would now cost $72,000 to construct. What per cent rise in cost does this represent?

18. The depreciation schedule for a knitting machine shows $2,500 as last year's value and $1,750 as the current value. What per cent decrease in value does this represent?

19. After an efficiency study, office expenses were reduced from $5,000 per month to $4,250 per month. What per cent savings were realized?

20. The cost-of-living index reveals that a standard market basket of food which cost $20 last year now costs $22.80 for the same items. What is the per cent increase in food costs?

21. What number increased by 40% of itself gives 49?

22. What number increased by $62\frac{1}{2}$% of itself yields 91?

23. What selling price reduced by 24% of itself yields $38?

24. What expense decreased by 36% of itself gives $1,600?

25. The cost of a lamp was increased by 15% of itself to get the selling price. What was the cost of the lamp, if the selling price was $23?

26. The cost of a bicycle was increased by 45% of itself to obtain the selling price. If the bicycle sold for $116, what was the dealer's cost?

27. After installing new equipment, the cost of manufacturing a machine was reduced by 10% of itself. If the new cost of manufacturing the machine is $144, what was the previous cost?

28. The sales quota required to qualify for a bonus was reduced by 6% of itself. What was the previous quota, if the revised quota is $235,000?

29. This year's sales are 13% more than last year's sales. If the current sales are $452,000, what were last year's sales?

30. The value of a certain stock dropped 16% last year, ending at $63. What was the value at the beginning of the year?

31. During a clearance sale, the regular price of a set of tires was reduced by 30%. What was the regular price, if the sale price of the tires was $112?

32. Within the past 5 years, the average selling price of a new car has increased by 40%. What was the average buyer paying then, if $4,200 is the current price?

PART TWO

33. Forty-two per cent of the workers in a plant took their vacations during July. If 63 employees took July vacations, how many people are employed at the plant?

34. Fifty-six per cent of a distributor's representatives met their sales quotas. How many representatives does the company employ if 84 people met their quotas?

35. Thirty-eight per cent of a firm's sales income is required to pay its overhead expenses (salaries, office supplies, utilities, etc.). If these overhead expenses totaled $22,800, how much were the company's sales?

36. Twenty-four per cent of an employee's gross wages were withheld for income tax, Social Security, and group insurance. How much were the gross wages, if $156 was deducted?

37. Following a 25% reduction in price, a cookware set was sold for $36. What was the regular price of the set?

38. The number of union employees at an electronics plant has increased by 20% during the past year. If the union now has 360 members, how many employees belonged to the union a year ago?

39. A 30% increase in the projected cost of opening a Mexican restaurant ran the total cost to $52,000. What was the original cost that had been budgeted?

40. After a 35% reduction in price, an office calculator sold for $156. What was the regular price of the calculator?

41. The value of a store's inventory increased from $30,000 to $32,400 during one 6-month period. What per cent rise in value did this represent?

42. The average price paid for a new home has increased from $30,000 to $42,000. By what per cent has the purchase price increased?

43. Over the years, the typical cost of a long distance telephone call has decreased from $3.50 to $1.75. What per cent decrease does this represent?

44. The number of building permits issued during June dropped from 360 in one year to 288 the following year. What per cent decrease in permits did this represent?

45. The salesman's commission on sales of $1,850 amounted to $148. What per cent of his sales was the commission?

46. The real estate agency's fee on the sale of a $125,000 building was $7,500. What per cent of the purchase price was the fee?

47. A gross profit of $160 was made on a sale of $480. What per cent of selling price was the gross profit?

48. The balance sheet of a pharmacy shows total assets of $225,000 and indicates that the owner's net worth is $90,000. What per cent of the total assets is the net worth?

SECTION 4
Aliquot Parts

A number that can be divided evenly (with no remainder) into another number is an **aliquot part** of that second number. Thus, 3 is an aliquot part of 6 (because it divides into 6 exactly 2 times); 5 is an aliquot part of 15 (divides into 15 exactly 3 times); $8\frac{1}{3}$ is an aliquot part of 25 (divides into 25 exactly 3 times); and $12\frac{1}{2}$ is an aliquot part of 100 (divides into 100 exactly 8 times).

For business applications, the aliquot parts of $1 and of 100 are particularly useful. The following table lists some of the most frequently used aliquot parts of 100% and their multiples. The student should be certain to memorize all of these equivalents, for they will prove extremely useful in future chapters, as well as in this section.

The advantage of using aliquot parts is that it permits the substitution of fractions for their decimal equivalents—a substitution that usually proves to be a significant time-saver as well.

Per Cent Equivalents of Common Fractions

The following per cents (many with fractional remainders) will be given in many problems so that students without calculating machines can conveniently use the exact fractional equivalents. (Students using calculators may also use the fractional equivalents by entering the numerators and denominators separately.)

$\frac{1}{2} = 50\%$

$\frac{1}{3} = 33\frac{1}{3}\%$ $\frac{2}{3} = 66\frac{2}{3}\%$

$\frac{1}{4} = 25\%$ $\frac{3}{4} = 75\%$

$\frac{1}{5} = 20\%$ $\frac{2}{5} = 40\%$ $\frac{3}{5} = 60\%$ $\frac{4}{5} = 80\%$

$\frac{1}{6} = 16\frac{2}{3}\%$ $\frac{5}{6} = 83\frac{1}{3}\%$

$\frac{1}{7} = 14\frac{2}{7}\%$ $\frac{2}{7} = 28\frac{4}{7}\%$ $\frac{3}{7} = 42\frac{6}{7}\%$

$\frac{1}{8} = 12\frac{1}{2}\%$ $\frac{3}{8} = 37\frac{1}{2}\%$ $\frac{5}{8} = 62\frac{1}{2}\%$ $\frac{7}{8} = 87\frac{1}{2}\%$

$\frac{1}{9} = 11\frac{1}{9}\%$ $\frac{2}{9} = 22\frac{2}{9}\%$ $\frac{4}{9} = 44\frac{4}{9}\%$ $\frac{5}{9} = 55\frac{5}{9}\%$

$\frac{1}{10} = 10\%$ $\frac{3}{10} = 30\%$ $\frac{7}{10} = 70\%$ $\frac{9}{10} = 90\%$

$\frac{1}{12} = 8\frac{1}{3}\%$

Example One

(a) Multiply 256 by \$.25.

$$\$.25 = \tfrac{1}{4} \text{ of } \$1 \quad \text{or} \quad \$\tfrac{1}{4}$$

Thus,

$$256 \times \$.25 = 256 \times \$\tfrac{1}{4}$$
$$= \$64$$

This can be computed in much less time than the standard multiplication of $256 \times \$.25$.

(b) Price 72 items at $\$.62\frac{1}{2}$. Since

$$\$.62\tfrac{1}{2} = \$\tfrac{5}{8}$$

Then

$$72 \times .62\tfrac{1}{2} = 72 \times \$\tfrac{5}{8}$$
$$= \overset{9}{\cancel{72}} \times \tfrac{5}{\cancel{8}}$$
$$= \$45$$

Sometimes it is more convenient to consider the number of items purchased as an aliquot of 100 items—that is, to price 100 items and then find the fractional part of that price.

Example Two   (a) Price 75 items at $.48.

$$75 \text{ items} = \tfrac{3}{4} \text{ of } 100 \text{ items}$$

Thus,

$$75 \times \$.48 = (\tfrac{3}{4} \text{ of } 100) \times \$.48$$

$$= \tfrac{3}{4} \times (100 \times .48)$$

$$= \tfrac{3}{4} \times \$48$$

$$= \tfrac{3}{\cancel{4}} \times \cancel{48}^{\,12}$$

$$= \$36$$

(b) What is the price of 40 items at $2.35?

$$40 \text{ items} = \tfrac{2}{5} \times 100 \text{ items}$$

$$40 \times \$2.35 = \tfrac{2}{5} \times 100 \times \$2.35$$

$$= \tfrac{2}{5} \times \$235$$

$$= \$94$$

SECTION 4 *Problems*

Price the following items.

1. 672 at $37\frac{1}{2}$¢
2. 356 at 25¢
3. 182 at $28\frac{4}{7}$¢

4. 228 at $33\frac{1}{3}$¢
5. 36 at $.75
6. 63 at $.55\frac{5}{9}$

7. 72 at $8\frac{1}{3}$¢
8. 48 at $.62\frac{1}{2}$
9. 168 at $.12\frac{1}{2}$

10. 462 at $66\frac{2}{3}$¢
11. 216 at $44\frac{4}{9}$¢
12. 128 at $.87\frac{1}{2}$

13. 120 at 30¢
14. 56 at $.42\frac{6}{7}$
15. 64 at $.62\frac{1}{2}$

16. 45 at $22\frac{2}{9}$¢
17. 152 at $87\frac{1}{2}$¢
18. 84 at $.14\frac{2}{7}$

19. 45 at $.33\frac{1}{3}$
20. 174 at $83\frac{1}{3}$¢
21. 10 at $1.80

22. 25 at $1.76
23. 50 at 48¢
24. 20 at $2.35

25. 25 at $2.16
26. 75 at 96¢
27. 20 at 85¢

28. 80 at $1.65
29. 75 at $1.28
30. 60 at 55¢

SUMMARY OF CONVERSIONS

GIVEN:	TO CONVERT TO:	
Per Cents	*A. Decimal*	*B. Fraction*
• Basic % (1% to 99%)	Basic per cents become the first two (hundredths) decimal places. (Other digits align accordingly.) Example: 76% = 76 hundredths = 0.76.	Per cent sign is dropped and given number is placed over a denominator of 100; reduce. Example: 76% = 76 hundredths = $\frac{76}{100} = \frac{19}{25}$.
• Decimal % (125.73%; 0.45%)	Digits representing per cents greater than 99% or less than 1% are aligned around the first two (hundredths) decimal places (see also "Basic Per Cents"). Example: 0.45% = 0.0045.	Convert the per cent to a decimal (as indicated at left). Pronounce the decimal value; then write this as a fraction and reduce. Example: 0.45% = 0.0045 = 45 ten-thousandths = $\frac{45}{10,000} = \frac{9}{2,000}$.
• Fractional % ($\frac{1}{4}$%; $\frac{7}{5}$%; $1\frac{2}{3}$%)	Convert the fractional per cent to a decimal per cent (by dividing the numerator by the denominator). Then convert this decimal per cent to an ordinary decimal (as shown above). Example: $\frac{7}{5}$% = 1.4% = 0.014.	Per cent sign is replaced by $\frac{1}{100}$; multiply and reduce. Example: $\frac{7}{5}$% = $\frac{7}{5} \times \frac{1}{100} = \frac{7}{500}$.

TO CONVERT TO PER CENT

C. Decimals (0.473; 1.2; 0.0015)	Isolate the first two (hundredths) decimal places to identify the basic per cents (1% to 99%). Other per cents will then be aligned correctly. Example: 0.473 = 0.⟨47⟩3 = 47.3%.
D. Fractions ($\frac{2}{9}$; $\frac{7}{3}$; $1\frac{1}{2}$)	Convert the fraction to a decimal (by dividing the numerator by the denominator. Then follow the above procedure for converting a decimal to per cent. Example: $\frac{2}{9}$ = $0.22\frac{2}{9}$ = $0.⟨22⟩\frac{2}{9}$ = $22\frac{2}{9}$%.

Aliquot part. For business purposes, an exact fractional part of 100 or of $1. (More strictly, any amount—either whole or fractional—which exactly divides into another number.)

Base. The number that a per cent multiplies; the first number in the basic per cent equation form. (The base represents 100%.)

Hundredths. Equals per cent; a value associated with the first two decimal places or with a common fraction having a denominator of 100.

Per cent. Means hundredths; indicates a common fraction with a denominator of 100 or a decimal fraction of two decimal places.

Percentage. A part of the base (a number or an amount) that is determined by multiplying the given per cent (rate) times the base.

Per cent equation form. The basic equation, ____% of ____ = ____; in words, What % of a first number (base) is a second number (percentage)?

Per cent of change. The equation, ____% of Original = Change; a variation of the basic equation form, used to find a per cent of increase or decrease.

Rate. The per cent that multiplies a base. See the figure below.

Example: 25% of 60 = 15.

Base

Base = 60

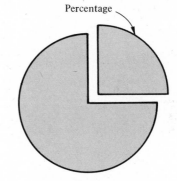

Percentage

Rate = 25%
Percentage = 15

PART

II

Accounting

Mathematics

CHAPTER 4

Basic Statistics
and Graphs

CHAPTER 4 OBJECTIVES

Upon completion of Chapter 4, the student will be able to:

1. Define and use correctly the terminology associated with each topic.
2. Compute the three simple averages—mean, median, and mode.
   (Section 1; Examples 1–7; Problems 1–18)
3. Use a frequency distribution to determine mean, median, and modal class for grouped data *(Section 2; Examples 1, 2; Problems 1–8).*
4. Using data that assume a normal curve distribution *(Section 3)*:
   a. Determine the per cents associated with various combinations of intervals $\pm 1\sigma$, $\pm 2\sigma$, and $\pm 3\sigma$ *(Example 1; Problems 1–14)*;
   b. Compute standard deviation for ungrouped data, using the formula

$$\sigma = \sqrt{\frac{\sum d^2}{n}}$$

   (Example 2; Problems 5–14).
5. Interpret index numbers and compute simple price relatives.
   (Section 4; Examples, 1, 2; Problems 1–6)
6. Construct the common types of graphs—bar, line, picture, and circle graphs. *(Section 5; Examples 1–4; Problems 1–16).*

4 Decisions about what course a business may take are rarely made without first consulting records indicating what past experience has been. When numerical records are involved, these data must be organized before they can present meaningful information. The process of collecting, organizing, tabulating, and interpreting numerical data is called **statistics**. The information presented as a result of this process is also known, collectively, as **statistics**. Statistics are invaluable to business in making comparisons, indicating trends, and analyzing facts affecting operations, production, profits, and so forth. However, the significance of statistics can often be realized more easily when the information is displayed in graph form. Thus, graphs are an integral part of statistics.

SECTION 1
Averages

If one attempted to analyze a large group of numbers simultaneously, it would usually be impossible to obtain much useful information. Thus, it is customary to condense such a group into a single number representative of the entire group. This representative number is generally some central value around which the other numbers seem to cluster; for this reason, it is called a **measure of central tendency** or an **average.** The three most common averages are the **arithmetic mean** (or just the "mean"), the **median**, and the **mode**, all of which we will consider briefly.

Mean

The **arithmetic mean** is the common average with which the student is already familiar. It is the average referred to in everyday expressions about average temperature, average cost, the average grade on a quiz, average age, and so on. The mean is found by adding the various numbers and dividing this sum by the number of items.

Example One

The five departments at Smith Sporting Goods made sales of the following amounts: A, $1,050; B, $1,200; C, $1,350; D, $1,800; E, $1,500. What were the average (mean) sales per department?

$$\frac{\$1,050 + \$1,200 + \$1,350 + \$1,800 + \$1,500}{5} = \frac{\$6,900}{5} = \$1,380$$

The mean sales per department were $1,380. Notice that there was not a single department which had sales of exactly $1,380. It is quite common for the "average" of a group of numbers to be a value not actually contained in the group. However, this mean is still representative of the entire group in that it is similar to most of the values in the group—some are somewhat larger and others somewhat smaller.

Further observe that if each department above had made sales of $1,380, the total sales would also have been $6,900. This kind of observation applies to any situation in which an arithmetic mean is utilized.

Weighted Mean   The ordinary mean will present a true picture only if the data involved are of equal importance. If they are not, a weighted mean is needed. A **weighted arithmetic mean** is found by "weighting" or multiplying each number according to its importance. These products are then added and that sum is divided by the total number of weights.

A weighted average of particular importance to students is the **grade-point average:**

Example Two   Listed below are Carol Dickerson's course credit and term grades for the spring quarter at West Ridge Community College. Each A carries 4 quality points; a B, 3 points; a C, 2 points; and a D, 1 point. Compute Carol's grade-point average (average per credit hour) for the quarter.

Credit Hours	Final Grade	Quality Points
4	A	4
3	C	2
3	B	3
3	C	2
2	C	2

If we simply computed the average of Carol's quality points

$$\left(\frac{4+2+3+2+2}{5} = \frac{13}{5} = 2.6\right)$$

the result would be misleading because her courses are not of equal importance from a credit standpoint. We must therefore weight the quality points for each course according to the number of credit hours

Example Two (cont.) each course carries:

Credit Hours		Quality Points		
4	×	4	=	16
3	×	2	=	6
3	×	3	=	9
3	×	2	=	6
+ 2	×	2	=	4
15				41

$$\tfrac{41}{15} = 2.733\ldots = 2.73$$

Carol's grade-point average for the quarter is thus 2.73. This is somewhat better than the 2.6 obtained by the ordinary averaging method.

Example Three The same model of microwave oven is available from several appliance stores. Prices and number of ovens sold are shown below. What is (a) the average price per store and (b) the average price per oven sold?

Store	Number Sold	Price
1	40	$450
2	60	400
3	120	350
4	80	375

It may help to first analyze the question. The word "per" indicates the division line of a fraction. The word following "per" tells which total number of objects to divide by. Hence, average price "per store" is found by dividing by the total number of stores; and average price "per oven" is found by dividing by the total number of ovens:

Solution (a) Average price per store = $\dfrac{\text{Sum of prices at all stores}}{\text{Total numbers of stores}}$

$$\frac{\$450 + \$400 + \$350 + \$375}{4} = \frac{\$1{,}575}{4}$$

$$= \$393.75 \quad \text{(average price per store)}$$

(b) Average price per oven = $\dfrac{\text{Sum of prices of all ovens}}{\text{Total number of ovens}}$

Example
Three
(cont.)
For this average, the various prices must be weighted according to the number of ovens sold at each price.

Number	Price	
40 ×	$450	= $ 18,000
60 ×	400	= 24,000
120 ×	350	= 42,000
+ 80 ×	375	30,000
300		$114,000

$$\frac{\$114,000}{300} = \$380 \quad \text{Average price per oven}$$

Example
Four
David Cohen invested $5,000 in a business on January 1. On May 1, he withdrew $200; on July 1, he reinvested $1,000; and on August 1, he invested another $1,400. What was his average investment during the year?

$$\text{Average investment} = \frac{\text{Sum of investments of all months}}{\text{Total number of months}}$$

Before we can find the average investment, we must first determine the new balance after each change. Each succeeding balance must then be multiplied (weighted) by the number of months it remained invested.

Date	Change	Amount of Investment	Months Invested	
January 1		$5,000 ×	4	= $20,000
May 1	− $200	4,800 ×	2	= 9,600
July 1	+ 1,000	5,800 ×	1	= 5,800
August 1	+ 1,400	7,200 ×	5	= 36,000
			12	$71,400

$$\frac{\$71,400}{12} = \$5,950 \quad \text{Average investment}$$

Median

Even when a group of numbers are of equal importance, the arithmetic mean may not convey an accurate description if the group contains a few values which differ greatly from the others. In such a case, the median may be the better average (or measure of central tendency). The **median** is the midpoint (or middle number) of a group of numbers. The median separates the group into two groups of equal size—one containing all the values larger than the median and the other containing all the values smaller than the median.

In order to find the median, we must arrange the numbers in order of size (such an arrangement is called an **ordered array**). If the group contains an odd number of entries, the median is the exact middle number. It may be determined quickly by dividing the number of entries by 2: the whole number next larger than the quotient indicates the position held by the median when the numbers are ordered in a series from smallest to largest.

When a group contains an even number of values, the median is also found by dividing the number of entries by 2: the median is then the arithmetic mean (average) between the number in this position and the next number when the numbers are ordered smallest to largest.

Example Five

The Wingate Insurance Agency has seven agents with the following respective years of experience: 5, 3, 22, 8, 6, 10, and 30. What is the median years' experience of these agents?

Notice that in this case the mean years of experience

$$\left(\frac{5+3+22+8+6+10+30}{7}=\frac{84}{7}=12 \text{ years}\right)$$

does not give a very good description, since only two of the seven agents have had at least that much experience.

Since there are seven numbers in the group,
divide 7 by 2: $\frac{7}{2}=3+$;

the median is the next, or fourth number when the numbers are arranged in order of size. Hence, in the series 3, 5, 6, 8, 10, 22, 30, the median is 8 years of experience.

Example Six

Wilcox & Co., a clothing store, employs six people (including Mr. Wilcox). Their monthly salaries are $640, $750, $560, $800, $850, and

Example Six (Cont.) $1,800. What is the median salary at the store?

$1,800
  850
  800⎤
  750⎦
  640
  560

Since there are six employees, there is no exact middle number. The median is the arithmetic mean of the third ($\frac{6}{2} = 3$) and fourth salaries:

$$\frac{\$800 + \$750}{2} = \frac{\$1,550}{2} = \$775$$

The median salary is $775. (The mean salary, however, is $900.)

A major difference between the mean and the median is that all the given values have an influence on the mean, whereas the median is determined basically by position. The median is often an appropriate measure of central tendency where the items can be ranked. However, if the number of items is quite large, it may be difficult to prepare the array necessary for determining the median. An alternative measure sometimes used in such circumstances is the **modified mean**, which is computed in the usual manner after the extremely high and low score(s) have been deleted. If each highest and lowest score was deleted from Examples 5 and 6, the modified means would be 10 years of experience and $760 per month, both of which are much nearer to the median scores than were the ordinary means.

Mode

The **mode** of a group of numbers is the value (or values) that occurs most frequently. If all of the values in a group are different, there is no mode. A set of numbers may have two or more modes when these all occur an equal number of times (and more often than the other values).

The mode may be quite different from the mean and the median, and it does not necessarily indicate anything about the quality of the group. Like the median, the mode is not influenced by all of the given values, and it may be very erratic. Unlike the other averages, however, the mode always represents actual items from the given data. The mode's principal application to business, from a production or sales standpoint, is in indicating the most popular items.

Example Seven The employees of Noland Construction Co. worked the following numbers of hours last week: 40, 48, 25, 36, 43, 48, 45, 60, 52, 43, 56, 54, 48, 33, and 53. What is the modal number of hours worked?

The total number of hours worked, arranged in order, are

60
56
54
53
52
48 ⎫
48 ⎬ There are three employees who worked
48 ⎭ exactly 48 hours last week; hence, 48
45 is the mode. If there were only two
43 employees with 48-hour weeks, then 48
43 and 43 would both be modes, since these
40 numbers would each be worked
36 by two employees.
33
25

SECTION 1 *Problems*

Find (1) *the arithmetic mean*, (2) *the median, and* (3) *the mode for each of the following groups of numbers.*

1. (a) $85, $106, $94, $110, $90, $98, $112, $105
    (b) 1,100, 1,450, 1,350, 1,500, 1,450, 250, 1,350, 1,600, 300, 1,350, 1,500, 1,450, 1,600

2. (a) 78, 37, 53, 46, 64, 53, 66, 48, 53, 49, 69
    (b) $110, $98, $85, $125, $107, $76, $114, $85, $112, $122, $109, $93

3. The credit hours and final grades for Ed Rothman's five courses are listed below. He has earned 4 quality points for each A, 3 points for a B, 2 points for a C, and 1 point for a D.

(a) What are Ed's average (mean) quality points per class?
(b) What is his quality-point average for the semester (average per credit hour)?

Credit Hours	Grade
5	A
3	C
4	C
2	B
1	C

4. Phil Preston has attained the scores listed below in his five classes, each of

which carries the number of credit hours indicated.

(a) What is his average (mean) score per course?

(b) What is his mean score per credit hour?

Credit Hours	Grade
3	90
2	95
4	80
3	84
3	86

5. The Super Drug Store carries eight brands of toothpaste. The price per tube (family size) and number of tubes sold last month are given below.

(a) What was the mean price per brand?

(b) What was the average price per tube sold?

Brand	Tubes Sold	Price
S	60	95¢
T	90	89
U	100	88
V	75	90
W	40	95
X (sale)	400	50
Y	120	85
Z	50	98

6. The same style of shoes is sold by several different stores at the prices shown below.

(a) What is the average price per store?

(b) What is the mean price per pair sold?

Store Number	Pairs Sold	Price
1	20	$25.00
2	60	22.50
3	15	28.00
4	14	27.50
5	10	30.00
6	20	26.00

7. The McNulty Furniture store employs 10 persons, whose positions and salaries are listed below.

(a) Compute the mean wage per position.

(b) What is the mean wage per person?

Position	Number in Position	Weekly Salary
Manager	1	$500
Salespeople	5	200
Delivery/ maintenance	2	110
Bookkeeper	2	150

8. The Food-Way Market employs 15 people in the positions and at the wages shown below.

(a) What is the mean wage per job?

(b) What is the mean wage per employee?

Job	Number in Job	Weekly Wages
Manager	1	$250
Cashiers	5	125
Department heads	3	175
Stock/ carryout	4	100
Office	2	135

9. Sam Winters invested $7,500 when he entered a partnership on January 1. On March 1, he withdrew $900. He reinvested $1,500 on August 1, but then he withdrew $300 on September 1. No other changes occurred until the end of the year. Find Winters' average (mean) investment during the year.

10. Mary Davis entered a partnership on January 1 with an investment of $4,500. On March 1, she invested another $500 and on June 1 she added $1,300. On October 1, she withdrew $400. Her investment then remained unchanged until the end of the year. What was Davis' mean investment for the year?

11. Last week's total sales at the five branches of Richmond's were as follows: $35,700, $25,600, $72,800, $38,400, and $29,200. What was the median sales figure for the Richmond's stores?

12. Chiles Decorators & Upholstery employs 10 people at the following monthly wages: $450, $525, $475, $1,250, $600, $850, $575, $525, $1,400, and $525. What is the median monthly wage?

13. Employees at Empire Corp. work on production. The women sewing pockets completed the following numbers last week: 1,600, 1,580, 1,640, 1,580, 1,620, 1,640, 1,560, 1,640, 1,620, and 1,580. What was the modal number of pockets sewn?

14. The 15 departments of Eastern Tool &

Dye Co. have safety records extending for the following number of weeks: 16, 23, 44, 13, 4, 23, 32, 28, 18, 36, 32, 21, 23, 40, and 27. What is the modal number of weeks without an accident?

15. The Smart Shop sold 12 dresses yesterday. The sales were $15, $18, $12, $20, $18, $60, $25, $20, $75, $18, $40, and $15. What was
(a) The mean?
(b) The median price per dress?
(c) Which price dress was most popular? (That is, what was the mode?)

16. Campus Casuals sold eight sweaters at the following prices: $25, $18, $30, $22, $25, $15, $25, and $22. Determine, for these prices:
(a) The arithmetic mean.
(b) The median.
(c) The mode.

17. The seven accountants in the Richfield Bank have had the following years of experience: 7, 4, 18, 24, 18, 6, and 10. Find, for these years of experience:
(a) The mean.
(b) The median.
(c) The mode.

18. The Insurance Exchange employs 13 agents whose ages are as follows: 47, 35, 28, 25, 33, 59, 33, 28, 48, 54, 63, 28, and 39. Compute, for these ages:
(a) The mean.
(b) The median.
(c) The mode.

SECTION 2
Averages
(Grouped Data)

Business statistics often involve hundreds or thousands of values. If a computer is not available, it would be extremely time-consuming to arrange each value in an array. It is easier to handle large numbers of values by organizing them into groups (or **classes**). The difference between the lower limit of one class and the lower limit of the next class is the **interval** of the class. (All classes of a problem usually have the same-sized interval.) Each class is handled by first determining the number of values within the class (the **frequency**) and then using the **midpoint** of the class as a basis for calculation. The end result of this classification and tabulation is called a **frequency distribution**.

The first step in making a frequency distribution is to decide what the class intervals shall be. For the sake of convenience, the intervals are usually round numbers. A tally is then made as each given value is classified; the total tally in each class is the frequency f of the class. After the midpoint of each class is computed, the frequency is multiplied by the midpoint value to obtain the final column of the frequency distribution.

Example One   Lady Fair Mills is a textile firm producing ladies' lingerie. Using a frequency distribution, determine (a) the mean and (b) the median number of garments processed last week in the sewing department. Production (in dozens) was as follows:

368	363	352	333
340	347	380	321
386	342	308	357
320	382	341	374
355	335	364	391
372	325	378	348

The smallest number is 308 and the largest is 391; thus, a table from 300 to 400 will include all entries. The difference between the upper and lower limits $(400 - 300)$ gives a **range** of 100. We can conveniently divide this range into 5 classes.* Since $\frac{100}{5} = 20$, each class interval will be 20.

Class Intervals	Tally	f	Midpoint	$f \times$ Midpoint
380–399	IIII	4	390	1,560
360–379	HHT I	6	370	2,220
340–359	HHT III	8	350	2,800
320–339	HHT	5	330	1,650
300–319	I	+ 1	310	+ 310
		24		8,540

*The choice of 5 classes is optional. Four classes with an interval of $\frac{100}{4} = 25$ could be chosen, as could 10 classes with an interval of $\frac{100}{10} = 10$.

Example One (cont.)   The midpoint of each interval is the arithmetic mean of the lower limit of that class and the lower limit of the next class.

$$\left(\text{Example:} \quad \frac{320+340}{2} = \frac{660}{2} = 330.\right)$$

Solution   (a) The arithmetic mean of the frequency distribution is found by dividing the $f \times$ midpoint total by the total number of items (the frequency total). Thus,

$$\frac{8,540}{24} = 355\tfrac{5}{6} \quad \text{or} \quad 356$$

The mean production in the sewing department was 356 dozen garments, to the nearest whole dozen.

The *median for grouped data* is found as follows:

Median for Grouped Data

1. Divide the total number of items (total frequency) by 2. This quotient represents the position which the median holds in the tally.

2. Counting from the smallest number, find the class where this item is located, and determine how many values within this class must be counted to reach this position.

3. Using the number of values that must be counted (step 2) as a numerator, and the *total* number within the class as a denominator, form a fraction to be multiplied times the class interval.

4. Add this result to the lower limit of the interval to arrive at the median.

Example One (cont.)   (b) The median for this example is thus determined as follows:

1. $\frac{24}{2} = 12$: we are concerned with the twelfth item from the bottom.

2. The bottom classes contain only $1+5=6$ items. We must therefore include 6 more items from the class 340–359.

3. There are 8 values in the class, and the class interval is 20. Hence,

$$\tfrac{6}{8} \times 20 = \tfrac{3}{4} \times 20$$

$$= 15$$

4. $340 + 15 = 355$.

The median of 355 is thus the dividing point where half of the employees obtained higher production and half had lower.

As a point of interest, compare the mean and median for the preceding example when the data are computed individually (without a frequency distribution). The mean is then 353.4 (as compared to the grouped data mean of 356) and the median is 353.5 (compared to the 355 obtained using a frequency distribution). The differences between these means and medians are small, even though we used a small number of items (24). For large numbers of items, the results obtained by the individual and by the grouped-data methods are almost identical.

Since a frequency distribution does not contain individual values, there is no single mode. However, the distribution may contain a *modal class* (the class containing the largest number of frequencies). The class interval 340–359 is the modal class of Example 1. This indicates that the most common production was between 340 and 359 dozen garments.

Example Two   What is the median production if a frequency distribution contains 25 items and is distributed at follows?

Class Intervals	f
2,000–2,399	3
1,600–1,999	4
1,200–1,599	10
800–1,199	7
400– 799	+ 1
	25

The steps for solution (see preceding rules) are as follows:

1. $\tfrac{25}{2} = 12.5$; we must locate the class containing the imaginary item numbered 12.5.

Example Two (Cont.)

2. The two bottom classes contain only $1 + 7 = 8$ entries. Thus 12.5 is in the next class, 1,200–1,599, and 4.5 more values from this class complete the required 12.5.

3. The class 1,200–1,599 contains 10 items and the interval is 400. Thus,

$$\frac{4.5}{10} \times 400 = 4.5 \times 40$$
$$= 180$$

4. The median production is $1,200 + 180 = 1,380$ pieces.

NOTE: The median can also be found by counting *down from the top* to the required item, multiplying the obtained fraction times the interval in the usual manner, and then *subtracting* this product from the *lower limit* of the adjacent class. For example, since the top two classes in Example 2 contain $3 + 4 = 7$ items, 5.5 more values from class 1,200–1,599 must be included. Now, $\frac{5.5}{10} \times 400 = 220$; and $1,600 - 220$ gives 1,380, as before.

SECTION 2 *Problems*

Use a frequency distribution to determine (a) the mean, (b) the median, and (c) the modal class for the following sets of data.

1. Use intervals of 0–19, 20–39, etc.

67	14	53	46	70	28
23	62	39	61	87	34
35	78	80	64	52	49

2. Use intervals of $50–$149, $150–$249, etc.

$275	$195	$240	$420	$385
160	425	295	335	405
330	345	380	365	75
215	60	115	150	430

3. Use intervals of $50, starting with $400.

$625	$420	$675	$615	$490	$470
580	435	530	465	595	495
465	565	405	540	485	440
515	480	500	680	565	515

4. Use intervals of 10, starting with 50.

75	94	78	64	71
88	71	84	75	63
62	69	60	85	59
80	53	57	95	68
78	83	98	67	82
77	79	76	65	74

5. The 30 sales representatives of Allied Business Machines are the ages listed below. Make a frequency distribution using intervals of 5 years (starting with 20 years), and determine (a) the mean, (b) the median, and (c) the most typical (modal) age group.

33	59	42	24	27	31
45	38	42	30	41	26
27	35	63	35	40	60
38	29	56	25	23	57
29	40	32	39	48	46

6. Bradford Laboratories employs 24 lab technicians whose years of experience are listed below. Use 3-year intervals in completing a frequency distribution, and compute (a) the mean, (b) the median, and (c) the most common interval (modal class) of experience.

8	10	14	6	13	4
18	5	2	0	6	2
3	9	4	19	22	8
11	6	10	7	3	12

7. The agents of McMann Insurance Agency sold policies last week in the amounts listed below. Use intervals of $10,000, starting with the lowest amount, in order to determine (a) the mean, (b) the median, and (c) the most common policy bracket (modal class).

$25,000	$55,500	$18,000	$50,000	$55,000
37,500	62,500	22,500	17,500	42,500
58,000	40,000	48,000	75,000	64,000
45,500	15,000	35,000	57,500	37,500
20,000	32,000	67,500	28,000	30,000

8. The 25 employees of Phillips Industries earn the annual salaries given below. Prepare a frequency distribution with $1,200 intervals, starting with the lowest amount. Compute (a) the mean, (b) the median, and (c) the most common salary bracket (modal class).

$ 9,600	$ 8,500	$ 7,200	$ 6,200	$ 9,000
6,800	8,200	6,500	7,500	12,800
12,500	10,500	9,800	6,000	8,000
7,400	13,100	8,600	7,000	7,100
7,000	9,200	12,400	7,800	6,900

SECTION 3
Standard
Deviation

Measures of central tendency—the arithmetic mean, median, and mode—are used to identify some typical value(s) around which the other values cluster. It is frequently also helpful to know something about how spread out the data are: Are many (or most) of the given amounts close in value to the measure of central tendency? Or do the amounts scatter out without concentrating near any particular value? To provide some indication of this scatteredness (or **variability**), we compute **measures of dispersion**. One simple measure of dispersion which has already been mentioned is the **range**—the difference between the upper and lower limits of a frequency distribution or between the highest and lowest values in a group of numbers. Probably the most widely used measure of dispersion is the **standard deviation**, which we will briefly consider.

The tally column of a frequency distribution provides a visual illustration of the central tendency and of the dispersion of a set of data. If a tally column were turned sideways and a smooth line drawn outlining the tallies, we could obtain a simple graph of the data, as shown in Figure 1. This example—with a heavy concentration of values in the middle and quickly tapering off symmetrically on both sides—is typical of the distribution for many sets of data. For example, the graphs of many human characteristics (such as height, weight, intelligence, athletic ability) would form such a graph, with most people obtaining some average, central score and those with higher and lower scores distributed evenly on both sides. Many sets of business-related data would also form a similar graph. For example, on quality-control tests of the chemical content of a medicine or on tests of the sizing accuracy of a mechanical part, most test results would match the desired standard, and variations higher and lower should taper off quickly. In business and industry, however, it is vital to know exactly how much variation exists.

When statistical data are collected on large groups of people who are typical of the entire population (rather than just some specialized group),

FIGURE 1

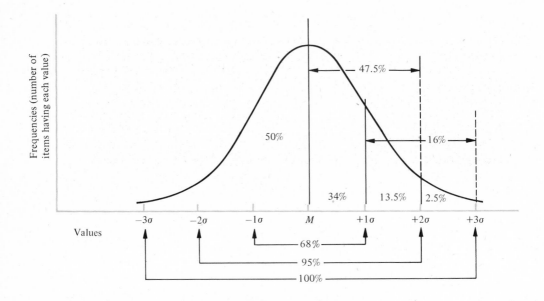

FIGURE 2:   *Normal Curve.*

the graph of this data would approach the perfect mathematical model known as the **normal curve** (or **bell curve**), shown in Figure 2. In this normal distribution, the mean, median, and mode all have the same value (*M*)—the value (on the horizontal line) which corresponds to the highest point on the curve. The range of values is evenly divided into six equal intervals, each of which represents one standard deviation, σ. The six intervals are marked off symmetrically around the mean at $\pm 1\sigma$, $\pm 2\sigma$, and $\pm 3\sigma$.*

The standard deviation is significant because we know what per cent of the total items (people) fall within each interval or combination of intervals. These per cent categories are indicated on the normal curve above (and apply symmetrically on each side of the mean). Thus, as illustrated in Figure 3, if the mean height of American males is 5′10″ and one standard deviation $\sigma = 2''$, then 68% of all men have heights between 5′8″ and 6′0″ tall; 95% of the men fall between 5′6″ and 6′2″; and 100% of the men fall between 5′4″ and 6′4″, as shown in Figure 3. (Obviously, there are men shorter than 5′4″ and taller than 6′4″. However, since less than 0.3% of the

*Technically, the normal curve continues infinitely in both directions, so that additional higher and lower values are possible. However, we assume for practical purposes that the given range of values lies entirely between $\pm 3\sigma$, since the area between $\pm 3\sigma$ includes 99.73% of all items depicted by the normal curve.

FIGURE 3

men would fall in either category, we assume for convenience that 100% have been included.)

Since the standard deviation for a set of data can be computed, industries can test their products to determine how accurate their manufacturing processes are and what per cent of their products fall into various tolerance categories. Clothing manufacturers or other firms whose products are sized may use the per cents associated with standard deviation as a guide in deciding how many items of each size to produce.

Example One   Assume that the mean size of women's dresses is size 12, with a standard deviation of 4, as shown in Figure 4. Use the per cent categories of the normal curve to answer each question.

FIGURE 4

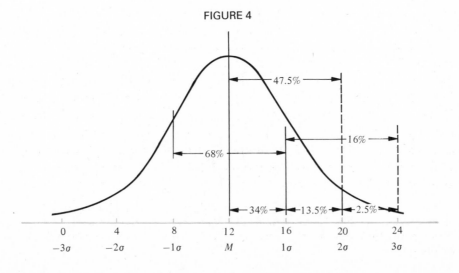

Example One (cont.)

(a) What per cent of the women are size 12 or larger? 50%

(b) What per cent of the women are size 16 or larger? 16%

(c) What per cent are size 24 or smaller? 100%

(d) What per cent are smaller than size 4? 2.5%

(e) What per cent are smaller than size 4 *or* larger than size 20? 2.5% + 2.5% = 5.0%.

(f) If a dress company plans to manufacture 5,000 dresses, how many of those should be in sizes 8 through 16? 68% × 5,000 = 3,400.

The computation of standard deviation from a set of grouped data in a frequency distribution requires more time and explanation than can be included in introductory business math. However, we can compute the standard deviation for a set of ungrouped values. Using this type of data, the formula for standard deviation is

$$\sigma = \sqrt{\frac{\sum d^2}{n}}$$

where $\sum d^2$ represents the sum of the squares of the deviations (differences) of each value from the mean, and n indicates the number of values given. (The symbol $\sum$ means "the sum of.") This procedure for finding standard deviation is outlined as follows:

Standard Deviation Procedure

1. Find the mean: add the given data and divide by n.

2. Find each deviation, d: subtract the mean from each given value, obtaining either a positive or negative difference. (The sum of these deviations must be 0.)

3. Square each deviation and find their sum, $\sum d^2$.

4. Apply the standard deviation formula, $\sigma = \sqrt{\frac{\sum d^2}{n}}$: divide $\sum d^2$ by n, and take the square root. (If the square root is not a whole number, let the standard deviation remain in $\sqrt{}$ form.)

Example Two

Find the standard deviation of the following values: 61, 62, 65, 67, 68, and 73.

Mean	Deviation, d	d^2	Standard Deviation
61	61–66 = −5	25	
62	62–66 = −4	16	$\sigma = \sqrt{\dfrac{\sum d^2}{n}}$
65	65–66 = −1	1	
67	67–66 = 1	1	$= \sqrt{\dfrac{96}{6}}$
68	68–66 = 2	4	
+73	73–66 = 7	49	$= \sqrt{16}$
6) 396 = 66	0	$\sum d^2 = 96$	$\sigma = 4$

The standard deviation is 4. Thus, the values associated with each interval would appear on a line graph as shown in Figure 5. The dots represent the six values given above. For a normal curve distribution, 68% of the values should fall between $\pm 1\sigma$; that is, 68% of the 6 numbers (or 4 numbers) should fall between 62 and 70. Four of our given numbers (62, 65, 67, and 68) fall between $\pm 1\sigma$. Between $\pm 2\sigma$ should be 95% of the 6 numbers, which equals 6 values to the nearest whole unit. All 6 of our given values do fall between $\pm 2\sigma$, which includes values from 58 through 74.

Our given set of data above contains too few numbers to include values in the two outside intervals under the normal curve. Sets of data containing many more values, however, would closely match the normal distribution. Industries using standard deviation for quality-control would thus use larger groups of data in order to obtain dependable statistical results.

FIGURE 5

Use the per cent categories associated with the normal curve in order to answer Problems 1–4.

1. Assume that the mean size for men's shoes is size 11, with a standard deviation of 2, as indicated in Figure 6.

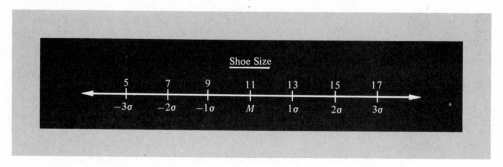

FIGURE 6

(a) What per cent of the men have feet size 13 or smaller?
(b) What per cent are size 15 or larger?
(c) What per cent are between size 9 and size 13?
(d) What per cent are size 7 through size 9?
(e) Suppose that a shoe company is manufacturing 4,000 pairs of shoes. How many of these pairs should be size 11 or larger?
(f) How many of the 4,000 pairs should be sizes 7 through 15?

2. Suppose that the mean size for a mechanical part is 5.00 centimeters (cm) with a standard deviation of 0.02, as shown in Figure 7.
(a) What per cent of the parts measure 5.00 cm or smaller?

FIGURE 7

(b) What per cent of the parts measure 5.02 cm or larger?

(c) What per cent measure between 4.96 and 5.00 cm?

(d) What per cent measure 4.98 through 5.04 cm?

(e) Suppose that 6,000 parts are manufactured. How many of these parts will measure between 4.98 and 5.02 cm?

(f) Suppose that all parts which exceed ±2σ will be unusable. How many of the 6,000 parts will have to be replaced?

3. Suppose that cans of processed meat contain 50 grams (g) of protein with a standard deviation of 1 g. Prepare a line graph (as in Problems 1 and 2) to show the grams associated with each deviation ±1σ, ±2σ, and ±3σ.

(a) What per cent of the meat contains 49 g of protein or less?

(b) What per cent contains at least 50 g?

(c) What per cent contains between 48 and 50 g?

(d) What per cent contains between 48 and 52 g?

(e) Assume that 8,000 cans are processed. How many of these cans contain between 49 and 52 g of protein?

(f) How many of the 8,000 cans do not fall within ±1σ of the expected 50 g?

(g) How many of the cans contain 51 g or less of protein?

4. Assume that bags of lawn fertilizer contain 5 pounds (lb) of nitrogen with a standard deviation of 0.2 lb. Prepare a line graph (as in Problems 1 and 2) to show the nitrogen weight associated with each deviation ±1σ, ±2σ, and ±3σ.

(a) What per cent of the bags contain 4.8 lb or more of nitrogen?

(b) What per cent of the bags contain 4.6 lb or less of nitrogen?

(c) What per cent of the bags contain between 4.4 and 5.6 lb of nitrogen?

(d) What per cent contain between 4.6 and 4.8 lb of nitrogen?

(e) Suppose that 2,000 bags of fertilizer are processed. How many of these bags contain 4.8 lb or less of nitrogen?

(f) How many of the 2,000 bags fall within ±1σ of the mean nitrogen weight?

(g) How many of the bags contain 4.6 lb or more of nitrogen?

For the following sets of data:

(a) Compute each standard deviation.

(b) Prepare a line graph showing the value associated with each deviation ±1σ, ±2σ, and ±3σ.

(c) Check each interval (between ±1σ, ±2σ, and ±3σ) to see whether it contains the expected number of given values.

5. 6, 10, 18, 19, 22.

6. 8, 10, 12, 16, 19.

7. 20, 21, 24, 26, 27, 32.

8. 32, 36, 41, 41, 42, 48.

9. 30, 32, 32, 35, 36, 39.

10. 40, 42, 45, 51, 55, 55.

11. 48, 51, 51, 52, 52, 53, 54, 55.

12. 57, 63, 64, 65, 65, 66, 68, 72.

13. 68, 72, 72, 73, 73, 73, 74, 75, 75, 75.

14. 74, 79, 80, 80, 81, 81, 82, 84, 84, 85.

SECTION 4
Index Numbers

An **index number** is similar to a per cent in both appearance and purpose. Like per cent, index numbers use a scale of 100 in order to show the relative size between certain costs or to indicate change in costs over a period of time, rather than showing the actual, numerical differences. Whereas the actual dollars-and-cents changes in costs often could not be readily analyzed, both the index number and per cent allow the reader to make comparisons between items more easily. Index numbers are often used in business to depict long-range trends in prices or volume (of sales, production, etc.).

The simplest index number which can be computed involves a single item. Such a simple price index is sometimes called a **price relative**. This index is simply the ratio of a given year's price to the base year's price, multiplied by 100:

$$\text{Index number (or price relative)} = \frac{\text{Given year's price}}{\text{Base year's price}} \times 100$$

Example One

Suppose that a half-gallon of milk cost 75¢ in 1976, 72¢ in 1977, and 81¢ in 1978. Compute the price relatives (or index numbers) for milk using 1976 as the base year.

Year	Price		Price Index (1976 = 100)
1976	75¢	Base year	100
1977	72¢	$\frac{72}{75} \times 100 = 0.96 \times 100 =$	96
1978	81¢	$\frac{81}{75} \times 100 = 1.08 \times 100 =$	108

The student should realize that this index is nothing more than a simple per cent, but written without the per cent sign. The question, "What per cent of the 1976 price was the 1978 price?" would be answered "108%."

An excellent example of the use of index numbers is the Consumer Price Index, published monthly by the U.S. Department of Labor (Bureau of Labor Statistics). The costs of a large number of goods and services are indexed for the United States as a whole and for selected cities and urban areas individually. Consider the example given in Table 1. (Assume that this index is for the present year.)

TABLE 1:   CONSUMER PRICE INDEX OF SELECTED EXPENSES IN
SELECTED URBAN AREAS

November–December, 19XX (1967 = 100)

Expense	U.S. Urban Average	Atlanta	Chicago	Dallas	Los Angeles	New York	Seattle
Food	180.7	187.8	180.9	176.7	175.3	185.1	173.8
Housing	172.2	171.0	158.3	162.7	172.2	178.1	168.7
Clothing	145.2	140.2	137.8	143.1	138.0	142.5	140.6
Transportation	157.6	148.1	157.5	162.3	158.5	177.4	140.8
Medical care	174.7	189.2	176.4	167.1	174.6	188.0	162.9

The index numbers show the "current" year-end costs of the major consumer expenses as compared to the cost of these same expenses in *that* locality during 1967. Thus, the same food which cost $100 in Atlanta in 1967 would cost $187.80 at the present time. Similarly, housing which cost $100 in Seattle in 1967 has now increased to $168.70. (These indexes may also be read, "Transportation that cost $10 in Chicago in 1967 would now cost $15.75.")

Various index numbers cannot be used for comparison among themselves unless they refer to the same base amount. For instance, Table 1 gives the price index for medical care in Dallas as 167.1 and in New York as 188.0. This means that medical care which cost $100 in Dallas in 1967 would now cost $167.10 and that medical care which cost $100 in New York in 1967 would now cost $188.00. It does *not* mean that $100 in 1967 would purchase the same medical services and drugs in both Dallas and New York.

Thus, Table 1 does not necessarily indicate that medical care in New York costs more than similar care in Dallas; it simply indicates that the cost of medical care in New York has *increased* more rapidly since 1967 than have medical expenses in Dallas (188.0 vs. 167.1). If a medical procedure in New York had cost substantially less in 1967 than did the same procedure in Dallas, then the New York medical procedure could still be less expensive than the Dallas procedure (although New York medical fees have increased faster than have the Dallas fees).

Hence, the actual cost of living in Los Angeles as compared with the cost of living in Chicago (or any other locality) cannot be determined from the Consumer Price Index, but would have to be obtained from some other statistical source which contains an index of comparative living costs. Such an index, released periodically by the Bureau of Labor Statistics, gives family budgets for a family of four covering the same purchases in various cities at low, intermediate, and high standards of living. The most recent budget available at the time of this

Example Two (cont.)

Compares Actual Prices Between Cities

TABLE 2: COMPARATIVE INDEX FOR SELECTED EXPENSES AT INTERMEDIATE STANDARD OF LIVING

(U.S. Urban Average = 100)

Expense	Atlanta	Chicago	Dallas	Los Angeles	New York	Seattle
Food	97	100	90	95	116	101
Housing	81	108	84	96	126	107
Clothing	97	102	94	100	102	108
Transportation	99	104	105	102	93	103
Medical care	95	105	114	121	110	106
Combined index	93	104	93	99	114	104

writing is given in Table 2 based on the U.S. urban average as 100. This comparative index enables us to determine that, for every $100 which the average urban family spends, the Atlanta and Dallas families spend $93, the Los Angeles family spends $99, the Chicago and Seattle families spend $104, and the New York family spends $114— all to maintain the same intermediate standard of living. As a matter of interest, notice on the comparative index of medical expenses that medical care in Dallas (114) is more expensive than in New York (110), despite the fact that the Consumer Price Index showed that medical costs have increased more rapidly in New York (188.0) than in Dallas (167.1).

Example 1 illustrated the computation of price relatives for only a single item—milk. Actually, the term "index number" is often reserved for a number derived by combining several related items, each weighted according to its relative importance. For instance, the index numbers for food expenses in Example 2 are a composite of many different grocery items, each weighted according to its portion of the total food budget in a typical family (as one consideration). There are many methods for constructing such composite index numbers, all of which require more statistical knowledge than can be acquired in basic business math. Even for the same data, these composite index numbers vary significantly according to the method used; hence, the best method to use depends upon careful analysis of the purpose that the index is intended to serve. Obtaining an accurate and meaningful composite index number is not a simple matter. Our index-number problems will therefore be limited to simple price relatives.

Answer the following questions, based on the Consumer Price Index and the Comparative Index in Example 2. (Include the appropriate index with each answer.)

1. (a) How much would a New York resident spend today for housing that cost $100 in 1967?

(b) How much does the average U.S. citizen pay today for clothing that cost $100 in 1967?

(c) If a medical fee was $10 in 1967, how much should a Seattle resident expect to pay now for the same service?

(d) In which area have food costs risen most rapidly?

(e) Where are groceries most expensive?

(f) In which area are transportation costs greatest?

(g) In which area are clothing expenses least?

(h) In which area have housing costs risen most slowly?

(i) In which urban area is housing least expensive?

2. (a) How much would the typical urban dweller pay today for medical expenses that cost $100 in 1967?

(b) How much does a Los Angeles resident spend today for transportation that cost $100 in 1967?

(c) If groceries cost $10 in 1967, what would these same groceries cost in Chicago now?

(d) In which urban area have housing expenses increased most rapidly?

(e) Where is housing most expensive?

(f) In which urban area is clothing most expensive?

(g) In which urban area is medical care least expensive?

(h) Which area has experienced the slowest increase in transportation costs?

(i) Where is transportation least expensive?

3. Determine index numbers (price relatives) for a gallon of regular gasoline, using 1970 as the base year.

Year	Price	Index 1970 = 100
1970	40¢	
1972	38	
1974	64	
1976	50	
1978	54	

4. Compute each price index for a 5-lb bag of sugar, using 1970 as the base year.

Year	Price	Index 1970 = 100
1970	80¢	
1972	76	
1974	180	
1976	116	
1978	92	

5. Calculate each price relative for a pound of T-bone steak, using 1971 as the base year.

Year	Price	*Index* 1971 = 100
1971	150¢	
1973	147	
1975	189	
1977	159	
1979	177	

6. Find each index number (price relative) for a dozen large eggs, using 1971 as the base year.

Year	Price	*Index* 1971 = 100
1971	75¢	
1973	72	
1975	69	
1977	78	
1979	84	

SECTION 5
Graphs

Many people read business statistics without fully realizing their significance. Statistics usually make a much stronger impression if they can be visualized. This is particularly true when the data are used to make comparisons among several items or when the statistics give the various parts that comprise a whole. The purpose of business graphs is to present such data in a manner that will be both accurate and easy to read. The most common **graphs**, which we will now consider, are *bar graphs*, *line graphs*, *picture graphs*, and *circle graphs*.

All graphs have certain things in common. Every graph should have a title so that the reader will know what facts are presented. A scale that will accurately present the information should be chosen; and the scale should be clearly labeled, starting at the point of origin (zero) for amounts of money, sales or production figures, and so on. Very large figures may be rounded off before graphing.

Bar Graphs

The *bar graph* uses either horizontal or vertical bars to compare several related values. These may be single items (sales, production, or income, for example) over a period of years; or they may be several different items during a single time period.

Graph paper should be used whenever possible for bar graphs. (If a large graph is to be constructed for display purposes, one should first devise a scale before attempting to draw the graph.) If the data cover a period of months or years, the time factor is usually labeled on the horizontal scale.

FIGURE 8

Example One

Capital Equipment Company's net sales during the past 5 years are as follows: 19X1—$225,000; 19X2—$250,000; 19X3—$235,000; 19X4—$263,000; 19X5—$275,000. Compare these net sales on a vertical bar graph.

The two graphs in Figure 8 present the same information. Notice that the graph on the right contains a break in the scale. A break may be used to eliminate unused space on a graph or, as shown here, to abbreviate noncrucial areas of the graph and allow a larger scale to be used, thus making it easier to determine the total amounts which the graph depicts. Breaks in the scale should be planned with care, however, for the differences between amounts may appear much greater proportionally than they actually are. To avoid giving a false impression and to help establish the scale for the reader, every graph should show the point of origin ($0 or 0%, for example) and some low value on the scale. (Many cost-of-living index graphs are notorious for starting at 100 rather than 0, so that a 2% increase from year 1 to year 2 falsely seems more like a 100% increase, as illustrated in Figure 9.)

Picture Graphs

The *picture graph* is a variation of the bar graph in which an appropriate picture is used to represent a specified quantity. The picture is then drawn the required number of times

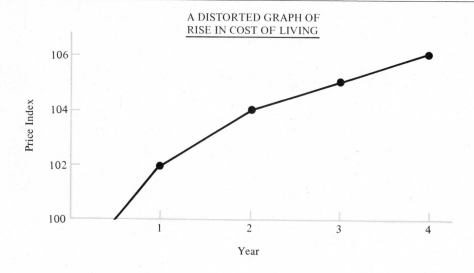

A DISTORTED GRAPH OF
RISE IN COST OF LIVING

to depict each of the totals included in the graph. The pictures thus simultaneously form horizontal bars which show the general relationships between totals.

Example Two A recent intermediate budget for a family of four ($14,500) includes expenditures (rounded to the nearest $100) as shown in the following categories: food—$3,600; housing—$3,300; clothing—$1,400; transportation—$1,200; medical care—$700; personal income tax—$2,000; social security—$800; all other unclassified expenses—$1,500. Illustrate these expenses on a horizontal picture graph. (See Figure 10.)

Line Graphs The *line graph* usually records change (in sales, production, income, etc.) over a period of time. The only basic difference between it and the vertical bar graph is that, instead of having bars that come up to the various values, the values are connected by a line. The line may be broken or unbroken, straight or curved. Two or more related statistics are often presented on the same line graph.

Line graphs should ordinarily be drawn on graph paper. After the scale of values has been labeled (time should be on the horizontal scale), locate the appropriate values and mark each with a dot. Finally, connect the dots

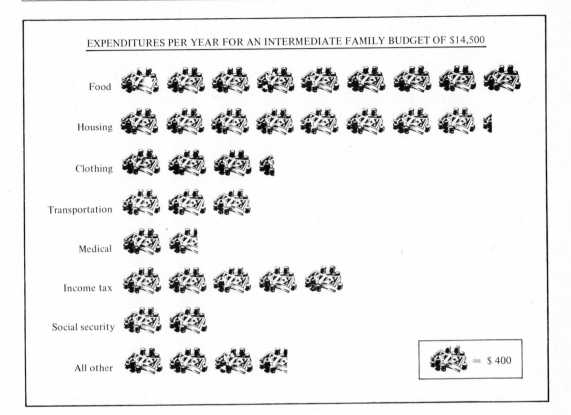

FIGURE 10

with a line. (When the graph contains more than one line, be sure to make each line distinct and to identify each.)

Example Three Koenig Building Distributors, Inc., experienced the following totals of net sales, cost of goods sold, and net profit during a 5-year period. Depict these data on a line graph. (See Figure 11.)

	19X1	19X2	19X3	19X4	19X5
Net sales	$180,000	$210,000	$160,000	$220,000	$237,000
Cost of goods sold	105,000	110,000	80,000	112,000	95,000
Net profit	25,000	32,000	8,000	10,000	42,000

Circle Graphs The *circle graph* (also called a "pie chart") presents the breakdown of a whole into its various parts. (For example, it may show what portion of a budget is spent for each

SALES ANALYSIS OF KOENIG BUILDING DISTRIBUTORS, INC., 19X1-19X5

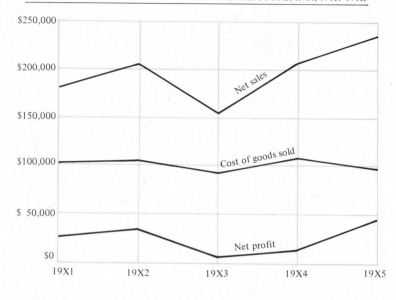

FIGURE 11

item.) Thus, the entire circle represents 100%, and each item should occupy an area proportional to its percentage of the total.

Before preparing the graph, convert each item to its corresponding per cent (if this is not given). Multiply each per cent times 360° to determine the number of degrees required for each item. Use a compass to draw the circle, and use a protractor to measure the number of degrees needed for each part of the graph.

Example Four   The $200,000 in total assets of Straiton Parts Co. are distributed on December 31, 19xx, as listed below. Represent these assets on a circle graph.

Current Assets		Fixed Assets	
Cash	$14,000	Plant	$40,000
Accounts receivable	36,000	Land	12,000
Inventory	70,000	Equipment	28,000

To prepare Figure 12, one must first convert each item to a rate (per cent) of the total assets by answering the question, "What per cent of the total assets is each separate item?"

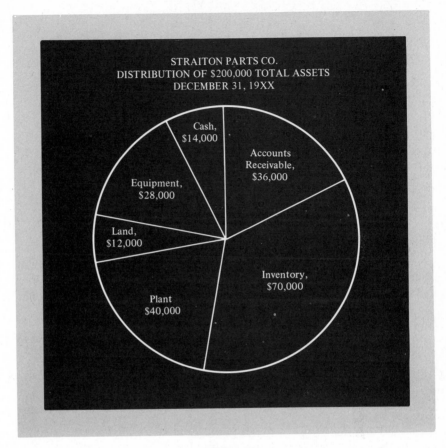

STRAITON PARTS CO.
DISTRIBUTION OF $200,000 TOTAL ASSETS
DECEMBER 31, 19XX

FIGURE 12

**Example
Four
(cont.)**

$$\text{\_\_\_\_}\% \text{ of Total assets} = \text{Each item}$$

$$\text{\_\_\_\_}\% \text{ of } \$200,000 = \text{Each item}$$

$$200,000r = \text{Each item}$$

$$r = \frac{\text{Each item}}{\$200,000}$$

Thus

$$\text{Cash} = \frac{\$14,000}{\$200,000} = 7\%; \quad \text{plant} = \frac{\$40,000}{\$200,000} = 20\%; \quad \text{etc.}$$

**Example
Four
(cont.)**

Each asset would require the following number of degrees:

Cash	7% of 360° = 25.2°	or	25°
Accounts receivable	18% of 360° = 64.8°	or	65°
Inventory	35% of 360° =		126°
Plant	20% of 360° =		72°
Land	6% of 360° = 21.6°	or	22°
Equipment	+ 14% of 360° = 50.4°	or	+ 50°
	100%		360°

SECTION 5 *Problems*

1. The Internal Revenue Service reports the following totals of personal income tax receipts during the period 1960–1974.* Represent these totals on a vertical bar graph. (Amounts are given in billions of dollars.) 1960—$41 billion; 1965—$49; 1970—$90; 1972—$95; 1973—$103; 1974—$119.

2. During 1960–1974, women represented the following per cents of the total U.S. labor force. Use a vertical bar graph to illustrate these data. 1960—28%; 1965—32%; 1970—40%; 1972—41%; 1973—42%; 1974—43%.

3. Use a horizontal bar graph to compare the various types of housing units built in 19XX by Coastal Construction Co.: Single-story homes, 225; two-story homes, 140; split-level homes, 75; duplex units, 150; townhouse apartment units, 250.

4. Prepare a horizontal bar graph on which to depict the average years of experience of the personnel in each job classification at Randolph Textiles:

Design	7 yr	Shipping	3 yr
Knitting	4 yr	Sales	10 yr
Inspection	8 yr	Office	6 yr
Maintenance	2 yr	Executive	15 yr

5. Given below are average budgets required to maintain the same intermediate standard of living for urban families of four in selected U.S. cities. Use this information to construct a horizontal picture graph, letting each symbol represent $2,000.

U.S. average	$14,600	Honolulu	$17,000
Atlanta	13,100	Los Angeles	14,100
Chicago	14,800	New York	16,600
Dallas	12,900	Seattle	14,500

*The national statistics pertaining to these years which are given in this set of problems are taken from the *Statistical Abstract of the United States, 1975* (U.S. Department of Commerce).

6. The average electrical consumption in kilowatt hours per month by selected household appliances is listed below. In preparing a horizontal picture graph, let each symbol represent 20 kilowatt hours. (A double row of symbols may be used for convenience.)

Appliance	Consumption (kWh)	Appliance	Consumption (kWh)
Dishwasher	40	Refrigerator	160
Dryer	140	Television	50
Freezer	160	Washer	15
Range/oven	100	Water heater	350

Listed below are the number of passenger cars and television sets (each to the nearest million) in use in selected nations.

7. Prepare a horizontal picture graph representing the number of passenger cars in use in each nation (except Russia). Let each symbol represent 2 million cars. (The United States had 101 million cars in use. If you wish to include this figure for a major graph comparison, double or triple rows of symbols may be used.)

8. Using a picture graph, depict the number of television sets in use in each country. Let each symbol represent 3 million televisions. (The United States had 110 million television sets. If you choose to include this figure on your graph, double or triple rows of symbols may be used for convenience.)

Nation	Passenger Cars (millions)	Televisions (millions)	Nation	Passenger Cars (millions)	Televisions (millions)
Canada	8	8	Netherlands	3	3
France	14	12	Russia	N/A	49
Italy	13	11	Sweden	3	3
Japan	14	25	United Kingdom	14	17
Mexico	2	4	West Germany	17	18

9. The total net sales of the Bradford Printing Co. over an 8-year period are given below. Prepare a line graph to compare these net sales.

19X1	$155,000	19X5	$188,000
19X2	$170,000	19X6	$195,000
19X3	$172,000	19X7	$203,000
19X4	$190,000	19X8	$210,000

10. On a line graph, compare the number of lawn mowers sold by National Mower Corp. over a 7-year period.

19X1	48,000	19X5	75,000
19X2	52,000	19X6	80,000
19X3	50,000	19X7	84,000
19X4	60,000		

11. The number of students (to the nearest million) enrolled in educational institutions in the United States during 1960–1974 is given below. Plot these enrollments on the same line graph.

Level	1960	1965	1970	1972	1974
Elementary (K–8)	32	35	37	35	34
High school (9–12)	10	13	15	15	15
Higher education	4	6	7	8	9

12. Prepare a line graph to show how the number of sales at The Discount Center were affected by the changing popularity of certain small appliances over a 6-year period.

	Blender	Toaster Oven	Blow-dryer	Drip Coffeemaker
19X1	125	30	20	0
19X2	150	40	30	10
19X3	130	50	75	30
19X4	100	40	110	75
19X5	80	25	100	150
19X6	75	30	90	175

13. The typical U.S. family currently budgets expenses as follows: food, 24%; housing, 33%; transportation, 13%; clothing, 13%; medical, 6%; other, 11%. Represent this distribution on a circle graph.

14. Net income at Noble Furniture Co. last year fell into the following categories: living room furniture, 30%; dining room furniture, 20%; bedroom furniture, 25%; home accessories, 15%; other, 10%. Use a circle graph to show this distribution.

15. The total floor space at Harbor Mills, Inc., is utilized as shown below. Prepare a circle graph to compare this utilization.

Receiving and raw materials	4,000 sq ft
Cutting and sewing	8,000
Inspecting	2,000
Shipping	5,000
Office	+ 1,000
	20,000 sq ft

16. The Jamison Co. Inc., had the following operating expenses last year. Construct a circle graph to compare these expenses.

Salaries		$30,000
Mortgage payments		7,500
Utilities		5,000
Depreciation		4,000
Taxes		2,500
Other	+	1,000
		$50,000

CHAPTER 4 *Glossary*

Arithmetic mean. (See "Mean.")

Array, ordered. A listing of numerical data in order of size.

Average. A typical value or measure of central tendency for a group of numbers; examples: mean, median, and mode.

Central tendency, measure of. A representative number around which the other numbers in a group seem to cluster; an average.

Classes. The groups (or intervals) into which given values are categorized in a frequency distribution.

Dispersion, measure of. A value that gives some idea of how spread out (or how scattered from the mean) a group of numbers are; examples: range and standard deviation.

Frequency. The number of values within a class interval of a frequency distribution.

Frequency distribution. A process for classifying large numbers of values and tabulating the data in groups (classes) rather than individually; used to compute measures of central tendency and/or dispersion.

Graph. A visual representation of numerical data.

Index number. A number based on a scale of 100 which shows the relative size between certain costs or indicates change in costs over a period of time. (Example: If $1967 = 100$ and the current index is 115, then $115 is

now required to purchase an item that cost $100 in 1967.)

Interval. On a frequency distribution, the difference between the lower limit of one class and the lower limit of the next class.

Mean, arithmetic. The most common average; the sum of all given values divided by the number of values.

$$\left(\text{Example:} \quad \frac{7+5+6}{3} = \frac{18}{3} = 6. \right)$$

Median. The midpoint (or middle value) of a group of numbers, which separates the group into two groups of equal size—one containing all values larger than the median and the other containing the smaller values. (Examples: Given 1, 2, 3, 7, and 9, the median is 3; given 1, 2, 3, 7, 9, and 10, the median is

$$\frac{3+7}{2} = \frac{10}{2} = 5. \right)$$

Midpoint. Of a class in a frequency distribution, the arithmetic mean of the lower limit of that class and the lower limit of the next class.

Mode. The value in a set of data that occurs most frequently. (Example: Given 1, 3, 3, 5, 5, 5, 7, 9, and 10, the mode is 5.)

Modified mean. An arithmetic mean computed after the extremely high and low value(s) have been deleted.

Normal (or bell) curve. A symmetrical, bell-shaped graph

associated with the expected distribution for many types of data; the graph for which standard deviation applies.

Price relative. A simple price index for one item $\left(= \dfrac{\text{current price}}{\text{base price}} \times 100 \right)$.

Range. The difference between the highest and lowest values in a group of numbers (or between the upper and lower limits in a frequency distribution); a simple measure of dispersion.

Standard deviation (σ). For a normal curve distribution, the deviation (difference) between the mean and two crucial points symmetrical to the mean, within which interval fall 68% of all the given values.

For ungrouped data, $\sigma = \sqrt{\dfrac{\Sigma\, d^2}{n}}$.

Statistics. Informally, the process of collecting, organizing, tabulating, and interpreting numerical data; also, the information presented as a result of this process.

Variability. Dispersion (or scatteredness) of data.

Weighted mean. A mean computed for data whose importance differs and where each value is weighted (or multiplied) according to its relative importance.

CHAPTER 5

Taxes

CHAPTER 5 OBJECTIVES

Upon completion of Chapter 5, the student will be able to:

1. Define and use correctly the terminology associated with each topic.

2. Compute sales tax (*Section 1; Problems 1–22*)
   a. Using a table (*Section 1; Example 1*); or
   b. Based on a percentage rate (*Section 1; Example 2*).

3. Find the marked price of an item, given (a) the sales tax rate and (b) the total tax or the total price (*Section 1; Examples 2–4*).

4. Express a given (decimal) property tax rate
   a. As a per cent;
   b. As a rate per $100;
   c. As a rate per $1,000.
   (*Section 2; Examples 1, 2; Problems 1–4*)

5. Using the property tax formula $R \cdot V = T$ and given two of the following items, determine the unknown
   a. Property tax;
   b. Tax rate; or
   c. Assessed value of property.
   (*Section 2; Examples 3–6; Problems 5–20*)

5	Increased government activity (at the federal, state, and local levels) has made taxes—personal as well as business—an integral part of modern life. Two of the most common taxes are the sales tax and the

property tax. The sales tax has become an everyday part of commerce. Property owners, including business organizations, must pay a property tax on their possessions. The following sections present the calculation of sales tax and property tax. (A third important tax is income tax. However, any significant study of income tax would require an entire course by itself and could not be accomplished in one unit of a business math course. Chapter 8, "Wages and Payrolls," includes the taxes that must be deducted from payrolls.)

SECTION 1
Sales Tax

A large majority of state legislatures has approved **taxes on retail sales** as a means of securing revenue. Retail merchants are responsible for collecting these taxes at the time of each sale and relaying them to the state. In some states, the legislatures have also allowed their cities the option of adopting a municipal sales tax in addition to the state tax, in order to obtain local funds.

There are two basic ways in which state sales taxes are established: (1) A few states have a tax which is a specified number of cents per whole dollar of the retail price, and tax on the extra cents is paid according to an arbitrarily adopted chart. (2) In most states, the sales tax is a specified per cent of the selling price. (Even in these states, however, the tax may follow a nonpercentage chart for sales under $1.)

Sales taxes ordinarily apply only to sales made within the jurisdiction of the taxing body. Thus, merchandise sold outside a state (such as by mail or by telephone) is not usually subject to that state's sales tax. Similarly, the municipal tax is not charged on goods delivered outside the city. In both instances, however, the tax would apply if merchandise were bought in person by a nonresident.

In areas subject to sales tax, charts are available so that the cashier may simply "look up" the tax. These charts eliminate the problem of rounding off the tax to the next cent by listing consecutive price intervals and indicating the tax to be charged in each interval. (Sales tax charts are used whether the intervals are calculated on a percentage basis or are arbitrarily fixed.) Table 5-1 illustrates a sales tax table with arbitrarily fixed intervals, including a municipal tax. Tax intervals for sales made in the city are on the right; and intervals for sales made in the state (but outside the city limits) are on the left.

TABLE 5-1: SALES TAX INTERVALS

SALES MADE WITHIN STATE		SALES MADE WITHIN CITY	
Amount of Sale or Interval	*Tax*	*Amount of Sale or Interval*	*Tax*
Per whole dollar	3¢	Per whole dollar	4¢
Additional cents:		Additional cents:	
$.00–$.09	0	$.00–$.09	0
.10– .39	1¢	.10– .39	1¢
.40– .69	2¢	.40– .49	2¢
.70– .99	3¢	.50– .69	3¢
		.70– .99	4¢

Excise taxes are taxes levied by the local, state, and/or federal government on the manufacture or sale of certain products and services. The excise tax is similar to sales tax and is paid in addition to sales tax; it may be either a per cent or a set amount. (Excise taxes paid by the manufacturer are passed on to the consumer as a higher marked price.) Most excise taxes are paid either on luxury items or to help finance projects related to the item taxed (such as highways financed by gasoline taxes). Other examples of excise taxes include taxes on automobiles, air transportation, telephone service, sporting and recreational equipment, firearms, alcoholic beverages and tobacco, entertainment, and business licenses.

Example One   Watts Plumbing Equipment, Inc. made the following sales: (a) an $18.65 faucet sold within the city; (b) an $85.50 pump, delivered to a plumbing company in a nearby city; and (c) a $23.72 valve ordered by mail from another state. How much sales tax must be charged for each sale? (Use the tax schedule in Table 5-1.)

Solution   (a) The municipal tax applies to this $18.65 sale made within the city:

$$18 \times 4\cent = \quad \$.72$$
$$\$.65 \text{ (see table)} = + \quad .03$$
$$\overline{\text{Total sales tax} = \quad \$.75}$$

(b) The $85.50 pump is subject only to the state sales tax:

$$85 \times 3\cent = \quad \$2.55$$
$$\$.50 \text{ (see table)} = + \quad .02$$
$$\overline{\text{Total sales tax} = \quad \$2.57}$$

(c) No sales tax is due on the $23.72 sale of the valve, since this purchase was delivered out of state.

Example Two   A 4% sales tax is charged on all retail sales made by Sun Country Pool Supplies. (a) How much tax must be charged on a $34.85 sale? (b) The sales tax on a case of pool chlorine was $2.16. What was the price of the case of chlorine?

Solution   (a) The sales tax is 4% of the price of the merchandise. (Sales tax is rounded to the next cent whenever the third decimal place is 5 or more.) Thus,

$$\text{Tax} = 4\% \times \text{Price}$$
$$= 0.04 \times \$34.85$$
$$\text{Tax} = \$1.39$$

The sales tax due is $1.39.

(b) The same formula is used to find the price when the sales tax is known. Since the tax was $2.16,

$$4\% \times \text{Price} = \text{Tax}$$
$$4\% \times \text{Price} = \$2.16$$
$$0.04p = \$2.16$$
$$p = \$54$$

The case of chlorine was priced $54; thus, the total price, including the sales tax, was $56.16.

Example Three The total price of a CB radio, including a 5% sales tax, was $136.50. What was the marked price of the CB?

$$\text{Marked price} + \text{Sales tax} = \text{Total price}$$

$$\text{Price} + 5\% \text{ of price} = \text{Total price}$$

$$p + 0.05p = \$136.50$$

$$1.05p = 136.50$$

$$p = \frac{136.50}{1.05}$$

$$p = \$130$$

The marked price of the CB was $130.

NOTE: Please observe that the sales tax is 5% of the marked price, *not* 5% of the total price. Therefore, problems of this type *cannot* be solved by taking 5% of the total price and subtracting to find the marked price. The results would be close, but they would always differ by a few cents; hence, they would always be wrong. (You are invited to try a few examples if you are still skeptical!)

Example Four The $51.30 total price of a target pistol includes a 4% sales tax and a 10% federal excise tax. What was the marked price of the pistol?

$$\text{Marked price} + \text{Sales tax} + \text{Excise tax} = \text{Total price}$$

$$\text{Price} + 4\% \text{ of price} + 10\% \text{ of price} = \$51.30$$

$$p + 0.04p + 0.10p = 51.30$$

$$1.14p = 51.30$$

$$p = \frac{51.30}{1.14}$$

$$p = \$45.00$$

SECTION 1 *Problems*

Compute the missing items in the following (a dash indicates that the item does not apply).

		Marked Price	Location	Sales Tax Rate	Sales Tax	Total Price
1.	(a)	$14.59	City	(Table 5-1)		
	(b)	89.25	State	(Table 5-1)		
	(c)	32.05	Out of state	(Table 5-1)		
	(d)	16.75	—	2%		
	(e)		—	4%	$.12	
	(f)		—	5%	.95	
	(g)		—	3%		$61.80
	(h)		—	2%		26.52
2.	(a)	$13.48	City	(Table 5-1)		
	(b)	25.36	State	(Table 5-1)		
	(c)	45.89	Out of state	(Table 5-1)		
	(d)	18.55	—	3%		
	(e)		—	4%	$1.12	
	(f)		—	5%	.68	
	(g)		—	5%		$33.60
	(h)		—	4%		50.96

3. Wilcox TV Sales Corp. is in an area subject to the sales tax shown in Table 5-1. Find the sales tax and the total price that must be collected on the following purchases:

(a) $219.50 within the city.

(b) $350.20 on a telephone order from another city in the state.

(c) $155.95 by an order from another state.

4. Fireplace Distributors, Inc., made the sales listed below in a location subject to the sales tax in Table 5-1. Compute the sales tax and total price (tax included) to be charged for each sale.

(a) A $59.60 fireplace set sold within the city.

(b) A $27.79 grate ordered by mail from another city.

(c) A $95.99 phone order for a custom screen from a dealer in an adjoining state.

5. If a 5% sales tax is collected, determine the sales tax and the total price on a toaster marked $16.95.

6. Determine the sales tax and the total price to be charged for an electronic calculator marked $29.95, if a 4% sales tax is required.

7. The 3% sales tax on a wall clock was $.54.

(a) Find the marked price of the clock.

(b) What was the total price of the clock, including the sales tax?

8. A 5% sales tax on a pair of prefaded jeans amounted to $1.15.

(a) What was the marked price of the jeans?

(b) What was the total price, including tax?

9. A sales tax of $14.60 was collected on the sale of a refrigerator where the sales tax rate was 4%.

(a) What was the marked price of the refrigerator?

(b) What was the total cost, including tax?

10. The import duty on a diamond pin was $52.50. If a 15% import duty was charged:

(a) What was the original value of the pin?

(b) What is the imported value, including tax?

11. The total cost of an iron, including a 3% sales tax, was $21.63.

(a) What was the marked price of the iron?

(b) How much was the sales tax?

12. The total cost of a cycle helmet was $17.51, including a 3% sales tax.

(a) What was the marked price of the helmet?

(b) How much sales tax was charged?

13. After a 4% sales tax was added, the total cost of a set of stainless steel flatware was $50.96.

(a) How much did the set cost before the tax?

(b) How much sales tax was paid?

14. An oil painting cost $182.00, including a 4% sales tax.

(a) What was the selling price of the painting?

(b) What amount of sales tax was paid?

15. The total cost of a blender was $25.74, including a 4% sales tax.

(a) How much was the blender before the tax was added?

(b) What amount of sales tax was required?

16. The total price for a set of radial tires was $176.40, including a 5% sales tax.

(a) How much were the tires before the tax was computed?

(b) How much tax did the total price include?

17. The total charge for a coat, including the 4% sales tax, was $54.34.

(a) What was the marked price of the coat?

(b) What amount of sales tax was paid?

18. After a 4% sales tax was added, a suitcase sold for $64.74.

(a) Determine the marked price of the luggage.

(b) How much tax did the total price include?

19. An airplane ticket cost $210. This included a 4% state sales tax and an 8% federal excise tax.

(a) What was the regular price of the ticket?

(b) How much was the state sales tax?

(c) How much federal excise tax was charged?

20. After a 5% state sales tax and a 10% federal excise tax on utilities, a telephone bill totaled $16.10.

(a) Compute the regular monthly charge for telephone service.

(b) How much state tax was paid?

(c) What was the federal tax?

21. A $5.75 theater ticket included a 5% state sales tax and a 10% entertainment (excise) tax.

(a) What was the basic price for the ticket?

(b) How much state sales tax was paid?

(c) What was the amount of excise tax?

22. The total cost of an automobile was $3,910, including a 4% sales tax and 11% in state and federal excise taxes.

(a) What was the basic price of the car?

(b) What amount of sales tax was paid?

(c) How much excise tax was included in the total cost?

SECTION 2
Property Tax

The typical means by which counties, cities, and independent public school boards secure revenue is the **property tax**. This tax applies to **real estate** (land and the building improvements on it), as well as to **personal property** (cash, cars, household furnishings, appliances, jewelry, etc.). Often, the real-property tax and personal-property tax are combined into a single assessment. Two things affect the amount of tax that will be paid: (1) the assessed value of the property, and (2) the tax rate.

Property tax is normally paid on the **assessed value** of property rather than on its market value. Assessed value in any given locality is usually determined by taking a per cent of the estimated fair market value of property. The per cent used varies greatly from locality to locality, although assessed valuations between 40% and 60% are probably most common.

Thus, the tax rate alone is not a dependable indication of how high taxes are in a community; one must also know how the assessed value of property is determined. Even though two towns have the same tax rate, taxes in one of the towns might be much higher if property there is assessed at a higher rate. Similarly, a community with a higher tax rate than surrounding areas might actually have lower taxes if property there is assessed at a much lower value. The recent trend has been for property to be assessed at higher per cents of market value and for tax rates to be reduced somewhat—with the net result that property taxes increase slightly. Assessed valuations equal to market value are becoming more common.

There are several ways in which the tax *rate* of an area might be expressed: as a per cent; as an amount per $100; or as an amount per $1,000. The latter method is less common than per cent or per $100 rates. (Another method now almost obsolete is a rate expressed in *mills*. In the same way that "per cent" means "hundredths," so "mills" indicates "thousandths." Thus, a rate of 15 mills means .015 and represents another way of expressing a rate per $1,000.)

The county commissioners, city councilmen, or other board responsible for establishing the tax rate use the following procedure: After the budget (total tax needed) for the coming year has been determined, and the total assessed value of property in the area is known, the rate is computed:

$$\text{Rate} = \frac{\text{Total tax needed}}{\text{Total assessed valuation}}$$

Example One

Markly County has an annual budget of $4,800,000. If the taxable property in the county is assessed at $300,000,000, what will be the tax rate for next year? Express this rate (a) as a per cent, (b) as an amount per $100, and (c) as an amount per $1,000.

$$\text{Rate} = \frac{\text{Total tax needed}}{\text{Total assessed value}}$$

$$= \frac{\$4,800,000}{\$300,000,000}$$

$$\text{Rate} = 0.016$$

Solution

(a) The property tax rate is 1.6% of the assessed value of property.

(b) When the rate is expressed per $100, the decimal point is marked off after the hundredths place. Thus, the rate is $1.60 per C (or per $100).

(c) The rate per $1,000 is found by marking off the decimal point after the thousandths place. Hence, the rate is $16.00 per M (or per $1,000).

In most instances, the tax rate does not divide out to an even quotient as in Example 1. When a tax rate does not come out even, the final digit to be used is always rounded off to the next highest digit, regardless of the size of the next digit in the remainder.

Example Two

The tax rate initially computed for the Richland Independent School District is 0.0152437+. Express this rate (a) as a per cent to two decimal places, (b) per $100 of valuation (correct to cents), and (c) per $1,000 of valuation (correct to cents).

Solution

(a) 1.53%   (b) $1.53 per C   (c) $15.25 per M

Property tax is found using the formula

$$\text{Rate} \times \text{Valuation} = \text{Tax}$$

The same basic formula is also used to find the rate or the valuation (assessed value) of property when either one is unknown.

Example Three   How much property tax will be due on a home assessed at $15,600 if the tax rate is 2%?

$$R = 2\% \qquad\qquad R \times \quad V \quad = T$$
$$V = \$15,600 \qquad 2\% \times \$15,600 = T$$
$$T = ? \qquad\qquad\qquad \$312 = T$$

The real property tax on this home is $312.

Example Four   A duplex apartment in Orange County is assessed at $9,500 and is subject to tax at the rate of $1.60 per C. Calculate the real property tax.

$$R = \$1.60 \text{ per C} \qquad R \times V = T$$
$$V = \$9,500 \qquad\qquad 1.60 \times 95 = T$$
$$\quad = \$95 \text{ hundred} \qquad \$152 = T$$
$$T = ?$$

A property tax of $152 is due on the duplex.

NOTE: When the tax formula is solved for valuation (*V*), the quotient obtained represents that many hundreds or thousands of dollars of valuation, according to whether the rate is per $100 or per $1,000. The original quotient must be converted to a complete dollar valuation. (For example, a solution of "$72" means "$72 hundred" when the rate is per $100; hence, the assessed value must be rewritten $7,200.)

Example Five   A property tax of $420 was paid in Brazos City, where the tax rate is $17.50 per M. What is the assessed value of the property?

$$R = \$17.50 \text{ per M} \qquad R \times V = T$$
$$V = ? \qquad\qquad\qquad 17.50\,V = \$420$$
$$T = \$420 \qquad\qquad\qquad V = \frac{420}{17.50}$$
$$\qquad\qquad\qquad\qquad = 24 \text{ thousand}$$
$$\qquad\qquad\qquad\qquad V = \$24,000$$

The property is assessed at $24,000.

Example Six The office building of Wesson & White, Inc., which is assessed at $86,500, was taxed $1,557. Determine the property tax rate per $1,000.

$$R = ? \text{ per M} \qquad\qquad R \times V = T$$
$$V = \$86,500 \qquad\qquad R \times \$86.5 = \$1,557$$
$$= \$86.5 \text{ thousand} \qquad\qquad 86.5\,R = 1,557$$
$$T = \$1,557 \qquad\qquad R = \frac{1,557}{86.5}$$
$$R = \$18 \text{ per M}$$

The tax rate is $18 per $1,000 of assessed valuation.

SECTION 2 *Problems*

In the following problems, express each tax rate as indicated.

	Tax Rate	Express the Rate
1.	0.0137229+	(a) As a per cent with one decimal place
		(b) As an amount per $100, correct to cents
		(c) As an amount per $1,000, correct to cents
2.	0.0174385+	(a) As a per cent with two decimal places
		(b) As an amount per $100, correct to cents
		(c) As an amount per $1,000, correct to cents
3.	0.0213724+	(a) As a per cent with three decimal places
		(b) As an amount per $100, correct to cents
		(c) As an amount per $1,000, correct to cents
4.	0.0225479+	(a) As a per cent with one decimal place
		(b) As an amount per $100, correct to cents
		(c) As an amount per $1,000, correct to cents

Find each missing factor relating to property tax.

	Rate	Assessed Value	Tax
5.	(a) 1.8%	$10,500	
	(b) $1.65 per C	14,000	
	(c) $13.50 per M	9,600	

	Rate	Assessed Value	Tax
(d)	2.2%		$187
(e)	$1.25 per C		95
(f)	$18.75 per M		330
(g)	?%	15,000	180
(h)	? per C	12,400	217
(i)	? per M	10,000	135
6. (a)	1.5%	$18,400	
(b)	$1.72 per C	15,000	
(c)	$13.60 per M	22,500	
(d)	2.8%		$266
(e)	$2.65 per C		371
(f)	$17.25 per M		414
(g)	?%	13,500	189
(h)	? per C	17,500	301
(i)	? per M	8,000	132

7. Citizens of Vista Heights pay a property tax of $12.50 per $1,000 of valuation. Compute the tax assessment on a home assessed at $11,200.

8. Williams County has a property tax rate of 2.3%. Determine the tax levied on a homeowner whose property is assessed at $22,000.

9. The property tax rate in Oakdale is $1.54 per C. Find the tax due on a home assessed at $15,000.

10. Residents of Hortonville are subject to a property tax of $1.85 per $100. How much tax will be due on a dental office building assessed at $38,000?

11. A resident of White Plains paid $168 property tax. If the tax rate was $1.60 per $100, what was the assessed value of his property?

12. The property tax rate in Springdale is $18.80 per $1,000. What is the assessed value of an unimproved lot on which the tax due is $141?

13. The school district in Anderson Mill taxes property at 1.8%. Determine the assessed value of a home for which $495 was due in property taxes.

14. A property owner paid $748 in property taxes to the Broughton school district. If the tax rate was $1.76 per C, what is the assessed value of the property?

15. A property owner in Phillips County paid $240 in property tax on an office building assessed at $16,000. What per cent is the county tax rate?

16. Property taxes cost a citizen of Port Nueces $535. If the property was assessed at $21,400, what per cent was the town's tax rate?

17. A tax of $369 was paid on a commercial property assessed at $16,400. Find the tax rate per $100 of assessed value.

18. A small manufacturing plant in Georgetown was assessed at $56,800 and was levied a property tax of $1,065. Determine the property tax rate per $1,000 in Georgetown.

19. The property tax was $396 on a store building when the tax rate was $16.50 per $1,000. During the succeeding year, the assessed value of the building was increased by $4,000 and the property tax amounted to $476. How much had the tax rate increased? (*Hint:* Solve each year separately.)

20. The property tax was $444 on a home assessed at $24,000. The following year, the tax rate was decreased $.25 per $100 and the property tax was $488. Determine how much the assessed value of the house had increased the second year.

CHAPTER 5   *Glossary*

Assessed value. A property value (usually computed as some per cent of true market value) which is used as a basis for levying property taxes.

Excise tax. A tax levied on the manufacture or sale of certain products and services, usually luxury items, or to finance projects related to the item taxed; paid in addition to sales tax.

Personal property. Possessions (such as cars, cash, household furnishings, appliances, jewelry, etc.) which together with real prop-

erty are subject to property tax.

Property tax. A tax levied on real property and personal property; the chief means by which counties, cities, and independent school districts obtain revenue.

Real property. Real estate (land and buildings) which together with personal property is subject to property tax.

Sales tax. Tax levied by states (and sometimes by cities) on the sale of merchandise and services.

CHAPTER 6

Insurance

CHAPTER 6 OBJECTIVES

Upon completion of Chapter 6, the student will be able to:

1. Define and use correctly the terminology associated with each topic.

2. a. Compute fire insurance premiums
   (*Section 1; Example 1; Problems 1–4, 11, 12*).
   b. Compute the premium refund due when policy is canceled (1) by the insured, or (2) by the carrier (*Examples 2, 3: Problems 1–4, 13, 14*).

3. a. Determine compensation due following a fire loss, if a coinsurance clause requirement is not met (*Example 4; Problems 5, 6, 15–20*).
   b. Find each company's share of a loss when full coverage is divided among several companies (*Example 5; Problems 7, 8, 21–24*).
   c. Find each company's share of a loss when a coinsurance requirement is not met (*Example 6; Problems 9, 10, 25–28*).

4. a. Compute the annual premium for (1) automobile liability and medical payment insurance, and (2) comprehensive–collision insurance
   (*Section 2; Examples 1, 3; Problems 1–12*).
   b. Find the compensation due following an accident
   (*Examples 2, 4; Problems 13–20*).

5. Determine premiums for the following life insurance policies: (a) term, (b) whole life, (c) 20-payment life, and (d) endowment.
   (*Section 3; Examples 1, 2; Problems 1, 2; Problems 1, 2, 9–14*).

6. Calculate the following nonforfeiture values: (a) cash value, (b) paid-up insurance, and (c) extended term insurance.
   (*Example 3; Problems 3, 4, 15–18*).

7. a. Determine (1) the interest adjusted net cost, and (2) the net cost index over the term of a life insurance policy.
   b. Compare the costs of different policies.
   (*Example 4; Problems 5, 6, 19–24*).

8. Compare the monthly (and total) annuities that a beneficiary could receive under various settlement options. (*Examples 5–7; Problems 7, 8, 25–32*).

6

All insurance is carried in order to provide financial compensation should some undesirable event occur. Insurance operates on the principle of shared risk. Many persons purchase insurance protection and their payments are pooled in order to provide funds with which to pay those who experience losses. Thus, rates are lower when many different people purchase the same protection and divide the risk; rates would be much higher if only a few people had to pay in enough money to provide reimbursement for a major loss.

The risk that an insurance company assumes by insuring an event always influences how high the rates will be. The company determines the mathematical probability that the insured event will occur and then sets its rates accordingly. The insurance company does not know which of its clients will suffer a loss, but it knows from experience how many losses to expect. The insurance rates must be high enough to pay the expected losses, to pay the expenses of operating the company, and to provide a reserve fund should losses exceed the expected amounts during any period.

The payment made to purchase insurance coverage is called a **premium**. Insurance premiums may usually be paid either annually, semiannually, quarterly, or monthly. The total cost of insurance is slightly higher when payments are made more frequently, in order to cover the cost of increased bookkeeping. An insurance contract, or **policy**, defines in detail the provisions and limitations of the coverage. The amount of insurance specified by the policy is the **face value** of the policy. Insurance premiums are paid in advance, and the **term** of the policy is the time period for which the policy will remain in effect. The insurance company is often referred to as the **insurer**, the **underwriter**, or the **carrier**. The person or business that purchases insurance is called the **insured** or the **policyholder**. When an insured loss occurs, the payment that the insurance company makes to reimburse the policyholder (or another designated person) is often called an **indemnity**.

As indicated above, insurance is sold in order to provide financial protection to the policyholder; it is not intended to be a profit-making proposition when a loss occurs. Thus, insurance settlements are always limited to either the actual amount of loss or the face amount of the policy, whichever is smaller.

Individual states have insurance commissions which regulate premium structure and insurance requirements (such as required automobile insurance) passed by their legislatures. Thus, insurance practices and premium computation vary widely from state to state.

SECTION 1
Business Insurance

Certain standard forms of insurance are carried by almost all businesses; these types of insurance are discussed on the following pages. Because of its importance to private citizens as well as to business organizations, fire insurance receives particular attention.

Fire Insurance

Basic fire insurance provides financial protection against property damage resulting from fire or lightning. (Insured property may be buildings and their contents, vehicles, building sites, agricultural crops, forest crops, etc.) Further damage resulting from smoke or from attempts to extinguish or contain a fire may be as costly as the fire damage itself. Therefore, **extended coverage** is usually included to provide protection against smoke, water, and chemical damage, as well as physical destruction caused by firemen having to break into the property or taking measures to keep a fire from spreading. Extended coverage also covers riot, civil commotion, hurricane, wind, and hail damage.

Homeowners often purchase a **comprehensive** "package" **policy**, which, in addition to the coverage above, also provides protection against loss due to theft, vandalism and malicious mischief, accidental loss or damage, and liability coverage in case of personal injury or property damage to visitors on the property. Similar protection may also be purchased by business firms, although it is sometimes obtained in separate policies.

Premiums

Historically, fire insurance policies have been written for several years in advance and reduced long-term rates have been given for premium prepayments. (For instance, a prepaid 3-year policy would have cost only 2.7 times as much as a 1-year

policy... ...ling costs for reimbursing fire losses
have ... ...these practices. Most fire
insu... ...3 years, and the prepaid
cost... ...e 1-year premium. If the
3-y... ...nts, interest may also be
cha... ...t this total cost would still
be... ...er, since rates have been
in...

...establishes its fire insurance
ra... every commercial property
a... ...ı. These rates vary greatly,
b... factors. The primary factors
...construction of the building,
...erein, (3) the quality of fire
...buildings, and (5) past experi-

Thus a building... ...on (all steel and concrete, and
...ch lower insurance rate than a
...larly, property located near fire
...re department in an area that
...e much lower premiums than
...me distance from a fire station.
...sprinkler systems would reduce
...normally have a lower rate than a
...nature of painting supplies; if the
...asoline storage area, however, its
...ly.

Fire insurance rates... ...e usually quoted from a table that
gives the exact amount to be paid for any specific level of coverage. Rates
for commercial properties, however, are often quoted as an amount per
$100 of insurance coverage, and the exact premium due is then obtained
by computation. (Separate rates are charged for insurance on the building
itself, on the furniture and fixtures, and on the stock or merchandise—
normally in that order of increasing premium expense.) Tables 6-1 and 6-2
and Example 1 illustrate the different ways in which premiums may be
determined.

Example One   Using Tables 6-1 and 6-2, determine the fire insurance premium due
for (a) a $25,000 home policy in the class B category, with contents
valued at $10,000; (b) a brick building in class C insured for $84,000.

TABLE 6-1: ANNUAL FIRE INSURANCE PREMIUMS FOR DWELLINGS

Amount of Insurance	STRUCTURE CLASS				CONTENTS CLASS			
	A	B	C	D	A	B	C	D
$ 5,000	$12	$18	$25	$30	$15	$17	$29	$31
10,000	15	21	29	36	18	25	32	40
15,000	20	32	45	50	24	35	48	54
20,000	24	37	49	55	29	38	55	60
25,000	28	40	52	58	32	43	57	64

TABLE 6-2: ANNUAL FIRE INSURANCE RATES FOR BUILDINGS PER $100 OF COVERAGE

Type of Construction	CLASS			
	A	B	C	D
Brick	$.15	$ .25	$ .325	$ .40
Frame	.875	1.15	1.40	1.625

Solution

(a) Class B structure, $25,000 policy = $40
Class B contents, $10,000 policy = <u> 25</u>
Total annual premium = $65

(b) For commercial properties, fire insurance premiums are computed using the procedure

$$\text{Premium} = \text{Rate} \times \text{Value of policy}$$

or simply

$$P = R \times V$$

Thus, the premium for the brick building above would be computed as follows:

$$R = \$.325 \text{ per } \$100 \qquad P = R \times V$$
$$V = \$84,000 \qquad\qquad\quad = \$.325 \times \$840$$
$$\quad = \$840 \text{ hundreds} \qquad P = \$273 \quad \text{Annual premium}$$
$$P = ?$$

The annual premium on the building itself is $273. The premium required to insure the contents would be separately computed in a similar manner, based on a rate per $100 and their value.

NOTE: Fire insurance premiums are rounded to the nearest whole dollar.

Short-Term
Policies

Sometimes a business may wish to purchase fire insurance for only a limited time in order to obtain coverage on merchandise which will soon be sold. Also, policies are sometimes canceled by the policyholder if he sells the insured property, if he moves, and so on. If, for any reason, a policy is in effect for less than 1 year, it is considered a short-term policy. The premium to be charged for such a policy is computed according to a short-rate table, such as Table 6-3. A very short policy is relatively expensive because of the cost to the insurance company of selling, writing, and processing the policy.

TABLE 6-3:   SHORT-TERM RATES INCLUDING
             CANCELLATIONS BY THE INSURED

Months of Coverage	Per Cent of Annual Premium Charged	Months of Coverage	Per Cent of Annual Premium Charged
1	20%	7	75%
2	30	8	80
3	40	9	85
4	50	10	90
5	60	11	95
6	70	12	100

Example
Two

Grant Avery owned a home on which he paid $45 for fire insurance. He moved after 8 months and canceled the insurance policy. How much refund will Avery receive?

Solution

For an 8-month premium, 80% of the annual premium will be charged:

Annual premium	$45
	× .8
8-month premium	$36

Annual premium	$45
8-month premium	− 36
Refund due	$ 9

Occasionally, it becomes necessary for an insurance company to cancel a policy. This might happen because of excessive claims or a refusal of the policyholder to accept higher rates when the fire risk has increased. The company ordinarily must give advance notice that the policy will be canceled, thus allowing the policyholder time to purchase another policy before the coverage ceases. When a company cancels, it may keep only that fraction of the annual premium equivalent to the time which has elapsed. Many companies compute this time precisely, using $\dfrac{\text{Exact days}}{365}$; however, we shall use approximate time for our calculations. The insurance company is not entitled to short-term rates when it cancels the policy.

Example Three

A $64,000 commercial fire policy, sold at the rate of $.75 per $100, is canceled by the company after 5 months. How much refund will the policyholder receive?

The annual premium is determined in the usual manner:

$$R = \$.75 \text{ per } \$100 \qquad \text{Annual premium } = \$.75 \times \$640$$
$$V = \$64,000 \qquad\qquad\qquad\qquad\qquad = \$480$$
$$ = \$640 \text{ hundreds}$$

Since the company canceled after 5 months, only $\frac{5}{12}$ of the annual premium may be retained:

$$\text{5-month premium} = \tfrac{5}{12} \times \$480 \qquad\qquad \text{Annual premium} \qquad \$480$$
$$= \$200 \qquad\qquad\qquad \text{5-month premium} \quad -\ 200$$
$$\text{Refund due} \qquad\qquad \$280$$

Compensation for Loss; Coinsurance Clause

Experience indicates that most fires result in the loss of only a small portion of the total value of property. Realizing that total destruction is relatively rare, many people would be tempted to economize by purchasing only partial coverage. However, to pay the full amount of these damages would be extremely expensive to an insurance company if most policyholders were paying premiums on only the partial value of their property. Therefore, to maintain an economically sound business operation, as well as to encourage property owners to purchase full insurance coverage, many policies contain a coinsurance clause. A **coinsurance clause** guarantees full payment after a loss (up to the face amount of the policy) only if the policyholder purchases coverage which is at least a specified per cent of the total value of the property at the time the fire occurs. (For example, if a house would cost $25,000 to replace, then this figure represents the total value, regardless of how much less money the house may have cost originally.)

Many policies contain coinsurance clauses requiring 80% coverage, although lower coverage is sometimes allowed, and higher (particularly for extended coverage policies) may often be necessary. If the required coverage is not carried, the company will pay damages equivalent only to the ratio of the required coverage that is carried; the policyholder must then bear the remaining loss. (In this respect, the policyholder "coinsures" the property. The term "coinsurance" implies that the insurance company and the policyholder each assume part of the total risk.) Most policies on homes do provide full coverage; businesses are more likely than home-owners to partially coinsure themselves.

A propertyowner may purchase more insurance than the minimum requirement, of course. However, in no case will payment for damages exceed the actual value of the property destroyed, no matter how much insurance is carried. The maximum payment is always the amount of damages or the face value of the policy, whichever is smaller. When a fire occurs, the policyholder must contact the insurance company, which sends out an *insurance adjuster* to inspect the damage and determine the indemnity to be paid. (The policyholder may also have to obtain repair or reconstruction estimates from several companies.)

Example Four
Centex Distributors, Inc., operates in a building valued at $75,000. The building is insured for $50,000 under a fire policy containing an 80% coinsurance clause. (a) What part of a fire loss will the company pay? (b) How much will the company pay on a $12,000 loss? (c) On a $42,000 loss? (d) On a $72,000 loss?

Solution
(a) According to the coinsurance clause, 80% of the property value must be insured:

$$\$75,000 \times 80\% = \$60,000 \text{ insurance required}$$

$$\frac{\text{Insurance carried}}{\text{Insurance required}} = \frac{\$50,000}{\$60,000} = \frac{5}{6}$$

Centex Distributors carries only $\frac{5}{6}$ of the insurance required by the coinsurance clause; therefore, the insurance company will pay only $\frac{5}{6}$ of any loss, up to the face value of the policy. By their failure to carry the required coverage, Centex has indirectly agreed to coinsure the remaining portion of any fire loss themselves.

(b) $\frac{5}{6} \times \$12,000$ loss $= \$10,000$ insurance reimbursement

Example Four (cont.)

(c) $\frac{5}{6} \times \$42,000$ loss $= \$35,000$ indemnity

(d) $\frac{5}{6} \times \$72,000$ loss $= \$60,000$

Preliminary calculations indicate the insurance company's share of this loss to be $60,000. However, this exceeds the face of Centex's policy; therefore, the insurance company will pay only the full value of the policy, or $50,000.

Multiple Carriers

Insurance coverage on property may often be divided among several companies. This may happen because the value of the property is so high that no single company can afford to assume the entire risk, because the owner wishes to distribute his business for public relations purposes, or simply because coverage on various portions of the property was purchased separately over a period of years.

When property is insured with multiple carriers, each company pays damages in the ratio that its policy bears to the total insurance coverage. As noted previously, the total amount paid by all carriers will never exceed the value of the damage, nor will any company's payment exceed the face value of its policy. Multiple policies may also contain coinsurance clauses.

Example Five

Farnsworth Equipment suffered a $180,000 fire. They were insured under the following policies: $150,000 with Company A, $100,000 with Company B, and $50,000 with Company C. What indemnity will each company pay? (Assume that Farnsworth meets the coinsurance requirement necessary to receive full coverage on a loss.)

Coinsurance Met

POLICIES

$150,000   A pays $\dfrac{\$150,000}{\$300,000}$ or $\frac{1}{2}$ of the loss

100,000   B pays $\dfrac{\$100,000}{\$300,000}$ or $\frac{1}{3}$ of the loss

50,000   C pays $\dfrac{\$\ 50,000}{\$300,000}$ or $\frac{1}{6}$ of the loss
_____

$300,000

The full $180,000 loss is insured; therefore, each company's payment is as follows:

Company A: $\frac{1}{2} \times \$180,000 = \$\ 90,000$

Company B: $\frac{1}{3} \times\ 180,000 =\ 60,000$

Company C: $\frac{1}{6} \times\ 180,000 =\ 30,000$

Total indemnity $= \$180,000$

Example Six

Centex Distributors' building (Example 4) is valued at $75,000 but is insured for only $50,000 under an 80% coinsurance requirement. Assume now that this $50,000 coverage is divided between Company A ($30,000) and Company B ($20,000). (a) What part of any loss is covered? (b) How much reimbursement will Centex receive after a $12,000 fire? (c) What is each insurance company's payment after the $12,000 loss?

Coinsurance Not met

(a) As in Example 4, the required coverage is $80\% \times \$75,000$, or $60,000. Thus, the part of any loss that is covered (up to the face value of the policy) as before is

$$\frac{\text{Insurance carried}}{\text{Insurance required}} = \frac{\$50,000}{\$60,000} = \frac{5}{6}$$

(b) Again, following a $12,000 fire,

$\frac{5}{6} \times \$12,000 = \$10,000$ Total indemnity

(to be shared by all insurance carriers)

(c) Each company's share of this $10,000 indemnity (due following the $12,000 loss) is in the ratio of its policy to the total insurance carried ($50,000):

Company A: $\dfrac{\$30,000}{\$50,000}$ or $\dfrac{3}{5} \times \$10,000 = \$\ 6,000$

Company B: $\dfrac{\$20,000}{\$50,000}$ or $\dfrac{2}{5} \times\ 10,000 =\ 4,000$

Total indemnity $= \$10,000$

Thus, with multiple carriers, the $10,000 will be reimbursed as $6,000 from Company A and $4,000 from Company B. Centex assumes the remaining $2,000 loss themselves.

Several other types of insurance are carried by most businesses. The following paragraphs give a brief description of this additional insurance.

Business Interruption   **Business interruption insurance** is purchased as a supplement to fire and property insurance. Whereas fire and property insurance provides coverage for the actual physical damage resulting from a fire or natural disaster (earthquake, flood, hurricane, tornado, etc.), business interruption insurance provides protection against loss of income until the physical damage can be repaired and normal business resumed. This insurance provides money to meet business expenses that continue despite the lapse in operations: interest, loan payments, mortgage or rent payments, taxes, utilities, insurance, and advertising, as well as the salaries of key members of the firm and ordinarily even the anticipated net profit.

Liability   Businesses may be held financially liable, or responsible, for many different occurrences; general **liability** insurance is a business essential in order to provide this protection. An accident causing personal injury to a customer often results in the customer's suing the business. When firms are declared negligent of their responsibility for the customer's safety, judgments of large sums of money are often granted by the courts. Hence, no well-managed company would operate without public liability insurance.

Another area in which court judgments have been quite large in recent years is bodily injury resulting from defective or dangerous products. Companies that manufacture mechanical products or food products that could conceivably be harmful can be insured by *product liability* policies.

Liability for the safety of employees is covered under **worker's compensation** policies. This insurance provides payments to an employee who loses work time because of sickness or accidental injury resulting directly from work responsibilities. Most worker's compensation policies also provide death benefits in case of a fatality. The labor statutes in many states require employers to carry this insurance; and some states have a state fund for worker's compensation, although in most cases it is purchased from commercial insurance companies. As would be expected, worker's compensation rates vary greatly according to the occupational hazards of different jobs. These rates are usually quoted as an amount per $100 in wages. The premiums are usually based only on regular wages; that is, premiums are not paid on overtime wages.

A business firm's liability for the operation of motor vehicles is similar to that of the general public; both are included in the following section of this chapter. Business policies, however, often contain special provisions covering fleets of cars, hired cars, or the cars of employees being used in company business.

Money and
Securities
The theft of money and securities (such as checks, stocks, titles of ownership, etc.) is a constant hazard in many businesses. A number of different policies cover the various conditions under which money and valuable securities may be stolen, such as burglary from an office safe or robbery of a messenger carrying money or securities to or from the business.

General theft policies do not cover the dishonesty of employees, which must be provided for by separate policies. *Fidelity bonds* protect against embezzlement or other loss by employees who handle large sums of money. These bonds are essential in banks, retail stores, and other offices where large amounts of cash or securities are involved.

The worst financial loss experienced by most retail stores results from shoplifting, a problem of major national proportion that is increasing annually. There is presently no insurance available that adequately protects against shoplifting losses; thus, the business's only means of recovery is to pass the loss along to consumers in the form of higher prices.

Life Insurance
Particularly in small businesses, the death of a partner or a key person in the firm may jeopardize the entire business operation. Many firms, therefore, purchase life insurance on critical personnel to protect against such financial loss. Such policies also enable the firm to buy from the estate the business interest of a deceased partner. Life insurance is discussed in more detail in a later section.

Group Insurance
Group insurance available at many companies provides life insurance and/or health and accident coverage for employees and their families. This coverage, unlike worker's compensation, provides coverage for illnesses or accidents not related to occupational duties. Most group life insurance plans offer term life insurance similar to the policies described later in this chapter. These group life policies are also available to many individuals through the official associations of their business or profession.

Typical group hospitalization plans provide basic benefits for either accidental injuries or medical/surgical care. Each policy contains a long list of covered hospital services and surgical procedures, each specifying the maximum amount that will be paid to the hospital and surgeon. Maternity benefits are generally included in group policies, although a specified waiting period is usually first required for this coverage, as well as for coverage of certain preexisting medical conditions.

Some group policies also include a major medical supplement, which provides for certain expenses not covered by the basic benefits. For example, major medical coverage will pay a specified per cent of the costs of physicians' fees, prescriptions, and many services or procedures not otherwise covered, as well as excess expenses above those reimbursed through the basic policy. All major medical plans and some basic policies specify a deductible amount which the patient must first pay before insurance coverage becomes effective.

The employer often pays half and sometimes all of the group insurance premiums as one of the organization's fringe benefits. Even when the employee pays the entire cost, group insurance is cheaper than similar coverage purchased privately. Also, group policies may usually be purchased without a physical examination, which permits some people to receive insurance protection when they would not ordinarily qualify. Coverage usually terminates immediately when a worker leaves the firm, although a group policy may often be converted to a private policy (at an increased rate, of course).

In many cases, group insurance provides standard coverage for all employees. However, certain benefits may sometimes be increased according to the employee's salary or years of service to the business.

SECTION 1 *Problems*

Compute the fire insurance premiums required for the following homes, using the premiums listed for dwellings in Tables 6–1 and 6–2.

		Structure Value	Contents Value	Class	Total Premium
1.	(a)	$20,000	$10,000	A	
	(b)	25,000	15,000	C	
2.	(a)	$15,000	$ 5,000	B	
	(b)	25,000	10,000	D	

Compute the premium and/or the refund due for the following amounts of insurance for the terms indicated. Use the short-term rates from Table 6-3 when applicable.

		Amount of Insurance	Annual Rate (per $100)	Term	Canceled by	Premium	Refund Due
3.	(a)	$25,000	$ .22	1 year	x		x
	(b)	20,000	.55	4 months	x		x
	(c)	15,000	.80	6 months	Insured		
	(d)	50,000	.72	5 months	Carrier		
4.	(a)	$60,000	$ .45	1 year	x		x
	(b)	24,000	.25	10 months	x		x
	(c)	45,000	.32	8 months	Insured		
	(d)	20,000	.18	4 months	Carrier		

Compute the compensation (indemnity) that will be paid under each of the following conditions.

		Property Value	Coinsurance Clause	Insurance Required	Insurance Carried	Amount of Loss	Indemnity
5.	(a)	$10,000	80%		$10,000	$ 3,000	
	(b)	30,000	90		24,000	18,000	
	(c)	25,000	80		16,000	15,000	
	(d)	90,000	90		45,000	90,000	
	(e)	80,000	70		48,000	49,000	
6.	(a)	$50,000	80%		$42,000	$25,000	
	(b)	75,000	80		45,000	36,000	
	(c)	80,000	90		48,000	60,000	
	(d)	45,000	80		30,000	18,000	
	(e)	60,000	75		35,000	54,000	

Determine the compensation to be paid by each carrier below (assume that coinsurance clause requirements are met).

		Company	Amount of Policy	Ratio of Coverage	Amount of Loss	Compensation
7.	(a)	A	$24,000		$15,000	
		B	16,000			
	(b)	L	12,000		20,000	
		M	30,000			
		N	18,000			

	Company	Amount of Policy	Ratio of Coverage	Amount of Loss	Compensation
8. (a)	C	$27,000		$24,000	
	D	45,000			
(b)	R	15,000		60,000	
	I	25,000			
	S	50,000			
	K	10,000			

Calculate the settlement due from each carrier below under the given coinsurance terms.

	Property Value	Coin-surance	Insur-ance Re-quired ($)	Insur-ance Car-ried ($)	Fire Loss	Total Indem-nity	Com-pany	Policy Value	Com-pany's Ratio	Pay-ment ($)
9. (a)	$150,000	80%			$80,000		A	$60,000		
							B	30,000		
(b)	80,000	70			28,000		P	20,000		
							Q	16,000		
10. (a)	$120,000	80%			$48,000		C	$20,000		
							D	60,000		
(b)	50,000	90			15,000		R	21,000		
							S	15,000		

11. King's Grant plantation purchased a 5-month fire insurance policy of $40,000 to insure their crops during the growing season. The annual rate for this coverage was $.15 per $100. Find the cost of the short-term policy.

12. Surf and Sand Casuals, located at a beach resort, needs a $30,000 fire insurance policy to protect its merchandise during the 7-month resort "season." Determine the short-term premium if the annual rate for this coverage is $.39 per $100.

13. The annual rate for fire insurance on a $15,000 store building was $.72 per $100.

Compute the premium charged and the refund due if the policy is canceled after 7 months.

(a) By the insured.
(b) By the carrier.

14. An annual rate of $.64 per $100 was charged on a $45,000 fire insurance policy. What are the cost and the refund due if the policy is canceled after 8 months.

(a) By the insured?
(b) By the carrier?

15. The fire insurance policy on a $90,000 manufacturing plant contains a 70% coinsurance clause. The plant is insured for

$75,000. How much should the insurance company pay following
(a) A $9,000 fire?
(b) A $27,000 fire?
(c) An $82,000 fire?

16. A $120,000 business office was insured for $105,000 with a fire policy requiring 85% coverage. Determine the amount to be paid if there is
(a) A $32,000 fire.
(b) A $75,000 fire.
(c) A $110,000 fire.

17. The coinsurance clause on a $150,000 plant required 80% fire coverage. The plant was insured for $100,000. What settlement should the company make following
(a) An $18,000 loss?
(b) A $42,000 loss?
(c) A total loss?

18. The owner of a $50,000 retail shop purchased a $36,000 fire insurance policy which included an 80% coinsurance clause. How much settlement would the company pay in event of
(a) A $6,000 loss?
(b) A $30,000 loss?
(c) A total loss?

19. The policy on an $80,000 office building requires 75% fire coverage. The building is insured for $48,000. What amount should the company pay following
(a) $3,500 fire damages?
(b) $27,500 damages?
(c) $65,000 damages?

20. A building valued at $160,000 is insured for $120,000. If the fire insurance policy includes a 90% coinsurance clause, determine the compensation due when a fire resulted in
(a) $18,000 damage.
(b) $72,000 damage.
(c) $150,000 damage.

21. A home is insured against fire under an $18,000 policy with Company M and a $12,000 policy with Company N, which meet coinsurance requirements. What settlement should each company make following
(a) A $7,500 fire?
(b) A $20,000 fire?

22. A food processing plant is insured for $250,000 with Company A; $200,000 with Company B; and $150,000 with Company C. The coinsurance requirements are met. Determine each company's indemnity following
(a) A $240,000 fire.
(b) A $480,000 fire.
(c) A $720,000 fire.

23. Fire protection on a retail store is provided by the following policies: $180,000 with Company R; $120,000 with Company S; and $60,000 with Company T. All coinsurance clauses are met. What is each company's share of
(a) A $15,000 loss?
(b) A $144,000 loss?
(c) A $420,000 loss?

24. A bakery has fire insurance policies with coverage at the levels specified in their coinsurance clauses. These policies include $200,000 with Company W; $150,000 with Company X; $50,000 with Company Y; and $100,000 with Company Z. Compute each company's liability for
(a) A $250,000 fire.
(b) A $400,000 fire.
(c) A $600,000 fire.

25. Fire inspectors valued Hines Clothing Shop at $40,000. Despite an 80% coinsurance clause, Hines' fire insurance policies total only $24,000 ($8,000 with Company A and $16,000 with Company B).

(a) What total indemnity will Hines receive after a $20,000 fire?

(b) How much will each company pay toward the $20,000 loss?

26. Winn's Variety Store was valued at $80,000. Their fire policies of $20,000 with Company P and $36,000 with Company Q include 80% coinsurance clauses.

(a) How much total compensation will Winn's be paid following $32,000 fire damages?

(b) What is the amount of each company's settlement?

27. The plant of Hillcrest Industries was valued at $200,000. Seventy-five per cent coinsurance clauses are attached to their fire policies of $15,000 with Company G; $60,000 with Company H; and $45,000 with Company K.

(a) What total settlement should the firm receive after an $80,000 fire?

(b) Determine each company's liability toward the settlement.

28. Star Manufacturing Co. has fire policies of $80,000 with Company L; $40,000 with Company M; and $120,000 with Company N. The plant was valued at $350,000 with 80% coinsurance clauses attached.

(a) What total indemnity should Star be paid after a $210,000 fire?

(b) What amount should each company pay toward this $210,000 loss?

SECTION 2
Motor Vehicle Insurance

Automobile and/or truck insurance is carried by responsible owners (private or industrial) of most vehicles. Insurance policies on motor vehicles are usually written only for a maximum term of 1 year. The primary reason for the 1-year policy is the alarmingly high, nationwide accident rate, which constantly increases rates for automobile insurance, since inflation causes repair costs to spiral. Since insurance rates always reflect the risk taken by the insurance company, the driving record (and age) of the operator is another major factor in determining the cost of vehicle insurance. This further accounts for the 1-year policies, since a driver's record may fluctuate over a period of years.

Insurance on motor vehicles is divided into two basic categories: (1) liability coverage, and (2) comprehensive–collision coverage.

Liability Insurance

Liability insurance provides financial protection for damage inflicted by the policyholder to the person or property of other people. As a protection to its citizens, some states require the owners of all vehicles registered in the state to purchase minimum amounts of liability insurance. Liability insurance covers **bodily injury liability** (liability for physical injury resulting from the policyholder's negligence) and **property damage liability** (liability for damage caused by the policyholder to another vehicle or other property.) Also available on an optional basis is **medical payment** insurance, which supplements other health and accident insurance the policyholder may carry. This insurance will begin paying medical costs immediately, without waiting for the courts to rule on a liability suit. "Medical pay" covers the insured driver as well as the person's immediate family and any injured passengers.

Minimum liability coverage is now often quoted as "10/20/5 coverage." This means that the policy will pay up to $10,000 for the bodily injury caused to a single person, or, when more than one person was involved in the accident, a maximum total of $20,000 for the injuries inflicted to all victims. Also, a maximum of $5,000 will be paid for the property damage resulting from a single accident. Much higher liability coverage is available at rates only slightly higher than those for minimum coverage. (Many states require higher coverage than the minimum 10/20/5 coverage.) Thus, many drivers purchase bodily injury coverage up to $300,000/$300,000 and property damage coverage up to $100,000.

If a court suit should result in a victim's being awarded a settlement that exceeds the policyholder's coverage, the additional sum would have to be paid by the insured. For example, suppose that a driver carried 10/20/10 liability insurance and a court awards $13,000 to one victim and $2,000 to each of three other victims. Even though the total awarded to all victims ($19,000) is less than the maximum total coverage ($20,000), the insurance company will not pay the total award: Since the maximum liability for a single victim is $10,000, the insurance company is responsible only for $16,000 ($10,000 to the first victim and $2,000 each to the other three victims). The remaining $3,000 of the $13,000 judgment must be paid by the policyholder.

Two factors determine the standard rates charged for liability insurance: the classification of the vehicle (according to how much it is driven, whether used for business, and the age of the driver) and the territory in which the vehicle is operated. (As would be expected, rates are higher in populous areas, since traffic congestion results in more accidents.) If a driver has a record of accidents and/or speeding tickets, insurance will be available only at greatly increased rates through an *assigned risk plan*, a joint underwriting association, or a reinsurance facility.

Table 6-4 contains excerpts of the driver classifications used to determine liability insurance premiums. As one can see from the table, drivers under 21 are intricately classified according to sex, age, and whether or not they have taken a driver training course. Males under 25 are classified according to marital status and whether they are the owners or principal operators of the automobiles. Unmarried males may continue to be so classified until they reach 30. Most mature drivers would be classified "all

TABLE 6-4: DRIVER CLASSIFICATIONS

Multiples of Base Annual Automobile Insurance Premiums

			Pleasure; Less than 3 Miles To Work Each Way	*Drives to Work, 3 to 10 Miles Each Way*	*Drives to Work, 10 Miles or More Each Way*	*Used in Business*
No young operators	Only operator is female, age 30–64		.90	1.00	1.30	1.40
	One or more operators age 65 or over		1.00	1.10	1.40	1.50
	All others		1.00	1.10	1.40	1.50
Young females	Age 16	DT[a]	1.40	1.50	1.80	1.90
		No DT	1.55	1.65	1.95	2.05
	Age 20	DT	1.05	1.15	1.45	1.55
		No DT	1.10	1.20	1.50	1.60
Young males (married)	Age 16	DT	1.60	1.70	2.00	2.10
		No DT	1.80	1.90	2.20	2.30
	Age 20	DT	1.45	1.55	1.85	1.95
		No DT	1.50	1.60	1.90	2.00
	Age 21		1.40	1.50	1.80	1.90
	Age 24		1.10	1.20	1.50	1.60

[a] "DT" indicates completion of a certified driver training course.

others." (An automobile is classified according to the status of the youngest person who operates the car or according to the person whose driver classification requires the highest multiple.)

Table 6-5 presents some typical base annual rates for automobile liability insurance (bodily injury and property damage) and medical payment insurance in three different territories. The total premium cost for two or more vehicles would be reduced by a certain per cent when the vehicles are covered under one insurance policy.

			Pleasure; Less than 3 Miles to Work Each Way	*Drives to Work, 3 to 10 Miles Each Way*	*Drives to Work, 10 Miles or More Each Way*	*Used in Business*
Young unmarried males (not principal operator)	Age 16	DT[a]	2.05	2.15	2.45	2.55
		No DT	2.30	2.40	2.70	2.80
	Age 20	DT	1.60	1.70	2.00	2.10
		No DT	1.70	1.80	2.10	2.20
	Age 21		1.55	1.65	1.95	2.05
	Age 24		1.10	1.20	1.50	1.60
Young unmarried males (owner or principal operator)	Age 16	DT	2.70	2.80	3.10	3.20
		No DT	3.30	3.40	3.70	3.80
	Age 20	DT	2.55	2.65	2.95	3.05
		No DT	2.70	2.80	3.10	3.20
	Age 21		2.50	2.60	2.90	3.00
	Age 24		1.90	2.00	2.30	2.40
	Age 26		1.50	1.60	1.90	2.00
	Age 29		1.10	1.20	1.50	1.60

[a] "DT" indicates completion of a certified driver training course.

TABLE 6-5: AUTOMOBILE LIABILITY AND MEDICAL PAYMENT
INSURANCE

Base Annual Premiums

	BODILY INJURY				PROPERTY DAMAGE		
Coverage	Territory 1	Territory 2	Territory 3	Coverage	Territory 1	Territory 2	Territory 3
10/20	$28	$37	$55	$ 5,000	$33	$45	$50
15/30	31	41	62	10,000	35	47	53
25/25	33	44	65	25,000	36	49	54
25/50	36	47	70	50,000	37	51	57
50/50	38	51	75	100,000	40	53	59
50/100	40	53	79				
100/100	41	54	81		MEDICAL PAYMENT		
100/200	44	58	86				
100/300	45	60	89	$1,000	$12	$13	$14
200/300	48	62	91	2,500	15	16	17
300/300	50	65	94	5,000	17	18	19

Example One

Edwin Carter is 32 years old and drives his car to work each day, a one-way distance of 6 miles. The area in which he lives is classified Territory 1. (a) Determine the cost of 15/30/10 liability coverage on his automobile and $2,500 medical payment insurance. (b) What would be Carter's premium if he increased his insurance to 50/100 bodily injury and $25,000 property damage coverage (with the same $2,500 medical pay coverage)?

Solution

(a) Table 6-5 is used to compute the base annual premium for Carter's liability ($15,000 single and $30,000 total bodily injury; $10,000 property damage) and medical payment ($2,500) coverage in Territory 1:

$31   Bodily injury (15/30)
  35   Property damage ($10,000)
+ 15   Medical payment ($2,500)
_____
$81   Total base premium

The base annual premium in Territory 1 is $81 for 15/30/10 liability and $2,500 medical pay coverage. Since Carter is 32, he falls into the category "all others" in the driver classification table. Because he drives 6 miles to work, Table 6-4 indicates that the

Example One (cont.)

multiple 1.10 should be used to compute Carter's annual premium:

$81	Base annual premium
× 1.10	
$89.10	Actual annual premium

(b) Increased coverage would cost as follows:

$40	50/100 Bodily injury
36	$25,000 Property damage
15	$2,500 Medical payment
$91	Base premium
× 1.10	
$100.10	Annual premium

Example Two

Bill Hold of Hold Construction Co. was driving a company truck when it struck an automobile, injuring a mother and her son. Hold Construction was subsequently sued for $120,000 personal injuries and $4,500 property damage. The court awarded the victims a $60,000 personal injury judgment and the entire property damage suit. Hold Construction carries 25/50/10 liability coverage. (a) How much will the insurance company pay? (b) How much of the award will Hold Construction have to pay?

Solution

(a) The insurance company will pay the $50,000 maximum total bodily injury converage ($25,000 maximum per person) and the total award for property damage ($4,500). Thus, the insurance company will pay a total of $54,500.

(b) Since the court awarded the claimants more than Hold Construction's bodily injury coverage, the firm will be responsible for the excess:

$60,000	Bodily injury awarded
− 50,000	Liability coverage for bodily injury
$10,000	Amount to be paid by Hold Construction

No-Fault Insurance

No-fault insurance of various types has been adopted in 16 states, and Congress has considered making a standard no-fault policy mandatory nationwide. Under **no-fault insurance,** each motorist collects for bodily injuries from his or her own insurance company after an accident, regardless of who is to blame. Reimbursement is made for medical expenses and the value of lost wages and/or services (such as the cost of a house-keeper for an injured mother). The victim then forfeits any right to sue, unless the accident was so severe that the damages exceed a certain specified amount.

No-fault insurance was proposed as a means whereby motorists could save money on insurance but still be protected financially in case of accident. However, the savings derived through no-fault insurance pertain only to reduced bodily injury premiums, since small suits are disallowed. Premiums for property-damage liability, as well as comprehensive and collision insurance on the driver's own vehicle (described below) are not reduced by the adoption of no-fault insurance. Furthermore, considerably more than half of a motorist's premiums apply toward these latter types of insurance. Thus, rising automobile repair costs, in particular, plus the tendency of victims to sue for large amounts, as well as the increased operating costs of the insurance companies themselves, have combined to produce continually increasing premiums in most areas, despite the adoption of no-fault insurance. Since the originally high expectations for no-fault insurance have not been achieved, enthusiasm for its adoption has also lessened. As this text was prepared, Congress failed to pass the no-fault bill it was debating.

Comprehensive and Collision Insurance   Comprehensive and collision insurance protect against damage to the policyholder's own automobile. **Comprehensive insurance** covers damage resulting from fire, theft, vandalism, acts of nature, falling objects, and so forth. Protection against collision or upset damage may be obtained through **collision insurance.** (That is, collision insurance also covers damage resulting from one-car accidents—including damage to runaway, driverless vehicles—where no collision of two vehicles occurred.) Collision insurance pays for repairs to the vehicle of the insured when the policyholder is responsible for an accident, when the insured's car was damaged by a hit-and-run driver, or when another driver was responsible for the collision but did not have liability insurance and was unable to pay the property damage caused. Since collision insurance (as well as comprehensive) will pay for damages regardless of who is at fault, it is in this respect already a type of no-fault insurance and thus is not affected whenever no-fault insurance is adopted in a state.

Also available is **uninsured motorists insurance,** which offers financial protection for the policyholder's own bodily injuries when hit by a driver who did not carry bodily-injury liability insurance.

Since comprehensive and collision insurance provides compensation only to the insured, it is not required by state law. Under certain circumstances, however, this coverage is mandatory. If an automobile is purchased by monthly installment payments, the institution financing the purchase retains legal title to the automobile until all installments are paid. In order to protect their investment, these financial agencies ordinarily require the purchaser to carry comprehensive and collision insurance.

A vehicle's owner may purchase collision insurance which pays the entire cost of repairing damage; however, such insurance is rather expensive. Most collision insurance is sold with a "deductible" clause, which means that the policyholder pays a specified part of any repair cost (an amount specified in the deductible clause). For instance, if "fifty-dollar-deductible" collision insurance is purchased, the insured must pay the first $50 in damage resulting from any one collision, and the carrier will pay the remaining cost, up to the value of the vehicle. (If damage is less than $50, the owner must pay the entire cost.) Collision policies are available with various deductible amounts specified; however, $100-deductible policies are now most common, and deductibles of $200 and $250 are becoming more frequent. Whereas comprehensive policies formerly were usually written without deductible amounts, such policies are now often $50-deductible. Both collision and comprehensive coverage become considerably less expensive as the policyholder pays a higher amount of each repair cost.

Recall that standard liability rates are determined by the classification of vehicle use and the territory in which the vehicle is operated. In addition to the previous considerations, comprehensive–collision rates also depend upon the make, model, and age of the vehicle (example: "Chevrolet, Bel Air, 2 years old"). Each automobile model is assigned an identification letter from A to Z. (Less expensive models are identified by letters near the beginning of the alphabet, and successive letters identify increasingly expensive models.)

The age of the automobile influences comprehensive and collision costs, since newer automobiles are more expensive to repair. Automobiles of the current model year classified as "Age group 1"; cars in Group 2 (the first preceding model year) and Group 3 (the second preceding model year) both pay the same rate; and models of three or more years old are classified in Group 4. Table 6-6 lists excerpts of base annual comprehensive and collision insurance rates in three territories for vehicles of various ages. As in the case of liability insurance, the base annual comprehensive–collision premiums must be multiplied by a multiple reflecting the driver's classification.

TABLE 6-6:   COMPREHENSIVE AND COLLISION INSURANCE

Base Annual Premiums

Model Class	Age Group	TERRITORY 1			TERRITORY 2			TERRITORY 3		
		Comprehensive	*$50 Deductible Collision*	*$100 Deductible Collision*	*Comprehensive*	*$50 Deductible Collision*	*$100 Deductible Collision*	*Comprehensive*	*$50 Deductible Collision*	*$100 Deductible Collision*
(1)	1	$15	$ 42	$36	$19	$ 52	$40	$23	$ 60	$ 51
A–G	2, 3	12	37	33	16	46	36	18	54	45
	4	9	31	27	11	39	30	14	45	38
(3)	1	23	71	61	29	88	68	35	101	87
J–K	2, 3	19	63	55	24	78	61	28	91	78
	4	14	53	46	17	66	51	21	76	65
(4)	1	28	83	72	36	103	80	43	119	102
L–M	2, 3	24	75	64	30	93	72	35	107	92
	4	17	62	54	22	77	60	26	89	77
(5)	1	37	100	86	46	124	96	55	143	122
N–O	2, 3	30	90	77	37	111	86	45	128	110
	4	22	75	65	28	93	72	33	107	92

Example Three

Juan Lopez, who is 26 and single, uses his car in business in Territory 3. His car is a Model K, less than 1 year old. Find his annual premium for the following insurance: 50/50/10 liability insurance; $1,000 medical payment; full comprehensive; and $100-deductible collision.

Table 6-5 is used to determine the base annual liability (bodily injury and property damage) and medical pay premiums, as before. The comprehensive and collision base premiums are shown in Table 6-6. The total of all these base annual premiums must then be multiplied by the driver classification multiple from Table 6-4 to obtain

Example Three (cont.)

the total annual premium:

$ 75	50/50 Bodily injury
53	$10,000 Property damage
14	$1,000 Medical pay
35	Comprehensive (Model K, Age Group 1, Territory 3)
+ 87	$100-deductible collision (classified as above)
$264	Base annual premium
× 2.00	Driver classification (unmarried male, age 26, business use)
$528	Total annual premium

Example Four

Harold Granger carries 10/20/5 liability insurance and $100-deductible collision insurance. Granger was at fault in an accident which caused $900 damage to his own car and $1,200 damage to the other vehicle. (a) How much of this property damage will Granger's insurance company pay? (b) Suppose that a court suit results in a $12,000 award for personal injuries to the other driver. How much would the insurance company pay and how much is Granger's responsibility?

Solution

(a) Property damage to the other car (under
    Granger's $5,000 property damage policy) $1,200
    Property damage to Granger's car (under his
    $100-deductible collision policy:
    $900–$100)   +   800
    ──────
    Total property-damage settlement $2,000

The insurance company will pay all property damage except the first $100 of repair costs for Granger's own car.

(b) Under Granger's $10,000 single and $20,000 total bodily injury policy, the maximum amount the insurance company will pay to any one victim is $10,000. Thus, Granger is personally liable for the remaining $2,000 of the $12,000 settlement.

SECTION 2   *Problems*

Compute the following motor vehicle insurance problems using the tables in this section.

Compute the total of liability and medical payment premiums for each of the following:

		Liability Coverage	Medical Payment	Territory	Driver Classification
1.	(a)	10/20/10	$1,000	2	Male, age 52, drives 15 miles to work
	(b)	50/100/10	2,500	1	Unmarried male, not principal operator, 16 (driver training), drives 4 miles to work
	(c)	100/200/25	5,000	3	Unmarried male, owner, 26, business use
2.	(a)	15/30/5	$1,000	3	Female, age 33, drives 7 miles to work
	(b)	50/50/25	2,500	1	Married male, 20 (no driver training), drives 5 miles to work
	(c)	100/300/50	5,000	2	Male, age 45, business use

Determine the total comprehensive–collision premiums for the following:

		Model	Age Group	Territory	Deductible on Collision	Driver Classification
3.	(a)	D	2	1	$ 50	Male, 48, drives 6 miles to work
	(b)	M	1	2	100	Female, 35, business use
	(c)	O	3	3	50	Male, 68, pleasure use
4.	(a)	N	1	3	$100	Male, 50, drives 2 miles to work
	(b)	K	3	2	50	Female, 20 (no driver training), drives 9 miles to work
	(c)	F	4	2	100	Male, 42, business use

5. Frank Belk, age 34, lives in Territory 3 approximately 7 miles from his work. His liability insurance covers a single bodily injury amounting to $50,000, total injuries of $50,000, property damage of $10,000, and $2,500 medical pay coverage. Calculate his annual premium.

6. Jennifer Bradly, age 34, lives in Territory 2 and drives 15 miles each way to the school where she teaches. How much will she pay for liability coverage that includes $15,000 for single bodily injuries, $30,000 for total injuries, and $5,000 for property damage, as well as $2,500 for medical payment coverage?

7. Johnson–Howard–Phelps Co. provides each salesman with a Model N automobile. These vehicles have a business-use classification and are in Age group 4, Territory 3. How much will the company pay for comprehensive and $50-deducible collision insurance on each automobile, if all salesmen are in the 30–50 age bracket?

8. Robert Wilson, age 41, lives in Territory 1 and operates a Model L, Age group 2 automobile for business use. Determine his annual premium for full comprehensive and $100-deductible collision coverage.

9. Ralph Kennedy, who lives in Territory 1, owns a Model M automobile in Age group 1. Kennedy is 24, married, and uses his car in business. His automobile insurance provides 100/300/50 liability protection and $5,000 medical pay, as well as comprehensive and $50-deducible collision coverage. Find the annual cost of Kennedy's automobile insurance.

10. Bob Riley is 21, married, and living in Territory 3. He has just purchased a new Model J automobile which he drives 6 miles each way to work. Bob wants to purchase 50/100/25 liability insurance and $5,000 medical pay. His bank requires that he carry comprehensive and $50-deductible collision insurance until his automobile loan is paid in full. What will be the cost of this insurance coverage?

11. Edward Ryan is 16 (with driver training) and lives in Territory 2. He is not the principal operator, using the family automobile (a Model K of Age group 3) only for pleasure. Ryan's father just purchased a 25/50/10 liability policy, $1,000 medical payment, comprehensive, and $100-deductible collision insurance. How much did he pay for this coverage?

12. Ronald Milburn is a semiretired businessman (age 67) who drives 5 miles from his home in Territory 2 to his part-time job. His car is a Model B of Age group 1. Calculate the annual premium that he must pay for 10/20/5 liability insurance, $1,000 medical payment, comprehensive, and $100-deductible collision.

13. Gary Campbell's automobile crossed

the center line on a curve and struck an oncoming car occupied by a mother and two children. Damage to the victims' car totaled $1,500. Following a court suit, the court awarded a judgment of $12,000 to the mother and $3,000 to each child for injuries they sustained. Campbell's automobile insurance included 10/20/5 liability coverage.

(a) How much of this amount will the insurance company pay?

(b) What amount of the judgment must Campbell finance himself?

14. Wayne Collier was liable in a head-on collision with a recreational vehicle which resulted in $7,500 damages to the vehicle. The other driver later sued and won a judgment of $25,000 for personal bodily injuries. Collier carried 15/30/10 liability insurance.

(a) How much of the cost of this accident will Collier's insurance pay?

(b) How much of the expense must Collier pay personally?

15. Vandals stole the hubcaps from Marilyn Hahn's automobile and also broke two side windows. The loss amounted to $160. If Marilyn carried comprehensive and $100-deductible collision insurance

(a) How much did the insurance cover?

(b) How much of the damage did Marilyn have to pay?

16. During a storm, a large tree limb fell onto David Robbins' car, badly denting the hood and fender. The paint and body shop's repair bill totaled $215. Robbins carries comprehensive and $50-deductible collision insurance.

(a) How much of the damage will Robbins' insurance cover?

(b) How much must Robbins pay?

17. Eric Flemming's car recently skidded on ice and sideswiped another vehicle. Damage to the other auto was $350 and $175 to his own car. The other driver suffered a neck injury; he sued Flemming for $15,000 bodily injuries and was awarded $7,500. Mr. Flemming carried 10/20/10 liability insurance, $1,000 medical payment, comprehensive, and $100-deductible collision insurance.

(a) For how much of the cost of Flemming's accident was the insurance company responsible?

(b) How much did Flemming have to pay?

18. The brakes on James Miller's truck failed at an intersection, causing a three-way collision with two cars. Damages included $500 to Miller's truck and $1,000 and $1,600 to the two automobiles. Court suits by both other drivers resulted in personal injury grants of $18,000 and $27,500. Miller's insurance includes 25/50/5 liability, $1,000 medical pay, comprehensive, and $100-deductible collision.

(a) What amount is the insurance company responsible for?

(b) How much of the court award is Miller personally responsible for?

19. A company car belonging to Phillips Sales, Inc., went out of control, left the road, and crashed into a private home. The car was a total loss ($2,000) and damage to the house was listed at $5,800. An occupant of the car, who was not an employee, sued Phillips Sales and was awarded $30,000 by the court for personal injuries.

(a) Determine what total amount the insurance company should pay if Phillips Sales carried 25/50/10 liability insurance, $2,500 medical pay, comprehensive, and $50-deductible collision insurance.

(b) How much will Phillips Sales have to pay in damages?

20. An accident whose cause was "driving at high speed while intoxicated" left a husband and wife dead and a badly injured child. A suit filed on behalf of the orphan won a court award of $90,000 because of the father's death, $60,000 for the mother's death, and $60,000 for the child. Property damages from the accident were $2,100 to the defendant's car, and the victims' recent-model car was a total loss ($5,400). The negligent driver carried liability insurance of 100/200/10, $5,000 medical pay, comprehensive, and $100-deductible collision.

(a) How much of the cost of this accident will the insurance company pay?

(b) For what amount is the guilty driver responsible?

SECTION 3
Life Insurance

The basic purpose of life insurance is to provide compensation to survivors following the death of the insured. Whereas other types of insurance pay damages only up to the actual value of the insured property, life insurance companies make no attempt to assign a specific value to any life. A person (in good health and with normal expectancy of survival) may purchase any amount of insurance corresponding to the policyholder's income and standard of living; and, when death occurs, the full value of the life insurance coverage will be paid.

The responsibility that most heads of households feel for the financial security of their families induces them to purchase life insurance. The Institute of Life Insurance reports that 92% of all married men with children under 18 are insured; where a household with children is headed by a woman, 72% are insured. A majority of wives and children also have some insurance coverage, at lesser amounts. Altogether, two-thirds of the people in the United States are insured. Excluding families with no life insurance, the average family's protection is now over $31,000, and the average size for new policies bought is approaching $15,000.

Many businesses purchase life insurance on key members of the firm whose death would cause a severe loss to the business. Partners sometimes carry insurance on each other so that, in event of a death, the surviving partners can purchase the deceased partner's share of the business from the estate.

There are four basic types of individually owned life insurance policies. In order of increasing premium rates, they are the (1) term policy, (2) whole life policy, (3) limited payment policy, and (4) endowment policy.

Term Insurance
The **term** policy is so named because it is issued for a specific period of time. The policyholder is insured during this time and, if the insured is still alive when the term expires, the coverage then ceases. Term insurance is considerably less expensive than the other types of policies. The principal reason for the low cost is that term policies do not build investment value for the policyholder. (Investment values are discussed in the section, "Nonforfeiture Options.")

Term policies are commonly issued for terms of 5, 10, or 15 years. Many heads of families feel that their need for insurance is greatest while they are younger and have children to support and educate. Term policies can provide maximum insurance protection during these years at a minimum cost. Another typical use of term policies is the life insurance purchased for a plane or boat trip; the term in this case is the duration of the trip.

Term policies may include the provision that, at the end of the term, the policy may be renewed for another term or converted to another form of insurance (both at increased premium rates). A variation of the ordinary term policy is *decreasing term* insurance; under this policy, the face value is largest when issued and decreases each year until it reaches zero at the end of the term. A typical example of decreasing term insurance is mortgage insurance, which decreases as the home loan decreases.

Whole Life   The **whole life** (or **ordinary life** or **straight life**) policy is by far the life insurance coverage most often purchased in the United States. In order to keep the original policy in force, premiums must be paid for as long as the insured lives.

Limited Payment   When a **limited payment life** policy is pur-
Life   chased, the policyholder makes payments for only a limited number of years. If the policyholder survives beyond this time, no further payments are required; however, the same amount of insurance coverage remains in force for the remainder of the policyholder's life. This coverage is similar to whole life insurance, except that the payments are sufficiently larger so that the policyholder will pay, during the limited payment period, an amount approximately equivalent to the total that would be paid during an average lifetime for whole life insurance.

Limited payment policies are frequently sold with payment periods of 20 or 30 years. Such policies are called "20-payment life" or "30-payment life" policies. The limited payment policy is also commonly sold with a payment period so that the policy is "paid up" at age 65.

Endowment   Like the term policy, the **endowment** policy pro-
vides insurance coverage for a specified number of years. It differs in that, if the insured is still alive when the policy period ends, the policyholder may then collect the full face value of the policy. (Of course, the insurance protection would terminate at that time.)

Typical of endowment policies are the policies sold to "provide for the college education of your children." Naturally, the cost of these policies is quite high, because the premiums not only purchase insurance protection during the term of the policy but must also build the amount required to pay the face value at the end of that time. Stated another way, insurance companies sell endowment policies knowing that all these policies must pay off in full at the end of the specified time period, if not before; thus, endowment policies are rather expensive.

Participating and   Insurance policies are further classified as par-
Nonparticipating   ticipating or nonparticipating. **Participating**
policies are so named because the policholders par-
ticipate in the profits earned on these policies. The premium rates charged

for participating policies are usually somewhat higher, because the insurance companies charge more than they expect to need in order to pay claims and operating expenses. However, the excess funds at the end of the year are then refunded to policyholders in the form of *dividends.* A large majority of the life insurance policies purchased in the United States are participating policies.

At the time a participating policy is purchased, the policyholder selects the form in which dividends will be paid. The usual choices available to the policyholder are that the dividends may be (a) paid in cash; (b) used to help pay the premiums; (c) used to purchase additional paid-up insurance (paid-up insurance is discussed in the section, "Nonforfeiture Options"); or (d) left invested with the company to accumulate with interest. A fifth option sometimes available is that the dividends may be (e) used to purchase a 1-year term insurance policy.

Nonparticipating policies, on the other hand, generally offer lower premium rates than participating policies; however, no dividends are paid on nonparticipating policies. Thus, the actual annual cost of life insurance is usually less for participating policyholders than for the owners of nonparticipating policies.

Most participating policies are sold by mutual companies. **Mutual life insurance companies** do not have stockholders, but are owned by the policyholders themselves. The companies are governed by a board of directors elected by the policyholders. Life insurance companies may also be *stock companies,* which are corporations operated for the purpose of earning profits and which are owned by stockholders. As is the usual case for corporations, the board of directors of a stock life insurance company is elected by the stockholders, and the profits earned by the company are paid to the stockholders. Thus, most stock companies issue nonparticipating policies, although a few do issue some participating policies.

Premiums The risk assumed by insurance companies for other types of policies (fire or automobile, for example) is the probability that a loss will occur times the expected size of the loss (it may be only a partial loss). With life insurance, however, the risk is not "whether" a loss will occur, but "when" the loss will occur; for death will inevitably come to all policyholders, and the full value of each effective policy will always be paid after a death.

Premium rates for life insurance are computed by an *actuary,* a highly skilled person trained in mathematical probability as well as business administration. To help calculate premiums and benefits, the actuary uses a *mortality table*; this is an extensive table showing, for a large number of people, how many persons are alive at each age from 0 to 99 years, how many people die at each age, and the death rate for each age. The data composing a mortality table are collected over a period of years by life insurance agents in all states.

The officially approved mortality table of the insurance industry is the Commissioner's 1958 Standard Ordinary Mortality Table, which is reprinted here as Table 6-7. If a group of people, all of the same age, take out insurance during the same year, the mortality table enables the actuary to know how many claims to expect during each succeeding year. Premium rates must be set so that the total amount paid by all policyholders is sufficient to pay all these claims, as well as to finance business expenses.

Almost all life insurance sold today is issued on the *level premium system.* This means that the policyholder pays the same premium each year for life insurance protection. Thus, the policyholders pay more than the expected claims during the early years of their policies, and during the later years they pay less than the cost of the claims. The excess paid during the early years is invested by the insurance company, and interest earned on these investments pays part of the cost of the insurance. Thus, the total premium cost over many years is less than if the policyholders paid each year only the amount which the company expected to need.

A physical examination is usually required before an individual life insurance policy will be issued. (Group policies, on the other hand, are generally issued without physical examinations.) Annual premiums on new policies are naturally less expensive for younger people, since their life expectancy is longer and the insurance company expects them to pay for more years than older persons would. (This emphasizes the advisability of setting up an adequate insurance program while one is still young. The high cost of insurance taken out at an older age makes new coverage too expensive for many older persons to afford.) Life insurance taken out at any given age is usually less expensive for women than for men, because women have a longer life expectancy.

Life insurance premiums on new policies are determined by the applicant's age to the nearest birthday. Thus, applicants who are $26\frac{1}{2}$ would pay premiums as if they were 27 at the time when the policy was issued.

Life insurance policies are written with face values in multiples of $1,000. The rate tables list the cost for a $1,000 policy; and this rate must be multiplied by the number of thousands of dollars in coverage that is

TABLE 6-7: COMMISSIONER'S 1958 STANDARD ORDINARY MORTALITY TABLE

Age	Number Living	Deaths Each Year	Deaths per 1,000	Age	Number Living	Deaths Each Year	Deaths per 1,000
0	10,000,000	70,800	7.08	50	8,762,306	72,902	8.32
1	9,929,200	17,475	1.76	51	8,689,404	79,160	9.11
2	9,911,725	15,066	1.52	52	8,610,244	85,758	9.96
3	9,896,659	14,449	1.46	53	8,524,486	92,832	10.89
4	9,882,210	13,835	1.40	54	8,431,654	100,337	11.90
5	9,868,375	13,322	1.35	55	8,331,317	108,307	13.00
6	9,855,053	12,812	1.30	56	8,223,010	116,849	14.21
7	9,842,241	12,401	1.26	57	8,106,161	125,970	15.54
8	9,829,840	12,091	1.23	58	7,980,191	135,663	17.00
9	9,817,749	11,879	1.21	59	7,844,528	145,830	18.59
10	9,805,870	11,865	1.21	60	7,698,698	156,592	20.34
11	9,794,005	12,047	1.23	61	7,542,106	167,736	22.24
12	9,781,958	12,325	1.26	62	7,374,370	179,271	24.31
13	9,769,633	12,896	1.32	63	7,195,099	191,174	26.57
14	9,756,737	13,562	1.39	64	7,003,925	203,394	29.04
15	9,743,175	14,225	1.46	65	6,800,531	215,917	31.75
16	9,728,950	14,983	1.54	66	6,584,614	228,749	34.74
17	9,713,967	15,737	1.62	67	6,355,865	241,777	38.04
18	9,698,230	16,390	1.69	68	6,114,088	254,832	41.68
19	9,681,840	16,846	1.74	69	5,859,253	267,241	45.61
20	9,664,994	17,300	1.79	70	5,592,012	278,426	49.79
21	9,647,694	17,655	1.83	71	5,313,586	287,731	54.15
22	9,630,039	17,912	1.86	72	5,025,855	294,766	58.65
23	9,612,127	18,167	1.89	73	4,731,089	299,289	63.26
24	9,593,960	18,324	1.91	74	4,431,800	301,894	68.12
25	9,575,636	18,481	1.93	75	4,129,906	303,011	73.37
26	9,557,155	18,732	1.96	76	3,826,895	303,014	79.18
27	9,538,423	18,981	1.99	77	3,523,881	301,997	85.70
28	9,519,442	19,324	2.03	78	3,221,884	299,829	93.06
29	9,500,118	19,760	2.08	79	2,922,055	295,683	101.19
30	9,480,358	20,193	2.13	80	2,626,372	288,848	109.98
31	9,460,165	20,718	2.19	81	2,337,524	278,983	119.35
32	9,439,447	21,239	2.25	82	2,058,541	265,902	129.17
33	9,418,208	21,850	2.32	83	1,792,639	249,858	139.38
34	9,396,358	22,551	2.40	84	1,542,781	231,433	150.01
35	9,373,807	23,528	2.51	85	1,311,348	211,311	161.14
36	9,350,279	24,685	2.64	86	1,100,037	190,108	172.82
37	9,325,594	26,112	2.80	87	909,929	168,455	185.13
38	9,299,482	27,991	3.01	88	741,474	146,997	198.25
39	9,271,491	30,132	3.25	89	594,447	126,303	212.46
40	9,241,359	32,622	3.53	90	468,174	106,809	228.14
41	9,208,737	35,362	3.84	91	361,365	88,813	245.77
42	9,173,375	38,253	4.17	92	272,552	72,480	265.93
43	9,135,122	41,382	4.53	93	200,072	57,881	289.30
44	9,093,740	44,741	4.92	94	142,191	45,026	316.66
45	9,048,999	48,412	5.35	95	97,165	34,128	351.24
46	9,000,587	52,473	5.83	96	63,037	25,250	400.56
47	8,948,114	56,910	6.36	97	37,787	18,456	488.42
48	8,891,208	61,794	6.95	98	19,331	12,916	668.15
49	8,829,410	67,104	7.60	99	6,415	6,415	1,000.00

being purchased. Table 6-8 gives typical annual premiums per $1,000 of face value for each type of life insurance policy, when taken out at various ages. (The policyholder would pay a slightly higher annual total if premiums were paid semiannually, quarterly, or monthly. Each semiannual premium is approximately 51.5% of the annual premium; quarterly premiums are approximately 26.3% of the annual; and each monthly premium would be approximately 8.9% of the annual.)

Actually, premiums vary greatly from company to company, as do the nonforfeiture values, which will be discussed later. The premiums in Table 6-8 represent an approximate average between participating and nonparticipating rates.

TABLE 6-8: ANNUAL LIFE INSURANCE PREMIUMS

Per $1,000 of Face Value for Male Applicants[a]

Age Issued	Term 10-Year	Whole Life	Limited Payment 20-Year	Endowment 20-Year
18	$ 6.81	$14.77	$24.69	$43.82
20	6.88	15.46	25.59	44.95
22	6.95	16.12	26.53	46.16
24	7.05	16.82	27.53	47.44
25	7.10	17.22	28.06	48.10
26	7.18	17.67	28.63	48.80
28	7.35	18.64	29.84	50.29
30	7.59	19.73	31.12	51.88
35	8.68	23.99	35.80	56.06
40	10.64	28.26	40.34	61.40
45	14.52	33.79	46.01	68.28
50	22.18	40.77	53.24	76.12
55	32.93	51.38	64.77	—
60	—	59.32	70.86	—

[a] Because of women's longer life expectancy, premiums for women approximately equal those of men who are 5 years younger.

Example One

Paul Kirkland is 30 and wishes to purchase $25,000 of life insurance. Determine the annual cost of (a) a whole life policy, and (b) a 20-payment life policy.

In each case, the insurance coverage is to be $25,000. Thus, each premium rate from Table 6-8 must be multiplied by 25.

Solution (a) <u>WHOLE LIFE</u>   (b) <u>20-PAYMENT LIFE</u>

$ 19.73   ← Premium per $1,000 → $ 31.12
× 25   × 25
─────   ─────
$493.25   ← Premium on $25,000 → $778.00

Kirkland would pay an annual premium of (a) $493.25 for a whole life policy or (b) $778 for similar coverage under a 20-payment life policy.

Example Two Suppose that Paul Kirkland (Example 1) lived for 38 years after purchasing his life insurance. (a) How much would he pay altogether in premiums for each policy? (b) Which policy's premiums would cost more, and how much more?

Solution (a) <u>WHOLE LIFE</u>   <u>20-PAYMENT LIFE</u>

$ 493.25	Annual premiums	$ 778.00
× 38	Number of premiums	× 20
$18,743.50	Total premium cost	$15,560.00

The total premium cost would be $18,743.50 for a $25,000 whole life policy and only $15,560 for an equivalent 20-payment life policy. Thus:

(b) $18,743.50   Total premium cost of whole life policy
   − 15,560.00   Total premium cost of 20-payment life policy
   ──────────
   $ 3,183.50   Extra premium cost of whole life policy

The whole life policy would cost Kirkland $3,183.50 more if he lived to be 68.

   Besides the basic life insurance coverage, several types of additional protection may be purchased at a slight increase in premiums. Among the additional features most frequently purchased are the **waiver of premium benefit** (the company agrees to assume the cost of the policyholder's insurance in case of total and permanent disability) and the **double indemnity benefit** (the insurance company will pay twice the face value of the policy if death results from accidental causes rather than illness.)

Nonforfeiture Options   The most obvious benefit from an insurance policy is the death benefit: the policyholder designates a person, called the **beneficiary**, to receive the face value of the policy following the death of the insured. However, there are a number of alternative benefits available to the policyholders themselves which should be taken into consideration when selecting a policy.

Whereas the premiums paid for other types of insurance policies purchase only protection, the premiums paid for life insurance policies (except term policies) also build an investment for the policyholder. This investment accumulates because the level premium system has caused excess funds to be paid into the company. Because of selling and bookkeeping costs, a policyholder is not usually considered to have accumulated any investment until 2 or 3 years after the policy was written. Any time thereafter, however, the policy possesses certain values, called **nonforfeiture values** (or **nonforfeiture options**) to which the policyholder is entitled. These values may often be claimed only if the insured stops paying premiums for some reason, or if the policyholder turns in the policy (and is thus no longer insured). The principal nonforfeiture options (cash value, paid-up insurance, and extended term insurance) are outlined briefly in the following paragraphs.

Included in each life insurance policy (excluding term policies) is a table showing the **cash value** of the policyholder's investment after each year. If the policyholder wishes to terminate the insurance coverage, (s)he may surrender the policy and receive this cash value. If the policyholder needs some money but prefers to maintain the insurance protection, (s)he may borrow up to the cash value of the policy. The loan must be repaid with interest at a moderate rate, and the full amount of insurance coverage will remain in force during this time.

Figure 13 compares the various life policies which earn nonforfeiture values and illustrates how their cash values build. The cash value of the 20-year endowment policy equals the face value ($1,000) at age 45. The 20-payment life policy builds cash value faster than the whole life policy during the first 20 years, but the cash values of both reach face value only at age 100. As expected, premiums are higher for the policies where cash value increases faster, as illustrated in the significant age bracket between 25 and 45 where payments are being made to all three policies.

If the insured wishes to stop paying premiums and surrender the policy, the cash value of the policy may be used to purchase a reduced level of **paid-up insurance**. This means that the company will issue a policy which has a smaller face value but which is completely paid for. That is, without paying any further premiums, the policyholder will have a reduced amount of insurance which will remain in effect for the remainder of his or her life. Life insurance policies (except term policies) also contain a table showing the amount of paid-up insurance which the cash value would purchase after each year.

FIGURE 13

When a policyholder simply stops paying premiums without notifying the company of any intent and without selecting a nonforfeiture option, the company usually automatically applies the third nonforfeiture option: **extended term** insurance. Under this plan the policy remains in effect, at its full face value, for a limited period of time. Stated another way, the cash value of the policy is used to purchase a term policy with the same face value and for the maximum time period that the cash value will finance. Each policy also includes a table indicating after each year the length of time that an extended term policy would remain in force. (This provision does not apply to term policies, since they do not build cash value.)

NOTE: Most insurance companies allow a *grace period* (usually 31 days following the date a premium is due) during which time the overdue premium may be paid without penalty. The policy remains in effect during this time.

Example Three

Carl Best purchased a $15,000 20-payment life insurance policy at age 25. Determine the following values for his policy after it had been in force for 10 years: (a) cash value, (b) the amount of paid-up insurance which he could claim, and (c) the time period for which extended term insurance would remain in effect.

TABLE 6-9: NONFORFEITURE OPTIONS[a] ON TYPICAL LIFE
INSURANCE POLICIES

Issued at age 25

Years in Force	WHOLE LIFE				20-PAYMENT LIFE				20-YEAR ENDOWMENT			
	Cash Value	Paid-up Insurance	EXT. TERM		Cash Value	Paid-up Insurance	EXT. TERM		Cash Value	Paid-up Insurance	EXT. TERM	
			Years	Days			Years	Days			Years	Days
3	$ 4	$ 14	1	174	$ 27	$ 89	10	84	$ 39	$ 104	14	42
5	26	82	9	71	69	213	19	184	90	227	23	126
10	88	243	18	46	182	502	28	186	316	515	30	131
15	157	382	20	148	314	763	32	164	590	772	35	290
20	246	530	21	137	465	1,000	Life		1,000	1,000	Life	
40	571	822	—	—	696	—	—	—	—	—	—	—

[a] The "cash value" and "paid-up insurance" nonforfeiture values are per $1,000 of life insurance coverage. The time period for "extended term insurance" applies as shown to all policies, regardless of face value.

Solution

(a) As shown in Table 6-9, the cash value per $1,000 of face value after 10 years on a 20-payment life policy issued at age 25 is $182. Therefore, the cash value of a $15,000 policy is

$ 182   Cash value per $1,000
× 15
————
$2,730   Cash value of a $15,000 policy

The cash value of Best's $15,000 policy would be $2,730 after the policy has been in effect for 10 years. Best could receive this amount by turning in his policy and foregoing his insurance coverage; or he could borrow this amount and pay it back with interest without losing his insurance protection.

(b) The amount of paid-up insurance available is

$ 502   Paid-up insurance per $1,000
× 15
————
$7,530   Paid-up insurance on a $15,000 policy

If Best surrenders his policy, he could receive a policy of $7,530, which would remain in force until his death without any premiums being required.

(c) From Table 6-9, we see that if Best stops paying premiums, for whatever reason, extended term insurance would allow his full $15,000 coverage to remain in effect for 28 years and 186 days.

Interest Adjusted
Net Cost

Except for term policies, the amount paid in premiums does not represent the true cost of insurance protection, because a sizable part of this money is building cash value for the insured and, for participating policies, part is refunded or invested as dividends. Since premiums as well as cash values and dividends vary widely among companies, consumers needed a method for determining the actual cost, or net cost, of just the insurance protection itself with the investment value removed. Traditionally, this has been computed by the **net cost** method shown below (as illustrated for a whole life policy after 20 years, where annual premiums were $16.50 per $1,000, cash value is $254, and dividends of $126 had accumulated).

$$
\begin{aligned}
\text{Net cost} &= \text{Total premiums} - (\text{Cash value} + \text{Dividends}^*) \\
&= (\$16.50 \times 20) - (\$254.00 + \$126.00) \\
&= \$330 - \$380 \\
&= -\$50 \quad \text{(or \$50 net profit of investment value} \\
&\qquad\qquad\quad \text{over premium cost)}
\end{aligned}
$$

As this illustration shows, when policies remained in force for many years, the cash value plus dividends (for a participating policy) often exceeded the total premiums, resulting in an apparent net profit or net return to the policyholder.

The net cost method was criticized, however, because it ignores the time value of money—the fact that $1 today is worth $1.04 one year from now (at 4% interest). That is, the net cost method compares investment value (Cash value + Dividends) existing at the end of 20 years with premiums paid over the 20-year interval. The investment value includes compound interest accumulated over the 20 years,† whereas the total premiums include no interest. The **interest adjusted net cost** method and **net cost index** (an annual cost) were thus developed to eliminate the interest included in the total investment value. This is now the accepted method of net cost calculation within the life insurance industry. Using the illustration above, interest adjusted net cost can be found by the formula

$$
\begin{aligned}
\text{I. A. Net Cost} &= \text{Total premiums} \\
&\quad - (\text{Cash value} + \text{Dividends}) \times \text{Interest Adjustment Factor} \\
&= \$330 - \$380(0.6458) \\
&= \$330 - \$245.40 \\
\text{I. A. Net Cost} &= \$84.60 \quad \text{(total cost for 20 years)}
\end{aligned}
$$

* For a participating policy; there are no dividends ($0) for a nonparticipating policy.

† We shall assume either that the dividends were left to accumulate with the insurance company or else that the policyholder personally invested all refunded dividends.

or

$$\text{I. A. Net Cost Index} = \frac{\text{I. A. Net Cost}}{\text{Years}}$$

$$= \frac{\$84.60}{20}$$

I. A. Net Cost Index = $4.23   (annual cost per $1,000)

The interest adjustment factor* (0.6458) corresponds to the 4% compound interest rate used by the insurance industry. Thus, if a set amount were deposited at the beginning of each year to earn interest at 4%, and the account contains $380 after 20 years, then the total of these deposits is $245.40; the remainder of the $380 is interest. Table 6-10 also gives interest adjustment factors for other periods of years.

TABLE 6-10: INTEREST ADJUSTMENT FACTORS FOR
INTEREST[a] ADJUSTED NET COST

Years in Force	Factor
5	0.88763
10	0.80087
20	0.64580

[a] Interest at 4% compounded annually.

Supposedly, money that a policyholder has available for investment purposes might be invested in something besides life insurance and still earn the same return. Thus, the investment value is not correctly part of the cost of insurance. However, it is first necessary to adjust the total investment value in order to find how much of the policyholder's money was deposited to build that investment value; only then can we subtract to determine how much could have been saved if the buyer had only wanted the insurance protection itself. Therefore, if a buyer is considering two similar insurance policies from equally reliable companies the better choice may well be the policy with the lower interest adjusted net cost.

Example Four   Harry Warren is considering a participating whole life policy for which the premiums are $18.75 per $1,000. After 10 years, the cash value will be $140 per $1,000 and guaranteed dividends will total $30 when

* The calculations shown here are a variation of the method used by life insurance companies, in order for students to avoid lengthy division. Using the 4% Amount of Annuity Table XV, Appendix C, for annuities due (annuities paid at the beginning of the period), the total investment principal is computed as $\frac{380}{31.969-1} \times 20$; for convenience $\frac{20}{31.969-1} = \frac{20}{30.969} = 0.6458$.

Example Four (cont')

accumulated at 4% interest. Determine (a) the interest adjusted net cost and (b) the interest adjusted cost index over the first 10 years of this policy.

Solution

(a) $\begin{pmatrix} \text{I.A.} \\ \text{Net} \\ \text{Cost} \end{pmatrix} = \begin{pmatrix} \text{Total} \\ \text{premiums} \end{pmatrix} - \left[\begin{pmatrix} \text{Cash} \\ \text{value} \end{pmatrix} + \text{Dividends} \right] \times \begin{pmatrix} \text{I.A.} \\ \text{Factor} \end{pmatrix}$

$$= (\$18.75 \times 10) - \quad (\$140 + \$30) \quad \times \quad (0.80087)$$

$$= \quad \$187.50 - \quad\quad \$170 \quad\quad \times \quad (0.80087)$$

$$= \quad \$187.50 - \quad\quad \$136.15$$

$$= \quad \$51.35 \quad (\text{total cost for 10 years})$$

(b) I. A. Cost Index $= \dfrac{\text{I. A. Net Cost}}{\text{Years}}$

$$= \dfrac{\$51.35}{10}$$

I. A. Cost Index $= \$5.14 \quad$ (annual cost per \$1,000)

Thus, the insurance protection alone cost \$51.35 altogether (per \$1,000) or \$5.14 annually during the 10-year period. The remaining \$13.61 of each annual premium (\$18.75 − \$5.14 = \$13.61) was used to build investment value.

Settlement Options   When a life insurance policyholder dies, there are several ways in which the death benefits may be paid, called **settlement options.** The beneficiary may receive the face value in one lump-sum payment; more than 90% of all death benefits are paid in this way. Or the benefits may be left invested with the company in order to earn interest. An alternative method of receiving benefits, which deserves consideration, is to receive the benefits in the form of an annuity. An **annuity** is a series of payments, equal in amount and paid at equal intervals of time. (We shall consider here only annuities paid monthly.) There are several options available to the beneficiary concerning the type of annuity (or installment) to choose; these choices are described briefly below.

1. The beneficiary may choose a monthly installment of a *fixed amount.* In this case, the specified amount will be paid each month for as long

as the insurance money (plus interest earned on it) lasts. (For example, a beneficiary may decide to receive a payment of $50 per month; this will continue until the account is depleted.)

2. The beneficiary may prefer the security of a monthly payment for a *fixed number of years.* (For example, the beneficiary may want to receive monthly payments for 15 years.) The insurance agent will then determine how much the beneficiary may receive monthly, in order for the funds to last the specified number of years.

3. A third choice is to take the benefits in the form of an *annuity for life.* That is, depending upon the age and sex of the beneficiary, the insurance company will agree to pay a monthly income to the beneficiary for as long as he or she lives.

4. The remaining possibility is to receive a *life annuity, guaranteed for a certain number of years.* (For example, if the beneficiary chooses a life annuity guaranteed for 15 years, a monthly annuity will be paid for a minimum of 15 years or as long thereafter as the beneficiary lives.) The monthly income from this annuity is somewhat lower than from the life annuity in plan 3, but a guaranteed annuity is selected much more often than an ordinary life annuity. The reason for this is that the unqualified life annuity is payable only to the beneficiary; when the beneficiary dies, even if only one annuity payment has been made, no further benefits will be paid. However, the guaranteed annuity is payable to the survivors or estate if the beneficiary should die before the specified time period has elapsed. Thus, most people with dependents naturally choose the guaranteed annuity. Even persons without dependents often select the guaranteed annuity, feeling that they would rather have someone receive the payments if they should die, instead of risking that most of the face value of the policy might be lost.

It should be noted that these settlement options are also available to policyholders themselves when an endowment policy matures. Also, older people often feel that they no longer need the amount of life insurance coverage carried since they were younger and had children to support. Therefore, many retired persons convert some of their life insurance policies to annuities in order to supplement other retirement income. (When whole life or limited payment life policies are converted to annuities, the monthly installment depends upon the cash value of the policy, rather than upon its face value.)

Table 6-11 lists the monthly income per $1,000 of face value available under the various settlement options. Life insurance policies also include tables similar to Table 6-11.

TABLE 6-11: SETTLEMENT OPTIONS

Monthly Installments per $1,000 of Face Value

OPTIONS 1 AND 2: FIXED AMOUNT OR FIXED NUMBER OF YEARS		OPTIONS 3 AND 4: INCOME FOR LIFE				
		AGE WHEN ANNUITY BEGINS			*Life with 10 Years Certain*	*Life with 20 Years Certain*
Years	*Amount*	*Male*	*Female*	*Life Annuity*		
10	$9.41	40	45	$3.80	$3.76	$3.64
12	8.03	45	50	4.15	4.09	3.90
14	7.05	50	55	4.58	4.50	4.18
15	6.65	55	60	5.14	5.01	4.47
16	6.31	60	65	5.86	5.61	4.75
18	5.74	65	70	6.82	6.30	4.98
20	5.29					

Example Five

Martha Donaldson, age 60 and the beneficiary of a $30,000 life insurance policy, has decided to receive the money as monthly payments rather than one lump sum. (a) Find the monthly payment if she chooses to receive payments for 15 years. (b) If Mrs. Donaldson arranges a monthly income of approximately $240, how many years will the payments continue?

Solution

(a) Table 6-11 shows that for a $1,000 policy, the monthly installment for the fixed number of years (15) would be $6.65. Thus, Mrs. Donaldson could receive $199.50 monthly for 15 years, as follows:

$$\begin{array}{r} \$ \ 6.65 \\ \times \ \ 30 \\ \hline \$199.50 \end{array}$$ Monthly installment per $1,000

$199.50   Monthly installment from $30,000 policy (for 15 years)

(b) Mrs. Donaldson will receive 30 times any amount shown in Table 6-11. Thus, $30 \times \$8.03$ will provide approximately $240 per month. The table indicates that she could receive $240.90 monthly for 12 years before the money (and interest paid by the insurance company) has been depleted.

NOTE: Notice that Mrs. Donaldson's age had no bearing on this problem, because she was not considering an annuity that would pay for the remainder of her life.

Example Six

Walter Carson became the beneficiary of a $25,000 life insurance policy at age 55. (a) What would be the monthly income from a life annuity? (b) From an annuity guaranteed for 20 years?

Solution

Carson's age affects both these options because either annuity pays until his death. (Notice that an older person would receive more per month because payments are not expected to be made for as many years.) From Table 6-11 for a male, age 55, the two annuities would pay as follows:

(a) *LIFE ANNUITY*

(b) *LIFE, 20-YEAR CERTAIN*

(a) LIFE ANNUITY		(b) LIFE, 20-YEAR CERTAIN
$ 5.14	←Monthly per $1,000→	$ 4.47
× 25		× 25
$128.50	← Monthly for $25,000 policy →	$111.75

Option (a) indicates Carson could receive $128.50 monthly for life. However, these payments would stop immediately upon his death, regardless of how few monthly installments might have been paid. Option (b) will pay $111.75 monthly for as long as Carson lives (even if this is more than 20 years). If he dies in less than 20 years, the payments will continue to his heirs until the guaranteed 20 years have passed.

Example Seven

Mary Reynolds was widowed at age 60, inheriting a $40,000 life insurance policy. She chose to receive all the benefits over a 10-year period. (a) What was her monthly installment? (b) How much would she have received monthly by choosing a life annuity guaranteed for 10 years? (c) Suppose that Mrs. Reynolds actually lived another 13 years. From which option above would she have received more total income, and how much more?

Solution

(a) 10-YEAR ANNUITY		(b) LIFE, 10-YEAR CERTAIN
$ 9.41	← Monthly per $1,000 →	$ 5.01
× 40		× 40
$376.40	← Monthly from $40,000 policy →	$200.40

Option (a) paid Mrs. Carson $376.40 per month for 10 years, although she lived longer. Had she chosen option (b), she would have received $200.40 monthly for the entire 13 years she lived.

(c) The total payments received under each settlement would have been as follows:

10-YEAR ANNUITY		LIFE ANNUITY GUARANTEED 10 YEARS
12	Months per year	12
×10	Years	×13
120	Payments	156
$ 376.40	Monthly annuity	$ 200.40
× 120	Payments	× 156
$45,168.00	Total received	$31,262.40

Mrs. Carson received $45,168 − $31,262.40 = $13,905.60 more income by selecting the fixed 10-year annuity, despite the fact that the guaranteed life annuity would have paid for 3 years longer. (Observe that no further payments would be made to her heirs, since the guaranteed period is past for both annuities.)

SECTION 3 *Problems*

Unless other rates are given, use the tables in this chapter to compute the following life insurance problems. Assume that each age given is the "insurable age" (age to the nearest birthday).

Using the information given and Table 6-8, compute the annual premium for each life insurance policy.

		Age	Type of Policy	Face Value
1.	(a)	24	Whole life	$20,000
	(b)	30	20-payment life	32,000
	(c)	35	10-year term	25,000
	(d)	50	20-year endowment	15,000
2.	(a)	28	10-year term	$50,000
	(b)	25	Whole life	30,000
	(c)	35	20-payment life	25,000
	(d)	40	20-year endowment	10,000

Determine the nonforfeiture values of the following policies, based on the rates in Table 6-9 (for policies issued at age 25).

		Years in Force	*Type of Policy*	*Face Value*	*Nonforfeiture Option*
3.	(a)	20	Whole life	$12,000	Extended term
	(b)	15	20-payment life	35,000	Paid-up insurance
	(c)	10	20-year endowment	40,000	Cash value
	(d)	10	20-payment life	25,000	Cash value
4.	(a)	10	Whole life	$45,000	Cash value
	(b)	5	20-payment life	30,000	Cash value
	(c)	20	Whole life	20,000	Paid-up insurance
	(d)	15	20-year endowment	15,000	Extended term

Use Tables 6-8, 6-9, and 6-10 to compute (1) the interest adjusted net cost (per $1,000), and (2) the net cost index for each policy for the given time period. (Assume that each policy earns the given accumulated dividends.)

		Policy	*Time Period*	*Acc. Div.–4%*			*Policy*	*Time Period*	*Acc. Div.–4%*
5.	(a)	Whole life	5 years	$ 8	**6.**	(a)	20-payment life	10 years	$ 58
	(b)	Whole life	10	$32		(b)	20-payment life	20	$205

Use Table 6-11 to find the monthly annuity (or total years of the annuity) which the beneficiary may select in settlement of the following policies.

		BENEFICIARY		*Face Value*	*Settlement Option Chosen*	MONTHLY ANNUITY	
		Sex	*Age*			*Years*	*Amount*
7.	(a)	F	57	$10,000	Fixed amount per month		$70
	(b)	M	60	25,000	Fixed number of years	12	
	(c)	M	50	50,000	Guaranteed annuity	20	
	(d)	F	45	25,000	Life annuity	—	
8.	(a)	F	58	$30,000	Fixed number of years	15	
	(b)	F	54	20,000	Fixed amount per month		$125
	(c)	F	55	60,000	Life annuity	—	
	(d)	M	50	25,000	Guaranteed annuity	10	

9. The small firm of Williams Electronics wished to insure the life of its owner, Jay Williams, for 10 years, until the firm could become well established and until additional personnel could be thoroughly trained. If Williams was 35 years old:

(a) What would the premiums on a $50,000 whole life policy cost for 10 years?

(b) How much would an equivalent 10-year term policy cost altogether?

(c) How much would be saved on premiums by purchasing the term policy?

(d) What other considerations would affect the choice of policy?

10. Arthur Simmons purchased a $20,000 20-payment life policy at age 28.

(a) What was the annual premium for this policy?

(b) What would be the annual premium on a whole life policy with the same face value?

Assume that Simmons lives for 40 years after buying this insurance. How much would he pay in total premiums

(c) For the 20-payment life policy?

(d) For the whole life policy?

11. Andrew Potter purchased a $30,000 whole life policy when he was 30.

(a) How much would premiums on this policy have cost until Potter was 65?

(b) If Potter had purchased a 20-payment life policy of the same face value, what would have been the total premiums on this policy to age 65?

12. When he was 45, Leonard Maxwell took out a $60,000, 10-year term policy.

(a) Compute the total cost of premiums for this policy.

(b) If Maxwell had purchased a 20-payment life policy of the same face value, what would those premiums have cost during this 10-year period?

(c) When deciding which of these policies to purchase, what besides premium cost should influence the decision?

13. Eric Johnson took out a $20,000 20-payment life policy when he was 40.

(a) How much would he have saved on the annual premium if he had purchased this policy at age 25?

(b) Find the total amount that would have been saved until the policy was fully paid for.

14. At age 40, Dennis Gerber purchased a $25,000 whole life policy.

(a) What would have been the annual savings on premiums if Gerber had taken out the policy at age 25?

(b) How much will the premiums cost for the whole life policy until Gerber reaches 65?

(c) What would the premiums have cost until 65 if the policy had begun at age 25?

15. When he was 25, Emory Crenshaw took out a $20,000 20-payment life insurance policy.

(a) Compute the annual cost of this policy.

(b) After the policy had been in force for 15 years, Crenshaw decided not to continue the policy. If he relinquishes all insurance protection, how much cash could he receive?

(c) If Crenshaw surrenders his policy in exchange for paid-up insurance, what amount of coverage would he have for the rest of his life?

(d) For how long could he continue the $20,000 coverage under an extended term policy?

16. James Avery took out a $50,000, 20-year endowment policy when he was 25.

(a) What was the annual premium?
(b) After 10 years, Avery decided he did not need this insurance coverage (since his business began offering group life insurance) and he felt he could make a better return by putting his money into other investments. If he terminates this coverage, what is the cash value of the policy?
(c) How much insurance, paid up for life, would this policy provide?
(d) For how long could the same $50,000 coverage be continued under extended term insurance?

17. Richard Sutton owned a $14,000 20-payment life policy which was issued when he was 25. Ten years later, Sutton needed some money but did not want to give up his insurance protection. What amount can he borrow from the insurance company and still keep the policy in force?

18. Edwin DeLany has made payments on a $24,000 whole life policy for 20 years, since he was 25. How much could he now borrow against this policy to help finance an addition to his home?

19. Larry Wynn, age 25, is considering a participating, 20-year endowment life policy for which the guaranteed dividends (accumulated at 4% interest) for 20 years are $300. Determine (a) the interest adjusted net cost (per $1,000) for 20 years and (b) the interest adjusted cost index.

20. At age 25, Sam Lyndstrom can purchase a participating, 20-payment life policy which at 4% will accumulate dividends of $17 over 5 years. Compute (a) the interest adjusted net cost (per $1,000) for this policy and (b) the net cost index which apply during the first 5 years.

21. Another policy which Larry Wynn (Problem 19) is considering is a participating, whole life policy on which the accumulated 20-year dividends total $134. Find for this policy (a) the interest adjusted net cost and (b) the net cost index. (c) For which of the two policies Wynn is considering does the insurance protection itself cost less?

22. Sam Lyndstrom (Problem 20) is also considering a 20-year endowment policy for which dividends of $20 will accumulate at 4% during the first 5 years. Calculate (a) the interest adjusted net cost and (b) the interest adjusted cost index for this policy. (c) Which of the policies has a lower cost for strictly the insurance protection during the first 5 years?

23. Compute per $1,000 (a) the interest adjusted net cost over the first 10 years and (b) the net cost index of a nonparticipating, whole life policy taken out at age 25.

24. If a nonparticipating, 20-payment life policy is purchased at age 25, determine per $1,000 (a) the interest adjusted net cost during the first 10 years and (b) the net cost index.

25. Grant Reid, 32, was the beneficiary of a $10,000 life insurance policy from his aunt.
(a) If Reid chooses to receive annuity payments for 18 years, how much will he receive each month?
(b) If Reid elects to receive a fixed annuity of approximately $95 per month, approximately how many years will the benefits last?

26. Barbara Templeton has become the beneficiary of a $100,000 life insurance policy at age 55.

(a) What will Mrs. Templeton receive each month if she selects the settlement option of a life annuity?

(b) How much will she receive monthly if she chooses a life annuity guaranteed for 20 years?

27. Loretta Trammell's husband died when she was 45, leaving $35,000 in life insurance.

(a) How much would Mrs. Trammell receive monthly if she selected a life annuity?

(b) If she decided to receive a life annuity guaranteed for 10 years, what annuity would Loretta Trammell receive monthly?

28. Michael O'Connor inherited a $20,000 life insurance policy when he was 60.

(a) Determine the monthly payment O'Connor will receive if he chooses the settlement option of a life annuity.

(b) What will he receive monthly from a life annuity guaranteed for 20 years?

29. Lawrence Armstrong became the beneficiary of a $10,000 life insurance policy when he was 50. Armstrong gave lengthy consideration to a 20-year annuity and to a life annuity guaranteed for 10 years. Finally, Armstrong decided to be optimistic and chose the guaranteed life annuity.

(a) How much did Armstrong receive altogether, if he lived to be 75?

(b) What total amount would he have received from the 20-year annuity?

(c) How much did Armstrong gain by selecting the guaranteed annuity?

30. When she was 50, Harriett Ausley inherited an $80,000 life insurance policy. After considering a 20-year annuity and a life annuity, Mrs. Ausley finally selected the 20-year fixed annuity. Mrs. Ausley lived to be 78.

(a) How much did Mrs. Ausley receive from the settlement she chose?

(b) Also determine the amount that she would have received from the life annuity.

(c) Did Mrs. Ausley gain or lose by her choice of settlement options, and how much?

31. When she was 60, Gretta Frost was the beneficiary of a $50,000 life insurance policy. Mrs. Frost selected a settlement option whereby she would receive a monthly annuity for 15 years.

(a) What was Mrs. Frost's monthly income from the insurance?

(b) If Mrs. Frost died at age 67, how much had she received at the time of her death?

(c) If Mrs. Frost had chosen a life annuity guaranteed for 10 years, how much would she have received monthly?

(d) What total amount would the guaranteed annuity have paid until her death?

(e) Did Mrs. Frost personally gain or lose by her choice of settlement methods, and how much?

32. At age 60, Constance Lindsay became the beneficiary of a $60,000 life insurance policy.

(a) If she chose to receive the benefits over 12 years, what was her monthly annuity?

(b) If Miss Lindsay lived to be 83, how much did she receive altogether from the insurance settlement?

(c) Suppose she had decided to have the benefits paid as a life annuity. What would her monthly installment have been?

(d) How much would the life annuity have paid until the time of her death?

(e) Did Miss Lindsay gain or lose by her choice of settlement options, and how much?

CHAPTER 6 *Glossary*

Annuity. The payment of a set amount at a regular interval. (Often used in settlement of a life insurance claim, either for a fixed number of years or for life—sometimes for life with 10 or 20 years certain.)

Beneficiary. The person designated to receive the face value of a life insurance policy after death of the insured.

Bodily injury liability. Portion of standard motor vehicle insurance which pays for physical injuries to other persons when the insured is at fault in an accident.

Business interruption insurance. Provides income after a fire to meet continuing business expenses and net income until business operations resume.

Carrier. An insurance company (also called an "underwriter" or an "insurer").

Cash value. An investment value earned by all life insurance policies except term, which may be borrowed against or may be paid in cash to a policyholder who terminates the policy.

Coinsurance clause. Clause in many fire policies requiring coverage of a stipulated per cent (often 80%) of value at the time of a fire in order to qualify for full reimbursement for damages.

Collision (and upset) insurance. Pays for damages to the policyholder's own vehicle (1) if the insured is at fault in an accident, or (2) if the insured's vehicle is damaged when there is no other responsible driver whose liability insurance will pay.

Comprehensive insurance. Pays for damages of any kind to the policyholder's own vehicle, except those caused by collision or one-vehicle upset.

Double indemnity. Optional provision of many life insurance policies which pays twice the face value in case of accidental death.

Endowment life insurance. Provides life insurance and builds cash value (or paid-up insurance) at maturity of the full face value of the policy.

Extended coverage. A supplement to standard fire policies which insures against related damages such as smoke and water damage.

Extended term. A nonforfeiture option earned by all life insurance policies except term, whereby the same level of coverage may be maintained for a specified time after premiums are terminated.

Face value. The full (maximum) amount of insurance specified by an insurance policy.

Group insurance. Life and/or health/accident insurance available at a reduced cost to employees of a business or to members of a business/professional organization.

Indemnity. Payment made by an insurance company after an insured loss.

Insured. A person or business that purchases insurance coverage (also called a "policyholder"), or a person whose life is covered by a life insurance policy.

Insurer. An insurance company (also called a "carrier" or an "underwriter").

Interest adjusted net cost. Method now used to determine cost of life insurance protection only, not including portion of premiums used to build investment value: Total premiums—(Cash value + Dividends) × Interest adjustment factor.

Interest adjusted net cost index. Annual cost of a life insurance policy: Total interest adjusted net cost ÷ Years.

Liability insurance. Portion of standard motor vehicle insurance and general business insurance which provides financial protection when the person or business is held legally responsible for personal injuries and/or physical damages.

Limited payment life insurance. Provides life insurance and, within the specified payment period, builds paid-up insurance of the full face value of the policy.

Medical payment insurance. Optional portion of standard motor vehicle insurance which pays medical costs (supplementing other policies) for injuries to the policyholder's own self, family, and passengers, regardless of who is at fault in an accident.

Mutual life insurance company. Life insurance company owned by policyholders rather than stockholders; sells participating policies which pay dividends to the policyholder.

Net cost of life insurance. Method formerly used to determine cost of life insurance protection only, not including investment value: Net cost = Total premiums − (Cash value + Dividends).

No-fault insurance. Variation of bodily injury liability insurance where damages (below a specified amount) are paid by each policyholder's own insurance company, regardless of who is at fault in an accident.

Nonforfeiture value (or option). The investment value (cash value, paid-up insurance, or extended term) available when any life insurance policy (except term) in terminated.

Nonparticipating policy. A life insurance policy which pays no dividends and usually has lower premiums than participating policies; type of policy usually sold by stock life insurance companies.

Ordinary life insurance. (See "Whole life insurance.")

Paid-up insurance. A nonforfeiture value earned by all life insurance policies except term whereby a specified level of insurance may be maintained after premiums are terminated.

Participating policy. A life insurance policy which pays dividends and usually has higher premiums than nonparticipating policies; type of policy usually sold by mutual life insurance companies.

Policy. An insurance contract that specifies in detail the provisions and limitiations of the coverage.

Policyholder. A person or business that purchase insurance (also called the "insured").

Premium. The payment made to purchase insurance coverage.

Property damage liability. Portion of standard motor vehicle insurance which pays for damages caused by the policyholder to another vehicle or other property.

Settlement option. Any of several types of annuities available to the beneficiary of a life insurance policy instead of a lump-sum payment.

Short-term policy. An insurance policy in force for less than 1 year (usually referring to a fire insurance policy).

Straight life insurance. (See "Whole life insurance.")

Term (of a policy). The time period for which a policy will remain in effect.

Term life insurance. Provides life insurance only and builds no nonforfeiture values for the policyholder; the least expensive type of life insurance policy.

Underwriter. An insurance company (also called "carrier" or "insurer").

Uninsured motorists insurance. Optional portion of standard motor vehicle insurance which provides financial protection for the policyholder's own bodily injuries when hit by a driver without bodily injury liability insurance.

Waiver of premium benefit. Optional provision of many life insurance policies whereby the company bears the cost of the premiums if the policyholder is totally and permanently disabled.

Whole (ordinary, or straight) life insurance. Most common type of policy, where premiums are paid for as long as the insured lives in order to maintain coverage of full face value.

Worker's compensation. Form of business liability insurance which pays employees for sickness or accidental injury resulting directly from work responsibilities.

CHAPTER 7

Checkbook and

Cash Records

CHAPTER 7 OBJECTIVES

Upon completion of Chapter 7, the student will be able to:

1. Define and use correctly the terminology associated with each topic.

2. Prepare a bank reconciliation *(Section 1; Example 1)*:
   a. Using given information *(Problems 1–6)*; or
   b. Using a check register and bank statement *(Problems 7–9)*.

3. Complete the following cash forms *(Section 2)*:
   a. Daily cash record *(Example 1; Problems 1, 2)*; and
   b. Over-and-short summary *(Example 2; Problems 3, 4)*.

Practically all business obligations today are paid by
check. Checks are not only more convenient and
safer than cash, but the canceled check also constitutes a legal receipt. Nevertheless, retail businesses
do handle a large amount of cash received on customer purchases. Both
checking and cash transactions require certain records, which are the
subject of this unit.

7

SECTION 1

Checkbook Records

A check, like a bank note, is a **negotiable
instrument**, which means that it may be transferred from one party to another for its equivalent
value; the second party then holds full title to the check. Most checks are
written on forms printed by the individual bank. A legal check may be
written on plain paper, however, provided the following requirements are
met: (1) it must be dated; (2) the bank (or **drawee**) must be positively
identified (with address, if necessary); (3) the check must name the **payee**
(the person, firm, "cash," or to whomever it is payable); (4) the amount
must be shown; and (5) the check must be signed by the **drawer** or
maker (the person writing the check). A **universal check** is shown in
Figure 14; this is a printed check that may be written on any bank, since it
contains blanks in which all the necessary information may be written.

Figure 15 illustrates the traditional commerical checks used by many
firms. Notice at the bottom of each check that the identifying numbers are
printed in magnetic ink so that the checks can be sorted electronically. The
check stub should always be kept current; all checks and deposits should
be recorded immediately and the new balance computed. The check stub
also provides space to record pertinent information about the check itself:
what the check was for, how much sales tax (or interest) was included, how
much cash discount was taken, and so on.

The **voucher check** (Figure 16) is often used in business today. The
"voucher" attached to the check itself explains which invoice the check
covers, itemizes any deductions, or otherwise accounts for the amount
shown on the check. The voucher is not negotiable and is torn off at the
perforation before the check is cashed or deposited. The company issuing
the check retains one or more carbon copies of the voucher for its records.

UNIVERSAL CHECK   DATE _June 12_   19___

Great Lakes Bank & Trust Co.
BANK
ADDRESS   Chicago, Illinois

PAY TO THE
ORDER OF   Gilbert and Son, Inc. $ 57.95

Fifty-seven and 95/100------------------------------------ DOLLARS

FOR VALUE RECEIVED, I REPRESENT THE ABOVE AMOUNT IS ON DEPOSIT IN SAID BANK
IN MY NAME, IS FREE FROM CLAIMS, AND IS SUBJECT TO THIS CHECK.

2405 W. Lansing Ave.
ADDRESS _Chicago, Illinois_   SIGNATURE _William F. Short_

ACCOUNT NO. 325-00-414

EFFICIENCY® LINE NO. 1230

FIGURE 14: *Universal Check*

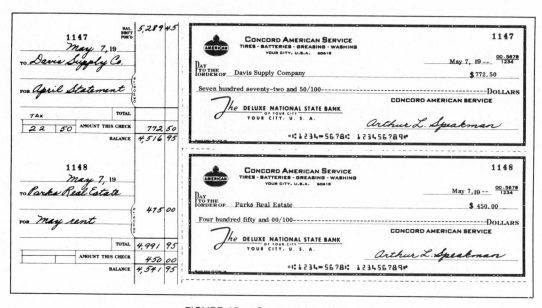

FIGURE 15: *Commercial Checks*

ORIGINAL			STATE BOARD OF EDUCATION		VOUCHER NO. / 1,308			
PAYEE SHOULD DETACH TOP AND DEPOSIT VOUCHER AT ONCE			DEPARTMENT OF COMMUNITY COLLEGES					
PURCHASE ORDER NO.	DATE OF INVOICE	BUDGET POS. NO.	PARTICULARS	CODE	GROSS AMOUNT	DEDUCTIONS	NET AMOUNT	
819	Sept. 23	14	30 Lab Stools	16-D	$345.00	$ 7.90	$337.10	
834	Sept. 26	21	60 #243A Desks	9-A	900.00	18.00	882.00	
							$1,219.10	

1BAA-35

DRAWN BY (NAME AND ADDRESS OF INSTITUTION)

Blue Ridge Community College
Asheville, North Carolina

STATE BOARD OF EDUCATION - DEPARTMENT OF COMMUNITY COLLEGES

PAYABLE AT PAR THROUGH THE FEDERAL RESERVE SYSTEM

PRESENT
TO STATE TREASURER—
STATE OF NORTH CAROLINA
RALEIGH, N. C.

66-1059
512

VOUCHER NO. 1,308

DATE November 9 ___19___

THIS CHECK VOID AFTER 60 DAYS FROM DATE

PAY Twelve hundred nineteen and 10/100 ------------------------- **DOLLARS** $ 1,219.10

TO THE ORDER OF
Whitman Technical Furniture, Inc.
Box 823
High Point, North Carolina

Specimen
Priscilla K. Stokes
AUTHORIZED SIGNATURE

William R. Morton
COUNTERSIGNED

G-185

⑈0512⑈1059⑈ 4⑈000⑈574⑈

FIGURE 16: *Voucher Check.*

Firms using voucher checks ordinarily also keep a **check register**, which is a concise record of checks and deposits. Figure 17 illustrates a typical check register.

FIGURE 17: *Check Register*

Date	Check Number	Order of	For	Amount Check	Amount Deposit	Balance
19 ___						$ 919.81
July 16	362	The May Co.	Brass fixtures	$ 86.15		833.66
18	363	Warren's, Inc.	Office supplies	15.83		817.83
18		Deposit			$840.00	1,657.83
19	364	Payroll	Weekly payroll	789.25		868.58
21	365	Carson's, Inc.	Equipment rental	27.44		841.14

Deposits Before a company can deposit or cash the checks it has received, the checks must be endorsed. There are three forms of **endorsement** in common use: the blank endorsement, the restrictive endorsement, and the special endorsement (Figure 18).

The **blank** endorsement is just the name of the person or the firm (and often the individual representing that firm) to which the check is made payable. This endorsement makes the check negotiable by anyone who has possession of it. That is, such a check could be cashed by anyone if it should become lost or stolen.

| Blank | Restrictive | Special |

FIGURE 18

The other two endorsements are somewhat similar. The **restrictive** endorsement is usually applied to indicate that the check must be deposited in the firm's bank account. Many firms endorse all their checks in this manner as soon as they are received, as a precautionary measure against theft. The **special** (or **full**) endorsement indicates a check is to be passed on to another person, firm, or organization. The special endorsement's great advantage over the blank endorsement is that, should the check be lost or stolen, it is negotiable only by the party named in the special endorsement.

After being endorsed, the checks are listed individually on a bank deposit slip. Checks are often listed according to the name of the bank on which they were written; however, many banks prefer that checks be listed by *bank number*. Most printed checks contain the complete identification number of the bank on which the check is written. For example,

$$\frac{66\text{-}1059}{512}$$

The "512" represents the Federal Reserve District within which the bank is located; the "66" identifies the location (state, territory, or city) of the bank; and the "1059" indicates the particular bank in that location. Notice in Figure 16 that the bank number "0512···1059" is coded in magnetic ink at the bottom of the check. Some checks contain only the numbers indicating location and official bank number (for example, 66-1059). It is sufficient to use this hyphenated number when listing checks on the deposit slip. A completed deposit slip is shown in Figure 19.

FIGURE 19: *Deposit Slip.*

Bank Statements   A monthly bank statement (Figure 20) is sent to the owner of each checking account. The bank statement is a chronological listing of all the checks, deposits, and other charges recorded by the bank during the month. It is a rare occurrence indeed when the balance shown on the bank statement is exactly the same as the checkbook balance. This does not mean that a mistake has been made in either record; usually neither figure indicates the true balance available to spend. For this reason, the bookkeeper should always prepare a bank statement **reconciliation**. Usually both the bank statement balance and the checkbook balance have to be adjusted; when these adjusted balances coincide, the account has been reconciled and the true balance found.

The bank statement usually contains several bank charges indicated by code letters which are explained at the bottom of the statement. Bank charges represent funds which the bank has deducted from the client's account. Typical bank charges are service charges for checks written, charges for printing new checks, corrections in deposits, returned checks, and so forth. (A **returned check** or **return item** is a check for which the writer's account did not contain sufficient funds. If a depositor submits a check for which the bank is unable to collect the funds, the amount must then be deducted from the depositor's account—the RT charge—and the check is returned to the depositor. The check may be redeposited after the maker [writer] has had time to replenish the funds in his/her account. The writer of the bad check will be charged a fee—the RC charge—which is deducted from the writer's account.) After the amount of all bank charges has been determined from the bank statement, the bookkeeper must also deduct this total from the checkbook balance.

Frequently, some checks and possibly a deposit (particularly those near the end of the month) will not have been processed in time to be recorded and returned with the bank statement. Such checks are known as **outstanding checks**. The bookkeeper should check the bank statement against the check stubs to determine which checks (and deposits) are outstanding. The bookkeeper must determine the amount of the outstanding checks and deduct this amount from the bank statement balance to obtain the adjusted bank balance. (A deposit not included on the bank statement must be added to the bank statement balance to determine the adjusted bank balance.)

After these adjustments have been made, the adjusted bank balance and the adjusted checkbook balance will be the same, provided that all transactions were recorded correctly and that there has been no mathematical mistake. This adjusted balance represents the true balance available to spend.

STATEMENT OF YOUR ACCOUNT WITH

ACCOUNT NO

Westwood Village

009 109817

CITY NATIONAL BANK

PERIOD ENDING   PAGE

May 27, 19XX   1

19

The Gates Company
Box 4490
Los Angeles Calif 90024

PLEASE NOTIFY US IMMEDIATELY
OF ANY CHANGE OF ADDRESS

CHECKS	CHECKS	CHECKS	DEPOSITS	DATE	NEW BALANCE
			BALANCE FORWARD		589.62
125.00				0430	464.62
			235.17	0501	699.79
186.45	92.07			0502	421.27
17.80	345.25			0506	58.22
			354.50	0508	412.72
118.44				0510	294.28
			649.89	0511	944.17
47.63	RT			0512	896.54
510.00	56.03	15.18			
43.67				0514	271.66
			1,359.26	0515	1,630.92
418.16	275.07			0519	937.69
106.19				0521	831.50
78.50	49.77			0523	703.23
2.40	SC			0525	700.83
27.89	345.80			0526	327.14

PLEASE EXAMINE THIS STATEMENT AND THE ENCLOSED ITEMS AT ONCE. IF NO ERROR IS REPORTED WITHIN
10 DAYS, THE STATEMENT WILL BE CONSIDERED CORRECT. ALL ITEMS CREDITED SUBJECT TO FINAL PAYMENT.
◄   FOR YOUR CONVENIENCE, A RECONCILEMENT FORM AND KEY CODES ARE ON THE REVERSE SIDE   ►

KEY

CM - Credit Memo   RC - Return Check Charges
CR - Credit Reversal   Bad check by depositor ($3.00 for NSF)
                          RT - Return Items – Check deducted
DM - Debit Memo   SC - Service Charges
DR - Debit Reversal   SR - Reverse Service Charge

FIGURE 20:   *Bank Statement*

Example One Reconcile the bank statement in Figure 20, based on the following information. The checkbook shows a balance of $771.93; a deposit was made on May 28 in the amount of $724.35; outstanding checks are for $174.89, $53.20, $16.42, and $85.08.

BANK RECONCILIATION

Bank balance	$ 327.14	Checkbook balance	$771.93
Add: outstanding deposit	+ 724.35		
	$1,051.49		
Less: outstanding checks			
$174.89		Less: bank charges	
53.20			
16.42		$47.63	
+ 85.08	− 329.59	+ 2.40	− 50.03
Adjusted balance	$ 721.90	Adjusted balance	$721.90

SECTION 1 *Problems*

Prepare a bank reconciliation for each of the following:

1. The checkbook balance was $752.70, and the bank statement balance was $845.19. Outstanding checks were in the amounts of $18.50, $6.98, $45.00, and $23.76. A service charge of $1.75 had been deducted.

2. The bank statement balance was $1,867.15, and the checkbook balance was $1,508.35. A bank service charge of $4.50 had been deducted. Outstanding checks were written for $85.25, $32.54, $127.91, and $117.60.

3. The bank statement balance was $1,375.25, and the checkbook balance was $1,313.76. A deposit of $106.44 had not been entered on the bank statement. A service charge was $1.50. New checks cost $2.15. A returned check was for $25.00.

Outstanding checks were for $8.95, $75.00, $47.81, $26.33, and $38.49.

4. The checkbook showed a balance of $2,128.42, while the bank statement indicated a balance of $1,945.33. A service charge was $2.74. A return item (check) totaled $43.06. A deposit of $725.36 was not shown on the statement. Outstanding checks amounted to $296.80, $9.45, $77.96, $136.51, and $67.35.

5. The checkbook showed a balance of $906.73, whereas the bank statement listed a balance of $684.37. An outstanding deposit totaled $308.82. Outstanding checks were for $41.85, $30.18, $7.95, and $26.63. A charge of $1.00 was shown to correct a deposit. A service charge was $1.65. A returned check amounted to $15.00. New checks cost $2.50 to print.

6. A bank statement indicated a balance of $3,418.89, and the checkbook gave a balance of $3,725.55. Outstanding checks were in amounts of \$366.59, \$85.01, \$56.14, \$128.37, and \$44.05. An addition of \$10 was made on the bank statement to correct an error in a deposit slip. A service charge was \$3.75. New checks cost \$5.19. A returned check was \$15.40. A deposit of \$972.48 was omitted from the bank statement.

7.–9. *Three check registers and bank statements are given on the following pages. (a) Find the final balance for each. Determine which checks and deposits have been processed, which are still outstanding, what bank charges have been made, and (b) reconcile each bank statement. (Use the "√" column of the register to check off items that appear on the bank statement. Some have already been checked the preceding month.) Each check register shows the adjustment made last month to balance the register. (c) How much must be deducted this month to balance each register? (See the forms on the next three pages.)*

7.

CHECK REGISTER

Check No.	Date	Check Issued To	Amount of Check	√	Amount of Deposit	Balance
						1,148 16
223	10/27	Allied Freight	18 53	√		1,129 63
224	10/28	Internal Revenue Service	57 49			1,072 14
225	10/28	Great Lakes Laboratories	24 21			1,047 93
	10/30	DEPOSIT			1,476 00	2,523 93
226	11/3	Heavenly Beauty Supplies	35 89			2,488 04
227	11/4	Payroll	442 12			2,045 92
	11/5	Adjustment for bank charges	3 59	√		2,042 33
228	11/10	Midwest Realty	315 00			
229	11/10	Barton Drug Supply	207 65			
230	11/10	Commercial Sales, Inc.	45 72			
231	11/10	Protective Insurance Agency	78 33	√		
232	11/10	Midwest Bell Telephone	21 41			
233	11/10	City of Chicago	86 64			
234	11/10	Health Products, Inc.	71 96			
235	11/11	Payroll	407 78			
	11/12	DEPOSIT			891 43	
236	11/15	Great Lakes Laboratories	169 35			
237	11/17	Nationwide Sales, Inc.	262 13	√		
	11/18	DEPOSIT			455 52	
238	11/18	Payroll	543 29			
239	11/23	Allied Freight	4 34	√		
	11/24	DEPOSIT			509 60	
240	11/25	Payroll	428 80			
241	11/27	Milford Laboratory	50 09			
	11/28	DEPOSIT			234 03	
242	11/29	Grange Drug Supply	361 15	√		

BANK STATEMENT

Checks and Other Debts		Deposits	Date	Balance
			10/31	1,126 04
24 21		1,476 00	11/5	
442 12	18 45 RT		11/8	
71 96	35 89		11/12	
86 64	315 00		11/15	
21 41			11/15	
		891 43	11/16	
407 78	45 72		11/17	
169 35		455 52	11/20	
543 29	207 65		11/21	
		509 60	11/26	
428 80	57 49		11/28	
50 09	2 40 SC		11/30	

8.

CHECK REGISTER

Check No.	Date	Check Issued To	Amount of Check	√	Amount of Deposit	Balance 1,788 43
189	7/30	Hillcrest Implements	45 37	√		1,743 06
190	7/31	Internal Revenue Service	121 82			1,621 24
	7/31	DEPOSIT			446 93	2,068 17
191	8/3	Payroll	905 56	√		1,162 61
192	8/3	Garner Realty Co.	275 00	√		887 61
	8/4	Adjustment for Bank Charges	3 27	√		884 34
193	8/6	City of San Gabriel	160 02			
194	8/7	Randolph-Hayes, Inc.	29 64			
195	8/7	Manor-Downes Corp.	57 75			
	8/7	DEPOSIT			1,028 54	
196	8/10	Payroll	877 97			
197	8/13	Truck City	68 53			
198	8/14	Milford Cleaning Supplies	88 10			
199	8/14	Jiffy Steam Supplies	140 68			
	8/17	DEPOSIT			1,662 75	
200	8/17	Payroll	918 04			
201	8/18	Carpet Care, Inc.	259 77			
	8/20	Fulbright Insurance	101 41			
202	8/24	Truck City	20 88			
	8/24	DEPOSIT			987 67	
203	8/24	Payroll	860 68			
204	8/26	Rayford-Holdings Corp.	25 17			
	8/27	DEPOSIT			1,443 36	
205	8/28	Milford Cleaning Supplies	58 18			

BANK STATEMENT

Checks and Other Debits		Deposits	Date	Balance
			8/4	559 23
		446 93	8/4	
160 02	29 64		8/10	
		1,028 54	8/11	
57 75			8/15	
121 82	5 00 DM		8/15	
877 97		1,662 75	8/18	
68 53	918 04		8/20	
259 77			8/24	
48 95 RT	101 41		8/25	
		987 67	8/26	
860 68			8/28	
88 10	3 75 SC		9/1	

9.

CHECK REGISTER

Check No.	Date	Check Issued To	Amount of Check	√	Amount of Deposit	Balance 2,591 84
582	9/15	Kramer Restaurant Supply	468 95			2,122 89
583	9/16	Gaines Produce Co.	78 36	√		2,044 53
	9/20	DEPOSIT			1,005 29	3,049 82
584	9/21	Payroll	645 18			2,404 64
585	9/22	Rexford Gas Co.	60 49			2,344 15
	9/23	Adjustment for Bank Charges	2 27	√		2,341 88
	9/24	DEPOSIT			567 82	
586	9/27	Longworth & Haynes	135 54			
587	9/28	Payroll	701 68			
588	9/30	Maxwell Wholesale Meats	346 76			
589	10/2	Capital Savings and Loan	429 33			
	10/3	DEPOSIT			1,134 67	
590	10/4	Mid-State Service Co.	15 85			
591	10/5	Payroll	689 21			
592	10/8	Karol Music Co.	26 57			
593	10/10	Steele Security, Inc.	40 00			
	10/10	DEPOSIT			989 43	
594	10/12	Whitworth Sales & Supply	159 78			
595	10/12	Payroll	671 60			
596	10/13	Falls River Light & Power	134 42			
	10/14	DEPOSIT			1,434 77	
597	10/15	Maxwell Wholesale Meats	453 73			

BANK STATEMENT

Checks and Other Debits		Deposits	Date	Balance
			9/18	2,511 21
		1,005 29	9/20	
60 49	645 18		9/24	
468 95			9/25	
34 18 RT		567 82	9/26	
701 68			9/30	
429 33		10 00 CM	10/4	
689 21	346 76	1,134 67	10/6	
26 57	4 78 SC		10/10	
40 00	15 85	989 43	10/13	
671 60			10/16	

SECTION 2

Cash Records

There is some variation, of course, but one good indication of business stability is the consistency of sales. These sales are recorded daily on the cash register tapes of a business and are given careful attention by officials of the company.

At the beginning of the business day, a stipulated amount is placed in each cash register drawer; this is the **change fund**, which must be available so that early customers may receive correct change. The fund (usually $20 to $50) will contain a certain number of the various denominations of money.

At the close of the business day, the clerk completes a **daily cash record**. (S)he counts each denomination of money separately, lists each check separately, and finds the total. The original change fund is then deducted from this total and the remaining sum (the **net cash receipts**) should equal the day's total cash sales shown on the cash register tape.

Human error being what it is, however, it frequently occurs that the cash receipts and the cash register total are not equal. If the cash receipts are smaller than the total sales, the cash is **short**. If there is more cash than the total of sales, the cash is **over**.

A summary of these daily cash records, commonly called an **over-and-short summary**, may be kept by the week or by the month. Over a period of time, the totals of the amounts in the "cash over" and in the "cash short" usually tend nearly to cancel each other.

Example One

THE PERFECT GIFT SHOP
Daily Cash Record

Date: February 8, 19X1
Register: 1–B
Clerk: Sharie Holmes

Pennies	$ .73
Nickels	1.85
Dimes	2.60
Quarters	6.75
Halves	10.50
Ones	18.00
Fives	45.00
Tens	40.00
Twenties	80.00
Other currency	
Checks (list separately): $ 5.15	
12.67	
23.80	
15.00	
32.50	89.12
Total	$294.55
Less: Change fund	− 30.00
Net cash receipts	$264.55
Cash over (subtract)	
Cash short (add)	+ .05
Cash register total	$264.60

Example Two

<table>
<tr><td colspan="5" align="center">THE PERFECT GIFT SHOP

Over-and-Short Summary</td></tr>
<tr><th>Date</th><th>Cash Register Totals</th><th>Net Cash Receipts</th><th>Cash Over</th><th>Cash Short</th></tr>
<tr><td>Feb. 8, 19X1</td><td>$ 552.69</td><td>$ 552.23</td><td></td><td>$ .46</td></tr>
<tr><td>9</td><td>615.87</td><td>616.12</td><td>$ .25</td><td></td></tr>
<tr><td>10</td><td>581.69</td><td>580.69</td><td></td><td>1.00</td></tr>
<tr><td>11</td><td>643.81</td><td>643.08</td><td></td><td>.73</td></tr>
<tr><td>12</td><td>577.16</td><td>578.25</td><td>1.09</td><td></td></tr>
<tr><td>13</td><td>601.12</td><td>601.62</td><td>.50</td><td></td></tr>
<tr><td>Totals</td><td>$3,572.34</td><td>$3,571.99</td><td>$1.84</td><td>$2.19</td></tr>
</table>

Total cash receipts	$3,571.99
Total cash short (add) +	2.19
	$3,574.18
Total cash over (subtract) −	1.84
Total cash register readings	$3,572.34

SECTION 2 *Problems*

1. Assume that you work at Wylder Hardware. Prepare your own daily cash report for today. The number of each denomination of money in your register drawer is as follows: pennies, 72; nickels, 58; dimes, 36; quarters, 28; halves, 7; ones, 21; fives, 9; tens, 9; twenties, 4; other currency—none. Checks were for $18.75, $6.50, $9.18, $4.75, $11.37, and $22.53. Your change fund is $20. The cash register total for the day is $306.70.

2. Prepare a daily cash report for clerk Terry Williams of The Clothes Closet on today's date. The number of each denomination of money is as follows: pennies, 83; nickels, 47; dimes, 27; quarters, 42; halves, 17; ones, 24; fives, 13; tens, 11; twenties, 4; other currency—one $2. Checks included $17.85, $30.00, $42.78, $24.41, $36.95, and $18.53. The change fund is $25. The cash register total for the day is $451.65.

3. Compute the weekly over-and-short summary for Green Garden Store. Each day's cash register totals and net cash receipts are as follows.

Date	Cash Register Totals	Net Cash Receipts
Sept. 18, 19X1	$ 943.52	$ 943.38
19	869.10	869.10
20	911.74	911.47
21	935.36	935.46
22	1,008.14	1,008.27
23	898.06	898.18

4. Complete an over-and-short summary for Wilson Drug Co., which had total sales and net cash receipts as follows.

Date	Total Sales	Net Cash Receipts
July 5, 19X2	$ 932.18	932.70
6	1,017.48	1,016.74
7	1,143.52	1,143.42
8	1,269.05	1,270.05
9	1,758.69	1,758.06
10	1,802.45	1,802.82

CHAPTER 7 *Glossary*

Blank endorsement. Name (signature) of person or firm to whom a check was payable and which transfers ownership of the check to anyone in possession of it.

Change fund. A set amount of money placed in a cash register at the start of each day, in order to provide change for early customers.

Check register. A record of checks and deposits made by the owner of a checking account.

Daily cash record. A form that compares the net cash receipts with the cash register's total cash sales, in order to determine whether the cash drawer is over or short.

Drawee. The bank from which funds of a check are drawn (paid).

Drawer (or Maker). The person (or firm) who draws funds (pays) by check.

Endorsement. Inscription on the back of a check (or negotiable instrument) by which ownership is transferred to another party.

Maker (or Drawer). The writer of a check.

Negotiable instrument. A document (check or bank note) that may be transferred from one party to another for its equivalent value.

Net cash receipts. A clerk's total (of money and checks) remaining after the change fund has been deducted; equals the total cash sales, if cash is neither over nor short.

Outstanding check. A check given in payment but not yet deducted from the writer's bank account.

Over. Term meaning that net cash receipts exceeded the cash register total.

Over-and-short summary. A weekly or monthly list of the total daily cash records of a business.

Payee. The party named to receive the funds of a check.

Reconciliation. Adjustments to the checkbook and the bank statement whereby the owner finds the actual spendable balance and determines that both accounts agree.

Restrictive endorsement. Endorsement restricting the use of a check; usually indicates that the check must be deposited to the endorser's account.

Returned check. A check returned to the party who deposited it because the check writer's account did not contain sufficient funds.

Short. Term meaning that net cash receipts were less than the cash register total.

Special (or full) endorsement. Endorsement naming the next party to whom a check is to be transferred.

Universal check. A check form that may be used by any owner of a checking account in any bank.

Voucher check. A check with a perforated attachment which explains or otherwise accounts for the amount shown on the check.

CHAPTER 8

Wages and Payrolls

CHAPTER 8 OBJECTIVES

Upon completion of Chapter 8, the student will be able to:

1. Define and use correctly the terminology in each topic.

2. Compute gross wages and payrolls based on
   a. Salary (*Section 1*);
   b. Commission (including quota and override)
      (*Section 2; Examples 1–3; Problems 1–18*);
   c. Hourly rates (*Section 3; Example 1; Problems 1, 2*); and
   d. Production (including incentives and dockings)
      (*Section 4; Examples 1, 3, 4; Problems 1–6, 9, 10*).

3. Complete the account sales and account purchase
   (*Section 2; Example 4; Problems 19–22*).

4. For overtime work, compute gross wages and payrolls using
   a. Hourly rates (at standard overtime or overtime excess)
      (*Section 3; Examples 2, 3, 5; Problems 3–12*);
   b. Salary (*Section 3; Example 4; Problems 7, 8*); or
   c. Production (*Section 4; Example 2; Problems 7, 8*).

5. Complete net weekly payrolls, including standard deductions for
   a. Social Security;
   b. Federal income tax; and
   c. Other common deductions, as given.
      (*Section 5; Examples 1–3; Problems 1–12*)

6. Complete the disbursement forms required for payrolls paid in cash: the
   change tally and change slip. (*Section 6; Example 1; Problems 1–4*).

7. a. Complete the basic portion of the Employer's Quarterly Federal Tax
      Return (*Section 7; Examples 1, 3; Problems 1–6; 11–14*).
   b. Determine employees' quarterly FICA taxable wages
      (*Example 2; Problems 7–10*).

8. a. Determine employees' taxable wages for unemployment
      (*Section 7; Example 4; Problems 15–18*).
   b. Compute employer's state and federal unemployment taxes
      (*Example 4; Problems 15–18*).

8

In any business math course, many topics apply primarily to certain types of businesses. The payroll, however, is one aspect of business math that applies to every conceivable type of business, no matter how small or how large.

There is probably no other single factor so important to company–employee relations as the negotiation of wages and completion of the payroll. Wage negotiation within a company—whether by a union or on an individual basis—is not a responsibility of the payroll clerk, however. We shall thus be concerned only with computation of the payroll, which is also a very important responsibility. To find a mistake in their pay is very damaging to employees' morale. It is imperative, therefore, that everyone connected with the payroll exercise extreme care to ensure absolute accuracy.

There are four basic methods for determining **gross wages** (i.e., before deductions): *salary, commission, hourly rate basis,* and *production basis.* We shall make a brief study of each.

SECTION 1
Computing Wages— Salary

Employees on a salary receive the same wages each pay period, whether this be weekly, biweekly, semi-monthly, or monthly. Most executives, office personnel, and many professional people receive salaries.

If a salaried person misses some work time because of illness or for personal reasons, (s)he will usually still receive the same salary on payday. However, if business conditions require a salaried person to work extra hours, the payment of additional compensation may vary according to the person's position in the firm. General office personnel who are subject to the Fair Labor Standards Act (a topic in Section 3) must receive extra compensation as though they were normally paid on an hourly-rate basis. However, highly paid executive and administrative personnel, whose positions are at the supervisory and decision-making level of the company, normally receive no additional compensation for extra work. Professional people (members of the medical professions, lawyers, accountants, educators, etc.) are similarly exempt from extra-pay provisions.

For the present time, we shall consider only a normal work week. In that case, once the payroll clerk has recorded the employee's salary on that person's paysheet, there is no further work required to determine the worker's gross wages. We shall, therefore, proceed directly to the next form of wage compensation.

SECTION 2
Computing Wages—
Commission

Business people whose jobs consist of buying or selling merchandise are often compensated for their work by means of a commission. The true (or **straight**) **commission** is determined by finding some per cent of the individual's net sales. Thus, we have another business formula based on the basic per cent form "____% of ____ = ____":

$$\text{____\% of Net sales} = \text{Commission}$$

or simply

$$\% \cdot S = C$$

Certain business people receive commissions without actually calling them commissions. For instance, a stockbroker's fee for buying stock is a certain percentage of the purchase price of that stock; however, this fee is called a **brokerage**. A lawyer's fee for handling the legal aspects of a real estate sale is generally some percentage of the value of the property; this constitutes a commission, although it probably will not be called one.

Straight Commission

Example One   (a) Edith Reilly receives an 8% commission on her net sales. Find her commission, if her gross (original) sales were $5,680 and sales returns and allowances were $180. (*Note:* "Sales returns and allowances" are first deducted from gross sales, because the customer either returned the merchandise or was later allowed some reduction in sales price.)

Gross sales	$5,580	$\% \, S = C$
Less: sales returns		$8\% \times \$5,500 = C$
and allowances	− 180	$\$440 = C$
Net sales	$5,500	

(b) A stock broker received a $240 commission on a stock sale. What was the value of the stock, if the broker charged 2%?

$$\% \, S = C$$

$$2\% \, S = \$240$$

$$\frac{0.02 \, S}{0.02} = \frac{240.00}{0.02}$$

$$S = \$12,000$$

Travel, meals, entertainment, and similar expenses of salespeople often remain approximately the same regardless of their sales. Thus, once a salesperson has made sufficient sales to cover expenses, the company may be willing to pay a higher commission on additional sales. A commission rate that increases as sales increase is known as a **sliding-scale commission**.

Example One *(cont.)* (c) Determine George Butler's commission on his net sales of $14,000. He receives 5% on his first $5,000 sales, 6% on the next $7,000, and 7.5% on all net sales over $12,000.

$$\% \, S = C$$

$$0.05 \, \times \$ \; 5{,}000 = \$250$$
$$0.06 \, \times \quad 7{,}000 = \quad 420$$
$$0.075 \times \quad 2{,}000 = \quad 150$$

Net sales $14,000 $820   Commission

Commission Variations *Salary.* Some salespeople are guaranteed a minimum income in the form of a salary. They are often then paid commissions at a lower rate than is usually earned by those on straight commission.

Example Two (a) Suppose that Edith Reilly [Example 1(a)] also receives a $100 salary. Her total gross wages would then be:

Salary	$100
Commission	+ 440
Gross wages	$540

Drawing Account. A salesperson on commission may be allowed a **drawing account** from which funds may be withdrawn to defray business or personal expenses. This is an advance on earnings, and the drawings are later deducted from the salesperson's commission. Like a salary, a drawing account assures a minimum income. However, the earned commission must consistently either equal or exceed the drawings, or else the employee would be released from the company.

Example Two *(cont.)* (b) Suppose that Edith Reilly [Example 1(a)] is entitled to a drawing account of $300. Her amount due would then be:

Commission	$440
Less drawings	− 300
Amount due	$140

Quota. Many persons on commission, particularly those who also receive a salary, are required to sell a certain amount (or **quota**) before the commission starts. This plan is designed to ensure the company a certain level of performance for the salary it pays.

Example Two *(cont.)* (c) Bob Hendrix has net sales of $9,000 and must meet a $3,000 quota. His 5% commission is then computed as follows:

Total sales	$9,000	$\% S = C$
Less: quota	− 3,000	$5\% \times \$6,000 = C$
Sales subject to commission	$6,000	$\$300 = C$

Override. Department heads in retail stores are often allowed a special commission on the net sales of all other clerks in their departments. This commission, called an **override**, is given to offset the time a department head must devote to nonselling responsibilities (such as pricing and stocking merchandise, taking inventory, placing orders, etc.). An override is computed exactly like an ordinary commission, but at a lower rate than the commission rate for one person's sales. The override is paid in addition to the department head's own commission and/or salary.

Example Three The following are examples of commission payrolls. The second example includes the calculation of net sales, as well as quotas and salaries.

(a)   TOP DRAWER FASHIONS

Payroll for week ending September 6, 19XX

| Name | NET SALES | | | | | | Comm. Rate | Gross Comm. |
	M	T	W	T	F	Total		
Albright, K.	$450	$675	$520	$570	$685	$2,900	5%	$145.00
Carver, D.	700	825	980	920	875	4,300	4	172.00
Foyt, B.	430	—	560	775	750	2,515	6	150.90
Gantt, M.	640	575	475	550	820	3,060	5	153.00
							Total	$620.90

(b)   VALLEY SALES DISTRIBUTORS, INC.

Payroll for week ending June 13, 19XX

| Name | SALES | | | Quota | Comm. Sales | Comm. Rate | Gross Comm. | Salary | Gross Wages |
	Gross	R&A	Net						
Barton, H.	$3,518	$18	$3,500	$1,200	$2,300	4%	$ 92.00	$ 75.00	$167.00
Dixon, R.	5,432	52	5,380	—	5,380	3	161.40	50.00	211.40
Hill, C.	4,776	86	4,690	2,000	2,690	4	107.60	80.00	187.60
Landers, J.	3,084	34	3,050	—	3,050	6	183.00	—	183.00
						Totals	$544.00	$205.00	$749.00

NOTE: On the bottom line, the total Commissions plus total Salaries must equal the total Gross Wages ($544 + $205 = $749).

Commission Agents   The entire operation of some agencies consists of buying and/or selling products for others. Agents employed for this purpose are known as **commission agents, commission merchants, brokers,** or **factors.** The distinguishing characteristic of such agents is that whereas they are authorized to act for another individual or firm, at no time do they become the legal owners of the property involved.

Many items—particularly foodstuffs—are produced in areas which are some distance from the market. The producer (or **consignor**) ships the goods "on consignment" to a commission agent (or **consignee**) who will sell them at the best possible price. The price obtained by the agent is the

gross proceeds. From these gross proceeds the agent deducts a commission, as well as any expenses incurred (such as storage, freight, insurance, etc.). The remaining sum, called the **net proceeds**, is then sent to the producer. Accompanying the net proceeds is an **account sales**, which is a detailed account of the sale of the merchandise and of the expenses involved. (Gross proceeds − Total charges = Net proceeds.)

Example Four

ACCOUNT SALES

HARCOURT & WYMAN
2519 South Shore Blvd.
Chicago, Illinois 60649

REC'D: Jan. 20, 19XX   NO: B27116
   VIA: Air freight   DATE: Feb. 1, 19XX

Aloha Floral Distributors
7401 Kamani Blvd.
Honolulu, Hawaii 96813

19- -		Sales		
Jan.	21	50 boxes — orchids @ $36	$1,800.00	
	22	25 boxes — bird of paradise @ $60	1,500.00	
	22	15 boxes — ti @ $40	600.00	
		Gross proceeds		$3,900.00
		Charges:		
		Commission, 6% of $3,900	$ 234.00	
		Refrigerator storage	24.75	
		Delivery charges	36.50	
				− 295.25
		Net proceeds		$3,604.75

Other commission agents act as buyers for their clients. When a store wishes to purchase an item not regularly carried in its inventory and not obtainable through regular wholesale distributors, the store may commission an agent to secure the items. Typical examples of such items might be art objects, specialized furniture, carpets, exclusive dry goods, exotic foods, etc., which are specialties of a particular locality or country. Much international as well as domestic purchasing is accomplished in this manner.

In general, a commission agent is employed whenever it is inconvenient to send a company buyer or when a special knowledge of the product or the market conditions is required. The agent submits an itemized account of the purchase, called an **account purchase**. The account purchase includes the actual price paid by the agent (**prime cost**) plus the agent's commission on the prime cost, as well as any expenses incurred during the purchase. This total (or **gross cost**) is the actual cost of the merchandise to the company and the amount to be remitted to the commission agent. (Prime cost + Total charges = Gross cost.)

Example Five

ACCOUNT PURCHASE

IMPORT SPECIALTIES, INC.
32714 Santa Monica Blvd.
Los Angeles, California 90037

BOUGHT FOR THE ACCOUNT OF:

The Import House
7709 Granville Rd.
St. Paul, Minnesota 55101

YOUR ORDER: #5415
DATE: April 9, 19XX

NO: G42081
DATE: May 1, 19XX

19XX		Purchases:		
April	18	15 — Philippine wicker fan chairs @ $96	$1,440.00	
	20	12 — Philippine wicker hooded swings @ $75	900.00	
	21	20 — Wicker chests @ $25	500.00	
		Prime cost		$2,840.00
		Charges:		
		Shipping	$ 78.85	
		Insurance	15.95	
		Import duty	56.80	
		Commission, 5% of $2,840	142.00	
				+ 293.60
		Gross cost		$3,133.60

Complete the following.

		Salary	Quota	Rate	Net Sales	Commission	Gross Wages
1.	(a)	x	x	5%	$2,100		x
	(b)	x	x	3		$ 78	x
	(c)	x	x		2,500	175	x
	(d)	$45	x	2	3,200		
	(e)	30	x		5,000		$155
	(f)	x	$ 500	6	2,100		x
	(g)	35	1,200	3	3,700		
	(h)	40	1,000	$1\frac{1}{2}$			118
	(i)		1,300	2	5,900		142
2.	(a)	x	x	6%	$5,400		x
	(b)	x	x	4		$312	x
	(c)	x	x		4,500	135	x
	(d)	$60	x	$4\frac{1}{2}$	2,000		
	(e)	50	x	5			$140
	(f)	x	$ 800	3	4,400		x
	(g)	40	1,500	4.	5,800		
	(h)	75	1,200	6			159
	(i)		1,000	5	3,600		175

3. A salesman in a furniture store sold furnishings totaling $11,935 during the month. Sales returns and allowances amounted to $135. What were his gross wages for the month, if his commission rate is 7%?

4. An office machines salesman made sales totaling $5,398, with sales returns and allowances of $198. What were his gross earnings, if his commission rate is 8%?

5. The brokerage paid to a stock broker for purchasing some stock was $48. If the sale price of the stock was $6,400, what is the broker's rate?

6. Beacon Realtors charges 6% of the selling price when they list a home for a client. If the firm received $2,880 after a sale, what was the price of the home?

7. Marshall Gaines is a salesman for a textile machine parts manufacturing company. He is allowed a monthly drawing account of $500. His commission is 3% of his first $10,000 of sales, 4% of the next $15,000, and $5\frac{1}{2}$% of all sales in excess of $25,000. Determine
(a) His total commission; and
(b) His amount due at the end of the month, if his sales were $31,600.

8. Karon Archibald is a sales representative for a cosmetics manufacturer, which allows her a $450 drawing account. Her sales commission is 4% on the first $4,000 in sales; 6% on the next $6,000; and $7\frac{1}{2}$%

on all sales over $10,000. Her sales this month totaled $12,400.

(a) What is her total commission?

(b) What amount will still be due at the end of the month?

9. Mike Nelson earned $148 for the week. This included a $50 salary and a 7% commission on his net sales. What were his net sales?

10. Arthur Ledbetter's $177 gross weekly wages included a salary of $45 and a commission on net sales of $2,200. What is his commission rate?

11. Phyllis Carpenter, a clerk in ladies ready-to-wear, earns $40 a week plus a 3% commission on all net sales in excess of $850. Determine her wages for a week in which she had gross sales of $2,922 and sales returns totaled $72.

12. Wayne Reich, a vacuum cleaner sales/repairman, is paid a $65 weekly salary plus a $12\frac{1}{2}$% commission on all sales in excess of $750. What were his wages last week, if he had sales of $1,523, and sales returns and allowances were $53?

13. As the parts manager of a large auto supply company, Tom Wallace receives a salary of $90 per week; a 3% commission on his sales in excess of $1,000; and a $\frac{1}{4}$% override on the sales of the other employees in his department. His sales last week were $2,443 with sales returns of $43. The other members of his department sold parts totaling $7,716, with sales returns of $116. Determine his total wages for the week.

14. Barbara Mayfield manages a large gift and stationery store, for which she receives a base weekly salary of $75. In addition, she receives a 4% commission on her net sales in excess of $500, plus a $\frac{1}{2}$% override on the net sales of the clerks she supervises. Last week her sales totaled $1,350. The other employees had sales of $4,326 with sales returns of $126. What were her gross wages for the week?

15. Compute the following commission payroll for Myers Men's Shop.

MYERS MEN'S SHOP

Payroll for week ending August 12, 19XX

| Name | NET SALES | | | | | | | Commission Rate | Gross Commission |
	M	T	W	T	F	S	Total		
Ball, J. W.		$375	$412	$390	$450	$478		6%	
Connor, Bill	$272		340	366	407	453		5	
Myers, Phil	285	320	378	398	410	425		8	
Owen, Mike	234	295		360	389	415		5	
Webb, J. E.	260	352	400		395	446		6	
								Total	

16. Complete the following payroll.

THE FASHION CORNER

Payroll for week ending January 6, 19XX

Name	\multicolumn{7}{c}{NET SALES}							Commission Rate	Gross Commission
	M	T	W	T	F	S	Total		
Belton, Clara	$325		$360	$415	$425	$410		5%	
Cruz, Delfina	275	$305		388	416	442		6	
Mercer, Linda		389	417	427	398	436		6	
Thomas, Mary	334		376	409	512	405		7	
Wesson, Kathy	380	355	382		450	467		8	
								Total	

17. Complete the following payroll.

NEWTON FURNITURE COMPANY

Payroll for week ending February 8, 19XX

Name	SALES			Quota	Commission Sales	Commission Rate	Gross Commission	Salary	Gross Wages
	Gross	R&A	Net						
Bame, Henry	$2,240	$30		$1,000		3%		$60.00	
Heavner, J. R.	3,587	37		1,500		6		—	
Ingram, Jerry	3,628	18		—		3		—	
Ramsey, Dan	4,656	26		1,200		2		75.00	
Ross, Ronald	4,214	24		—		2		50.00	
Wise, L. K.	3,945	15		1,800		4		45.00	
						Total			

18. Calculate the following commission payroll.

CARSON WHOLESALE DISTRIBUTORS

Payroll for week ending June 17, 19XX

Name	SALES			Quota	Commission Sales	Commission Rate	Gross Commission	Salary	Gross Wages
	Gross	R&A	Net						
Ammons, Roy	$3,179	$49		$1,200		4%		$70.00	
Dickens, P. T.	2,853	83		—		3		55.00	
Long, Harry	3,795	75		1,000		8		—	
Perry, Joe	2,434	64		750		5		60.00	
Steele, James	2,628	58		—		7		—	
Wyatt, J. R.	2,562	82		900		5		75.00	
						Total			

19. Complete the following account sales:

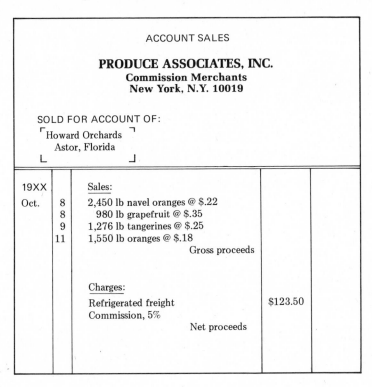

ACCOUNT SALES

PRODUCE ASSOCIATES, INC.
Commission Merchants
New York, N.Y. 10019

SOLD FOR ACCOUNT OF:

⌐Howard Orchards ⌐
   Astor, Florida
L   ⌐

19XX				
Oct.	8	Sales:		
	8	2,450 lb navel oranges @ $.22		
	9	980 lb grapefruit @ $.35		
	11	1,276 lb tangerines @ $.25		
		1,550 lb oranges @ $.18		
		Gross proceeds		
		Charges:		
		Refrigerated freight	$123.50	
		Commission, 5%		
		Net proceeds		

20. Prepare an account sales for the following:

Sunshine Peach Orchards, Allendale, S.C., consigned a shipment to Empire Commission Merchants, New York, N.Y. The shipment contained 260 bushels of Albertas sold on June 15 at $6.50; 120 bushels of Freestones sold on June 16 at $6.25; 225 bushels of Clings sold on June 17 at $6.00; and 150 bushels of Georgia belles sold on June 17 at $6.50. Storage fees were $27.50 and cartage charges totaled $45. The commission agents' charge was 2%.

21. Complete the account purchase at top of p. 202.

22. Prepare an account purchase for the following:

Pierre Seibert, an independent agent, was employed by The Import House, Newark, N.J., to purchase European art work. Seibert secured 240 original Roman oils on October 19 at $45; 170 pieces of Venetian crystal on October 22 at $8; and 50 Swiss clocks on October 30 at $25. His charges were $370 for freight and shipping, $230 for insurance, $350 for travel expenses, and 5% commission.

ACCOUNT PURCHASE

DAMON & RATHBORNE

Commission Merchants   San Francisco, California

BOUGHT FOR ACCOUNT OF:

Sullivan Interiors
Denver, Colorado

19XX		Purchases:		
June	17	18 – ginger jar lamps @ $72.50		
	17	36 – Ming vases @ $58.75		
	18	12 – 5 x 7' Oriental carpets @ $87.50		
	19	5 – 9 x 12' Oriental carpets @ $346.00		
			Prime cost	
		Charges:		
		Shipping	$ 89.70	
		Insurance	53.20	
		Commission, 7%		
			Gross cost	

SECTION 3

Computing Wages—
Hourly-Rate Basis

The hourly-rate basis for determining wages is the method under which the wages of the majority of the American working force are computed. Under this plan, the employee receives a stipulated amount for each hour's work. One or more of several factors may determine the hourly rate: the individual's ability, training, and experience, as well as federal minimum-wage laws or union contracts. Once the hourly rate has been established, however, the employees' quality of performance or amount of production in no way influence their wages.

The **Fair Labor Standards Act** governs the employment of more than 57 million workers. Previously affecting primarily workers engaged in some form of interstate, international, or other large-scale commercial enterprises, the Act has now been extended to include a wide range of occupations. Among newly covered workers are nonprofessional employees of hospitals and nursing homes, public or private schools, cleaners and laundries, all levels of government, transportation services, and small-scale construction, as well as domestic workers. It is expected that the act will eventually be extended to cover essentially all full-time workers.

Effective in 1978, the Act prescribed a 40-hour work week and set the minimum wage for all covered employees at $2.65 per hour. Many states have also established minimum wages (usually somewhat lower than the federal minimum) for employees not subject to the federal regulations. The federal act applies equally to men and women. It should be emphasized, however, that certain employees are specifically excluded from the provisions of the act—executive and administrative personnel in businesses, professional people (such as medical personnel, educators, lawyers, etc.), as well as outside salesworkers, employees of many small retail or service establishments, and many seasonal and small-farm workers.

Overtime   In accordance with the federal law covering the 40-hour work week, most employees' regular week consists of five 8-hour working days. Under the federal regulation, **overtime** must be paid to covered employees for work in excess of 40 hours. Many employers, even though not subject to the federal act, follow this policy voluntarily.

The standard overtime rate is $1\frac{1}{2}$ times the worker's regular hourly rate ("time-and-a-half"). "Double time" is often paid for work on Sundays or on holidays. It should be noted, however, that the Fair Labor Standards Act does *not* require extra pay for Saturdays, Sundays, or holidays (except for hours in excess of 40); neither does it require pay for time off during vacations or holidays. Whether premium rates are paid or time off is granted depends entirely on the employment (or union) agreement.

In some instances, overtime is paid when an employee works more than 8 hours on any one day. (Some union contracts contain this provision.) As a general practice, however, a worker is required to have worked 40 hours before receiving any overtime compensation; otherwise, the worker might be paid some overtime without having completed the prescribed 40-hour week. If a company nonetheless pays overtime on a daily basis, the payroll clerk must keep a careful record of each employee's hours to ensure that the same time is not counted twice; that is, hours which qualify as daily overtime must not be applied toward the regular 40-hour week, after which all work would be at overtime rates.

Union contracts often contain overtime provisions regarding any number of other situations, such as working two complete shifts in one day or working six or seven consecutive days.

Large firms usually have timeclocks that record entering and leaving times on each employee's timecard. Total work hours are then calculated from this record. Just as employees are compensated for overtime work, they are likewise penalized for tardiness. In smaller firms, a supervisor may record the whole crew's hours; or, in some instances employees report their own hours. Total hours worked are usually kept to the nearest quarter-hour each day.

Example One

Compute the gross wages of each employee:

DAVIS HARDWARE

Payroll for week ending May 9, 19XX

Name	M	T	W	T	F	S	Total Hours	Rate per Hour	Gross Wages
Anderson, James	9	7	8	8	8	0	40	$2.50	$100.00
Bailey, Carl	8	8	10	0	10	4	40	3.75	150.00
Carson, W. J.	8	6	0	5	8	4	31	2.80	86.80
Davis, Willard	9	8	8	8	6	0	39	4.00	156.00
								Total	492.80

Example Two

Compute the gross wages of each comployee of Milford Roofing Co. Overtime is paid at $1\frac{1}{2}$ times the regular rate on hours in excess of 40 per week.

MILFORD ROOFING CO.
Payroll for week ending December 12, 19XX

Name	M	T	W	T	F	S	Total Hours	Regular Hours	Rate per Hour	Overtime Hours	Overtime Rate	Regular Wages	Overtime Wages	Total Gross Wages
Elliott, D. R.	8	8	10	9	10	4	49	40	$3.00	9	$4.50	$120.00	$40.50	$160.50
Farmer, Ray	10	8	9	7	7	4	45	40	2.60	5	3.90	104.00	19.50	123.50
Givens, Troy	8	8	8	8	8	0	40	40	4.75	—	7.13	190.00	—	190.00
Harper, Tony	5	8	6	7	8	4	38	38	2.50	—	3.75	95.00	—	95.00
Ivey, Marion	9	8	6	8	9	4	44	40	3.50	4	5.25	140.00	21.00	161.00
											Totals	$649.00	$81.00	$730.00

NOTE: The total of the Regular Wages plus the total of the Overtime Wages must equal the total Gross Wages ($649 + $81 = $730).

Example Three

Compute William Kurio's gross wages, based on the following: overtime at time-and-a-half is paid daily on work in excess of 8 hours and weekly on work in excess of 40 regular hours; double time is paid for all Sunday work. His hours each day were as follows:

	M	T	W	T	F	S	S
Kurio, Wm.	8	9	7	10	7	5	5

		M	T	W	T	F	S	S	Total Hours	Rate per Hour	Base Wages	Total Gross Wages
Kurio, Wm.	RTª	8	8	7	8	7	2		40	$2.80	$112.00	
	1½		1		2		3		6	4.20	25.20	$165.20
	DT							5	5	5.60	28.00	

ªRT indicates "Regular time"; 1½, "Time-and-a-half"; and DT, "Double time."

Overtime for Salaried Personnel

The following example illustrates the computation of gross wages for salaried personnel who must be paid overtime wages. This procedure is required under the Fair Labor Standards Act for salaried personnel subject to overtime provisions. (Refer also to Section 1, "Computing Wages—Salary," p. 191).

Example Four

(a) A file clerk receives a $100 salary for her regular 40-hour week. What should be her gross wages for a week when she works 44 hours?

The clerk's regular wages are equivalent to $\dfrac{\$100}{40 \text{ hours}}$ or $2.50 per hour. She must be paid overtime at 1½ times this rate, or $3.75 per hour. Her wages for a 44-hour week would thus be $115:

40 hours @ $2.50 = $100	Regular salary
4 hours @ $3.75 = 15	Overtime
44-hour week = $115	Gross wages

(b) An administrative assistant receives a $112 weekly salary. If a regular work week contains 35 hours, how much compensation would she receive when she works 43 hours?

$$\frac{\$112}{35 \text{ hours}} = \$3.20 \text{ per hour}$$

Overtime rate = $1\frac{1}{2} \times \$3.20 = \$4.80$ per hour

40 hours @ $3.20 = $128.00	
3 hours @ $4.80 = 14.40	
43-hour week = $142.40	Gross wages

Example Four (cont.)

(c) A service manager's base salary is $162, although his hours vary each week. What are his gross wages for a week when he works 45 hours?

$$\frac{\$162}{45 \text{ hours}} = \$3.60 \text{ per hour}$$

$$\text{Overtime rate} = 1\tfrac{1}{2} \times \$3.60 = \$5.40 \text{ per hour}$$

$$
\begin{array}{lll}
40 \text{ hours @ } \$3.60 = & \$144.00 \\
\underline{\;5 \text{ hours @ } \$5.40 =} & \underline{\;\;\;27.00} \\
45\text{-hour week} & = \$171.00 & \text{Gross wages}
\end{array}
$$

Observe that, for any employee whose hours vary each week as do this man's hours, the employee's regular rate per hour will also vary each week. That is, his regular rate is $3.60 per hour only during a week when he works 45 hours. If he works 54 hours the following week, then his regular rate that week will be

$$\frac{\$162}{54} = \$3 \text{ per hour on the 40 hours,}$$

plus overtime for 14 hours at $4.50 per hour.

Overtime Excess

All the examples above show regular rates for 40 hours and an overtime rate of $1\tfrac{1}{2}$ times the regular rate. An alternative method will produce the same result: Calculate the total hours at the regular rate plus the overtime hours at one-half the regular rate. The additional compensation calculated by this method (overtime hours times one-half the regular rate) is called the **overtime excess**.

Example Five

A worker who earns $3 per hour works 46 hours. Compare these earnings (a) by standard overtime and (b) by overtime excess.

Solution

(a)
$$
\begin{array}{lll}
40 \text{ hours @ } \$3.00 = & \$120.00 & \text{Straight-time wages} \\
\underline{\;6 \text{ hours @ } \$4.50 =} & \underline{\;\;\;27.00} & \text{Overtime wages} \\
46 \text{ hours} & = \$147.00 & \text{Total gross wages}
\end{array}
$$

(b) One-half the regular rate is $\tfrac{1}{2}$ of $3.00 = $1.50 per hour for the excess hours over 40.

$$
\begin{array}{lll}
46 \text{ hours @ } \$3.00 = & \$138.00 & \text{Regular-rate wages} \\
\underline{\;6 \text{ hours @ } \$1.50 =} & \underline{\;\;\;\;9.00} & \text{Overtime excess} \\
46 \text{ hours} & = \$147.00 & \text{Total gross wages}
\end{array}
$$

Some firms prefer the overtime excess method for their own cost accounting, since it emphasizes the extra expense (and lost income) resulting from overtime work. (Notice above that, if the extra 6 hours' work could have been delayed until the following week and all done at the regular rate, the company's cost would have been only $138, rather than $147.)

Use of the overtime excess method is becoming more widespread. Although either overtime method is permitted under the Fair Labor Standards Act, the Wage and Hour division (which enforces the act) uses the overtime excess method. A major reason for using overtime excess is that workers' compensation insurance premiums are based on a worker's regular-rate wages (that is, the $138 above).

SECTION 3 *Problems*

1. Compute the following gross earnings.

LIGHTING SUPPLY HOUSE

Payroll for week ending May 25, 19XX

Name	M	T	W	T	F	S	Total Hours	Rate per Hour	Gross Wages
Abbot, Robert	7	8	8	7	8	0		$3.20	
Davis, Jim	8	8	8	5	7	4		2.85	
Eagles, A. C.	8	8	8	8	8	0		3.35	
Garcia, Al	6	7	8	8	9	0		2.75	
Melton, Tony	7	7	8	4	6	5		3.40	
Rogers, Glenn	9	8	5	5	8	4		4.20	
Slaton, Terry	7	7	7	8	7	4		2.95	
								Total	

2. Complete the following gross payroll.

LIBERTY FENCE CO.

Payroll for week ending October 21, 19XX

Name	M	T	W	T	F	S	Total Hours	Rate per Hour	Gross Wages
Conover, Ray	8	6	7	7	9	0		$3.10	
Evans, D. L.	9	8	4	8	8	3		3.45	
Hotchkiss, S. P.	7	7	8	6	8	3		2.80	
Myers, Andrew	8	8	8	8	8	0		3.15	
Overton, Ross	9	8	8	6	6	0		2.90	
Royer, Robert	8	7	7	8	6	4		2.85	
Young, Steven	6	7	8	8	7	3		3.00	
								Total	

3. The employees of The Wiley Company receive overtime at time-and-a-half for all work in excess of 40 hours per week. Calculate their gross wages from the following payroll.

THE WILEY COMPANY

Payroll for week ending November 4, 19XX

Name	M	T	W	T	F	S	Total Hours	Regular Hours	Rate per Hour	Over-time Hours	Over-time Rate	Regular Wages	Overtime Wages	Total Gross Wages
Gleason, Marvin	8	9	8	8	7	5			$3.20					
Jackson, Cathy	9	9	9	9	8	0			2.80					
Nunis, Todd	8	8	7	7	9	3			3.10					
Peavey, Carole	8	8	7	6	7	4			3.60					
Wendt, Thomas	9	9	8	9	8	0			3.00					
											Totals			

4. The employees of Textile Parts, Inc., are required to work a regular 40-hour week, after which they receive standard overtime for any additional hours. Compute the gross payroll below.

TEXTILE PARTS, INC.

Payroll for week ending March 30, 19XX

Name	M	T	W	T	F	S	Total Hours	Regular Hours	Rate per Hour	Over-time Hours	Over-time Rate	Regular Wages	Overtime Wages	Total Gross Wages
Berry, Paul	8	10	7	7	8	0			$3.50					
Horton, Ken	9	8	8	6	7	5			2.80					
Lewis, Robert	9	7	6	8	8	4			3.30					
Rogers, J. M.	7	8	5	8	6	4			3.20					
Wyatt, Paul	10	8	7	9	8	4			4.20					
											Totals			

5. The employees listed on the payroll excerpt below receive daily overtime for work in excess of 8 hours. Weekly overtime is paid after they have completed 40 regular hours. Work done on Sundays or holidays receives double-time wages. From the total hours listed each day, divide the time into the correct category and complete the gross payroll. Monday of the week shown was a national holiday.

	M	T	W	T	F	S	S
Dixon, Sara	0	8	9	9	10	5	2
Ingles, Michael	4	9	9	8	8	8	0
Stoner, Kent	2	9	7	8	9	5	3

Name		M	T	W	T	F	S	S	Total Hours	Rate per Hour	Base Wages	Total Gross Wages
Dixon, Sara	RT $1\frac{1}{2}$ DT									$3.00		
Inglis, Michael	RT $1\frac{1}{2}$ DT									3.40		
Stoner, Kent	RT $1\frac{1}{2}$ DT									3.25		
											Total	

6. Daily overtime (in excess of 8 hours) and weekly overtime (after a 40-hour week) are paid to the employees listed below. They also receive double time for Sunday work. From the total daily hours given, determine the number of hours in each category and compute the gross wages.

	M	T	W	T	F	S	S
Coley, Jack	8	9	9	10	7	5	0
Hart, Bill	7	8	10	8	10	5	4
Puett, Ira	9	8	8	6	10	5	4

Name		M	T	W	T	F	S	S	Total Hours	Rate per Hour	Base Wages	Total Gross Wages
Coley, Jack	RT $1\frac{1}{2}$ DT									$3.60		
Hart, Bill	RT $1\frac{1}{2}$ DT									3.50		
Puett, Ira	RT $1\frac{1}{2}$ DT									2.75		
											Total	

Compute the gross weekly wages for the salaried employees shown below, who are all subject to the Fair Labor Standards Act.

	Position	Regular Hours per Week	Regular Salary	Hours Worked	Gross Wages
7. (a)	Keypunch operator	40	$120	42	
(b)	Receptionist	36	90	44	
(c)	Data programmer	(varies)	190	50	
8. (a)	Administrative assistant	40	$140	44	
(b)	Typist	35	98	45	
(c)	Branch manager	(varies)	243	54	

For each of the employees listed below, compute gross earnings (a) with overtime at time-and-a-half and (b) using overtime excess.

	Employee	Hours	Rate per Hour
9.	A	44	$4.00
	B	46	3.70
	C	47	3.20
10.	X	45	$3.60
	Y	48	2.90
	Z	43	3.00

11. Complete the following payroll register, where the overtime excess method is used for work above 40 hours per week.

WESTPORT SMALL ENGINE REPAIR

Payroll for week ending August 11, 19XX

Name	M	T	W	T	F	S	Total Hours	Rate per Hour	Over-time Hours	Over-time Excess Rate	Regu-lar Rate Wages	Over-time Excess	Total Gross Wages
Ford, G. R.	10	8	9	12	11	5		$3.00					
Jones, B. O.	9	9	11	10	12	4		3.20					
Moyer, E. L.	8	10	10	12	9	5		3.40					
Ramsey, E. L.	9	11	9	9	8	5		2.80					
Thomas, M. E.	9	10	11	12	9	4		3.60					
										Totals			

12. Use the overtime excess method in computing the following gross payroll.

MIDWEST MANUFACTURING CO., INC

Payroll for week ending May, 5, 19XX

Name	M	T	W	T	F	S	Total Hours	Rate per Hour	Over-time Hours	Over-time Excess Rate	Regu-lar Rate Wages	Over-time Excess	Total Gross Wages
Archer, D. O.	8	9	9	10	10	6		$2.60					
Barnes, V. L.	9	9	9	9	9	4		3.00					
Doss, P. R.	9	10	12	12	9	5		3.80					
Goforth, L. L.	10	11	8	9	11	3		4.20					
Neeley, N. E.	9	11	12	9	11	4		2.80					
										Totals			

SECTION 4

Computing Wages—Production Basis

In many factories, each employee's work consists of repeating the same task—either some step in the construction of a product, or inspecting or packing finished products. The employee's value to the company can thus be measured by how often this task is completed. Therefore, many plants compensate employees at a specified rate per unit completed; this constitutes the **production** basis of computing wages. This type of wage computation is also known as the **piecework** or **piece-rate** plan.

Naturally, some steps in the production of a product require more time than others. Thus, the rate per unit for that step would be more than the rate on another task which could be completed much more quickly. In order to keep the entire plant production moving at an even pace, more employees are hired to perform time-consuming tasks and fewer workers are employed to perform easier tasks.

On the straight production plan, the employee receives the same rate for each piece; thus,

62 pieces at $1.55 = $96.10 wages

Incentives (Premium Rates)

At first glance, the production plan would seem to be quite acceptable to employees, since compensation is determined entirely by individual performance. Such has not been the case, however. Most companies that use the piecework plan have established quotas or minimum production standards for each job. As an extra incentive to production, workers receive a higher rate per unit on all units which they complete in excess of this minimum. It is these quotas which historically have caused such dissatisfaction with the production plan. In the past, many companies set "production" (quotas) at such high levels that only a few of the most skillful and experienced employees could attain them. Furthermore, employees complained that when they finally did master the task well enough to "make production," the company would reassign them to a new, unfamiliar task.

As a result of the general dissatisfaction over piecework plans, many union contracts now contain provisions that members must be paid on the hourly-rate basis. Those plants which do still use the production basis have tended to reestablish quotas which are more in line with the production that average employees can attain.

Dockings   Although companies are willing to pay premium
(Spoilage   rates as incentives to high production, they also
Chargebacks)   wish to discourage haste resulting in carelessness
and mistakes. An employee who makes an uncorrectable mistake has destroyed not only the raw materials involved but has also wasted the work done previously by other employees. Thus, an unreasonably high amount of spoilage would be quite expensive to a company. In order to discourage carelessness, many plants require employees to forfeit a certain amount for each piece they spoil. These penalty **dockings** (or **chargebacks**) are generally at a lower rate than the employee ordinarily receives for each task, since a small amount of spoilage is to be expected. In general,

$$\text{Gross wages} = \text{Base production} + \text{Premium} - \text{Chargeback}$$

Overtime   Piecework employees who are subject to the Fair
              Labor Standards Act must likewise be paid time-and-a-half for work in excess of 40 hours per week. This overtime may be computed similarly to that of salaried workers (by finding the hourly rate to which their regular-time earnings are equivalent and paying $1\frac{1}{2}$ this hourly rate for overtime hours.) However, the overtime wages of a production worker may be computed at $1\frac{1}{2}$ times the regular rate per piece, provided that certain standards are met to ensure that workers are indeed being paid the required minimum wage for regular-time hours, as well as time-and-a-half for overtime hours. This method is preferred because it is simpler to compute and will therefore be used for our

problems. We shall not, however, attempt to compute overtime where premium production is also involved.

Example One

The following example shows a payroll based on straight production:

TEXAS BOOT CO.

Payroll for week ending April 5, 19XX

Name	NET PIECES PRODUCED						Total Net Pieces	Rate per Piece	Gross Wages Earned
	M	*T*	*W*	*T*	*F*	*S*			
Cruz, Ramon	17	14	18	19	16	8	92	$1.85	$170.20
Gelernter, Art	39	46	39	37	34	19	214	.65	139.10
Kearns, D. M.	125	138	140	131	129	65	728	.18	131.04
Lotus, Kim	71	67	74	79	70	34	395	.40	158.00
Steiner, Lois	76	82	81	77	80	40	436	.40	174.40
								Total	$772.74

Example Two

In the following production payroll, all work performed on Saturday is overtime and is paid at $1\frac{1}{2}$ times the regular piece rate.

PRECISION INSTRUMENTS, INC.

Payroll for week ending August 30, 19XX

Name	NET PIECES PRODUCED						Regular Time Prod.	Rate Per Piece	Over-time Prod.	Over-time Rate	Regular Wages	Over-time Wages	Total Gross Wages
	M	*T*	*W*	*T*	*F*	*S*							
Ball, A. J.	214	220	218	216	219	112	1087	$.09	112	$.135	$ 97.83	$15.12	$112.95
Grange, N. R.	94	90	97	99	101	51	481	.20	51	.30	96.20	15.30	111.50
Mills, P. D.	68	70	72	69	71	30	350	.25	30	.375	87.50	11.35	98.85
Trent, S. M.	151	155	153	150	152	75	761	.14	75	.21	106.54	15.75	122.29
										Totals	$388.07	$57.52	$445.59

Example Three

Cynthia Simmons sews zippers into dresses for a garment manufacturer. Her base rate is 45¢ per dress, and a premium rate of 52¢ per dress is paid after she exceeds the weekly production quota of 240 zippers. She is docked 35¢ for each zipper that does not pass inspection. Compute her gross earnings for the week:

Example Three (*cont.*)

	M	T	W	T	F	Total
Gross production	54	51	55	53	52	265
Less: spoilage	2	0	0	3	1	− 6
Net production	52	51	55	50	51	259

Cynthia will receive the premium rate on 259−240 = 19 zippers. Her Gross wages = Base production + Premium − Chargeback:

	Total Net Production	×	Rate	=	Gross Wages
Base production	240	@	$.45		$108.00
Premium production	19	@	.52	+	9.88
					$117.88ᵃ
Spoilage chargeback	6	@	.35	−	2.10
					$115.78

ᵃ Wage computation would end at this point for any production tasks not subject to chargeback.

Example Four

Complete the following production payroll, which includes incentive and penalty chargeback rates

Gross wages = Base wages + Premium − Chargeback:

HANOVER GAME CO.
Payroll for week ending October 17, 19XX

Name		DAILY PRODUCTION M	T	W	T	F	Total Production	Net Quota	Production	Rate (cents)	Base Wages	Total Gross Wages
Eaton, C. C.	GPᵃ	159	162	152	155	158	786		Base: 750	15¢	$112.50	
	S	7	3	0	2	2	14		Premium: 22	21	4.62	$115.72
	NP	152	159	152	153	156	772	750	Chargeback: 14	10	1.40	
Gray, N. S.	GP	126	128	131	125	129	639		Base: 632	17¢	107.44	
	S	2	1	3	0	1	7		Premium: —	24	—	106.60
	NP	124	127	128	125	128	632	650	Chargeback: 7	12	.84	
Spann, B. R.	GP	143	141	145	142	144	715		Base: 700	16¢	112.00	
	S	2	0	0	1	2	5		Premium: 10	23	2.30	113.75
	NP	141	141	145	141	142	710	700	Chargeback: 5	11	.55	
											Total	$336.07

ᵃ GP indicates "Gross production"; S, "Spoilage"; and NP, "Net production."

SECTION 4 *Problems*

1. Ronald Forbes works in a shipping department of a sweater factory. His base rate is 48¢ per dozen sweaters. He receives a premium rate of 55¢ per dozen when he has packed more than 200 dozen sweaters per week. Determine his wages for the following week.

	M	T	W	T	F	Total
Forbes, Ronald	42	38	36	44	43	

2. Sue Lackey is an inspector in a hosiery mill, for which the quota is 500 dozen hose per week. She is paid 21¢ per dozen regularly and 28¢ per dozen after she has exceeded production. Determine her gross wages for the following week's production.

	M	T	W	T	F	Total
Lackey, Sue	98	105	107	108	102	

3. John Tyler operates a machine which bolts together two pieces of a motor. He is paid 1¢ per bolt on net production, and a premium rate of $1\frac{1}{4}$¢ per bolt in excess of 9,600 bolts per week. His spoilage chargeback rate is $\frac{3}{4}$¢ per bolt. Compute his gross wages for the following week.

	M	T	W	T	F	Total
Gross production	2,005	1,980	1,972	1,978	1,994	
Less: spoilage	12	11	8	10	11	
Net production						

4. Andrew White operates a machine which cuts the notches that fit together the pieces of a drawer. The furniture factory pays 6.5¢ per dozen on net production up to 1,600 dozen pieces, and an incentive of 8.5¢ per dozen thereafter. He is docked 4.5¢ per dozen when his work fails to pass inspection. Calculate his gross wages for the following week, given production in dozens.

	M	T	W	T	F	Total
Gross production	323	330	332	326	325	
Less: spoilage	5	1	2	0	2	
Net production						

5. Complete the following payroll based on straight production.

WARING BOLT & SCREW CO.
Payroll for week ending January 24, 19XX

Name	NET PIECES PRODUCED					Total Net Pieces	Rate per Piece	Gross Wages Earned
	M	T	W	T	F			
Bufort, Maude	157	162	165	161	169		12¢	
Duncan, Willis	301	310	315	298	307		7	
Eaves, Norris	90	93	97	94	95		20	
Norwood, E. L.	315	320	318	317	321		6	
Putnam, C. W.	270	275	268	273	269		7	
Summey, Jane	345	346	347	344	352		6	
Tillman, O. R.	278	280	275	278	283		8	
							Total	

6. Complete the following production payroll.

WAINWRIGHT MANUFACTURING CO.
Payroll for week ending December 9, 19XX

Name	NET PIECES PRODUCED					Total Net Pieces	Rate per Piece	Gross Wages Earned
	M	T	W	T	F			
Berry, R. J.	152	148	157	153	149		14¢	
Fine, Ralph	286	291	302	295	293		7	
Gore, L. C.	97	103	107	104	105		23	
Knapp, D. F.	65	67	66	64	70		32	
Lane, Sara	28	25	30	33	34		82	
Thorne, M. B.	112	118	123	115	123		19	
Yount, A. M.	81	84	82	90	86		26	
							Total	

7. Compute the following production payroll. Work performed on Saturday is overtime and should be reimbursed at $1\frac{1}{2}$ times the standard rate per piece.

BARNHART FURNITURE CO.
Payroll for week ending March 6, 19XX

Name	NET PIECES PRODUCED						Regular Time Production	Rate Per Piece	Overtime Production	Overtime Rate	Reg. Wages	Overtime Wages	Total Gross Wages
	M	T	W	T	F	S							
Castle, Mary	75	78	80	81	78	38		$.30					
Givens, John	107	110	108	111	119	54		.18					
Hall, Troy	188	190	185	192	186	93		.12					
Martin, D. I.	116	110	120	116	118	64		.20					
Quinn, S. E.	89	84	90	85	87	48		.25					
										Totals			

8. Complete the following production payroll. Overtime will be paid for all Saturday work.

COMFORT-KNIT SLACKS, INC.

Payroll for week ending June 23, 19XX

Name	M	T	W	T	F	S	Regular Time Production	Rate Per Piece	Overtime Production	Overtime Rate	Regular Wages	Overtime Wages	Total Gross Wages
			NET DAILY PRODUCTION										
Daly, R.	90	94	93	95	98	45		$.22					
Goff, J.	155	160	161	158	156	78		.14					
Jones, B.	170	178	180	176	182	94		.12					
Land, M.	70	69	68	70	72	35		.30					
Phipps, D.	150	148	147	152	155	72		.15					
										Totals			

9. Find the gross wages for the following payroll.

QUALICRAFT MILLS, INC.

Payroll for week ending September 3, 19XX

Name		M	T	W	T	F	Total Production	Net Quota	Production	Rate	Base Wages	Total Gross Wages
		DAILY PRODUCTION										
Camp, Ann	GP	112	115	114	116	115			Base:	20¢		
	S	2	3	2	2	3			Premium:	26		
	NP							550	Chargeback:	15		
Horn, Hazel	GP	85	90	93	90	91			Base:	24¢		
	S	2	0	2	1	0			Premium:	30		
	NP							425	Chargeback:	20		
Macon, Ina	GP	79	82	86	89	88			Base:	28¢		
	S	3	1	0	0	1			Premium:	35		
	NP							375	Chargeback:	24		
Steele, Wm.	GP	58	54	55	56	55			Base:	45¢		
	S	4	1	0	1	2			Premium:	54		
	NP							240	Chargeback:	40		
Tuttle, Lee	GP	143	156	160	152	157			Base:	18¢		
	S	5	3	5	4	7			Premium:	25		
	NP							600	Chargeback:	15		
										Total		

10. Complete the following gross wages.

BEST HOSIERY
Payroll for week ending August 4, 19XX

Name		DAILY PRODUCTION M	T	W	T	F	Total Production	Net Quota	Production	Rate	Base Wages	Total Gross Wages
Orvin, Glenn	GP	40	42	45	48	47			Base:	45¢		
	S	3	0	1	2	0			Premium:	54		
	NP							220	Chargeback:	30		
Pealer, E. R.	GP	75	78	73	76	80			Base:	34¢		
	S	0	0	2	1	2			Premium:	42		
	NP							300	Chargeback:	25		
Rhyne, Mary	GP	108	106	103	98	110			Base:	20¢		
	S	3	5	0	1	4			Premium:	24		
	NP							525	Chargeback:	14		
St. John, Jane	GP	86	93	90	93	89			Base:	24¢		
	S	2	5	1	0	2			Premium:	30		
	NP							400	Chargeback:	16		
Watts, David	GP	56	59	65	62	64			Base:	34¢		
	S	4	2	7	2	2			Premium:	42		
	NP							300	Chargeback:	25		
										Total		

SECTION 5

Net Weekly Payrolls

Employers are required by law to make certain deductions from the gross earnings of their employees. The amount remaining after deductions have been withheld is known as **net wages.** (The same methods are used to arrive at net wages from gross wages regardless of which payroll plan has been used to compute gross wages.)

Two compulsory, federal deductions are made in all regular payrolls: Social Security and personal income tax. In many states, the employer is also required to withhold state income tax. Certain other deductions, either compulsory or voluntary, may also be made. The following paragraphs discuss important aspects of the various deductions.

Social Security or FICA (Federal Insurance Contributions Act)

The original **Federal Insurance Contributions Act** was one of the emergency measures passed during the Great Depression of the 1930s; it has since been amended and extended many times and now draws payments from approximately 100 million workers. **Social Security**—as the Federal Insurance Contributions

Act program has come to be called—is not a tax in the normal sense; it could more accurately be described as a compulsory savings or insurance program. Social Security funds are used to pay monthly benefits to retired or disabled workers, to pay benefits to the surviving spouse and minor children of a deceased worker, and to finance the Medicare program enacted by Congress in 1965. Some 30 million Americans currently receive Social Security benefits.

This text uses the 1977 withholding rate for Social Security, which was 5.85% of the first $16,500 earned by each worker.* All FICA deductions must be matched by an equal contribution from the employer (making the total rate 11.7%). Self-employed persons paid 7.9% of the first $16,500. Both the rate and the base income for FICA withholdings are considered annually by Congress. The rate has remained at 5.85% since 1973; however, the base income subject to FICA has been increased each year, so that a majority of workers now pay Social Security on their entire year's earnings.

The Social Security deduction to be withheld may be computed by finding 5.85% of the employee's gross wages. To save time, however, most payroll clerks use Social Security tax tables furnished by the government. These tables list wage intervals and the deduction to be made within each interval.

Example One
(a) Ewald Straiton earns a gross salary of $180 each week. What FICA deduction must be made? By percentage:

$$5.85\% \text{ of } \$180 = \$10.53$$

By the Social Security Table (Table XI, Appendix C): Under the "Wages" heading, consult the interval where gross earnings are "at least $179.92, but less than $180.09" The next column shows the "tax to be withheld" is $10.53.

(b) Mary Gibson earned gross wages of $123. What is her Social Security deduction?

By the table: $123 appears on two lines of the table. On the first line, however, Gibson's wages appear under the heading "but less than $123." This does not apply, because Gibson did not earn "less than $123." We must use the second line, where the wages earned were "at least $123." The "Tax to be withheld" column indicates Gibson's deduction will be $7.20.

* The 1978 rate was 6.05% of the first $17,700.

Although the $16,500 base for FICA means that most workers make contributions from their entire year's earnings, most executives and many highly paid workers have earnings above $16,500 that are not subject to FICA. The payroll clerk should thus be alert so that no FICA deductions are made on earnings in excess of $16,500.

Federal
Income Tax

Employers are required to make deductions from each worker's wages for federal **income tax**. As in the case of Social Security, most businesses use federal **withholding** tables to determine income tax deductions. Immediately after a new employee is hired, the payroll clerk should ask the worker to complete Form W-4, the **Employee's Withholding Allowance Certificate**. This form indicates the employee's marital status and the total number of dependents or allowances (including the worker) which are claimed.

Married and single persons are subject to different income tax rates, the rates being higher for single persons. The Income Tax Withholding Tables (pp. 597–599) therefore contain separate listings for married and single persons. The tax to be withheld is thus dependent upon three factors: (1) the worker's gross earnings, (2) whether married or single, and (3) the number of allowances claimed.

One allowance may be claimed on Form W-4 for each member of the family. This total number may include a grandparent or other persons who live with the family and/or qualify as dependents.* Additional allowances may also be claimed if the worker (or spouse) is over 65 or is blind. These allowances are the same ones that are claimed on the personal income tax return, Form 1040.

Since the income tax withholding tables (of 1977, in this text) would withhold more tax than many workers actually owe, the Internal Revenue Service has taken steps to ensure that the tax withheld more nearly equals the amount owed for the year. Thus, in addition to the allowances cited above, Form W-4 may include certain other allowances that are not permitted on a personal tax return. The withholding tables assume that the worker will claim a standard deduction for personal income tax purposes.

---

* To qualify, the persons (1) must either be specified relatives or reside with the taxpayer; (2) must have received more than one-half their support from the taxpayer; (3) must have earned less than a certain gross income of their own (except youths under 19 or qualified students); (4) must not have filed a joint return with a spouse; and (5) must be a citizen of the United States or of certain other specified places.

However, people who itemize deductions (because their deductions exceed the standard 15%) typically owe less income tax than the tables withhold. Therefore, the W-4 permits extra allowance(s) according to the worker's itemized-deductions bracket. A special allowance is also permitted for persons who only have one employer (if the worker is single or is married to a nonworking spouse), since these workers also usually owe less tax than the tables would normally withhold.

The total of these W-4 allowances may all be claimed by a husband; or, if the wife works, she may claim her own allowance and also some of the children's allowances. The principal restriction is that the total number of allowances claimed by both husband and wife may not exceed the total allowances to which the family is entitled. Also, persons with more than one job may not claim the same allowance(s) with more than one employer at the same time.

Any worker holding more than one job is also responsible for assuring that enough tax has been withheld (since these wages may yield a total for which the tax rate is higher). The usual means by which workers have more tax withheld is to claim fewer allowances than they are entitled to. (Any employees may claim *fewer* but may never claim more allowances than they are entitled to. Many workers claim fewer allowances as a forced, short-term savings plan, so that they will receive a refund when their annual income tax return is filed.)

Example Two

Sharie Chiles and Sue Watson both earn salaries of $150 per week. Each claims only herself as a dependent; however, Chiles is married and Watson is single. How much income tax will be withheld from each salary?

Solution

Since Sharie Chiles is married and claims only herself, the exemption indicated on her payroll sheet is "M-1." Using the income tax withholding table for "Married Persons" paid on a "Weekly Payroll Period," we find the gross wage interval containing wages that are "at least $150 but less than $160." The columns at the right have headings indicating the number of exemptions that may be claimed. For Chiles, we use the column which shows "1 exemption claimed" and see that the tax to be withheld is $17.10. If Chiles' salary does not change, she will have income tax of $17.10 withheld each week during the entire year.

Sue Watson's payroll sheet indicates that her exemption is "S-1." Using the income tax table for "Single Persons" paid on a "Weekly"

Example Two (*cont.*) basis, we find the same gross wage interval of "at least $150 but less than $160." In the column for "1 exemption claimed," we see that income tax of $22.20 will be deducted from Watson's salary each week. Thus, Watson, because she is single, pays $22.20 − $17.10, or $5.10 more income tax each week than Chiles pays.

State Deductions In many states, state income tax is also a compulsory deduction. Withholding tables are usually available for the state tax, which is typically at a considerably lower rate than the federal income tax.

The Social Security (FICA) Act contains provisions for an **unemployment insurance tax.** The funds from this tax provide compensation to ablebodied workers who are willing to work, but who have been "laid off" by their employers because there is no work available. Under the federal act, this unemployment tax is paid by the *employer only*, with most of the funds being collected by the individual states. (That is, no deduction is made from the worker's pay for federal unemployment tax.) In a few states, however, the state has levied its own unemployment tax in addition to the federal tax. In these states, a compulsory unemployment tax may be deducted from the worker's wages.

Other Deductions There are any number of other deductions which may be withheld from the worker's wages. One of the most common is group insurance. Many firms sponsor a group policy whereby employees may purchase health, accident, hospitalization, and sometimes even life insurance at rates substantially lower than they could obtain individually.

Union dues or dues to professional organizations may be deducted. Employees often contribute to a company or state retirement plan which will supplement their Social Security retirement benefits. Contributions to charitable causes (such as the United Fund or Community Chest) may be withheld. Some businesses participate in a payroll savings plan whereby deductions are made to purchase U.S. Savings Bonds. Numerous other examples could be cited.

Example Three Below is a net payroll of Everett Paint Co. In addition to the standard deductions, 1.5% of each employee's gross wages is withheld for a company retirement plan.

EVERETT PAINT CO.

Payroll for week ending June 3, 19XX

| Employee | Allow-ances | Gross Wages | DEDUCTIONS | | | | | Total Deductions | Net Wages Due |
			FICA	Federal Income Tax	Other (Ret.)	Other	Other		
Camden, S. R.	M-3	$145.00	$ 8.48	$ 9.80	$ 2.18			$ 20.46	$124.54
Duncan, E. M.	M-2	145.00	8.48	12.80	2.18			23.46	121.54
Hager, Wm.	S-2	145.00	8.48	17.10	2.18			27.76	117.24
Ingles, Carl	M-1	128.00	7.49	11.60	1.92			21.01	106.99
Mott, Craig	M-3	137.50	8.04	7.80	2.06			17.90	119.60
Reid, Mark	S-1	120.00	7.02	14.90	1.80			23.72	96.28
Trent, Brian	M-4	160.00	9.36	10.40	2.40			22.16	137.84
	Totals	$980.50	$57.35	$84.40	$14.72			$156.47	$824.03

HINT: A net payroll can be completed more efficiently if all deductions of the same type are done at one time. That is, list FICA for all employees, then determine federal income tax for all employees, etc.

NOTE: The totals of the individual deductions, when added together, must equal the total in the "Total Deductions" column. ($57.35 + $84.40 + $14.72 = $156.47.) The Total Gross Wages minus the Total Deductions must give the Total Net Wages Due. ($980.50 − $156.47 = $824.03.) The payroll clerk should always verify these totals before writing the paychecks.

SECTION 5 *Problems*

1.   Complete the following salary payroll. Withhold Social Security and income tax. All workers also contribute 1% of their gross salary toward a company retirement plan.

CAPITAL CREDIT UNION

Payroll for week ending April 7, 19XX

| Employee | Allow-ances | Gross Salary | DEDUCTIONS | | | | | Total Deductions | Net Wages Due |
			FICA	Federal Income Tax	Other (Ret.)	Other	Other		
Aronson, Sol	M-4	$165.00							
Cline, Kathryn	S-1	150.00							
Michaels, J. D.	M-3	190.00							
Prentice, M. B.	M-1	110.00							
Wyatt, Krystin	M-2	125.00							
	Totals								

2. Compute each person's net wages due. Deduct FICA and federal income tax. All employees also pay $4.50 for their own group insurance plus $1.00 for each additional dependent. (The number of "additional dependents" for each employee is shown in parentheses beside their names.)

JONES & RUDOLPH, INC.

Payroll for week ending January 3, 19XX

Employee (Addl. Deps.)	Allow- ances	Gross Salary	DEDUCTIONS						Net Wages Due
			FICA	Federal Income Tax	Other (Insurance)	Other	Other	Total Deductions	
Garrett, Nina (0)	M-2	$167.50							
Jones, Richard (3)	M-4	150.00							
Kelly, Phyllis (0)	S-2	130.00							
Rudolph, K. T. (1)	M-3	150.00							
Styres, R. L. (2)	M-3	140.00							
	Totals								

3. Compute the net payroll of Grier Textile Machines, Inc., whose employees are paid on an hourly basis. Deductions are made for Social Security, income tax, and union dues. These dues are deducted according to the employee's rate per hour as follows:

Rate per Hour	Dues	Rate per Hour	Dues
$2.50–$2.99	$3.00	$4.00–$4.49	$4.50
3.00– 3.49	3.50	4.50– 4.99	5.00
3.50– 3.99	4.00	5.00– 5.99	6.00

GRIER TEXTILE MACHINES, INC.

Payroll for week ending May 13, 19XX

Employee Number	Allow- ances	Total Hours	Rate per Hour	Gross Wages	DEDUCTIONS					Net Wages Due
					FICA	Income Tax	Other	Other	Total Deds.	
101	M-2	40	$2.75							
103	M-4	38	2.85							
105	M-3	40	3.25							
107	S-2	40	3.50							
109	M-3	38	4.50							
			Totals							

4. Complete the weekly payroll of the Automotive Specialties Co. The employees are paid on an hourly basis, and deductions are withheld for FICA, income tax, and union dues. (These employees belong to the same union discussed in Problem 3—see Problem 3 for the dues rates.)

AUTOMOTIVE SPECIALTIES CO.

Payroll for week ending August 19, 19XX

Employee Number	Allow-ances	Total Hours	Rate per Hour	Gross Wages	FICA	Income Tax	Other	Other	Total Deds.	Net Wages Due
					DEDUCTIONS					
121	M-2	35	$2.80							
136	S-3	40	3.75							
149	M-3	39	3.20							
173	M-5	40	5.25							
192	M-2	40	4.75							
Totals										

5. The following commission payroll has standard deductions for FICA and Social Security. The sales representatives have each pledged 10% of their gross wages for the week as contributions to the United Fund campaign. Determine the net payroll for the week.

ROCKFORD DISTRIBUTORS, INC.

Payroll for week ending January 16, 19XX

Employee Number	Allow-ances	Net Sales	Comm. Rate	Gross Wages	FICA	Income Tax	Other	Other	Total Deds.	Net Wages Due
					DEDUCTIONS					
K-5	M-3	$5,700	3%							
L-8	M-1	4,500	4							
L-10	M-2	8,500	2							
R-3	S-1	8,000	2							
R-6	M-5	4,200	4							
Totals										

6. Employees at Acme Sales Corp. are paid on the commission basis. Standard deductions are made. In addition, all employees have pledged a "day's pay" to the Community Chest. (That is, deduct $\frac{1}{5}$ or 20% of each employee's gross wages for their pledges.) Complete the net payroll on page 226.

ACME SALES CORP.

Payroll for week ending June 23, 19XX

Employee Number	Allow- ances	Net Sales	Comm. Rate	Gross Wages	FICA	Income Tax	Other	Other	Total Deds.	Net Wages Due
						DEDUCTIONS				
NE-3	M-2	$3,500	4%							
NE-7	M-1	2,900	6							
MA-3	M-4	4,000	3							
MA-5	S-3	4,500	3							
SE-2	M-3	3,500	5							
			Totals							

7. Hughes Processing, Inc., pays its employees on the production basis. Complete their net payroll, which includes the standard deductions as well as group insurance deducted at the rate of $5.00 for each worker and $1.50 for each additional dependent. (The total number of additional dependents is listed in parentheses beside each "employee number.")

HUGHES PROCESSING, INC.

Payroll for week ending November 5, 19XX

Employee Number (Dependents)	Allow- ances	Net Produc- tion	Rate per Piece	Gross Wages	FICA	Income Tax	Other	Other	Total Deds.	Net Wages Due
						DEDUCTIONS				
A1(3)	M-6	1925	8¢							
A2(0)	M-2	650	16							
B1(1)	M-4	850	18							
B2(1)	S-3	880	15							
B3(2)	M-5	712	25							
			Totals							

8. The production plan is used by Winfield, Inc., to pay its employees. Deductions are made for Social Security and income tax, plus a 1% withholding for the company retirement plan. Compute the net payroll.

WINFIELD, INC.

Payroll for week ending August 19, 19XX

Employee Number	Allow-ances	Net Produc-tion	Rate per Piece	Gross Wages	DEDUCTIONS					Net Wages Due
					FICA	Income Tax	Other	Other	Total Deds	
#28	M-1	350	32¢							
#30	M-0	200	55							
#34	S-2	260	45							
#38	S-1	220	55							
#41	M-4	450	34							
			Totals							

9. The employees of Kiser Associates are salaried and work 40 hours during a normal week. Since end-of-the-month pressures required extra work, it will be necessary to compute overtime for the additional hours. Complete the net payroll, including a 1% deduction made for company retirement.

KISER ASSOCIATES

Payroll for week ending December 19, 19XX

Employee	Allow-ances	Hours Worked	Regular Salary	Over-time Wages	Total Gross Wages	DEDUCTIONS				Net Wages Due
						FICA	Income Tax	Other	Total Deds.	
A	M-3	45	$120.00							
B	M-5	50	180.00							
C	M-1	46	100.00							
D	M-2	44	140.00							
		Totals								

10. Marvel Industries pays standard overtime after 40 hours per week. Group insurance of $7.50 will be withheld for each employee. Determine the company's net payroll for the week on page 228.

MARVEL INDUSTRIES, INC.

Payroll for week ending August 14, 19XX

Employee Number	Allow- ances	Total Hours	Rate per Hour	Regular Wages	Over- time Wages	Total Gross Wages	DEDUCTIONS				Net Wages Due
							FICA	Income Tax	Other	Total Deds.	
#20	M-3	42	$3.20								
#21	M-2	44	3.50								
#22	M-4	46	4.60								
#23	M-2	45	3.80								
			Totals								

11. Compute the net payroll for Mayfair Sales & Service. Standard overtime will be paid. Deduct 2% for a company retirement policy.

MAYFAIR SALES & SERVICE, INC.

Payroll for week ending May 8, 19XX

Employee Number	Allow- ances	Total Hours	Rate per Hour	Regular Wages	Over- time Wages	Total Gross Wages	DEDUCTIONS				Net Wages Due
							FICA	Income Tax	Other	Total Deds.	
#1	M-3	42	$4.20								
#2	S-1	45	4.80								
#3	M-4	46	3.60								
#4	M-4	43	4.00								
			Totals								

12. Compute the net payroll for Bentwood Furniture Manufacturing Co. Overtime is paid at $1\frac{1}{2}$ times the regular piece rate. In addition to the standard deductions, union dues of 5% of the worker's gross wages are to be collected.

BENTWOOD FURNITURE MANUFACTURING CO.

Payroll for week ending December 20, 19XX

Employee	Allow- ances	Net Regular Production	Over- time Production	Regular Piece Rate	Regular Wages	Over- time Wages	Total Gross Wages	DEDUCTIONS				Net Wages Due
								FICA	Income Tax	Other	Total Deds.	
L	M-4	495	40	$.30								
M	M-4	446	42	.40								
N	M-2	558	54	.20								
P	M-3	264	24	.50								

SECTION 6
Disbursement
Forms

Most businesses today pay their employees by check. This is more convenient and also eliminates the hazard of having large amounts of cash on the premises. However, there are a significant number of firms—usually smaller companies—which still pay their employees in cash. When a firm pays its employees in cash, two disbursement forms— the *change tally* and the *change slip*—must first be completed.

Before pay envelopes can be filled, the payroll clerk must determine exactly how many bills and coins of each denomination will be required for each employee. This computation is done on a **change tally**. In listing the number of bills and coins for each employee, it is customary to use the largest possible denominations that will give the correct total. (For example, $50 due should be paid in 2 twenties and 1 ten, rather than 5 tens.) This means that fewer actual pieces of money will be handled, with less likelihood of an error.

The columnar totals of each denomination of money are then transferred to a **change slip**, which verifies that these individual totals results in the correct net payroll. A single payroll check is then written for the total net wages due. This check and the change slip are presented to the bank teller, who will cash the check using the number of each denomination of money indicated on the change slip. The payroll clerk then fills the pay envelopes, using the change tally as a guide.

Example
One
Verify the figures in the following change tally and change slip:

CHANGE TALLY

Name	Net Wages Due	$20	$10	$5	$1	50¢	25¢	10¢	5¢	1¢
Barger, Frances	$125.42	6		1			1	1	1	2
Earle, Robert	138.90	6	1	1	3	1	1	1	1	
Horton, Mark	143.24	7			3			2		4
Long, Elaine	147.65	7		1	2	1		1	1	
Nueces, Ron	104.73	5			4	1		2		3
Totals	$659.94	31	1	3	12	3	2	7	3	9

**Example
One
(cont.)**

CHANGE SLIP

Denomination	No.	Amount
$20.00	31	$620.00
10.00	1	10.00
5.00	3	15.00
1.00	12	12.00
.50	3	1.50
.25	2	.50
.10	7	.70
.05	3	.15
.01	9	.09
	Total	$659.94

SECTION 6 *Problems*

1. Complete a change tally listing the following employees' net wages:

A $114.18   B $146.56   C $130.71
D 155.98   E 121.83   F 148.24

2. Complete a change tally for the following payroll:

U $136.45   V $102.70   W $167.13
X 153.94   Y 144.59   Z 132.27

3. Complete a change slip for Problem 1.

4. Complete a change slip for Problem 2.

SECTION 7

***Quarterly Earnings
Records and
Returns***

*Employee's
Earnings Records*

Employers must keep an individual payroll record showing each employee's earnings, deductions, and other pertinent information. Figure 21 presents a typical **employee's earnings record.** An earnings record shows quarterly (and sometimes monthly) totals, which are used in computing the state and federal quarterly payroll reports that every company must file. In addition, the individual earnings record enables the payroll clerk to know whether the employee's earnings reach the current year's cutoff point for Social Security. It also

Employee's Earnings Record

DATE EMPLOYED 7-15-68		SOCIAL SECURITY NUMBER 123-45-6789		FULL NAME Craig Logan Williams			CLOCK OR BADGE NO. R-19
TERMINATED		DEPARTMENT Office		ADDRESS 1035 Duval St.			
Allowances: M-4							

PAY PERIOD ENDING		TIME WORKED		RATE		EARNINGS				DEDUCTIONS					NET AMOUNT PAID
Mo.	Wk. 19	Regular	Over-time	Regu-lar	Over-time	Regular	Overtime	Total	Total To Date	Withholding Tax	F.I.C.A.	L. Dues	Insurance	Total Deductions	
FORWARD				480	7.20				502040	44410	29367	60-	105-	90279	411761
JULY	1 6	32	-			15360	-	15360		840	899			1739	13621
	2 13	40	4			192-	2880	22080		2240	1292		1750	5282	16798
	3 20	40	2			192-	1440	20640		1840	1207			3047	17593
	4 27	40	4			192-	2880	22080		2240	1292	100		4532	17548
	5														
MONTHLY TOTAL						80160	5822-			7160	4690	100	1750	14600	65560
AUGUST	1 3	Vacation													
	2 10	40	3			192-	2160	21360		2040	1250		1750	5040	16320
	3 17	40	1			192-	720	19920		1640	1165			2805	17115
	4 24	40	6			192-	4320	23520		2430	1376	100		4806	18714
	5 31	40	4			192-	2880	22080		2240	1292			3532	18548
MONTHLY TOTAL						86880	66980			8350	5083	100	1750	16183	70697
SEPTEMBER	1 7	32	4			15360	2880	18240		1440	1067			2507	15733
	2 14	40	-			192-		192-		1640	1123		1750	4513	14687
	3 21	40	2			192-	1440	20640		1840	1207			3047	17593
	4 28	40	8			192-	5760	24960		26-	1460	100		5060	19900
	5														
MONTHLY TOTAL						83040	752120			7520	4857	100	1750	15127	67913
QUARTERLY TOTAL						250080	752120			23030	14630	300	5250	45910	204170
OCTOBER	1 5	40	-			192-		192-		1640	1123			2763	16437
	2 12	40	-			192-		192-		1640	1123		1750	4513	14687
	3 19	40	5			192-	36-	228-		2240	1334			3574	19226
	4 26	40	4			192-	2880	22080		2240	1292	100		4532	17548
MONTHLY TOTAL						83280	8354-			7760	4872	100	1750	15382	67898
NOVEMBER	1 2	40	2			192-	1440	20640		1840	1207			3047	17593
	2 9	36	-			17280		17280		1240	1011		1750	4001	13279
	3 16	40	2			192-	1440	20640		1840	1207			3047	17593
	4 23	40	4			192-	2880	22080		2240	1292	100		4532	17548
	5 30	24	-			11520		11520		0-	674			874	10646
MONTHLY TOTAL						92160	927560			7360	5391	100	1750	15501	76659
DECEMBER	1 7	40	5			192-	36-	228-		2240	1334			3574	19226
	2 14	40	-			192-		192-		1640	1123		1750	4513	14687
	3 21	40	3			192-	2160	21360		2040	1250			3290	18070
	4 28	24	8			11520	5760	17280		1240	1011	100		3251	14029
	5														
MONTHLY TOTAL						80640	10082-			7160	4718	100	1750	14628	66012
QUARTERLY TOTAL						256080	10082-			22280	14981	300	5250	45511	210569
TOTAL TO DATE							10082-			89720	589.80	120-	210-	1817-	8,265-

FIGURE 21: *Employee's Earnings Record.*

contains the yearly totals of earnings and deductions required for personal income tax purposes, which are distributed to the employee and the Internal Revenue Service on Form W-2, the Wage and Tax Statement.

Quarterly Payroll Returns

There are several payroll reports which must be completed at the end of each quarter. The exact reports vary somewhat from state to state, but there are two types which must be completed in every state: the *Employer's Quarterly Federal Tax Return* (Form 941), as well as state *unemployment returns* required under the Federal Insurance Contributions Act.

Employer's Quarterly Federal Tax Return. This form reports the amount of Social Security paid (by both the employer and employee) and the income tax that has been withheld by the company. Figure 22 shows a completed Form 941, **Employer's Quarterly Federal Tax Return.**

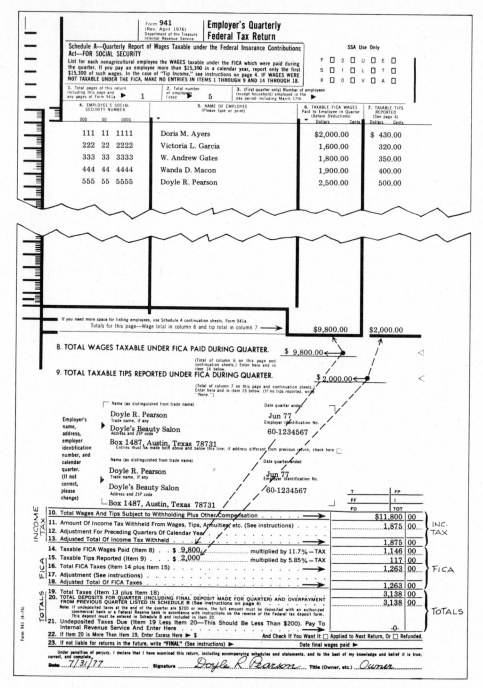

FIGURE 22: *Employee's Quarterly Federal Tax Return.*

* As revised in 1978, Form 941 no longer requires that employees be listed individually as they are at the top of this figure. However, the company totals of FICA taxable wages and tips (lines 8 and 9) are still required.

At the top of the quarterly return (columns 4–7) is a list of the employees who earned FICA taxable wages and tips during the quarter. (That is, the return lists only wages and tips *earned during that quarter* which apply toward the first $16,500* for the year. If the combined total of an employee's wages and tips for the year reaches $16,500, then additional earnings are no longer listed under "6. Taxable FICA Wages" or "7. Taxable Tips." Thus, any employee who had already earned $16,500 before the quarter began would not be listed. If an employee's total earnings reached $16,500 during the quarter, only the first part of that quarter's earnings would be listed. For most workers, however, all earnings for the entire year will be subject to FICA deductions.) For a small company where all employees can be listed on one sheet, line 8 is the total of taxable wages from column 6, and line 9 is the total of taxable tips from column 7.

Lines 10–21 compose the basic part of the return. (Notice that dashed lines and brackets have been inserted in Figure 22 to emphasize the lines pertaining to income tax, FICA, and totals.) Line 10 is the total of *all* gross wages earned and tips reported during the quarter which were "subject to (income tax) withholding." (Notice this line applies to *income tax* wages, rather than the Social Security wages listed at the top. There is no cutoff point for income tax, of course. Thus, if any employees are no longer paying Social Security, the total earnings on line 10 will be *more* than the amounts listed in columns 6 and 7 above.) Line 11 is the total income tax withheld from all employees (even any not listed on the top portion of the return).

As the arrows in Figure 22 emphasize, line 14 is the total of all FICA taxable wages from item (or line) 8 above; these wages are multiplied by 11.7% to obtain the total Social Security obligation from both the employees and the employer. Line 15 is the total of all FICA taxable tips from item 9 above; these tips are multiplied by 5.85% to obtain the employee's FICA liability. (Employees must pay income tax, as well as FICA, on tips. Employers are not required to match the FICA due on tips, however, since these tips were not paid by the employer.)

Whenever the Social Security (of both the employee and the employer) plus income tax withheld during 1 month exceeds $200, the employer is required to deposit these funds in an authorized commercial or Federal Reserve bank on a monthly basis, rather than waiting until the quarter

---

* $16,500 is the 1977 cutoff point used in this text. Students may be instructed to substitute the current year's FICA base amount for the problems in this chapter.

ends. (Similarly, the taxes must be deposited when the cumulative total for 2 or 3 months exceeds $200.) Most firms with as many as four to six employees will have at least $200 in taxes for any one month and will thus have already deposited all taxes before the 941 Quarterly Return is completed.

Line 20 of the quarterly return asks for the total of these deposits.* This deposit total is then deducted from the total taxes due for the whole quarter (line 19), to obtain any undeposited taxes still due (line 21). (These undeposited taxes should always be less than $200, since a deposit is required after any month when the cumulative taxes due total $200 or more.) A check for any undeposited taxes less than $200 may either be submitted with the quarterly return or deposited in the regular manner. (Normally, no taxes are due except for a very small firm or if some adjustment has been made on lines 12 or 17.)

Example One Complete lines 10–21 of the Employer's Quarterly Federal Tax Return for Warren Carpet Sales, based on the following information: total wages (all FICA taxable) for the quarter totaled $12,000; income tax of $1,572 was withheld; monthly deposits of $987, $1,012, and $977 have been made. (No tips are earned by these employees.)

Solution The total monthly deposits for the quarter (line 20) are $987 + $1,012 + $977 = $2,976. The completed lower portion (lines 10–21) of the quarterly return is shown in Figure 23 on page 235.

Most employee earnings records include (after the end of each month and each quarter) a total of the worker's cumulative earnings and deductions for the year (see Figure 21). Most of the figures required for the quarterly return can thus be obtained simply by computing company totals from these earnings records—the total gross wages (and tips, if applicable) for line 10, and the total income tax withheld for line 11. During the early quarters, all wages earned are FICA taxable; thus, line 14 will be the same as the company's gross wages. When any employee's yearly earnings exceed the current base amount for FICA, however, the payroll clerk must compute the worker's FICA taxable wages (included in column 6 and on the total lines 8 and 14).

To reemphasize: When any employees pass the $16,500 level, the top

---

* Large firms whose total taxes exceed $2,000 in less than 1 month must deposit their taxes immediately after the $2,000 level is reached. Our study will not include such larger firms. Companies so equipped are also encouraged to use magnetic tape reporting rather than filing a paper Form 941.

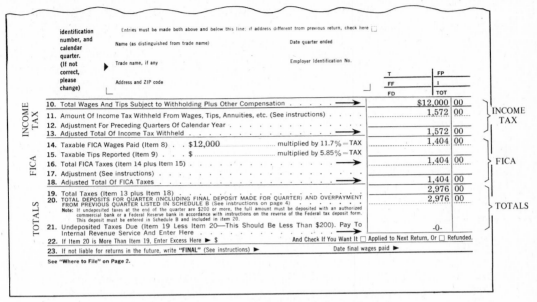

FIGURE 23: *Lower Portion of Form 941*

portion of the quarterly report will list only that portion of their wages (and tips) *earned during that quarter* which brought their total earnings for the year to $16,500. An employee who passes the $16,500 maximum for FICA *during* a quarter will be listed on the quarterly return (columns 4–7, etc.) for that quarter but will *not* be listed there for any succeeding quarter. (However, the employee's gross wages and tips and the income tax paid on those earnings will continue to be included on lines 10 and 11.)

Example Two

(a) William Harris of Harris Electronics earned $15,000 during the first two quarters of the year. How much of his third quarter's wages will be listed as "taxable FICA wages" in column 6?

In general,

$$\$16,500 - \begin{pmatrix} \text{Cumulative total} \\ \text{at end of} \\ \text{previous quarter} \end{pmatrix} = \begin{pmatrix} \text{FICA taxable} \\ \text{wages for} \\ \text{current quarter} \end{pmatrix}$$

$$\$16,500 - \quad \$15,000 \quad = \quad \$1,500$$

Thus, $1,500 of Harris' third-quarter wages will be listed in column 6 as FICA taxable. During the fourth quarter, Harris will not be listed at the top of Form 941. (However, *all* of Harris'

Example Two (*cont.*)

wages for each quarter will still be included on line 10, and the income tax deducted will be included on line 11.)

(b) The quarterly wages of Al Gibbons, a real estate agent, were $5,500, $5,200, $5,400, and $5,900. When did he exceed the FICA base amount, and how much of that quarter's wages were FICA taxable?

The quarterly totals of Gibbons' earnings were

$5,500 + $5,200   = $10,700   End of 2nd quarter

$5,500 + 5,200 + $5,400   = 16,100   End of 3rd quarter

$5,500 + 5,200 + 5,400 + $5,900
                                = 22,000   End of 4th quarter

Since he had earned $16,100 at the end of the 3rd quarter, Gibbons passed the $16,500 FICA base amount during the 4th quarter. Thus,

$16,500 − $16,100 = $400   FICA taxable wages
                              for 4th quarter

During the 4th quarter, Gibbons paid Social Security on only $400, which is the amount to be listed beside his name at the top of Form 941. However, income tax was withheld on his entire $5,900 earnings; and the entire $5,900 was included on line 10, as part of the "total wages subject to (income tax) withholding" for all employees in his office.

Example Three

Complete lines 10–21 of the quarterly return for the 4th quarter of the real estate office above. Assume that the *other* employees in the office earned gross wages (all FICA taxable) of $8,500. [See Example 2(b) for Al Gibbons' taxable wages.] Income tax (for everyone) of $1,950 was withheld. Monthly deposits were made in the amounts of $1,000, $1,000, and $991.30.

Solution

Line 10 of the completed Form 941 in Figure 24 contains the "total (gross) wages subject to (income tax) withholding" for the other employees and Gibbons ($8,500 + $5,900 = $14,400). Line 14 computes 11.7% on "taxable FICA wages" of $8,500 + $400 = $8,900. Total monthly deposits (line 20) are $1,000 + $1,000 + $991.30 = $2,991.30.

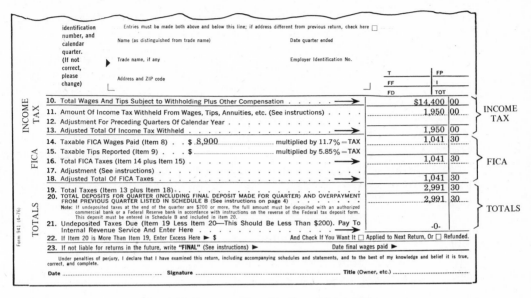

FIGURE 24: *Lower Portion of Form 941*

Unemployment Tax Returns. As mentioned earlier the employer's **unemployment insurance tax** was passed as part of the FICA Act. The funds collected under this tax are used to provide limited compensation, for a limited period of time, to workers who are unemployed because there is no work available to them. The federal tax is levied only against employers, with most of the funds being collected by the states; the federal unemployment tax is *not* deducted from workers' earnings. (Only a few states have levied additional unemployment taxes of their own, which may be deducted from the workers' gross earnings.) The portion of unemployment taxes paid to the state must be reported quarterly; the federal return, Form 940, is submitted each January for the preceding calendar year, although deposits may be required quarterly. Since unemployment forms are not uniform from state to state, however, we shall omit any forms and study only the computation of these taxes.

At the time of this 1977 revision, the conditions and base wages for the unemployment tax had not changed for several years. Employers were subject to unemployment tax if they employed one or more persons during any 20 weeks of the year or if they paid $1,500 in salaries during any quarter. The unemployment tax is similar to the FICA tax in that it applies only on wages up to a specific maximum—currently the first $4,200 earned by each employee. The federal rate effective in 1977 became

2.7%	Paid to the state (quarterly)
0.7%	Paid to the federal government (annually)
3.4%	Total federal unemployment rate

Employers who have a good history of stable employment may have their state rates substantially reduced, while still paying only 0.7% to the federal government, so that their actual rate is well below 3.4%. Conversely, employers with a history of high unemployment may be required to pay substantially more than 2.7% for the state portion of their unemployment insurance. However, 2.7% is the maximum that could be claimed against the 3.4% federal unemployment rate; that is, all employers must pay 0.7% to the federal government. The following example illustrates computation of the federal unemployment tax.

Example Four   Martha Mattox is a salaried employee who earned $1,800 each quarter.

(a) Determine the amount of her wages that are subject to unemployment tax each quarter.

   The cumulative totals of Ms. Mattox's earnings after each quarter are:

$$1 \times \$1,800 = \$1,800 \quad \text{End of 1st quarter}$$
$$2 \times 1,800 = 3,600 \quad \text{End of 2nd quarter}$$
$$3 \times 1,800 = 5,400 \quad \text{End of 3rd quarter}$$
$$4 \times 1,800 = 7,200 \quad \text{End of 4th quarter}$$

   She had earned $3,600 at the end of the 2nd quarter; thus, her wages passed the $4,200 cutoff point for unemployment tax during the 3rd quarter. In general,

$$\$4,200 - \begin{pmatrix} \text{Cumulative total} \\ \text{at end of} \\ \text{previous quarter} \end{pmatrix} = \begin{pmatrix} \text{Unemployment-} \\ \text{taxable wages,} \\ \text{current quarter} \end{pmatrix}$$

   Thus,

$$\$4,200 - \$3,600 = \begin{pmatrix} \$600 \text{ Unemployment-} \\ \text{taxable wages} \\ \text{for 3rd quarter} \end{pmatrix}$$

   Ms. Mattox's employer must pay unemployment tax on $600 of the wages she earns during the 3rd quarter. No tax will be due on her 4th quarter earnings.

(b) Assume that the employer in part (a) has a reduced state unemployment tax rate of 2.0%. Compute the company's state unemployment taxes for each quarter, based on the following wages:

	TAXABLE WAGES FOR UNEMPLOYMENT			
	1st Quarter	*2nd Quarter*	*3rd Quarter*	*4th Quarter*
Other employees	$5,000	$3,600	$3,000	0
Ms. Mattox	1,800	1,800	600	0
Totals	$6,800	$5,400	$3,600	0

$6,800 × 2.0% = $136   Due to state for 1st quarter
5,400 × 2.0% = 108   Due to state for 2nd quarter
3,600 × 2.0% =   72   Due to state for 3rd quarter

No unemployment tax will be owed to the state during the 4th quarter.

(c) Find the federal unemployment tax due at the end of the year.
   The company's total taxable wages for the year (for unemployment) are the sum of the firm's quarterly totals:

$6,800 + $5,400 + $3,600 + $0 = $15,800   Total wages subject to unemployment tax

Since every firm must pay 0.7% to the federal government, $15,800 × 0.7% = $110.60 due to federal government for entire year.

SECTION 7 *Problems*

Complete lines 10–21 *of the Employer's Quarterly Federal Tax Return (Form* 941) *shown on page* 240 *as Figure* 25, *based on the following information.* (*Assume that only* taxable FICA wages and tips were earned, unless otherwise indicated.)

	Taxable FICA Wages	*Taxable Tips*	*Income Tax Withheld*	*Monthly Deposits*		
1.	$ 5,000	—	$ 650	$ 425;	$ 410;	$ 400
2.	16,000	—	2,300	1,390;	1,400;	1,382
3.	8,000	$ 2,000	1,200	750;	750;	753
4.	25,000	8,000	3,600	2,350;	2,330;	2,313
5.	6,000[a]	14,000	2,500	1,350;	1,340;	1,331
6.	12,000[a]	6,000	2,100	1,285;	1,280;	1,290

[a] Assume that income tax was deducted on an additional $2,000 in earnings that were not FICA-taxable.

identification number, and calendar quarter. (If not correct, please change)	Entries must be made both above and below this line; if address different from previous return, check here ☐

Name (as distinguished from trade name)   Date quarter ended

Trade name, if any   Employer Identification No.

Address and ZIP code

	T		FP
	FF		I
	FD		TOT

10. Total Wages And Tips Subject to Withholding Plus Other Compensation . . . . . ➤ — *5,000*
11. Amount Of Income Tax Withheld From Wages, Tips, Annuities, etc. (See instructions) *650*
12. Adjustment For Preceding Quarters Of Calendar Year . . . .
13. Adjusted Total Of Income Tax Withheld . . . . ➤ *650*
14. Taxable FICA Wages Paid (Item 8) . . . $ ....*5,000*.... multiplied by 11.7% = TAX *585*
15. Taxable Tips Reported (Item 9) . . . $ .... multiplied by 5.85% = TAX
16. Total FICA Taxes (Item 14 plus Item 15) . . . . ➤ *585*
17. Adjustment (See instructions) . . . .
18. Adjusted Total Of FICA Taxes . . . . ➤ *585*
19. Total Taxes (Item 13 plus Item 18) . . . . ➤ *1,235*
20. TOTAL DEPOSITS FOR QUARTER (INCLUDING FINAL DEPOSIT MADE FOR QUARTER) AND OVERPAYMENT FROM PREVIOUS QUARTER LISTED IN SCHEDULE B (See instructions on page 4) *1,235*
    Note: If undeposited taxes at the end of the quarter are $200 or more, the full amount must be deposited with an authorized commercial bank or a Federal Reserve bank in accordance with instructions on the reverse of the Federal tax deposit form. This deposit must be entered in Schedule B and included in item 20.
21. Undeposited Taxes Due (Item 19 Less Item 20—This Should Be Less Than $200). Pay To Internal Revenue Service And Enter Here ➤   *0*
22. If Item 20 is More Than Item 19, Enter Excess Here ➤ $ And Check If You Want It ☐ Applied to Next Return, Or ☐ Refunded.
23. If not liable for returns in the future, write **"FINAL"** (See instructions) ➤   Date final wages paid ➤

Under penalties of perjury, I declare that I have examined this return, including accompanying schedules and statements, and to the best of my knowledge and belief it is true, correct, and complete.

Date .... Signature .... Title (Owner, etc.) ....

Form 941 (4–76)

FIGURE 25: *Employee's Quarterly Federal Tax Return.*

Quarterly earnings for three executives are listed in each problem below. Determine how much of each person's earnings during the following quarter will be subject to FICA tax deductions.

$16,500 → ceiling for FICA withhold

	Employee	GROSS WAGES EARNED			
		1st Quarter	2nd Quarter	3rd Quarter	4th Quarter
7.	U	$4,000	$5,000	$7,000	*500*
	V	3,800	5,600	5,800	
	W	6,200	6,200		*$4100*
8.	X	$4,000	$6,000	$5,000	
	Y	3,500	7,000	5,200	
	Z	6,500	6,800		

Listed in each problem on the facing page are all the employees of a small business, along with their total gross earnings and income tax deductions for each quarter.

(*a*) *Determine each employee's FICA taxable wages for each quarter.*
(*b*) *Find the firm's total FICA taxable wages for each quarter.*

	Employee	1ST QUARTER Gross Wages	Income Tax	2ND QUARTER Gross Wages	Income Tax	3RD QUARTER Gross Wages	Income Tax	4TH QUARTER Gross Wages	Income Tax
9.	A	$3,000	$370	$3,200	$400	$3,500	$420	$3,100	$390
	B	4,100	490	3,900	470	4,100	490	4,800	580
	C	1,800	160	2,000	180	2,500	240	2,500	240
	D	4,000	500	4,500	580	6,000	750	5,500	690
	Totals								
10.	E	$2,000	$240	$2,000	$240	$2,000	$240	$2,000	$240
	F	3,800	430	4,200	480	4,800	530	4,000	440
	G	4,600	600	5,000	650	5,200	680	5,400	700
	H	1,600	150	2,000	180	1,800	160	2,400	220
	Totals								

Compute lines 10–21 of the 941 Employer's Quarterly Federal Tax Return for each indicated problem and quarter, given the monthly deposits of withheld income tax and Social Security.

	Refer to Problem	Quarter to Compute	Monthly Deposits
11.	# 9	2nd	$1,075; $1,080; $1,066.20
12.	#10	3rd	$1,060; $1,200; $ 964.60
13.	# 9	4th	$1,250; $1,050; $1,004.00
14.	#10	4th	$1,100; $ 950; $ 696.60

15. Refer to the employees in Problem 7.

  (a) Determine the taxable wages for unemployment of each worker for each quarter.
  (b) Find the total taxable wages for unemployment of the company for each quarter, assuming that these are the only employees.
  (c) How much unemployment tax will the company pay to its state each quarter? What are the annual taxes due to the federal government? Assume that the firm in Problem 7 has a state rate of 1.6%. (The federal rate is never reduced.)

16. Repeat parts (a), (b), and (c) from the preceding problem; this time refer to the employees in Problem 8. Assume that the company in Problem 8 has a reduced state employment tax rate of 1.2%.

17. Again answer the questions of Problem 15, this time based on the employee wages given in Problem 9. Assume that the company in Problem 9 has a reduced state unemployment rate of 2.1%.

18. Repeat the steps of Problem 15, basing your answers on the employees in Problem 10. Assume that the business in Problem 10 must pay state unemployment at the rate of 3.5%.

CHAPTER 8 *Glossary*

Account purchase. Itemized statement (Prime cost + Charges = Gross cost) for merchandise bought by a commission agent.

Account sales. Itemized statement (Gross proceeds – Charges = Net proceeds) for the merchandise sold by a commission agent.

Broker. (See "Commission agent.")

Brokerage. (See "Commission.")

Change slip. A list of the total pieces (and corresponding value) of each denomination of money that are required to disburse a net cash payroll.

Change tally. A computation that determines how many pieces of each denomination of money are required to pay each individual employee.

Chargeback (or docking). A deduction made from base production or base earnings, because of production work that did not pass inspection.

Commission. Wages computed as a per cent of the value of items sold or purchased; this is also called "straight commission" or "brokerage."

Commission agent. One who buys or sells merchandise for another party without becoming legal owner of the property; also called a "commission merchant," "broker," or "factor."

Consignee. Agent to whom a shipment is sent in order to be sold.

Consignor. Party who sends a shipment to an agent who will sell it.

Docking. (See "Chargeback.")

Drawing account. Fund from which a salesperson may receive advance wages to defray business or personal expenses.

Employee earnings record. The tabulation of an employee's gross wages, itemized deductions, and net wages for each pay period of the year.

Employee's Withholding Allowance Certificate (Form W-4). Federal form on which an employee lists marital status and computes the number of qualified allowances for income tax withholding.

Employer's Quarterly Federal Tax Return (Form 941). Quarterly form on which a company reports wages and tips earned (taxable and total), and the amount of Social Security and income tax that has been withheld (and matched, for FICA).

Factor. (See "Commission agent.")

Fair Labor Standards Act. Federal law requiring the payment of a minimum wage ($2.30 per hour) and overtime (at "time-and-a-half" for hours worked in excess of 40 per week) to all employees covered.

Federal Insurance Contributions Act (FICA or "Social Security"). Deduction of a specified per cent made on a base amount of each worker's yearly wages (and matched by the employer) to fund benefits for retired or disabled workers, for surviving spouses and children, and for Medicare.

Gross cost. Total cost, after commission and other charges are added, of merchandise purchased by a commission agent.

Gross proceeds. Initial sales value, before commission and other charges are deducted, of merchandise sold by a commission agent.

Gross wages. Wages earned by an employee before FICA, income tax, or other deductions.

Income tax (federal). Tax withheld from each employee's pay, as determined by the person's gross earnings, marital status, and number of allowances.

Net proceeds. Remaining sales value, after commission and other charges are deducted, of merchandise sold by a commission agent.

Net wages. The actual wages (after all deductions) paid to a worker.

Override. A small commission on the net sales of all other salespersons, paid to reimburse a supervisor for nonselling duties.

Overtime. (See "Fair Labor Standards Act.")

Overtime excess. The extra amount (at one-half the regular rate) that must be paid for work done during overtime hours.

Piecework or piece-rate. (See "Production.")

Premium rates. Higher-than-regular rates, paid for overtime work or work that exceeds a quota.

Prime cost. Initial cost, before commission and other charges are added, of merchandise purchased by a commission agent.

Production. Wage computation determined by the number of times a task is completed; also called the "piecework" or "piece-rate" method.

Quarterly return. (See "Employer's Quarterly Federal Tax Return.")

Quota. Minimum sales or production level required in many jobs (usually in order to qualify for pay at a higher rate).

Sliding-scale commission. A commission rate that increases, once sales exceed the specified level(s), on all sales above the set level(s).

Social Security. (See "Federal Insurance Contributions Act.")

Straight commission. (See "Commission.")

Unemployment insurance tax. Federal tax (paid partially to the state) to provide some compensation to workers who are unemployed because there is no work available; paid by the employer only.

Withholding. Deductions made by employers from the gross earnings of their employees—including required FICA and income tax deductions. (See also "Employee's Withholding Allowance Certificate.")

CHAPTER 9

Depreciation and Overhead

CHAPTER 9 OBJECTIVES

Upon completion of Chapter 9, the student will be able to:

1. Define and use correctly the terminology associated with each topic.

2. Compute depreciation (including additional first-year allowance and net salvage value) by the following three methods *(Section 1)*:
   a. Straight-line *(Examples 1, 4–6; Problems 1–6, 11–12, 19–22)*;
   b. Sum-of-the-digits *(Examples 2, 4, 5; Problems 1–4, 7, 8, 13–14)*; and
   c. Declining balance *(Examples 3–5; Problems 1–4, 9, 10, 15–18)*.

3. Compute overhead as a ratio of (Section 2)
   a. Floor space per department *(Example 1; Problems 1, 2, 7, 8)*;
   b. Net sales *(Example 2; Problems 3, 4, 9, 10)*; and
   c. Employees per department *(Example 3; Problems 5, 6, 11, 12)*.

9

When expenses are calculated tor a business, two of the most important items are depreciation and overhead. To determine these expenses, you will have to learn certain mathematical techniques. The procedures you will need to know will be explained in the following sections.

SECTION 1

Depreciation

The **fixed assets** of a business are its buildings, machinery, equipment, and similar properties that will be used for more than 1 year. Such fixed assets always experience **depreciation**—loss in value because of pyhsical deterioration (from age, use, or the effects of weather) or obsolescence (due to a change in style or because of the invention of more efficient models). Eventually, the low value, inefficiency, or maintenance required for these assets makes it necessary to replace them.

Because a fixed asset will be used for several years, the Internal Revenue Service does not allow a business to list the entire business cost of the asset as an expense during the year in which it was obtained. However, a business is permitted to distribute the depreciation of a fixed asset over all the years of its use. Thus, depreciation currently claimed does not normally represent money actually spent during the present year; rather, it represents this year's share of a larger expenditure that occurred during some previous year. However, depreciation is considered an operating expense (just as are salaries, rent, insurance, etc.) and is deducted from business profits when determining the year's taxable income. Because depreciation is a tax-deductible item on business income tax returns, the Internal Revenue Service regulates carefully the conditions under which depreciation may be computed.

There are several acceptable methods for computing depreciation. We shall consider here the three most common methods: the *straight-line method*, *the sum-of-the-digits method*, and the *declining-balance method*. In general, a business is not required to use any particular method and may in fact depreciate different assets by different methods. As a rule, a business must obtain prior permission in order to change its method of

247

computing depreciation on any item; a change from the sum-of-the-digits or the declining-balance method to the straight-line method is possible without prior permission, but any other change may never be made without authorization. Before depreciation can be computed, however, several aspects must be considered.

First, the **useful life** (in years) of the property to the business must be determined. This will vary from business to business, depending upon company policy. (Some firms prefer to use machinery as long as possible, whereas others prefer to replace it more frequently.) The Internal Revenue Service provides information regarding the normal life expectancy of many typical business properties.

Second, the value of the property at the end of its useful life must be estimated. This may be the **trade-in value** if the equipment will be traded, or the **salvage** (or **scrap**) **value** if it is simply to be junked after use. In order to allow for the expense of removing a machine or similar property, a business may deduct up to 10% of the cost of an item from the salvage value. Salvage, when reduced by the cost of removal, is called *net salvage.* Either salvage or net salvage may be used in determining depreciation, so long as one policy is consistently followed. (We will use salvage in all problems unless net salvage is clearly indicated.)

Finally, the **wearing value** is the difference between the original business cost and the scrap value. The total amount of depreciation charged may never exceed this wearing value. (That is, a firm may never depreciate an asset below a reasonable scrap value. Observe also that the "business cost" could differ from the original retail price, if a used asset is brought into the business.)

A **depreciation schedule** or **depreciation account** is kept for each asset. This is a record showing the amount of depreciation claimed each year, the total amount of depreciation claimed to date, and the current **book value** (calculated value after depreciation) of the asset. The book value is then used in determining the company's capital assets for the year.

NOTE: Depreciation may never be claimed on land and may not ordinarily be claimed by an individual on personal property. However, some fixed assets, particularly automobiles, are frequently used for both business and pleasure. Records must be kept of the amount of business use, and a corresponding portion of standard depreciation may then be claimed by the owner (unless IRS-approved reimbursement has been paid for the business use).

Furthermore, if a business fails to claim depreciation for a given year, that depreciation may not be claimed later except by filing an amended tax return for the given year. If a fixed asset is eventually sold for more than its book value (calculated value), the gain must be reported as income; similarly, a loss may be deducted from taxable income.

Straight-Line
Method

The **straight-line method** is the simplest and most frequently used method for computing depreciation. By this method, the total wearing value is divided evenly among the years of useful life. (That is, the same amount of depreciation is charged each year.)

Example One

A copying machine is purchased for $5,100. It is expected to last for five years and have a trade-in value of $900. Prepare a depreciation schedule by the straight-line method.

Solution

First, the wearing value must be computed and divided by the years of use to determine each year's depreciation charge:

Original cost	$5,100
Trade-in value	− 900
Wearing value	$4,200

$$\frac{\text{Wearing value}}{\text{Years}} = \frac{\$4,200}{5}$$

$$= \$840 \text{ Annual depreciation}$$

Next, the depreciation schedule is completed as follows:

1. A year "0" is marked down to indicate when the asset was new, and the original cost is entered under "book value." Of course, no depreciation has yet occurred when the asset is new; thus, depreciation columns have no entries on line 0.

2. Each year the "annual depreciation" is entered.

3. The "accumulated depreciation" is found each year by adding the current year's depreciation to the previous year's accumulated depreciation.

4. The "book value" is determined by subtracting the current year's (annual) depreciation from the previous year's book value.

DEPRECIATION SCHEDULE

Straight-Line Method

Year	Book Value (End of Year)	Annual Depreciation	Accumulated Depreciation
0	$5,100	—	—
1	4,260	$840	$ 840
2	3,420	840	1,680
3	2,580	840	2,520
4	1,740	840	3,360
5	900	840	4,200

NOTE: If a mistake is made at any point in a depreciation schedule, all succeeding entries will also be incorrect. Therefore, the student should use the following checks: (1) For any year, the sum of all the annual depreciations to that point should equal that year's accumulated depreciation. (Example: Year 3—$840+$840+$840 = $2,520.) (2) During any year, the book value plus the accumulated depreciation must equal the original cost. (Example: Year 4—$1,740+$3,360 = $5,100.) (3) The final book value should equal the salvage value of the asset. (4) The final accumulated depreciation should equal the total wearing value.

Sum-of-the-Digits Method

The straight-line method (depreciating the same amount each year) proves satisfactory provided the asset is kept for the expected number of years. However, most machinery actually undergoes greater depreciation during its early years and less depreciation during later years. If for some reason the machine is disposed of earlier than expected, the book value on a straight-line depreciation schedule may be considerably higher than the actual market value. In order to apportion the depreciation more realistically, the **sum-of-the-digits method** may be used. This method distributes the wearing value unevenly among the years, with the greatest depreciation occurring during the first years. (This method is also called the *sum-of-the-years'-digits* or the *sum-of-the-periods method.*)

The fact that depreciation is a tax deductible item also accounts for the popularity of depreciation methods which offer greater depreciation during early years. (Both the sum-of-the-digits method and the declining-balance method offer this advantage.) When depreciation is accelerated, net income and resulting tax obligations of the business are reduced; this tax savings means available cash is increased, since depreciation is not an "out-of-pocket" expense. This money can then be used in the business in order to increase future income.

Example Two

Prepare a depreciation schedule for Example 1 using the sum-of-the-digits method. (A $5,100 copying machine was expected to be worth $900 after 5 years.)

The sum-of-the-digits method derives its name from step 1 in the following procedure:

1. The digits comprising the life expectancy of the asset are added.* Thus, since the life expectancy is 5 years,

$$1+2+3+4+5 = 15$$

2. This sum becomes the denominator of a series of fractions. The years' digits, taken in reverse order, are the numerators of the fractions.

3. The fractions derived in step 2 are then multiplied times the wearing value to compute each year's depreciation:

$$\text{Wearing value} = \$5,100 - \$900 = \$4,200$$

Year	Annual Depreciation
1	$\frac{5}{15} \times \$4,200 = \$1,400$
2	$\frac{4}{15} \times 4,200 = 1,120$
3	$\frac{3}{15} \times 4,200 = 840$
4	$\frac{2}{15} \times 4,200 = 560$
5	$\frac{1}{15} \times 4,200 = 280$

NOTE: In textbook problems, the final year's depreciation may be found first (carrying it out to three decimal places if it does not come out even). Depreciation for the other years can then be computed, in reverse order, by multiplying the final year's depreciation by 2, 3, 4, etc.

* The sum of the year's digits may also be found by applying the formula: $\frac{n(n+1)}{2}$, where $n =$ the number of years. That is, $\frac{5(5+1)}{2} = \frac{5 \times 6}{2} = \frac{30}{2} = 15$. This formula is of particular advantage when the number of years is large.

**Example
Two
(cont.)** A depreciation schedule according to the sum-of-the-digits method is then completed in the same manner described in Example 1, and the same checks apply.

DEPRECIATION SCHEDULE

Sum-of-the-Digits Method

Year	Book Value (End of Year)	Annual Depreciation	Accumulated Depreciation
0	$5,100	—	—
1	3,700	$1,400	$1,400
2	2,580	1,120	2,520
3	1,740	840	3,360
4	1,180	560	3,920
5	900	280	4,200

*Declining-Balance
Method* A third method frequently used for computing depreciation is the **declining-balance method** (sometimes called the *constant per cent method*). This method also offers the advantage of greatest annual depreciation during the early years, progressively declining as time passes.

When the declining-balance method is used, depreciation is computed using the same rate (per cent) each year. Each year's depreciation is found by multiplying this per cent times the previous year's book value. Thus, the annual depreciation decreases in direct proportion to the decrease in book value.

This method does not require estimating a salvage value in advance.* The general rule for determining the per cent to be used for a new asset is to double the reciprocal of the number of years. For example, the rate for a new asset that will be used for 6 years is

$$2 \times \tfrac{1}{6} = \tfrac{2}{6} = \tfrac{1}{3} \quad \text{or} \quad 33\tfrac{1}{3}\% \text{ annually}$$

This is the *maximum rate* allowed; a lower rate may be used. (The maximum rate for used assets is $1\tfrac{1}{2}$ times the reciprocal of the years. If the preceding asset were used prior to purchase, the maximum depreciation is $\tfrac{3}{2} \times \tfrac{1}{6} = \tfrac{3}{12} = \tfrac{1}{4}$ or 25% annually.)

---

*If one wishes to use a rate so that a specific scrap value will be obtained, the required per cent can be found using the formula $r = 1 - \sqrt[n]{\dfrac{s}{c}}$, where r = rate, n = number of years, s = salvage value, and c = original cost. Practical use of this formula requires a knowledge of logarithms.

Example Three

A new vending machine that cost $4,800 has an expected life of 5 years. Prepare a depreciation schedule by the constant per cent method.

Since the machine will be used for 5 years, it can be depreciated at a rate of

$$2 \times \tfrac{1}{5} = \tfrac{2}{5} = 40\% \text{ annually}$$

Each succeeding book value will be multiplied by 40% (or .4) to find the next annual depreciation. (For example, $4,800 \times 40\% = \$1,920$.)

DEPRECIATION SCHEDULE

Declining-Balance Method

Year	Book Value (End of Year)	Annual Depreciation	Accumulated Depreciation
0	$4,800.00	—	—
1	2,880.00	$1,920.00	$1,920.00
2	1,728.00	1,152.00	3,072.00
3	1,036.80	691.20	3,763.20
4	622.08	414.72	4,177.92
5	373.25	248.83	4,426.75

Additional First-Year Depreciation Allowance

Recognizing the rapid early depreciation which machinery and equipment undergo, the Internal Revenue Service allows businesses to elect during the first year an extra depreciation of 20% of the cost. This extra 20% depreciation is over and above the depreciation claimed by any of the standard methods and may be claimed on either new or used assets which qualify. The additional 20% first-year depreciation applies only to machinery and equipment, not to buildings. Also, the asset must have a useful life of at least 6 years; and the maximum cost on which the additional depreciation may be computed is $10,000, as the total of all assets which qualify. That is, $2,000 is the maximum amount of additional first-year depreciation that a firm may claim in any 1 year.

When the 20% additional depreciation allowance is taken, this depreciation, as well as the scrap value, must be deducted from the original cost to find the base amount used for computing depreciation by the straight-line or the sum-of-the-digits method. When the declining-balance method is used, only the additional first-year's depreciation is subtracted from the cost, and the remaining balance is then multiplied by the annual depreciation rate.

<table><tr><td>Example
Four</td><td>A new machine for canning and sealing paint cost Wondercote Paint Manufacturers $10,000. The machine will be used for 8 years, after which its trade-in value will be $800. (a) Find the 20% additional first year's depreciation. Then compute the annual depreciation by (b) the straight-line method, (c) the sum-of-the-digits method (with depreciation schedule), and (d) the declining-balance method (with depreciation schedule).</td></tr></table>

(a) The **additional first-year depreciation** is 20% of cost:

$$\$10,000 \times 20\% = \$10,000 \times 0.2$$
$$= \$\ 2,000$$

The additional first-year depreciation amounts to $2,000, regardless of which depreciation method is used.

Straight-Line Method

(b) The $2,000 additional first-year depreciation and the salvage value must be deducted from the cost before calculating the yearly depreciation.

Original cost	$10,000
Additional depreciation	− 2,000
	$ 8,000
Salvage value	− 800
Remaining wearing value	$ 7,200

The remaining wearing value of $7,200, distributed evenly among all the years, gives

$$\frac{\$7,200}{8} = \$900$$

Depreciation by the straight-line method will be $900 each year after the first year. (During the first year, the additional $2,000 depreciation will bring the total first-year depreciation to $2,900.)

Sum-of-the-Digits Method

(c) As in part (b), the additional first-year's depreciation and the scrap value must first be deducted. The remaining wearing value would then be the same as in part (b)—$7,200.

The sum of the digits is $1+2+3+4+5+6+7+8=36$. Thus,

depreciation by the sum-of-the-digits me

Year	Annual Deprec
1	$\frac{8}{36} \times \$7,200 = \$1,600 +$
2	$\frac{7}{36} \times 7,200 = 1,400$
3	$\frac{6}{36} \times 7,200 = 1,200$
4	$\frac{5}{36} \times 7,200 = 1,000$
5	$\frac{4}{36} \times 7,200 = 800$
6	$\frac{3}{36} \times 7,200 = 600$
7	$\frac{2}{36} \times 7,200 = 400$
8	$\frac{1}{36} \times 7,200 = 200$

During the first year, the $1,600 regular depreciation plus the $2,000 additional depreciation brings the total first-year's depreciation to $3,600.

DEPRECIATION SCHEDULE

Sum-of-the-Digits Method with Additional First-Year Allowance

Year	Book Value (End of Year)	Annual Depreciation	Accumulated Depreciation
0	$10,000	—	—
1	6,400	$3,600	$3,600
2	5,000	1,400	5,000
3	3,800	1,200	6,200
4	2,800	1,000	7,200
5	2,000	800	8,000
6	1,400	600	8,600
7	1,000	400	9,000
8	800	200	9,200

Declining-Balance Method

(d) The balance remaining after the additional first year's depreciation is deducted from the cost is $10,000–$2,000 = $8,000. This is the base used for computing depreciation by the declining-balance method.

Since the paint canning machine will be used for 8 years, it is depreciated at a maximum rate (for new equipment) of $2 \times \frac{1}{8} = \frac{1}{4}$, or

25% per year. The normal first-year's depreciation is $8,000 $\times$ 25%, or $2,000. The total first-year's depreciation is thus $4,000 ($2,000 normal depreciation plus $2,000 additional depreciation). This leaves a balance of $10,000–$4,000 = $6,000 to be multiplied by 25% to obtain the second year's depreciation ($1,500).

DEPRECIATION SCHEDULE

Declining-Balance Method with
Additional First-Year Allowance

Year	Book Value (End of Year)	Annual Depreciation	Accumulated Depreciation
0	$10,000	—	—
1	6,000	$4,000	$4,000
2	4,500	1,500	5,500
3	3,375	1,125	6,625
4	2,531.25	843.75	7,468.75
5	1,898.44	632.81	8,101.56
6	1,423.83	474.61	8,576.17
7	1,067.87	355.96	8,932.13
8	800.90	266.97	9,199.10

Summary   The calculation of depreciation is sometimes confusing if the methods are thought of as three unrelated procedures; therefore, the following section is offered to help the student consolidate the straight-line, sum-of-the-digits, and declining-balance methods.

Regardless of the depreciation method employed, the annual depreciation can be thought of as the product of the **depreciable value** of the asset times the annual depreciation rate. That is,

Depreciable value $\times$ Rate = Annual depreciation

Before performing this operation, the depreciable value must first be determined. The depreciable value is computed identically for the straight-line and sum-of-the-digits calculations; the declining-balance calculation differs only by omitting the salvage value:

$$\text{Cost} - \underset{\text{(if elected)}}{20\% \text{ 1st year allowance}} - \underset{\text{(if any)}}{\text{Salvage value}} = \underset{\substack{\text{(or remaining} \\ \text{wearing value)}}}{\text{Depreciable value}}$$

The depreciable value (or remaining wearing value) is then multiplied by the appropriate rate. The rate changes each year in the sum-of-the-digits method; the rate remains constant for the entire time in the straight-line and declining-balance methods. The declining-balance method further requires that, in each succeeding year, the depreciable value be reduced by the previous annual depreciation.

After each annual depreciation is computed, these amounts are then used to complete the depreciation schedules already presented.

Example Five   A new machine was purchased for $5,625 and will be used for 6 years, after which its salvage value will be $300. The 20% additional first-year depreciation allowance is to be used. Compare the annual depreciation that would be claimed under (a) the straight-line method, (b) the sum-of-the-digits method, and (c) the declining-balance method at the maximum rate.

Solution   First, the 20% additional first-year depreciation allowance must be computed:

$$\$5,625 \times 20\% = \$1,125$$

The additional first-year depreciation is $1,125 in each case.

Next, the depreciable value is computed for each depreciation method:

	(a) Straight-Line	(b) Sum-of-Digits	(c) Declining-Balance
Cost	$5,625	$5,625	$5,625
−1st-year allowance	− 1,125	− 1,125	− 1,125
	$4,500	$4,500	$4,500
−Salvage value	− 300	− 300	—
Depreciable value (or remaining wearing value)	$4,200	$4,200	$4,500

Finally, annual depreciation is computed for each depreciation method. The rate to be used in each case is summarized as follows:

(a) The **straight-line rate** is the reciprocal of the number of years; in this case, $\frac{1}{6}$. (A fraction is often converted to its equivalent per cent for computing depreciation by machine.)

(b) The sum-of-the-digits $1+2+3+4+5+6=21$.

(c) The maximum declining-balance rate for new assets is twice the straight-line rate; that is, $2 \times \frac{1}{6} = \frac{2}{6} = \frac{1}{3}$.

Therefore,

(a) Straight-line:

	Depreciable Value	$\times$ Rate $=$	Annual Depreciation
(1)	$4,200	$\times \frac{1}{6}$ =	$700 + $1,125 = $1,825
(2)	4,200	$\times \frac{1}{6}$ =	700
.			
.			
.			
(6)	4,200	$\times \frac{1}{6}$ =	700

Each year is the same, after the first year.

(b) Sum-of-the-digits:

	Depreciable Value	$\times$ Rate $=$	Annual Depreciation
(1)	$4,200	$\times \frac{6}{21}$ =	$1,200 + $1,125 = $2,325
(2)	4,200	$\times \frac{5}{21}$ =	1,000
(3)	4,200	$\times \frac{4}{21}$ =	800
(4)	4,200	$\times \frac{3}{21}$ =	600
(5)	4,200	$\times \frac{2}{21}$ =	400
(6)	4,200	$\times \frac{1}{21}$ =	200

(c) Declining balance:

Depreciable Value	× Rate =	Annual Depreciation

(1) $4,500.00 × $\frac{1}{3}$ = $1,500.00 + $1,125 = $2,625
       − 1,500.00

(2)   3,000.00 × $\frac{1}{3}$ = 1,000.00
       − 1,000.00

(3)   2,000.00 × $\frac{1}{3}$ =   666.67
       − 666.67

(4)   1,333.33 × $\frac{1}{3}$ =   444.44
       − 444.44

(5)   888.89 × $\frac{1}{3}$ =   296.30
       − 296.30

(6)   592.59 × $\frac{1}{3}$ =   197.53
       − 197.53
       $ 395.06

The following example illustrates an asset whose purchase price exceeds the $10,000 maximum allowable for the 20% additional first-year depreciation, and also includes net salvage value.

Example Six A knitting machine cost Bradford Sox, Inc., $14,000 when new and will be used for 7 years, after which its second-hand value will be $2,200. (a) Compute the 20% additional first-year depreciation. (b) Determine the *net* salvage value for the machine. (c) Use the net salvage value to compute the annual depreciation by the straight-line method.

Solution (a) The additional first-year depreciation on this $14,000 machine is the maximum allowable: 20% of $10,000 = $2,000.

(b) Net salvage is found by reducing the normal salvage by 10% of the cost.

Salvage	$2,200
10% of cost (10% of $14,000)	− 1,400
Net salvage	$ 800

(c) The $2,000 additional first-year depreciation and the $800 net salvage value must be deducted from the cost of the machine before the annual depreciation can be determined:

Original cost	$14,000
Additional depreciation	− 2,000
	$12,000
Net salvage value	− 800
Remaining wearing value (or Depreciable value)	$11,200

The remaining wearing value of $11,200 distributed evenly among the years, gives

$$\text{Depreciable Value} \times \text{Rate} = \text{Annual Depreciation}$$

$$\frac{\$11,200}{7} = \$1,600 \qquad \text{or} \qquad \$11,200 \times \tfrac{1}{7} = \$1,600$$

The depreciation will be $1,600 annually for each year after the first year. Depreciation for the first year will be $3,600 (the $1,600 annual amount plus the $2,000 additional allowance.)

The depreciation problems in this text each pertain to a single item that is used for a whole number of years. In actual practice, however, an asset is often acquired in midyear, in which case the first- (and/or last-) year's standard depreciation charge would normally be limited to that corresponding portion of the whole year's depreciation (although the entire 20% additional first-year allowance may be claimed, if it applies). Also, in order to simplify depreciation record keeping for business firms, the IRS allows assets with the same or even different useful lives to be combined into one account, which is then depreciated by any acceptable method as though it were a single item. We will also assume that all given assets are acquired new unless otherwise stated. However, the only way in which an asset's being new or used affects depreciation computation is in determining the maximum rate allowable by the declining-balance method. (The maximum rate should be used unless another rate is given.)

Compute the annual depreciation and complete a depreciation schedule for each of the following, using the data and method indicated:

		Cost	Scrap Value	Useful Life	Depreciation Method
1.	(a)	$2,200	$700	5 yr	Straight line
	(b)	2,200	700	5	Sum of digits
	(c)	4,800 (new)	—	4	Declining balance
	(d)	6,400 (used)	—	3	Declining balance
2.	(a)	$2,000	$800	4 yr	Straight line
	(b)	2,000	800	4	Sum of digits
	(c)	2,000 (new)	—	5	Declining balance
	(d)	2,000 (used)	—	3	Declining balance

If the additional 20% first-year depreciation allowance were elected, compute the annual depreciation that would be charged during (1) the first year, and (2) the second year:

		Cost	Scrap Value	Useful Life	Depreciation Method
3.	(a)	$7,500	$600	6 yr	Straight line
	(b)	8,000	800	7	Sum of digits
	(c)	6,000 (new)	—	8	Declining balance
	(d)	4,500 (used)	—	9	Declining balance
4.	(a)	$2,000	$200	7 yr	Straight line
	(b)	5,000	400	8	Sum of digits
	(c)	2,250 (new)	—	6	Declining balance
	(d)	9,000 (used)	—	9	Declining balance

5. The building in which Warwick Paint Co. is located cost $80,000. They estimate that in 30 years it will be worth approximately $5,000 and will have to be replaced. What will be the annual depreciation charge by the straight-line method during this time?

6. The Eye Center spent $3,600 to furnish its waiting room. After 6 years of use, the furniture will have a second-hand value of about $600. Prepare a straight-line depreciation schedule for these furnishings.

7. Chateau Restaurant purchased a new,

high-speed, electronic oven for $1,200. They plan to use the oven for 5 years, after which they expect to receive about $300 on a trade-in. Complete a depreciation schedule for the oven using the sum-of-the-digits method.

8. Comfortzone Insulation paid $7,000 for the truck and equipment used to blow insulation into houses. It is expected that this equipment will last for 7 years, when it will be worth $1,400. Construct a depreciation schedule by the sum-of-the-digits method, in order to determine how much income tax deduction can be claimed each year.

9. A new television camera cost station WXYZ $4,800. Such cameras are usually obsolete in 4 years.
(a) Make a depreciation schedule using the declining-balance method at a constant yearly rate of 30%
(b) How much will the camera supposedly be worth on trade-in at that time?

10. The company president's new station wagon, will cost Langley Processing $7,500, will be driven for 3 years.
(a) Depreciate the station wagon on a declining-balance schedule, using a constant yearly rate of 40%.
(b) What will be the book value of the wagon when it is traded?

11. The knitting machine at Lytton Fabrics cost $6,500. After 7 years, Lytton expects to receive approximately $1,000 when they trade in on a newer model. Using the straight-line method and claiming the additional 20% first-year allowance, construct a depreciation schedule for the machine.

12. Yummy Cereal Co. paid $5,500 for a new packaging machine. After 8 years of use, the machine's value will be $400. Con-struct a depreciation schedule by the straight-line method, including the 20% additional first-year depreciation allowance.

13. Gardner's Sheet Metal Shop paid $4,000 for a machine used to construct ducts. The machine is expected to last for 7 years, and it will then be valued at $400. Complete a depreciation schedule by the sum-of-the-digits method, and elect the 20% additional first-year allowance.

14. New freezing cases cost Handy Mart Grocery $8,000. The store expects to use the cases for 8 years, after which their trade-in value will be about $1,000. In order to obtain more tax savings during early years, Handy Mart decided to claim the 20% additional first-year allowance and to depreciate the cases using the sum-of-the-digits method. Prepare this depreciation schedule.

15. Dr. Steven Lindley purchased $8,000 worth of new dental equipment for his office. The equipment will be used for 8 years. Dr. Lindley wants to claim the additional first-year allowance and thereafter to depreciate at the maximum yearly rate by the declining-balance method. Prepare his depreciation schedule.

16. An automatic assembly machine cost Electrical Motors, Inc., $6,750. The machine is expected to operate for 6 years. Make a depreciation schedule for the machine using the declining-balance method at the maximum rate and including the additional first-year allowance.

17. A set of used cash registers with magnetic-ink readers cost Handy Building Supplies $3,200. They expect to use the registers for 6 years in order to qualify for the additional first-year depreciation allowance. Prepare a depreciation schedule using the declining-balance method.

18. A-1 Equipment Rentals paid $6,000 for a used bulldozer. They wish to claim the 20% additional first-year depreciation on the machine, which will be used for 6 years. Use the declining-balance method to prepare the depreciation schedule.

In each of the following problems, determine (a) the 20% additional first-year depreciation allowance, (b) the net salvage value of the asset, and (c) compute the annual depreciation by the straight-line method for the first year and for succeeding years. (Depreciation schedules are not necessary.)

19. Processing equipment at a cannery cost $11,000. After 13 years of use, the machinery will be worth $3,600 second-hand.

20. The ice cream processing equipment at a dairy cost $18,000 new and will be used for 15 years, when its salvage value will be $2,800.

21. A machine to mold hand tools cost a manufacturer $18,000. The machine's salvage value will be $5,300 after 10 years.

22. The machines and pneumatic pipes for a drive-in banking system cost $21,000. If the system is used for 12 years, the bank can expect $3,100 on a trade-in.

SECTION 2
Overhead

In addition to the cost of materials or merchandise, other expenses are incurred in the operation of any business. Examples of such *operating expenses* are salaries, rent, utilities, office supplies, taxes, depreciation, insurance, and so on. These additional expenses are known collectively as **overhead.**

Overhead contributes indirectly to the actual total cost of the merchandise being manufactured or sold by the concern. In order to determine the efficiency of various departments, to determine the total cost of manufacturing various items, or to determine whether certain items are being sold profitably, a portion of the total plant overhead is assigned to each department. From the many methods of distributing overhead, we shall consider three: according to total floor space, according to total net sales, and according to the number of employees in each department.

Example One

The mean monthly overhead of $96,000 at Johnson Manufacturing Corp. is distributed *according to the total floor space* of each department. The floor space of each department is as follows:

Department	Floor Space (sq ft)
A—Receiving and raw materials	4,000
B—Assembling	9,000
C—Inspecting and shipping	8,000
D—Administration	+ 3,000
	Total = 24,000

Example One (cont.) Each department therefore has the following ratio of floor space and is assigned the following amount of overhead expense:

Dept.	Ratio of Floor Space	Overhead Charge
A	$\dfrac{4,000}{24,000} = \dfrac{1}{6}$	$\dfrac{1}{6} \times \$96,000 = \ \$16,000$
B	$\dfrac{9,000}{24,000} = \dfrac{3}{8}$	$\dfrac{3}{8} \times \$96,000 = \ 36,000$
C	$\dfrac{8,000}{24,000} = \dfrac{1}{3}$	$\dfrac{1}{3} \times \ 96,000 = \ 32,000$
D	$\dfrac{3,000}{24,000} = \dfrac{1}{8}$	$\dfrac{1}{8} \times \ 96,000 = +\ 12,000$
		Total overhead = $\ \$96,000$

NOTE: Students using machines may convert ratios to their decimal equivalents. However, nonterminating decimals must be carried out to at least as many significant digits as there are digits in the given overhead. For instance, $\frac{1}{6} = 0.16667$, since \$96,000 has five digits (to the nearest dollar).

Example Two Avery Hardware wishes to distribute its \$20,000 July overhead *according to the total net sales* of each department. These sales and the overhead distribution are as follows:

Department	Net Sales	Ratio of Sales	Overhead Charge
Lumber/glass	\$24,000	$\dfrac{\$24,000}{\$80,000} = \dfrac{3}{10}$	$\dfrac{3}{10} \times \$20,000 = \$\ 6,000$
Tools/electricity	16,000	$\dfrac{\$16,000}{\$80,000} = \dfrac{1}{5}$	$\dfrac{1}{5} \times \ 20,000 = \ 4,000$
Building supply	20,000	$\dfrac{\$20,000}{\$80,000} = \dfrac{1}{4}$	$\dfrac{1}{4} \times \ 20,000 = \ 5,000$
Housewares	8,000	$\dfrac{\$8,000}{\$80,000} = \dfrac{1}{10}$	$\dfrac{1}{10} \times \ 20,000 = \ 2,000$
Sports equipment	+ 12,000	$\dfrac{\$12,000}{\$80,000} = \dfrac{3}{20}$	$\dfrac{3}{20} \times \ 20,000 = +\ 3,000$
Total net sales = \$80,000			Total overhead = \$20,000

Example Three

The $15,000 monthly office overhead at White Plumbing & Heating is charged to the various divisions *according to the number of employees* in the office who work directly with each division. This results in the following overhead charge:

Division	Number of Employees	Ratio of Employees	Overhead Charge	
Plumbing	3	$\frac{3}{10}$	$\frac{3}{10} \times \$15,000 =$	$ 4,500
Heating	1	$\frac{1}{10}$	$\frac{1}{10} \times \ 15,000 =$	1,500
Air conditioning	4	$\frac{4}{10} = \frac{2}{5}$	$\frac{2}{5} \times \ 15,000 =$	6,000
Appliance	+ 2	$\frac{2}{10} = \frac{1}{5}$	$\frac{1}{5} \times \ 15,000 = +$	3,000
	Total = 10		Total overhead =	$15,000

SECTION 2 *Problems*

In each of the following problems, distribute overhead according to floor space, net sales, or number of employees, depending on the information given.

		Dept.	Floor Space (sq ft)	Total Overhead		Dept.	Floor Space (sq ft)	Total Overhead
1.	(a)	A	7,500	$90,000	(b)	#1	500	$40,000
		B	2,500			2	3,500	
		C	3,000			3	5,000	
		D	1,500			4	1,000	
		E	500					
2.	(a)	W	2,500	$60,000	(b)	#50	3,000	$48,000
		X	500			60	6,000	
		Y	5,000			70	2,000	
		Z	2,000			80	4,000	
						90	1,000	

	Dept.	Net Sales	Total Overhead		Dept.	Net Sales	Total Overhead
3. (a)	R	$15,000	$8,000	(b)	1B	$20,000	$18,000
	S	8,000			2D	15,000	
	T	12,000			3G	25,000	
	U	5,000			4M	30,000	
					5S	10,000	
4. (a)	#1	$2,000	$4,800	(b)	J	$10,000	$90,000
	2	2,500			K	15,000	
	3	4,500			L	5,000	
	4	3,000			M	25,000	
					N	20,000	

	Dept.	Number of Employees	Total Overhead		Dept.	Number of Employees	Total Overhead
5. (a)	H	10	$120,000	(b)	B-1	4	$ 14,000
	I	20			B-2	5	
	J	5			B-3	9	
	K	10			B-4	2	
	L	25					
	M	30					
6. (a)	A	10	$ 72,000	(b)	MT	9	$140,000
	B	12			PR	18	
	C	8			GR	12	
	D	6			FF	6	
					DL	15	

7. Jensen Manufacturing Co. wishes to distribute their annual overhead of $150,000 among their separate departments according to floor space allotted to each. Divide their overhead among the following departments:

Department	Floor Space (sq ft)
Office	800
Raw materials	1,200
Casting	2,500
Assembling	4,000
Warehouse	1,500

8. Logan's allocates overhead expenses according to the total floor space occupied by each department. Determine the overhead to be assigned to each department, if total overhead for January was $72,000.

Department	Floor Space (sq ft)
Women	9,000
Juniors	6,000
Men	7,500
Children	4,000
Shoes	2,000
Linens	4,500
Housewares	3,000

9. The Little Something (a ladies' clothing store) wishes to distribute its September overhead of $9,600 according to each department's portion of the total net sales. Compute the operating expense to be assigned each of the following departments.

Department	Net Sales
Dresses and coats	$16,000
Sportswear	12,000
Shoes	6,000
Hats	2,000
Accessories	4,000
Lingerie	8,000

10. The Furniture Warehouse apportions overhead to its various departments according to each department's ratio of total net sales. If their annual operating expenses were $30,000, what was each department's share of the overhead?

Department	Net Sales
Living room furniture	$25,000
Dining room furniture	15,000
Bedroom furniture	20,000
Patio and other furniture	6,000
Home accessories	4,000
Carpets	10,000
Appliances	12,000
TV/stereos	8,000

11. Expenses at Garden Fresh Grocers are distributed according to the number of people working in each department. If their December overhead was $18,000, how much should be charged to each department?

Department	Number of Employees
Meat and dairy	6
Produce	3
Grocery items	4
Frozen foods	2
Bakery products, dietary and gourmet foods	1
Cashiers, bagboys, and management	8

12. Georgetown Motors charges operating expenses according to the number of employees in each department. Overhead during April totaled $45,000. Assign the overhead expense to each department.

Department	Number of Employees
New cars	8
Used cars	5
Trucks	2
Repair	9
Paint/body	6

CHAPTER 9 *Glossary*

Additional first-year depreciation allowance. Twenty per cent of cost (up to a total of $2,000 on all items) permitted along with other standard depreciation during the first year of ownership on certain fixed assets that will be used at least six years.

Book value. The calculated value of a fixed asset after depreciation has been deducted.
Declining-balance method. Depreciation method where a constant per cent is annually multiplied times book value (starting with cost).

Depreciable value. The base value on which annual depreciation is computed:

Depreciable value = Cost
  − 20% Additional
    allowance*
  − Salvage value.*

Depreciation. The loss in value experienced by a fixed asset; the expense of a fixed asset distributed over its useful life and claimed as overhead to reduce a business' taxable income.

Depreciation schedule. A record showing annual depreciation, current book value, and accumulated depreciation of a fixed asset.

Fixed asset. A business possession that will be used for more than 1 year. (Examples: buildings, vehicles, machinery, equipment.)

Overhead. Business expenses other than the cost of materials or merchandise. (Examples: Salaries, rent, utilities, supplies, advertising.)

* If applicable

Salvage (scrap) value. The value of the materials in a fixed asset at the end of its useful life; the lowest value to which an asset may be depreciated.

Straight-line method. Depreciation method in which the wearing value of an asset is evenly divided among the years.

Straight-line rate. Depreciation rate that is the reciprocal of the number of years of useful life. (Example: for an asset used 5 years, the annual straight-line rate is $\frac{1}{5}$.)

Sum-of-the-digits method. Accelerated depreciation method where wearing value is multiplied by a series of fractions whose denominators are the total of the years' digits and whose numerators are the years' digits taken in reverse order.

Useful life. The number of years that a fixed asset is efficiently used and depreciated in a business.

Wearing value. The total amount of depreciation that may be claimed: Wearing value = Business cost − Scrap value.

CHAPTER 10

Financial Statement

Analysis

CHAPTER 10   OBJECTIVES

Upon completing Chapter 10, the student will be able to:

1. Define and use correctly the terminology in each topic.

2. On an income statement with the individual amounts given
   a. Compute the net profit; and
   b. Find the per cent of net sales that each item represents.
   (*Section 1; Examples 1, 2; Problems 1, 2*)

3. On comparative income statements, compute
   a. Subtotals and totals;
   b. Per cents of net sales for each year; and
   c. Increase or decrease between years (amounts and per cent).
   (*Example 3; Problems 3, 4*)

4. On a balance sheet with individual amounts given, compute
   a. Total assets;
   b. Total liabilities;
   c. Net worth; and
   d. Per cent each item represents.
   (*Section 2; Example 4; Problems 5, 6*)

5. On comparative balance sheets, compute the
   a. Subtotals and totals;
   b. Per cents of total assets for each year; and
   c. Increase or decrease between years (amounts and per cent).
   (*Example 5; Problems 7, 8*)

6. Select from income statements and balance sheets the amounts required to compute common business ratios:
   a. Working capital ratio;
   b. Acid-test ratio;
   c. Rate (per cent) of net income (after taxes) to average net worth;
   d. Ratio of net sales to average total assets;
   e. Accounts receivable turnover;
   f. Average age of accounts receivable; and
   g. Other percentage relationships where the items required are specifically named.
   (*Example 6; Problems 9–12*)

10	At least once each year (sometimes more often), the bookkeeping records of every business are audited to determine the financial condition of the business: what the volume of business was, how much profit

(or loss) was made, how much these things have changed in the past year, how much the business is actually worth, and so on. As a means of presenting this important information, two financial statements are normally prepared and analyzed: the *income statement* and the *balance sheet*.

SECTION 1
The Income
Statement

The **income statement** shows a business' sales, expenses, and profit (or loss) during a certain period of time. (The time might be a month, a quarter, 6 months, or a year.) The basic calculations of an income statement are these:

$$\begin{array}{l} \text{Net sales} \\ - \text{ Cost of goods sold} \\ \hline \text{Gross profit} \\ - \text{ Operating expenses} \\ \hline \text{Net profit (or net loss)} \end{array}$$

Notice that **gross profit** (also known as **margin** or **markup**) is the amount that would remain after the merchandise has been paid for. Out of this gross profit must be paid all the **operating expenses (overhead,** such as salaries, rent, utilities, supplies, insurance, etc.). The amount that remains is the clear or spendable profit—the **net income** or **net profit**.

In order to effectively analyze expenses or to compare an income statement with preceding ones, it is customary to convert the dollar amounts to per cents of the total net sales. These per cents are computed as follows:

$$-\% \text{ of Net sales} = \text{Each amount}$$

$$\frac{-\% \times \text{Net sales}}{\text{Net sales}} = \frac{\text{Each amount}}{\text{Net sales}}$$

$$-\% = \frac{\text{Each amount}}{\text{Net sales}}$$

Example One During April, Williams Pharmacy had net sales of $60,000. The drugs and merchandise cost $45,000 wholesale, and operating expenses totaled $12,000. How much net profit was made during April, and what was the per cent of net sales for each item?

WILLIAMS PHARMACY

Income Statement for Month Ending April 30, 19XX

Net sales	$60,000	100%
Cost of goods sold	− 45,000	− 75%
Gross profit	$15,000	25%
Operating expenses	− 12,000	− 20%
Net profit	$ 3,000	5%

The per cents above were obtained as follows:

$$-\% = \frac{\text{Each amount}}{\text{Net sales}}$$

(1) $\dfrac{\text{Cost of goods}}{\text{Net sales}} = \dfrac{\$45,000}{\$60,000} = 75\%$

(2) $\dfrac{\text{Gross profit}}{\text{Net sales}} = \dfrac{\$15,000}{\$60,000} = 25\%$

(3) $\dfrac{\text{Operating expenses}}{\text{Net sales}} = \dfrac{\$12,000}{\$60,000} = 20\%$

(4) $\dfrac{\text{Net profit}}{\text{Net sales}} = \dfrac{\$ 3,000}{\$60,000} = 5\%$

Thus, we find that 75% of the income from sales was used to pay for the drugs and merchandise itself, leaving a gross profit ($15,000) of 25% of sales. Another 20% of the income from sales was used to pay the $12,000 operating expenses. This leaves a clear, net profit of $3,000, which is 5% of the sales income.

NOTE: Observe that the cost of goods, the overhead, and the net profit account for all of the income from sales. Also, the overhead (operating expenses) and the net profit comprise the margin (gross profit). In equation form,

$$\text{Cost} + \text{Overhead} + \text{Net profit} = \text{Sales}$$
$$\$45,000 + \ \$12,000 \ + \ \$3,000 \ = \$60,000$$

$$\begin{array}{ccc} \text{Cost} + & \text{Margin} & = \text{Sales} \\ \$45,000 + & \$15,000 & = \$60,000 \end{array}$$

This fundamental relationship is the basis for the equation $C + M = S$, which is applied by merchants to determine the selling price of their merchandise. (This is the subject of Chapter 13.)

These relationships, which are true for the amounts of money shown on the income statement, are also true of the per cents for each item:

$$
\begin{array}{llll}
\text{Cost} + \text{Overhead} + \text{Net profit} & = \text{Sales} \\
75\% + \quad\ 20\% \quad + \quad 5\% & = 100\% \\
\\
\text{Cost} + \qquad \text{Margin} & = \text{Sales} \\
75\% + \qquad \quad 25\% & = 100\%
\end{array}
$$

The foregoing income statement was a highly simplified example. In actual practice, the basic topics used to calculate profit (net sales, cost of goods sold, and operating expenses) are broken down in detail, showing the contributing factors of each. The next example presents a more complete income statement.

Of the various topic breakdowns, only cost of goods sold needs particular mention. To the value of the inventory on hand at the beginning of the report period is added the total of all merchandise bought during the period (less returned merchandise and plus freight charges paid separately). This gives the total value of all merchandise that the company had available for sale during the period. Since some of this merchandise is not sold, however, the value of the inventory on hand at the end of the period must be deducted, in order to obtain the value of the merchandise which was actually sold.

Notice that, just as the individual amounts are added or subtracted to obtain subtotals, so may their corresponding per cents be added or subtracted to obtain the per cents of the subtotals. This is possible because each amount is represented as a per cent of the same number (net sales).

The per cents indicated in the right-hand column are the ones of particular interest to management and potential investors: (1) What per cent of sales was the cost of goods? (2) What per cent of sales was the gross profit (margin)? (3) What per cent of sales was the operating expense (overhead)? But most important by far to the owners and possible investors is the final per cent: (4) What per cent of sales was the net profit? This is usually the first question asked by anyone considering investing money in a business.

RANIER ELECTRONICS, INC.

Income Statement for Year Ending December 31, 19XX

Income from sales:				
Total sales		$123,000		102.5%
Less: sales returns and				
allowances		− 3,000		− 2.5
Net sales			$120,000	100.0%
Cost of goods sold:				
Inventory, January 1		$ 31,300		
Purchases	$71,600			
Less: returns and				
allowances	− 1,300			
Net purchases	$70,300			
Add: freight in	+ 800			
Net purchase cost		+ 71,100		
Goods available for sale		$102,400		
Inventory, December 31		− 27,400		
Cost of goods sold			− 75,000	−62.5%
Gross profit on sales			$ 45,000	37.5%
Operating expenses:				
Office salaries		$ 24,000		20.0%
Rent and utilities		4,800		4.0
Office supplies		1,200		1.0
Insurance		720		0.6
Advertising		1,800		1.5
Depreciation		3,000		2.5
Miscellaneous		+ 480		+ 0.4
Total operating expenses			− 36,000	− 30.0
Net income from operations			$ 9,000	7.5%

The per cents derived in the foregoing examples represent **vertical analysis**. That is, each separate item is represented as a per cent of the total during a *single* time period. In order to analyze business progress and potential more effectively, however, recent figures should be compared with corresponding figures from the previous period (or periods). When comparisons are made between corresponding items during a *series* of two or more time periods, this is known as **horizontal analysis.**

The following example illustrates horizontal analysis. On this comparative income statement, both the dollar increase (or decrease) and the per cent of change are shown. Figures for the earlier year are used as the basis for finding the per cent of change, using the formula "—% of original = change?"

**Example
Three**

GOLDSTEIN'S, INC.

*Comparative Income Statement
for Fiscal Years Ending June* 30, 19X2 *and* 19X1

	19X2	19X1	INCREASE OR (DECREASE) Amount	Per Cent	PER CENT OF NET SALES 19X2	19X1
Income:						
Net sales	$275,000	$250,000	$25,000	10.0%	100.0%	100.0%
Cost of goods sold:						
Inventory, July 1	$ 60,000	$ 70,000	($10,000)	(14.3%)	21.8%	28.0%
Purchases	205,000	165,000	40,000	24.2	74.5	66.0
Goods available						
for sale	$265,000	$235,000	$30,000	12.8%	96.4%	94.0%
Inventory, June 30	75,000	60,000	15,000	25.0	27.3	24.0
Cost of goods sold	190,000	175,000	15,000	8.6	69.1	70.0
Gross margin	$ 85,000	$ 75,000	$10,000	13.3%	30.9%	30.0%
Expenses:						
Administration	$ 50,000	$ 45,000	$ 5,000	11.1%	18.2%	18.0%
Occupancy	7,500	5,000	2,500	50.0	2.3	2.0
Sales	16,000	10,000	6,000	60.0	5.8	4.0
Miscellaneous	1,500	2,500	(1,000)	(40.0)	0.5	1.0
Total expenses	75,000	62,500	12,500	20.0	27.3	25.0
Net income (before taxes)	$ 10,000	$ 12,500	($2,500)	(20.0%)	3.6%	5.0%

The example below (for net sales) illustrates how the preceding
per cents of change were computed. Net sales increased from
$250,000 to $275,000, a "change" of $25,000. The "original" is
the first year, 19X1. Thus,

$$\text{----}\% \text{ of Original} = \text{Change}$$
$$\text{----}\% \text{ of } \$250,000 = \$25,000$$
$$\frac{250,000x}{250,000} = \frac{25,000}{250,000}$$
$$x = 10\%$$

Notice that, whereas the "amounts" of increase or decrease may be added
or subtracted to obtain the amounts of the subtotals, the "per cents" of

increase or decrease *cannot* be added or subtracted to obtain the per cents of change in the subtotals. This is because each per cent of change is based on a different number (the 19X1 amount of that particular item).

SECTION 2

The Balance Sheet

The purpose of a **balance sheet** is to give an overall picture of what a business is worth at a specific time: how much it owns, how much it owes, and how much the owners' investment is worth. On a balance sheet are listed all of a business' **assets** (possessions and money owed to the business) and all its **liabilities** (money which the business owes to someone else). The balance remaining after the liabilities are subtracted from the assets is the **net worth** of the business. Thus, the assets must balance the liabilities and net worth; or

$$\text{Assets} = \text{Liabilities} + \text{Net worth}$$

The general headings of assets and liabilities on a balance sheet are ordinarily broken down into current and fixed (long-term) categories, as follows:

Current Assets	*Fixed Assets*
Cash	Buildings
Bank accounts	Furnishings
Accounts receivable	Machinery
Notes receivable	Equipment
Merchandise inventory	Land

Accounts receivable are accounts owed to the business by customers who have bought merchandise "on credit." Notes receivable indicates money owed by customers who have signed a written promise to pay by a certain date. The fixed assets are listed on a balance sheet at their current book value after depreciation, except for land (which may not be depreciated).

The liabilities of a business are separated according to current liabilities and fixed (long-term) liabilities, as indicated:

Current Liabilities	*Fixed Liabilities*
Accounts payable	Mortgages
Notes payable	Bonds
Accrued interest	
Accrued taxes	

Accounts payable are accounts owed to others for goods or services bought on credit. "Accrued" interest or taxes means that these items are due within a short time. Fixed liabilities, by contrast, would not have to be paid in full within the near future.

Other common terms used instead of net worth are **net ownership, net investment, proprietorship** (for an individually owned business), **owner's equity,** and **stockholders' equity** (for a corporation).

The following balance sheet again illustrates vertical analysis. That is, each asset is represented as a per cent of the total assets; and each liability, as well as the net worth, is presented as a per cent of the total liabilities plus net worth (which is the same as the total assets).

Example Four

COLLIER-WHITWORTH CORP.

Balance Sheet December 31, 19X1

Assets			%	
Current assets:				
Cash on hand		$ 500	0.2%	
Cash in bank		9,000	3.6	
Accounts receivable		42,000	16.8	
Inventory		23,500	9.4	
Total current assets		$ 75,000		30.0%
Fixed assets:				
Plant site		$25,000	10.0%	
Building	$150,000			
Less: depreciation	− 55,000			
		95,000	38.0	
Equipment	$ 75,000			
Less: depreciation	− 20,000			
		55,000	22.0	
Total fixed assets		175,000		70.0
Total assets		$250,000		100.0%
Liabilities and Net Worth				
Current liabilities				
Accounts payable	$37,500		15.0%	
Notes payable	10,000		4.0	
Total current liabilities		$ 47,500		19.0%
Fixed liabilities:				
Mortgage		102,500		41.0
Total liabilities		$150,000		60.0%
Net worth		100,000		40.0
Total liabilities and net worth		$250,000		100.0%

Just as horizontal analysis was helpful in studying the income statement, so is it useful in determining the significance of a balance sheet. The next example presents such a balance sheet.

Example Five

THE DANVILLE CORP.

Comparative Balance Sheet, January 31, 19X2 and 19X1

	19X2	19X1	INCREASE OR (DECREASE) Amount	INCREASE OR (DECREASE) Per Cent	PER CENT OF TOTAL ASSETS 19X2	PER CENT OF TOTAL ASSETS 19X1
Assets						
Cash	$ 11,000	$ 14,000	($ 3,000)	(21.4%)	4.6%	7.0%
Accounts receivable	32,000	28,000	4,000	14.3	13.3	14.0
Inventory	57,000	38,000	19,000	50.0	23.8	19.0
Current assets	$100,000	$ 80,000	$20,000	25.0%	41.7%	40.0%
Fixed assets (net)	140,000	120,000	20,000	16.7	58.3	60.0
Total assets	$240,000	$200,000	$40,000	20.0%	100.0%	100.0%
Liabilities and Stockholders' Equity						
Current liabilities	$ 45,000	$ 36,000	$ 9,000	25.0%	18.7%	18.0%
Fixed liabilities	90,000	74,000	16,000	21.6	37.5	37.0
Total liabilities	$135,000	$110,000	$25,000	22.7	56.2%	55.0%
Common stock	$ 75,000	$ 65,000	$10,000	15.4%	31.3%	32.5%
Retained earnings	30,000	25,000	5,000	20.0	12.5	12.5
Total stockholders' equity	105,000	90,000	15,000	16.7	43.8	45.0
Total liabilities and stockholders' equity	$240,000	$200,000	$40,000	20.0%	100.0%	100.0%

Business Ratios

In addition to the analysis possible from single or comparative financial statements, a number of other business ratios are commonly used to provide a more thorough indication of a business' financial condition. These ratios are computed using figures readily available from the income statement and the balance sheet. The next example contains an explanation and example of some of the more common ratios.

Example Six

The ratios (a) through (f) given below are based on the balance sheet of The Danville Corp. in Example Five. Their income statement for

19X2 was as follows:

THE DANVILLE CORP.

*Condensed Income Statement
for Fiscal Year Ending January* 31, 19X2

Net sales	$300,000	100.0%
Cost of goods sold	− 195,000	− 65.0
Gross margin	$105,000	35.0%
Operating expenses	− 90,000	− 30.0
Net income (before taxes)	$ 15,000	5.0%
Income taxes	− 5,000	− 1.7
Net income (after taxes)	$ 10,000	3.3%

*Working
Capital
Ratio*

(a) The **working capital ratio** is often called the **current ratio,** because it is the ratio of current assets to current liabilities. Thus, the Danville Corp.'s 19X2 current ratio is

$$\frac{\text{Current assets}}{\text{Current liabilities}} = \frac{\$100,000}{\$45,000}$$

$$= \frac{2.2}{1} \quad \text{or} \quad 2.2 \text{ to } 1$$

The Danville Corp.'s current ratio is 2.2 to 1. A current ratio of $2:1$ is generally considered the minimum acceptable ratio; bankers would probably hesitate to lend money to a firm whose working capital ratio was lower than $2:1$.

*Acid-Test
Ratio*

(b) The current ratio included all current assets. In order to provide some measure of a firm's ability to obtain funds quickly, the **acid-test** or **quick ratio** is computed. This is a ratio of the quick assets to the current liabilities. **Quick assets** (sometimes called **liquid assets**) are those which can be easily and quickly converted to cash; for example, accounts receivable and notes receivable, as well as cash itself. (The inventory is not included in the acid-test ratio, because it often proves difficult to convert the inventory to cash quickly.)

$$\frac{\text{Quick assets}}{\text{Current liabilities}} = \frac{\$43,000}{\$45,000}$$

$$= \frac{0.96}{1} \quad \text{or} \quad 1.0 \text{ to } 1$$

Example Six *(cont.)*

As an indication of a firm's ability to meet its obligations the acid-test ratio should be at least $1:1$. The Danville Corp. barely meets this minimum requirement in 19X2. This may be only a temporary drop, however (from 1.2 to 1 the previous year). Observe that during 19X2 Danville greatly increased its inventory, with a corresponding increase in current liabilities and a drop in cash. If the increased inventory results in higher net sales and an improved cash position, the acid-test ratio may also soon improve.

Net Income (after taxes) to Average Net Worth

(c) Since businesses are oganized to make profits, of primary concern to the owners is the return on their investment. The **ratio of net income (after taxes) to average net worth** indicates the rate of return on the average owners' equity. Using the 19X1 and 19X2 figures for total stockholders' equity of The Danville Corp.,

$$\text{Average net worth} = \frac{\$90,000 + \$105,000}{2}$$

$$= \frac{\$195,000}{2}$$

$$= \$97,500$$

$$\frac{\text{Net income (after taxes)}}{\text{Average net worth}} = \frac{\$10,000}{\$97,500}$$

$$= 10.3\%$$

Net Sales to Average Total Assets

(d) The **ratio of net sales to average total assets** gives some indication of whether a business is using its assets to best advantage—that is, of whether its sales volume is in line with what the company's capital warrants. This ratio (sometimes called the **total capital turnover**) would indicate inefficiency if it is too low. (NOTE: The "total assets" used here should exclude any assets held by the company which do not contribute to the business operation.)

$$\text{Average total assets} = \frac{\$200,000 + \$240,000}{2}$$

$$= \frac{\$440,000}{2}$$

$$= \$220,000$$

$$\frac{\text{Net sales}}{\text{Average total assets}} = \frac{\$300,000}{\$220,000}$$

$$= \frac{1.4}{1} \quad \text{or} \quad 1.4 \text{ to } 1$$

The ratio of net sales to average total assets at The Danville Corp. is 1.4 to 1; or, the turnover of total capital was 1.4 times during 19X2.

Accounts Receivable Turnover

(e) **Accounts receivable turnover** is the ratio of net sales to average accounts receivable. (Notes receivable, if they are held, should also be included with the accounts receivable.)

$$\text{Average accounts receivable} = \frac{\$28,000 + \$32,000}{2}$$

$$= \frac{\$60,000}{2}$$

$$= \$30,000$$

$$\frac{\text{Net sales}}{\text{Average accounts receivable}} = \frac{\$300,000}{\$\ 30,000}$$

$$= 10 \text{ times}$$

Accounts receivable are not actually an asset to a business until they are collected. Prompt collection of the accounts receivable makes funds available to the business to meet its own obligations and to take advantage of cash discounts and special offers. Furthermore, the older an account becomes, the less the likelihood that it will be collected. Thus, a minimum of the firm's assets should be tied up in receivables, and they should turn over frequently.

Average Age of Accounts Receivable

(f) This ratio, the **average age of accounts receivable,** in conjunction with the preceding one, indicates whether a business is keeping its accounts receivable up to date. The average age in days is found by dividing 365 days by the turnover in accounts receivable.

$$\frac{365}{\text{Accounts receivable turnover}} = \frac{365}{10}$$

$$= 36.5 \text{ days}$$

The average age of the accounts receivable is 36.5 days. If The Danville Corp. has an allowable credit period of 30 days, this average age of 36.5 days indicates that they are not keeping up with collections.

There are quite a few other ratios of interest to owners and management. One of these, the equity ratio, is already indicated on the balance sheet; the equity ratio is the ratio of owners' equity to total assets (52.9%). The ratio of current liabilities to net worth and the ratio of total liabilities to net worth are ratios based on balance sheet figures. Other common ratios relating to net sales are the ratio of net sales to net worth, the fixed property turnover (the ratio of net sales to fixed assets), the ratio of net sales to net working capital

$$\frac{\text{Net sales}}{\text{Current assets} - \text{Current liabilities}}$$

and the inventory turnover (the ratio of net sales to average inventory, which is discussed in Chapter 14, "Markdown and Turnover").

Additional ratios involving net income are the ratio of net income to total assets and the rate (per cent) of return per share of common stock

$$\frac{\text{Net income after taxes} - \text{Preferred dividends}}{\text{Average common stockholders' equity}}$$

Of interest also is the book value of the stock when there is only one type of stock, this is computed: $\left(\dfrac{\text{Owners' equity}}{\text{Number of shares of stock}} \right)$. Any number of other ratios could be computed if it were thought they would be useful.

Although the financial statements and the ratios that can be computed from them are of great value in evaluating the overall efficiency and financial condition of a business, such reports are not foolproof. Similar information from other businesses of the same type, as well as the general economic condition of the country as a whole, must also be taken into consideration as part of any thorough analysis by management or by a potential investor. On this basis, reports which originally seemed acceptable might appear less acceptable or might indicate the business did unusually well in comparison with competing firms.

SECTIONS 1 AND 2 *Problems*

Copy and complete the following financial statements, computing per cents to the nearest tenth.

1.   ARDMORE WHOLESALERS, INC.

Income Statement for Fiscal Year Ending March 31, 19X2

Income from sales:				
Gross sales		$615,000	*%	
Sales returns and allowances		15,000	*	
Net sales		$		*%
Cost of goods sold:				
Inventory, April 1, 19X1		$200,000		
Purchases	$432,500			
Less: returns and allowances	6.000			
Net purchases	$			
Add: freight in	3,500			
Net purchase cost				
Goods available for sale		$		
Inventory, March 31, 19X2		180,000		
Cost of goods sold			*	
Gross margin on sales		$		*%
Operating expenses:				
Office salaries		$ 20,000	*%	
Occupancy		25,000	*	
Selling		45,000	*	
Buying		15,000	*	
Insurance		6,000	*	
Depreciation		12,000	*	
Miscellaneous		3,000	*	
Total operating expense			*	
Net income on operations		$		*%
Income taxes		5,000	*	
Net income (after taxes)		$		*%

* Compute per cents at the indicated points only.

2.

MAYFIELD ROOFING CO.

Income Statement for Fiscal Year Ending June 30, 19X2

Income from sales:			
Gross sales	$408,000		*%
Sales returns and allowances	8,000		*
Net sales		$	*%
Cost of goods sold:			
Inventory, July 1	$ 95,500		
Purchases	$272,000		
Less: returns and allowances	6,500		
Net purchases	$		
Add: freight in	1,200		
Net purchase cost			
Goods available for sale	$		
Inventory, June 30	102,200		
Cost of goods sold:			*
Gross profit on operations		$	*%
Expenses:			
Salaries	$ 52,000		*%
Rent and utilities	16,000		*
Office supplies	2,000		*
Maintenance	12,000		*
Advertising	4,800		*
Insurance	5,600		*
Depreciation	6,400		*
Other	1,200		*
Total operating expenses			*
Net profit on operations		$	*%
Income taxes		12,000	*
Net income		$	*%

3.

SMITH PENCIL CO.

Balance Sheet, April 1, 19X1

Assets				
Current assets:				
Cash		$14,000	*%	—
Accounts receivable		36,000	*	
Stock on hand		70,000	*	
Total current assets		$		*%
Fixed assets:				
Plant	$60,000			
Less: depreciation	20,000			
		$		
Land		15,000		
Equipment	$40,000			
Less: depreciation	15,000			
Total fixed assets				*
Total assets		$		*%
Liabilities and Net Worth				
Current liabilities:				
Accounts payable		$33,000	*%	
Note payable		6,000	*	
Interest payable		1,000	*	
Total current liabilities		$		*%
Fixed liabilities:				
Bonds (due 19X9)		25,000		*
Total liabilities:		$		*%
Net worth:				
Retained earnings		$35,000	*%	
6% preferred stock		54,000	*	
Common stock		46,000	*	
Total net worth				*
Total liabilities and net worth		$		*%

4.

WILSON SUPPLY CO.

Balance Sheet, November 30, 19X1

Assets				
Current assets:				
Cash	$ 3,600		*%	
Accounts receivable	18,000		*	
Note receivable	2,400		*	
Merchandise inventory	42,000		*	
Total current assets		$		*%
Fixed assets:				
Building	$55,000			
Less: depreciation	25,000			
		$	*%	
Furnishings and fixtures	$ 9,000			
Less: depreciation	3,000			
			*	
Delivery van	$ 7,500			
Less: depreciation	2,700			
			*	
Land	13,200		*	
Total fixed assets				*
Total assets		$		*%
Liabilities and Proprietorship				
Current liabilities:				
Accounts payable	$14,400		*%	
Taxes payable	2,400		*	
Note payable	1,200		*	
Total current liabilities		$		*%
Fixed liabilities:				
Mortgage (amortizes 19X7)		30,000		*
Total liabilities		$		*%
Proprietorship:				
R. B. Wilson, capital				*
Total liabilities and proprietorship		$		*%

5.

SIMS UPHOLSTERY SHOP

Comparative Income Statements
for Fiscal Years Ending March 31, 19X2 and 19X1

	19X2	19X1	INCREASE OR (DECREASE)		PER CENT OF NET SALES	
			Amount	*Per Cent*	19X2	19X1
Income from sales:						
Net sales	$66,000	$60,000				
Cost of goods sold:						
Inventory, April 1	$24,000	$20,000				
Purchases	42,000	44,000				
Goods available for sale	$	$				
Inventory, March 31	21,000	24,000				
Cost of goods sold						
Gross margin	$	$				
Operating expenses:						
Salaries	$12,000	$10,000				
Occupancy	3,300	3,000				
Depreciation	400	600				
Insurance	300	500				
Other	500	900				
Total expenses						
Net income on operations	$	$				

6.

HAND-KRAFTED GIFTS, INC.

Comparative Income Statements
for Fiscal Years Ending September 30, 19X1 and 19X0

	19X1	19X0	INCREASE OR (DECREASE)		PER CENT OF NET SALES	
			Amount	Per Cent	19X1	19X0
Income:						
Net sales	$108,000	$100,000				
Cost of goods:						
Inventory, October 1	$ 25,000	$ 20,000				
Purchases	58,000	75,000				
Goods available for sale	$	$				
Inventory, September 30	20,000	25,000				
Cost of goods sold	$	$				
Gross profit	$	$				
Expenses:						
Salaries	$ 17,000	$ 12,000				
Occupancy	5,400	3,000				
Promotion	2,400	2,000				
Depreciation	400	600				
Miscellaneous	1,800	400				
Total expenses						
Net profit on operations	$	$				

7.

ARDMORE WHOLESALERS, INC.
Comparative Balance Sheet, March 31, 19X2 and 19X1

	19X2	19X1	INCREASE OR (DECREASE)		PER CENT OF TOTAL ASSETS	
			Amount	Per Cent	19X2	19X1
Assets						
Cash	$ 40,000	$ 32,000				
Accounts receivable	60,000	48,000				
Inventory	180,000	200,000				
Current assets	$	$				
Fixed assets (net)	120,000	100,000				
Total assets	$	$				
Liabilities and Owner's Equity						
Current liabilities	$ 80,000	$ 70,000				
Fixed liabilities	140,000	170,000				
Total liabilities	$	$				
J. D. Ardmore, equity	180,000	140,000				
Total liabilities and owner's equity	$	$				

8.

MAYFIELD ROOFING CO.
Comparative Balance Sheet, June 30, 19X2 and 19X1

	19X2	19X1	INCREASE OR (DECREASE)		PER CENT OF TOTAL ASSETS	
			Amount	Per Cent	19X2	19X1
Assets						
Cash	$ 22,000	$ 15,000				
Accounts receivable	60,000	50,000				
Inventory	68,000	80,000				
Current assets	$	$				
Fixed assets (net)	125,000	105,000				
Total assets	$	$				
Liabilities and Net Worth						
Current liabilities	$ 72,600	$ 75,000				
Fixed liabilities	81,400	80,000				
Total liabilities	$	$				
Common stock	$ 77,000	$ 70,000				
Retained earnings	44,000	25,000				
Total net worth						
Total liabilities and net worth	$	$				

9. Compute the following ratios or per cents, based on the balance sheet in Problem 3:

(a) Working capital ratio
(b) Acid-test ratio
(c) What per cent of total assets are current assets?
(d) What per cent of total assets are fixed assets?
(e) What per cent of total assets are the total liabilities?
(f) What per cent of total assets is the owners' equity?

10. Determine the ratios or per cents in Problem 9(a)–(f), based on the balance sheet in Problem 4.

11. Calculate the ratios or per cents requested below, which pertain to the 19X2 business year of Ardmore Wholesalers, Inc. Use the income statement in Problem 1 and the balance sheet in Problem 7.
(a) Working capital ratio
(b) Acid-test ratio
(c) Rate (per cent) of net income (after taxes) to average net worth

(d) Ratio of net sales to average total assets
(e) Accounts receivable turnover
(f) Average age of accounts receivable
(g) What per cent of net sales was the cost of goods?
(h) What per cent of net sales was the gross profit?
(i) What per cent of net sales were the operating expenses?
(j) What per cent of net sales was net profit (both before and after taxes)?
(k) What per cent of total assets were current assets?
(l) What per cent of total assets were fixed assets?
(m) What per cent of total assets were total liabilities?
(n) What per cent of total assets was total net worth?

12. Compute the ratios or per cents listed in Problem 11(a)–(n), concerning the fiscal year ending June 30, 19X2, of Mayfield Roofing Co. The figures needed to compute these ratios are found in Problems 2 and 8.

CHAPTER 10 *Glossary*

Accounts receivable (or payable). Money owed to a business (or owed by a business) for merchandise or services bought on credit.

Accounts receivable turnover. The ratio of net sales to average accounts receivable.

Accrued interest or taxes. Interest or taxes that must be paid within a short time; a current liability.

Acid-test ratio. Ratio of quick assets to current liabilities; the minimum acceptable ratio is 1 to 1.

Assets. Possessions owned by a business and money owed to it.

Average age of accounts receivable. In days: 365 divided by the accounts receivable turnover.

Balance sheet. A financial statement indicating how much a business is worth on a specific date: Assets = Liabilities + Net worth.

Current assets or liabilities. Assets or liabilities due or payable within a short time.

Fixed assets or liabilities. Long-term assets or

liabilities that will continue for more than 1 year.

Gross profit (margin or markup). Amount remaining when cost of merchandise is subtracted from sales income: $S - C = M$.

Horizontal analysis. Financial statement analysis where each item in one year is compared (amount and/or per cent) with that same item in the previous year.

Income statement. A financial statement showing a business' sales, expenses, and profit (or loss) during a specified time period: Sales − Cost of goods − Expenses = Net profit.

Liabilities. Money that a business owes to others.

Margin or markup. (See "Gross profit.")

Net income (or net profit). Amount remaining after both cost of goods and operating expenses are deducted from sales income.

Net income (after taxes) to average net worth. A business ratio that indicates the owners return on investment.

Net sales to average total assets. A ratio indicating whether sales volume is in line with the capital assets of a business.

Net worth (net ownership or net investment). Owners share of a firm's assets; amount remaining when liabilities are sub-

tracted from assets.

Operating expenses (or overhead). Business expenses other than the cost of materials or merchandise. (Examples: Salaries, occupancy expenses, advertising, office supplies, etc.)

Owners equity. (See "Net worth.")

Proprietorship. Net worth where one individual owns a business.

Quick (or liquid) assets. Assets that can easily and quickly be converted to cash; all current assets except inventory.

Retained earnings. That part of net profit that is kept for use in the business (rather than being distributed to the owners).

Stockholders' equity. Net worth owned by stockholders of a corporation.

Total capital turnover. (See "Net sales to average total assets").

Vertical analysis. Financial statement analysis (pertaining to one year only) where each item is compared to one significant figure on the statement (that is, as a per cent of net sales on the income statement or a per cent of total assets on the balance sheet).

Working capital (or current) ratio. Ratio of current assets to current liabilities; the minimum acceptable ratio is 2 to 1.

CHAPTER 11

Distribution
of
Profit and Loss

CHAPTER 11 OBJECTIVES

Upon completion of Chapter 11, the student will be able to:

1. Define and use correctly the terminology associated with each topic.

2. Compute the dividend to be paid per share of common and preferred stock, given the total dividend declared and information about the number and types of stock. (*Section 1; Examples 1–3; Problems 1–12*)

3. Distribute profits (or losses) to the members of a partnership, given the total profit (or loss) and information about each partner's investment. Distributions will be according to (*Section 2*)
   a. Agreed ratios (*Examples 1–3, 5; Problems 1–12*);
   b. Salaries (*Examples 5, 6; Problems 1, 2, 11, 12, 17–20*);
   c. Interest on investments (*Example 6; Problems 1, 2, 15–20*);
   d. Average investments per month (*Example 4; Problems 13–16*); and
   e. Combinations of these methods
      (*Examples 5, 6; Problems 1, 2, 11, 12, 15–20*).

Within our system of free enterprise, businesses are operated for the ultimate purpose of making a profit. After the amount of net profit (or loss) of a business has been determined, it is necessary to apportion that amount among the owners. Methods of distribution depend largely upon the type of business. In general, there are three categories of private business organization: *sole proprietorship*, *partnership*, and *corporation*.

Sole Proprietorship

Sole **proprietorship** is the simplest form of business. A single person makes the initial investment and bears the entire responsibility for the business. If a profit is earned, the entire profit belongs to the individual owner. By the same token, the sole proprietor must assume full responsibility for any loss incurred. (One principal disadvantage of this form of business is that the owner's liability extends even to personal possessions not used in business; for instance, the proprietor's home might have to be sold to discharge business debts.)

Sole proprietorships are usually small businesses, since they are limited to the resources of one person. There often is no formal organization or operating procedure; an individual with sufficient skill or financial resources simply goes into business by making services available to potential clients.

Since all profit (or loss) resulting from a sole proprietorship belongs to the individual owner, there is no mathematical distribution required. Hence, the problems in this section will be limited to those concerning partnerships and corporations.

Partnerships

A **partnership** is an organization in which two or more persons engage in business as co-owners. A partnership may provide the advantages of increased investments and more diversified skills, as well as more manpower available to operate the business. (For example, partners A, B, and C might form a partnership because A had the funds to start the business, B had the skill and experience required to manufacture their product, and C was an expert in salesmanship and marketing. Thus, by pooling their resources, both financial and personal, a profitable business can be formed; however, none of the partners could have established a profitable business independently.) Partnerships often include a **silent partner**—one who takes no active part in the business operations, whose contribution to the partnership is entirely financial, and whose very existence as a partner may not be known outside the business.

A partnership may be entered into simply by mutual consent. To avoid misunderstanding and disagreement, however, all partners should sign a legal agreement (called *articles of copartnership*) setting forth the responsibilities, restrictions, procedures, method of distribution of profits and losses, etc., of the partnership. (For instance, the abrupt withdrawal of a partner, if not prohibited by written agreement, might place the entire partnership in bankruptcy.)

Taking into consideration the contribution made by each partner, a partnership is permitted to distribute profits or losses in any way that is acceptable to the partners involved. In the absence of any formal written agreement, the law would require that profits be shared equally among the partners. Despite whatever agreement the partners may have among themselves, however, in most states the partners are responsible jointly and separately for the liabilities of the partnership. This means that if the personal resources of the partners together (jointly), when calculated according to their terms of agreement, are not sufficient to meet the partnership's liabilities, then a single partner with more personal wealth will have to bear the liabilities of the partnership individually (separately). Also, a business commitment made by any partner, even if it is not within that person's agreed area of responsibility, is legally binding upon the entire partnership.

A partnership is automatically dissolved whenever there is any change in the partners involved, such as when a partner withdraws from the business, sells to another person, or dies, or when an additional person enters the partnership. However, a new partnership may be created immediately to reflect the change, without any lapse in business operations.

Corporations
The **corporation** is the most complex form of business. It is considered to be an artificial person, created according to state laws. Its capital is derived from the sale of

stock certificates, which are certificates of ownership in the business. A person's ownership in a corporation is measured according to the number of shares of stock which (s)he owns. Figure 26 illustrates a stock certificate.

The corporation offers a distinct advantage over both the sole proprietorship and the partnership in that its liability extends only to the amount invested in the business by the stockholders. That is, the personal property of the owners (**stockholders**) may not be confiscated to meet business liabilities. (It should be noted that even small businesses may be incorporated in order to provide this protection. However, the ethics of certain professions—legal, medical, accounting, and others—permit only partnerships, not corporations.) The corporation also differs from the sole proprietorship and the partnership in that the firm must pay income taxes on its net operating income.

When a corporation is formed, it receives a *charter* from the state,

FIGURE 26: *Specimen Stock Certificate*

authorizing the operation of business, defining the privileges and restrictions of the firm, and specifying the number of shares and type of stock which may be issued. The stockholders elect a **board of directors,** which selects the *administrative officers* of the corporation. Although it is ultimately responsible to the stockholders, the board actually makes decisions regarding policy and the direction which the business will take, and the officers are responsible for carrying out the board's decisions. The board of directors also makes the decision to distribute profits to the stockholders; the income declared on each share of stock is called a **dividend.**

When a corporation issues stock, the certificates may be assigned some value, called the **par** or **face value.** The par value may be set at any amount, although it is typically some round number. Stock is usually sold at par value when a corporation is first organized. After the firm has been in operation for some time, the *market value* (the amount for which stockholders would be willing to sell their stock) will increase or decrease, depending upon the prosperity of the business, and the par value becomes insignificant. Thus, stock is often issued without any face value, in which case it is known as **non-par-value** or **no-par-value stock.**

There are two main categories of stock: *common stock* and *preferred stock.* Since there are fewer methods for distributing profits to stockholders than to partners, we shall consider first the distribution of corporate profits.

SECTION 1

Distribution of Profits in a Corporation

Common Stock

Common stock carries no guaranteed benefits in case a profit is made or the corporation is dissolved. It does entitle its owner to one vote in a stockholders meeting for each share (s)he owns. Many corporations issue only common stock. In this case, distributing the profits is simply a matter of dividing the profit to be distributed by the **outstanding stock** (the number of shares of stock which have been issued).

Example One

The board of directors of the Wymore Corp. authorized $258,000 of the net profit to be distributed among their stockholders. If the corporation has issued 100,000 shares of common stock, what is the dividend per share?

$$\frac{\text{Total dividend}}{\text{Number of shares}} = \frac{\$258,000}{100,000} = \$2.58 \text{ per share}$$

A dividend of $2.58 per share of common stock will be declared.

Preferred Stock   The charters of many corporations also authorize the issuance of **preferred stock.** This stock has certain advantages over common stock; most notably, preferred stock carries the provision that dividends of a specified per cent of par value (or of a specified amount per share, on non-par-value stock) must be paid to preferred stockholders before any dividend is paid to common stockholders. For example, a share of 6%, $100 par-value stock would be expected to pay a $6 dividend each year (usually as quarterly payments of $1.50 each).

Also, in the event that the corporation is dissolved, the corporation's assets may first have to be applied toward refunding the par value of preferred stock, before any compensation is returned to common stockholders. Holders of preferred stock usually do not have a vote in the stockholders' meeting. Also, most preferred stock is **nonparticipating,** which means it cannot earn dividends above the specified rate. (However, some preferred stock is **participating,** which permits dividends above the stated per cent when sufficient profits exist. Participating stock is frequently restricted so that additional earnings above the specified rate are permitted only after the common stockholders have received a dividend equal to the special preferred dividend.)

Even when a net profit exists, a board of directors may not think it advisable to declare a dividend. Thus, the owners of a corporation may receive no income on their investment during some years. **Cumulative preferred stock** provides an exception to this situation, however. As the name implies, unpaid dividends accumulate; that is, dividends due from previous years, when no dividend was declared, must first be paid to owners of cumulative preferred stock before any dividends are paid to other stockholders.

As an alternative to paying cash dividends, boards of directors often declare *stock dividends*, where each stockholder receives an additional share for each specified number of shares already owned. The stockholders thus obtain an increased investment but do not have to pay income taxes as they would on cash dividends. When a stock dividend is declared, the dividend for many stockholders would include a fractional share. Thus, the board assigns a value to each whole share (often slightly less than market value) and either pays the stockholder this value for any fractional share or else allows the stockholder to purchase the remaining portion of another whole share.

Example Two   Artcraft Sales, Inc., has 1,000 shares of 5%, $100 par-value preferred stock outstanding and 10,000 shares of common stock. The board declared a $50,000 dividend. What dividends will be paid on (a) the preferred stock and (b) the common stock?

Solution (a) Dividends on preferred stock are always computed first, as follows:

$$\text{Total preferred dividend} = \underbrace{\% \times \text{Par value}}_{} \times \left(\begin{array}{c}\text{Number of} \\ \text{preferred shares}\end{array}\right)$$

$$= \left(\begin{array}{c}\text{Dividend} \\ \text{per share}\end{array}\right) \times \left(\begin{array}{c}\text{Number of} \\ \text{preferred shares}\end{array}\right)$$

$5\% \times \$100$ par value $= \$5$	Dividend on each share of preferred stock
$\$5$ per share $\times 1{,}000$ shares $= \$5{,}000$	Required to pay dividends on all preferred stock

(b)

$50,000	Total dividend
− 5,000	Dividend on all preferred stock
$45,000	Dividend allotted to common stock

$$\frac{\text{Total common stock dividend}}{\text{Number of common shares}} = \frac{\$45{,}000}{10{,}000} = \$4.50 \qquad \text{Dividend per share of common stock}$$

Hence, the preferred stockholders receive their full dividend of $5 per share; and a dividend of $4.50 per share will be paid to common stockholders.

Example Three No dividend was paid last year by McGill, Inc. A dividend of $325,000 has now been declared for the current year. Stockholders own 100,000 shares of common stock and 25,000 shares of 6%, $50 par-value cumulative preferred stock. How much dividend will be paid on each share of stock?

Dividends for 2 years must first be paid on the cumulative preferred stock.

$6\% \times \$50$ par value $=$	$3	Dividend per year on each share of cumulative preferred stock
	× 2	Years
	$6	Dividend due on each share of cumulative preferred stock

$6 per share $\times$ 25,000 shares = $150,000   Payable to
preferred stockholders

$325,000	Total dividend
$-$ 150,000	Dividend on preferred stock
$175,000	Total dividend on common stock

$$\frac{\$175,000}{100,000 \text{ shares}} = \$1.75$$ Dividend per share of common stock

Thus, a 2-year dividend of $6 per share will be paid to owners of the cumulative preferred stock, and $1.75 per share will go to the common stockholders.

SECTION 1 *Problems*

Determine the dividend that should be paid on each share of stock.

		Number of Shares	Type of Stock	Total Dividend Declared
1.	(a)	80,000	Common	$ 28,000
	(b)	10,000	Common	$ 60,000
		2,000	8%, $50 par-value preferred	
	(c)	400,000	Common	$380,000
		10,000	6%, $100 par-value preferred, cumulative for 3 years	
2.	(a)	40,000	Common	$130,000
	(b)	12,000	Common	$ 36,000
		2,000	6%, $50 par-value preferred	
	(c)	100,000	Common	$700,000
		5,000	7%, $200 par-value preferred, cumulative for 2 years	

3. The board of directors of Sigfield Corp. declared a $150,000 dividend. What is the dividend per share for their 60,000 shares of common stock?

4. Following a successful business year, the board of directors of Travis Manufacturing, Inc., declared a $360,000 dividend. The corporation has 80,000 shares of common stock outstanding. What is the dividend on each share?

5. There are 50,000 shares of common stock and 5,000 shares of 7%, $100 par-value preferred stock outstanding at Transit Freight. If the board declared a $410,000 dividend, how much will be paid on each share of stock?

6. Midland Distributors, Inc., has issued 100,000 shares of common stock and 15,000 shares of 8%, $50 par-value preferred stock. Determine the amount to be paid on each share, if the board voted a $350,000 dividend.

7. Golden West Sales, Inc., approved a $160,000 dividend. Determine the dividend per share for their 150,000 outstanding shares of non-par-value common stock and 20,000 shares of 5%, $100 par-value preferred stock.

8. Collier-Clark, Inc., has 45,000 outstanding shares of common stock and 6,000 shares of 7%, $50 par-value preferred stock. The board voted to pay $174,000 in dividends to all stockholders of record. What dividend will each share earn?

9. Due to the costs of plant expansion, Lyttaker Corp. declared no dividend during the past 2 years. This year a $53,000 dividend was declared. Compute the dividend payable on each share of the 80,000 shares of common stock and 5,000 shares of 6%, $10 par-value cumulative preferred stock.

10. The Winfield Corp. has 40,000 shares of common stock outstanding and 7,500 shares of 5%, $100 par-value cumulative preferred stock. No dividend was declared during the past year. This year the board approved a $225,000 dividend. Compute the earnings for each share of stock.

11. A decline in sales resulted in no dividend being declared last year by Macomb, Inc. This year, however, a $46,000 dividend was declared. What dividend per share will be paid on each category of stock, if there are 10,000 shares of common stock and 1,000 shares of 8%, $100 par-value cumulative preferred stock?

12. In order to increase retained earnings, the board of directors of Barger Textiles, Inc., has not declared a dividend for the past 2 years. This year, however, the board has approved a $261,000 dividend. What dividend per share will be paid, if there are 50,000 shares of common stock and 4,500 shares of 6%, $100 par-value cumulative preferred stock?

SECTION 2
Distribution of Profits in a Partnership

There are numerous ways in which the profits or losses of a partnership may be divided. We shall consider some of the typical methods. Recall that profits and losses are shared equally among partners unless another specific agreement is made.

Example One

Equal Distribution

The partnership of Wynn, Bright & Phillips was organized without a formal agreement regarding the distribution of profits. A net profit of $39,000 was earned during the business year now ending. Their individual investments included $14,000 by Wynn, $8,000 by Bright, and $11,000 from Phillips. How much should each partner receive?

$$\frac{\$39,000}{3} = \$13,000 \text{ each}$$

Chapter 11: Distribution of Profit and Loss **303**

In the absence of a formal agreement, each partner would receive an equal distribution of $13,000.

Example Two

Agreed Ratio

After considering both the capital investment and the time devoted to the business by each partner in Example 1, partners Wynn (W), Bright (B), and Phillips (P) agreed to share profits (or losses) in the ratio 4:3:6. Divide their $39,000 profit.

The sum of $4+3+6 = 13$ indicates the profit will be divided into 13 shares; W will receive 4 of the 13 shares, B will receive 3 shares, and P will receive 6 shares. Thus, W receives $\frac{4}{13}$ of the profit, B gets $\frac{3}{13}$, and P earns $\frac{6}{13}$ of the profit.

$$\text{W:} \quad \tfrac{4}{13}(\$39,000) = \$12,000*$$
$$\text{B:} \quad \tfrac{3}{13}(\$39,000) = 9,000$$
$$\text{P:} \quad \tfrac{6}{13}(\$39,000) = \underline{18,000}$$
$$\text{Total profit} = \$39,000$$

Partner W will receive $12,000, B will receive $9,000, and P gets $18,000. Notice that the sum of all partners' shares equals the total profit of the partnership.

NOTE: Agreed distributions are also often expressed as per cents, such as a 30%/20%/50% distribution. The given per cents must total 100% of the profit, and finding each partner's share is simply a matter of calculating that given per cent of the total profit (or loss).

Example Three

Original Investment

Partners A and B opened a business with a $10,000 investment from A and an $8,000 investment by B. Partner B later invested another $6,000. Their partnership agreement stipulated that profits or losses would be divided according to the ratio of their original investments. What portion of a $7,200 profit would each partner receive?

$$\$10,000 + \$8,000 = \$18,000 \qquad \text{Total original investment}$$

$$\text{A had } \frac{\$10,000}{\$18,000} \quad \text{or} \quad \frac{5}{9} \text{ of the original investment}$$

$$\text{B had } \frac{\$8,000}{\$18,000} \quad \text{or} \quad \frac{4}{9} \text{ of the original investment}$$

*Students using machines may convert fractions to their decimal equivalents. However, nonterminating decimals must be carried out to at least as many significant digits as the net income (or loss) being distributed. For instance, the $\frac{4}{13}$ ratio must have five significant digits: $0.30769 \times \$39,000 = \$12,000$ to the nearest dollar.

Example Three *(cont.)*

Thus, A will receive $\frac{5}{9}$ of the profit and B receives the other $\frac{4}{9}$:

$$A: \quad \frac{5}{9}(\$7{,}200) = \quad \$4{,}000$$
$$B: \quad \frac{4}{9}(\$7{,}200) = + \ 3{,}200$$
$$\overline{\qquad\qquad\qquad \$7{,}200} \quad \text{Total profit}$$

A's share is $4,000 and B has earned $3,200.

Investment at Beginning of the Year

A variation of the foregoing "original-investment" distribution is to divide profits according to each partner's investment at the beginning of the year. Suppose that partners A and B (above) use this method during their second year of operations. Partner A still has $10,000 invested, while B's investment is now $8,000 + $6,000 = $14,000, giving a total investment by both partners of $24,000.

Therefore, following the second year of operations,

$$A \text{ would receive} \quad \frac{\$10{,}000}{\$24{,}000} \quad \text{or} \quad \frac{5}{12} \text{ of the profit}$$

$$B \text{ would receive} \quad \frac{\$14{,}000}{\$24{,}000} \quad \text{or} \quad \frac{7}{12} \text{ of the profit}$$

Example Four

Average Investment per Month

When partners C and D began operations on January 1, C had $4,000 invested, which did not change during the year. D had $5,800 invested on January 1; on May 1, he withdrew $200; and on August 1, he reinvested $800. If profits are to be shared according to each partner's average investment per month, how much of a $12,500 profit should each receive?

Partner C's average investment is $4,000, since his investment did not change during the year. D's average investment is computed as follows:

Date	Change	Amount of Investment		Months Invested		
January 1	—	$5,800	×	4	=	$23,200
May 1	−$200	5,600	×	3	=	16,800
August 1	+$800	6,400	×	+5	=	+ 32,000
				12		$72,000

$$\frac{\$72{,}000}{12} = \$6{,}000 \quad \text{Average investment per month}$$

$ 4,000	C's average investment
+ 6,000	D's average investment
$10,000	Total of average investments

Thus, C receives $\dfrac{\$4,000}{\$10,000}$ or $\dfrac{2}{5}$ of the profit. D's investment earns

$\dfrac{\$\ 6,000}{\$10,000}$ or $\dfrac{3}{5}$ of the profit.

$$
\begin{aligned}
\text{C:} \quad & \tfrac{2}{5}(\$12,500) = \$\ 5,000 \\
\text{D:} \quad & \tfrac{3}{5}(\$12,500) = \underline{\quad 7,500} \\
& \qquad\qquad\qquad \$12,500 \quad \text{Total profit}
\end{aligned}
$$

C earns $5,000 of the total profit and D receives $7,500.

Example Five

Salary and Agreed Ratio

Partners X, Y, and Z agreed to pay X a salary of $10,000, to pay Y a salary of $12,000, and to divide the remaining profit or loss in the ratio of $4:3:5$. If the partnership earned a $40,000 net profit, how much will each partner receive?

The salaries should be deducted first, and the remaining profit then divided into $4+3+5 = 12$ shares:

Salaries: $\$10,000 + \$12,000 = \$22,000$

$$
\begin{array}{rl}
\$40,000 & \text{Total net profit} \\
-\ \ 22,000 & \text{Salaries} \\
\hline
\$18,000 & \text{To be divided in the ratio } 4:3:5
\end{array}
$$

X receives $\tfrac{4}{12}$ or $\tfrac{1}{3}$ of the $18,000 $\tfrac{1}{3}(\$18,000) = \quad \$\ 6,000$

Y gets $\tfrac{3}{12}$ or $\tfrac{1}{4}$ of the $18,000 $\tfrac{1}{4}(\$18,000) = \quad\quad 4,500$

Z has earned $\tfrac{5}{12}$ of the $18,000 $\tfrac{5}{12}(\$18,000) = +\quad 7,500$

$$\qquad\qquad\qquad\qquad\qquad\qquad\qquad\qquad\qquad \$18,000$$

The total net profit is distributed as follows:

	X	Y	Z		*Check*
Salary	$10,000	$12,000	—	$16,000	X's share
Ratio	6,000	4,500	$7,500	16,500	Y's share
Total	$16,000	$16,500	$7,500	7,500	Z's share
				$40,000	Total net profit

Thus, X's share of the net profit is $16,000, Y earns $16,500, and Z receives $7,500.

Example Six

Interest on Investment, Salary, and Agreed Ratio

Partners R and S began operations with an investment of $15,000 by R (a silent partner) and $5,500 by S. They agreed to pay 8% interest on each partner's investment, to pay S a $10,000 salary, and to divide any remaining profit or loss equally. (a) Divide a profit of $18,640. (b) Distribute a $10,840 net profit.

(a) The various methods of distribution are computed in the same order in which the agreement is stated. The interest earned by each partner is thus

	R	S
Investment	$15,000	$5,500
Interest rate	×8%	×8%
Interest	$1,200	$440

The interest is deducted from the net profit and then the salary is paid:

INTEREST
$1,200
+   440
$1,640   Total interest

$18,640   Total profit
− 1,640   Interest
$17,000
− 10,000   Salary
$ 7,000   To be shared equally

$$\frac{\$7,000}{2} = \$3,500 \quad \text{Additional profit due each partner}$$

Each partner thus receives the following portion of the net profit:

	R	S		Check
Interest	$1,200	$ 440		$ 4,700 R's share
Salary	—	10,000		13,940 S's share
Ratio	3,500	3,500		$18,640 Total net profit
Total	$4,700	$13,940		

R receives $4,700 of the net profit, and S earns $13,940.

(b) The same interest and salary would be due each partner as computed in part (a). The remaining calculations would then be

$10,840   Total profit
− 1,640   Interest
$ 9,200
− 10,000   Salary
−$ 800   Shortage to be shared equally

The net profit of the partnership is $800 less than the interest and salary due. According to the terms of their agreement, this shortage will be shared equally by the partners. That is, $800 ÷ 2 or $400 of the amount due each partner will not be paid. Each partner's share is thus computed as follows:

	R	S	Check	
Interest	$1,200	$ 440	$ 800	R's share
Salary	—	10,000	10,040	S's share
	$1,200	$10,440	$10,840	Total profit
Ratio (shortage)	− 400	− 400		
Total	$ 800	$10,040		

SECTION 2 *Problems*

Divide the net profit among the partners according to the conditions given.

		Partners	Investment	Method of Distribution	Net Profit
1.	(a)	A	$ 4,000	Ratio of 5:3:4	$18,000
		B	9,000		
		C	7,000		
	(b)	D	$ 6,000	Ratio of their investments	$24,000
		E	10,000		
	(c)	F	$ 7,000	$5,000 salary to F;	$16,000
		G	8,000	$3,000 salary to G; and remainder divided equally	
	(d)	H	$ 6,000	7% interest on investment;	$14,330
		I	8,000	$4,000 salary to J; and	
		J	5,000	remainder in ratio 3:4:2	

		Partners	Investment	Method of Distribution	Net Profit
2.	(a)	Q	$ 7,500	Ratio of 3:4	$14,000
		R	6,000		
	(b)	S	$ 9,000	Ratio of their	$25,000
		T	15,000	investments	
		U	6,000		
	(c)	V	$ 8,000	8% interest on	$26,200
		W	12,500	investment and ratio	
		X	7,000	of 3:1:2	
	(d)	Y	$ 7,500	6% interest on investment;	$21,200
		Z	12,500	$8,000 salary to Y; and	
				the remainder 40%/60%	

3. P, Q, and R entered into a partnership without making any arrangement for the distribution of profits. P invested $5,000 as a silent partner. Q invested $3,000 and devoted his full time to the business. R invested $6,000 and worked half-time in the business. How much of a $13,500 net profit should each partner receive?

4. Partners L and M began operations without making specific arrangements regarding the distribution of profits or losses. L invested $7,000 and M contributed $5,000. L worked half-time in the business and M devoted three-fourths time. How much of their $15,000 net profit will go to each partner?

5. Partners A, B, C, and D agreed on a ratio of 3:4:5:4 to distribute profits or losses.

(a) Divide a net profit of $19,200.

(b) How much of a $9,600 loss must be assumed by each partner?

6. Partners G, H, and K formed a partnership and decided to divide profits or losses in the ratio of 5:3:7.

(a) Determine each partner's share of a $12,000 net profit.

(b) How much obligation must each partner assume for a $3,000 loss?

7. The partnership formed by X and L agreed to pay X an $8,000 salary, to pay L a $5,000 salary, and to divide any remaining profit 25%/75%. Distribute a profit of $19,000.

8. Partners I, O, and U began a business after deciding to pay $6,000 salaries to I and O, a $10,000 salary to U, and to distribute any remaining profits or losses 30%/20%/50%. What is each partner's share of a $30,000 net profit?

9. X and Y are partners. X's original investment was $5,000, and he later invested $3,000 more. Y invested $7,000 in the partnership. If their agreement was to distribute profits and losses according to the ratio of their original investments, how much of a $16,800 net profit should go to each partner?

10. When M and R formed a partnership, M invested $10,000. R invested $5,000 initially and several months later invested $3,000 more. Their partnership agreement stated that the net profit or loss would be divided according to the ratio of each partner's original investment. If the partnership earns $21,000, how much will each partner receive?

11. Partners X and Y (see Problem 9) amended their agreement so that during the second year their net profit was divided as follows: X would get a salary of $4,500, Y received a $6,500 salary, the remaining profit or loss was to be divided in the ratio of their investment at the beginning of the second year. How much of a $26,000 profit would each partner receive?

12. During the second year of M and R's business operations (see Problem 10), their profit distribution agreement was changed as follows: M would draw a $9,000 salary, R would receive an $11,500 salary, and the remaining profit or loss would be divided in the ratio of their investments at the beginning of the year. Disburse their second year's profit of $25,000.

13. S and T agreed to divide profits from their partnership according to their average investments. On January 1, S invested $5,000. On June 1, he withdrew $1,000. On September 1, he reinvested $550 and did not change his investment thereafter. T's original investment of $5,400 remained unchanged.

(a) What is S's average investment per month?
(b) What part does each partner get of their $15,000 profit?

14. Partners A and Z decided that profits from their business would be distributed according to their average investments per month. A's original investment of $10,000 remained unchanged during the year. Z had invested $5,000 on January 1. On April 1, she invested another $1,200. On

September 1, she deposited $300 more, and her investment then remained the same until the end of the year.

(a) Determine Z's average investment per month.
(b) Divide a net profit of $24,000 between A and Z.

15. P and T are partners. P had $6,000 invested and did not change his investment. On January 1, T had $5,100 invested; on May 1, he withdrew $600; and on October 1, he reinvested $1,200.

(a) What was T's average investment?
(b) P and T agreed to distribute profits by paying 6% interest on their average investments and dividing the remaining profit or loss equally. What is each partner's share of a $17,660 net profit?

16. Q and T are partners. Q's investment of $9,000 did not change during the year. T had $8,500 invested on January 1. On March 1, he withdrew $700. On September 1, he reinvested $250, after which his investment did not change again.

(a) What average investment per month did T maintain?
(b) The partnership agreement stipulates that each partner will receive 9% interest on his average investment and that the remaining profit or loss will be shared equally. How much will each partner receive if a net profit of $18,730 was earned for the year?

17. T and V are partners, T having invested $6,000 and V having $8,000 invested. They agreed to pay 7% interest on investment, to pay T a salary of $7,500, and to divide the remaining profit or loss equally.

(a) Divide a net profit of $16,480.

(b) What would be each partner's share of an $8,240 profit?

18. The partnership of N and P was formed with a $6,500 investment by N and an $8,500 investment by P. The terms of their agreement are that each will receive 6% interest on investment, P will be paid a $9,600 salary, and the remaining profit or loss will be shared equally.

(a) What is each partner's share of an $18,500 net profit?
(b) Distribute a $10,000 profit.

19. H and J are partners. H invested $7,200 and J invested $8,400. They agreed to pay 5% interest on investment, to pay H a salary of $4,000 and J a salary of

$5,000, and to distribute the remaining profit or loss in the ratio 3:4.

(a) Divide a net profit of $13,280.
(b) What is each partner's share of an $8,380 net profit?

20. V invested $15,000 and W added $14,500 to fund their partnership venture. By their agreement, each would receive 8% interest on investment, salaries of $7,500 to V and $9,000 to W would be paid, and the remaining profit or loss would be divided in the ratio of 3:2.

(a) Compute each partner's share of a $21,360 profit.
(b) How much would V and W each receive from a $17,860 profit?

CHAPTER 11 *Glossary*

Board of directors. Officials elected by stockholders to set policy and decide direction of a corporation, including determining whether/when dividends will be paid.
Common stock. A share of corporation ownership that includes no guarantee about size of dividend.
Corporation. A business established as an artificial person according to state law and owned by stockholders, whose liability for the business is limited to the amount invested in the stock.
Cumulative preferred stock. Preferred stock which guarantees that dividends unpaid in any year(s) will accumulate and will all be paid the next time a dividend is declared.
Dividend. The return on owner's investment (cash or additional stock) paid per share of stock in a corporation.
Nonparticipating stock. Preferred stock which stipulates that dividends will not exceed the specified rate.

Non-par-value stock. Stock issued without a par (face) value printed on it.
Outstanding stock. The number of shares of stock that a corporation has sold.
Participating stock. Preferred stock that may earn dividends above the specified rate.
Partnership. A business for which two or more individuals legally are jointly and separately liable, although responsibilities and profits may be divided in any way that is mutually agreeable.
Par (or face) value. A value assigned to and printed on a share of stock when a corporation is organized (or when it issues new stock at a later time).
Preferred stock. Stock for which the dividend is preset as a certain per cent of the par value, and on which dividends must be paid before dividends are paid on common stock.
Proprietorship. A business having a single (sole) owner who is also personally liable for the business' debts.

Silent partner. A member of a partnership who invests financially but takes no active part in a business.

Stock certificate. A certificate of ownership in a corporation; classified as either common or preferred stock.

Stockholder. A person who owns stock (and thus owns a portion of a corporation).

PART

Retail Mathematics

CHAPTER 12

Commercial

Discounts

CHAPTER 12 OBJECTIVES

Upon completion of Chapter 12, the student will be able to:

1. Define and use correctly the terminology associated with each topic.

2. When a series of trade discount per cents are given
   (*Section 1; Problems 1, 2*)
   a. Find net cost rate factor (*Examples 2, 5; Problems 7, 8*); and
   b. Use it to compute
      (1) Net cost (*Examples 2, 3*); and
      (2) Single equivalent discount per cent
      (*Examples 4, 5; Problems 7–10, 15–22*)

3. Using the trade discount formula "% Paid × List = Net" and given two of
   the following amounts, find the unknown
   a. Net cost (*Examples 1–3; Problems 1–10*);
   b. List price (*Example 5; Problems 11–14*); or
   c. Discount per cent (*Examples 6, 7; Problems 15–22*).

4. Use sales terms given on an invoice to determine
   a. Cash discount; and
   b. Net payment due. (*Section 2; Examples 1–4; Problems 1–12*)

5. Use sales terms and the formula "% Paid × List = Net" to find list price
   when net payment is given. (*Example 5; Problems 3, 4, 13, 14*)

12

A business that purchases merchandise that is then sold directly to the **consumer** (user) is known as a **retail** business or store. The retailer may have purchased this merchandise either from the manufacturer or from a **wholesaler** (a business that buys goods for distribution only to other businesses and does not sell to the general public). The purchasing, pricing, and sale of merchandise in a retail store requires a certain kind of mathematics, which is the subject of this unit.

Competition for the customer has led to a widespread use of discounts, both in wholesale and retail sales. The following sections examine two of these commercial discounts—*trade discounts* and *cash discounts.*

SECTION 1
Trade Discounts

Manufacturers and wholesalers usually issue catalogs to be used by retailers. These catalogs are often quite bulky, containing photographs, diagrams and/or descriptions of all items sold by the company. As would be expected, the prices of items shown in the catalogs are subject to change periodically. To reprint an entire catalog each time there is a price change would be unduly expensive; thus, several methods have been developed whereby a business can keep the customer informed of current prices without having to reprint the entire catalog.

Some catalogs are issued in looseleaf binders, and new pages are printed to replace only those pages where a price change has occurred. Other catalogs contain no prices at all; instead, a separate price list, which is revised periodically, accompanies the catalog.

We shall be concerned in this course with a third type of catalog. The prices shown in this catalog are the **list prices** or **suggested retail prices,** usually the prices which the consumer pays for the goods. The retailer buys these goods at a reduction of a certain percentage off the catalog price. This reduction is known as a **trade discount.** The actual cost to the retailer, after the trade discount has been subtracted, is the retailer's **net cost** or **net price** of the item. The per cents of discount that are to be allowed (which may vary from item to item in the catalog) may be printed on a discount sheet which supplements the catalog, or they may be quoted directly to a company placing a special order.

It should be noted that these discounts apply only to goods; the full amount must be paid for freight, telephone, or other charges.

Example One

A tape recorder/radio is shown at a catalog list price of $60. The discount sheet indicates a 25% trade discount is to be allowed. What is the net price to the retail store?

(a)

List price	$60
Less trade discount (25% × $60)	− 15
Net price	$45

Observe that when a 25% reduction is allowed, this means that the retailer still pays the other 75% of the list price. Indeed, the per cent of discount subtracted from 100% (the whole list price) will always indicate what per cent of the list price is still being paid for the goods. For example,

$$10\% \text{ discount means} \quad 100\% - 10\% = 90\% \text{ paid}$$

$$35\% \text{ discount means} \quad 100\% - 35\% = 65\% \text{ paid}$$

$$18\% \text{ discount means} \quad 100\% - 18\% = 82\% \text{ paid}$$

The **complement** of any given per cent (or of its decimal or fractional equivalent) is some number such that their sum equals a whole, or 100%. Each "per cent paid" above is thus the complement of the corresponding discount per cent. By using the complement of the given discount, the previous problem can be solved by a shorter method, applying the formula %Paid × List = Net. (Keep in mind that per cents must be converted to their decimal or fractional equivalent before being used. Many problems can be worked more conveniently when per cents are changed to fractions.)

(b) A 25% discount on the tape recorder/radio above means that $100\% - 25\% = 75\%$ of the list price is still being paid. (The complement of 25% is 75%.)

USING DECIMALS	USING FRACTIONS
% Paid × List = Net	% Paid × List = Net
75% × $60 = Net	75% × $60 = Net
0.75 × 60 = Net	$\frac{3}{4}$ × 60 = Net
$45 = Net	$45 = Net

Two or more successive trade discounts are often quoted on the same goods; these multiple discounts are known as **series** or

chain discounts. If discounts of 25%, 20%, and 10% (often written 25/20/10) are offered, the net price may be found by calculating each discount in succession. (However, the order in which the discounts are taken does not affect the final result.)

Example Two

An upholstered chair is advertised at \$200 less 20%, 10%, and $12\frac{1}{2}\%$. Find the net cost to the furniture store.

(a)
List	\$200
Less 20%	$-\quad40$ (20% × \$200 = \$40)
	\$160
Less 10%	$-\quad16$ (10% × \$160 = \$16)
	\$144
Less $12\frac{1}{2}\%$	$-\quad18$ ($12\frac{1}{2}\%$ × \$144 = \$18)
Net cost	\$126

This net cost may be computed much more quickly using the method % Paid × List = Net.

(b) 20%, 10%, and 12.5% discounts have complements of 80%, 90%, and 87.5% paid:

$$(0.8)(0.9)(0.875)(\$200) = N$$

$$(0.63)200 = N$$

$$\$126 = N$$

The number that is the product of all the "per cents paid" is very significant and is called the **net cost rate factor.** As demonstrated above, the net cost rate factor is a number that can be multiplied times the list price to determine the net cost. All items subject to the same discounts have the same net cost rate factor. Thus, instead of reworking the entire problem for each item, the buyer determines the net cost rate factor that applies and then uses it to find the net price of all the items.

Example Three

A coffee table subject to the same discount rates given in Example 2 lists for \$80. What is the net cost?

Solution

From Example 2, the net cost rate factor = 0.63.

$$0.63 \times \$80 = \$50.40 \qquad \text{Net cost}$$

For purposes of cost comparison, it is often desirable to know what single discount rate is equivalent **(single equivalent discount)** to a series of discounts. This is also an application of the complement, found by subtracting the per cent paid (the net cost rate factor) from 100%, as follows.

Example Four

What single discount rate is equivalent to the series 20/10/12.5 offered in Example 2?

Solution

The net cost rate factor, 0.63, means that 63% of the list price was paid. Finding the complement indicates that

$$100\% - 63\% = 37\% \qquad \text{Single equivalent discount rate}$$

Observe that series discounts of 20%, 10%, and 12.5% are *not* the same as a single discount of 42.5%.

Example Five

Following trade discounts of 20% and 15%, a furnace cost a dealer $374. (a) What is the list price? (b) What is the net cost rate factor? (c) What single discount per cent is equivalent to discounts of 20% and 15%?

Solution

(a) $\quad \% \text{Pd} \times L = N$

$$(0.8)(0.85)L = 374$$

$$0.68L = 374$$

$$\frac{0.68L}{0.68} = \frac{374}{0.68}$$

$$L = \$550$$

(b) Net cost rate factor $= 0.68$

(c) The single discount equal to discounts of 20% and 15% is

$$100\% - 68\% = 32\%$$

Example Six

The suggested retail price of a television set is $400. If the net cost is $320, what single discount rate was offered?

$\% \text{Pd} \times L = N$

$x \cdot 400 = 320$

$\dfrac{400x}{400} = \dfrac{320}{400}$

OR

$x = \frac{4}{5}$

$x = 80\%$

But $x = \% \text{Pd}$. Thus, a 20% discount was given.

The price changed by $400 - \$320 = \$80$:

—% of Original = Change?

$x \cdot 400 = 80$

$\dfrac{400x}{400} = \dfrac{80}{400}$

$x = \frac{1}{5}$

$x = 20\%$ discount

Example Seven

A rifle lists for $80. The distributor had originally allowed a 15% discount. In order to meet his competitor's price of $61.20, the distributor later offered a second discount. Find the second discount per cent.

$$\% \, Pd \times L = N$$

$$(0.85)(x)(\$80) = \$61.20$$

$$68x = 61.20$$

$$x = 0.9$$

But x represents 90% paid. The additional discount is thus the complement, or $100\% - 90\% = 10\%$ additional discount.

SECTION 1 *Problems*

Complete the following.

		Trade Discounts	% Paid (or Net Cost Rate Factor)	List Price	Net Cost	Single Equivalent Discount %
1.	(a)	20%		$15		X
	(b)	15%		40		X
	(c)	30%			$ 31.50	X
	(d)		76%		38.00	X
	(e)	25%, 20%		55		
	(f)	$14\frac{2}{7}$, $33\frac{1}{3}$%		35		
	(g)	40%, 15%			43.35	
	(h)	20%, 15%, 10%			91.80	
2.	(a)	40%		$65		X
	(b)	25%		48		X
	(c)	15%			$102.00	X
	(d)		65%		39.00	X
	(e)	20%, 5%		50		
	(f)	$22\frac{2}{9}$, $28\frac{4}{7}$%		45		
	(g)	30%, 10%			50.40	
	(h)	25%, 20%, 10%			81.00	

3. Determine net cost on the following items.
   (a) A pencil sharpener listed at \$9.60, less 20%.
   (b) A desk lamp listed at \$12.00, less 35%.
   (c) A typewriter table listed at \$27.00, less $33\frac{1}{3}$%.
   (d) A typewriter chair listed at \$36.00, less $16\frac{2}{3}$%.

4. Compute the net cost for the following items.
   (a) A desk set listed at \$20, less 15%.
   (b) A bookcase listed at \$75, less 28%.
   (c) A typewriter cover listed at \$3.20, less $37\frac{1}{2}$%.
   (d) A secretary's desk listed at \$140, less $14\frac{2}{7}$%.

5. Complete the invoice for the Carver Drapery Supply Co.

CARVER DRAPERY SUPPLY
P.O. Box 2160
Austin, Texas 78767

To: A-1 Blind & Drapery
1311 Woods Dr.
San Marcos, Tex. 78666

INVOICE NO.: 4387
DATE: July 8, 19XX

YOUR ORDER NO.	RECEIVED	SHIPPED	VIA	TERMS
1228	6/30/XX	7/7/XX	Truck	Net

QUANTITY	CAT NO.	DESCRIPTION	LIST	EXTENSION
10	D111	Single pull rods, black	\$ 7.50	
12	D121	Double pull rods, black	9.75	
6	R408	Roman shades, green/gold	32.50	
8	R418	Roman shades, brown/orange	B.O.*	
5 doz	S234	Boxes, drapery hooks	12.20 doz	
4 doz	P354	Tassel tie backs, gold	9.75 doz	
2 doz	X674	Metal holdbacks, brass	26.50 doz	
			Total list	
			Less 30% discount	
			Net	
			Freight	\$ 12.75
			Total	

---

*"B.O." indicates "Back Order" and means that, although the item listed is not currently in stock, the order will be held and the item will be shipped as soon as it becomes available.

6. Find the total cost of the following goods. All are subject to a 15% discount. Freight charges are \$4.75.

5 dozen aspirin at \$4.50 per dozen
3 dozen lozenges at \$4.20 per dozen
2 dozen boxes adhesive tape at \$4.80 per dozen
$\frac{1}{2}$ dozen elastic arch supports at \$1.50 each
3 sets aluminum crutches at \$10.00 each

7. Find (1) the net cost on each of the following items. Also, tell (2) the net cost rate factor and (3) the single equivalent discount rate.
(a) A pair of pliers listed for $2, less 20% and 25%.
(b) A handsaw listed for $10, less 20%, and $12\frac{1}{2}$%.
(c) A toolbox listed for $12, less 30%, 20%, and 5%.
(d) An electric drill listed for $30, less 20%, 10%, and 10%.

8. Determine (1) the net cost for each of the following items. Also, find (2) the net cost rate factor and (3) the single equivalent discount rate.
(a) A grass clipper listed for $15, less 20% and 10%.
(b) A lawn mower listed for $96, less $12\frac{1}{2}$% and $14\frac{2}{7}$%.
(c) An electric edger listed for $80, less 25%, 20%, and 5%.
(d) An evaporative cooler listed for $60, less 20%, 20%, and 5%.

9. Williams Company advertises discounts of 20/10/5. Young, Inc., offers 15% and 20%. Which company sells at the lower price? (HINT: Compare single equivalent discount rates.)

10. Mayfair Wholesalers offers trade discounts of 30% and 10%. Their chief competitor, Avery Distributing, Inc., advertises 20/15/5. Which firm offers the better discount?

11. The net price of an article is $18 after discounts of 20% and 10% have been allowed. What was the list price?

12. After discounts of 25% and 10%, the dealer's net cost for a wall clock was $27. Find the list price.

13. Find the list price of a garden rake if, after discounts of 30% and 20%, the net cost is $2.80.

14. Determine the suggested retail price of a framed mirror for which the net price was $16 after discounts of 20% and 20%.

15. What single discount per cent has been allowed if a garden tractor that lists for $84 is sold for $70?

16. The dealer's net cost was $72 on a chandelier that retails for $108. What single discount per cent had been allowed?

17. Jones Hardware Distributors have their best sprinklers listed at $15, less 20%. In order to reduce their net price to $10.20, what extra discount per cent must they now offer? What single discount rate would give the same net price?

18. Academy Wholesale Tools has been advertising bench saws for $200 less 40%. The saws are now available from their competitor for $114. What additional discount will Academy have to give in order to meet the competition's net price? What single discount would produce the same price?

19. Crown Jewelers have watches listed for $50 less 40% and 20%. The Jewel Box carries the same watches for $45 less $33\frac{1}{3}$%.
(a) What are the net prices offered by each company?
(b) What further discount per cent must The Jewel Box allow so that their net price will be the same as the Crown Jewelers?

20. Colony Business Supply has a stamp machine listed for $75 less 20% and 15%. ABC Office Products distributes the same machine for $80 less 25%.
(a) What net price does each company offer now?

(b) What additional discount will ABC Office Products have to allow in order to meet Colony's price?

21. Williams Company carries a yard furniture group at $30, less 20%. Young, Inc., advertises the same group for $36, less $33\frac{1}{3}$% and 10%.

(a) What are the net prices offered by each company?

(b) What is the additional discount rate that must be allowed by the higher

company in order to meet the competitor's price?

22. Warren Specialties carries a window cooler that wholesales for $300 less 25% and 20%. American A.C. Distributors offers the same unit for $250 less 20/15/10.

(a) Find the current net price of each wholesaler.

(b) What further discount rate must be offered by the higher company in order to meet the competitor's price?

SECTION 2
Cash Discounts

Merchants who sell goods on credit often offer the buyer a reduction on the amount due as an inducement to prompt payment. This reduction is known as a **cash discount.** The cash discount is a certain percentage of the price of the goods, but it may be deducted only if the account is paid within a stipulated time period. The invoice or the monthly statement contains **sales terms** which indicate the cash discount rate and allowable time period. There are several variations of the ordinary method, as described below.

Ordinary Dating

By the most common method, **ordinary dating,** the discount period begins with the date on the invoice. A typical example would be "Terms: 2/10, n/30." These sales terms are read "two ten, net thirty." This means a 2% discount may be taken if payment is made within 10 days from the invoice date; from the eleventh to thirtieth days, the net amount is due; after 30 days, the account is overdue and may be subject to interest charges. (If given sales terms do not specify the day by which the net amount must be paid, which is typical in several of the following methods, it is commonly assumed that the net amount is due within 30 days after the discount period began.)

Contrary to the way it sounds, "cash discount" does not generally refer to a discount allowed only for the payment of cash on the day of purchase. On the other hand, cash discounts may be taken only on the net cost of goods, not on freight or other charges.

*End-of-Month,
or Proximo*

Some monthly statements, sent out during the last week of a month, contain terms such as "1/10, E.O.M." This means the 1% discount may be taken if paid within 10 days following the "end of the month"; that is, if paid by the tenth of the coming month. Terms of "1/10, PROX." mean essentially the same thing, as "proximo" is a Latin word indicating the next month after the present. In actual practice, many businesses assume this to be the meaning of sales terms on a statement of account, even though the abbreviations E.O.M. or PROX. may not appear.

Example One Determine the amount due on the following statement of account.

STATEMENT

NAPIER FURNITURE DISTRIBUTORS
3608 Longworth Blvd.
Los Angeles, California 90069

Phone:
213-767-8445

Golden West Furniture Co.
Box 4018
Pasadena, California 90472

DATE: November 25, 19XX
TERMS: 3/10, E.O.M.

Date	Invoice No.	Charges	Credits	Balance
11/1				$545.50
11/8	5391	$239.20		784.70
11/12			$545.50	239.20
11/16	5437	137.35		376.55
11/20	5562	123.45		500.00
11/25	Less 20% and 10% trade discount		140.00	360.00
11/25	Total Ppd. Fgt.*	25.80		385.80

PAY LAST
AMOUNT IN
THIS COLUMN

*"Ppd. Fgt." indicates "prepaid freight."

The charges shown for merchandise are $239.20+$137.35+$123.45, or $500 list. This is reduced by the trade discounts allowed. If the bill is paid by December 10, the 3% cash discount may be taken on the $360 net cost of the merchandise. (If no trade discount were given, the cash discount would be computed on the full $500 cost of the merchandise.) Recall that the cash discount does not apply to the freight.

Net cost of goods	$360.00		Due on goods	$349.20
Less discount (3% × $360)	− 10.80		Freight	+ 25.80
Payment due on goods	$349.20		Total amount due	$375.00

Example
One
(cont.)

A check for $375 will be mailed with a notation or a voucher indicating that a $10.80 cash discount has been taken. The next statement will show a credit for the full $385.80. If the statement is paid December 11 or after, a check for the entire $385.80 must be sent.

Example
Two

Three invoices from L. R. Hinson & Co. are to be paid on May 15. Sales terms on these invoices are 4/15, 2/30, n/60. The invoices are dated April 8 for $93.00, April 23 for $112.50, and May 9 for $297.50. What total amount must be paid to retire the entire obligation?

AMOUNT DUE

No discount may be taken on the April 8 invoice, since it is over 30 days old: $ 93.00

The April 23 invoice is less than 30 days old, so a 2% discount may be taken:

$112.50
(2% × $112.50) −   2.25

110.25

The third invoice is less than 15 days old, so the full 4% discount may be taken:

$297.50
(4% × $297.50) − 11.90

+ 285.60

Total payment due $488.85

Receipt of Goods

Sales terms such as 3/10, R.O.G. (**receipt of goods**) indicate that the discount period begins on the day the merchandise arrives. These terms are used especially when the goods are likely to be in transit for a long while, such as a shipment by cross-country rail freight or by boat from a foreign country.

Postdating or
AS OF

Distributors may sometimes induce additional sales by guaranteeing that payment can be postponed without penalty. However, an invoice is dated and mailed on the same day as the order is shipped (which notifies the buyer that the order has been filled), and the distributor's ordinary sales terms (such as 2/10, 1/30, n/60) may already be printed on the invoice. Thus, another date must also be given to indicate how long the extended discount period applies, for example "Date: January 12 AS OF March

15." This **postdating** means that the buyer may wait until March 15 to start applying the given sales terms. (The 2% discount could be taken any time on or before March 25, and so on.)

Extra　　　　　　　　The **extra** method also allows payment to be post-
poned and the cash discount still be taken. For example, terms of 3/10–80X (or 3/10–80 extra, or 3/10–80 ex.) indicate the discount is permitted if paid within 10 days plus 80, or a total of 90 days from the date of the invoice.

Extended cash discount periods, as described in the previous two paragraphs, are particularly popular in the sale of seasonal goods, such as lawn mowers or Christmas decorations. With delayed payments possible, retailers are willing to place orders sooner. The distributor can then spread shipments to all retailers over a wider period of time, which is easier for the wholesaler. The retailer may also benefit, since in many cases the merchandise can be sold before the cash discount period expires.

**Example
Three**　　　An order arrived June 4. What is the last day on which a cash discount may be claimed, given the following conditions? (a) The invoice is dated April 27, with sales terms of 3/15, R.O.G. (b) The invoice is dated April 27 AS OF July 7, with sales terms of 3/15, n/30.

Solution　　(a) The cash discount may be taken through June 19 (or 15 days after June 4, when the goods were received).

(b) The last day for the discount will be July 22 (or 15 days after the July 7 postdate).

On occasion it may not be possible to pay an entire invoice during the discount period. Whatever payment is made, however, is considered to be the net payment due after the discount had been calculated on some part of the debt. That is, given a 3% cash discount, each 97¢ paid reduces the amount due by $1. These partial payment problems may be solved using the formula %Paid × List = Net (payment).

**Example
Four**　　An invoice dated August 3 for $450 has terms 3/20, n/60. What payment must the buyer make to reduce the obligation by $100, if paid by August 23?

Solution   The $100 portion of the account is subject to the 3% discount, as illustrated previously.

<table>
<tr><td></td><td></td><td></td><td>3% discount means
97% was paid:</td></tr>
<tr><td>Portion paid off</td><td>$100</td><td rowspan="3">OR</td><td>% Pd × L = N</td></tr>
<tr><td>Less (3% × $100)</td><td>− 3</td><td>0.97 × $100 = N</td></tr>
<tr><td>Net payment</td><td>$ 97</td><td>$97 = N</td></tr>
</table>

Thus, a payment of $97 will deduct $100 from the balance due. That is, by paying $97 of the $450 account, $450−$100 = $350 remains to be paid.

Example Five   Sales terms of 2/15, n/30 were given on an invoice for $380 dated February 12. If a $245 payment is made on February 27, by how much has the debt been reduced? What amount is still due?

Solution   A 2% discount means 98% was paid:

$$\% \text{ Pd} \times L = N$$

$$0.98L = \$245$$

$$L = \frac{245}{0.98}$$

$$L = \$250$$

Since $250 has been deducted from the debt by a $245 payment, $380−$250 = $130 remains to be paid.

Business firms ordinarily pay invoices on the last day a cash discount is allowed, or on the final due date if no cash discount is offered, in order to have the use of their money for the longest possible time. In some industries, early payment is encouraged by offering another discount, known as **anticipation,** which is deducted in addition to any cash discount available. Anticipation is computed at the annual rate of interest currently being offered by most financial institutions (approximately 8%) and for the number of days (over a denominator of 360) by which the payment is early (that is, for the time until the end of the cash discount period; or else the time until the final due date, if no cash discount is offered). If the seller offers cash discounts, the necessary anticipation agreement between buyer and seller will specify whether the anticipation is to be computed on

1. The full (net) invoice *before* a cash discount is taken, or

2. The adjusted invoice *after* a cash discount is deducted.

Anticipation is calculated exactly like bank discounts, which are the subject of Chapter 16; hence, no anticipation problems will be included here. It should be pointed out that cash discounts result in considerably larger deductions than does anticipation, since cash discount rates convert to much larger annual rates than do any annual rates offered for anticipation. (For example, given the sales terms 2/10, n/30, the 2% full discount corresponds to an equivalent annual rate of 36%.)

SECTION 2 *Problems*

Determine the amount due on each invoice if paid on the date indicated.

		Date of Invoice	Amount	Date Goods Received	Sales Terms	Date Paid
1.	(a)	June 16	$320	June 21	3/10, n/30	June 24
	(b)	July 19	650	July 28	2/15, n/30	Aug. 4
	(c)	Sept. 25	462.50	Oct. 3	2/15, 1/30, n/60	Oct. 9
	(d)	Feb. 25	538.42	Mar. 5	2/10, n/30, E.O.M.	Mar. 10
	(e)	Apr. 11	420.75	May 2	4/15, R.O.G.	May 15
	(f)	Jan. 20 AS OF Mar. 15	480	Mar. 6	3/15, 1/30, n/60	Mar. 30
	(g)	Aug. 10	725	Sept. 8	2/10–50X	Oct. 5
2.	(a)	Oct. 20	$580	Oct. 25	1/10, n/30	Oct. 29
	(b)	Mar. 28	450	Apr. 3	2/10, 1/30, n/45	Apr. 5
	(c)	Nov. 14	742.75	Nov. 30	4/15, 2/30, n/60	Jan. 2
	(d)	July 18	238.60	July 26	3/15, PROX	Aug.12
	(e)	Feb. 6	342.50	Mar. 23	4/10, R.O.G.	Apr. 1
	(f)	Sept. 27 AS OF Nov. 25	270	Nov. 16	2/15, 1/30, n/60	Dec. 20
	(g)	Apr. 15	375	June 22	2/10–80X	July 2

Find the following, if partial payment was made on each invoice within the discount period:

		Amount of Invoice	Sales Terms	Credit Toward Account	Net Payment Made	Amount Still Due
3.	(a)	$400	3/10, n/30	$250		
	(b)	670	2/10, n/30	335		
	(c)	800	4/10, n/20			$200
	(d)	765	2/10, n/30		$392	
	(e)	580	3/15, n/30		368.60	
4.	(a)	$500	2/10, n/30	$350		
	(b)	720	3/15, n/30	420		
	(c)	700	2/15, n/30			$150
	(d)	575	3/20, n/45		$339.50	
	(e)	630	3/10, n/30		271.60	

5. Trade discounts of $33\frac{1}{3}\%$ and 10% are to be allowed on the following items. The items were listed on an invoice dated September 24 and which contained terms 3/10, n/30. Find the amount due if paid on October 4. Prepaid freight and insurance totaled $5.45.

15 dozen packages drapery pins at $7.00 per dozen
15 dozen packages drapery hooks at $.40 each
150 yd drapery cord at $.25 per yd
200 yd pleating tape at $.30 per yd
10 dozen curtain rods at $.75 each

6. The following items were listed on an invoice dated August 24. The supplier offers trade discounts of 25% and 20%. Prepaid freight of $10.70 was included on the invoice, which contains sales terms of 2/15, n/30. Compute the remittance due on September 3.

2 dozen lantern batteries at $1.50 each
4 dozen replacement bulbs at $14.00 per dozen

17 camp lanterns at $4.00 each
6 dozen 150-watt floodlights at $2.50 each
5 fluorescent ceiling fixtures at $27

7. The Wilson Company decides to pay four invoices simultaneously on May 12. Each contains sales terms 3/15, 1/30, n/60. What amount does Wilson owe, if the invoices are dated March 20 for $225, April 15 for $170, April 21 for $405, and April 27 for $618?

8. Sales terms of 2/10, 1/30, n/45 were given on three invoices received from Gable Wholesale Distributors. The invoices total $267 on November 13, $457 on December 2, and $635 on December 6. If the invoices are all paid on December 16, how much is due?

9. Jones Furniture wants to reduce a $600 debt by $300. The charge was on an invoice dated June 17 and containing terms 2/10, R.O.G. The shipment arrived on June 21. How much must Jones remit on July 1 in order to receive the $300 credit?

10. Capital Plumbing Co. received an $820 invoice dated March 18 and containing sales terms of 3/15–45X. On May 10, Capital decided to pay enough to reduce the account by $400. What amount must be paid?

11. Wilson, Inc., owes Grant Distributors $1,200, according to Grant's August 26 statement with terms 2/10, 1/20, n/30, E.O.M.
(a) What must be the amount of Wilson's payment on September 10 in order to credit his account for two-thirds of his debt?
(b) If Wilson finds he can pay the remainder of the account on September 18, what will be his second payment?
(c) What will be the total he has paid to discharge his $1,200 debt?

12. An invoice dated Feb. 22 for $480 contains sales terms of 2/15, 1/30, PROX. On March 9, the buyer wishes to make a payment that will discharge half of her obligation.
(a) How much should be remitted on March 9?
(c) On March 18, the buyer is able to pay the remainder of the debt. How much is the second payment?
(c) What is the total amount that was paid to discharge this $480 account?

13. On March 3, Drexel Mills received a $735 partial payment from Jones Furniture Company. Drexel had sent an invoice for $1,500 on February 22, with temrs 2/10, n/30.
(a) How much credit on account will Jones Furniture receive for this partial payment?
(b) How much more does Jones owe Drexel?

14. R. T. Harris Interiors owes Scarborough Fair Imports $870, according to an invoice dated May 4 AS OF July 10, and bearing sales terms of 3/10, n/30.
(a) If Scarborough Fair receives Harris' July 18 check for $455.90, how much credit should be given to the Harris account?
(b) How much does Harris Interiors still owe?

CHAPTER 12 *Glossary*

Anticipation. A discount on the invoice cost of merchandise that is computed at a current annual interest rate, prorated for the period of time by which payment is early. Anticipation may be claimed in addition to a cash discount.

AS OF (or Postdating). A later date shown on an invoice, at which time the given sales terms may begin.

Cash discount. A discount given for early payment of an invoice or monthly statement.

Complement (of a %). 100% minus the given per cent; a per cent such that the sum of the two per cents equals 100%. (Their fractional or decimal equivalents are also complements.)

Consumer. An individual who buys a product for personal use.

End-of-month (E.O.M.). Sales terms that start at the beginning of the following month. (Same as "proximo" terms.)

Extra (–X). Sales terms in which the discount

period extends for a specified additional number of days. (Example: 2/10–50X indicates a total of 60 days.)

List price. A suggested retail price; price paid by the consumer.

Net cost. Total (invoice) cost after trade discounts and before cash discounts.

Net cost rate factor. Factor that multiplies times list price to produce net cost; the product of the "per cents paid" in a trade discount.

Ordinary sales terms. Sales terms where the cash discount period begins on the date shown on the invoice.

Postdated sales terms. (See "AS OF.")

Proximo (PROX.). (See "End-of-month.")

Receipt of goods (R.O.G.). Sales terms where the cash discount period begins on the day the merchandise arrives.

Retailer. A business that sells directly to consumers.

Sales terms. A code on an invoice or monthly statement which specifies the rate and the allowable time period for a cash discount, if offered.

Series (chain) discounts. Two or more trade discounts where each succeeding discount is applied to the balance remaining after the previous discount.

Single equivalent discount. One trade discount that produces the same net cost as does a group of series discounts.

Trade discount. A discount off the list (suggested retail) price of merchandise, given to obtain the wholesale price.

Wholesaler. A business that buys merchandise from the manufacturers and sells it to retail stores.

CHAPTER 13

Markup

CHAPTER 13 OBJECTIVES

Upon completing Chapter 13, the student will be able to:

1. Define and use correctly the terminology in each topic.

2. Given a percentage markup based on cost (C) or on selling price (S), use the formula "$C + M = S$" to find
   a. Selling price;
   b. Cost; and
   c. Dollar markup.
   [(C) *Section 1; Examples 1–4; Problems 1–16;*
   [(S) *Section 2: Examples 1–3; Problems 1–18*]

3. a. Determine per cent of markup based on cost using the formula "?% of $C = M$". [(C) *Section 1; Example 5; Problems 7, 8*]
   b. Similarly, compute per cent of markup based on selling price using the formula "?% of $S = M$". [(S) *Section 2; Example 5; Problems 1, 2, 7–14*].

4. a. Calculate selling price factor ($\overline{Spf}$)
   [(C) *Section 1; Example 6; Problems 5, 6, 9, 10*].
   b. Use "$\overline{Spf} \times C = S$" to find selling price or cost
   [(S) *Section 2; Example 3; Problems 3, 4, 7, 8, 13–16*].

5. Use "$C + M = S$," "%Pd $\times L = N$," and "__% $S = M$" to find
   a. Regular selling price;
   b. Reduced sale price;
   c. Per cent of sale or regular markup; and/or
   d. Net cost (when trade discounts are offered). (The order in which the formulas are used depends on which information is given and which must be computed.) (*Section 3; Examples 1–4; Problems 1–10*)

6. a. Find the selling price required on perishable items so that the goods expected to sell will provide the desired profit on the entire purchase (*Section 4; Example 1; Problems 1, 2, 5–10*).
   b. Similarly determine the regular selling price when some of the items will be sold at a given reduced price (*Example 2; Problems 3, 4, 11, 12*).

13   In accordance with the American economic philosophy, merchants offer their goods for sale with the intention of making a profit. If a profit is to be made, the merchandise must be marked high enough so that the cost of the goods and all selling expenses are recovered. On the other hand, a merchant cannot mark his goods so as to include an unreasonably high profit, or else he will not be able to meet his competition from other merchants in our free enterprise system. In order to stay within this acceptable range, therefore, it is important that business people have a thorough understanding of the factors involved and the methods used to determine the selling price of their merchandise. The first step in this direction should be to become familiar with the terms involved.

The actual *cost* of a piece of merchandise includes not only its catalog price but also insurance, freight, and any other charges incurred during the process of getting the merchandise to the store.

The difference between this cost and the selling price is known as **gross profit.** Other names for gross profit are **markup** and **margin.**

Gross profit is not all clear profit, however, for out of it must be paid business expenses, or **overhead.** Examples of overhead are salaries, rent, office equipment, lights and water, heat, advertising, taxes, insurance, and so on. Whatever remains after these expenses have been paid constitutes the clear or **net profit.** The net profit remaining is often quite small; indeed, expenses sometimes exceed the margin, in which case there is a loss.

Figure 27 illustrates the breakdown on selling price. Markup (or gross profit) may be computed as a percentage of cost, or it may be based on sales. But regardless of which method is used, the same relationship

	Selling Price	
Cost	Markup	
	Overhead	Net profit

FIGURE 27

between cost and markup always exists as shown in the diagram; specifically, Cost plus Markup (or margin or gross profit) always equals Selling price. From this relationship we obtain our fundamental selling price formula:

$$C + M = S$$

where $C = $ Cost, $M = $ Markup, and $S = $ Selling price.

Since the markup (or Margin) is composed of Overhead plus net profit, the same formula can be restated

$$C + (\overline{OH} + P) = S$$

where $\overline{OH} = $ overhead and $P = $ net profit.

SECTION 1
Markup Based
on Cost

Before attempting to calculate selling price, let us consider the following examples.

Example One

Suppose that a furniture store bought a lamp table for $50 and sold it for $70. Assume that the store's expenses (overhead) run 30% of cost. (a) How much margin (or markup or gross profit) did the store obtain? (b) What were the store's expenses related to this sale? (c) What amount of profit was made?

Solution   (a)

$$C + M = S$$
$$\$50 + M = \$70$$
$$M = \$20$$

The markup (or margin or gross profit) on the sale was $20.

(b) Overhead averages 30% of cost; thus,

$$30\% \times C = \overline{OH}$$
$$0.3(\$50) = \overline{OH}$$
$$\$15 = \overline{OH}$$

The furniture store's expenses for this sale were $15.

(c) Since the overhead plus net profit make up the margin, then

$$\overline{\text{OH}} + P = M$$
$$\$15 + P = \$20$$
$$P = \$5$$

A net profit of $5 was obtained on the lamp table. Using our previous diagram, the $70 selling price would be broken down as shown in Figure 28.

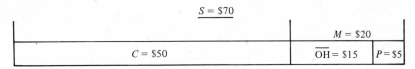

$S = \$70$

| $C = \$50$ | $M = \$20$ | |
| | $\overline{\text{OH}} = \$15$ | $P = \$5$ |

FIGURE 28

Example Two

The wholesale cost of a winter coat was $80. A clothing store sold the coat for $100. According to the store's last income statement, expenses have averaged 27% of sales income. (a) What was the markup on the coat? (b) How much overhead should be charged to this sale? (c) How much profit or loss was obtained on the coat?

Solution   (a)

$$C + M = S$$
$$\$80 + M = \$100$$
$$M = \$20$$

The selling price produced a markup of $20.

(b) The expected overhead was 27% of the selling price; thus,

$$27\% \, S = \overline{\text{OH}}$$
$$0.27(\$100) = \overline{\text{OH}}$$
$$\$27 = \overline{\text{OH}}$$

Business expenses related to this sale would be $27.

(c) One can immediately realize that, if expenses were $27 while only $20 was bought in by the sale, there was obviously a $7 loss on the transaction. This calculation is shown in the following series of equations.

$$\overline{OH} + P = M$$

$$\$27 + P = \$20$$

$$\$27 - \$27 + P = \$20 - \$27$$

$$P = -\$7$$

The calculation produces a negative difference, and a negative profit ($-\$7$) indicates a \$7 loss on the sale.

Example 2 illustrates a vital fact about selling—just because an item sells for more than it costs does not necessarily mean that any profit is made on the sale. Thus, it is essential that business people have the mathematical ability to take their expenses into consideration and price their merchandise to obtain the required markup.

Now let us consider some examples where the markup is based on cost.

**Example
Three**   A merchant has found that his expenses plus the net profit he wishes to make usually run $33\frac{1}{3}\%$ of the cost of his goods. For what price should he sell a dress that cost him \$36?

(a) We know that the markup equals $33\frac{1}{3}\%$ or $\frac{1}{3}$ of the cost. Since $\frac{1}{3}$ of $\$36 = \$12$, then

$$C + M = S$$

$$\$36 + \$12 = S$$

$$\$48 = S$$

(b) This same problem can be computed in another way. Since markup equals $\frac{1}{3}$ of the cost $(M = \frac{1}{3}C)$, by substitution

$$C + M = S$$

$$C + \tfrac{1}{3}C = S$$

$$\tfrac{4}{3}C = S$$

but since cost equals \$36,

$$\tfrac{4}{3}(\$36) = S$$

$$\$48 = S$$

It is customary in business to price merchandise as shown in Example 3(b), primarily because this is quicker than the method in Example 3(a), where markup was computed separately and then added to the cost (an extra step). In using method (b), the student should form the habit of combining the C's before substituting the dollar value of the cost. Another advantage of method (b) is that it allows one to find the cost when the selling price is known. The following example illustrates how cost is found (as well as why the C's should be combined before substituting for cost).

Example Four A home improvement center marks up its merchandise 30% of cost. (a) What would be the selling price of a screen door that cost $40? (b) What was the cost of a weed trimmer selling for $65?

Solution (a) Markup is 30% of cost, or $0.3C$.

$$C + M = S$$
$$C + 0.3C = S$$
$$1.3C = S$$
$$1.3(\$40) = S$$
$$\$52 = S$$

The door should sell for $52 in order to obtain a gross profit (markup) of 30% on cost.

(b)
$$C + M = S$$
$$C + 0.3C = S$$
$$1.3C = S$$
$$1.3C = \$65$$
$$C = \$50$$

The weed trimmer cost $50.

One can quickly see that markup based on cost is quite different from margin based on sales. For instance, suppose that an article cost $1.00 and sold for $1.50. The 50¢ markup is 50% of the cost but only $33\frac{1}{3}\%$ of the selling price.

A merchant may wish to know what margin based on sales is equivalent to his margin based on cost, or vice versa. To find the percent markup based on cost, he would use the formula

$$\underline{?}\% \text{ of } C = M$$

where C = cost and M = markup or margin. To determine the per cent of margin based on selling price, he would use the formula

$$\underline{\ ?\ }\% \text{ of } S = M$$

where S = selling price and M = markup.

Example Five

A circular saw cost $57 and required a $3 freight charge. It sold for $75. (a) What per cent markup on cost did this represent? (b) What was the per cent of margin based on selling price?

Solution

The actual cost of the saw was $57 + $3 = $60. The margin is then

$$C + M = S$$
$$\$60 + M = \$75$$
$$M = \$75 - \$60 = \$15$$

(a)
$$\underline{\quad}\% \, C = M$$
$$\underline{\quad}\% \times \$60 = \$15$$
$$60x = 15$$
$$x = \tfrac{1}{4} = 25\% \text{ markup, based on cost}$$

(b)
$$\underline{\quad}\% \, S = M$$
$$\underline{\quad}\% \times \$75 = \$15$$
$$75x = 15$$
$$x = \tfrac{1}{5} = 20\% \text{ markup, based on selling price}$$

To summarize, the $75 selling price is composed of a $60 cost plus a $15 markup. This $15 overhead can be expressed as a per cent either of the cost or of the selling price, as shown in Figure 29. Notice that,

FIGURE 29

for the given dollar markup, the per cent based on cost (25% C) is larger than the per cent based on selling price (20% S). This illustrates a general rule: The markup per cent is always larger when based on the cost than when based on the selling price. Figure 30 will help to visualize why: Since cost is smaller than selling price, the $15 represents a larger portion of the cost than it does of the selling price.

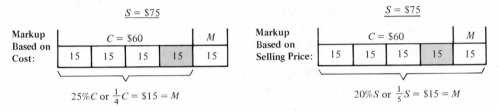

FIGURE 30

NOTE: In all cases where the same markup is used, the beginning calculations would be the same. Suppose that the markup is 25% of cost $(M = \frac{1}{4}C)$; then

$$C + M = S$$
$$C + \tfrac{1}{4}C = S$$
$$\tfrac{5}{4}C = S$$

When the margin is 25% of cost, the basic calculation would always yield $\frac{5}{4}C = S$. This $\frac{5}{4}$ is called the selling price factor. The **selling price factor** $(\overline{\text{Spf}})$ is a number that can be multiplied times the cost to obtain the selling price. This definition can be expressed by the formula

$$\overline{\text{Spf}} \times C = S$$

Thus, in actual practice, a retail store would not price each item by the complete process, starting with $C + M = S$. Rather, any store which uses a markup of 25% on cost would know that its selling price factor is $\frac{5}{4}$. (The selling price factor of $\frac{5}{4}$ could be expressed in any equivalent form: $1\frac{1}{4}$, 1.25, or 125%.) Hence, the store would eliminate the first steps of the markup formula and start with the selling price factor.

Example Six   Use $\mathrm{Spf} \times C = S$ to price an item that cost $24, if the markup is 25% on cost.

In order to price an item that cost $24, the store above would perform only the following calculation:

$$\overline{\mathrm{Spf} \times C = S}$$
$$\tfrac{5}{4}C = S$$
$$\tfrac{5}{4}(\$24) = S$$
$$\$30 = S$$

The item should sell for $30.

NOTE: After trying a few examples, the student will observe that, when markup is based on cost, the selling price factor can be found simply by adding "1" ("one") to the decimal or fractional equivalent of the markup. (This is *not* true when markup is a per cent of sales.)

A word to the wise: Don't forget that many per cents can be handled easier when converted to fractions instead of to decimals. If review is needed, refer to the table of Per Cent Equivalents of Common Fractions on page 58.

SECTION 1   *Problems*

Answer the following questions about each problem.

(1) *How much markup does each sale include?* (2) *How much are the overhead expenses?* (3) *Is a **profit** or loss made on the sale, and how much?*

		Cost	Selling Price	Overhead
1.	(a)	$40	$48	15% of cost
	(b)	25	28	20% of cost
	(c)	30	36	$11\tfrac{1}{9}$% of selling price
	(d)	10	12	25% of selling price
	(e)	65	72	$16\tfrac{2}{3}$ of selling price
2.	(a)	$16	$24	25% of cost
	(b)	20	25	35% of cost
	(c)	36	48	$12\tfrac{1}{2}$% of selling price
	(d)	25	30	20% of selling price
	(e)	28	35	$28\tfrac{4}{7}$% of selling price

Find the missing information. (Compute the selling price before finding the markup.)

		Per Cent Markup on Cost	Cost	Selling Price	Markup	Per Cent Markup on Selling Price
3.	(a)	50%	$18			
	(b)	20	45			
	(c)	$12\frac{1}{2}$	56			
	(d)	40 ⟶		$35		
	(e)	$22\frac{2}{9}$		55		
	(f)	28%⁄₇⁹⁰	63	81	18	
		25%				
	(g)		48	60	$12	20%
4.	(a)	25%	$32			
	(b)	60	45			
	(c)	$33\frac{1}{3}$	42			
	(d)	30		$91		
	(e)	$37\frac{1}{2}$		77		
	(f)		25	35		
	(g)			30	$ 9	

Handwritten notes at right:
$$\frac{markup}{cost} = \text{\% markup on cost}$$
$$C + M = S$$
$$C + .40C = 35$$

5. (a) If a markup of 35% on cost is used, what would be the selling price factor? 1.35

  (b) What would be the selling price of an article that cost $80? 80 × 1.35

  (c) How much gross profit would be made? 108 − 80 = 28

6. (a) What would be the selling price factor for a markup of 32% on cost?

  (b) What would be the selling price of an item costing $50?

  (c) What dollar markup does this yield?

7. Hosiery costs a department store $9 per dozen and sells for $1.00 a pair. N × 9 = 3

  (a) What per cent of cost is the margin?

  (b) What per cent of selling price is the margin? N × 12 = 3

8. Fiberglass hammers cost a hardware store $48 a dozen and sell for $6 each.

  (a) What per cent of cost is the markup?

  (b) What per cent of selling price is the markup?

9. (a) What selling price factor is equivalent to a margin of 40% on cost?

  (b) Determine what selling price should be marked on goods which have the following costs: $3.95, $7.90, $5.45, and $4.85.

  (c) What per cent markup on selling price does this correspond to?

10. (a) Find the selling price factor corresponding to a 20% markup on cost.

  (b) Price items which cost as follows: $3.50, $5.00, $7.75, and $4.45.

  (c) What per cent markup on selling price does this correspond to?

11. (a) Using a margin of 35% on cost, a store priced an article at $3.24. What was the cost of this item?

(b) A markup of $42\frac{6}{7}\%$ on cost was used to price an item that sold for $3.00. Find the cost of this item; and find what per cent markup on sales this represents.

12. (a) An item selling for $46.40 was marked to obtain a gross profit of 45% on cost. Find the cost of this item.

(b) After an article was marked up $16\frac{2}{3}\%$ on cost, it sold for $4.20. What was its cost; and what was the equivalent per cent markup on sales?

13. A lawnmower has a catalog list price of $60. The Discount Barn buys the mowers at a 40% discount.

(a) What is their per cent markup on cost, if they sell the mowers at a 25% discount off this list price?

(b) What per cent markup on sales does this represent?

14. The catalog list price of a metal stor-

age shed is $175. Miller's Discount Center buys the sheds at a 40% discount and sells them at a 20% discount off the list price. find

(a) The cost and the selling price.

(b) The per cent markup based on cost.

(c) The per cent markup based on selling price.

15. Freight and insurance on a shipment of 10 lamps was $8; the catalog price of the 10 lamps was $172.

(a) If the merchant is to make a gross profit of 25% on cost, what should be the selling price of each lamp?

(b) What would be the equivalent per cent markup on selling price?

16. A shipment of 8 barbeque grills cost $114. Freight on the shipment amounted to $6.

(a) At what price should each grill be marked in order to obtain a margin of 40% on cost?

(b) What per cent markup on selling price does this represent?

SECTION 2
Markup Based on Selling Price

Many business expenses are calculated as a per cent of net sales. For example, salesmen's commissions are based on their sales. Sales taxes, of course, are based on sales. When deciding how much to spend for advertising or research and development, a firm may designate a certain per cent of sales. Many companies take inventory at its sales value. The income statement, which is one of two key reports used to indicate the financial condition of a company, lists the firm's sales, all its expenses, and its net profit; each of these items is then computed as a per cent of net sales.

With so many other items calculated on the basis of sales, it is not surprising, then, that most businesses prefer to price their merchandise so that markup will be a certain per cent of the selling price. Markup based on sales also offers a merchant the added advantage of being able to refer to his daily cash register tape and immediately estimate his gross profit.

Example One Using a markup of 30% on sales, price an item that costs $42.

As before, we start with the equation $C + M = S$. We know that the markup equals 30% of sales, or $M = \frac{3}{10}S$. Thus, we substitute $\frac{3}{10}S$ for M in the formula $C + M = S$:

$$C + M = S$$
$$C + \tfrac{3}{10}S = S$$
$$C + \tfrac{3}{10}S - \tfrac{3}{10}S = S - \tfrac{3}{10}S$$
$$C = \tfrac{7}{10}S$$

It is essential that the student understand the preceding calculations. When $\frac{3}{10}S$ is substituted for M, there are then S's on both sides of the equation. When an equation contains the same variable on both sides of the equal signs, the variables cannot be combined directly. So, in order to combine the S's, "$\frac{3}{10}S$" must be subtracted from both sides of the equation. (When markup is based on selling price, it will always be necessary to subtract on both sides of the equation. This should be done before the actual dollar value is substituted for the cost.)

Now we are ready to find the selling price. The $42 is substituted for the cost C:

$$C = \tfrac{7}{10}S$$
$$\$42 = \tfrac{7}{10}S$$

In order to find S, we must eliminate the $\frac{7}{10}$. This is accomplished by multiplying both sides of the equation by the reciprocal, $\frac{10}{7}$:

$$\$42 = \tfrac{7}{10}S$$
$$\tfrac{10}{7}(\$42) = \tfrac{10}{7}(\tfrac{7}{10}S)$$
$$\$60 = S$$

Thus, the selling price is $60. (In this example, $\frac{10}{7}$ is the selling price factor, because $\frac{10}{7}$ multiplied times the cost, $42, produces the selling price, $60.) Notice that the $60 selling price, which includes a markup of $60 - \$42 = \$18$, meets the stated requirement that markup be 30% of sales, as illustrated in Figure 31 on page 346.

Sometimes it is more convenient to convert the markup per cent to a decimal than to a fraction. The following example illustrates such a problem.

FIGURE 31

Example Two

A department store prices its merchandise so as to obtain a gross profit of 24% of the selling price. What selling price will be shown on a redwood picnic table that cost $38?

Solution

The markup is to be 24% of sales ($M = 0.24S$). Recall that $S = 1S = 1.00S$; thus,

$$C + M = S$$
$$C + 0.24S = S$$
$$C + \cancel{0.24S} \cancel{- 0.24S} = S - 0.24S$$
$$C = 0.76S$$
$$\$38 = 0.76S$$
$$\frac{38}{0.76} = \frac{\cancel{0.76}S}{\cancel{0.76}}$$
$$\$50 = S$$

The table would sell for $50. The gross profit is $50 − $38 = $12, which is 24% of the $50 selling price, as required.

Note: The value of the selling price factor ($\overline{Spf}$) when markup is based on sales can be obtained as follows:

1. Compute the complement of the given markup; then

2. Find the reciprocal of that complement.

In Example 1, the given markup based on sales is $30\% S$ or $\frac{3}{10}S$. The complement is $\frac{7}{10}$; therefore, $\overline{Spf} = \frac{10}{7}$. Similarly in Example 2, the given markup is 24% of sales, or $0.24S$. The complement is 0.76; thus, the selling price factor would be the reciprocal of the complement, or $\overline{Spf} = \frac{1}{.76} = 1.3158$. (That is, $\overline{Spf} \times C = 1.3158 \times \$38 = \$50$, to the nearest cent.)

Example Three

A set of patio furniture sold for $120. The store's expenses run 19% of sales and net profit has been 6% of sales. (a) What was the cost of the set? (b) What per cent markup on cost does this represent?

Solution

(a) Recall that markup (gross profit) equals expenses plus net profit. Thus,

$$M = \overline{OH} + P$$
$$= 19\% S + 6\% S$$
$$M = 25\% S$$

Since $M = \frac{1}{4}S$, then

$$C + M = S$$
$$C + \frac{1}{4}S = S$$
$$C + \frac{1}{4}S - \frac{1}{4}S = S - \frac{1}{4}S$$
$$C = \frac{3}{4}S$$
$$= \frac{3}{4}(\$120)$$
$$C = \$90$$

The markup was $120 - $90 = $30. The selling price of $120 would then be broken down as shown in Figure 32.

$S = \$120$

$M = \$30$

$C = \$90$　　$\overline{OH}$　P

$P = 6\%S = 6\% \times \$120 = \$\ 7.20$
$\overline{OH} = 19\%S = 19\% \times \$120 = \ \ 22.80$
$M = \overline{OH} + P = \$30.00$

FIGURE 32

(b) Using the $90 cost and $30 markup, the markup per cent (based on cost) is

$$\_\_\% C = M$$
$$\_\_\% (\$90) = \$30$$
$$90x = 30$$
$$x = \frac{30}{90} = \frac{1}{3}$$
$$x = 33\frac{1}{3}\% \text{ markup on cost}$$

That is, $33\frac{1}{3}\% C = 33\frac{1}{3}\% \times \$90 = \$30$, which is the known markup.

Complete the following.

		Per Cent Markup on Selling Price	Cost	Selling Price	Markup	Per Cent Markup on Cost
1.	(a)	$33\frac{1}{3}$%	$18	27	9	
	(b)	$22\frac{2}{9}$	49			
	(c)	25		$52		
	(d)	$14\frac{2}{7}$		84		
	(e)		21		$9	
2.	(a)	20%	$32			
	(b)	$37\frac{1}{2}$	35			
	(c)	40		$90		
	(d)	$33\frac{1}{3}$		72		
	(e)		18		$18	

3. (a) What would be the selling price factor for a markup of $44\frac{4}{9}$% on selling price?

(b) Find the selling price of an item that cost $35.

(c) How much dollar markup does this yield?

4. (a) If a markup of $12\frac{1}{2}$% on sales is used, what would be the selling price factor?

(b) What would be the selling price of an article that cost $63?

(c) What gross profit would be made?

5. A margin of 45% on selling price resulted in a gross profit of $54.
(a) What was the selling price?
(b) What was the cost?

6. A gross profit of $24 is made on a sale. If the margin was 32% on selling price,
(a) What was the selling price?
(b) What was the cost?

7. (a) What selling price factor is equiv-

alent to a margin of $33\frac{1}{3}$% on sales?

(b) Determine the selling price of goods which cost as follows: $4.90, $7.50, $2.85, and $5.00.

(c) What per cent markup on cost does this correspond to?

8. (a) Find the selling price factor corresponding to a 25% markup on sales.

(b) Price items which cost $2.40, $6.00, $5.40, and $9.75.

(c) What per cent markup on cost does this represent?

9. The Chapeaux bought 250 spring hats at a total cost of $1,500. They sold 25 for $14 each, 50 for $11 each, 80 for $10 each, 75 for $8 each, and the remaining 20 were reduced and sold at $5 each.
(a) How much gross profit was made on the entire transaction?
(b) What was the per cent of margin based on cost?

(c) What per cent markup on selling price did they make?

10. The Mod Shop purchased 100 knit shirts at a total cost of $600. They sold 15 shirts for $12 each, 40 for $10 each, 25 for $8 each, and the remaining 20 in a special "at cost" promotion for $6 each.
(a) How much gross profit was made on the entire transaction?
(b) What per cent markup on cost was made?
(c) What per cent markup on selling price was made?

11. (a) Would 25% on cost or 25% on selling price yield a larger gross profit? (HINT: Compare selling price factors.)
(b) Which is better, 40% on cost or 30% on selling price?

12. (a) Which would give a better markup, $37\frac{1}{2}$% on cost or $37\frac{1}{2}$% on selling price?
(b) Which is better, 50% on cost or 40% on selling price?

13. Using a margin of $28\frac{4}{7}$% on sales, a company sold an item for $49. Find their
(a) Selling price factor.
(b) Cost.
(c) Corresponding per cent markup based on cost.

14. An item selling for $75 was priced using a markup of 20% of sales.
(a) What was the selling price factor?
(b) What was the cost of the item?
(c) What is the equivalent per cent markup on cost?

15. The Grande Shoppe requires a margin of $16\frac{2}{3}$% on sales.
(a) What is the most they could pay for some roll brim hats which will sell for $18?
(b) What is their selling price factor?

16. Crown Jewelers wishes to purchase some birthstone rings that can retail for $70. They must obtain a gross profit of 50% on sales.
(a) What is the largest wholesale price Crown can pay for the rings they buy?
(b) What is the firm's selling price factor?

17. The Old Gate Antiques figures its expenses to be 20% of sales and wants to make a net profit of $13\frac{1}{3}$% of sales. At what price should they sell a picture frame which cost them $40 less 30%?

18. Leather World paid $450 less 20% for a silver-trimmed saddle. Their last income statement showed expenses to be 16% of sales and their net profit to be 9% of sales. At what price should the saddle be sold?

SECTION 3

Markup Based on Selling Price (Continued)

Few, if any, retail merchants are able to sell their entire stock at its regular marked prices. Clearance sales and "store-wide discounts" are common. The following problems involve markup when merchandise is sold at a sale or discount price.

Both the **regular** and the **reduced prices** of merchandise are commonly known by several different terms that are used interchangeably, as follows:

Price Before Reduction	Price After Reduction
Regular marked price	Reduced price
Regular selling price	Sale price
Marked price	Actual selling price
List price	Net selling price (after trade discounts)

When $M = \_\_\%\,S$ is used for per cent of markup based on sales, S may represent either the regular or the reduced selling price, depending on the information given. Figure 33 shows the breakdown of selling price (S) both for a regular marked price (similar to previously given diagrams) and for a reduced sale price.

FIGURE 33

Example One

The regular marked price of a suitcase is $35, including a markup of 25% on *cost*. During a special sale, the case was reduced so that the store obtained a $12\frac{1}{2}\%$ markup on sales at the clearance sale price. What was (a) the cost and (b) the sale price?

Solution

(a) When $M = 25\%$ of cost,

$$C + M = S$$
$$C + \tfrac{1}{4}C = S$$
$$\tfrac{5}{4}C = S$$
$$\tfrac{5}{4}C = \$35$$
$$C = \$28$$

(b) When $M = \frac{1}{8}$ of sales, then

$$C + M = S$$
$$C + \tfrac{1}{8}S = S$$
$$C + \tfrac{1}{8}S - \tfrac{1}{8}S = S - \tfrac{1}{8}S$$
$$C = \tfrac{7}{8}S$$
$$\$28 = \tfrac{7}{8}S$$
$$\tfrac{8}{7}(28) = \tfrac{8}{7}(\tfrac{7}{8}S)$$
$$\$32 = S$$

The sale price was \$32, giving a margin of \$32 − \$28 = \$4. Notice that this \$4 markup is $12\frac{1}{2}\% \, S = 12\frac{1}{2}\% \times \$32$, as stipulated.

For situations in which a "sale" price is involved, the student may often find it helpful to think through the entire pricing process from the time an item enters the store until it is sold "on sale."

Example Two

A markup of 40% on the selling price was used to obtain the regular marked price of a suede jacket which had cost \$48. During an end-of-season clearance, the jacket was reduced by 25% off the marked price. (a) What was the regular marked price of the coat? (b) What was the sale price? (c) What per cent markup on sales was made at the clearance sale price?

Solution

(a) First, the jacket is priced using a markup of 40% on sales $(M = \frac{2}{5}S)$:

$$C + M = S$$
$$C + \tfrac{2}{5}S = S$$
$$C = S - \tfrac{2}{5}S$$
$$C = \tfrac{3}{5}S$$
$$\$48 = \tfrac{3}{5}S$$
$$\tfrac{5}{3}(48) = \tfrac{5}{3}(\tfrac{3}{5}S)$$
$$\$80 = S$$

The regular marked price (or regular selling price) of the jacket was \$80.

(b) Later this regular price was reduced: A 25% discount means 75% (or $\frac{3}{4}$) of the regular marked price (or list price) was paid:

$$\% \, \text{Pd} \times L = \text{Net sale price}$$
$$\tfrac{3}{4}(\$80) = N$$
$$\$60 = N$$

The clearance sale price of the jacket was $60.

(c) Before finding the per cent markup based on sales at the sale price, we must first determine the actual dollar markup at the sale price:

$$C + M = S \qquad\qquad \_\% \, S = M$$
$$M = S - C \qquad\qquad \_\% \, (\$60) = \$12$$
$$= \$60 - \$48 \qquad\qquad 60x = 12$$
$$M = \$12 \qquad\qquad x = \tfrac{12}{60} \;\; \text{or} \;\; \tfrac{1}{5}$$
$$x = 20\%$$

Thus, 20% of the sale price ($20\% \times \$60 = \$12$) was gross profit.

During a special promotion, Avery Jewelers marked a watch down 30%, selling it for $42. Even at this reduced sale price, Avery still made a gross profit (markup) of $14\tfrac{2}{7}\%$ on sales. What per cent markup on sales would Avery have made if the watch had sold at its regular marked price?

Before we can use the formula $\_\% \, S = M$ to determine (d) the per cent markup on sales at the regular price, we must first know M and S (at the regular marked price). Thus, we must first calculate (a) the cost and (b) the regular marked price. From these we can determine (c) the regular markup.

(a) At the clearance sale price of $42, the $M = \tfrac{1}{7}S$:

$$C + M = S$$
$$C + \tfrac{1}{7}S = S$$
$$C = S - \tfrac{1}{7}S$$
$$= \tfrac{6}{7}S$$
$$= \tfrac{6}{7}(\$42)$$
$$C = \$36$$

The watch cost the jeweler $36.

(b) The watch was reduced by 30% off the regular price to obtain the $42 sale price:

$$\% \,\mathrm{Pd} \times \mathrm{List} = \text{Net sale price}$$
$$0.7L = \$42$$
$$L = \frac{\$42}{0.7}$$
$$L = \$60$$

The regular marked price (or list price) was $60.

(c) Since the watch was regularly priced at $60, the regular markup was $60 - \$36 = \$24$.

(d) Thus

$$\underline{\quad}\% \, S = M$$
$$\underline{\quad}\% \, (\$60) = \$24$$
$$60x = 24$$
$$x = \tfrac{24}{60} \quad \text{or} \quad \tfrac{2}{5}$$
$$x = 40\%$$

The regular markup, based on sales, was 40% of the regular marked price ($40\% \, S = 40\% \times \$60 = \$24$). The regular price and the reduced (sale) prices are illustrated in Figure 34.

Many businesses deal in discounts every day. These merchants must price their goods very carefully, so they can allow the customer a "discount" off the marked price and still make their desired markup on the

FIGURE 34

sale. The discount price thus appears to be a "sale" price (and is computed similarly), although in reality this is the price at which the goods are always expected to sell; the business never expects to obtain the "regular marked price" for its merchandise.

Example Four

Caldwell Furniture paid a wholesale distributor $750 less 20% and 20% for a dining room suite. Caldwell must obtain a markup of $33\frac{1}{3}\%$ on their actual selling price. At what price must the dining room suite be marked so that Caldwell can allow 20% and 10% off this marked price and still make their $33\frac{1}{3}\%$ markup?

Solution

This solution involves three parts: (a) to find the cost; (b) to determine what the actual selling price (the apparent "sale" price) will be, and (c) to determine what "regular" marked price, less discounts of 20% and 10%, will leave the actual (net) selling price that Caldwell needs.

(a)
$$\% \text{Pd} \times L = \text{Net cost}$$
$$(0.8)(0.8)(\$750) = N$$
$$0.64(750) = N$$
$$\$480 = N$$

The dining room suite cost $480 after trade discounts.

(b) A $33\frac{1}{3}\%$ markup on sales ($M = \frac{1}{3}S$) is used to determine the actual selling price (which will later be made to appear as a "sale" price):

$$C + M = S$$
$$C + \tfrac{1}{3}S = S$$
$$C = S - \tfrac{1}{3}S$$
$$C = \tfrac{2}{3}S$$
$$\$480 = \tfrac{2}{3}S$$
$$\tfrac{3}{2}(480) = \tfrac{3}{2}(\tfrac{2}{3}S)$$
$$\$720 = S$$

Caldwell Furniture will actually sell the suite for $720.

(c) Finally, we compute a "regular" marked (or list) price which, after discounts of 20% and 10%, will leave the actual $720 net selling

Marked Price:

S = Marked price = $1,000

Cost	Markup
C = $480	$240

Markdown = 20% and 10%

Actual Price:

Actual $M = 33\frac{1}{3}\%S = \frac{1}{3} \times \$720 = \$240$

S = Actual price = $720

FIGURE 35

price (the apparent "sale" price):

$$\%\,Pd \times L = \text{Net selling price}$$
$$(0.8)(0.9)L = \$720$$
$$0.72L = \$720$$
$$L = \$1,000$$

The marked price on the dining room suite will be $1,000 (although Caldwell knows the suite will never be sold at that price). These marked and actual prices are illustrated in Figure 35.

SECTION 3 *Problems*

Compute the missing items in the following problems.

		Cost	Per Cent Regular Markup	Regular Price	Per Cent Discount	Sale Price	Per Cent Sale Markup
1.	(a)		25% of C	$90	X		10% of S
	(b)		35% of C	54	X		$16\frac{2}{3}\%$ of S
	(c)	$32	20% of S		10%		?% of S
	(d)	60	25% of S		20%		?% of S
	(e)		?% of S		20%	$32	$12\frac{1}{2}\%$ of S
	(f)		?% of S		25%	45	20% of S
	(g)	$400 less 30/10 = ?	X		20/10		30% of S
	(h)	$250 less 20/10 = ?	X		25/20		$33\frac{1}{3}\%$ of S

	Cost	Per Cent Regular Markup	Regular Price	Per Cent Discount	Sale Price	Per Cent Sale Markup
2. (a)		50% of C	$90	X		20% of S
(b)		30% of C	52	X		$11\frac{1}{9}$% of S
(c)	$45	40% of S		20%		?% of S
(d)	25	$37\frac{1}{2}$% of S		25%		?% of S
(e)		?% of S		10%	$54	$16\frac{2}{3}$% of S
(f)		?% of S		25%	90	$11\frac{1}{9}$% of S
(g)	$540 less 25/20 = ?	X		20/10		25% of S
(h)	$425 less 20/20 = ?	X		20/15		20% of S

3. The Style Shoppe sold coats for $49, representing a markup of 40% on cost. At a clearance sale, the coats are to be re-marked with a new price giving a margin of $12\frac{1}{2}$% on selling price.
(a) What did the coats cost? **35**
(b) What will be the sale price? **40**

4. The regular marked price of a wrench/tool set at The Tool Chest was $108, which included a markup of 35% on cost. During an anniversary sale, the set was reduced so that the sale price produced an $11\frac{1}{9}$% gross profit on sales.
(a) What was the cost of the socket wrench set?
(b) What was the sale price?

5. A raincoat that cost $24 was priced to make a gross profit of 40% on sales at the regular marked price. The marked price was later reduced by 25% before the coat was sold.
(a) What was the regular price of the rain-coat? **40**
(b) What was the sale price of the rain-coat? **30**
(c) What per cent of the sale price was the markup? **20%**

6. The regular marked prices at Harcourt-Myers Menswear include a gross profit that is $33\frac{1}{3}$% on sales. During a pre-inventory sale, a sports coat that cost $40 received a 20% reduction off its regular price.
(a) What was the regular marked price of the coat?
(b) What was the sale price of the sports coat?
(c) What per cent of the sale price was the markup?

7. A merchant marked a cookware set down 30%, clearing it out on sale for $35. At this sale price, he still obtained a margin of $14\frac{2}{7}$% on sales. What were his
(a) Regular marked price? **50**
(b) Cost? **30**
(c) Per cent of gross profit based on sales at the regular list price? **40%**

8. During a clearance sale, a sporting equipment store marked a trampoline down 10%, making the sale price $450. At this sale price, the store made a $22\frac{2}{9}$% gross profit on sales. Determine
(a) The regular price of the trampoline.
(b) The cost.

(c) The per cent markup on sales at the regular price.

9. A chair cost a dealer $150 less 20% and 15%. He marked the chair so that he could allow a "discount" of 20% off his marked price; but he still made a gross profit of 25% on sales. What had been
(a) The cost? *102*
(b) The actual selling price? *136*

(c) The marked price? *170*

10. A food freezer cost a dealer $480 less 25/20. After marking the freezer so that he could allow a "20/10 discount," the dealer still obtained a markup of 20% of the actual selling price. What had been
(a) The cost of the freezer?
(b) The actual selling price?
(c) The marked price?

SECTION 4
Markup on Perishables

A number of businesses handle products that perish in a short time if they are not sold. Examples of such businesses would be produce markets, bakeries, florists, dairies, and so forth. To a lesser extent, many other businesses would fall into this category, since styles and seasons change and the demand for a certain product diminishes. Clothing stores, appliance stores, and automobile dealers would be typical of this category.

These merchants know that not all of their goods will sell at their regular prices. The remaining items will have to be sold at a reduced price or else discarded altogether. Experienced businessmen know approximately how much of their merchandise will sell. They must, therefore, price the items high enough so that those which do sell will bring in the gross profit required for the entire stock.

The selling price on perishable merchandise is computed by the following basic procedure:

1. Determine the *cost* of the entire purchase.

2. Determine the *total selling price* of the entire purchase.

3. Determine the *amount of merchandise* that is expected to sell.

4. Express a *pricing equation*; divide the total sales in (2) by the amount of merchandise in (3) to obtain the selling price (per item or per pound).

Example One A grocer bought 100 lb of bananas at 12¢ per pound. Experience indicates that about 10% of these will spoil. At what price per pound must the bananas be priced in order to obtain a margin of 50% on cost?

The bananas cost 100 lb × 12¢, or $12. Since the markup will be

Example One (cont.)   50% on cost ($M = 0.5C$), then

$$C + M = S$$
$$C + 0.5C = S$$
$$1.5C = S$$
$$1.5(\$12) = S$$
$$\$18 = S$$

At least $18 must be made from the sale of the bananas.

The grocer expects 10%, or 10 lb of bananas to spoil; thus, his needed $18 in sales must come from the sale of the other 90 lb. Now, if p = price per pound of bananas, then

$$90p = \$18$$
$$p = \frac{\$18}{90}$$
$$p = 20\text{¢ per pound}$$

NOTE: When a fraction of a cent remains, retail merchants customarily mark the item to the next penny even though the fraction may have been less than one-half cent. It should also be observed in the preceding example that, on all sales above the expected 90 lb, the entire selling price will be additional profit.

Example Two   A delicatessen made 40 snack cakes at a cost of 25¢ each. About 15% of these will be sold "day old" at 10¢ each. Find the regular price in order that the delicatessen can make 25% on cost.

Solution   The snack cakes cost 40×25¢, or $10 to bake, and the delicatessen uses a markup of 25% on cost ($M = 0.25C$). Thus,

$$C + M = S$$
$$C + 0.25C = S$$
$$1.25C = S$$
$$1.25(\$10) = S$$
$$\$12.50 = S$$

Now, 15%, or 6 cakes will probably be sold at 10¢ each, which means that 60¢ will be earned at the reduced price. This leaves 34 cakes to be sold at the regular price. The regular sales and the "old" sales together must total $12.50; thus, if $p=$ regular price per cake,

$$\text{Regular} + \text{Old} = \text{Total}$$
$$\text{Regular} + 60\text{¢} = \$12.50$$
$$\text{Regular} = \$11.90$$
$$34p = 11.90$$
$$p = 35\text{¢ per cake}$$

SECTION 4 *Problems*

Find the missing information.

		Number Bought	Cost Per Item	Total Cost	Markup on Cost	Total Sales	Amount to Spoil	Number to Sell	Selling Price
1.	(a)	100 lb	40¢ $40		50% $60		4%	96 lbs.	63¢
	(b)	25	$16	400	30 $520		8	23	44.23
	(c)	30 dozen	$ 5		$33\frac{1}{3}$		10		22.61
2.	(a)	100 lb	25¢		44%		4%		
	(b)	20 dozen	$ 3		25		5		
	(c)	75	$ 2.80		$28\frac{4}{7}$		4		

Complete the following, which involves part of the goods being sold at the regular price and the remainder at the reduced price.

		Number Bought	Cost per Item	Total Cost	Markup on Cost	Total Sales	No. at Reg. Price	Amt. at Red. Price	No. at Red. Price	Red. Price	Reg. S.P.
3.	(a)	20 dozen	$4 $80		25% $100		18	10%	2	$2.75	
	(b)	120 lb	15¢		35			5			6¢
4.	(a)	250 lb	40¢		39%			8%		28¢	
	(b)	60 dozen	$5		35			5		$2	

5. Suppose in Example 1 (Section 4), that 95 lb of bananas actually sold.
(a) How much gross profit would the grocer make?
(b) What per cent markup on cost would he obtain? 58.3%
(c) What per cent markup on selling price would that be? 36.8%

6. Suppose that in Example 2 (Section 4), the delicatessen actually sold 38 snack cakes at the regular price, and the remainder at 10¢ each.

(a) What gross profit would be obtained?
(b) What per cent markup on cost does that represent?
(c) What per cent markup on selling price does that represent?

7. Supreme Florists purchased 40 chrysanthemum plants at $2 each. Previously, about 5% have remained unsold. What must they charge per plant in order to make 30% on cost?

8. The Farmer's Market purchased 175 lb of peaches at a cost of 36¢ per pound. Experience indicates that 4% of the peaches will probably not sell. At what price per pound should the peaches be sold in order for the market to make $33\frac{1}{3}$% on cost?

9. A grocery purchased 10 crates of berries at $4.80 per crate. Each crate con-

28¢ per box

tained 24 boxes of strawberries. The grocer has found that about 10% of the berries spoil and do not sell. What should he charge for each box of berries to realize a gross profit of 25% on cost?

10. A grocery bought 5 crates of cherry tomatoes at $9.60 per crate. Each crate contains 16 boxes of tomatoes. Approximately 10% of the tomatoes will spoil prior to sale. At what price per box will the grocery realize a 20% gross profit on cost?

11. The Sunshine Dairy purchased 200 quarts of Jersey milk at a cost of 25¢ each. Their operating margin is 22% of cost. If $7\frac{1}{2}$% of the milk has to be sold after 4 days at a reduced price of 18¢ per quart, what is their regular price per quart? *32¢ per quart*

12. The Clothes Rack purchased 60 bathing suits at a cost of $15 each. The buyer expects that 25% of the suits will eventually be sold at a clearance sale price of $18. What must be the regular price of the bathing suits if the store is to make 60% on cost for the entire purchase?

CHAPTER 13 *Glossary*

Gross profit. (See "Markup.")

Margin. (See "Markup.")

Markup (or gross profit or margin). The difference between cost and selling price of merchandise; the overhead and net profit combined: $C + M = S$; $M = \overline{OH} + P$. Markup is usually stated as a per cent of cost: $M = \_\_\% \ C$ or of selling price $M = \_\_\% \ S$.

Net profit (P). The spendable profit remaining after cost of merchandise and overhead are deducted from selling price.

Overhead (OH). Business expenses other than cost of merchandise.

Reduced price. Selling price after a deduction or discount off the regular (higher) marked price; also called sale price, actual selling price, or net selling price.

Regular price. Selling price at which merchandise would normally be marked; also called regular marked price, regular selling price, marked price, or list price.

Selling price factor (Spf). A number (usually greater than 1) that multiplies times cost to produce selling price: $\overline{Spf} \times C = S$.

CHAPTER 14

Markdown and Turnover

CHAPTER 14 OBJECTIVES

Upon completion of Chapter 14, the student will be able to:

1. Define and use correctly the terminology associated with each topic.

2. a. Using "—% of Original = Change," compute
   (1) Amount of markdown; and/or
   (2) Per cent of markdown.
   (Section 1; Examples 1, 4; Problems 1–4, 11, 12)
   b. When necessary, first use appropriate markup formulas to determine cost and regular selling price *(Examples 4, 5; Problems 1–4, 9–14)*.

3. When a markdown has occurred, find the total handling cost and use it to determine the amount and per cent of
   a. Operating profit;
   b. Operating loss; or
   c. Absolute loss.
   (Examples 2, 3, 5; Problems 1–4, 5–10, 13, 14)

4. Compute (both at cost and at retail) *(Section 2)*
   a. Average inventory *(Example 1; Problems 1–4, 9)*; and
   b. Inventory turnover *(Examples 2, 3; Problems 5–10)*.

5. a. Evaluate inventory by the methods of
   (1) Weighted average;
   (2) FIFO;
   (3) LIFO.
   b. On an income statement, compare gross profit (amount and per cent) under each inventory method. *(Section 3; Example 1; Problems 1–6)*

<table>
<tr><td>**14**</td><td>Two other significant aspects of retail business are markdown and turnover. Almost all retail concerns must sell at least some of their merchandise at a reduced selling price, while stock turnover reflects</td></tr>
</table>

the selling efficiency of an organization. The following sections explain the mathematics required to compute markdown and turnover.

<table>
<tr><td>**SECTION 1**
Markdown</td><td>In the previous chapter, we saw that merchandise must often be sold at a reduced price. This reduction may be expected and planned for well in ad-</td></tr>
</table>

vance, as in the case of seasonal clearance sales on clothing. Other reductions may be less predictable, as when the merchants' association decides to have a special city-wide promotion or when the competition has unexpectedly lowered its price.

Regardless of what motivates a price reduction, there are guidelines which merchants generally follow in determining how much to mark down their merchandise. The wholesale cost plus the overhead on a sale is known as the **total handling cost**. Businesses prefer to recover this total handling cost $(C + \overline{OH})$ if possible; in this case, no net profit would be made, but there would be no loss either. This critical value between profit and loss is often called the **breakeven point**.

If the merchant fails to recover the wholesale cost plus all of the operating expenses, there has been an **operating loss**. If not even the wholesale cost of the article was recovered, the transaction resulted in an **absolute loss** (or **gross**). These various sales conditions are shown in Figure 36, on page 364, which assumes a sale price lower than cost.

As described above, the following relationships* exist among actual selling (or sale) price (ASP), total handling cost (THC), and wholesale cost (C):

If ASP > THC, then a net profit exists.

If ASP = THC, then breakeven exists.

If ASP < THC, then an operating loss exists.

If ASP < C, then an absolute loss exists.

* The symbol ">" indicates "is greater than," and "<" denotes "is less than."

FIGURE 36

We will be interested here in determining whether or not any profit was made following a markdown, as well as certain percentages related to markdown.

Example One

A chair that sold for $120 was reduced to $84. (a) What was the markdown on the chair? (b) By what per cent was the price reduced?

Solution

(a) The chair was reduced by $120 - $84 = $36.

(b) __% of Original selling price = Change?

$$\_\%(\$120) = \$36$$

$$120x = 36$$

$$x = \tfrac{36}{120} \quad \text{or} \quad \tfrac{3}{10}$$

$$x = 30\% \quad \text{Reduction on selling price}$$

Example Two

The chair in Example 1 had cost the furniture store $75. The store's operating expenses run 20% of cost. Was an operating profit (net profit) or an operating loss made on the chair?

Solution

The breakeven point or total handling cost $= C + \overline{OH}$. Since $\overline{OH} = 20\%$ of cost and $C = \$75$, then

$$\text{Total handling cost} = C + \overline{OH}$$
$$= C + 0.2C$$
$$= 1.2C$$
$$= 1.2(\$75)$$
$$\overline{THC} = \$90$$

In order to recover all operating expenses, the chair's actual selling price (or sale price) should have been $90. Since the chair sold for less than this breakeven figure, the store's operating loss on the chair was the difference between total handling cost and actual selling price:

Total handling cost	$90
Actual selling price	− 84
Operating loss	$ 6

Example Three

The regular marked price of a man's suit was $144. The suit cost $120, and related selling expenses were $18. The suit was later marked down by 25% during a clearance sale. (a) What was the operating loss? (b) What was the absolute loss? (c) What was the per cent of gross loss (based on wholesale cost)?

Solution

The total handing cost $(C + \overline{OH})$ of the suit was $120 + $18 = $138. The actual net selling price (or sale price) of the suit was

$$\% \,\mathrm{Pd} \times L = \mathrm{Net}$$

$$0.75(\$144) = \mathrm{Net}$$

$$\$108 = \mathrm{Net}\ \text{selling price}$$

(a) Since the suit sold for less than its total handling cost:

Total handling cost =	$138
Actual selling price =	− 108
Operating loss =	$ 30

(b) The absolute or gross loss is the difference between wholesale cost and the actual selling price:

Wholesale cost =	$120
Actual selling price =	− 108
Absolute (or gross) loss =	$ 12

(c) Absolute loss is always computed as some per cent of the wholesale cost, as follows:

What per cent of wholesale cost was the absolute loss?

$$\_\_\% (\$120) = \$12$$

$$120x = 12$$

$$x = \tfrac{12}{120} \quad \text{or} \quad \tfrac{1}{10}$$

$$x = 10\%\ \text{gross loss}$$

The operating and gross loss incurred in this sale may be visualized by referring to Figure 37 on page 366.

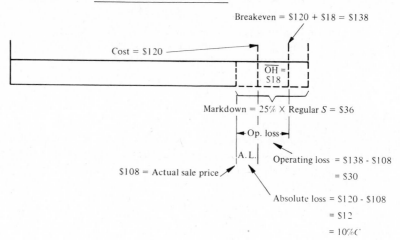

Regular S = $120 + $24 = $144

Breakeven = $120 + $18 = $138

Cost = $120

$\overline{OH}$ = $18

Markdown = 25% × Regular S = $36

Op. loss

A.L.

$108 = Actual sale price

Operating loss = $138 - $108

= $30

Absolute loss = $120 - $108

= $12

= 10% C

FIGURE 37

Example Four

A dress cost a department store $40. The store's operating expenses are 35% on cost and normal profit is 15% on cost. (a) What is the regular selling price of the dress? (b) What is the maximum per cent of markdown that can be offered without taking an operating loss?

Solution

(a) The normal markup of overhead plus net profit is

$$M = \overline{OH} + P$$

$$= 35\% \, C + 15\% \, C$$

$$M = 50\% \, C$$

Therefore, using $M = 50\% \, C$ and Cost = $40, the regular selling price is

$$C + M = S$$

$$C + \tfrac{1}{2}C = S$$

$$\tfrac{3}{2}C = S$$

$$\tfrac{3}{2}(\$40) = S$$

$$\$60 = S \qquad \text{(Regular selling price)}$$

(b) The operating expenses are 35% or $\frac{7}{20}$ of cost; thus,

Total handling cost $= C + \overline{\text{OH}}$

$\qquad\qquad\quad = C + 0.35C$

$\qquad\qquad\quad = 1.35C$

$\qquad\qquad\quad = 1.35(\$40)$

$\qquad \overline{\text{THC}} = \$54$

Regular selling price	$60
Total handling cost	$- \;54$
Maximum markdown	$ 6

The lowest sale price the store could offer without taking any operating loss would be the breakeven point, $54. This means the dress could be marked down $6 from its regular selling price. The per cent of reduction would be

$$\_\% \text{ of Original} = \text{Change}$$

$$\_\% \text{ of } \$60 = \$6$$

$$60x = 6$$

$$x = \tfrac{6}{60} \quad \text{or} \quad \tfrac{1}{10}$$

$$x = 10\% \text{ reduction in price}$$

Example Five

A variety store bought 200 pen sets at $2 each. The regular price of $2.50 included 15% on cost for overhead. After 180 sets were sold at the regular price, the remaining 20 sets were closed out at $1 each. (a) How much net profit, operating loss, or absolute loss was made? (b) What per cent of wholesale cost was it?

Solution

(a)   Cost: $200 \times \$2 = \$400$

Total sales:	$180 \times \$2.50 =$	$450
	$20 \times \$1.00 =$	$+ \;\;\; 20$
		$470

Total handling cost:

$\overline{\text{THC}} = C + \overline{\text{OH}}$

$\qquad\;\; = C + 0.15C$

$\qquad\;\; = 1.15C$

$\qquad\;\; = 1.15(\$400)$

$\overline{\text{THC}} = \$460$

Total sales	$470
Total handling cost	$- \;460$
Net profit	$ 10

(b) $\_\%$ of wholesale cost $=$ Net profit

$\qquad\;\; \_\%(\$400) = \$10$

$\qquad\qquad\;\; 400x = \;\; 10$

$\qquad\qquad\quad\;\; x = \;\;\; 2.5\%$

Complete the following.

		Regular Selling Price	MARKDOWN Per cent	MARKDOWN Amount	Sale Price	Whole-sale Cost	Over-head	Total Han-dling Cost	Operating Profit or (Loss)
1.	(a)	$36		$ 8		$24	$ 3		
	(b)	20	15%				4	$19	
	(c)	75			$60	50			($5)
	(d)	32			24	20		25	
	(e)			9	21		5		(4)
	(f)		20				3	10	2
2.	(a)	$50		$10		$32	$6		
	(b)	48	25%				6	$40	
	(c)	27			$18		3		$5
	(d)	12					2	9	1
	(e)			7		25		31	(3)
	(f)		$22\frac{2}{9}$		42		8		(4)

Insert the missing entries in the following table.

		Regular Selling Price	MARKDOWN Per Cent	MARKDOWN Amount	Sale Price	Whole-sale Cost	Over-head	Total Han-dling Cost	Opera-ting Loss ($)	GROSS LOSS Amount	GROSS LOSS Per Cent
3.	(a)	$24	$33\frac{1}{3}$%			$20	$3				
	(b)	5		$ 2		3		$ 4			
	(c)	50			$37		5	45			
	(d)		25		30		4		($2)		
4.	(a)	$60		$24		$40	$5				
	(b)	88	25%			75		$83			
	(c)		36		$16		2	22			
	(d)		30		28		3		($4)		

5. A $33\frac{1}{3}$% discount was offered on a tape recorder which usually sold for $96. The recorder cost $50 and operating expenses were 15% of cost.

How much operating profit or loss was made on this sale?

6. During a Labor Day special, a $50 tennis racquet was reduced by 30%. If the racquet had originally cost $32, and selling expenses were 25% of cost, how much operating profit or loss was made on the racquet?

7. A $120 rotary antenna was closed out for $75.

(a) What per cent markdown did this represent?

(b) The dealer had paid $100 less 30% and 10% for the antenna, and operating expenses are 10% of the regular selling price. How much operating profit or loss was made?

8. A CB radio which usually retails for $200 was sold during a special promotion for $160.

(a) What per cent markdown did the store allow?

(b) If the CB had cost the store $180 less 25% and 20%, and selling expenses had been $27, how much operating profit or loss was made?

9. A hardware store paid $40 for a set of Teflon-coated aluminum cookware. On regular sales, their overhead is 15% of sales and the net profit is $13\frac{4}{7}\%$ of sales. For a Dollar Days special, the store sold the set at a 40% discount.

(a) What would be the regular price of the cookware?

(b) What was the operating loss on this sale?

(c) How much and what per cent gross or absolute loss did the store suffer?

10. A discount store paid $60 for an automobile tape deck. Normal markup there includes expenses that are 30% of regular selling price and a net profit that is 10% of regular selling price. As a "door-buster" special, the tape deck was advertised at a 50% discount.

(a) What is the regular selling price of the tape deck?

(b) How much operating loss did the store have on this sale?

(c) How much and what per cent gross or absolute loss did they experience?

11. A shoe store buys textured hosiery for $18 per dozen, less $33\frac{1}{3}\%$ and 10%. The marked price of the hose includes 20% on cost for expenses and 30% on cost for net profit.

(a) What does a pair of hose regularly sell for?

(b) What is the largest markdown which would be allowed on a pair of hose without experiencing an operating loss?

(c) What per cent markdown would this represent?

12. Eight-track tapes cost a record shop $100 per dozen, less 25% and 20%. The shop marks up the tapes to cover expenses of 40% on cost and a net profit of 20% on cost.

(a) What is the regular marked price of each tape?

(b) What is the maximum markdown which the shop could allow on each tape and still break even (that is, have no operating loss)?

(c) What per cent markdown would this be?

13. A cloth store bought 120 pairs of scissors. They sold 100 pairs for $1.95 each, which included 10% on cost for expenses and 20% on cost for net profit. The remaining 20 pairs were sold on Dollar Day for $1 each.

(a) What were the total wholesale cost, total handling cost, and total sales?

(b) Was a net profit, operating loss, or absolute loss made on the entire transaction?

(c) How much was it, and what per cent of wholesale cost did it represent?

14. A drugstore sold 120 boxes of color

film for $2.75 each. This regular price included a markup of 20% on cost for overhead and $17\frac{1}{2}$% on cost for net profit. Another 30 boxes of the film were sold during a special promotion for $1.50 each.
(a) What were the total wholesale cost, total handling cost, and total sales?

(b) Was a net profit, operating loss, or gross loss made on the 150 boxes of film?

(c) How much was it, and what per cent of wholesale cost did it represent?

SECTION 2

Inventory

Turnover

One indication of a business's stability and efficiency is the number of times per year that its inventory is sold—its **inventory** (or **stock**) **turnover**. This varies greatly with different types of businesses. For instance, a florist might maintain a relatively small inventory but sell the complete stock every few days. A furniture dealer, on the other hand, might stock a rather large inventory and have a turnover only every few months.

Regardless of what might be considered a desirable turnover for a business, the methods used to calculate this turnover are similar. One business statistic that is used in this calculation is the average value of the store's inventory. Inventory may be evaluated at either its cost or its retail value, although it is probably more often valued at retail.

Average inventory for a period is found by adding the various inventories and dividing by the number of times the inventory was taken.

Example One

Inventory at retail value at the Village Bookstore was $15,950 on January 1; $14,780 on June 30; and $17,240 on December 31. Determine the average inventory.

$$
\begin{array}{r}
\$15,950 \\
14,780 \\
17,270 \\
\hline
\end{array}
$$
$3\,)\,\overline{\$48,000} = \$16,000$ Average inventory (at retail) for the year

Stock turnover is found as follows:

$$\text{Turnover (at retail)} = \frac{\text{Net sales}}{\text{Average inventory (at retail)}}$$

$$\text{Turnover (at cost)} = \frac{\text{Cost of goods sold}}{\text{Average inventory (at cost)}}$$

Turnover is more frequently computed at retail than at cost. Many modern stores mark their goods only with retail prices, which makes it almost impossible to take inventory at cost. Another reason is that turnover at cost does not take into consideration the markdown on merchandise which was sold at a reduced price or the loss on goods which were misappropriated by shoplifters—a constant problem in many retail businesses. Turnover at retail and at cost will be the same only if all merchandise is sold at its regular price; ordinarily, the turnover at retail is slightly less than at cost.

Example Two

The bookstore in Example 1 above had net sales during the year of $56,800. What was the stock turnover for the year at retail?

$$\text{Turnover} = \frac{\text{Net sales}}{\text{Average inventory (at retail)}} = \frac{\$56,800}{\$16,000}$$

Turnover = 3.55 at retail

Example Three

The bookstore above had used a markup of 25% on sales to price its books. Find the turnover at cost, if the cost of goods sold for the year was $43,200.

Solution

The average inventory at retail value was $16,000. The markup used was 25% or $\frac{1}{4}$ of selling price. The cost of this average inventory is computed

$$C + M = S$$

$$C + \tfrac{1}{4}S = S$$

$$C = \tfrac{3}{4}S$$

$$= \tfrac{3}{4}(\$16,000)$$

$$C = \$12,000$$

The average inventory at cost was $12,000. Thus, turnover at cost is

$$\text{Turnover} = \frac{\text{Cost of goods}}{\text{Average inventory (at cost)}} = \frac{\$43,200}{\$12,000}$$

Turnover = 3.6 at cost

1. The following inventories were taken at cost during the year: $19,170, $17,840, $15,990, $16,870, and $20,130. What was the average inventory?

2. The following inventories were taken at cost: $39,734, $41,825, $45,209, and $41,232. Determine the average inventory.

3. A store uses a markup of 25% on cost to price its merchandise. Having taken an inventory of $14,200 at cost, a store took subsequent inventories at retail. If later inventories were for $16,820 and $17,330, what was the average inventory at retail?

4. An inventory of $22,500 was taken at cost. It was then decided that future inventories would be taken at retail. The next inventories were valued at $33,470 and $32,530. If the store uses a regular markup of 40% on cost, compute the average inventory at retail.

5. Net sales at the shop in Problem 1 were $66,000 and the cost of goods sold had been $50,400. What was the shop's turnover at cost?

6. The store in Problem 2 had net sales for the year of $267,600; their merchandise had cost $189,000. Determine their turnover at cost.

7. The shop discussed in Problems 1 and 5 priced all its merchandise using a markup of 25% on selling price. Find its turnover at retail.

8. The store described in Problems 2 and 6 had used a markup of 30% on selling price to mark its merchandise. What was its turnover at retail value?

9. During the year, a store took inventories at cost of $7,980, $9,630, $11,550, and $10,840. Their income statement showed that net sales for the year were $43,750 and the cost of goods sold was $35,200. What was their inventory turnover at cost?

10. The store in Problem 9 used a markup of 20% on sales to price its merchandise. Determine its turnover at retail.

SECTION 3
Inventory Valuation

We have used inventory values without previously considering the process by which the inventory was evaluated. Some firms (particularly those with computers) keep a **perpetual inventory**: each new inventory item is cost-coded and its subsequent sale is recorded, so that the firm knows at all times the exact content and value of its inventory. Most firms, however, take a **periodic inventory**: at regular intervals a physical count is made of inventory items. Four methods by which a periodic inventory may be taken are described as follows.

If each item is cost-coded, the periodic inventory may be taken by the **specific identification** method, where the inventory value is simply the total of each individual item. Evaluating items is not always an obvious process, however; inventories often contain many indistinguishable items that have been purchased at different times and for different amounts (such as valves in a plumbing supply house). If the items are small, it may be impractical to cost-code each item; thus, there would be some question about what value to attach to each. (This is a primary reason for the popularity of taking inventory at retail value—the current selling price of merchandise is always known.) One solution is to use the **weighted average method** of inventory valuation, where an average cost is computed like the weighted means we studied in Chapter 4.

The **first-in, first-out method** (usually called the **FIFO method**), is probably most commonly used. This method assumes that those items which were bought first were also sold first, and that the items still in the inventory are those which were purchased most recently. (This method conforms to actual selling practice in most businesses.) The number of items on hand are valued according to the invoice prices most recently paid for the corresponding number of items.

The **last-in, first-out** (or **LIFO**) **method** assumes that the items most recently bought are those items which have been sold, and that the items still in stock are the oldest items. Although this method is contrary to most actual selling practice, there is certain justification from an accounting standpoint: on the income statement, the LIFO method uses "current" costs (which are usually higher) for the cost of goods sold and thus produces a smaller gross profit, which many accountants argue is more realistic in an inflationary economy. Accepted accounting procedure requires that income statements specify the method(s) used to evaluate the inventories listed.

Example One Assume that a new valve came on the market this year and that the following purchases were made during the year: 15 at $5; 9 at $6; and 12 at $8. Twenty valves were sold (leaving 16 in inventory) for a total net sales of $300. Evaluate the ending inventory by the following methods: (a) weighted average, (b) FIFO, and (c) LIFO. (d) Compare the effect of each inventory method on the income statement.

Weighted Average Method (a)

$$
\begin{array}{rl}
15 @ \$5 = & \$\ 75 \\
9 @ \$6 = & 54 \\
+12 @ \$8 = +& 96 \\
\hline
36 \text{ items} & \$225 \text{ Total cost} \\
\text{purchased} &
\end{array}
$$

$$\frac{\$225}{36} = \$6.25 \quad \text{Average cost}$$

$$16 \text{ items} @ \$6.25 = \$100 \quad \begin{array}{l}\text{Inventory value at cost} \\ \text{by weighted average method}\end{array}$$

FIFO
Method

(b) The 16 items remaining are assumed to be the last 12 plus 4 from the previous order:

$$
\begin{array}{rl}
12 @ \$8 = & \$\ 96 \\
+\ 4 @ \$6 = + & 24 \\
\hline
16 & \$120 \quad \text{Inventory value} \\
& \qquad\ \ \text{at cost by FIFO}
\end{array}
$$

LIFO
Method

(c) The 16 items remaining are assumed to be the first 15 plus 1 from the second order:

$$
\begin{array}{rl}
15 @ \$5 = & \$75 \\
+\ 1 @ \$6 = + & 6 \\
\hline
16 & \$81 \quad \text{Inventory value} \\
& \qquad\ \text{at cost by LIFO}
\end{array}
$$

Income
Statements

(d)

	Weighted Average		FIFO		LIFO
Net sales		$300		$300	$300
Cost of goods sold:					
Beginning inventory	$ 0		$ 0		$ 0
Purchases	+ 225		+ 225		+ 225
Goods available	$225		$225		$225
Ending inventory	− 100		− 120		− 81
Cost of goods		− 125		− 105	− 144
Gross profit		$175		$195	$156
Gross profit as a % of Net sales		58.3%		65%	52%

SECTION 3 *Problems*

Evaluate the following inventories by (1) weighted average, (2) FIFO, and (c) LIFO:

		Purchases	Ending Inventory		Purchases	Ending Inventory
1.	(a)	9 @ $ 8 10 @ $10 6 @ $13	12 items	(b)	10 @ $20.00 8 @ $22.25 9 @ $24.00	13 items
2.	(a)	4 @ $10.50 5 @ $12.00 6 @ $13.00	7 items	(b)	12 @ $2.00 8 @ $3.25 10 @ $4.00	14 items

3. A variety store has made the following purchases of a decorated window shade: 4 at $19; 10 at $20; and 6 at $24. An inventory taken December 31 reveals that 8 shades are still in stock. Evaluate this inventory at cost by the following methods: (a) weighted average, (b) FIFO, and (c) LIFO.

4. A toy shop has bought a newly marketed space module on the following orders: 20 at $7.50, 18 at $10, and 25 at $12. Their recent inventory counted 30 modules still on hand. Evaluate this item at cost by the (a) weighted average, (b) FIFO, and (c) LIFO inventory methods.

5. Assume that the window shade in Problem 3 is a new product not in previous inventories. The 12 shades that sold have produced total net sales of $400. Prepare an income statement showing the gross profit (dollars and per cent) earned on the window shades, under each inventory method above.

6. Total net sales of the 33 space modules sold in Problem 4 have been $500. Complete an income statement showing the gross profit (dollars and per cent) made on sales of the space module, for each of the preceding inventory methods.

CHAPTER 14 *Glossary*

Absolute (or gross) loss. Loss resulting when the sale price of merchandise is less than cost: Absolute loss = Cost − Sale price.

Breakeven point. A sale price that produces neither profit nor loss; same as Total handling cost.

First-in, first-out (FIFO) method. Inventory costing method which assumes that the first items purchased were also sold first, and that present inventory items are the ones most recently purchased.

Gross loss. (See "Absolute loss.")

Last-in, first-out (LIFO) method. Inventory costing method which assumes that the items most recently bought are the ones that have been sold, and that present inventory contains the oldest items.

Operating loss. Loss resulting when the sale price of merchandise is less than the total handling cost: Operating loss = Total handling cost − Sale price.

Periodic inventory. An inventory taken at a regular interval by a physical count of items.

Perpetual inventory. An inventory that is continuously updated by recording the purchase and subsequent sale of each item.

Specific identification. Inventory costing method where each item is cost-coded and the total inventory is the sum of these costs.

Total handling cost. The wholesale cost plus the related overhead on a sale $(C + OH)$.

Turnover. The number of times per year that the average inventory is sold:

$$\left(\begin{array}{c}\text{Turnover}\\\text{at cost}\end{array}\right) = \frac{\text{Cost of goods sold}}{\text{Average inventory (at cost)}}$$

$$\left(\begin{array}{c}\text{Turnover}\\\text{at retail}\end{array}\right) = \frac{\text{Net sales}}{\text{Average inventory (at retail)}}$$

Weighted average method. Inventory costing method where each item is valued at the weighted average (or mean) of all costs paid during the time interval.

PART

IV

Mathematics of Finance

CHAPTER 15

Simple Interest

CHAPTER 15 OBJECTIVES

Upon completing Chapter 15, the student will be able to:

1. Define and use correctly the terminology in each topic.

2. a. Use the simple interest formula $I = Prt$ to find any variable, when the other items are given
   (*Section 1; Examples 1, 3, 4; Problems 1, 2, 5–10, 13, 14*).
   b. Use the amount formula $S = P + I$ to find amount or interest
   (*Examples 1, 2, 4; Problems 1–4, 7–10*).
   c. Use the amount formula $S = P(1 + rt)$ to find amount or principal
   (*Examples 2, 5; Problems 3, 4, 11–14*).

3. a. Compute ordinary or exact interest using ordinary or exact time
   (*Section 2, Examples 1–4, Problems 1–6; Section 3, Examples 1, 2, Problems 1–8*).
   b. Predict how a given change in rate or time will affect the amount of interest (*Section 3; Problems 9–12*).

4. Apply the 6 %, 60-day method of interest calculation
   (*Section 4; Examples 1, 2; Problems 1–22*).

5. Given information about a simple interest note, use any of the above formulas required to compute the unknown
   a. Interest;
   b. Maturity value;
   c. Rate;
   d. Time; or
   e. Principal
   (*Section 5; Examples 1–3; Problems 1–20*).

6. Compute present value of a simple interest note (*Section 6*), either
   a. On the original day (*Examples 1, 2; Problems 1–4, 7–10*); or
   b. On some other given day prior to maturity
   (*Example 3; Problems 5, 6, 11–14*).

15

The borrowing and lending of money is a practice that dates far back into history. Never, however, has the practice of finance been more widespread than it is today. Money may be loaned at a simple interest or a simple discount rate. The loan may be repaid in a single payment or a series of payments, depending upon the type of loan. When money is invested with a financial institution, compound interest is usually earned on the deposits. The following chapters explain the basic types of loans, important methods of loan repayments, and fundamental investment procedures.

SECTION 1
Basic Simple Interest

Persons who rent buildings or equipment expect to pay for the use of someone else's property. Similarly, those who borrow money must pay rent for the use of that money. Rent paid for the privilege of borrowing another's money is called **interest**. The amount of money that was borrowed is the **principal** of a loan.

A certain percentage of the principal is charged as interest. The per cent or **rate** is quoted on a yearly (per annum) basis, unless otherwise specified. The **time** is the number of days, months, or years for which the money will be loaned. (In order to make rate and time correspond, time is always converted to years, since rate is always given on a yearly basis.) When simple interest is being charged, interest is calculated on the whole principal for the entire length of the loan. Simple interest is found using the formula

$$I = Prt$$

where I = interest, P = principal, r = rate, and t = time. The **amount** due at the end of the loan (also called **maturity value**) is the sum of the principal plus the interest. This is expressed by the formula

$$S = P + I$$

where $S =$ amount (or maturity value or sum), $P =$ principal, and $I =$ interest.

Example One A loan of \$800 is made at 6% for 5 months. Determine (a) the interest and (b) the maturity value of this loan.

Solution (a) $P = \$800$

$r = 6\%$ or 0.06 or $\frac{6}{100}$

$t = 5$ months* $= \frac{5}{12}$ year

$I = Prt$

$= \$800 \times \frac{6}{100} \times \frac{5}{12}$

$I = \$20$

(b) $S = P + I$

$= \$800 + \$20$

$S = \$820$

The two formulas in Example 1 can be combined, allowing the maturity value to be found in one step. Since $I = Prt$, by substitution in the formula

$$S = P + I$$
$$\downarrow$$
$$= P + Prt$$
$$S = P(1 + rt)$$

If the formula $S = P(1 + rt)$ is used to calculate the amount, the interest may be found by taking the difference between maturity value and principal.

Example Two Rework Example 1 using the maturity value formula $S = P(1 + rt)$. As before, $P = \$800$, $r = \frac{6}{100}$, and $t = \frac{5}{12}$ year.

(a) $S = P(1 + rt)$

$= \$800(1 + \frac{6}{100} \times \frac{5}{12})$

$= 800(1 + \frac{5}{200})$

$= 800(\frac{200}{200} + \frac{5}{200})$

$= 800(\frac{205}{200})$

$S = \$820$

(b) $P + I = S$

$I = S - P$

$= \$820 - \$800$

$I = \$20$

* Keep in mind that, for periods less than 1 year, time must be expressed as a fraction of a year.

Example Three

At what rate will $480 earn $28 in interest after 10 months?

$$P = \$480 \qquad\qquad I = Prt$$

$$r = ? \qquad\qquad \$28 = \$480r \times \tfrac{5}{6}$$

$$t = \tfrac{10}{12} \text{ or } \tfrac{5}{6} \text{ year} \qquad\qquad 28 = 4\overset{80}{\cancel{80}}(\tfrac{5}{6})r$$

$$I = \$28 \qquad\qquad 28 = 400r$$

$$r = \tfrac{28}{400} \text{ or } \tfrac{7}{100} \text{ or } 0.07$$

$$r = 7\%$$

Example Four

How long will it take for $950 to amount to $988 at an 8% simple interest rate?

Solution

This problem may be worked using the maturity value formula $S = P(1 + rt)$. However, the simple interest formula $I = Prt$ is easier to work with and should be used whenever possible. The student should notice that the formula $I = Prt$ may be used to find a missing variable whenever the interest is given or can be found quickly.

In this case, the interest may be computed easily, since

$$I = S - P \qquad\qquad I = Prt$$

$$= \$988 - \$950 \qquad\qquad \$38 = \$950(\tfrac{8}{100})t$$

$$I = \$38 \qquad\qquad 38 = 76t$$

$$\tfrac{38}{76} = t$$

$$P = \$950 \qquad\qquad t = \tfrac{38}{76} \text{ or } \tfrac{1}{2}$$

$$r = 8\% \text{ or } \tfrac{8}{100} \qquad\qquad t = \tfrac{1}{2} \text{ year} \text{ or } 6 \text{ months}$$

$$t = ?$$

Example Five

What principal would have a maturity value of $636 in 8 months if the interest rate is 9%?

Solution

In this problem the interest is not given and is impossible to determine because the maturity value and principal are not both known. Thus, the amount formula $S = P(1 + rt)$ must be used to find the principal.

$$P = \$?$$
$$r = 9\% \quad \text{or} \quad \tfrac{9}{100}$$
$$t = \tfrac{8}{12} \quad \text{or} \quad \tfrac{2}{3} \text{ year}$$
$$S = \$636$$

$$S = P(1 + rt)$$
$$\$636 = P(1 + \tfrac{\overset{3}{\cancel{9}}}{100} \times \tfrac{2}{\cancel{3}})$$
$$= P(1 + \tfrac{6}{100})$$
$$= P(\tfrac{100}{100} + \tfrac{6}{100})$$
$$= P(\tfrac{106}{100})$$
$$\tfrac{100}{\cancel{106}} \times \overset{6}{\cancel{636}} = P(\tfrac{\cancel{106}}{\cancel{100}})(\tfrac{\cancel{100}}{\cancel{106}})$$
$$\$600 = P$$

SECTION 1 *Problems*

Find the interest and amount—

1. (a) $400 at 10% for 6 months
   (b) $400 at 5% for 6 months
   (c) $630 at 8% for 9 months
   (d) $840 at $6\frac{1}{2}$% for 7 months
   (e) $540 at 8% for 3 months

2. (a) $500 at 6% for 1 year
   (b) $500 at 6% for 6 months
   (c) $600 at 9% for 5 months
   (d) $750 at 8.5% for 4 months
   (e) $680 at 7% for 9 months

3. Find the interest and amount of parts (a), (c), and (e) in Problem 1, using the maturity value formula $S = P(1 + rt)$.

4. Utilize the amount formula $S = P(1 + rt)$, to find both interest and amount of parts (a), (c), and (e) of Problem 2.

5. What was the interest rate if the interest due on a 10-month loan of $780 was $32.50?

6. What is the interest rate if $38.40 is due in interest on a $640 loan after 9 months?

7. How long would it take for a loan of $1,200 at 7% to acquire a maturity value of $1,270?

8. How long will it take for $800 to amount to $840 at a 10% interest rate?

9. If $600 is worth $609 after 4 months, what was the interest rate?

10. If $600 is worth $615 after 4 months, what interest rate was charged?

11. What principal will amount to $832 after 8 months at 6%?

12. What principal will have a maturity value of $1,449 after 6 months at 7% interest?

13. At what simple interest rate will an investment double itself in 8 years?
(HINT: Choose any principal; what is the interest after 8 years?)

14. How long would it take for an investment to double at 10% simple interest?

SECTION 2

Ordinary Time and
Exact Time

The problems given in Section 1 were limited to those with time periods of even months or years. This is not always the case, as many loans are made for a certain number of days. Suppose that a loan is made on July 5 for 60 days; do we consider 60 days to be 2 months and consider the loan due on September 5, or do we take the 60 days literally and consider the amount due on September 3? Suppose this loan made on July 5 is for a time of 2 months; would we consider the time to be $\frac{2}{12} = \frac{1}{6}$ year or should we use the actual 62 days between July 5 and September 5? The answers to these questions depend upon whether ordinary time or exact time is being used.

When **ordinary time** is being used, each month is assumed to have 30 days. Thus, any 5-month period would be considered as $5 \times 30 = 150$ days. Similarly, 90 days would be considered as 3 months. In actual practice, however, ordinary time is seldom used, as we shall see later.

If **exact time** is being used, the specific number of days within the time period is calculated. Thus, 90 days would usually be slightly less than 3 months. Exact time may be calculated most conveniently using Table XIII, The Number of Each Day of the Year, in Appendix C. In this table, each day of the year is listed in consecutive order and assigned a number from 1 to 365. The following examples demonstrate use of the table.

Example One

Using exact time, find (a) the due date of a loan made on April 15 for 180 days and (b) the exact time between February 10 and July 23.

Solution

(a) From the table of each day of the year, we see that April 15 is the 105th day. Thus,

$$
\begin{array}{rl}
\text{April 15} = & 105 \text{ day} \\
+ & 180 \text{ days} \\
\hline
\end{array}
$$

285th day is October 12, the due date of
the note using exact time

(b) From March 10 to July 23:

$$
\begin{array}{rl}
\text{July 23} = & 204 \text{ day} \\
\text{March 10} = - & 69 \text{ day} \\
\hline
\end{array}
$$

135 days between March 10 and July 23,
using exact time

Example Two

A loan is taken out on June 1 for 5 months. Determine (a) the due date and (b) the number of days in the term of the loan, using both ordinary and exact time.

Solution   (a) Five months after June 1 is November 1. The loan (principal plus interest) will be due on November 1 regardless of which kind of time is used.*

(b) From June 1 to November 1:

ORDINARY TIME	*EXACT TIME*
5 months = 5 × 30	November 1 = 305 day
= 150 days	June 1 = − 152 day
	153 days

Sometimes the time period of a loan includes a leap year. This does not affect the calculation of ordinary time, of course, since all months are considered to have 30 days. The leap year must be given consideration, however, when exact time is being used. During a leap year, February 29 becomes the 60th day of the year; thus, from March 1 on, the number of each day is one greater than is shown in the table. For example, during a leap year, March 15 is the 75th day, instead of the 74th day as the table shows. This change in the number of the day must be made before the exact time is calculated.

A simple test allows one to determine whether any given year is a leap year: Leap year always falls on a year evenly divisible by the number 4. That is, 1976 is divisible by 4; so 1976 was a leap year. The year 1978 is not divisible by 4; thus, 1978 is not a leap year. Presidential election years also fall on leap years.

Example Three   Find the exact time between January 16, 1980, and May 7, 1980. Since 1980 is a leap year, May 7 is the 128th day:

$$\begin{array}{rl} \text{May 7} = & 128 \text{ day} \\ \text{January 16} = - & 16 \text{ day} \\ \hline & 112 \text{ days between January 16, 1980,} \\ & \text{and May 7, 1980} \end{array}$$

Example Four   Find the exact time between November 16 of one year and April 3 of the next.

---

* *Note*: If the given number of months ends on a day that does not exist, the due date would be the last day of the month. For example, a loan on March 31 for 8 months would be due on November 30, since there is no November 31.

We must find the remaining days in the present year and then add the days in the following year:

$$\begin{aligned} \text{Present year} &= 365 \text{ days} \\ -\text{ November } 16 &= 320 \text{ day} \\ \hline &\ 45 \text{ days remaining in present year} \\ +\text{ April } 3 &= 93 \text{ day} \\ \hline &138 \text{ days between November 16 and April 3} \end{aligned}$$

SECTION 2 *Problems*

Fine the exact time from the first date to the second date.

1. (a) March 15 to November 26
  (b) January 4 to April 19
  (c) May 26 to October 17
  (d) August 16 to December 1
  (e) Jan. 16, 1976, to May 20, 1976
  (f) February 20, 1980, to April 8, 1980
  (g) September 12, 1977, to January 30, 1978
  (h) November 23, 1979, to March 17, 1980

2. (a) March 4 to October 23
  (b) June 10 to November 21
  (c) April 19 to August 5
  (d) July 29 to November 12
  (e) February 11, 1976, to May 18, 1976
  (f) January 10, 1980, to September 3, 1980
  (g) July 4, 1977, to Feb. 15, 1978
  (h) October 14, 1983, to May 25, 1984

Determine the due date, using both ordinary and exact time.

3. (a) 60 days after August 13
  (b) 180 days after June 10
  (c) 120 days after July 23

4. (a) 30 days after August 25
  (b) 90 days after April 10
  (c) 150 days after June 3

Find the due date and both the ordinary and exact times (in days) for loans made on the given dates.

5. (a) April 24 for 5 months
  (b) January 17 for 7 months
  (c) February 20, 1980, for 6 months
  (d) January 31, 1979, for 3 months
  (e) October 25, 1977, for 4 months

6. (a) September 15 for 3 months
  (b) May 19 for 6 months
  (c) February 16, 1980, for 9 months
  (d) January 8, 1979, for 8 months
  (e) June 10, 1978, for 10 months

SECTION 3
Ordinary Interest and Exact Interest

It has been seen that the time of a loan is frequently a certain number of days. As stated previously, a time of less than one year must be expressed as a fraction of a year. The question then arises: When converting days to fractional years, are the days placed over a de-nominator of 360 or 365? It is this question with which ordinary and exact interest are concerned.

The term "interest" here refers to the number of days representing one year. Just as ordinary time indicated 30 days per month, **ordinary interest** indicates interest calculated using 360 days per year. Similarly, the term **exact interest** indicates interest calculated using 365 days per year. (A 366-day year is not used in business even for leap year.)

We have now discussed two ways of determining time (days in the loan period) and two types of interest (days per year). There are four possible combinations of these to obtain t for the interest formula:

1. Ordinary time over ordinary ~~interest~~ year: $$t = \frac{\text{Approximate days}}{360}$$

2. Ordinary time over exact ~~interest~~ year: $$t = \frac{\text{Approximate days}}{365}$$

3. Exact time over ordinary ~~interest~~ year: $$t = \frac{\text{Exact days}}{360}$$

4. Exact time over exact ~~interest~~ year: $$t = \frac{\text{Exact days}}{365}$$

Example One

A $730 loan is made at 8% for 135 days. Compute (a) the ordinary interest and (b) the exact interest.

Solution

(a) $P = \$730$ $I = Prt$

$r = \frac{8}{100}$ $= \$730 \times \frac{8}{100} \times \frac{3}{8}$

$t = \frac{135}{360}$ or $\frac{3}{8}$ $I = \$21.90$ (ordinary interest)

$I = ?$

(b) $P = \$730$ $I = Prt$

$r = \frac{8}{100}$ $= \$730 \times \frac{8}{100} \times \frac{135}{365}$

$t = \frac{135}{365}$ $I = \$21.60$ (exact interest)

$I = ?$

Example Two

A four-month loan of $720 with interest at 9% is originated on August 15. Find the interest due on this loan using (a) ordinary time and (b) exact time. (Use ordinary interest—a 360-day year—for both parts.)

Solution   (a) $P = \$720$ $I = Prt$

$r = \frac{9}{100}$ $= \$720 \times \frac{\overset{3}{\cancel{9}}}{\cancel{100}} \times \frac{1}{\cancel{3}}$

$t = \frac{120}{360}$ or $\frac{1}{3}$ $I = \$21.60$

$I = ?$ (ordinary time/ordinary interest)

(b) Four months after August 15 is December 15; the exact time is

$$December\ 15 = \ \ 349\ day$$
$$August\ 15 = -227\ day$$
$$\overline{\hspace{1.5cm}122\ days}$$

$P = \$720$ $I = Prt$

$r = \frac{9}{100}$ $= \$\overset{2}{\cancel{720}} \times \dfrac{9}{\cancel{100}} \times \dfrac{\cancel{122}}{\cancel{360}}$

$t = \frac{122}{360}$ $I = \$21.96$ (exact time/

$I = ?$ ordinary interest)

Example 1 showed that for the same number of days, *ordinary interest* (360-day year) results in more interest due on a loan. Using this ordinary interest in both cases, Example 2 then demonstrated that *exact time* brings more interest on a loan. Thus, of the four possible combinations, the combination of exact time and ordinary interest results in the most interest due to the lender and is, therefore, the combination most often used.

This combination of exact time and ordinary interest (number 3 in our list) is known as the **Bankers' Rule**, a name derived from the fact that banks (as well as other financial institutions) generally compute their interest in this way.

SECTION 3 *Problems*

Find the ordinary interest and exact interest

1. (a) On \$730 for 120 days at 6%.
   (b) On \$1,095 for 160 days at 9%.

2. (a) On \$730 for 90 days at 8%.
   (b) On \$1,460 for 180 days at 10%.

3. A loan of \$365 was made on April 2 for 6 months at 5%. Calculate the interest

on this loan using each of the four combinations of time and interest.

4. If \$365 was loaned on May 19 for 4 months at 9%, determine the interest due by each of the four combinations of time and interest.

5. Compute ordinary interest on \$720 for

152 days at the given rates. Study your answers carefully.

(a) 10%   (b) 5%
(c) 2½%   (d) 7.5%

6. Find the ordinary interest on $900 for 123 days at each of the given interest rates. Carefully observe the relationships among your answers.

(a) 8%   (b) 4%
(c) 2%   (d) 6%

7. Compute the ordinary interest on a $600 loan at 8% for each of the given time periods. Observe carefully the relationship between time and interest due.

(a) 90 days   (b)   45 days
(c) 30 days   (d) 120 days

8. Determine the ordinary interest on a $1,200 loan at 11% for each of the given time periods. Notice the relationship between change in time and the change in interest due.

(a) 120 days   (b)   60 days
(c)   30 days   (d) 180 days

9. The ordinary interest on a sum of money for a certain number of days at 6% was $6.40. Applying what you discovered in Problem 5, find the ordinary interest on this sum for the same number of days at

(a) 3%   (b) 9%   (c) 4.5%

10. The ordinary interest on a loan for a certain number of days at 8% was $12.60. Using what you learned in Problem 6, compute the ordinary interest on this loan for the same time at

(a) 4%   (b) 12%   (c) 6%

11. Interest of $9.30 was due on a 150-day loan at a certain rate. Applying what you learned in Problem 7, compute the interest on the same principal and at the same rate, if the time were

(a)   50 days   (b) 120 days
(c) 180 days

12. When interest was computed at a certain rate, the interest due on a 180-day loan was $15.60. Using your conclusions from Problem 8, find the interest due on the same principal and at the same rate if the time were

(a)   90 days   (b) 120 days
(c) 270 days

The **6%, 60-day method** is a frequently used shortcut for computing interest. When the time of a loan is 60 days ($=\frac{1}{6}$ year) and the interest rate is 6%, the time and rate will always cancel each other, as follows:

$$I = P \times \frac{\cancel{6}}{100} \times \frac{1}{\cancel{6}} = \frac{P}{100}$$

Thus, the interest charged will always be exactly $\frac{1}{100}$ or 1% of the principal. The interest on a 6%, 60-day loan can therefore be calculated very quickly by mentally moving the decimal point of the principal two places to the left.

Example One   Find the interest on $675 at 6% for 60 days, using the 6%, 60-day method.

The interest at 6% for 60 days is 1% of the principal.

$$I_{6\text{-}60} = 1\% \text{ of } \$675 = \$6.75$$

The problems in Section 3 pointed out that if the interest rate is halved, the interest will be cut in half. The same is true of time; if time is reduced to one-third as long, the interest will be only one-third as much. These facts are also employed as part of the 6%, 60-day method, in order to compute interest for other rates and times.

Example Two   Find the interest as indicated.

(a) $400 at 9% for 60 days.

Interest at 6% for 60 days is $I_{6\text{-}60} = \$4.00$.
Since 9% is $\frac{9}{6}$ or $\frac{3}{2}$ of 6%, the interest due is

$$\tfrac{3}{2}(\$4.00) = \$6.00$$

(b) $300 at 6% for 30 days.

$I_{6\text{-}60} = \$3.00$. Since 30 days is $\frac{30}{60}$ or $\frac{1}{2}$ of 60 days, the interest due is

$$\tfrac{1}{2}(3.00) = \$1.50$$

(c) $520 at 7.5% for 180 days.

$I_{6\text{-}60} = \$5.20$. Both the rate and time factors (multipliers) are different from 6% or 60 days, as follows:

$$7.5\%: \quad \frac{7.5}{6} = \frac{7.5}{6.0} = \frac{75}{60} = \frac{5}{4} \quad (\text{of } 6\%)$$

$$180 \text{ days}: \quad \tfrac{180}{60} = 3 \quad (60\text{-day periods})$$

Thus, the interest due is

$$(\tfrac{5}{4})(\tfrac{3}{1})(\$5.20) = \$19.50$$

Use the 6%, 60-day method to find the interest, and also find the amount on each of the following.

	Principal	Rate	Time		Principal	Rate	Time
1.	$1,850	6%	60 days	**12.**	1,260	8	40
2.	575	6	60	**13.**	360	9	45
3.	1,200	8	60	**14.**	600	5	150
4.	420	9	60	**15.**	436	7	90
5.	750	6	30	**16.**	596	7.5	120
6.	320	6	45	**17.**	780	7.5	80
7.	380	6	180	**18.**	1,275	9	48
8.	350	6	108	**19.**	664.73	9	40
9.	450	8	20	**20.**	764.36	8	45
10.	460	12	75	**21.**	206.25	7.5	48
11.	600	10	30	**22.**	482.18	4.5	80

SECTION 5
Simple Interest Notes

When a person borrows money, (s)he usually signs a written promise to repay the loan; this document is called a **promissory note**, or just a **note**. The money value that is specified on a note is the **face value** of the note. If an interest rate is mentioned in the note, the face value of this simple interest note is the principal of the loan. Interest is computed on the whole principal for the entire length of the loan, and the **maturity value** (principal plus interest) is repaid in a single payment on the **due date** (or maturity date) stated in the note. If no interest is mentioned, the face value is the maturity value of the note. The person who borrows the money is called the **maker** of the note, and the one to whom the money will be repaid is known as the **payee**.

The use of simple interest notes varies from state to state; the banks in some states issue simple interest notes, whereas others normally use another type of note. Figure 38 shows a simple-interest bank note. [The

NAME George D. Rogers   DUE DATE Oct. 5 No. 08335   July 7   , 19 —— $510.00

P ON DEMAND, or if no demand is made, then ____90 days____ after date, without grace, for value received, I, we, and
R each of us, as principals, promise to pay to the order of NORTH AUSTIN STATE BANK, at Austin, Texas,
I the sum of __Five hundred and no/100__————————————————————————————————————DOLLARS,
N with a __FINANCE CHARGE__ of __$10__ which is an __ANNUAL PERCENTAGE RATE__ of ____8____ % from __July 7__
   until maturity, and if not then paid, at the rate of 10% per annum until paid.
      In the event of default in the payment of this note, when due, or in the performance of any agreement contained in the security agreement if any is taken to secure
   payment hereof, or in the event the holder deems itself insecure, then the holder of this note shall have the option, without demand or notice, to declare the principal and
   interest at once due and payable and to exercise any and all other rights or remedies provided in this note and in the security agreement, if any, including the right to set
   off against this note and all other liabilities of the undersigned to the holder, all money or other property in its possession held for or owed to the undersigned.
      Each maker, surety, endorser, and guarantor of this note hereby waives presentment for payment or acceptance, notice of non-payment or dishonor, protest, notice of or
   protest, and diligence in the collection hereof or in filing suit herein and agrees that liability for the payment hereof shall not be affected or impaired by any release of or
   change in the security, if any, or by any extension in the time for payment; and further agrees to pay all costs and expenses of collection incurred by the holder, and if this
   note is placed in the hands of an attorney for collection after maturity, or is collected by legal proceedings of any kind, to pay a reasonable attorney's fee, which shall not in
   any event be less than the sum of $50.00 and shall bear interest at the rate of 10% per annum from the date of its accrual.
      Payment of this note is secured by all money or other property of the undersigned now or at any time hereafter in the possession of the holder in any capacity and also

by _____

                              INSURANCE AGREEMENT

CREDIT LIFE INSURANCE is not required to obtain this loan. No charge is made for credit insurance and no credit insurance is provided
unless the borrower checks the appropriate statement below:
   (a) The cost for Credit Life Insurance alone will be $_____ for the term of credit.   ☐ I desire Credit Life Insurance.

                                                                                                   ☒ I do not desire Credit Life Insurance.

                                    Signature for Insurance Acknowledgment

          Date _____   ___George D. Rogers___
I   Address: _4206 Running Brook Lane_
N   Phone: Bus. __472-8911__ Res. _____
S   Age ____ Filing Fee ____ __CO-SIGNERS ARE EXPECTED TO PAY IN THE EVENT THE BORROWER DOES NOT.__

X

$5
0 0

$1
0 0

FIGURE 38: Interest-Bearing Promissory Note.

393

face value of this note is $500. Notice that the maturity value ($510) is entered in the top margin for the bank's convenience.] Notes between individuals are usually simple interest notes also.

Another use is that of a customer giving a creditor a note which promises to pay an account on a specified date, either with or without interest. Figure 39 illustrates a customer's promise to pay without interest.

Before loaning money, a bank may require the borrower to provide **collateral**—some item of value which is used to secure the note. Thus, if the loan is not repaid, the bank is entitled to obtain its money by selling the collateral. (Any excess funds above the amount owed would be returned to the borrower.) Some items commonly used as collateral are cars, real estate, insurance policies, stocks and bonds, as well as savings accounts. Figure 40 illustrates a simple interest note in which a savings account is the collateral.

Most promissory notes are short-term notes—for 1 year or less. The most common time period for notes is one quarter (or 90 days), after which the interest due must be paid and the note may usually then be renewed for another quarter at the current rate.

In many localities, short-term loans from banks are almost exclusively either installment loans or simple discount loans. For an installment loan, the maturity value is calculated as for a simple interest loan; however, this

---

$250.00   Des Moines, Iowa   May 10, 19-

_____ Thirty days _____ after date _____ we _____ promise to pay

to the order of   Wilson Lumber Company

Two hundred fifty and no/100 -- Dollars

at   Wilson Lumber Company

for value received.

Due   June 9, 19-   (Seal) *Mason Jones*

                              (Seal) *Gladys P. Jones*

FIGURE 39: *Non-Interest-Bearing Promissory Note.*

DATE	CREDITS	BALANCE

DUE Oct. 13   **No.** 10411   **$ 1,242.00**

COLLATERAL NOTE

Austin, Texas, _____ April 16 ____, 19--

ON DEMAND, or if no demand be made, then ____ 180 days ____ after date, without grace, for value received, the undersigned (including all makers, endorsers, sureties, and guarantors) promise(s) to pay to the order of NORTH AUSTIN STATE BANK, at Austin, Texas

the sum of $1,200.00 with a FINANCE CHARGE of 542.00 which is an ANNUAL PERCENTAGE RATE OF 7% from April 16 until maturity, and if not then paid, at the rate of 10% per annum until paid.

The undersigned has pledged and deposited herewith as collateral security for the payment of this and any other liability or liabilities, joint or several, contingent or absolute, to the holder hereof, now due or to become due or that may hereafter be contracted or incurred, and hereby creates in favor of holder, a security interest in the following property, including all income and all cash, stock, and other dividends paid thereon, all securities received in addition thereto or in exchange therefor, and all rights to subscribe for securities incident to such property, hereinafter called collateral:

Savings account #42-6749

INSURANCE AGREEMENT

CREDIT LIFE INSURANCE is not required to obtain this loan. No charge is made for credit insurance and no credit insurance is provided unless the borrower checks the appropriate statement below:

(a) The cost for Credit Life Insurance alone will be $_____ for the term of credit.

☐ I desire Credit Life Insurance.
☒ I do not desire Credit Life Insurance.

_____   _____
Date   Signature for Insurance Acknowledgment

ADDRESS 7808 Silverlake Drive

PHONE: BUS. _____ RES. 345-7741

FILING FEE _____ AGE _____

James F. Wasson
Karen R. Wasson

FIGURE 40: *Interest-Bearing Promissory Note.*

amount is repaid in weekly or monthly payments rather than being repaid in one lump sum, as is the case for simple interest notes. (The simple discount loan and the installment loan are both discussed in detail in later topics.)

Example One

A note for $450 was dated June 12 and repaid in three months with interest at 8%. Find (a) the due date and (b) the amount repaid.

Solution

(a) The due date was September 12. Using the Banker's Rule, interest and maturity value were as follows:

(b) Sept. 12 = 255 day
$\underline{\text{June 12} = 163 \text{ day}}$
$t = \quad 92 \text{ days} \quad \text{or} \quad \frac{92}{360} \text{ year}$

$P = \$450$

$r = 8\%$

INTEREST	MATURITY VALUE
$I = Prt$	$S = P + I$
$= \$450 \times \frac{8}{100} \times \frac{92}{360}$	$= \$450 + \$9.20$
$I = \$9.20$	$S = \$459.20$

Example Two

The maturity value of a 60-day simple interest note was $976, including interest at 10%. What was the face value of the note?

$S = \$976$

$r = \frac{10}{100}$

$t = \frac{60}{360} \quad \text{or} \quad \frac{1}{6}$

$P = ?$

$S = P(1 + rt)$

$\$976 = P(1 + \frac{10}{100} \times \frac{1}{6})$

$976 = P(1 + \frac{5}{300})$

$976 = P(\frac{305}{300})$

$(\frac{300}{305})976 = P(\frac{305}{300})(\frac{300}{305})$

$\$960 = P$

Example Three

A $750 note drawn at 9% interest had a maturity value of $777. What was the time of the note?

$S = \quad \$777$
$\underline{P = - \quad 750}$
$I = \quad \$ \ 27$

$r = \frac{9}{100}$

$t = ?$

$I = Prt$

$\$27 = \$750 \times \frac{9}{100} \times t$

$27 = 67.5t$

$0.4 \text{ year} = t$

$t = 0.4 \text{ year} \times 360 \text{ days per year}$

$t = 144 \text{ days}$

NOTE: Since the Banker's Rule is used by financial institutions, the student should also use the Bankers' Rule at all times, unless other directions are given or unless it is impossible to compute exact time from the information given. (For example, if a problem involves a 3-month loan but no date is included, it is impossible to compute exact time; thus, ordinary time would have to be used. However, if a problem states that a 3-month loan began on some specific date, then the exact days during that particular 3-month interval would be used.) The 6%, 60-day method may also be used whenever it is convenient.

SECTION 5 *Problems*

1. Identify each part of the first note (Figure 38) shown previously.
   (a) Face value
   (b) Maker
   (c) Payee
   (d) Date
   (e) Due date
   (f) Principal
   (g) Rate
   (h) Time
   (i) Interest
   (j) Maturity value

2. Identify each part of the third note (Figure 40) shown previously.
   (a) Face value
   (b) Maker
   (c) Payee
   (d) Date
   (e) Due date
   (f) Principal
   (g) Rate
   (h) Time
   (i) Interest
   (j) Maturity value

Complete the following simple interest problems, using the Bankers' Rule whenever possible.

		Principal	Rate	Date	Due Date	Time	Interest	Maturity Value
3.	(a)	$600	8%	3/27	8/24			
	(b)	480	6%	4/17		6 months		
	(c)	288	5%	10/23		61 days		
	(d)		9%		9/23	140 days	$14	
4.	(a)	$800	7%	3/21	12/16			
	(b)	900	8%	5/3		92 days		
	(c)	840	9%	9/18		2 months		
	(d)		10%		11/20	108 days	$36	

5. A note dated May 15, 1979, reads: "Three months from date, I promise to pay $450 with interest at 8%." What will be the interest on the note and the maturity value?

6. A note dated February 8, 1979, calls for payment on June 8, 1979. Find the interest and the amount to be repaid, if the principal is $350 and the interest rate is 9%.

7. A note dated January 20, 1980, is due on April 9, 1980, with interest at 7%. If the principal is $270, what amount will be due?

8. A note dated April 2, 1980, reads: "Six months from date, I promise to pay $600 with interest at 12%." Find the maturity value.

9. Find the maturity value of an 8%, 7-month note with a face value of $720.

10. A 10-month note is drawn for $750 with interest at 8%. What amount will be repaid on the due date?

11. Find the interest rate charged if $307.50 was paid on October 17 to cancel a $300 debt incurred on April 20.

12. A note dated March 31 was due in 1 month. If the face value of the note was $840 and $847 was paid to discharge the debt, what interest rate was charged?

13. How long will it take $400 to earn $10 at 6% interest?

14. How much time is required for $900 to earn $27 interest at a 7.5% interest rate?

15. What time is required for $300 to amount to $304.50 at 5% interest?

16. How long will it take for $800 to amount to $855 at 11% interest?

17. The interest on a 183-day note is $12.81. If interest was computed at 6%, find the principal of the note.

18. A four-month note dated June 10 earned interest at 9%. If the interest due was $36.60, what was the face value of the note?

19. A 6-month note dated May 5 is discharged on the due date by a payment of $738.40. What was the principal of the note, if 5% interest was charged?

20. If $369.18 is paid on December 15 to discharge a note dated July 15, find the face value of the 6% note.

SECTION 6

Present Value

In the last two problems of the previous section, we were told that the maturity value of a note and asked to find what principal had been loaned. When the principal is being found, this is often referred to as finding the **present value**. Present value can also be explained by answering the question: What amount would have to be invested today (at the present) in order to obtain a given maturity value? This "X" amount that would have to be invested is the present value.

Present value at simple interest can be found using the same maturity value formula that has been used previously: $S = P(1 + rt)$. However, when present value is to be found repeatedly, the formula is usually altered slightly by dividing by the quantity in parentheses.

$$S = P(1 + rt)$$

$$\frac{S}{1+rt} = \frac{P\cancel{(1+rt)}}{\cancel{(1+rt)}}$$

$$\frac{S}{1+rt} = P$$

or

$$P = \frac{S}{1+rt}$$

The formula can be used more conveniently in this form, since it is set up to solve for the principal or present value. However, Example One illustrates a present-value problem solved with both versions of the formula, and either form may be used for this type of problem.

Example One If the maturity value of a 6%, 3-month note dated March 11 was $609.20, find the present value (or principal, or face value) of the note (see Figure 41).

$$S = P(1 + rt)$$

$$\$609.20 = P\left(1 + \frac{\cancel{6}}{\cancel{100}} \times \frac{\overset{92}{\cancel{92}}}{\underset{60}{360}}\right)$$

$$\$609.20 = P\left(1 + \frac{0.92}{60}\right)$$

$$609.20 = P\left(\frac{60}{60} + \frac{0.92}{60}\right)$$

$$609.20 = P\left(\frac{60.92}{60}\right)$$

$$\left(\frac{60}{60.92}\right)\overset{10}{\cancel{609.20}} = P\left(\frac{\cancel{60.92}}{\cancel{60}}\right)\left(\frac{\cancel{60}}{\cancel{60.92}}\right)$$

$$\$600 = P$$

$$P = \frac{S}{1+rt}$$

$$= \frac{\$609.20}{1 + \frac{\cancel{6}}{\cancel{100}} \times \frac{\overset{92}{\cancel{92}}}{\underset{60}{360}}}$$

$$= \frac{609.20}{\frac{60}{60} + \frac{0.92}{60}}$$

$$= \frac{609.20}{\frac{60.92}{60}}$$

$$= \overset{10}{\cancel{609.20}}\left(\frac{60}{60.92}\right)$$

$$P = \$600$$

FIGURE 41: *Determining the present value of the note in Example 1.*

Example 1 involved only one interest rate. Many investments, however, involve two interest rates. To illustrate present value at two interest rates, consider the following case.

Suppose that I find a place where I can earn 10% on my investment. The most I have been offered any other place is 6%, so I immediately invest $1,000 in this "gold mine." On the way home, I meet a friend who offers to buy this investment for the same $1,000 I just deposited. Would I sell the investment for $1,000, knowing I could not earn 10% interest on any other investment I might make? No! My $1,000 is really worth more than $1,000 to me, because I would have to deposit more than $1,000 elsewhere in order to earn the same amount of interest.

This case demonstrates that an investment is not always worth its exact face value; it may be worth more or less than its face value, when compared to the average rate of interest being paid by most financial institutions. This typical, or average, interest rate is referred to as the **rate money is worth**. Thus, if most financial institutions are paying 7%, then money is worth 7%.

If an investment is made at a rate that is not the prevailing rate money is worth, then the present value of the investment is different—either greater or less—than the principal. We therefore find what investment, made at the rate money is worth, would have the same maturity value that the actual investment has. The size of this "rate-money-is-worth investment" is the present or true value of the actual investment.

Example Two

A 90-day note for $1,000 is drawn on November 12 at 6%. If money is worth 8%, find the present value of the note on the day it was drawn.

The solution to this kind of problem involves two steps:

(a) Find the *actual maturity value* of the note and **(b)** find the *present value at the rate money is worth* of that calculated amount (Figure 42).

Solution

(a) $P_1 = \$1,000$

$r = 6\%$

$t = \frac{90}{360}$ or $\frac{1}{4}$

$S = ?$

$S = P(1 + rt)$

$= 1,000(1 + \frac{3\cancel{6}}{100} \cdot \frac{1}{\cancel{4}}_2)$

$= 1,000(1 + \frac{3}{200})$

$= 1,000(\frac{203}{200})$

$S = \$1,015$

(b) $S = \$1,015$

$r = 8\%$

$t = \frac{90}{360}$ or $\frac{1}{4}$

$P_2 = ?$

$P = \dfrac{S}{1 + rt}$

$= \dfrac{\$1,015}{1 + \frac{2\cancel{8}}{100} \cdot \frac{1}{\cancel{4}}}$

$= \dfrac{1,015}{1 + \frac{2}{100}}$

$= \dfrac{1,015}{\frac{102}{100}} = 1,015(\frac{100}{102})$

$P_2 = \$995.10$

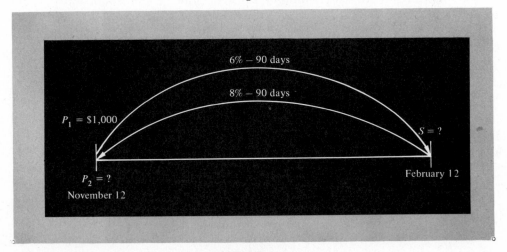

FIGURE 42

The present value of the note on the day it was drawn was $995.10. This means that the lender (payee) could have invested only $995.10 at the rate money is worth (8%) and would achieve the same maturity value ($1,015) that will be obtained on the $1,000 note at only 6% interest. That is, $995.10 invested at 8% would earn $19.90 interest ($995.10 + $19.90 = $1,015), producing the same $1,015 maturity value as $1,000 plus $15 interest. Thus, the $1,000 is really worth only $995.10 to the lender.

When computing present value of an investment where two interest rates are involved, one should know beforehand whether the present value is more or less than the principal. In general, the present value is less than the principal when the investment rate is less than the rate money is worth. That is, when the actual rate is less, then the present value is less. The reverse is also true: If the actual rate is more than the rate money is worth, then the present value is more than the principal.

Previous examples have required finding the present value on the day a note was drawn. It is often desirable to know the worth of an investment on some day nearer the due date. The worth of an investment on any day prior to the due date is also called present value. The procedure for finding this present value is the same as that already discussed, except that in the second step the time as well as the rate will be different. It should be emphasized that present value is:

1. Computed using the maturity value.

2. Computed for an exact number of days *prior* to the due date.

3. Computed using the rate money is worth.

Example Three Find the (present) value on October 11 of a $720, 4-month note taken out on July 10 at 10%, if money is worth 8% (Figure 43).

(a) $P_1 = \$720$ $I = Prt$ $S = P + I$

$r = 10\%$ $= \$720 \times \dfrac{10}{100} \times \dfrac{123}{360}$ $= \$720 + \$24.60$

$t = \frac{123}{360}$ $S = \$744.60$

$S = ?$ $I = \$24.60$

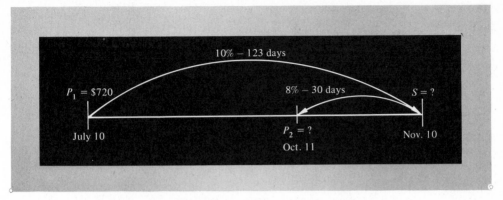

FIGURE 43: *Finding the present value of the note in part (a)*

(b) $S = \$744.60$

$P = \dfrac{S}{1+rt}$

$r = 8\%$

$t = \dfrac{30}{360}$ or $\dfrac{1}{12}$

$= \dfrac{\$744.60}{1 + \frac{\cancel{2}8}{100} \cdot \frac{1}{\cancel{12}_3}}$

$P_2 = ?$

$= \dfrac{744.60}{1 + \frac{2}{300}}$

$= \dfrac{744.60}{\frac{302}{300}}$

$= 744.60\left(\dfrac{300}{302}\right)$

$P_2 = \$739.67$

   This means that if the note were sold on October 11, it would be sold for \$739.67; this money could then be invested at 8% interest, and on Nobember 10 the maturity value of the new investment (\$739.67 plus \$4.93 interest) would also be \$744.60.

NOTE: Any convenient method may be used to find the amount in the following problems: $I = Prt$ and $S = P + I$; the 6%, 60-day method; or $S = P(1+rt)$.

Complete the following, using the Bankers' Rule.

		Maturity Value	Rate	Time	Present Value
1.	(a)	$820	6%	150 days	
	(b)	357	8%	90	
2.	(a)	$515	9%	120 days	
	(b)	828	7%	180	

Complete the following, finding the present value on the day of investment.

		Principal	Rate	Time	Maturity Value	Rate Money Is Worth	Present Value
3.	(a)	$1,000	7%	72 days		5%	
	(b)	800	5%	45		6%	
4.	(a)	$1,000	6%	60 days		9%	
	(b)	600	8%	90		5%	

Find the present value on the day indicated.

		Principal	Rate	Time	Maturity Value	Rate Money Is Worth	Days Before Maturity Date	Present Value
5.	(a)	$500	5%	72 days		6%	20 days	
	(b)	200	9%	100		6%	30	
6.	(a)	$600	8%	180 days		10%	72 days	
	(b)	800	12%	90		8%	15	

7. The maturity value was $465.30 on an 8% note. If the 5-month note was dated June 10, find its face value.

8. On August 4, $936 was paid in settlement of a note dated March 13. If interest was charged at 10%, what was the principal of the note?

9. A 10-month note for $600 was drawn on January 15 at 6%. If money is worth 9%, find the present value of the note on the day it was issued.

10. A 2-month note for $300 was drawn on May 28 at 6%. If money is worth 8%, find the present value of the note on the day it was made.

11. On April 10, a 3-month note for $450 is taken out at 8%. If money is worth 5%, find the present value of the note on June 4.

12. A 4-month note dated August 16 is made at 9% for $800. What is the present value of the note on November 1, if money is worth 8%?

13. A realtor received the following bids on a lot he was offering: $9,900 cash right now; $10,200 in 4 months; or $10,500 in 12 months. What is the best offer, if money is worth 6%? (HINT: Compare the present values of the three amounts.)

14. The following offers were made on a house: $39,500 cash; $41,000 in 3 months; or $42,500 in 9 months. Which offer should be accepted, if money is worth 10%?

CHAPTER 15 *Glossary*

Amount. (See "Maturity value at simple interest.")

Bankers' Rule. Commonly used method of interest calculation, where time is expressed in exact days over 360 days per year.

Collateral. An item of value which is pledged by a borrower in order to insure that a note will be repaid or equivalent value received.

Date (of a note). The date on which a note is drawn (or signed).

Due date (of a note). The date on which a note is to be repaid; the maturity date.

Exact interest. Interest calculated using 365 days per year.

Exact time. The time period of a loan expressed in the specific number of calendar days.

Face value. The money value specified on a promissory note; the principal of a simple interest note.

Interest. Rent paid for the privilege of borrowing money: $I = Prt$, where I = interest, P = principal, r = rate, and t = time.

Maker. A person who signs a note promising to repay a loan.

Maturity value (at simple interest). The total amount (principal plus interest) due after a simple interest loan; also called "amount" or "sum": $S = P + I$, or $S = P(1 + rt)$, where S = maturity value, P = principal, I = interest, r = rate, and t = time.

Maturity value (of a note). The amount to be repaid on the due date of a note (which may or may not include interest).

Note. A written promise to repay a loan (either with or without interest, and with or without collateral).

Ordinary interest. Interest calculated using 360 days per year.

Ordinary time. The time period of a loan where each month is assumed to have 30 days.

Payee. The person (or bank or firm) to whom the maturity value of a note will be paid.

Present value. (1) Principal; also (2) the value of another investment which, if made (on any given date) at the rate money is worth, would have the same maturity value as has an actual, given investment: $P = \dfrac{S}{1 + rt}$, where P = principal or present value, S = maturity value, r = rate, and t = time.

Principal. The original amount of money that is loaned or borrowed; the investment value on which interest is computed.

Promissory note. (See "Note.")

Rate. An annual per cent at which simple interest is computed.

Rate money is worth. An average or typical rate currently being used at most financial institutions.

1.0049999

Simple interest. Interest that is computed on the original principal of a loan and is then added to the principal to obtain the maturity value. (See also "Interest.")

Six-per-cent, 60-day method. This method of interest calculation is a shortcut based on the fact that simple interest at 6% for 60 days equals 1% of the principal.

Sum. (See "Maturity value at simple interest.")

Time. The duration of a simple interest investment. (Time must be expressed as a fractional year, in order to correspond with the annual percentage rate at which interest is calculated.)

CHAPTER 16

Bank Discount

CHAPTER 16 OBJECTIVES

Upon completion of Chapter 16, the student will be able to:

1. Define and use correctly the terminology associated with each topic.

2. a. Determine the proceeds of a simple discount note, using the simple discount formulas
   (1) $D = Sdt$; and
   (2) $p = S - D$. *(Section 1; Examples 1, 2; Problems 1-18)*
   b. Also, apply $p = S(1 - dt)$ to compute
   (Section 1; Example 3; Problems 7, 8, 17, 18)
   (1) Proceeds; or
   (2) Maturity value *(Section 2; Example 1; Problems 1, 2, 7–10)*.

3. a. Rediscount a simple discount note (or a simple interest note) on a given day prior to the maturity date
   (Section 2; Examples 2, 3; Problems 3–6, 11–16).
   b. Also, determine the amount of interest made
   (1) By original lender; and
   (2) By the second lender.

4. Compute the savings gained by signing a discount note on the last day allowed by invoice sales terms, in order to take advantage of the cash discount. (The bank note will be repaid on the same due date specified by the sales terms.) *(Section 3; Example 1; Problems 1–6)*

5. Explain the similarities and differences of simple interest and discount notes. *(Section 4; Problems 1–20)*

16

The preceding chapter discussed the simple interest note. Many banks, however, use the simple discount note (illustrated in the following section) for short-term loans of 1 year or less. There are some similarities and several major differences between the two types which it is imperative that the student understand. (The two notes will also be summarized in Section 4.)

SECTION 1
Simple Discount Notes

The student will recall that the face value of the simple interest note is the principal of the loan. Interest is computed on this principal and added to it to obtain the maturity value.

The **face value** of a discounted note, however, is the **maturity value**—the amount that will be repaid to the payee. As in the case of the simple interest note, the maturity value is repaid in a single payment at the end of the loan.

The interest on a discounted note is called **bank discount**. Bank discount is computed on the **maturity value** (face value) of the note and is then *subtracted* from the maturity value. (As opposed to simple interest, which is computed on the *principal* and then *added* to the principal to *obtain* the maturity value.) The amount remaining after the bank discount has been subtracted from the maturity value of the note is called **proceeds**. The proceeds is the actual amount which the borrower will receive from the bank and which can then be spent. Because the bank discount is subtracted from the face value before the borrower receives any money, this is often referred to as paying "interest in advance."

To reemphasize: the distinguishing aspect of the simple discount note is that interest is charged on the amount that is to be paid back, rather than on the amount that was actually borrowed.

Figures 44 and 45 illustrate typical simple discount notes. Figure 44 is an unsecured or signature note; that is, the loan is made simply on the basis of the borrower's good credit standing. Banks often establish some maximum amount which they will lend on an unsecured note. Figure 45

Int. = $20.00

$ 1,000.00 _____ March 19 ____, 19--

90 days _____ after date, for value received and with interest discounted to maturity

at __8__ % per annum, the undersigned promise(s) to pay

to **NORTH CAROLINA NATIONAL BANK** or Order

One thousand and no/100--------------------------------------Dollars

PAYABLE AT ANY OFFICE OF THE NORTH CAROLINA NATIONAL BANK IN NORTH CAROLINA. INTEREST HEREON SHALL ACCRUE AFTER MATURITY OR DEMAND, UNTIL PAID, AT THE RATE STATED ABOVE.

The holder of this note may accelerate the due date hereof or require the pledging of collateral as security herefor, or both, at any time the holder deems itself insecure. In the event the indebtedness evidenced hereby be collected by or through an attorney at law after maturity, the holder shall be entitled to collect reasonable attorneys' fees. The Bank is hereby authorized at any time to charge against any deposit accounts of any parties hereto any and all liabilities hereunder whether due or not. All persons bound on this obligation, whether primarily or secondarily liable as principals, sureties, guarantors, endorsers or otherwise, hereby waive the benefits of all provisions of law for stay or delay of execution or sale of property or other satisfaction of judgment against any of them on account of liability hereon until judgment be obtained and execution issued against any other of them and returned unsatisfied or until it can be shown that the maker or any other party hereto has no property available for the satisfaction of the debt evidenced by this instrument, or until any other proceedings can be had against any of them, also their right, if any, to require said Bank to hold as security for this note any collateral deposited by any of said persons as security for this demand, or any other demands. Demand, presentment, protest, notice of protest and notice of dishonor waived by all parties bound hereon. Witness my/our hand(s) and seal(s)

_____Charles N. Oxford_____ (Seal)

Address __3016 N. Enfield Drive_____

_____ (Seal)

Due __June 17____ No.__20842__

NCNB 2151 REV 10-69

FIGURE 44: *Simple Discount Note.*

INT = $30

$2,400.00   September 20 , 19--

60 days   after date, for value received and with interest discounted to maturity

at 7.5 % per annum, the undersigned promise(s) to pay

to   **NORTH CAROLINA NATIONAL BANK**   or Order

Two thousand four hundred and no/100--Dollars

PAYABLE AT ANY OFFICE OF THE NORTH CAROLINA NATIONAL BANK IN NORTH CAROLINA. INTEREST HEREON SHALL ACCRUE AFTER MATURITY OR DEMAND, UNTIL PAID, AT THE RATE STATED ABOVE.

To secure the payment of this note and liabilities as herein defined, the parties hereto hereby pledge and grant to said Bank (the word "Bank" wherever used herein shall include any holder or assignee of this note) a security interest in the collateral described as follows:

10 shares - IBM stock

and any collateral added thereto or substituted therefor, including shares issued as stock dividends and stock splits and dividends representing distribution of capital assets. The Bank is hereby authorized at any time to charge against any deposit accounts of any party hereto any and all liabilities whether due or not. The Bank may declare all liabilities due at once in the event any party hereto becomes subject to any proceedings for the relief of creditors including but not limited to proceedings under the Bankruptcy Act or otherwise, or if in the judgment of Bank the collateral decreases in value so as to render Bank insecure and Bank demands additional collateral which is not furnished, or if Bank at any time otherwise deems itself insecure. In the event the indebtedness evidenced hereby or liabilities as defined herein be collected by or through an attorney at law, the holder shall be entitled to collect reasonable attorneys' fees.

Upon failure to pay any liability when due, Bank may sell the collateral at public or private sale, for cash or on credit, as a whole or in parcels, without notice, and Bank may at any such sale purchase the collateral or any part thereof for its own account, and the proceeds of any such sale shall be applied first to the costs of such sale and the expenses of collection, including reasonable attorneys' fees, and then to the outstanding balance due on said liabilities, the application to be made in the manner and proportions as Bank elects. The Bank may forbear from realizing on the collateral or any part thereof, by sale or otherwise, all as the parties hereto may decide, and the liabilities of the parties hereto shall not be released, discharged or in any way affected by any such forbearance, nor shall any of the parties hereto have any rights or recourse against the Bank by reason of any action the Bank may take or omit to take under this note, by reason of any deterioration, waste, or loss of any of the collateral unless such deterioration, waste, or loss be caused by the willful act or willful failure to act of the Bank. Upon payment of this note the Bank may release the collateral but shall have the right to retain the same to secure any unpaid liabilities. Upon any transfer of this note and the collateral, the Bank shall be fully relieved of responsibility with reference thereto. Liabilities' as herein used, shall include this note and all obligations of every kind of any party hereto in whatever capacity to Bank, now or hereafter existing, whether arising directly or acquired from others as collateral or otherwise, whether absolute or contingent, joint or several, secured or unsecured, due or not due, direct or indirect, including, but not limited to, liabilities arising by operation of law, contractual or tortious, liquidated or unliquidated or otherwise.

All persons, who are now or hereafter bound hereon on this obligation, whether primarily or secondarily liable as principals, sureties, guarantors, endorsers or otherwise, hereby waive presentment, protest, notice of dishonor and of acceleration of maturity and any right to require the Bank to retain any collateral pledged as security for this note or any other liabilities and agree that any extension of time for payment with or without notice shall not affect their joint and several liabilities.

Witness our/my hand(s) and seal(s).

_____ (Seal)

_____ (Seal)

Address   619 Winding Way

Due November 19   No. 62275

NCNB 2155 REV. 10-69

FIGURE 45:   Collateral Discount Note.

411

illustrates a collateral note, which requires the maker (borrower) to secure the note with some item of value.

Bank discount is computed using the formula

$$D = Sdt$$

where D = discount, S = maturity value (face value) of the discount note, d = discount rate, and t = time. As would be expected, the Bankers' Rule is used for all discount notes.

Proceeds p are then found using the formula

$$p = S - D$$

Let us consider the difference between the amount of money one would be able to spend if (s)he borrows at a discount rate versus the amount available to spend when borrowing at an interest rate. (The following discount computation illustrates Figure 44.)

Example One The face values of two notes are $1,000 each. The discount rate and interest rate are both 8%, and the time of each is 90 days.

INTEREST NOTE	*DISCOUNT NOTE*
$P = \$1,000$	$S = \$1,000$
$r = 8\%$	$d = 8\%$
$t = \frac{90}{360}$ or $\frac{1}{4}$	$t = \frac{90}{360}$ or $\frac{1}{4}$
$I = Prt$	$D = Sdt$
$= \$1,000 \times \frac{8}{100} \times \frac{1}{4}$	$= \$1,000 \times \frac{8}{100} \times \frac{1}{4}$
$I = \$20$	$D = \$20$
$S = P + I$	$p = S - D$
$= \$1,000 + \$20$	$= \$1,000 - \$20$
$S = \$1,020$	$p = \$980$

Notice on the simple interest note that the borrower pays $20 for the use of $1,000. On the simple discount note, however, the borrower pays $20 for the use of only $980. Thus, based on the actual amount of money the borrower has available to spend, more interest is paid at a discount rate than at an interest rate. Or stated another way, the borrower is really paying slightly more than 8% on the money (s)he actually uses, since 8% of $980 for 90 days would be only $19.60 interest due, not $20.

From this example we can conclude that, when a borrower obtains money at a discount rate, (s)he will always be paying somewhat more than the stated rate on the money actually received. In addition, the **Truth in Lending Law**, enacted in 1969, enables the borrower to be more informed about the true rate being paid. The law requires the lender to reveal both the amount of interest and the annual percentage rate charged on the money received, correct to the nearest $\frac{1}{4}\%$. Banks have available tables which enable them to determine this true rate very easily. We will not study this procedure here, but will cover Truth in Lending rates more thoroughly in Chapter 17 as part of our study of installment buying. (The difference between the stated rate and the true rate is much greater when multiple payments are involved.)

It will be of interest here to know the true rate required under the Truth in Lending Law for the examples above. Figure 46 shows the Truth in Lending disclosure statement which corresponds to the note illustrated in Figure 44 and Example 1. We see that the true annual percentage rate paid for the $980 which the borrower received is actually 8.25%. For the note in Figure 45, the true rate is the stated rate of 7.5%, correct to the nearest $\frac{1}{4}\%$.

The bank discount formulas given above can be combined into a single formula for finding proceeds. By substituting Sdt for D, we have

$$p = S - D$$

$$= S - Sdt$$

$$p = S(1 - dt)$$

Example Two

A $3,000 note dated January 31 is to be discounted at 10% for 5 months. Find the bank discount and the proceeds using (a) $D = Sdt$, (b) the 6%, 60-day method, and (c) $p = S(1 - dt)$.

TRUTH IN LENDING DISCLOSURE STATEMENT
NORTH CAROLINA NATIONAL BANK
COMMERCIAL BANKING DEPARTMENT

DATE OF NOTE
March 19

BORROWER'S NAME
Charles N. Oxford

AMOUNT OF NOTE
$ 1,000.00

FINANCE CHARGES		AMOUNT FINANCED	
Interest	$ 20.00	Paid to Borrower	$ 980.00
Fees	$ --	Credit life Insurance Prem. (if any)	$ --
	$	Financing Statement Filling Fee (if any)	$ --
	$		$
Total FINANCE CHARGE	$ 20.00		$
ANNUAL PERCENTAGE RATE	8.25 %		$
Prepaid Finance Charge (if any)	$ --	TOTAL AMOUNT FINANCED	$ 980.00

No. of Payments	Due Dates or Periods	Amount of Regular Payment	Amount of Final Payment	Balloon Payment (if any)	Total of Payments
1	June 17	--	--	--	$ 1,000.00

SECURITY INTEREST IN THE FOLLOWING COLLATERAL (if applicable) _____

NOTE: The Security Agreement will secure future or other indebtedness and will cover after-acquired property.

☐ If checked, the collateral includes the principal residence of the borrower, and two (2) copies of the Notice of Right to Rescind are attached hereto.

REBATE OF UNEARNED FINANCE CHARGE IN EVENT OF PREPAYMENT   ☐ NO REBATE   ☐ OTHER (specify)_____

PROPERTY INSURANCE, IF REQUIRED, MAY BE PURCHASED FROM ANY REPUTABLE INSURER SELECTED BY THE BORROWER.

ADDITIONAL INFORMATION_____

Receipt of the foregoing statement fully completed and any attachments referred to therein is hereby acknowledged.

Charles N. Oxford
Customer's Signature

CREDIT LIFE INSURANCE ELECTION (if applicable)
I understand that Credit Life insurance is not required as a condition of this loan but may be purchased at a cost of $ _____ . I hereby affirm my desire to purchase such insurance.

NCNB 2260 REV. 2-70

Date _____

Customer's Signature for Credit Life Insurance _____

FIGURE 46: *Truth in Lending Disclosure Statement (for Figure 44).*

Solution   The Bankers' Rule should be applied when computing bank discount, as follows.

$$
\begin{array}{ll}
\text{June } 30 = & 181 \text{ day} \\
\text{January } 31 = - & 31 \text{ day} \\
\hline
\text{time} = & 150 \text{ days}
\end{array}
$$

$$S = \$3,000$$
$$d = 10\%$$
$$t = \tfrac{150}{360} \quad \text{or} \quad \tfrac{5}{12}$$

(a) $D = Sdt$

$\qquad = \$3,000 \times \tfrac{10}{100} \times \tfrac{5}{12}$

$\quad D = \$125$

$p = S - D$

$\qquad = \$3,000 - \$125$

$p = \$2,875$

(b) $\qquad D_{6-60} = \$30$

rate: $\quad \tfrac{10}{6} = \tfrac{5}{3}$

time: $\tfrac{150}{60} = \tfrac{5}{2}$

$D = (\tfrac{5}{3})(\tfrac{5}{2})(\$30)$

$D = \$125$

$p = S - D$

$\qquad = \$3,000 - \$125$

$p = \$2,875$

(c) $p = S(1 - dt)$

$\qquad = \$3,000(1 - \overset{5}{\tfrac{10}{100}} \times \underset{6}{\tfrac{5}{12}})$

$\qquad = \ 3,000(1 - \tfrac{25}{600})$

$\qquad = \ 3,000(\tfrac{600}{600} - \tfrac{25}{600})$

$\qquad = \ 3,000(\tfrac{575}{600})$

$p = \$2,875$

$D = S - p$

$\qquad = \$3,000 - \$2,875$

$D = \$125$

Although bank discount and proceeds may be found in any of the above ways, one would probably use method (a) or (b), since the computation would be easier.

It was shown in Example 1 that, when interest and bank discount are equal, the borrower has less spendable money from a discounted note. In that example, however, the maturity values of the two notes were not the same. We will now consider a simple interest and a simple discount note which both have the same maturity value, and compare the amounts which the borrower would have available to spend.

Example Three
A simple interest note and a simple discount note both have a maturity value of \$1,000. If the notes both had interest computed at 9% for 120 days, find (a) the principal of the simple interest note, and (b) the proceeds of the discount note.

Solution

(a) *SIMPLE INTEREST NOTE*

$S = \$1,000$

$r = 9\%$

$t = \frac{120}{360}$ or $\frac{1}{3}$

$P = ?$

$$P = \frac{S}{1 + rt}$$

$$= \frac{\$1,000}{1 + \frac{3\cancel{9}}{100} \times \frac{1}{\cancel{3}}}$$

$$= \frac{1,000}{\frac{100}{100} + \frac{3}{100}}$$

$$= \frac{1,000}{\frac{103}{100}}$$

$$= 1,000(\tfrac{100}{103})$$

$$P = \$970.87$$

(b) *SIMPLE DISCOUNT NOTE*

$S = \$1,000$

$d = 9\%$

$t = \frac{120}{360}$ or $\frac{1}{3}$

$p = ?$

$$p = S(1 - dt)$$

$$= \$1,000(1 - \tfrac{3\cancel{9}}{100} \times \tfrac{1}{\cancel{3}})$$

$$= 1,000(1 - \tfrac{3}{100})$$

$$= 1,000(\tfrac{100}{100} - \tfrac{3}{100})$$

$$= \cancel{1,000}(\tfrac{\overset{10}{97}}{\cancel{100}})$$

$$p = \$970$$

In this case, the maker of the note would have 87¢ more to spend if the note were a simple interest note. If \$970.87 were invested at 9% for 120 days, the maturity value would be \$1,000.

Example Four
A note discounted for 90 days had proceeds of \$786. If the face value of the note were \$800, what discount rate was charged?

$S = \quad \$800$
$p = - \quad 786$
$\overline{}$
$D = \quad \$\ 14$

$t = \frac{90}{360}$ or $\frac{1}{4}$

$d = ?$

$D = Sdt$

$\$14 = \$800 \times d \times \tfrac{1}{4}$

$14 = 200d$

$\dfrac{14}{200} = \dfrac{200d}{200}$

$0.07 = d$

$d = 7\%$

1. Identify the parts of the first discounted note (Figure 44) shown previously

(a)	Face value		(f)	Rate
(b)	Maker		(g)	Time
(c)	Payee		(h)	Bank discount
(d)	Date		(i)	Proceeds
(e)	Due date		(j)	Maturity value

2. Identify each part of the second discounted note (Figure 45) shown previously on page 411.

(a)	Face value		(f)	Rate
(b)	Maker		(g)	Time
(c)	Payee		(h)	Bank discount
(d)	Date		(i)	Proceeds
(e)	Due date		(j)	Maturity value

Supply the missing entries for Problems 3 and 4. Complete the table by using the Bankers' Rule.

		Maturity Value	Discount Rate	Date	Due Date	Time	Bank Discount	Proceeds
3.	(a)	$800	6%	3/5	6/3			
	(b)	640	7.5	1/10		150 days		
	(c)	300	5	7/19		120		
	(d)	450	8		12/16	60		
4.	(a)	$850	6%	8/11		120 days		
	(b)	480	7.5	5/20		60		
	(c)	550	8	4/16	7/15			
	(d)	600	9		10/7	180		

For Problems 5 and 6, use the 6%, 60-day method to find bank discount and to find proceeds.

5. (a) $400 at 5.5% for 90 days
    (b) 240 at 6% for 135 days
    (c) 840 at 7% for 30 days

6. (a) $540 at 8% for 75 days
    (b) 500 at 9% for 144 days
    (c) 360 at 7.5% for 108 days

Complete the following, using the Bankers' Rule.

		Maturity Value	Discount Rate	Date	Due Date	Time	Proceeds
7.	(a)	$420	6%	1/14		5 months	
	(b)	600	7	4/19		120 days	
	(c)	240	9	2/4		7 months	
	(d)	450	8	6/9		3 months	
8.	(a)	$450	8%	5/9		4 months	
	(b)	840	6	8/23		90 days	
	(c)	360	10	10/16		2 months	
	(d)	640	9	1/5		6 months	

9. A borrower signs a 120-day note for $600. If the bank discounts the note at 5%, what will be the amount of the check he receives from the bank?

10. A bank discounts notes at 8%. How much did a borrower receive from the bank after signing a $1,200 note for 150 days?

11. A note had a face value of $800. When the note was discounted at 6%, the bank discount was $12. What was the time of the note?

12. The bank discount was $15 on a note with a maturity value of $500. If the note was discounted at 9%, what was the time of the note?

13. The proceeds of a 60-day note were $296. If the discount was computed on a maturity value of $300, what discount rate was used?

14. The face value of a note was $840 and the proceeds were $819. What discount rate was charged on this 90-day note?

15. A note with maturity value of $900 is dated March 10 for 6 months. If a bank discount at 7.5% is deducted, what are the proceeds?

16. A 9-month note dated February 18 is discounted the same day at 9%. If the face value is $800, what are the proceeds?

17. The maturity values of two 3-month notes are both $714. Compare the present value at 8% interest with the proceeds at 8% discount.

18. Two 4-month notes both have maturity values of $1,560. Compare the present value at 12% interest with the proceeds at 12% discount.

SECTION 2

Maturity Value (and Rediscounting Notes)

It often happens that the proceeds of a simple discount note are known and one wishes to find the maturity value of the note. When problems of this type are to be computed, it is customary to use an altered version of the basic discount formula $p = S(1 - dt)$. The formula is altered by dividing both sides of the equation by the expression in parentheses:

$$p = S(1 - dt)$$

$$\frac{p}{1 - dt} = \frac{S(\cancel{1 - dt})}{(\cancel{1 - dt})}$$

$$\frac{p}{1 - dt} = S \qquad \text{or} \qquad S = \frac{p}{1 - dt}$$

Thus, the formula is set up to solve for the maturity value S. Example 1, however, shows a problem worked by both versions of the discount formula, and either form may be used to solve the assignment problems.

Example One

The proceeds were $440.80 on a 3-month note dated August 29 and discounted at 8%. What is the maturity value?

$p = \$440.80$

$d = 8\%$

$t = \frac{92}{360}$

$S = ?$

$$p = S(1 - dt)$$

$$\$440.80 = S\left(1 - \frac{8}{\cancel{100}} \times \frac{\cancel{92}^{45}}{\cancel{360}}\right)$$

$$= S\left(1 - \frac{0.92}{45}\right)$$

$$= S\left(\frac{45}{45} - \frac{0.92}{45}\right)$$

$$= S\left(\frac{44.08}{45}\right)$$

$$\left(\frac{45}{\cancel{44.08}}\right)\cancel{440.80}^{10} = S\left(\frac{\cancel{44.08}}{\cancel{45}}\right)\left(\frac{\cancel{45}}{\cancel{44.08}}\right)$$

$$\$450 = S$$

$$S = \frac{p}{1 - dt}$$

$$= \frac{\$440.80}{1 - \frac{8}{\cancel{100}} \times \frac{\cancel{92}^{45}}{\cancel{360}}}$$

$$= \frac{440.80}{1 - \frac{0.92}{45}}$$

$$= \frac{440.80}{\frac{45}{45} - \frac{0.92}{45}}$$

$$= \frac{440.80}{\frac{44.08}{45}}$$

$$= \cancel{440.80}^{10}\left(\frac{45}{\cancel{44.08}}\right)$$

$$S = \$450$$

The maturity value is $450 on November 29.

A promissory note, like a check or currency, is a negotiable instrument. That is, it can be sold to another party (a person, a business, or bank), or it can be used to purchase something or to pay a debt.

If the payee of a discounted note (usually some financial institution) sells the note to another bank, the note has been **rediscounted**. In that case, the second bank also uses the maturity value of the note as the basis for determining the proceeds which it will pay for the note. It should be observed that the discount rates which financial institutions charge each other are somewhat lower than those which banks ordinarily charge businesses and individuals.

When a note is rediscounted, the actual amount of interest earned by the original lender is determined as follows:

Rediscounted proceeds	(Amount received when note sold)
− Original proceeds	(Amount originally loaned)
Actual interest earned	(By original payee)

Example Two

City National Bank was the holder (payee) of a $1,200, 120-day note discounted at 9%. Thirty days before the note was due, City Bank rediscounted (or sold) the note to Capital Mortgage and Trust at 6%. (a) How much did City Bank receive for the note? (b) How much did City actually make on the transaction? (See Figure 47.)

ORIGINAL NOTE

Solution

$$S = \$1,200 \qquad\qquad D = Sdt$$

$$d = 9\% \qquad\qquad\qquad = \$1,200 \times \tfrac{9}{100} \times \tfrac{1}{3}$$

$$t = \tfrac{120}{360} \quad \text{or} \quad \tfrac{1}{3} \qquad\qquad D = \$36$$

$$p_1 = ? \qquad\qquad\qquad p = S - d = \$1,200 - \$36$$

$$\qquad\qquad\qquad\qquad p_1 = \$1,164$$

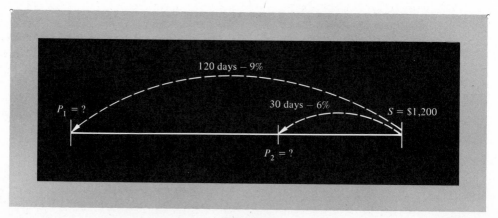

FIGURE 47

The proceeds of the original note (the amount which City Bank loaned to the maker) were $1,164.

REDISCOUNTED NOTE

$$S = \$1,200 \qquad\qquad p = S(1 - dt)$$

$$d = 6\% \qquad\qquad = \$1,200(1 - \tfrac{\overset{6}{\cancel{6}}}{100} \times \tfrac{\overset{1}{\cancel{1}}}{\cancel{12}})$$

$$t = \tfrac{30}{360} \quad \text{or} \quad \tfrac{1}{12} \qquad\qquad = 1,200\left(1 - \frac{1}{200}\right)$$

$$p_2 = ? \qquad\qquad = 1{,}\overset{6}{\cancel{200}}\left(\frac{199}{\cancel{200}}\right)$$

$$p_2 = \$1,194$$

(a) The proceeds of the rediscounted note were $1,194. That is, City Bank received $1,194 when they sold the note to Capital Mortgage and Trust.

(b) City Bank made $1,194 − $1,164 or $30 on the transaction. This is only $6 less than the entire $36 interest that City would have earned if they had kept the note, although only $\tfrac{3}{4}$ of the time had elapsed.

Discounting Simple Interest Notes

It is also possible that the payee of a simple interest note may wish to sell the note at a bank before the due date. The amount that the bank would pay is determined as follows:

1. Find the maturity value of the simple interest note.

2. Discount the maturity value of the note using the bank's rate and the time until the due date. The proceeds remaining is the amount that the bank would pay for the note.

3. The interest that the original payee has made is the difference between what the note was sold for (the discounted proceeds) and the original amount loaned (the principal of the simple interest note).

Example Three

A-1 Appliance Sales was the payee of an $800, 90-day note with interest at 12%. Forty days before the due date, A-1's bank discounted the note at 9%. (a) How much did A-1 receive for the note? (b) How much did A-1 make on the transaction? (See Figure 48.)

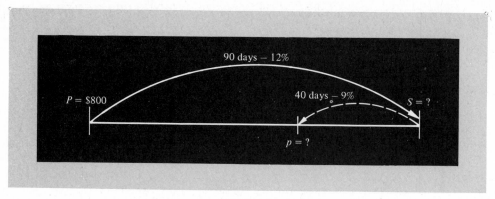

FIGURE 48

SIMPLE INTEREST NOTE (FINDING MATURITY VALUE)

Solution

$P = \$800$ $I = Prt$

$r = 12\%$ $= \$\cancel{800}^{8} \times \frac{\cancel{12}^{3}}{\cancel{100}} \times \frac{1}{4}$

$t = \frac{90}{360}$ or $\frac{1}{4}$ $I = \$24$

$S = ?$ $S = P + I$

                       $= \$800 + \$24$

                       $S = \$824$

DISCOUNT NOTE (FINDING PROCEEDS)

$S = \$824$ $D = Sdt$

$d = 9\%$ $= \$8.24 \times \frac{\cancel{9}}{\cancel{100}} \times \frac{1}{\cancel{9}}$

$t = \frac{40}{360}$ or $\frac{1}{9}$ $D = \$8.24$

$p = ?$ $p = S - D$

                       $= \$824 - \$8.24$

                       $p = \$815.76$

(a) A-1 received \$815.76 when the note was sold.

(b) Since they had loaned \$800 originally, A-1 made \$15.76 in interest. This is nearly $\frac{2}{3}$ of the \$24 interest which the maker will pay on the note, although only $\frac{5}{9}$ of the time has passed.

Complete the following.

		Proceeds	Discount Rate	Date	Due Date	Time	Maturity Value
1.	(a)	$714	5%	Jan. 25		60 days	
	(b)	770	9	July 12		150 days	
	(c)	295.40	6	Aug. 4		3 months	
	(d)	437.80	8	Apr. 25		4 months	
2.	(a)	$882	8%	Sept. 2		90 days	
	(b)	780	7.5	Apr. 26		120 days	
	(c)	581.60	6	Mar. 19		6 months	
	(d)	707.80	10	June 30		2 months	

Find the additional information.

		ORIGINAL NOTE				REDISCOUNTED NOTE			
		Maturity Value	Rate	Time	Proceeds	Rate	Time	Proceeds	Net Interest Earned
3.	(a)	$ 400	6%	270 days		5%	72 days		
	(b)	900	7	120		4	40		
	(c)	1,200	9	180		5	90		
4.	(a)	$ 500	8%	90 days		6%	60 days		
	(b)	600	10	150		8	45		
	(c)	1,500	6	96		5	48		

Find the net interest made on the following.

		SIMPLE INTEREST NOTE				DISCOUNTED NOTE			
		Principal	Rate	Time	Maturity Value	Discount Rate	Time	Proceeds	Net Interest Earned
5.	(a)	$500	6%	120 days		9%	40 days		
	(b)	600	5	180		8	75		
6.	(a)	$900	8%	150 days		6%	60 days		
	(b)	800	6	90		9	30		

7. On January 19, the proceeds of a 10-month note were $839.20. If "interest in advance" had been deducted at 8%, what was the face value of the note?

8. The proceeds of a 3-month note dated May 8 were $350.80. If the discount rate was 10%, what was the maturity value of the note?

9. A 4-month note was discounted at 6% on May 20. If the proceeds of the note were $411.39, what was the maturity value?

10. On January 31, the proceeds of a 5-month note were $1,155. If bank discount had been computed at 9%, what was the face value of the note?

11. On June 1, the First State Bank issued a 150-day note for $450, discounted at 8%. On September 19, First State rediscounted the note with the Bank of the West at 6%.
(a) What amount had First State loaned the maker?
(b) How much did First State receive when they rediscounted the note?
(c) How much did First State make on the transaction?
(d) How much more would First State have received if they had kept the note?

12. Community State Bank was the payee of a $600, 60-day note dated June 13 and discounted at 9%. On July 23, the note was rediscounted at First National Bank at 6%. Find
(a) The amount originally loaned by Community Bank.
(b) The amount received when the note was sold.
(c) The amount that Community Bank made on the transaction.
(d) How much less interest this was than

Community would have earned had they kept the note.

13. Andrew Gaines was the holder of a $400, 108-day note dated June 21, with interest at 5%. On September 7, Gaines' banker discounted the note at 6%.
(a) How much did Gaines receive when he sold the note?
(b) How much interest did Gaines make on the note?
(c) How much interest did Gaines lose by selling the note before the due date?

14. Luxury Carpet Center was the payee of an $800, 90-day note dated August 20, with interest at 10%. On October 4, Luxury Carpet discounted this note at their bank at 8%.
(a) How much did Luxury Carpet receive for the note?
(b) How much interest did Luxury Carpet earn on the note?
(c) How much interest did Luxury Carpet lose by not holding the note until maturity?

15. Blackman Furniture Co. was the payee of a $1,500, 120-day note dated April 30, with interest at 8%. On June 29, Blackman Furniture discounted the note at their bank at 6%.
(a) How much did the bank pay Blackman Furniture for the note?
(b) How much interest did Blackman Furniture earn on the note?
(c) How much more interest would Blackman Furniture have made by keeping the note until maturity?

16. Industrial Bank was the payee of a $1,000 180-day note dated May 19 and discounted at 11%. On September 4, the note was rediscounted with Jefferson Savings and Loan at a 7% discount rate.

(a) What amount did Industrial Bank lend to the maker of the note?

(b) What amount did Industrial Bank receive when they sold the note?

(c) How much interest did Industrial Bank earn on the note?

(d) How much interest did Industrial lose by not keeping the note to maturity?

SECTION 3

Discounting Notes to Take Advantage of Cash Discount

In Chapter 12, we learned that many merchants offer cash discounts as inducements to buyers to pay their accounts promptly. These discounts typically are a full 1% to 2% in only 10 days. When businesses do not have sufficient cash available on the last day of a cash discount period, they often sign a bank note in order to take advantage of the cash discount. Although the bank charges interest on the note, the business still "comes out ahead" if they borrow for only a short term. Remember that a bank rate of 9% means 9% for an entire year; for a 20-day note, the actual interest charge would be only $\frac{1}{2}$%. Thus, the business would still save $1\frac{1}{2}$% by borrowing to take advantage of a 2% cash discount.

The business would save money by borrowing provided that they borrowed for any short enough period of time so that the bank discount they must pay is less than the cash discount. However, we will consider only the situation when the maximum amount will be saved: On the *last* day of the cash discount period, a note is discounted so that the proceeds exactly equal the amount required to take advantage of the cash discount. The note will be for only the time remaining until the net amount of the invoice would have been due.

Example One

An invoice dated July 2 covers merchandise of $655 and freight of $4.85. Sales terms on the invoice are 2/10, n/30. A note is discounted at 9% in order to take advantage of the cash discount. (a) What will be the face value of the note? (b) How much will be saved by borrowing the necessary cash?

The last day of the discount period is July 12; the full net amount will be due 20 days later on August 1. Therefore, to obtain maximum savings, a discounted note will be signed on July 12 for 20 days.

Solution

(a)

	$655.00	Goods
×	0.02	
	$ 13.10	Cash discount

	$655.00	Goods
−	13.10	Cash discount
	$641.90	
+	4.85	Freight
	$646.75	Amount needed to take advantage of cash discount (proceeds needed)

Example One *(cont.)*

$p = \$646.75$

$d = 9\%$

$t = 20$ days

$\quad = \frac{20}{360}$ or $\frac{1}{18}$

$S = ?$

$$S = \frac{p}{1 - dt}$$

$$= \frac{\$646.75}{1 - \frac{9}{100} \times \frac{1}{18}}$$

$$= \frac{646.75}{1 - \frac{1}{200}}$$

$$= \frac{646.75}{\frac{199}{200}}$$

$$= 646.75\left(\frac{200}{199}\right)$$

$$S = \$650$$

The required note will have a face (maturity) value of $650.

(b)
$655.00	Goods
+ 4.85	Freight
$659.85	Amount due August 1 if a note is not signed
− 650.00	Maturity value of note due August 1
$ 9.85	Amount saved by discounting a note

SECTION 3 *Problems*

Complete the following.

		Amount of Invoice	Sales Terms	Amount Needed (Proceeds)	Time of Note	Discount Rate	Face Value of Note	Amount Saved
1.	(a)	$366.12	2/10, n/30			6%		
	(b)	814.29	2/15, n/30			6		
	(c)	923.71	3/10, n/30			8		
2.	(a)	$406.12	2/10, n/30			9%		
	(b)	912.24	2/15, n/45			8		
	(c)	616.49	3/15, n/30			8		

3. A bank note is discounted at 8% in order to take advantage of the cash discount on an invoice for $1,232.99 with terms of 3/15, n/30.
(a) What is the maturity value of the note?
(b) How much will be saved by borrowing to take the cash discount?

4. An invoice for $1,626.53 has terms 2/15, n/30. If a bank note is discounted at 9% in order to take advantage of the cash discount.
(a) What will be the face value of the note?
(b) How much will be saved by taking out the note?

5. An invoice shows merchandise of $612.50 and shipping charges of $7.00. A 10% bank note is discounted in order to take advantage of the 4/15, n/45 sales terms.
(a) What will be the face value of the note?
(b) How much will be saved by signing the note?

6. Freight and extra charges totaled $12.20 on an invoice for merchandise of $1,408.98. The invoice contains sales terms of 2/10, n/30.
(a) What would be the amount of a bank note discounted at 9% in order to take advantage of the cash discount?
(b) How much will be saved by borrowing in order to pay within the discount period?

SECTION 4

Summary of
Simple Interest
and Simple Discount

It is essential that the student understand the identifying characteristics of both the simple interest and simple discount notes, as well as the differences between the two. Both kinds of *promissory notes* are:

1. Generally for 1 year or less.

2. Repaid in a single payment at the end of the time.

As for their differences, the following are characteristic of the *simple interest note* (Figure 49):

1. The face value is the principal of the note. The face value is the actual amount which was loaned.

2. Interest is computed on the face value of the note at the rate and for the time which appear on the note.

3. The maturity value of the simple interest note is the sum of the face value plus interest.

4. A simple interest problem will contain one or more of these identifying characteristics: "*interest* rate of $x\%$"; "with *interest* at $x\%$"; a maturity value which exceeds the face value; "*amount*".

$400

_____

6%   interest

FIGURE 49:   *Simple Interest Note.*

$600

_____

6%   Interest discounted to maturity

FIGURE 50:   *Simple Discount Note.*

5. The solution of simple interest problems requires one or more of the following formulas:

(a) $I = Prt$

(b) $S = P + I$

(c) $S = P(1 + rt)$

(d) $P = \dfrac{S}{1 + rt}$

The following are characteristic of the *simple discount note* (a sample of which is shown in Figure 50):

1. The face value of the simple discount note is the maturity value—the amount that will be repaid.

2. Discount notes may contain a rate quoted as a certain per cent "discounted to maturity." The interest (called "bank discount") is computed on the face value of the note. (That is, the borrower pays interest on the amount that will be repaid, rather than on the amount actually borrowed.)

3. The actual amount which the borrower (maker) receives from the lender (payee) is called the "proceeds." The proceeds are found by subtracting the bank discount from the face value. This is often called paying interest in advance.

4. Simple discount problems may be distinguished from simple interest problems by the use of one or more of the following terms: "*discount rate of x%*"; *discounted* at *x%*; "*proceeds*"; maturity value equals the face value; "interest in advance."

5. The solution of simple discount problems requires one or more of the

following formulas:

(a) $D = Sdt$

(b) $p = S - D$

(c) $p = S(1 - dt)$

(d) $S = \dfrac{p}{1 - dt}$

SECTION 4 *Problems*

1. An $800 note is taken out for 120 days at 7.5%. Find the interest and the amount.

2. Find the interest and amount on a $600 note for 90 days at 8%.

3. The face value of a 150-day note is $480. Compute the bank discount at 10% and find the proceeds.

4. A bank discounts a 180-day note for $1,000 at 9%. Find the bank discount and the proceeds.

5. The face value is $600 on both a simple interest and a simple discount note. If both notes have interest charged at 10% for 90 days:

(a) How much interest will be charged on each note?

(b) How much will each maker have to spend?

(c) How much will the payee receive on the maturity date in each case?

6. A simple interest and a simple discount note both have face values of $450. Both notes are for 60 days, and both have interest charged at 8%.

(a) Find the interest which will be paid on each.

(b) Find the amount the borrower will actually receive in each note.

(c) Find the maturity value of each note.

7. The proceeds of a 6%, 75-day note are $790. Find the maturity value; the face value.

8. Find the face value of an 11%, 45-day note if the proceeds are $789. What is the maturity value?

9. A 144-day note with interest at 7% has a maturity value of $514. Find the principal of the loan. What is the face value of the note? What amount did the maker receive on the loan?

10. The maturity value is $412 on a 108-day note with interest at 10%. What is the face value of this note? How much did the maker receive on the loan?

11. Two 4-month notes both have maturity values of $721.

(a) Compare the present value at 9% interest with the proceeds at 9% discount.

(b) What amount does the maker receive from each note?

(c) How much interest is paid on each note?

12. The maturity values of two 6-month notes are both $820.

(a) Compare the present value at 5% interest with the proceeds at 5% discount.

(b) How much would the maker have to spend in each case?

(c) What amount of interest is paid on each?

13. On April 12, a $360, 5-month note is drawn with interest at 7%. If money is worth 9%, what is the (present) value of the note on the day it was drawn?

14. A $540 note was issued on May 30 for 2 months at 6% interest. If money is worth 9%, what was the (present) value of the note on the day it was drawn?

15. On May 15, a $420 note is drawn for 7 months, with interest to be charged at 6%. Find the present value of the note 90 days before it is due, if most investments are earning interest at 8%.

16. On June 9, a 4-month note is signed for $450 with interest at 8%. If the standard rate of interest is 10%, find the present value of the note 72 days before it is due.

17. Capital Furniture Co. was the payee of a $600, 3-month note dated September 15, with interest at 12%. Twenty days before it was due, Capital Furniture sold the note to their bank, which discounted it at 9%.
(a) What did Capital Furniture receive for the note?
(b) How much did Capital make on the note?
(c) How much interest did the bank earn?

18. William Lacy was the holder of a 5-month, $600 note dated April 20 with interest at 6%. Forty-five days before the note was due, Lacy discounted the note at his bank at 8%.
(a) How much did Lacy receive for the note?
(b) How much interest did he earn?
(c) How much interest did the bank make?

19. On March 11, the Columbia State Bank became the holder of a 2-month note for $720, discounted at 10%. Thirty days before the due date, Columbia rediscounted the note with a trust company at 6%.
(a) How much were the proceeds loaned to the maker of the note?
(b) What amount did Columbia Bank receive for the note?
(c) How much interest did Columbia make on the note?
(d) How much interest did the trust company earn?

20. Citizens Bank was the payee of an $800 note dated June 9 for 6 months, discounted at 9%. The Citizens Bank rediscounted the note at 6% at another bank 60 days before it was due.
(a) What amount had the Citizens Bank loaned to the maker?
(b) How much did Citizens Bank receive when they sold the note?
(c) How much interest did Citizens Bank earn?
(d) How much interest did the second bank make?

CHAPTER 16 *Glossary*

Bank (or simple) discount. Interest that is computed on the maturity value of a loan and is then subtracted to obtain the proceeds; often called "interest in advance": $D = Sdt$, where D = bank discount, S = maturity value, d = discount rate, and t = time.

Face value. The money value specified on any promissory note, the maturity value of a simple discount note.

Maturity value. The total amount (Proceeds plus Bank discount) due after a simple discount loan; the value on which simple discount is computed.

Proceeds. The amount remaining after bank

discount is subtracted from maturity value; the amount actually received by a borrower: $p = S - D$ or $p = S(1 - dt)$, where $p =$ proceeds, $S =$ maturity value, $D =$ bank discount, $d =$ discount rate, and $t =$ time.

Rediscounted note. A simple discount note that is sold for a value equal to the proceeds of the note at the buyer's discount rate.

Simple discount. (See "Bank discount.")

Truth in Lending. A federal law requiring lenders to disclose both their total finance charge and corresponding annual percentage rate (based on the amount actually received by a borrower).

CHAPTER 17

Multiple Payment

Plans

```
╔══════════════════════════════════════════════════╗
║         CHAPTER 17   OBJECTIVES                    ║
╚══════════════════════════════════════════════════╝
```

Upon completion of Chapter 17, the student will be able to:

1. Define and use correctly the terminology associated with each topic.

2. Apply the United States rule to
   a. Compute the credit to be given for partial payments made on a note; and
   b. Find the balance due on the maturity date.
   (*Section 1; Example 1; Problems 1–6*)

3. On an open-end charge account,
   a. Compute the interest due monthly and
   b. Determine the total amount required to pay off the account.
   (*Section 2; Example 1; Problems 1, 2, 9, 10*)

4. Determine for an installment plan purchase the
   a. Down payment;
   b. Finance charge; and
   c. Regular monthly or weekly payment.
   (*Examples 2, 3; Problems 3, 4, 11–14*)

5. a. Compute "finance charge per $100" (or "rate×time") and
   b. Consult a table to determine the annual percentage rate charged on an installment purchase. (*Examples 3–5; Problems 5, 6, 15–30*)

6. Construct a table to verify that the annual percentage rate (Objective 5) would actually result in the amount of interest charged.
   (*Examples 4, 5; Problems 7, 8, 27–30*)

The simple interest and simple discount notes studied earlier are normally repaid in a single payment at the end of the time period. However, a borrower may prefer to repay part of a debt before the entire loan is due. The lender, in order to give the borrower proper credit for payments made prior to the maturity date, should apply the United States rule. Also, many firms, when extending credit, feel that the entire debt will more likely be repaid if the borrower is required to make regular installment payments which begin immediately, rather than a single payment, which is not due for some time. Partial payments may thus be made under the *United States rule* or on basic *installment plans*, both of which are discussed in the following sections.

SECTION 1
United States Rule

A person who has borrowed money on a note may sometimes wish to pay off part of the debt before the due date, in order to reduce the amount of interest paid. Such partial payments are not required (as they would be for an installment loan) but may be made whenever the borrower's financial condition permits. The United States rule, which we shall study, is used to calculate the credit which should be given for partial payments and to determine how much more is owed on the debt.

The **United States rule** derives its name from the fact that this method has been upheld by the United States Supreme Court, as well as by a number of state courts. It is the method used by the federal government in its financial transactions.* The Banker's rule should be used to determine "time" for the interest calculations in this section.

Basically, the U.S. rule is applied in the following manner:

1. Interest is computed on the principal from the first day until the date of the first partial payment.

---

* It might also be noted that interest calculations by the U.S. government use exact interest: t = exact days over 365 or 366. However, exact interest is not an essential part of the U.S. rule.

2. The partial payment is used first to pay the interest, and the remaining part of the payment is deducted from the principal.

3. The next time a payment is made, interest is calculated on the adjusted principal from the date of the previous payment up to the present. The payment is then used to pay the interest due and to reduce the principal, as before. (This step will be repeated for each payment made prior to the maturity date.)

4. The balance due on the maturity date is found by computing interest due since the last partial payment and adding this interest to the unpaid principal.

Example One On April 1, Mary Carrington Interiors took out a 90-day note for $1,500 bearing interest at 8%. On May 1, Carrington paid $700 toward the obligation; and on May 16, she paid another $300. How much remains to be paid on the due date?

(a) Using the 6%, 60-day method of interest calculation, interest is computed on the original $1,500 from April 1 until the day of the first partial payment (May 1):

$$\begin{array}{ll} \text{May } 1 = \quad 121 \text{ day} & I_{6-60} \quad \$15 \\ \text{April } 1 = - \quad 91 \text{ day} & \\ \hline \quad\quad\quad 30 \text{ days} & 8\%: \quad \frac{8\%}{6\%} = \frac{4}{3} \text{ (of 6\%)} \\ & 30 \text{ days}: \quad \frac{30}{60} = \frac{1}{2} \text{ (of 60 days)} \end{array}$$

$$I = \$15 \times \tfrac{4}{3} \times \tfrac{1}{2}$$
$$I = \$10$$

(b) The $700 is first applied to pay the interest, and the remaining amount ($700 − $10 = $690) is then deducted from the principal:

Principal	$1,500
Less: payment to principal	− 690
Adjusted principal	$ 810

(c) Interest is computed on the $810 adjusted principal from May 1 until May 16. The $300 payment first pays this interest, and the remainder of the payment is then subtracted from the current principal:

$$\begin{array}{ll} \text{May } 16 = \quad 136 \text{ day} & I_{6-60} = \$8.10 \\ \text{May } \;\; 1 = - 121 \text{ day} & \\ \hline \quad\quad\quad\quad 15 \text{ days} & 8\%: \quad \tfrac{4}{3} \\ & 15 \text{ days}: \quad \frac{15}{60} = \frac{1}{4} \text{ (of 60 days)} \end{array}$$

$$I = \$8.10 \times \tfrac{4}{3} \times \tfrac{1}{4}$$

$$I = \$2.70$$

Partial payment	$300.00	Current principal	$810.00
Less: interest	− 2.70	Payment to principal	− 297.30
Payment to principal	$297.30	Adjusted principal	$512.70

(d) No other payment is made until the maturity date; therefore, interest is computed on $512.70 from May 16 until the 90-day period ends on June 30. The maturity value $(P + I)$ is the final payment:

June 30 = 181 day	$I_{6-60} = \$5.13$
May 16 = 136 day	8%: $\tfrac{4}{3}$
45 days	45 days: $\tfrac{45}{60} = \tfrac{3}{4}$ (of 60 days)

$$I = \$5.13 \times \tfrac{4}{3} \times \tfrac{3}{4} \qquad S = \quad P \quad + \quad I$$

$$I = \$5.13 \qquad\qquad = \$512.70 + \$5.13$$

$$S = \$517.83$$

Thus, $517.83 remains to be paid on June 30. The total interest paid was $10 + $2.70 + $5.13 = $17.83. With no partial payments, interest on the note would have been $30. Thus, $30 − $17.83 = $12.17 was saved by making early payments.

The entire process required in the foregoing application of the United States rule is summarized below:

Original principal, 4/1		$1,500.00
1st partial payment, 5/1	$700.00	
Less: interest ($1,500, 8%, 30 days)	− 10.00	
Payment to principal		− 690.00
Adjusted principal		$ 810.00
2nd partial payment, 5/16	$300.00	
Less: interest ($810, 8%, 15 days)	− 2.70	
Payment to principal		− 297.30
Adjusted principal		$ 512.70
Interest due ($512.70, 8%, 45 days)		+ 5.13
Balance due, 6/30		$ 517.83

Complications arise from the United States rule if the partial payment is not large enough to pay the interest due. The unpaid interest cannot be added to the principal, for then interest would be earned on interest; this would constitute compound interest, and the charging of compound interest on loans is illegal. This problem is solved simply by holding the payment or payments (without giving credit for them) until the sum of these partial payments is large enough to pay the interest due to that date. The procedure then continues as usual. (Note that the borrower does not save any interest unless the partial payment is sufficiently large to pay the interest due and reduce the principal somewhat.)

SECTION 1 *Problems*

Using the United States rule, determine the balance due on the maturity date of each of the following notes. (Use the Bankers' Rule and compute interest by either the 6%, 60-day method or I = Prt.)

		NOTE		PARTIAL PAYMENTS	
	Principal	Rate	Time	Amount	Day
1. (a)	$1,800	10%	180 days	$615	30th day
				630	120th
(b)	1,000	9	120	405	20th
				206	60th
(c)	1,500	8	270	530	90th
				310	135th
2. (a)	$1,000	9%	120 days	$415	60th day
				203	80th
(b)	1,500	6	150	410	40th
				511	100th
(c)	1,200	8	205	320	75th
				468	165th

3. On March 3, Andrew Myer signed a $3,000 note with interest at 8% for 270 days. Myer made payments of $680 on July 1 and $932 on August 30. How much will he owe on the due date?

4. Randolph Distributors Inc. borrowed $2,500 on a note dated April 18, with interest at 9% for 180 days. A payment of $825 was made toward the note on May 28, and $734 was paid on August 16. Find the balance due on the day the note matures.

5. Henderson Paving Co. was the maker of a 10.5% note for $4,000, dated June 20 for 150 days. The firm made partial payments of $835 on July 20 and $1,642 on September 3. What payment will be required when the note is due?

6. On February 20, Albert Rogers borrowed $1,200 by signing a 7.5%, 240-day note. He made a $415 partial payment on April 21 and paid $210 on June 20. Determine the amount he still owes at the end of the loan period.

SECTION 2

Installment

Plans

The student undoubtedly already has some knowledge of that uniquely American tradition, the **installment plan**. Almost all department stores, appliance stores, and furniture stores, as well as finance companies and banks, offer some form of installment plan whereby a customer may take possession of a purchase immediately and, for an additional charge, pay for it later by a series of regular payments. Americans pay exhorbitant rates, as we shall see, for the privilege of buying on credit; but, because the dollar amounts involved are not extremely large, many people are willing to pay them.

The installment plan actually provides a great boost to the American economy, because many families buy things on the spur of the moment on the installment plan that they would never buy were they compelled to save the money required for a cash purchase. The lure of the sales pitch—"nothing down; low monthly payments," "budget terms," "go now, pay later," "buy now; no payment for 60 days," "small down payment; 3 years to pay," "consolidate all your bills into one low, monthly payment"—has caused many families to feel that they will never miss that small extra amount each month. The result is that many families soon find themselves saddled with so many of these "small monthly payments" that they cannot make ends meet and are in danger of bankruptcy. The Chamber of Commerce or the Family Service Agency in many cities provides inexpensive counseling to help such families learn to budget their incomes and "get back on their feet" financially.

The **Truth in Lending Law** (officially entitled Regulation Z), which took effect in 1969, enables consumers to determine how much the privilege of credit buying actually costs, thereby allowing them to make intelligent decisions when faced with the question of when to buy on the installment plan. Indeed, the question has become "when to buy" rather than "whether to buy," because almost all Americans take advantage of time-payment plans at one time or another. The single item most often purchased in this way (other than homes) is the automobile, which is followed by other durable items, such as furniture and appliances. Even realizing the expense of these plans, most people feel that the added convenience at times justifies the additional cost.

The high rate of interest charged by companies offering installment plans is not without justification. The merchant incurs numerous additional operating expenses as a result of the installment plan: the costs of investigating the customer's credit standing, discounting bank notes, buying extra insurance, paying cashiers and bookkeepers for the additional work, collection costs necessitated by buyers who do not keep up with payments, as well as "bad debts" loss from customers who never finish paying. And, of course, the merchant is entitled to interest, since the business has capital invested in the merchandise being bought on the time-payment plan. Thus, the installment plan is expensive for the seller as well as the buyer.

Basically, there are two types of installment plans: open end accounts and accounts with a set number of payments, which are described in the following paragraphs.

Open End
Accounts

The first plan is called **open end credit,** because the time period of the credit account is not definite and the customer may receive additional credit before the first credit is entirely repaid. Under this plan, interest is computed each month on the unpaid balance (or sometimes on an average balance). Each payment is applied first toward the interest and then toward the balance due, in accordance with the United States rule of partial payments.

This plan is used by most department stores and other retail businesses offering "charge accounts" and "credit cards." The monthly interest rate is usually 1% (= 12% per year) to $1\frac{1}{2}$% (= 18% per year). Customer accounts at these stores usually vary quite a bit from month to month, because the account results from a number of small purchases rather than one large purchase. Many accounts of this type are never actually paid off, because new purchases continue to be made. These accounts are therefore often called **revolving charge accounts.** There may be a limit to the amount a customer is entitled to charge; and a prescribed minimum monthly payment may be required according to the amount owed. (For instance, suppose the maximum balance that a charge account may reach is $200. The customer may be required to pay at least $10 per month if her balance is under $100 and must pay at least $15 per month if she owes $100 or more.)

Example One

Installment Plan Having Monthly Rate

Mrs. Cohen's charge account at Butler-Stohr has a balance of $100. Interest of 1% per month is charged on unpaid customer accounts. Mrs. Cohen has decided to pay off her account by making monthly payments of $25. (a) How much of each payment is interest, and how much will apply toward her account? (b) What is the total amount Mrs. Cohen will pay, and how much of this is interest?

The following schedule computes the interest and payment that applies toward the balance due each month. "Interest" is found by taking 1% of the "balance due." This interest must then be deducted from the "monthly payment" in order to determine the "payment (that applies) toward the balance due." The "payment toward balance due" is then subtracted from the "balance due" to find the "adjusted balance due," which is carried forward to the next line as the "balance due."

Solution (a)

Payment Number	Balance Due	1% Interest Payment	Monthly Payment	Payment Toward Balance Due	Adjusted Balance Due
1	$100.00	$1.00	$25.00	$24.00	$76.00
2	76.00	.76	25.00	24.24	51.76
3	51.76	.52	25.00	24.48	27.28
4	27.28	.27	25.00	24.73	2.55
5	2.55	.03	2.58	2.55	.00
		$2.58	$102.58	$100.00	

(b) During the last month, Mrs. Cohen paid only the remaining balance due plus the interest due. She thus paid a total of $102.58 in order to discharge her $100 obligation, which included total interest of $2.58.

Accounts with Set Number of Payments

This second type of installment plan is used when a single purchase (automobile, suite of furniture, washing machine, etc.) is made. In this case, the account will be paid in full in a specified number of payments; hence, finance charges for the entire time are computed and added to the cost at the time of purchase.

The typical procedure for an installment purchase is as follows. The customer makes a **down payment** (sometimes including a trade-in) which is subtracted from the cash price to obtain the **outstanding balance.** A **carrying charge** (or **time payment differential**) is then added to the outstanding balance. The resulting sum is divided by the number of payments (usually weekly or monthly) to obtain the amount of each installment payment.

This type of time payment loan is also used by finance companies and by banks in their installment loan, personal loan, and/or automobile loan departments. The only variations in the plan as described above are that there is no down payment made (the amount of the loan becomes the outstanding balance) and the interest charged corresponds to the carrying charge. Bank interest rates are usually lower, because banks will lend money only to people with acceptable credit ratings. Finance companies cater to persons whose credit ratings would not qualify them for loans at more selective institutions. Many states allow these small-loan agencies to charge up to $3\frac{1}{2}\%$ per month (or 42% per year). Their profits are not so high as their rates might indicate, however, for these companies have a high percentage of bad debts from uncollected loans.

As noted above, high-powered advertising has often misled buyers into making financial commitments that were substantially greater than they realized beforehand. The Truth in Lending Law protects against false impressions by requiring that if a business mentions one feature of credit in its advertising (such as the amount of down payment), it must also mention all other important features (such as the number, amount, and frequency of payments that follow.) If an advertisement states "Only $2 down," for example, it must also state that the buyer will have to pay $10 a week for the next 2 years.

The principal accomplishment of the law is that it enables the buyer to know both the **finance charge** (the total amount of extra money paid for buying on credit) and the **annual percentage rate** to which this is equivalent. Some merchants may require a carrying charge, a service charge, interest, insurance, or other special charges levied only upon credit sales; the finance charge is the sum of all these items. The annual percentage rate correct to the nearest quarter of a per cent must then be determined by one of the two methods approved in the law. Tables are available from the government which enable the merchant to determine the correct percentage rate without extensive mathematical calculations.

It is important to understand the distinction between the interest rates required under the law and simple interest rates such as we studied previously. Formerly, merchants often advertised a simple interest rate, and interest was computed on the original balance for the entire payment period. Consider the following, however: On a simple interest note, the borrower keeps all the money until the due date; thus, the borrower rightfully owes interest on the original amount for the entire period. On an installment purchase at simple interest, on the other hand, the buyer must immediately begin making payments. As the credit period expires, therefore, the buyer has repaid most of the obligation and then owes very little, yet the latter payments would still include just as much interest as the early payments did. This means the buyer would be paying at a much higher interest rate than on the early payments. A simple interest rate would thus be deceiving; however, the Truth in Lending Law permits the buyer to know the true rate that is paid. (Examples in this section will illustrate the differences in these rates.) Since the rates required under the law are quite complicated to compute, the Federal Reserve System publishes tables which merchants can use to determine annual percentage rates. These tables contain rates corresponding to both monthly and weekly payments; however, this text will include tables only for monthly payments.

It should be pointed out that the Truth in Lending Law does not establish any maximum interest rates or maximum finance charges or otherwise restrict what a seller may charge for credit. Neither are there restrictions on what methods the seller may use to determine the finance charge. The law only requires that the merchant fully inform the buyer what (s)he is paying for the privilege of credit buying. In addition to the finance charge and the annual percentage rate, other important information must also be itemized for the buyer, including penalties (s)he must pay for not conforming to the provisions of the credit contract.

NOTE: The term "installment plan," as used in this section, describes high-interest payment plans which run for a limited period. (The maximum time is usually 3 years.) The chapter on amortization includes the periodic payments made to repay home loans or other real estate loans, to repay long-term personal bank loans, or to repay other loans when a relatively low interest rate is computed only on the balance due at each payment (such as credit union loans or loans on insurance policies).

The following examples all pertain to installment plans of a set period of time, where the finance charge (carrying charge, interest, etc.) is calculated at the time the contract is made.

Example Two

The Appliance Warehouse will sell a garden weeder for $64 cash or on the following "easy-payment" terms: a $\frac{1}{4}$ down payment, a full 10% carrying charge, and monthly payments for 6 months. (a) Find the monthly payment. (b) What is the total cost of the weeder on the time payment plan? (c) How much more than the cash price will be paid on the installment plan?

Solution

(a)

Cash price	$64.00	
Down payment	− 16.00	($\frac{1}{4}$ of $64)
Outstanding balance	$48.00	
Carrying charge	+ 4.80	(10% of $48)
Total of payments	$52.80	

$$\frac{\$52.80}{6} = \$8.80 \qquad \text{Monthly payment}$$

A payment of $8.80 per month is required. Notice that the finance (carrying) charge was a full 10% of the outstanding balance (without multiplying by $\frac{1}{2}$ for the 6 months' time period). The merchant may use this or any convenient method for determining the finance charge; however, this 10% rate is much lower than the rate the seller is required to disclose to the credit buyer. Since these payments cover only half a year, this rate is equivalent to simple interest at 20% per year. However, the rate which the merchant must reveal to the buyer is the rate that applies when interest is computed only on the balance due at the time each payment is made. Thus, the merchant must tell the buyer that an annual percentage rate of 33.5% is being charged. (Later examples will further illustrate these rates.)

The student should also observe the following. If the finance charge is given as a rate (either a fraction or a per cent), the finance charge is found by multiplying this rate times the outstanding balance remaining *after* the down payment has been made.

(b) The total cost of the weeder, when bought on the installment plan, is $68.80, as follows:

Down payment	$16.00
Total of monthly payments	52.80
Total installment plan cost	$68.80

(c) The $4.80 carrying charge represents the additional cost to the credit customer:

Total installment plan price	$68.80
Cash price	− 64.00
Time payment differential	$ 4.80

This $4.80 finance charge, along with the 33.5% annual percentage rate, represent the two most important items the merchant must disclose to the credit buyer under the Truth in Lending Law, although several other things are also required.

Example Three

Gerald Wood bought a new color television that sold for $675 cash. He received a $35 trade-in allowance on his old set and also paid $40 cash. The store arranged a 2-year payment plan, including a finance charge computed at regular 8% simple interest. (a) What is Wood's monthly payment? (b) What will be the total cost of the TV? (c) How much extra will he pay for the convenience of installment buying? (d) What annual percentage rate must be disclosed under the Truth in Lending Law?

Solution

(a) Wood's regular payment of $29 per month is computed as follows:

Cash price	$675	
Down payment	− 75	($35 trade-in + $40 cash)
Outstanding balance	$600	
Finance charge	+ 96	$\left(\begin{array}{l} I = Prt \\ = \$600 \times \frac{8}{100} \times \frac{2}{1} \end{array}\right)$
Total of monthly payments	$696	

$$\frac{\$696}{24} = \$29 \text{ per month}$$

(b) The total cost of the TV will be $771:

Down payment:	Trade-in	$ 35
	Cash	40
Total of monthly payments		696
Total cost		$771

(c) The $771 total cost includes an extra $96 interest (or finance or carrying) charge above the cash price.

(d) The annual percentage rate which the dealer must disclose is found using Table XXII, Appendix C. First, the finance charge should be

Example Three *(cont.)* divided by the amount financed (the outstanding balance) and the result multiplied by 100. This gives the finance charge per $100 of amount financed:

$$\frac{\text{Finance charge}}{\text{Amount financed}} \times 100 = \frac{\$96}{\$600} \times 100 = 0.16 \times 100 = 16$$

Thus, the credit buyer pays $16 interest for each $100 being financed. (Note that this result is also the total simple interest per cent charged; that is, the "rate × time": 8% × 2 years = 16%. This relationship will always exist, so either method could be used to determine the table value.)

To use Table XXII, look in the left-hand column headed "Number of Payments" and find line 24, since this problem includes 24 monthly payments. Look to the right until you find the column containing the value nearest to the 16.00 we just computed. The per cent at the top of that column will then be the correct annual percentage rate. In this example, the value nearest to our 16.00 is the entry 16.08. (In case a computed value is midway between two table values, the larger table value should be used.) Thus, the per cent at the top of the column indicates that the annual percentage rate is 14.75%.

For practical purposes, this means that if interest were computed at 14.75% only on the remaining balance each month and the United States rule were used so that the $29 applied first to the interest due and then to reduce the principal, then 24 payments of $29 would exactly repay the $600 loan and the $96 interest.* Thus, it is the 14.75% rate that the merchant must state is being charged.

When simple interest is calculated on the *original balance* for the entire length of a loan, this rate is often called a **nominal interest rate.** The interest computed in this way is frequently called **add-on interest.** By contrast, an annual rate which is applied only to the *balance due at the time of each payment* is called an **effective interest rate.** The annual

---

* Strictly speaking, there is a mathematical distinction between the annual percentage rates in Table XXII and the annual rates that one should use to apply the United States rule (as was done here), although either rates are acceptable under the Truth in Lending law. The U.S. rule computes interest on the amount financed from the original date until the day payments are made. The rates in Table XXII, however, are applied in the opposite direction: the present value on the original day of all the payments must equal the amount financed. Although this is a distinct difference in mathematical procedure, the difference in the actual percentage rates is insignificant for our purposes. Thus, since a table of rates applicable to the U.S. rule was not available, we shall use the rates from Table XXII in applying the U.S. rule.

rates determined for the Truth in Lending Law by Table XXII are known as **actuarial rates,** which are almost identical to effective rates. It is this actuarial (or effective) rate which must be disclosed to the buyer by the merchant.

Example Four

(a) What actuarial (or effective) interest rate is equivalent to a nominal (or simple) interest rate of 10%, if there are six monthly installments? (b) How much simple interest would be required on a $400 loan at a nominal 10% for 6 months? What is the monthly payment? (c) Verify that the actuarial rate would produce the same amount of interest, if six monthly payments were made.

Solution

(a) The value we look for in the table is found by multiplying "rate × time":

$$10\% \times \tfrac{1}{2}\,\text{year} = 5$$

This indicates that the interest due is 5% of the amount borrowed. It also means the borrower pays $5 interest for each $100 borrowed.

Since this is a 6-month loan, we look on line 6 for the column containing the value nearest to 5.00. The nearest value is 5.02. We thus find that a simple (nominal) interest rate of 10% for 6 months corresponds to an actuarial (effective) rate of 17.00%, correct to the nearest $\tfrac{1}{4}$%. It is this actuarial rate* that is required under the Truth in Lending Law.

(b) A loan of $400 at 10% simple interest for 6 months would require interest as follows:

$$I = Prt$$
$$= \$400 \times \underbrace{10\% \times \tfrac{1}{2}}$$
$$= \$400 \times \quad 5\% \qquad \text{[as in part (a)]}$$
$$I = \$20$$

<u>OR</u> At $5 per $100 financed,

4 hundreds
×$ 5 per $100
———————
$20 interest

---

*A very similar rate can be computed without tables using the formula $e = \dfrac{2nr}{n+1}$, where e = effective rate, r = annual simple interest rate, and n = number of payments (either monthly or weekly). Thus, for Example 4, $e = \dfrac{2(6)(10)}{6+1} = 17.14\%$.

Example Four *(cont.)*

If the \$400 principal plus \$20 interest were repaid in six monthly payments, then

$$\frac{\$420}{6} = \$70 \text{ per month}$$

(c) The United States rule is used to verify the 17.00% actuarial rate. Each month, the interest due is subtracted from the \$70 payment. The remainder of the payment is then deducted from the outstanding principal to obtain the adjusted principal upon which interest will be calculated at the time of the next payment.

Month	$Prt = I$	Payment to Principal
1st	$\$400.00 \times \frac{17}{100} \times \frac{1}{12} = \$\ 5.67$	\$ 64.33
2nd	$335.67 \times \frac{17}{100} \times \frac{1}{12} = \ 4.76$	65.24
3rd	$270.43 \times \frac{17}{100} \times \frac{1}{12} = \ 3.83$	66.17
4th	$204.26 \times \frac{17}{100} \times \frac{1}{12} = \ 2.89$	67.11
5th	$137.15 \times \frac{17}{100} \times \frac{1}{12} = \ 1.94$	68.06
6th	$69.09 \times \frac{17}{100} \times \frac{1}{12} = \ .98$	69.02
	$\$20.07 \ + $	$\$399.93 \ = \$420.00$

Thus we see that a rate of 17.00%, applied only to the unpaid balance each month, would result in interest of \$20.07 over 6 months' time. This is 7¢ more than the \$20 simple interest that would be due at a 10% nominal rate. (The difference results from rounding and from the use of Table XXII in applying the U.S. rule. Recall that Table XXII is correct only to the nearest quarter of a per cent.)

Example Five

To repay a loan of \$160 from IOU Finance Co. requires six payments of \$29 each.

Determine (a) the amount of interest that will be paid and (b) the annual (actuarial) percentage rate charged.

(c) Verify that this annual percentage rate would actually result in the amount of interest charged.

Solution

(a) The six payments of \$29 will total \$174 altogether. The interest charged will thus be $14:

$ 29	Total of payments	$174
× 6	Amount of loan	− 160
$174	Interest (finance charge)	$ 14

(b) Before finding the actuarial rate, we first find the finance charge per $100 of amount financed:

$$\frac{\text{Finance charge}}{\text{Amount financed}} \times 100 = \frac{\$14}{\$160} \times 100 = 0.0875 \times 100 = 8.75$$

Then on line 6 of the table, we find that the value nearest to 8.75 is the entry 8.78. Thus, IOU Finance Co. must inform the borrower that (s)he is paying interest at an annual percentage rate of 29.5%.

(c) As before, the monthly payment applies first to the interest due, and the remainder of the payment is then deducted from the outstanding principal.

Month	$Prt = I$	Payment to Principal
1st	$160.00 \times \frac{29.5}{100} \times \frac{1}{12} = \ \$3.93$	$ 25.07
2nd	$134.93 \times \frac{29.5}{100} \times \frac{1}{12} = \ 3.32$	25.68
3rd	$109.25 \times \frac{29.5}{100} \times \frac{1}{12} = \ 2.69$	26.31
4th	$82.94 \times \frac{29.5}{100} \times \frac{1}{12} = \ 2.04$	26.96
5th	$55.97 \times \frac{29.5}{100} \times \frac{1}{12} = \ 1.38$	27.62
6th	$28.35 \times \frac{29.5}{100} \times \frac{1}{12} = \ .70$	28.30

$$\$14.06 \quad + \quad \$159.94 \ = \$174.00$$

Thus, we find that an effective rate of 29.5%, applied only to the unpaid balance each month, would require $14.06 in interest on a $160 loan. (This calculation contains a 6¢ rounding error.) The $14 interest on this loan would be equivalent to simple interest at the rate of only 17.5%, which illustrates well how misleading advertised installment rates could be before the Truth in Lending Law was passed.

NOTE: In verifying rates as in part (c), the "rate × time" will be the same each month (in this case, $\frac{29.5}{100} \times \frac{1}{12}$). In doing calculations of this kind, therefore, it is easiest to find the product $(\frac{29.5}{100} \times \frac{1}{12} = .02458)$ and use this factor to multiply times the principal each month. (Be sure you carry the factor out to enough places to obtain correct cents. Review Section 1, "Accuracy of Computation," in Chapter 1.)

As a general rule, the shorter the period of time, the higher installment rates tend to be. Customers seem to be willing to pay these very high rates, since the actual dollar amounts for shorter periods are not as large.

SECTION 2 *Problems*

For each account, complete a table (as in Example 1) that shows both the monthly interest due on the unpaid balance and the amount of each payment that applies to the balance due.

		Amount of Account	Monthly Payment	Interest per Month
1.	(a)	$ 70	$15	$1\frac{1}{2}$%
	(b)	220	50	1
2.	(a)	$ 50	$10	1%
	(b)	150	40	$1\frac{1}{2}$

Find the regular (monthly or weekly) payment required to pay for the following installment purchases.

		Cash Price	Down Payment Required	Finance Charge	Time Period
3.	(a)	$165	None	$15	15 months
	(b)	120	30%	$12	32 weeks
	(c)	400	10%	8% simple interest	36 months
4.	(a)	$250	$25	$15	8 months
	(b)	150	20%	$10	26 weeks
	(c)	675	$\frac{1}{3}$	12% simple interest	18 months

911 13

For the following installment problems, determine the annual (actuarial) percentage rate charged.

page 623

		Amount Financed	Finance Charge	Months
5.	(a)	$100	$16	12
	(b)	280	$70	24
	(c)	—	8% simple interest	36
	(d)	—	18% simple interest	6
6.	(a)	$80	$6	6
	(b)	125	$50	30
	(c)	—	12% simple interest	24
	(d)	—	15% simple interest	4

Compute monthly interest and payment to principal to verify that the following annual percentage rates would produce the given interest.

	Principal	Interest	Monthly Payment	Months	Annual Rate
7.	$200	$12	$ 53	4	28.50%
8.	400	20	105	4	23.75

9. Oakdale Department Store charges 1% per month interest on charge accounts. David Anderson charged a $70 suit and agreed to pay $13 monthly toward his account. How much interest will he pay?

10. William Harrison charged to his account a $170 CB radio during a special promotion at Austin Electronics. The store charges 1% per month on the unpaid balance, and Harrison is paying $30 per month. How much interest will he pay?

11. A portable color television sells for $240 cash; or a $\frac{1}{3}$ down payment, a carrying charge of $20, and the balance in 12 payments. What is the monthly installment payment?

12. A microwave oven sells for $480 cash; or a $\frac{1}{4}$ down payment, a finance charge of $54, and the balance in 18 monthly installments. Compute the monthly payment.

13. A washing machine sells for $260; or 15% down, a carrying charge of $25, and the balance in 12 equal installments. What amount is required each month?

14. A used motorcycle is priced at $600. On the time payment plan, a 20% down payment is required, and the 15 monthly payments include a $75 finance charge. Find the amount of each monthly installment.

15. A stereo is priced at $500. The time payment plan requires a 10% down payment and 24 monthly payments. For simplicity, the finance charge is computed at 6% nominal (simple) interest.
(a) How much is the finance charge?

(b) Determine the monthly payment on the stereo.

(c) What is the total cost of the stereo when bought on the installment plan?

(d) Find the annual percentage rate that the seller must reveal under the Truth in Lending Law.

16. The cash price of a sailboat and trailer is $3,000. The equipment may be purchased for a 10% down payment and 36 monthly payments. For convenience, the dealer computes the finance charge at 8% simple interest.

(a) What is the finance charge on the boat and trailer?

(b) How much is the monthly payment?

(c) Determine the total cost of the outfit on the installment plan.

(d) What annual percentage rate must the dealer disclose to the buyer?

17. Eighteen monthly payments of $5.75 are required to repay a $90 loan. Determine

(a) The finance charge the borrower pays.

(b) The annual percentage rate charged on the loan.

18. A loan of $60 is repaid in 12 monthly payments of $5.80 each. Find

(a) The finance charge on the loan.

(b) The annual percentage rate the lender must disclose.

19. A $600 loan requires payments of $31 each for 24 months.

(a) What is the finance charge on the loan?

(b) At what annual percentage rate is interest paid?

20. A $450 loan is repaid in 18 monthly payments of $31 each.

(a) What is the finance charge on the loan?

(b) At what annual percentage rate is interest paid?

21. A room air conditioner sells for $550. On the time payment plan, after a down payment of $50, 12 monthly installments of $45 each are required.

(a) How much is the total cost of the air conditioner when purchased on credit?

(b) What is the carrying charge?

(c) At what annual percentage rate is interest paid?

22. A frostproof freezer costs $800 cash. It may also be purchased for $50 down and 24 payments of $37 each.

(a) What is the total cost of the freezer on the installment plan?

(b) How much does the buyer pay to finance this purchase?

(c) What annual percentage rate is paid for the convenience of credit buying?

23. Dennis Jones made 18 monthly payments of $46.60 to pay for a used car. The car had originally been priced to sell for $1,000, and Jones made a cash down payment of $280.

(a) What was the total cost of the car?

(b) How much extra did Jones pay in order to finance the car?

(c) At what annual percentage rate was interest paid?

24. Sharon Lewis received a $1,300 allowance when she traded her old car for a $3,800 import. Her payments are $75 per month for 42 months.

(a) How much did Lewis pay altogether for her car?

(b) What was the finance charge for this time payment purchase?

(c) What annual percentage rate must be disclosed?

25. The State Appliance Co. finds it

easiest to determine finance charges by computing 12% simple interest. Determine the rate they must disclose under the Truth in Lending Law for
(a) A 12-month installment purchase.
(b) An 18-month installment purchase.
(c) An 8-month installment purchase.

26. For their own convenience, the Thrif-T-Loan Co. computes interest at 18% simple interest. What annual percentage rate must they reveal under the Truth in Lending Law on
(a) A 1-year loan?
(b) A 24-month loan?
(c) A 6-month loan?

27. A loan company computes 12% nominal interest on a loan of $200 to be repaid in 5 monthly payments.
(a) How much interest will the borrower pay?
(b) What is the monthly payment required?
(c) At what annual actuarial rate is interest paid?
(d) Verify that the actuarial rate you found will result in the same amount of interest.

28. (a) What amount of interest would be due on a 6-month loan of $300 if a nominal rate of 8% were charged?
(b) How much will the monthly payment be?
(c) What annual actuarial rate is charged on the loan?
(d) Verify that this actuarial rate is correct.

29. Suppose that $600 was borrowed under the conditions in Problem 5(d).
(a) How much interest would be charged?
(b) How much is the monthly payment?
(c) Verify that the annual rate determined in Problem 5(d) would produce the required amount of interest.

30. Assume that $160 was borrowed at the rate and time of Problem 6(d).
(a) How much interest would the borrower pay?
(b) What amount is his monthly payment?
(c) Verify that the annual rate you found in Problem 6(d) would actually result in the correct amount of interest.

CHAPTER 17 *Glossary*

Actuarial interest rate. The annual percentage rate required by the Truth in Lending Law; a rate computed on the balance due at the time of each installment payment.

Add-on interest. Simple interest.

Annual percentage rate. Annual rate required by the Truth in Lending Law; an actuarial or effective rate.

Carrying charge. An extra charge paid for the privilege of buying on the installment plan; a time payment differential or interest.

Down payment. An initial payment made at the time of purchase and deducted from the cash price before an installment payment is computed.

Effective interest rate. (See "Actuarial interest rate.")

Finance charge. Total amount of extra money paid for credit buying—carrying charge plus service charge, insurance, or any other required charges; the amount that must be disclosed under the Truth in Lending Law.

Installment plan. Payment plan that requires periodic payments for a limited time, usually at a relatively high interest rate; either (1) an open end account or (2) an account with a set number of payments.

Nominal (or simple) interest rate. An interest rate computed on the original balance for the entire time, without regard to the decreasing balance due after each payment to an installment account.

Open end credit. An account without a definite payment period and to which additional credit may be added before the first credit is entirely repaid; a revolving charge account.

Outstanding balance. On an installment purchase, the portion of the cash price remaining after the down payment and before the carrying charge is added.

Revolving charge account. An open end charge account offered by many retail businesses, where new charges may be added up to a set maximum, and minimum monthly payments (depending on the balance due) are made, with interest at 1% to $1\frac{1}{2}$% monthly computed on the unpaid balance.

Simple interest rate. (See "Nominal interest rate.")

Time payment differential. (See "Carrying charge.")

Truth in Lending Law. A federal regulation requiring sellers to inform buyers of (1) the finance charge, and (2) the effective annual percentage rate paid on any credit account (installment purchase, installment loan, promissory note, etc.).

United States rule. Standard method used to give credit for partial payments; each payment is first used to pay the interest due, and the remainder is then deducted from the principal, to obtain an adjusted principal upon which future interest will be computed.

CHAPTER 18

Compound

Interest

CHAPTER 18 OBJECTIVES

Upon completion of Chapter 18, the student will be able to:

1. Define and use correctly the terminology associated with each topic.

2. Compute compound amount without use of a table for short periods. *(Section 1; Examples 1–4; Problems 1–10)*

3. Compute compound interest and amount using the formula $S = P(1 + i)^n$ and the compound amount table. *(Section 2; Examples 1–3; Problems 1–20)*

4. a. Find compound interest and amount at institutions paying interest compounded daily from date of deposit to date of withdrawal, including deposits that earn from the first of a month if deposited by the tenth. *(Section 3; Examples 1–4; Problems 1–12)*

    b. Also, compare this with interest and amount that would be earned if interest were not compounded daily. *(Problems 5, 6)*

    c. The formulas $I = P \times$ Dep. tab. and $I = W \times$ W/D tab. are used for computing interest compounded daily.

5. Compute present value at compound interest of investments made at either simple or compound interest. The formula $P = S(1 + i)^{-n}$ and the present value table will be used.

    (Section 4; Examples 1–3; Problems 1–14)

18

It was previously noted that money invested with a financial institution earns compound interest. Compound interest is more profitable than simple interest to the investor because, at compound interest, "interest is earned on interest." That is, interest is earned, not only on the principal, but also on all interest accumulated since the original deposit. Most compound interest is calculated using prepared tables. To be certain you clearly understand compound interest, however, you should compute a few problems yourself.

NOTE: Pages 513–517 contain a summary of Chapters 18–20, which all contain topics involving interest at a compound rate. You may refer to the summary to identify the characteristics of each topic.

SECTION 1

Compound Interest (By Computation)

Recall that for a simple interest investment, interest is paid on the *original principal* only; at the end of the time, the maturity value is the total of the principal plus the simple interest. Now consider the following example.

Example One

Suppose that investor A makes a $1,000 investment for three years at 8% simple interest. Then,

$$P = \$1,000 \qquad I = Prt \qquad\qquad S = P + I$$
$$r = 8\% \qquad\qquad = \$1,000 \times \tfrac{8}{100} \times \tfrac{3}{1} \qquad = \$1,000 + \$240$$
$$t = 3 \text{ years} \qquad I = \$240 \qquad\qquad S = \$1,240$$

Mr. A would earn $240 interest on this investment, making the total maturity value $1,240.

Now suppose that Ms. B invests $1,000 for only 6 months, also at 8% interest. Then,

$$P = \$1,000 \qquad\qquad I = Prt \qquad\qquad\qquad S = P + I$$
$$r = 8\% \qquad\qquad\qquad = \$1,000 \times \tfrac{8}{100} \times \tfrac{1}{2} \qquad = \$1,000 + \$40$$
$$t = 6 \text{ months} \quad \text{or} \quad \tfrac{1}{2} \text{ year} \qquad I = \$40 \qquad\qquad S = \$1,040$$

Ms. B. would have $1,040 at the end of this 6-month investment.

Assume that Ms. B then reinvests this $1,040 for another 6 months at 8%; she would earn $41.60 on her second investment, making the total amount $1,081.60. If this total were then deposited for another 6 months, the interest would be $43.26 and Ms. B would have $1,124.86. If this procedure were repeated each 6 months until 3 years had passed, Ms. B. would have made six investments and the computations would be as follows:

FIRST 6 MONTHS

$I = Prt$

$= \$1,000 \times \frac{8}{100} \times \frac{1}{2}$

$I = \$40$

$$S = \$1,040$$

SECOND 6 MONTHS

$I = Prt$

$= \$1,040 = \frac{8}{100} \times \frac{1}{2}$

$I = \$41.60$

$$S = \$1,081.60$$

THIRD 6 MONTHS

$I = Prt$

$= \$1.081.60 \times \frac{8}{100} \times \frac{1}{2}$

$I = \$43.26$

$$S = \$1,124.86$$

FOURTH 6 MONTHS

$I = Prt$

$= \$1,124.86 \times \frac{8}{100} \times \frac{1}{2}$

$I = \$44.99$

$$S = \$1,169.85$$

FIFTH 6 MONTHS

$I = Prt$

$= \$1,169.85 \times \frac{8}{100} \times \frac{1}{2}$

$I = \$46.79$

$$S = \$1,216.64$$

SIXTH 6 MONTHS

$I = Prt$

$= \$1,216.64 \times \frac{8}{100} \times \frac{1}{2}$

$I = \$48.67$

$$S = \$1,265.31$$

Thus, after 3 years, Ms. B's original principal would have amounted to $1,265.31. Since Mr. A had only $1,240 after his single, 3 year investment, Ms. B made $1,265.31 − $1,240 or $25.31 more interest by making successive, short-term investments.

The example above illustrates the idea of **compound interest:** Each time that interest is computed, the interest is added to the previous principal; that total then becomes the principal for the next interest period. Thus, money accumulates faster at compound interest because *interest is earned on interest*, as well as on the principal.

Interest is said to be "compounded" whenever interest is computed and added to the previous principal. This is done at regular intervals known as **conversion periods** (or just **periods**). Interest is commonly compounded annually (once a year), semiannually (twice a year), quarterly (four times a year), or monthly. The total value at the end of the investment (original principal plus all interest) is the **compound amount**. The *compound interest* earned is the difference between the compound amount and the original principal. The length of the investment is known as the **term**. The quoted interest rate is always the nominal (or yearly) rate.

Before compound interest can be computed, (1) the term must be expressed as its total number of periods, and (2) the interest rate must be converted to its corresponding rate per period.

Example Two   Determine the number of periods for each of the following investments: (a) 7 years compounded annually; (b) 5 years compounded semiannually; (c) 6 years compounded quarterly; (d) 3 years compounded monthly.

In general, the number of periods is found in this way:

$$\text{Years} \times \text{Number of periods per year} = \text{Total number of periods}$$

Thus,

Solution   (a) 7 years compounded annually
$$= 7 \text{ years} \times 1 \text{ period per year} = 7 \text{ periods}$$
(b) 5 years compounded semiannually
$$= 5 \text{ years} \times 2 \text{ periods per year} = 10 \text{ periods}$$
(c) 6 years compounded quarterly
$$= 6 \text{ years} \times 4 \text{ periods per year} = 24 \text{ periods}$$
(d) 3 years compounded monthly
$$= 3 \text{ years} \times 12 \text{ periods per year} = 36 \text{ periods}$$

Example Three   Determine the rate per period for each investment: (a) 7% compounded annually; (b) 9% compounded semiannually; (c) 5% compounded quarterly; (d) 6% compounded monthly.

Keep in mind that the stated interest rate is always the yearly rate. Thus, if the rate is 4% compounded quarterly, the rate per period is 1% (since 1% paid four times during the year is equivalent to 4%).

Example Three
(cont.)

One may find rate per period as follows:

$$\frac{\text{Yearly rate}}{\text{Number of periods per year}} = \text{Rate per period}$$

Hence,

Solution

(a) 7% compounded annually

$$= \frac{7\%}{1 \text{ period per year}}$$

$$= 7\% \text{ per period (or 7\% each year)}$$

(b) 9% compounded semiannually

$$= \frac{9\%}{2 \text{ periods per year}}$$

$$= 4\tfrac{1}{2}\% \text{ per period (or } 4\tfrac{1}{2}\% \text{ each six months)}$$

(c) 5% compounded quarterly

$$= \frac{5\%}{4 \text{ periods per year}}$$

$$= 1\tfrac{1}{4}\% \text{ per period (or } 1\tfrac{1}{4}\% \text{ each quarter)}$$

(d) 6% compounded monthly

$$= \frac{6\%}{12 \text{ periods per year}}$$

$$= \tfrac{1}{2}\% \text{ per period (or } \tfrac{1}{2}\% \text{ each month)}$$

Now let us compute a problem at compound interest:

Example Four

Find the compound amount and the compound interest for the following investments:

(a) $1,000 for 3 years at 6% compounded annually:

$$3 \text{ years} \times 1 \text{ period per year} = 3 \text{ periods}$$

$$\frac{6\%}{1 \text{ period per year}} = 6\% \text{ per period}$$

First period: Principal $1,000.00
            Interest   +   60.00   (6% of $1,000)

Second period: Principal $1,060.00
             Interest   +   63.60   (6% of $1,060)

Third period: Principal $1,123.60
             Interest   +   67.42   (6% of $1,123.60)

Compound amount $1,191.02

Compound amount	$1,191.02
Less: original principal	− 1,000.00
Compound interest	$ 191.02

(b) $1,000 for 1 year at 8% compounded quarterly:

$$1 \text{ year} \times 4 \text{ periods per year} = 4 \text{ periods}$$

$$\frac{8\%}{4 \text{ periods per year}} = 2\% \text{ per period}$$

First period: Principal $1,000.00
             Interest   +   20.00   (2% of $1,000)

Second period: Principal $1,020.00
             Interest   +   20.40   (2% of $1,020)

Third period: Principal $1,040.40
             Interest   +   20.81   (2% of $1,040.40)

Fourth period: Principal $1,061.21
             Interest   +   21.22   (2% of $1,061.21)

Compound Amount $1,082.43

Compound amount	$1,082.43
Less: original principal	− 1,000.00
Compound interest	$ 82.43

NOTE: Compare this $1,082.43 compound amount with Example 1, where the compound amount after 1 year at 8% compounded semiannually was $1,081.60.

all odd problems

Determine the number of periods and the rate per period for each of the following in Problems 1 and 2.

		Rate	Compounded	Years
1.	(a)	6%	Semiannually	4
	(b)	9	Quarterly	3
	(c)	5	Monthly	5
	(d)	7	Annually	15
	(e)	8	Monthly	6

		Rate	Compounded	Years
2.	(a)	6%	Monthly	7
	(b)	5	Quarterly	4
	(c)	8	Semiannually	12
	(d)	9	Annually	14
	(e)	7	Quarterly	5

Find the compound amount and the compound interest for each of the following:

3. $500 invested for 3 years at 8% compounded (a) annually; (b) semiannually.

4. $500 invested for 1 year at 8% compounded (a) semiannually; (b) quarterly.

5. $800 invested for 1 year at 6% compounded (a) annually; (b) quarterly.

6. $800 invested for 3 years at 6% compounded (a) annually; (b) semiannually.

7. $1,000 invested for $\frac{1}{2}$ year at 6% compounded (a) quarterly; (b) monthly.

8. $400 invested for 6 months at 9% compounded (a) quarterly; (b) monthly.

9. Study carefully your answers to parts (a) and (b) of the preceding problems. What conclusion seems to be indicated?

10. Suppose you are given the principal, rate, and years of a compound interest problem. What else must you know in order to work the problem?

SECTION 2
Compound Amount (Using Tables)

Example 1 in the previous section illustrated the advantage of a compound interest investment over a simple interest investment. All banks and savings institutions in the United States pay compound interest on savings accounts. There are several factors that an investor should consider before opening an account, however, as various types of accounts are available, often at considerably different rates and under different conditions.

In an **open account,** the owner may deposit or withdraw funds at any time. The most common type of open account is a **passbook account,** where each transaction is entered in a record book kept by the account owner. (Deposits to bank savings accounts may be made using deposit slips similar to those for checking accounts.) Formerly, interest was paid on the lowest balance that open accounts contained any time during an interest period. Thus, interest was not earned on funds deposited after a period began or on funds withdrawn during a period. Dissatisfaction with this procedure led to the immediate popularity of interest compounded daily, where interest is paid on all funds for the exact number of days during each period that they are on deposit. Most savings institutions now offer daily conversion periods for all passbook accounts.

Funds deposited for a specific period of time may be used to purchase a **certificate of deposit** (commonly called a **CD**). CD's offer higher rates than passbook accounts, and their rates increase as funds are committed for longer periods of time. CD's are commonly available for 90 days (one quarter); 6 months; and 1, 2, 4, or 6 years. Minimum deposits of $1,000 or more are usually required for CD's. If funds are withdrawn early from a CD, the owner forfeits the higher interest rate and is usually paid only at the institution's passbook rate.

The problems in the previous section demonstrated the advantage of more frequent compounding. Thus, if two accounts offer $5\frac{1}{2}$% interest, but one compounds daily and the other compounds quarterly, the depositor would earn slightly more interest in the account compounded daily. (Most CD's have their interest compounded quarterly, even though the CD is for a longer period of time.)

While computing the problems in Section 1, it no doubt became obvious to the student that this procedure can become quite long and tedious. Compound amount may also be found using the formula

$$S = P(1+i)^n$$

where S = compound amount, P = original principal, i = interest rate per period, and n = number of periods.

Example One   (a) Using the formula for compound amount, compute the compound amount and compound interest on $1,000 invested for 3 years at 8% compounded semiannually.

$$P = \$1,000 \qquad\qquad S = P(1+i)^n$$

$$i = 4\% \text{ per period} \qquad = \$1,000(1+4\%)^6$$

$$n = 6 \text{ periods} \qquad\quad = \ 1,000(1+0.04)^6$$

$$S = ? \qquad\qquad\quad S = \ 1,000(1.04)^6$$

Recall that the exponent (i.e., "6") tells how many times the factor 1.04 should be written down before being multiplied. Thus, 1.04

Example
One
(cont.)

should be used as a factor 6 times:

$$S = \$1{,}000(1.04)^6$$
$$= 1{,}000\underbrace{(1.04)(1.04)(1.04)(1.04)(1.04)(1.04)}$$

$$= 1{,}000 \quad \times \quad (1.2653190\ldots)$$
$$= 1{,}000(1.2653190\ldots)$$
$$S = \$1{,}265.32$$

Therefore, the maturity value (compound amount) would be $1,265.32. The compound interest is $1,265.32–$1,000, or $265.32.

Even using this formula, however, the calculation of compound amount would still be quite tedious if the number of periods (the exponent) were very large. The computation is greatly simplified through the use of a compound amount table—a list of the values obtained when the parenthetical expression $(1+i)$ is used as a factor for the indicated numbers of periods.

Example
One
(cont.)

(b) Using the compound amount formula and table, rework part (a).

$$P = \$1{,}000 \qquad S = P(1+i)^n$$
$$i = 4\% \qquad\qquad = \$1{,}000(1+4\%)^6$$
$$n = 6$$

To find compound amount, turn to Table XIV, Amount of 1 (at Compound Interest), Appendix C. Various interest rates per period are given at the top outside margin of each page; find the page headed by 4%. The lines of the columns correspond to the number of periods, and these are numbered on both the right-hand and left-hand sides of the page. Go down to line 6 of the Amount column on the 4% page and there read "1.2653190185"; this is the value of $(1.04)^6$. Now,

$$S = P(1+i)^n \qquad\qquad I = S - P$$
$$= \$1{,}000(1+4\%)^6 \qquad = \quad \$1{,}265.32$$
$$= 1{,}000(1.2653190185) \qquad - \quad 1{,}000.00$$
$$S = \$1{,}265.32 \qquad\qquad I = \quad \$ \ \ 265.32$$

NOTE: The value in the table includes the "1" from the parenthetical expression $(1+i)$. It is *not* correct to add "1" to the tabular value before multiplying by the principal. (The student should now review Section 1, "Accuracy of Computation," in Chapter 1, which demonstrates how many digits from the table must be used in order to ensure an answer correct to the nearest penny.)

Example Two

Find the compound amount and compound interest on $2,000 invested at 7% compounded quarterly for 6 years.

$$P = \$2,000 \qquad S = P(1+i)^n \qquad\qquad I = S - P$$
$$i = 1\tfrac{3}{4}\% \qquad\quad = \$2,000(1 + 1\tfrac{3}{4}\%)^{24} \qquad = \quad \$3,032.89$$
$$n = 24 \qquad\qquad = \ 2,000(1.5164428) \qquad \underline{- \ \ 2,000.00}$$
$$\qquad\qquad\qquad = \ 3,032.8856 \qquad\qquad I = \ \ \$1,032.89$$
$$\qquad\qquad S = \$3,032.89$$

After 6 years, the $2,000 investment would thus be worth $3,032.89, of which $1,032.89 is interest.

CD = certificate of deposit

Example Three

Ray Copeland opened a passbook savings account on April 1, 19X1, with a deposit of $800. The account paid 6% compounded quarterly. On October 1, 19X1, Ray closed that account and added enough additional money to purchase a 6-month CD earning interest at 7% compounded monthly. (a) How much did Ray deposit on October 1? (b) What was the maturity value of his CD on April 1, 19X2? (c) How much total interest was earned? (See Figure 51.)

Solution

(a) Banking quarters usually begin on the first days of January, April, July, and October. This means that Ray's $800 deposit earned

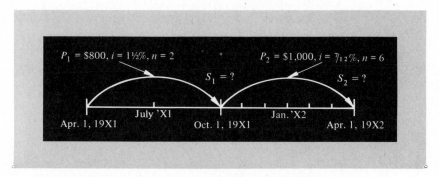

FIGURE 51

interest for two quarters. Hence,

$$P_1 = \$800 \qquad S = P(1+i)^n$$
$$i = 1\tfrac{1}{2}\% \qquad = \$800(1 + 1\tfrac{1}{2}\%)^2$$
$$n = 2 \qquad = 800(1.030225)$$
$$= 824.1800$$
$$S_1 = \$824.18$$

$$\begin{array}{r} \$1,000.00 \\ -\ \ \ 824.18 \\ \hline \$\ \ 175.82 \quad \text{Deposit} \end{array}$$

Nelda partied too much again.

(b) On October 1, Ray's passbook account contained $824.18. A deposit of $175.82 more on October 1 was required to purchase a $1,000 CD. There were then 6 months (two quarters) until the CD matured on April 1, during which time the $1,000 principal earned interest at 7% compounded monthly:

$$P_2 = \$1,000 \qquad S = P(1+i)^n$$
$$i = \tfrac{7}{12}\% \qquad = \$1,000(1 + \tfrac{7}{12}\%)^6$$
$$n = 6 \qquad = 1,000(1.0394004)$$
$$= 1,039.4004$$
$$S_2 = \$1,039.40$$

The maturity value of Ray's CD was $1,039.40 on April 1, 19X2.

(c) The total interest may be found in either of two ways:
(1) By adding the interest paid on each of the principals, or
(2) By finding the difference between the final balance and the total of all deposits.

(1)
$$I = S - P \qquad\qquad I = S - P$$
$$= \ \ \$824.18 \qquad = \ \ \$1,039.40$$
$$\underline{-\ \ 800.00} \qquad \underline{-\ 1,000.00}$$
$$I_1 = \ \ \$\ \ 24.18 \qquad I_2 = \ \$\ \ \ 39.40$$

$$\begin{array}{r} \$24.18 \quad \text{Interest} \\ +\ 39.40 \quad \text{Interest} \\ \hline \$63.58 \quad \text{Total interest} \end{array}$$

(2)
$$\begin{array}{r} \$800.00 \\ +\ 175.82 \\ \hline \$975.82 \quad \text{Total deposits} \end{array}$$

$$\begin{array}{r} \$1,039.40 \quad \text{Final balance} \\ -975.82 \quad \text{Total deposit} \\ \hline \$\ \ \ \ 63.58 \quad \text{Total interest} \end{array}$$

How Long Does It Take to Double an Investment?

For a sum of money invested at various interest rates compounded quarterly, the following table shows how long it takes (to the nearest quarter after the money doubles).

Quarterly Rate	Years to Double	Quarterly Rate	Years to Double	Quarterly Rate	Years to Double
5%	14	7%	10	9%	8
$5\frac{1}{2}$%	$12\frac{3}{4}$	$7\frac{1}{2}$%	$9\frac{1}{2}$	$9\frac{1}{2}$%	$7\frac{1}{2}$
6%	$11\frac{3}{4}$	8%	9	10%	$7\frac{1}{4}$
$6\frac{1}{2}$%	11	$8\frac{1}{2}$%	$8\frac{1}{4}$		

SECTION 2 *Problems*

1–6. Rework Problems 3–8 of the previous section, using the compound amount formula and Table XIV. (Some answers may vary by a few cents because the tables are not rounded off after each period.)

Compute the following compound amounts and compound interest, using Table XIV.

$847.78

$4,921.55

		Principal	Rate	Compounded	Years
7.	(a)	$ 600	5%	Semiannually	7
	(b)	950	6	Monthly	4
	(c)	1,500	8	Quarterly	15
	(d)	2,400	7	Quarterly	9
	(e)	400	9	Semiannually	20
8.	(a)	$1,000	7%	Monthly	4
	(b)	500	6	Semiannually	15
	(c)	1,200	9	Quarterly	7
	(d)	750	8	Monthly	8
	(e)	2,400	5	Quarterly	13

9. Compute compound amount and interest on the following at 5% compounded monthly for 7 years.
(a) $100
(b) $200
(c) $400
(d) What is your conclusion regarding the principal?

10. Find compound amount and compound interest on the following at 6% compound monthly for 5 years.
(a) $500
(b) $1,000
(c) $2,000
(d) What conclusion can be reached about the principal?

11. Calculate compound amount and interest (compounded semiannually for 10 years) on $1,000 at
(a) 4%.
(b) 8%.
(c) 16%.
(d) Does the interest exactly double when the rate is doubled?

12. Determine compound amount and interest on $1,000 with interest compounded quarterly for 5 years at the following rates.
(a) 5%
(b) 10%
(c) 20%
(d) Does doubling the rate exactly double the interest?

13. Determine compound amount and interest on $1,000 at 6% compounded semiannually for
(a) 6 years.
(b) 12 years.
(c) 24 years.
(d) Does doubling the time exactly double the interest?

14. Compute compound amount and compound interest on $1,000 at 9% compounded quarterly for
(a) 4 years.
(b) 8 years.
(c) 16 years.
(d) Does the interest exactly double when the time is doubled?

15. On July 1, 19X1, Sharon White deposited $1,000 in a savings bank. The institution paid 5% compounded semiannually.
(a) What was the value of Sharon's account on January 1, 19X2?
(b) On that day, Sharon made a deposit which brought the balance in her account to $1,200. What was the amount of her deposit?
(c) What was Sharon's account worth on January 1, 19X3?
(d) How much total interest did her account earn?

16. Juan Hernandez opened a passbook savings account on January 1, 19X1, with a deposit of $1,000. On October 1, 19X1, he deposited enough money to make his account total $1,300. If the account earned 5% compounded quarterly,
(a) What was the value of his account on October 1, 19X1, prior to his deposit?
(b) What amount did he deposit on that day?
(c) How much was Hernandez's account worth on July 1, 19X2?
(d) How much total interest had been earned?

17. Bill Carson's passbook account contained $800 on March 1, 19X1. The bank paid 5% compounded monthly.
(a) What was the value of Carson's account on July 1, 19X1?
(b) On that day, Carson made a deposit which brought the balance in his

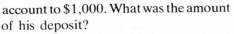

account to $1,000. What was the amount of his deposit?

(c) Also on that day, Carson transferred his funds to a 6-month CD, which paid 6% compounded monthly. What was the maturity value of the CD?

(d) What total amount of interest was earned?

18. Frank Scranton had $1,000 on deposit on April 1, 19X1, in a passbook account which paid 5% compounded quarterly. On October 1, 19X1, Scranton made a deposit which brought his balance to $1,200.

(a) What was the value of Scranton's account on October 1, before his deposit was made?

(b) How much did Scranton deposit?

(c) On October 1, Scranton used his account to purchase a 1-year CD, which earned interest at 6% compounded quarterly. What was the value of his CD on the maturity date?

(d) How much interest was earned altogether?

19. On May 1, James Salmon purchased a $1,500, 6-month CD, which earned interest at 6% compounded quarterly.

(a) What was the maturity value of Salmon's CD?

(b) On November 1, Salmon cashed his CD and added the extra funds necessary to purchase a $2,000, 1-year CD paying interest at 6% compounded monthly. How much additional deposit was required?

(c) What was the maturity value of Salmon's 1-year CD?

(d) How much total interest was earned by the two CD's?

20. On January 2, Mary Anne Phillips purchased a $1,000, 90-day CD earning interest at 6% compounded monthly.

(a) What was the maturity value of the CD?

(b) On April 2, Phillips added enough additional money to buy a $1,400, 6-month CD which paid interest at 7% compounded quarterly.

    How much was Phillips' additional deposit?

(c) How much will Phillips' CD be worth on the maturity date?

(d) What total amount of interest did the two CD's earn?

SECTION 3

Interest Compounded Daily

Most financial institutions now pay "daily interest" (interest compounded daily) on all open accounts (passbook or similar savings accounts where deposits or withdrawals may be made at any time). Some institutions pay interest for the exact number of days that money has been on deposit, while many others offer the added inducement of interest paid from the first of the month for all deposits made by the tenth of the month.

Interest on deposits is compounded daily; but to eliminate excessive bookkeeping, most institutions enter interest in the depositor's account only once each quarter. (For this reason, the daily interest table contains factors for one quarter. In accordance with the practice followed by most savings institutions, it is a 90-day quarter; deposits made on the 31st of any month earn interest as if they were made on the 30th. Recall that quarters begin in January, April, July, and October.)

In the previous section, it was pointed out that depositors formerly lost interest at many institutions because deposits or withdrawals were made sometime during an interest period. The primary advantage of interest compounded daily is that interest is never lost—money earns interest for every day it is on deposit, regardless of when it is deposited or withdrawn.

Interest on Deposits   Our study will be limited to 5% interest compounded daily. Interest is found by multiplying the principal (deposit) times the appropriate value from Table XX, Interest from Date of Deposit, Appendix C. That is,

$$\text{Interest} = \text{Principal} \times \text{Deposit table}$$

which might be abbreviated

$$I = P \times \text{Dep. tab.}$$

In the daily interest deposit table, there is a column for each of the three months of the quarter; each column (month) contains entries for 30 days. To use the table, one looks for the date on which a deposit was made; the factor beside that date is the number to be multiplied by the amount of deposit in order to obtain the interest (provided the money remained on deposit until the quarter ended). If interest is paid from the first of the month and a deposit was made by the tenth of the month, then one should use the factor given beside the first day of the month rather than beside the actual day of deposit.

Example One   Find the interest which would be earned at 5% compounded daily, if $1,000 were deposited in a savings and loan association paying interest from the first on deposits made by the tenth (a) on July 17 and (b) on March 9.

Solution   (a) July is the first month of the quarter; therefore, we refer to the "1st Month" column of the deposit table and to the 17th line under that heading:

$$I = P \times \text{Dep. tab.}$$

$$= \$1,000(0.010330)$$

$$= 10.330$$

$$I = \$10.33$$

When the quarter ends, interest of \$10.33 will be added to the depositor's account.

(b) March is the third month of the quarter. Since the deposit was made by the tenth of March, we use the factor beside the "1" (the first) under "3rd Month":

$$I = P \times \text{Dep. tab.}$$

$$= \$1,000(0.004175)$$

$$= 4.175$$

$$I = \$4.18$$

The deposit will earn interest of \$4.18 during the remaining part of the quarter.

Example Two   Richard Chiles has an account in a savings and loan association where deposits made by the tenth earn interest from the first at 5% compounded daily. When the quarter began on January 1, Chiles' account contained \$750. He made the following deposits during the quarter: \$250 on January 10; \$200 on February 7; and \$300 on March 13. (a) How much interest will the account earn during the quarter? (b) What will be the balance in Chiles' account at the end of the quarter?

If a deposit is made by the tenth of the first month of a quarter, that deposit can be added to the beginning balance and interest computed on that principal for the entire quarter. For deposits made after the tenth of the first month, interest should be computed separately for each deposit. The total interest for the quarter is the sum of all interest of the various deposits.

Solution (a) Since \$250 was added to his \$750 balance by January 10, Chiles will earn interest on \$1,000 for the entire quarter:

$$I = P \times \text{Dep. tab.}$$

$$= \$1,000(0.012578)$$

$$= 12.578$$

$$I = \$12.58$$

The \$200 deposit on February 7 would earn interest from the first of the second month:

$$I = P \times \text{Dep. tab.}$$

$$= \$200(0.008368)$$

$$= 1.6736$$

$$I = \$1.67$$

Interest on the \$300 deposit made March 13 (the third month) is:

$$I = P \times \text{Dep. tab.}$$

$$= \$300(0.002503)$$

$$= 0.7509$$

$$I = \$0.75$$

The transactions for the entire quarter would thus be summarized as follows:

PRINCIPAL	INTEREST	
\$ 750 ⎱	\$12.58	
250 ⎰		
200	1.67	
300	.75	
\$1,500 +	\$15.00 = \$1,515.00	Balance, end of quarter

The account would earn total interest of \$15.00 during the quarter.

(b) Chiles' account would have a balance of $1,515 at the end of the quarter.

Interest on Withdrawals

When withdrawals are involved, interest may be calculated in the following manner:

1. Subtract the withdrawals from the opening principal. Compute interest on this remaining balance for the entire quarter.

2. Determine the interest which would be earned on the withdrawn funds until the date they were withdrawn. This interest is found as follows, using Table XXI, Interest to Date of Withdrawal, Appendix C:

$$\text{Interest} = \text{Withdrawal} \times \text{Withdrawal table}$$

which may be abbreviated

$$I = W \times W/D \text{ tab.}$$

(The daily interest withdrawal table is similar to the daily interest deposit table in that it is divided into the 3 months of the quarter, and one uses the factor beside the appropriate date.)

3. Total interest for the quarter is the sum of the various amounts of interest found in steps 1 and 2.

Example Three

On July 1, a savings account in a credit union contained $1,250. A withdrawal of $250 was made on September 5. (a) How much interest did the account earn for the quarter, if interest was paid at 5% compounded daily? (b) What was the ending balance in the account?

Solution

(a) Since $250 was withdrawn from the $1,250 account, only $1,000 earned interest for the entire quarter. In the preceding example, we found that the interest on $1,000 for one quarter is $12.58.

Next, we compute interest on the $250 between the beginning of the quarter and September 15, when the funds were withdrawn. Since September is the third month of the quarter, we use the 15th line in the "3rd Month" column in the withdrawal table:

$$I = W \times W/D \text{ tab.}$$
$$= \$250(0.010470)$$
$$= 2.6175$$
$$I = \$2.62$$

Example Three *(cont.)*   The $250 will earn interest of $2.62 before it is withdrawn on September 15. Total interest for the quarter is thus

INTEREST

$12.58
+   2.62
$15.20   total interest for the quarter

(b) The balance in this account at the end of the quarter was

Opening balance	$1,250.00
Withdrawal	− 250.00
	$1,000.00
Interest	+ 15.20
	$1,015.20 Balance, end of quarter

Example Four   Compute the (a) interest and (b) balance at the end of the quarter after the following transactions, when daily interest is compounded at 5%:

Balance	April 1	$1,500
Deposit	April 8	300
Withdrawal	May 18	200
Deposit	June 14	400
Withdrawal	June 21	200

Solution   (a) Since a $300 deposit was made on April 8, the account would have earned interest on $1,500 + $300 or $1,800 for the entire quarter, if there had been no withdrawals. Since there were two withdrawals of $200, however, only $1,800 − $400, or $1,400 will earn interest for the whole quarter:

WITHDRAWALS

May 18	$200	Opening balance	$1,500
June 21	200	Deposit, April 8	+ 300
	$400	Effective opening balance	$1,800
		Withdrawals	− 400
		Principal earning interest for entire quarter	$1,400

Interest for the quarter is thus computed as follows:

$1,400 principal for the entire quarter:

$$I = P \times \text{Dep. tab.}$$
$$= \$1,400(0.012578)$$
$$= 17.6092$$
$$I = \$17.61$$

$400 deposit on June 14 (third month):

$$I = P \times \text{Dep. tab.}$$
$$= \$400(0.002364)$$
$$= 0.9456$$
$$I = \$0.95$$

The following interest was earned prior to the two withdrawals:

$200 withdrawal on May 18 (second month):

$$I = W \times \text{W/D tab.}$$
$$= \$200(0.006688)$$
$$= 1.3376$$
$$I = \$1.34$$

$200 withdrawal on June 21 (third month):

$$I = W \times \text{W/D tab.}$$
$$= \$200(0.011313)$$
$$= 2.2626$$
$$I = \$2.26$$

Thus, total interest for the quarter is:

	INTEREST
Interest on funds on deposit for the entire quarter	$17.61
Interest on $400 deposited June 14	.95
Interest on $200 withdrawn May 18	1.34
Interest on $200 withdrawn June 21	2.26
Total interest for quarter	$22.16

(b) The balance after the quarter ended would be:

DEPOSITS	*WITHDRAWALS*
$300	$200
400	200
$700	$400

Opening balance		$1,500.00
Deposits	+	700.00
		$2,200.00
Withdrawals	−	400.00
		$1,800.00
Interest	+	22.16
Balance, end of quarter		$1,822.16

The savings account would contain $1,822.16 after the quarter ended.

The following problems are all for interest paid at 5% compounded daily. Unless otherwise stated in the problem, interest is to be paid from the first of the month on deposits made by the tenth of the month.

Find (1) the amount of interest, and (2) the balance at the end of the quarter for the following deposits.

1. (a) $ 100 on May 17
    (b) 2,000 on January 7
    (c) 1,500 on December 3
    (d) 400 on July 29

2. (a) $1,000 on August 19
    (b) 600 on April 20
    (c) 1,200 on June 5
    (d) 4,000 on October 9

In the following problems, compute the interest that would be earned (1) if interest is paid from the exact date of deposit, and (2) if interest is paid from the first of the month on deposits made by the tenth.

3. (a) $1,000 on November 6
    (b) 5,000 on January 8
    (c) 700 on June 4

4. (a) $1,000 on December 7
    (b) 500 on July 10
    (c) 2,000 on February 5

In the following problems, compute the interest that would be earned for one quarter (1) at 5% compounded daily, and (2) at 5% compounded quarterly on the given principals.

5. (a) $10,000
    (b) 2,500

6. (a) $1,000
    (b) 3,600

Find (1) the total amount of interest, and (2) the balance after the quarter ended for the following accounts.

	Opening Balance	Deposits
7. (a)	$2,500 on January 1	$ 500 on January 7
		50 on February 27
		400 on March 6
(b)	$4,000 on October 1	$ 80 on October 20
		200 on November 2
		1,000 on December 10
8. (a)	$2,000 on April 1	$ 600 on April 22
		1,000 on May 6
		100 on June 12
(b)	$2,800 on July 1	$ 200 on July 10
		500 on August 16
		300 on September 7

476

Compute (1) the interest for the quarter and (2) the balance when the quarter ended for the following problems:

	Opening Balance	Withdrawals
9. (a)	$3,400 on July 1	$400 on August 16
(b)	$1,800 on April 1	$500 on May 1
		300 on June 7
10. (a)	$1,500 on January 1	$500 on March 3
(b)	$5,800 on October 1	$600 on October 10
		200 on December 18

Transactions for an entire quarter are given below. Calculate (1) the total interest each account would earn and (2) the balance in each account after the quarter ends. (Hint: Be alert for deposits made before the tenth of a month.)

	Opening Balance	Deposits	Withdrawals
11. (a)	$ 900 on January 1	$300 on January 10	$200 on March 25
(b)	$2,400 on October 1	$200 on November 18	$300 on October 3
		50 on December 6	100 on December 13
(c)	$4,700 on April 1	$400 on April 8	$200 on April 27
		70 on May 9	900 on June 20
12. (a)	$ 800 on October 1	$400 on October 8	$200 on November 30
(b)	$3,500 on July 1	$500 on August 7	$200 on August 24
		100 on September 1	300 on September 9
(c)	$1,800 on January 1	$700 on January 4	$400 on February 28
		50 on January 25	100 on March 17

SECTION 4
Present Value (At Compound Interest)

It often happens that one wishes to know how much would have to be deposited now (at the present) in order to obtain a certain maturity value. The principal that would have to be deposited is the **present value.**

The formula for obtaining present value at compound interest is a variation of the compound amount formula. The formula is rearranged to solve for *P* rather than *S*, by dividing both sides of the equation by the parenthetical expression $(1+i)^n$:

$$S = P(1+i)^n$$

Divide by $(1+i)^n$:

$$\frac{S}{(1+i)^n} = \frac{P\cancel{(1+i)^n}}{\cancel{(1+i)^n}}$$

$$\frac{S}{(1+i)^n} = P$$

or, reversing the order,

$$P = \frac{S}{(1+i)^n}$$

Therefore, present value could be found by dividing the known maturity value S by the appropriate value from the compound amount table (Table XIV) which we have already been using. However, division using such long decimal numbers would be an extremely long and cumbersome operation; hence, present-value tables have been developed which allow present value to be computed by multiplication.

Just as $\frac{12}{3} = 12 \cdot \frac{1}{3}$, so

$$\frac{S}{(1+i)^n} = S \cdot \frac{1}{(1+i)^n}$$

The entries in Table XVII, Present Worth of 1, Appendix C, are the quotients obtained when the numbers from the compound amount table are divided into "1." These quotients (the present-value entries) may then be multiplied by the appropriate maturity value to obtain the present value.

Since present value is usually computed using multiplication, the formula is commonly written in a form that indicates multiplication and uses a negative exponent. Recall that a negative exponent indicates the factor actually belongs in the opposite part of the fraction. (That is, $3x^{-2}$ means $\dfrac{3}{x^2}$.) Thus,

$$P = \frac{S}{(1+i)^n}$$

is usually written

$$P = S(1+i)^{-n}$$

The following examples will illustrate that present value may be found using either the compound amount table (Table XIV) or the present-value table (Table XVII). As a general rule, however, the student should use the present-value table (Table XVII) when computing present value at compound interest.

Example One

An investment made for 6 years at 9% compounded monthly is to have a maturity value of $1,000. Determine the present value using (a) the compound amount table (Table XIV) and (b) the present-value table (Table XVII). Also, (c) find how much interest will be included.

Solution

(a) $S = \$1,000$ $P = \dfrac{S}{(1+i)^n}$

$i = \frac{3}{4}\%$

$n = 72$ $= \dfrac{\$1,000}{(1+\frac{3}{4}\%)^{72}}$

$P = ?$ $= \dfrac{\$1,000}{1.712553}$

$= 583.924$

$P = \$583.92$

(b) $P = S(1+i)^{-n}$ (c) $I = S - P$

$= \$1,000(1+\frac{3}{4}\%)^{-72}$ $= \$1,000.00$

$= 1,000(0.583924)$ $-\quad 583.92$

$P = \$583.92$ $I = \overline{\quad\$\ \ 416.08}$

Thus, $583.92 invested now at 9% compounded monthly will earn $416.08 interest and mature to $1,000 after 6 years.

Example Two

Charles and Sue Baker would like to have $6,000 in 4 years for a down payment on a condominium. (a) What single deposit would have this maturity value if CD's earn 7% compounded quarterly? (b) How much of the final amount will be interest?

Solution (a) $S = \$6,000$ $P = S(1+i)^{-n}$ (b) $I = S - P$

$n = 16$ $= \$6,000(1 + 1\frac{3}{4}\%)^{-16}$ $= \quad \$6,000.00$

$i = 1\frac{3}{4}\%$ $= 6,000(0.7576163)$ $\frac{- \quad 4,545.70}{}$

$P = ?$ $= \$4,545.698$ $I = \quad \$1,454.30$

                 $P = \$4,545.70$

If the Bakers purchase a $4,545.70 CD now, it will earn interest of $1,454.30 during 4 years at 7% compounded quarterly and have a $6,000 maturity value.

As was true of simple interest problems, present value (or present worth) may on occasion differ from principal. The actual amount of money that is invested is always the principal; it may or may not be invested at the interest rate currently being paid by most financial institutions. The present value of the investment is the amount that would have to be invested at the rate money is worth (the rate being paid by most financial institutions) in order to obtain the same maturity value that the actual investment will have. If an investment is sold before its maturity date, it should theoretically be sold for its present value at that time.

Example Three Arthur Levy has made a $12,000 real estate investment which he expects will have a maturity value equivalent to interest at 12% compounded monthly for 5 years. If most savings institutions are currently paying 8% compounded quarterly on 5-year CD's, what is the least amount for which Levy should sell his property?

Solution This is a two-part problem. We must first determine the maturity value of the $12,000 investment. Then, using the rate money is actually worth, we must compute the present worth of the maturity value obtained by step 1 (Figure 52).

1. $P = \$12,000$ $S = P(1+i)^n$

    $i = 1\%$ $= \$12,000(1 + 1\%)^{60}$

    $n = 60$ $= 12,000(1.81669670)$

    $S = ?$ $= \$21,800.3604$

                  $S = \$21,800.36$

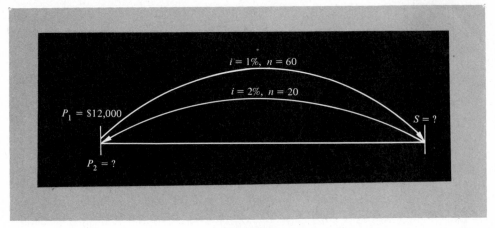

FIGURE 52

2. $S = \$21,800.36$ $P = S(1+i)^{-n}$
    $i = 2\%$ $= \$21,800.36(1+2\%)^{-20}$
    $n = 20$ $=\ \ 21,800.36(0.67297133)$
    $P_2 = ?$ $=\ \ 14,671.017$
                             $P_2 = \$14,671.02$

Levy should not sell the property for less than $14,671.02, for he would have to purchase a CD of this value, paying interest at 8% compounded quarterly, in order to have $21,800.36 in 5 years.

SECTION 4   *Problems*

Compute present value at compound interest, using the data given in each part of Problems 1 and 2. Also determine the amount of interest that will be earned before maturity.

		Maturity Value	Rate	Compounded	Years
1.	(a)	$1,000	7%	Quarterly	15
	(b)	2,800	5	Semiannually	18
	(c)	500	9	Monthly	8
	(d)	1,400	6	Quarterly	11
	(e)	2,000	8	Semiannually	10

		Maturity Value	Rate	Compounded	Years
2.	(a)	$1,000	9%	Quarterly	15
	(b)	2,500	8	Monthly	6
	(c)	3,000	7	Semiannually	12
	(d)	1,200	6	Monthly	4
	(e)	800	5	Quarterly	8

3. Watkins Associates expects to need $5,000 in 8 years to replace some machinery. If they can make an investment which pays 7% compounded semiannually:

(a) How much should Watkins invest in order to have this maturity value?

(b) What amount of interest will their investment earn?

4. Fred Stewart wants to have $10,000 in savings when his young son reaches college age in 16 years. If his savings and loan will pay 9% compounded semiannually on long-term certificates of deposit:

(a) What single deposit now will obtain Stewart's goal?

(b) How much interest will the investment earn during this time?

5. Far West Motor Freight Lines expect to replace a van in 5 years at a cost of $8,000. If they can make an investment now at 6% compounded monthly:

(a) How much must be deposited now to obtain the desired maturity value?

(b) How much of the $8,000 will be interest?

6. Kathy Tippett wants to have $1,000 in 3 years for a down payment on a new car. Passbook accounts earn 5% compounded monthly.

(a) What single deposit now will mature to $1,000?

(b) How much interest will the account earn?

7. William Farmer will retire in 15 years, and he would like to have $10,000 at that time.

(a) What single deposit made now will mature to $10,000 if money is worth 6% compounded quarterly?

(b) How much interest will the deposit earn in 15 years?

8. A manufacturing plant expects to expand its production in 5 years at a cost of $60,000. On an investment of this size, the savings and loan will pay 10% compounded quarterly.

(a) What single deposit would produce the desired maturity value?

(b) How much interest will be included?

9. A $4,000 investment is made at 8% compounded monthly, for a term of 7 years.

(a) What is the maturity value of the investment?

(b) If money is generally worth 7% compounded quarterly, what is the present worth of the investment? [Round S to nearest $10 for part (b).]

10. A 7-year, $4,000 investment is made at 7% compounded quarterly.

(a) Find the maturity value of this investment.

(b) What is the present worth of the investment, if 8% compounded monthly is usually paid on similar investments? (Use S rounded to nearest $10.)

11. Wayne Redmond is the payee of a $500 note at 6% simple interest for 3 years. Most financial institutions pay 5% compounded monthly.
(a) What maturity value must the maker repay?
(b) How much should Redmond have received if he had sold the note on the day it was issued?

12. Smith Supply Co. holds a 5-year, 8% simple interest note for $1,000. Money is worth 6% compounded quarterly.
(a) How much will be due when the note matures?
(b) If Smith Supply had sold the note on the day it was drawn, how much should they have received?

13. A $1,000 note was issued for 2 years at 5% simple interest.
(a) How much will be owed on the maturity date of the note?
(b) What was the present worth of this note on the day it was drawn, if money is worth 8% compounded monthly?

14. A $1,600, simple interest note was drawn at $6\frac{1}{4}$% for 4 years.
(a) What will be the total amount due when the note matures?
(b) If money is worth 7% compounded semiannually, what was the present worth of the note on the day it was drawn?

CHAPTER 18 *Glossary*

Certificate of deposit (CD). A savings contract that offers a slightly higher rate when a (minimum $1,000) deposit is made for a specified time period. (An early withdrawal would forfeit the higher rate.)

Compound amount. The total value at the end of a compound interest investment (original principal plus all interest).

Compound interest. Interest computed periodically and then added to the previous principal, so that this total then becomes the principal for the next interest period. "Interest earned on (previous) interest." The difference between final maturity value and original principal.

Conversion period. A regular time interval at which interest is compounded (or computed and added to the previous principal). Interest is commonly compounded daily, monthly, quarterly, semiannually, or annually.

Open account. A savings account where deposits or withdrawals may be made at any time.

Passbook account. An open account where each transaction is entered in a record book kept by the account owner.

Period. (See "Conversion period.")

Present value. The amount of money that would have to be deposited (on some given date prior to maturity) in order to obtain a specified maturity value.

Term. The length of time for a compound interest investment.

CHAPTER 19

Annuities

CHAPTER 19 OBJECTIVES

Upon completion of Chapter 19, the student will be able to:

1. **Define and use correctly the terminology associated with each topic.**

2. **Determine amount and compound interest earned on an annuity, using** $S = \text{Pmt.} \times \text{Amt. ann. tab.}_{\overline{n}|i}$ **and the amount of annuity table.**
   (Section 1; Example 1; Problems 1–10)

3. **a. Compute present value of an annuity, using** $\text{P.V.} = \text{Pmt.} \times \text{P.V. ann tab.}_{\overline{n}|i}$
   and the present value of annuity table. (That is, determine the original value required in order for one to withdraw the given annuity payments.) *(Section 2; Examples 1, 2; Problems 1–12)*
   b. Also, determine
      (1) The total amount received; and
      (2) The interest included.

4. **Use the same procedure (Objective 3) to determine**
   a. The total amount paid for a real estate purchase; and
   b. The equivalent cash price. *(Section 2; Example 3; Problems 13–16)*

19 Notice that the compound interest problems in the previous chapter basically involved making a *single deposit* which remained invested for the entire time. There are few people, however, who have large sums available to invest in this manner. Most people must attain their savings goals by making a series of regular deposits. This leads to the idea of annuities.

An **annuity** is a series of payments (normally equal in amount) that are made at regular intervals of time. Most people typically think of an annuity as the regular payment received from an insurance policy when it is cashed in after retirement. This is one good example, but there are many other everyday examples that are seldom thought of as annuities. Besides savings deposits, other common examples are rent, salaries, Social Security payments, installment plan payments, loan payments, insurance payments—in fact, any payment made at regular intervals of time.

There are several time variables that may affect an annuity. For instance, some annuities have definite beginning and ending dates; such an annuity is called an **annuity certain**. Examples of an annuity certain are installment plan payments or the payments from a life insurance policy converted to an annuity of a specified number of years.

If the beginning and/or ending dates are uncertain, the annuity is called a **contingent annuity**. Monthly Social Security retirement benefits and the payments on an ordinary life insurance policy are examples of contingent annuities for which the ending dates are unknown, because both will terminate when the person dies. If a person provides in a will that following death a beneficiary is to receive an annuity for a fixed number of years, this is a contingent annuity for which the beginning date is uncertain. A man with a large estate might provide that his surviving wife receive a specified yearly income for the remainder of her life and that the balance then be donated to some charity; this contingent annuity would then be uncertain on both the beginning and ending dates.

Another factor affecting annuities is whether the payment is made at the beginning of each time interval (such as rent or insurance premiums, which are normally paid in advance) or at the end of the period (such as salaries or Social Security retirement benefits). An annuity for which payments are made at the beginning of each period is known as an **annuity due**. When payments come at the end of each period, the annuity is called an **ordinary annuity**.

We shall be studying *investment annuities*—annuities that earn compound interest (rather than rent or installment payments, for example, which earn no interest). An annuity is said to be a **simple annuity** when the date of payment coincides with the conversion date of the compound interest.

The study of contingent annuities requires some knowledge of probability, which is not within the scope of this text. Thus, since our purpose is just to give the student a basic introduction to annuities, our study of annuities will be limited to simple, ordinary annuities certain—annuities for which both the beginning and ending dates are fixed, and for which the payments are made on the conversion date at the end of each period.

SECTION 1
Amount of an Annuity

The **amount of an annuity** is the maturity value which an account will have after a series of equal payments into it. As in the case of other compound interest problems, amount of an annuity is usually found by using the appropriate table for the appropriate rate per period and number of periods. Thus, we shall compute amount of an annuity by using Table XV, Amount of Annuity, Appendix C, and the following procedure:

$$\text{Amount} = \text{Payment} \times \text{Amount of annuity table}_{\overline{n}|i}$$

where n = number of periods and i = interest rate per period. For simplicity, the procedure* might be abbreviated,

$$S = \text{Pmt.} \times \text{Amt. ann. tab.}_{\overline{n}|i}$$

The total amount of deposits is found by multiplying the periodic payment times the number of periods. Total interest earned is then the difference between the maturity value and the total deposits made into the account.

*Many texts give the procedure for amount of an annuity in the form $S = Ps_{\overline{n}|i}$, where S = maturity value, P = payment, and $s_{\overline{n}|i}$ indicates use of the amount of an annuity table. Strictly speaking, $S = Ps_{\overline{n}|i}$ is also a procedure, not a formula. The actual formula is $S = P \cdot \dfrac{(1+i)^n - 1}{i}$.

Example One

(a) Determine the amount of an annuity, if Leonard Feldman deposits $100 each quarter for 6 years into an account earning 8% compounded quarterly. (b) How much of this total will Feldman deposit himself? (c) How much of the final amount is interest?

Solution

(a) (Notice that deposits are made each quarter to coincide with the interest conversion date at the bank; we would not be able to compute the annuity if they were otherwise.)

$$\text{Pmt.} = \$100 \qquad S = \text{Pmt.} \times \text{Amt. ann. tab.}_{\overline{n}|i}$$

$$n = 24 \qquad\qquad\quad = \$100 \times \text{Amt. ann. tab.}_{\overline{24}|2\%}$$

$$i = 2\% \qquad\qquad\quad = 100(30.42186)$$

$$S = \$3,042.19$$

Feldman's account will contain $3,042.19 after 6 years.

(b) There will be 24 deposits of $100 each, totaling $24 \times \$100$ or $2,400.

(c) The interest earned during this annuity period is

Amount of annuity	$3,042.19
Total deposits	− 2,400.00
Interest	$ 642.19

SECTION 1 *Problems*

Using the amount-of-an-annuity procedure, find the maturity value that would be obtained if one makes the payments given below. Also determine the total deposits and the total interest earned.

		Periodic Payment	Rate	Compounded	Years
1.	(a)	$ 100	6%	Monthly	7
	(b)	1,500	7	Semiannually	8
	(c)	80	6	Quarterly	16
	(d)	600	5	Quarterly	5
	(e)	200	8	Monthly	6
2.	(a)	$ 500	7%	Quarterly	4
	(b)	1,000	9	Semiannually	10
	(c)	300	8	Quarterly	15
	(d)	100	5	Monthly	6
	(e)	1,800	6	Semiannually	5

3. A "rich uncle" gave his niece $100 each Christmas through her 18th Christmas. If the savings bank paid 7% annual interest:

(a) What was the value of the account after the last Christmas?

(b) How much had actually been deposited?

(c) How much was interest?

4. A father deposited $100 into his son's savings account on each birthday through his 21st birthday.

(a) How much did the father give his son?

(b) What amount was in the account after the 21st deposit, if the account earned 6% annual interest?

(c) How much interest was earned during the time of the annuity?

5. Each month Harry Wise deposits $50 into his savings and loan account. The association has been paying 5% compounded monthly.

(a) How much will Harry's account be worth in 7 years?

(b) How much of this total will Wise have deposited?

(c) How much will be interest?

6. Each 6 months, Lynn Grayson purchases a $1,000 CD that earns 7% compounded semiannually. Each certificate (principal plus interest) is then renewed when it matures.

(a) What will be the value of Grayson's savings after 5 years?

(b) How much of this total will Grayson have invested himself?

(c) How much interest will the CD's have earned?

7. Lytle Industries are investing $5,000 each 6 months with the intention of expanding their plant facilities in 5 years. The money is being invested in a mutual fund paying 8% compounded semiannually.

(a) How much will Lytle invest during the 5 years?

(b) What will be the amount of their account?

(c) How much interest will the account have drawn?

8. Capital Mobile Home Sales is budgeting $2,000 quarterly in order to open a second sales location in 4 years. Their investments are earning 9% compounded quarterly.

(a) How much will Capital invest over 4 years?

(b) What will be the value of their account then?

(c) How much will be interest?

9. In order to finance the production of a new product, Natural Cosmetics, Inc., is investing $10,000 each 6 months.

(a) How much will the firm invest in 2 years?

(b) If their CD's earn 9% compounded semiannually, what will be the maturity value of this annuity?

(c) How much interest will be included?

10. The city of Fort Milton is investing $1,000 each month in order to meet its obligation for a new swimming pool, which is due in 3 years. The city's savings certificates pay 8% compounded monthly.

(a) How much will the city deposit during 3 years?

(b) What will their investment be worth then?

(c) How much of the maturity value will be interest on the annuity?

SECTION 2

Present Value of
an Annuity

Observe that our study of amount of an annuity involved starting with an empty account and making payments into it so that the account contained its largest amount at the end of the term. The study of present value of an annuity is exactly the reverse: The account contains its largest balance at the beginning of the term and one receives payments from the account until it is empty. This balance which an account must contain at the beginning of the term is the **present value** or **present worth of an annuity**.

Rather than studying the actual formula for present value of an annuity, we will use an informal procedure as we did for amount of an annuity. **By consulting Table XVIII, Present Value of Annuity, Appendix C**, present value may be computed as follows:

$$\text{Present value} = \text{Payment} \times \text{Present value of annuity table}_{\overline{n}|i}$$

where, as before, n = number of payments and i = interest rate per period. The procedure* may be abbreviated

$$\text{P.V.} = \text{Pmt.} \times \text{P.V. ann. tab.}_{\overline{n}|i}$$

The total amount to be received from an annuity is found by multiplying the payment times the number of periods. As long as there are still funds in the account, it will continue to earn interest; thus, even though the balance of the account is declining during the term of the annuity, the account will still continue to earn some interest until the final payment is received. The total interest which the account will earn is found by subtracting the beginning balance (the present value) from the total payments to be received.

**Example
One**

Elaine Shaw wishes to receive a $100 annuity each quarter for 6 years while attending college and graduate school. Her account earns 8% compounded quarterly. (a) What must be the (present) value of Elaine's account when she starts to college? (b) How much will Elaine actually receive? (c) How much interest will these annuity payments include?

---

*The procedure for present value of an annuity is often indicated as $A = Pa_{\overline{n}|i}$, where A = present value, P = payment, and $a_{\overline{n}|i}$ indicates use of the present-value-of-an-annuity table.

Solution
(a) Pmt. = \$100

$\quad n = 24$

$\quad i = 2\%$

P.V. = Pmt. $\times$ P.V. ann. tab.$_{\overline{n}|i}$

$\quad = \$100 \times$ P.V. ann. tab.$_{\overline{24}|2\%}$

$\quad = 100(18.91393)$

P.V. = \$1,891.39

Elaine's account must contain \$1,891.39 when she enters college.

(b) She will receive 24 annuity payments of \$100 each, for a total of \$2,400.

(c) The account will earn interest of

Total payments	\$2,400.00
Present value	− 1,891.39
Interest	\$ 508.61

Thus, from an account containing \$1,891.39, Elaine may withdraw \$100 each quarter until a total of \$2,400 has been withdrawn. During this time, the declining fund will have earned \$508.61 interest. After the final payment is received, the balance in her account will be exactly \$0.

Example Two

Grover Campbell would like to receive an annuity of \$5,000 semiannually for 10 years after he retires; he will retire in 18 years. Money is worth 9% compounded semiannually. (a) How much must Campbell have when he retires in order to finance this annuity? (b) What single deposit made now would provide the funds for the annuity? (c) How much will Campbell actually receive from the annuity? (d) How much interest will the single deposit earn before the annuity ends?

Solution

This is a two-part problem: (1) to find the beginning balance (present value) required for the 10-year annuity, and (2) to find what single deposit (present value at compound interest) would produce a maturity value equal to the answer obtained in step 1 (Figure 53).

(a) Pmt. = \$5,000

$\quad n = 20$

$\quad i = 4\frac{1}{2}\%$

P.V. = Pmt. $\times$ P.V. ann. tab.$_{\overline{n}|i}$

$\quad = \$5,000 \times$ P.V. ann tab.$_{\overline{20}|4\frac{1}{2}\%}$

$\quad = 5,000(13.0079365)$

$\quad = 65,039.6825$

P.V. = \$65,039.68

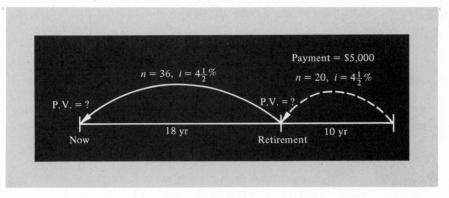

FIGURE 53

The account must contain \$65,039.68 at Campbell's retirement, in order for him to receive \$5,000 each 6 months for 10 years.

(b) We next find what single deposit, made now, would reach a maturity value of \$65,039.68 when Campbell retires in 18 years.

$$S = \$65,039.68 \qquad P = S(1+i)^{-n}$$
$$n = 36 \qquad\qquad = \$65,039.68(1+4\tfrac{1}{2}\%)^{-36}$$
$$i = 4\tfrac{1}{2}\% \qquad\qquad = \ 65,039.68(0.2050281740)$$
$$\qquad\qquad\qquad\qquad = \ 13,334.9668\ldots$$
$$P = \$13,334.97$$

A single deposit of \$13,334.97 now will be worth \$65,039.68 after 18 years at 9% compounded semiannually.

(c) Campbell will receive 20 payments of \$5,000 each, for a total of \$100,000 during the term of his annuity.

(d) The total interest is the difference between what he will actually receive from the annuity (\$100,000) and the original amount invested (\$13,334.97):

Total received	\$100,000.00
Principal invested	− 13,334.97
Interest	\$ 86,665.03

The original investment of \$13,334.97 would produce interest of \$86,665.03 before the annuity expires. (Campbell will receive approximately 7.5 times the original amount invested.)

Equivalent Cash Price. Keep in mind that "present value" often refers to the value of an investment on the first day of the term. (It always refers to the value on some day prior to the maturity date.) This fact will help clarify the following example.

Example Three

A home buyer made a down payment of $7,000 and will make payments of $2,000 each 6 months for 25 years. Money is worth 8% compounded semiannually. (a) What would have been the equivalent cash price of the house? (b) How much will the buyer actually pay for the house?

Solution

(a) The "cash price" would have been the cost on the original day. This value on the beginning day of the term indicates that present value is required.

$$\text{Cash price} = \text{Down payment} + \text{Present value of the periodic payments}$$

$$\text{Pmt.} = \$2,000 \qquad \text{P.V.} = \text{Pmt.} \times \text{P.V. ann. tab.}_{\overline{n}|i}$$
$$n = 50 \qquad\qquad\quad = \$2,000 \times \text{P.V. ann. tab.}_{\overline{50}|4\%}$$
$$i = 4\% \qquad\qquad\quad = 2,000(21.4821846)$$
$$\qquad\qquad\qquad\qquad\quad = 42,964.3692$$
$$\qquad\qquad\qquad \text{P.V.} = \$42,964.37$$

Thus,

Down payment	$ 7,000.00
Present value of	
periodic payments	+ 42,964.37
Cash price	$49,964.37

(b) The buyer will actually make a down payment of $7,000 plus 50 payments of $2,000 each, for a total cost of $107,000:

Down payment	$ 7,000
Total of periodic	
payments	+ 100,000
Total cost	$107,000

The equivalent cash price was $49,964.37 because that sum, invested in an account earning 8% semiannual interest, would have the same maturity value ($355,080.95) as if the $7,000 down payment and each semiannual payment were deposited at the same rate. Notice the buyer's total cost ($107,000) will be more than twice the cash price. This is not an uncommon ratio for the payment of home loans. This subject is discussed in more detail in Section 2 on "Amortization" in the next chapter.

SECTION 2 *Problems*

HINT: Remember that the basic problems of amount and present value at compound interest involve a *single* deposit for some period of time, whereas the annuity problems involve a *series* of payments.

Using the present-value-of-an-annuity procedure, determine (1) *the present value required in order to receive each of the annuities given below,* (2) *the total amount that each annuity would pay, and* (3) *how much interest would be included.*

		Payment	Rate	Compounded	Years
1.	(a)	$ 100	7%	Quarterly	7
	(b)	50	6	Monthly	8
	(c)	1,500	8	Semiannually	10
	(d)	400	6	Quarterly	18
	(e)	80	5	Monthly	5
2.	(a)	$1,000	5%	Quarterly	8
	(b)	60	7	Monthly	3
	(c)	1,200	8	Semiannually	6
	(d)	800	9	Quarterly	15
	(e)	2,000	6	Semiannually	10

(1) *Calculate the amount of an annuity (as in Section* 1) *and the interest included if one makes deposits as given below. Also,* (2) *determine the present value (as in Section* 2) *required in order to receive the given annuity payments, and the total interest that would be included in the annuity.*

		Payment	Rate	Compounded	Years
3.	(a)	$ 100	5%	Quarterly	10
	(b)	500	6	Semiannually	15
	(c)	60	7	Monthly	4
4.	(a)	$1,000	7%	Semiannually	12
	(b)	100	9	Monthly	5
	(c)	500	8	Quarterly	7

5. James Carson wishes to purchase an annuity of $100 monthly for 3 years. If the current interest rate is 6% compounded monthly:
(a) How much would be required to finance the annuity?
(b) How much will Carson actually receive from the annuity?
(c) How much interest will the annuity include?

6. A widow wishes to use part of her insurance settlement to purchase an annuity of $1,000 quarterly for 20 years. She can invest the funds at 7% compounded quarterly.
(a) How much must be in her account when the annuity starts?
(b) How much will the annuity pay?
(c) How much interest will be earned before the account is exhausted?

7. Gary Post would like to receive a $50 monthly annuity during the 4 years he is in college. If his savings and loan association pays 5% compounded monthly:
(a) How much would Gary have to have on deposit when he starts to college, in order to be able to withdraw $50 each month?
(b) What will be the total of Gary's withdrawals?
(c) How much interest will be earned during his college years?

8. Charles Greer wants to provide an annuity to pay himself $4,000 semiannually for 16 years after he retires.
(a) What amount must Greer have at retirement, if money is worth 8% compounded semiannually?
(b) How much will Greer receive from the annuity?
(c) How much interest will be included?

In the following problems, round your solution to each part to the nearest $100 for use in succeeding parts.

9. A man would like to receive $1,000 each 6 months for 10 years after he retires. He can invest his money at 7% compounded semiannually.
(a) How much money must he have when he retires in order to receive the annuity?
(b) The man will retire in 20 years. What deposit could he make today that will provide the funds for the annuity?
(c) How much interest would this deposit earn before the annuity ends?

10. Karen Wilson's parents want to set up an annuity that will pay $100 each month for 4 years while she attends college. They can make an investment paying 8% compounded monthly.
(a) What must be the balance in the account when Karen enters college?
(b) What single investment made now would be sufficient to provide the annuity, if Karen will enter college in 6 years?
(c) How much interest would the initial deposit earn before the annuity terminates?

11. William Jennings' son will be ready for college in 12 years. Jennings wants to provide for an annuity of $400 quarterly during his son's 4 years in college. His money can be invested at 7% compounded quarterly.
(a) What amount must be on deposit when the son enters college in order to receive this annuity?
(b) How much would Jennings have to deposit today in order to provide for the annuity?

(c) How much total interest will this deposit earn before the son finishes college?

12. Walter Harrison will retire in 11 years. He wants to fund an annuity that will pay $300 each quarter for 15 years after retirement.

(a) If money is worth 9% compounded quarterly, how much will be required at retirement in order to finance the annuity?

(b) What amount deposited today would provide the funds for the annuity?

(c) How much total interest would be earned before the annuity expires?

13. Mr. and Mrs. Horton purchased a home for $12,000 down and semiannual payments of $2,000 for 20 years.

(a) How much will the Hortons pay altogether?

(b) What cash price deposited at 8% compounded semiannually would yield the owner the same maturity value he would have after 20 years of depositing the Hortons' payments?

14. Richardson Corporation bought a tract of land for $8,000 down and monthly payments of $1,000 for 5 years.

(a) How much will Richardson pay altogether for the land?

(b) What cash price invested at 8% compounded monthly would give the former owner the same total after 5 years that he would have by depositing Richardson's payments?

15. A business property was purchased for $15,000 down and monthly payments of $1,000 for 6 years.

(a) What was the total cost to the buyer?

(b) What would have been the equivalent cash price, if money were worth 9% compounded monthly?

16. Purchase agreements for the Grants' new home include a $5,000 down payment and $1,000 quarterly payments for 25 years.

(a) What is the total cost to the Grants?

(b) What would have been the equivalent cash price, if money were worth 9% compounded quarterly?

CHAPTER 19 *Glossary*

Amount (of an annuity). The maturity value of an account after a series of equal (annuity) payments into it.

Annuity. A series of equal payments made at regular intervals of time (either with or without interest).

Annuity certain. An annuity with definite beginning and ending dates.

Annuity due. An annuity paid (or received) at the beginning of each time interval. (Example: Rent or insurance premiums.)

Contingent annuity. An annuity for which the beginning and/or ending dates are uncertain.

Ordinary annuity. An annuity paid (or received) at the end of each time period. (Example: Salaries or stock dividends.)

Present value (of an annuity). The beginning balance an account must contain in order to receive an annuity from it.

Simple annuity. An annuity where the date of payment coincides with the conversion date of the compound interest.

CHAPTER 20

Sinking Funds and Amortization

CHAPTER 20 OBJECTIVES

Upon completion of Chapter 20, the student will be able to:

1. Define and use correctly the terminology associated with each topic.

2. Using $\text{Pmt.} = S \times \text{S.F. tab.}_{\overline{n}|i}$ and the sinking fund table, determine
   a. The regular payment required to finance a sinking fund;
   b. The total amount deposited; and
   c. The interest earned. *(Section 1; Example 1; Problems 1–8)*

3. Prepare a sinking fund schedule to verify that the payments (Objective 2) will result in the required maturity value. *(Example 2; Problems 9, 10)*

4. Using $\text{Pmt.} = \text{P.V.} \times \text{Amtz. tab.}_{\overline{n}|i}$ and the amortization table, compute
   a. The periodic payment required to amortize a loan;
   b. The total amount paid; and
   c. The interest included. *(Section 2; Example 1; Problems 1–10)*

5. Prepare an amortization schedule to verify that the payments (Objective 4) pay off the loan correctly. *(Example 2; Problems 11, 12)*

6. Explain the characteristics of the six basic types of compound interest and annuity problems. *(Section 3; Problems 1–24)*

| 20 | Far-sighted investors may wish to establish a savings plan whereby regular deposits will achieve a specified savings goal by a certain time. An account of this type is known as a sinking fund. |

In the loan plans studied in previous chapters, either simple interest or simple discount was charged. For large loans that take many years to repay, however, ordinary simple interest would not be profitable to lenders, as later examples will show. Thus, long-term loans must be repaid in a series of payments which include all interest due since the previous payment. This loan repayment procedure is known at amortization.

Sinking funds and amortization are the subject of the following sections; both topics involve finding a required periodic payment (or annuity).

SECTION 1

Sinking Funds

The section in the preceding chapter on amount of an annuity dealt with making given periodic payments into an account (at compound interest) and finding what the maturity value of that account would be. It frequently happens that businesses know what amount will be needed on some future date and are concerned with determining what periodic payment (annuity) would have to be invested in order to obtain this amount. When a special account is established so that the maturity value (equal periodic deposits plus compound interest) will exactly equal a specific amount, such a fund is called a **sinking fund**.

Sinking funds are often used to finance the replacement of machinery, equipment, facilities, and so forth, after depreciation, or to finance the redemption of bonds. **Bonds** are somewhat similar to promissory notes in that they are written promises to repay a specified debt on a certain date. The primary difference is that interest on bonds is typically paid periodically, whereas the interest on a note is all repaid on the maturity date. Large corporations, municipalities, and state governments usually finance long-term improvements by selling bonds. The study of bonds themselves is not within the scope of this text; we shall be concerned here only with setting up a sinking fund to provide the face value (or redemption value) of the bonds at maturity. (Payment of any periodic interest due on bonds will be disregarded.)

The object of a sinking fund problem, then, is to determine what periodic payment, invested at compound interest, will produce a given maturity value. Since amount-of-annuity problems also involve building a fund that would contain its largest amount at maturity, we can see that sinking fund problems are a variation of amount-of-annuity problems. The difference is that in this case we are concerned with finding the periodic payment of the annuity rather than the maturity value. (The periodic payment to a sinking fund is often called the **rent**.)

The periodic payment to a sinking fund can be found using the amount-of-annuity procedure $S = \text{Pmt.} \times \text{Amt. ann. tab.}_{\overline{n}|i}$ and solving for Pmt. Since use of this procedure would involve long and tedious division, however, the student will normally find the periodic payment by using Table XVI, Sinking Fund, Appendix C, and the following procedure:

$$\text{Payment} = \text{Maturity value} \times \text{Sinking fund table}_{\overline{n}|i}$$

where $n = $ number of payments and $i = $ interest rate per period. This procedure* may be abbreviated

$$\text{Pmt.} = S \times \text{S.F. tab.}_{\overline{n}|i}$$

Example One

Brandon County issued bonds totaling $100,000 in order to build an addition to the courthouse. The county commissioners set up a sinking fund at 9% compounded quarterly in order to redeem the 5-year bonds. (a) What quarterly rent must be deposited to the sinking fund? (b) How much of the maturity value will be deposits? (c) How much interest will the sinking fund earn?

Solution

(a) $S = \$100,000$

$n = 20$

$i = 2\frac{1}{4}\%$

$\text{Pmt.} = S \times \text{S.F. tab.}_{\overline{n}|i}$

$= \$100,000 \times \text{S.F. tab.}_{\overline{20}|2\frac{1}{4}\%}$

$= 100,000(0.04014207)$

$\text{Pmt.} = \$4,014.21$

---

*The procedure for finding the payment to a sinking fund is often given as $P = S \times \dfrac{1}{s_{\overline{n}|i}}$, where $P = $ payment, $S = $ maturity value, and $\dfrac{1}{s_{\overline{n}|i}}$ indicates use of the sinking fund table. The procedure $P = S \times \dfrac{1}{s_{\overline{n}|i}}$ indicates that it is a variation of the amount-of-annuity procedure $S = P s_{\overline{n}|i}$.

A payment of $4,014.21 must be deposited into the sinking fund quarterly in order to have $100,000 at maturity.

(b) There will be 20 deposits of $4,014.21 each, making the total deposits $80,284.20.

(c) The interest earned is thus

Maturity value	$100,000.00
Total deposits	− 80,284.20
Interest	$ 19,715.80

When a sinking fund is in progress, businesses often keep a **sinking fund schedule**. The schedule shows how much interest the fund has earned during each period and what the current balance is. The schedule also verifies that the periodic payments will result in the desired maturity value.

Example Two

Prepare a sinking fund schedule to show that semiannual payments of $949 for 2 years will amount to $4,000 when invested at 7% compounded semiannually.

Solution

The "interest" earned each period is found by multiplying the previous "balance at end of period" by the periodic interest rate i. (Example: $949 \times 3\frac{1}{2}\% = \$33.22$.)

Payment	Periodic Interest $(i = 3\frac{1}{2}\%)$	Periodic Payment	Total Increase	Balance at End of Period
1	$ 0	$ 949.00	$ 949.00	$ 949.00
2	33.22	949.00	982.22	1,931.22
3	67.59	949.00	1,016.59	2,947.81
4	103.17	949.00	1,052.17	3,999.98
Totals	$203.98	$3,796.00		

$3,999.98   Final balance

Notice that the final balance in the sinking fund will be 2¢ less than the $4,000 needed, because of rounding.

Using the sinking fund table, determine the periodic payment necessary to finance the sinking fund. Also calculate the total deposits and the total amount of interest contained in the maturity value.

		Maturity Value	Rate	Compounded	Years
1.	(a)	$100,000	8%	Semiannually	12
	(b)	20,000	7	Annually	5
	(c)	5,000	9	Annually	3
	(d)	75,000	5	Semiannually	8
	(e)	150,000	6	Quarterly	12
2.	(a)	$ 30,000	6%	Quarterly	9
	(b)	10,000	9	Monthly	4
	(c)	8,000	5	Semiannually	7
	(d)	120,000	7	Quarterly	10
	(e)	400,000	8	Annually	15

3. Bearington and Styres, Inc., expects to need $10,000 in 5 years to purchase new office equipment.

(a) What quarterly rent would have to be paid into a sinking fund invested at 8% compounded quarterly?

(b) What part of the maturity value would be deposits?

(c) How much interest will the fund draw?

4. World Enterprises is planning to open a a new plant in 6 years at a cost of $900,000. To finance the project, the corporation will establish a sinking fund at 9% compounded quarterly.

(a) What payment should World Enterprises make to the sinking fund each quarter?

(b) What will be the total of these payments?

(c) How much interest will the fund contain at maturity?

5. The voters of Kensington passed an $80,000 bond referendum for new playground equipment for its parks. An 8-year sinking fund was established at 7% compounded annually to redeem the bonds.

(a) What annual payment must be made to finance the fund?

(b) How much interest will the account contain at maturity?

6. Robert Harris would like to buy a new car in 3 years by paying cash. He expects to need $6,000.

(a) If Harris starts a sinking fund earning 6% compounded monthly, what is the monthly payment that will provide the cash he needs?

(b) How much of the maturity value will be Harris' deposits?

(c) How much interest will be included?

7. The city of River Bend sold bonds worth $400,000 at maturity in order to

504

build a new library. To provide for redemption of the bonds, a sinking fund was established at 10% compounded semiannually for 12 years.

(a) What will be the semiannual payment to the fund?

(b) How much will the city invest for the library?

(c) How much interest will the mature fund include?

8. The citizens of Bradley Heights voted to issue bonds totaling $100,000 to build an addition to the high school. The bonds will mature in 10 years. If a sinking fund is set up earning 9% compounded semiannually:

(a) How much must be deposited each 6 months to finance the fund?

(b) How much of the final amount will be interest?

Find the periodic payment necessary to finance each of the following sinking funds. Then prepare a sinking fund schedule to verify that these periodic payments will result in the desired maturity value.

		Maturity Value	Rate	Compounded	Years
9.	(a)	$ 1,000	7%	Annually	4
	(b)	5,000	8	Semiannually	3
10.	(a)	$10,000	6%	Annually	4
	(b)	4,000	8	Quarterly	2

SECTION 2
Amortization

Bank Loans

In our study of simple interest, it was pointed out that simple interest notes are usually for short periods of time—a year or less. Example 1 in Section 1 of Chapter 18 (p. 457) was given to illustrate the advantage to the depositor of compound interest over simple interest. The same example can be used to illustrate that simple interest notes for long periods are not profitable to bankers. Suppose the investors in that example are replaced by bankers who are each lending $1,000. Banker A lends $1,000 at 8% simple interest for 3 years, for which he would receive $240 interest.

Banker B, on the other hand, lends $1,000 at 8% for only 6 months. When the borrower repays the loan after 6 months, banker B then lends both the principal and the interest for another 6 months. This process is repeated for 3 years; so, in effect, banker B earns compound interest on the $1,000 he originally lent.

That is, banker B would earn $265.31 total interest, or $25.31 more than banker A. One can easily understand that banks would prefer to invest their money in successive short-term loans rather than tying it up in single long-term loans. If carried to its logical conclusion, the result would be that no one could borrow money for long-term projects such as building a home or starting a business.

Therefore, a borrower who receives a large bank loan makes periodic, partial payments. (That is, at regular intervals payments are made that include both a payment to reduce the principal and also the interest due on the principal still owed.) This procedure is the same as paying on the installment plan at an annual percentage rate required by the Truth in Lending Law (that is, an effective interest rate—interest paid only on the balance due.) At the same time, it enables the bank, in effect, to earn compound interest (by reloaning the interest just repaid).

NOTE: It should be pointed out that financial institutions are prohibited from *charging* compound interest on a single loan. That is, a single borrower could not be charged $265.31 "interest" for a $1,000 3-year loan at 8%. The lender earns "interest on interest" only by reloaning each borrower's interest to other borrowers.

As mentioned above, it is usual to repay a large loan by making a series of equal periodic payments that include both principal and interest; this process is known as *amortization.* Perhaps the best example of amortization is the monthly payment homeowners make to pay off real estate mortgages. However, equal periodic payments may be used to amortize a long-term loan taken out for any purpose—such as to start a business, to purchase equipment or machinery, to modernize facilities, and so on.

NOTE: It should be emphasized that the interest rates associated with amortization are effective rates; that is, the interest rate each period is applied to the outstanding balance only. To put it another way: The borrower receives credit for the principal which has been repaid, and interest is paid only on the amount still owed.

Since the bulk of the debt exists at the beginning of the time period, and the problem is to determine what periodic payment is necessary to discharge the debt, amortization is thus a variation of the present-value-of-an-annuity problem already studied. The debt itself is the present (beginning) value of the annuity. The payment may be found by using the present-value-of-annuity procedure $P.V. = Pmt. \times P.V.$ ann. tab.$_{n|i}$ and solving for Pmt.

This procedure, however, necessitates dividing by a number from the present-value-of-an-annuity table. In order to simplify the calculations, financial institutions usually use Table XIX: Amortization, Appendix C, which is an amortization table for regular payments scheduled each period. This table can be used in the following procedure:

$$\text{Payment} = \text{Present value} \times \text{Amortization table}_{\overline{n}|i}$$

As before, $n =$ number of periods and $i =$ interest rate per period. The procedure* may be abbreviated

$$\text{Pmt.} = \text{P.V.} \times \text{Amtz. tab.}_{\overline{n}|i}$$

The total amount paid to amortize a loan is found by multiplying the periodic payment by the number of payments. The total amount of interest is then the difference between the total paid and the original loan (present value).

Example One

Marge and Gary Thomas bought a $13,000 residential lot by making a $3,000 down payment and making equal semiannual payments for 4 years. (a) How much was each payment if they had a 9% loan? (b) What was the total of their payments? (c) How much interest did the payments include? (d) How much did they pay altogether for the lot?

Solution

(a) Following the $3,000 down payment, the principal (or present value) of the loan was $10,000.

$$\text{P.V.} = \$10,000 \qquad \text{Pmt.} = \text{P.V.} \times \text{Amtz. tab.}_{\overline{n}|i}$$

$$n = 8 \qquad\qquad\qquad = \$10,000 \times \text{Amtz. tab.}_{\overline{8}|4\frac{1}{2}\%}$$

$$i = 4\tfrac{1}{2}\% \qquad\qquad\quad = 10,000(0.1516097)$$

$$\text{Pmt.} = \$1,516.10$$

A payment of $1,516.10 each 6 months would repay both the principal and the interest due on a $10,000 loan.

(b) There were eight payments of $1,516.10 each, making a total (principal plus interest) of $12,128.80.

---

*This procedure may also be indicated by $P = A \times \dfrac{1}{a_{\overline{n}|i}}$, where $P =$ payment, $A =$ present value, and $\dfrac{1}{a_{\overline{n}|i}}$ denotes use of the amortization table. (This table is often entitled "Annuity Whose Present Value is 1.") The form $P = A \times \dfrac{1}{a_{\overline{n}|i}}$ indicates that it is a variation of the present-value-of-an-annuity procedure $A = Pa_{\overline{n}|i}$.

(c)   Interest would be computed each 6 months on the balance still owed (times $4\frac{1}{2}\%$). The total interest would be

Total payments	$12,128.80
Principal	− 10,000.00
Interest	$ 2,128.80

(d)   The total cost of the lot, including the down payment, was thus

Total cost of loan	$12,128.80
Down payment	+ 3,000.00
Total cost of lot	$15,128.80

Persons making payments to amortize a loan are often given an **amortization schedule**, which is a period-by-period breakdown showing how much of each payment goes toward the principal, how much is interest, the total amount of principal and interest that has been paid, the principal still owed, and so forth. Figure 54 illustrates an actual amortization schedule of a $30,000 loan at 9% interest for 30 years, which will be repaid in monthly payments of $241.39.

Monthly Payment per $1,000 of Mortgage

Since our amortization table (Table XIX) contains only 100 periods, we are only able to determine monthly payments for loans with terms no longer than $8\frac{1}{3}$ years. However, the following table will enable the student to compare the monthly payments required at various prevailing rates for mortgages of the most common lengths—20, 25, and 30 years.

Rate	20 Years[a]	25 Years[a]	30 Years[a]
8 %	$8.37	$7.72	$7.34
$8\frac{1}{4}$	8.53	7.89	7.52
$8\frac{1}{2}$	8.68	8.06	7.69
$8\frac{3}{4}$	8.84	8.23	7.87
9	9.00	8.40	8.05
$9\frac{1}{4}$	9.16	8.57	8.23
$9\frac{1}{2}$	9.33	8.74	8.41
$9\frac{3}{4}$	9.49	8.92	8.60

[a] Monthly payments including principal and interest.

Prepared by Financial Publishing Company, Boston

PAYMENT NUMBER	PAYMENT ON INTEREST	PRINCIPAL	BALANCE OF LOAN	PAYMENT NUMBER	PAYMENT ON INTEREST	PRINCIPAL	BALANCE OF LOAN
1	225.00	16.39	29,983.61	61	215.73	25.66	28,738.18
2	224.88	16.51	29,967.10	62	215.54	25.85	28,712.33
3	224.75	16.64	29,950.46	63	215.34	26.05	28,686.28
4	224.63	16.76	29,933.70	64	215.15	26.24	28,660.04
5	224.50	16.89	29,916.81	65	214.95	26.44	28,633.60
6	224.38	17.01	29,899.80	66	214.75	26.64	28,606.96
7	224.25	17.14	29,882.66	67	214.55	26.84	28,580.12
8	224.12	17.27	29,865.39	68	214.35	27.04	28,553.08
9	223.99	17.40	29,847.99	69	214.15	27.24	28,525.84
10	223.86	17.53	29,830.46	70	213.94	27.45	28,498.39
11	223.73	17.66	29,812.80	71	213.74	27.65	28,470.74
12	223.60	17.79	29,795.01	72	213.53	27.86	28,442.88
13	223.46	17.93	29,777.08	73	213.32	28.07	28,414.81
14	223.33	18.06	29,759.02	74	213.11	28.28	28,386.53
15	223.19	18.20	29,740.82	75	212.90	28.49	28,358.04
16	223.06	18.33	29,722.49	76	212.69	28.70	28,329.34
17	222.92	18.47	29,704.02	77	212.47	28.92	28,300.42
18	222.78	18.61	29,685.41	78	212.25	29.14	28,271.28
19	222.64	18.75	29,666.66	79	212.03	29.36	28,241.92
20	222.50	18.89	29,647.77	80	211.81	29.58	28,212.34
21	222.36	19.03	29,628.74	81	211.59	29.80	28,182.54
22	222.22	19.17	29,609.57	82	211.37	30.02	28,152.52
23	222.07	19.32	29,590.25	83	211.14	30.25	28,122.27
24	221.93	19.46	29,570.79	84	210.92	30.47	28,091.80
25	221.78	19.61	29,551.18	85	210.69	30.70	28,061.10
26	221.63	19.76	29,531.42	86	210.46	30.93	28,030.17
27	221.49	19.90	29,511.52	87	210.23	31.16	27,999.01
28	221.34	20.05	29,491.47	88	209.99	31.40	27,967.61
29	221.19	20.20	29,471.27	89	209.76	31.63	27,935.98
30	221.03	20.36	29,450.91	90	209.52	31.87	27,904.11
31	220.88	20.51	29,430.40	91	209.28	32.11	27,872.00
274	115.36	126.03	15,255.27	334	44.07	197.32	5,678.26
275	114.41	126.98	15,128.29	335	42.59	198.80	5,479.46
276	113.46	127.93	15,000.36	336	41.10	200.29	5,279.17
277	112.50	128.89	14,871.47	337	39.59	201.80	5,077.37
278	111.54	129.85	14,741.62	338	38.08	203.31	4,874.06
279	110.56	130.83	14,610.79	339	36.56	204.83	4,669.23
280	109.58	131.81	14,478.98	340	35.02	206.37	4,462.86
281	108.59	132.80	14,346.18	341	33.47	207.92	4,254.94
282	107.60	133.79	14,212.39	342	31.91	209.48	4,045.46
283	106.59	134.80	14,077.59	343	30.34	211.05	3,834.41
284	105.58	135.81	13,941.78	344	28.76	212.63	3,621.78
285	104.56	136.83	13,804.95	345	27.16	214.23	3,407.55
286	103.54	137.85	13,667.10	346	25.56	215.83	3,191.72
287	102.50	138.89	13,528.21	347	23.94	217.45	2,974.27
288	101.46	139.93	13,388.28	348	22.31	219.08	2,755.19
289	100.41	140.98	13,247.30	349	20.66	220.73	2,534.46
290	99.35	142.04	13,105.26	350	19.01	222.38	2,312.08
291	98.29	143.10	12,962.16	351	17.34	224.05	2,088.03
292	97.22	144.17	12,817.99	352	15.66	225.73	1,862.30
293	96.13	145.26	12,672.73	353	13.97	227.42	1,634.88
294	95.05	146.34	12,526.39	354	12.26	229.13	1,405.75
295	93.95	147.44	12,378.95	355	10.54	230.85	1,174.90
296	92.84	148.55	12,230.40	356	8.81	232.58	942.32
297	91.73	149.66	12,080.74	357	7.07	234.32	708.00
298	90.61	150.78	11,929.96	358	5.31	236.08	471.92
299	89.47	151.92	11,778.04	359	3.54	237.85	234.07
300	88.34	153.05	11,624.99	360	1.76	234.07	235.83*

The final payment is usually somewhat different from the regular payment, and is shown starred on the last line.

360	12	********	56894.84		3000000	758597545

FIGURE 54: *Schedule of Direct Reduction Loan.*

Example Two

Prepare a simplified amortization schedule for Example 1, which found that a semiannual payment of $1,516.10 would amortize a $10,000 loan at 9% for 4 years.

Solution

The "interest" due each period is found by multiplying the "principal owed" by the periodic interest rate i. (Example: $10,000 × 4\frac{1}{2}\% = $450.) The next period's principal is found by subtracting the "payment to principal." (Example: $10,000 − $1,066.10 = $8,933.90.)

Payment	Principal Owed	Interest $(i = 4\frac{1}{2}\%)$	Payment to Principal ($1,516.10 − Interest)
1	$10,000.00	$ 450.00	$ 1,066.10
2	8,933.90	402.03	1,114.07
3	7,819.83	351.89	1,164.21
4	6,655.62	299.50	1,216.60
5	5,439.02	244.76	1,271.34
6	4,167.68	187.55	1,328.55
7	2,839.13	127.76	1,388.34
8	1,450.79	65.29	1,450.81
Totals		$2,128.78	$10,000.02

Total cost of loan $12,128.80

Notice there is a 2¢ difference in the total amounts of interest and principal derived in this example and in Example One, which results from rounding interest to the nearest cent each period. In actual practice, the final payment is usually slightly different from the regular payment, in order to have the total amounts come out exact.

Effective vs. Simple Interest

The advantage to the borrower of effective interest over simple interest is obvious from the following example, which compares 8% simple interest $(I = Prt)$ with effective interest at 8% compounded semiannually $(i = 4\%)$ on a $25,000 loan for 10, 20, and 30 years.

EFFECTIVE VS. SIMPLE INTEREST ON A $25,000 LOAN AT 8%

Term (years)	Total Effective Interest $(i = 4\%)$	Total Simple Interest (8%)	Extra Interest at Simple Rate
10	$11,790.80	$ 20,000	$ 8,209.20
20	25,523.60	40,000	14,476.40
30	41,303.00	60,000	18,697.00

Observe on the 10-year loan that there would be 70% more interest at the simple rate. The percentage difference decreases with longer terms, but on the 30-year loan there would still be 45% more interest at the simple rate. The simple interest alone on the 30-year loan would be 2.4 times as much as the principal that was borrowed. It is easy to see that no one could afford to buy a home or start a business if it were necessary to borrow money at simple interest.

The illustration at the beginning of this section pointed out that long-term simple interest notes (with a single payment at maturity) would not be profitable to bankers. We now see that such notes would also be unreasonably expensive to borrowers. Thus effective interest with periodic payments works to the advantage of both the borrower and the lender. (If financial institutions could charge simple interest and also receive periodic payments—as is frequently done on installment purchases and loans (although the Truth in Lending Law does require that the equivalent effective annual percentage rate be disclosed)—this would be the most profitable arrangement for the lender; however, this is not done on long-term loans from banking institutions.)

SECTION 2   *Problems*

Using the amortization table (Table XIX), find the payment necessary to amortize each loan. Also compute the total amount that will be repaid and determine how much interest is included.

		Principal (P.V.)	Rate	Compounded (Paid)	Term (Years)
1.	(a)	$100,000	6%	Semiannually	25
	(b)	30,000	5	Monthly	8
	(c)	8,000	8	Quarterly	3
	(d)	25,000	7	Quarterly	20
	(e)	70,000	9	Annually	12
2.	(a)	$ 10,000	7%	Semiannually	15
	(b)	80,000	6	Quarterly	20
	(c)	7,000	8	Monthly	5
	(d)	50,000	5	Annually	30
	(e)	32,000	9	Quarterly	25

3. William White borrowed $10,000 in order to build a new den on his home. He will repay the 9% loan in monthly payments for 7 years.
(a) What is White's monthly payment?
(b) How much total interest will be paid?

4. Eric Grayson borrowed $60,000 in order to go into business for himself. His loan was at 8% with semiannual payments for 23 years.
(a) How much will he pay each 6 months?
(b) How much total interest will Grayson pay?

5. A $70,000 loan at 6% was signed by Apex Corp. in order to build a new warehouse. If payments were made quarterly for 10 years:
(a) What payment was necessary to discharge the loan?
(b) How much interest was included in the payments?

6. Oven-Fresh Bakeries, Inc. borrowed $40,000 in order to purchase new packaging equipment. Quarterly payments will be made for 8 years in order to amortize the 8% loan.
(a) What is the amount of each payment?
(b) How much total interest will be charged?

7. Mr. and Mrs. Garrison paid $3,000 down on a $33,000 house and made quarterly payments for 25 years on a 5% loan.

(a) What payment did the Garrisons make each quarter?
(b) How much interest did their loan include?
(c) What was the total cost of their home to the Garrisons?

8. Mr. and Mrs. Dotson purchased a $56,000 home by paying $6,000 down and signing a 9% mortgage for 25 years.
(a) How much is each semiannual payment?
(b) How much interest will the Dotsons pay?
(c) What will be the total cost of the home?

9. The contractor's price for a new building was $63,000. The Snyder Co. paid $13,000 down and financed the balance for 6 years at 6%.
(a) What monthly payment was necessary to repay the loan?
(b) How much interest was included in the payments?
(c) What was the actual total cost of the building to Synder Co.?

10. Quality Carpet Mills invested $14,000 immediately and made monthly payments for 8 years in order to finance a $114,000 plant expansion.
(a) How much was each payment, if the loan was drawn at 7%?
(b) What amount of interest was paid?
(c) What was the actual total cost of the expansion?

Find the periodic payment required for each of the following loans. Then verify your answer by preparing an amortization schedule similar to the one in Example Two, showing how much of each payment is interest and how much applies toward principal.

		Principal (P.V.)	Rate	Compounded (Paid)	Term (Years)
11.	(a)	$10,000	9%	Annually	4
	(b)	8,000	6	Semiannually	3
12.	(a)	$ 1,000	7%	Annually	4
	(b)	6,000	8	Semiannually	2

SECTION 3
Review

The following criteria may help enable the student to distinguish between the basic types of problems studied in Chapters 18–20. The first step is to determine whether the problem is a compound interest problem or an annuity problem. (If a series of regular payments is involved, it is an annuity; otherwise, it is a compound interest problem.) The next step is to decide whether amount or present value is required. (In general, if the *question* in the problem refers to the *end* of the time period, it is an *amount* problem; if the question relates to the *beginning* of the time period, it is a *present-value* problem.)

NOTE: This review includes only the basic problems of each type so that the student can confidently identify each without its being listed under a section heading. This is not intended to be a complete review of the entire unit; the student's personal review should also include the variations of the basic problems studied in each section. The chart on page 514 identifies each basic type of problem and the corresponding formula for each.

Compound Interest	*Annuity*
The basic problem involves a *single* deposit invested for the entire time.	The problem involves a *series* of *regular* payments (or deposits).

The basic problem involves a *single* deposit invested for the entire time.

1. *Amount* at compound interest: A single deposit is made and one wishes to know how much it will be worth at the *end* of the time. $[S = P(1 + i)^n]$

2. *Present value* at compound interest: One wishes to find what single deposit must be invested at the *beginning* of the time period in order to obtain a given maturity value. $[P = S(1 + i)^{-n}]$

The problem involves a *series* of *regular* payments (or deposits).

1. *Amount* of an annuity: Regular deposits are *made* and one wishes to know the value of the account at the *end* of the time. $[S = \text{Pmt.} \times \text{Amt. ann. tab.}_{\overline{n}|i}]$

2. *Present value* of an annuity: Regular payments are to be *received* and one wants to find how much must be on deposit at the *beginning* from which to withdraw the payments. $[\text{P.V.} = \text{Pmt.} \times \text{P.V. ann. tab.}_{\overline{n}|i}]$

If the problem involves *finding a periodic payment*, one of the following applies:

3. *Sinking fund*: One is asked to find what regular payment must be made to *build up* an account to a given amount. $[\text{Pmt} = S \times \text{S.F. tab.}_{\overline{n}|i}]$

4. *Amortization*: One is asked to determine what regular payment must be made to *discharge* a debt. $[\text{Pmt.} = \text{P.V.} \times \text{Amtz. tab.}_{\overline{n}|i}]$

Use the following information to complete Problems 1–8.

		Value	Rate	Compounded	Term (Years)
Odd	(a)	$ 1,000	6%	Monthly	5
	(b)	5,000	7	Quarterly	8
Even	(a)	$10,000	8%	Quarterly	12
	(b)	2,000	9	Semiannually	10

1–2. Assume that each value given above is the principal of an investment. Find the compound amount and compound interest.

3–4. Assume that each value given above is the maturity value of an investment. Compute the present value and compound interest.

5–6. Assume that each value given above is the desired maturity value of a sinking fund. (1) Find the periodic payment required to finance the fund. (2) How much of the final value will be actual deposits? (3) How much interest will be included?

7–8. Assume that each value given above is the principal (present value) of a loan. (1) Compute the periodic payment required to amortize each debt. (2) What total amount will be paid to discharge each obligation? (3) How much interest will be included?

Use the following information to complete Problems 9–12.

		Periodic Payment	Rate	Compounded	Term (Years)
Odd	(a)	$1,000	6%	Semiannually	8
	(b)	100	9	Quarterly	10
Even	(a)	$1,000	7%	Semiannually	20
	(b)	100	8	Monthly	6

9–10. (1) Determine the maturity value if one makes (invests) each annuity payment above. (2) How much would be deposited during the time period? (3) How much of the maturity value is interest?

11–12. (1) Find the present value required in order to receive each annuity payment above. (2) How much would be received during the term of the annuity? (3) How much interest would be included?

13. Tom Freeman plans to replace his pickup truck in 4 years at a cost of $4,000. His savings and loan pays 7% compounded quarterly on 4-year CD's.
(a) How much deposited now would provide the $4,000?
(b) How much of the $4,000 will be interest?

14. Harry Banks wants to have $6,000 available in 3 years in order to remodel his home. Money is worth 6% compounded monthly.
(a) How much must he deposit now in order to achieve his savings goal?
(b) How much interest will the account earn?

15. Samuel Green deposits $100 each month into his savings account, which earns 5% compounded monthly.
(a) How much will Sam have after 5 years?
(b) How much of this amount will be interest?

16. Valley Produce Distributors is investing $2,000 each quarter, planning to enlarge their refrigerated truck line in 4 years. Their investment earns 9% compounded quarterly.
(a) What amount will the account contain in 4 years?
(b) How much of this amount will be interest?

17. In order to purchase a $5,000 boat, Fred Graham made quarterly payments for 4 years. He had a 6% loan.
(a) What was the amount of each payment?
(b) How much total interest did Fred's payments include?

18. Insurance Associates purchased an $80,000 office building by signing an 8%, 20-year loan and making semiannual payments.
(a) How much does Insurance Associates pay each 6 months?
(b) How much interest will be paid during the 20 years?

19. Instructor Myers plans to return to graduate school for 3 years and would like to receive $1,000 each 6 months during this time. He can invest his money at 7% compounded semiannually.
(a) What amount must Mr. Myers' account contain when he returns to school if he is to receive these payments?
(b) How much will he receive while in school?
(c) What part of these payments will be interest?

20. Archie Stanford would like to receive $10,000 annually for 15 years after he retires. He can invest in savings certificates earning 7% compounded annually.
(a) How much must Stanford's account contain at retirement in order to provide these payments?
(b) How much would he receive before the fund is exhausted?
(c) How much interest would be earned during this time?

21. In order to extend curb and gutter facilities, the town of Roxbury sold bonds worth $100,000 at maturity. The city council plans to make deposits for 15 years in order to provide the $100,000 to redeem the bonds. If money is worth 8% compounded quarterly:
(a) What quarterly payment will the town have to make to finance the fund?

(b) How much of the $100,000 will be actual deposits?

(c) How much interest will the $100,000 include?

22. David and Frances Furr want to have $10,000 when he retires in 7 years, in order to purchase a recreational vehicle. Money is currently worth 8% compounded monthly.

(a) What amount must the Furrs save each month to reach their goal?

(b) How much of the $10,000 will be their deposits?

(c) How much interest will the mature account contain?

23. Jason Wright invested $10,000 in a fund that was earning 9% compounded quarterly. If the fund continues to earn at the same rate:

(a) What will be the value of his investment after 10 years?

(b) How much interest will the account contain then?

24. Marian Rogers purchased a $1,000 CD which pays 7% compounded quarterly when held for 6 years.

(a) How much will the CD be worth at maturity?

(b) How much interest will the certificate earn?

CHAPTER 20 *Glossary*

Amortization. The process of repaying a loan (principal plus interest) by equal periodic payments.

Amortization schedule. A listing of the principal and interest included in each periodic loan payment, as well as a statement of the balance still owed.

Bond. A written promise to repay a specified debt on a certain date, with periodic interest to be paid during the term of the bond. Bonds are typically sold by large corporations and by city and state governments when they borrow money.

Rent. The periodic payment to a sinking fund.

Sinking fund. An annuity account established so that the maturity value (equal periodic deposits plus interest) will exactly equal a specific amount.

Sinking fund schedule. A periodic listing of the growth (in principal and interest) of a sinking fund.

Appendices

APPENDIX A

Arithmetic

APPENDIX A OBJECTIVES

Upon completing Appendix A, the student will be able to:

1. Define and use correctly the terminology in each topic.

2. a. Identify the place value associated with each digit in a whole number or a decimal number (*Sections 1, 4*).
   b. Pronounce the complete number.

3. a. Express the basic number properties:
      (1) Commutative for addition and multiplication;
      (2) Associative for addition and multiplication; and
      (3) Distributive.
      (*Section 2*)
   b. Verify each property using
      (1) Whole numbers (*Section 2*);
      (2) Common fractions (*Section 3*); and
      (3) Decimal fractions (*Section 4*).

4. Perform accurately the arithmetic operations (addition, subtraction, multiplication, and division) using whole numbers, common fractions, and decimal fractions. (*Sections 2–4*)

5. Manipulate common fractions accurately (*Section 3*):
   a. Reduce;
   b. Change to higher terms (least common denominator);
   c. Convert mixed numbers to improper fractions; and
   d. Convert common fractions to their equal decimal value (*Section 4*).

6. Manipulate decimal fractions accurately:
   a. Convert to common fractions (including decimals with fractional remainders); and
   b. Multiply and divide by powers of 10 by moving the decimal point.
   (*Section 4*)

| A |

Although machines are used in most businesses to perform arithmetic computations, it is still advantageous for the student to have a certain facility with computation. The following topics are presented to give the student an opportunity to develop or practice the necessary skills.

SECTION 1

Reading Numbers

The Hindu–Arabic number system which we use is known as the "base 10" system. This means that it is organized by 10 and powers of 10. Any number can be written using combinations of 10 basic characters called **digits:** 0, 1, 2, 3, 4, 5, 6, 7, 8, and 9. When combined in a number, each digit represents a particular value according to its rank in the order of digits and to the position it holds in the number (the latter is known as its **place value**). Figure 55 shows what place value (and power of 10) is represented by each place in a number. Larger place values are on the left and smaller values are toward the right.

NOTE: Each power of 10 is indicated (or abbreviated) by an **exponent,** which is a small number written after the 10 in a raised position. The exponent indicates the number of tens that would have to be multiplied together in order to obtain the unabbreviated place value. Thus, in the expression 10^4, the exponent "4" indicates the complete number is found by multiplying together four 10's: $10^4 = 10 \times 10 \times 10 \times 10 = 10,000$. It should also be observed that the exponent indicates the number of zeros that the complete number contains. That is, 10^5 is equal to a "1" followed by 5 zeros: $10^5 = 10 \times 10 \times 10 \times 10 \times 10 = 100,000$.

The "2" in the number in Figure 55, because of the place it occupies, represents "two 10's" or 20. Similarly, the "4" represents "four 10,000's" or 40,000. The last three digits in the chart, "528," are read "five hundred twenty-eight."

For convenience in reading, large numbers are usually separated with commas into groups of three digits, starting at the right. Each three-digit group is then read as the appropriate number of hundreds, tens, and

523

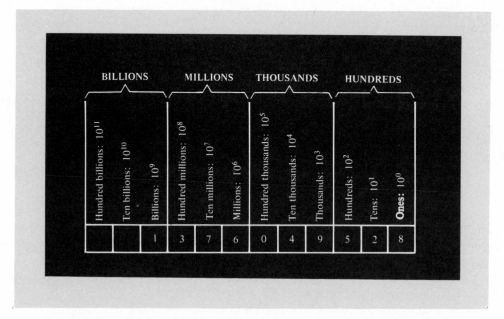

FIGURE 55

units, followed by the family name of the groupings. Thus, the digits "376" in Figure 55 are read "three hundred seventy-six million." The entire number, written with commas, would appear 1,376,049,528 and would be read "one billion, three hundred seventy-six million, forty-nine thousand, five hundred twenty-eight." Commas in a number have no mathematical significance and are used merely to separate the family groupings and indicate the point at which one should pronounce the family name.

When preparing to read a large number, the student should never have to name every place value (smallest to largest) in order to determine the largest value; rather, one should point off the groups of three, reading the family names as he proceeds, until the largest family grouping is reached. Thus, the largest value of the number 207,XXX,XXX,XXX is quickly identified, reading right to left:

$$\overset{\displaystyle B \quad\ M \quad\ T \quad\ H}{207,XXX,XXX,XXX}$$

The 207 represents "two hundred seven billion," and succeeding values would be read in decreasing order.

In reading the value of a number, it is incorrect to use the word "and" except to designate the location of a decimal point. The number 16,000,003 is pronounced "sixteen million, three."

SECTION 1 *Problems*

In the number 62,508,390,147 *identify the place value of each digit.*

1. (a) 1   (b) 2   (c) 3   **2.** (a) 5   (b) 6   (c) 7
     (d) 4   (e) 5   (d) 8   (e) 9

Write in words the values of the following numbers.

3. (a)   6,411,293,857   (b)   123,625,819,743   (c)   205,100,416
     (d)   15,063,008,760   (e)   9,301,000,065   (f)   620,000,090,050
     (g)   30,000,000,700

4. (a)   733,416,952   (b)   14,007,389,520   (c)   811,054,623,905
     (d)   69,373,800,017   (e)   8,500,006,034   (f)   563,042,000,960
     (g)   27,000,000,008

SECTION 2
Whole Numbers

The simplest set of numbers in our number system are those used to identify a single object or a group of objects. These are the **counting numbers** or **natural numbers** or positive **whole numbers.** The counting numbers, along with zero and the negative whole numbers (whole numbers less than zero), comprise the set known as the **integers.** Earliest "mathematics" consisted simply of using the integers to count one's possessions—sheep, cattle, tents, wives, and so on. As civilization advanced and became more complex, the need for more efficient mathematics also increased. This led to the perfection of the four arithmetic **operations:** addition, subtraction, multiplication, and division. (This review includes operations only with nonnegative numbers.)

Addition

This operation provides a shortcut which eliminates having to count each item consecutively until the total is reached. The names of the numbers in an operation of addition are as follows:

$$
\begin{array}{lr}
\text{Addend} & 23 \\
\text{Addend} & +16 \\
\hline
\text{Sum} & 39
\end{array}
$$

Addition functions under two basic mathematical laws, expressed as (1) the commutative property of addition, and (2) the associative property of addition. The **commutative property of addition** means that the *order* in which *two* addends are taken does not affect the sum. More simply, if two numbers are to be added, it does not matter which is written down first. The commutative property is usually written in general terms (terms which apply to all numbers) as

$$\text{CPA:} \qquad a + b = b + a$$

The commutative property of addition can be illustrated using the numbers 2 and 3:

$$2 + 3 \overset{?}{=} 3 + 2$$
$$5 = 5$$

The **associative property of addition** applies to the *grouping* of *three* numbers; it means that, when three numbers are to be added, the sum will be the same regardless of which two are grouped together to be added first. The associative property is expressed in the following general terms:

$$\text{APA:} \qquad (a + b) + c = a + (b + c)$$

The associative property can be verified as follows. Suppose that the numbers 2, 3, and 4 are to be added. By the associative property,

$$(2 + 3) + 4 \overset{?}{=} 2 + (3 + 4)$$
$$5 + 4 \overset{?}{=} 2 + 7$$
$$9 = 9$$

By applying both the commutative and associative properties of addition, one can verify other groupings or the addition of more addends.

An excellent way in which the student can speed addition is by adding in groups of numbers which total 10. The student should be thoroughly familiar with the combinations of two numbers which total 10 ($1 + 9$; $2 + 8$; $3 + 7$; $4 + 6$; $5 + 5$) and should be alert for these combinations in problems.

For example,

3	This should not be added "3 plus 7 is 10 plus 6 is 16	3⟩ 10
7	plus 4 is 20." Rather, one should immediately recog-	7⟩
6	nize the two groups of 10 and add "10 plus 10 is 20,"	6⟩ 10
4	as:	4⟩
		20

Most problems do not consist of such obvious combinations, but the device may frequently be employed if one is alert for it. For instance,

8⟩	10	4	(added "4 plus 10
4⟩		5⟩	is 14 plus 9 is 23,"
2⟩	10	9⟩	or "4 plus 9 is 13
6		5	plus 10 is 23")
20		23	

9⟩	(added "10	8	(added "8 plus 10
6⟩	plus 6 is 16	6⟩	is 18 plus 10 is 28
1⟩	plus 10 is	4⟩	plus 5 is 33")
4⟩	26")	3	
6		5⟩	
		7⟩	
26		33	

This technique, like many others, can be carried to extremes. It is intended to be a time-saver; it will be provided that the student is alert for combinations adding up to 10 when they are conveniently located near each other. However, a problem may take longer to add if one wastes time searching for widely separated combinations. Also, it is easy to miss a number altogether if one is adding numbers from all parts of the problem rather than adding in nearly consecutive order. Therefore, students should use the device when they can but should not expect it to apply to every problem.

If a first glance at a problem reveals that the same digit appears several times in a column, the following device is useful: Count the number of times the digit appears and multiply this number by the digit itself; the remaining digits are then added to this total. For example,

$$
\begin{array}{l}
7 \\
4 \\
7 \\
7 \\
8 \\
\underline{7} \\
40
\end{array}
$$

(added "four 7's
are 28 plus 4 is
32 plus 8 is 40")

As the student probably knows, addition problems may be checked either by adding upward in reverse order or simply by re-adding the sum.

Horizontal addition problems seem harder because the numbers being added are so far apart. More mistakes are made in horizontal problems because a digit from the wrong place is often added. However, many business forms require horizontal addition. The following hint may make such addition easier:

1. A right-handed person should use his left index finger to cover all the larger digits in the first number, down to the digit currently being added. (Unfortunately, left-handed persons will have to forego this aid.)

2. As digits from succeeding numbers are added, place the pencil point beneath the digit currently being added. Mentally repeat the current subtotal frequently as you proceed.

For example, while the tens' digits are being added in the following problem, the left index finger should cover the digits "162" of the first number. The pencil point should be placed under the 5, 1, 2, and 7 as each is added.

$$16,2)83 + 22,054 + 40,611 + 7,927 + 19,670 = \underline{\ldots 45}$$

Subtraction This operation is the opposite of addition. (Since subtraction produces the same result as when a negative number is added to a positive, subtraction is sometimes defined as an extension of addition.) The parts of a subtraction operation have the following names:

Minuend	325
Subtrahend	− 198
Difference or Remainder	127

A subtraction problem can be checked mentally by adding together the subtrahend and difference; if the resultant sum equals the minuend, the operation is verified.

The student can easily determine that neither the commutative nor the associative property applies to subtraction. For example, it makes a great deal of difference whether we find $17 − $8 or $8 − $17. And any example will show that the associative property does not hold:

$$(7-5)-2 \overset{?}{=} 7-(5-2)$$

$$2 \quad -2 \overset{?}{=} 7- \quad 3$$

$$0 \neq 4$$

As the student knows, subtraction often necessitates "borrowing," or regrouping of the place values. For example, the number 325 in our first example of subtraction—which represents three 100's, two 10's, and five 1's—had to be regrouped into two 100's, eleven 10's, and fifteen 1's. Both groupings equal 325, as the following examples show:

ORIGINAL	_REGROUPED_		_SUBTRACTION_
300	200	(two 100's)	(two 100's)
20	110	(eleven 10's)	(eleven 10's)
5	15	(fifteen 1's)	(fifteen 1's)
325	325		

$$\begin{array}{ccc} 2 & 11 & \\ \not{3} & 2 & \overset{1}{5} \\ -1 & 9 & 8 \\ \hline 1 & 2 & 7 \end{array}$$

The student is also aware that addition problems often contain many numbers, whereas subtraction problems contain only two numbers. Subtraction problems could just as well contain more numbers were it not for the fact that regrouping becomes so complicated. Many office calculators, which can regroup repeatedly when necessary, can perform a series of subtractions before indicating a total. (This is usually not possible with multiplication or division.)

Multiplication This operation was developed as a shortcut for addition. Suppose that a student has three classes on each of five days; the week's total classes could be found by addition:

$$\frac{M}{3} + \frac{T}{3} + \frac{W}{3} + \frac{T}{3} + \frac{F}{3} = \frac{TOTAL}{15}$$

This approach to the problem would become quite tedious, however, if we wanted to know the total receipts at a grocery store from the sale of 247 cartons of soft drinks at $1.49 each.

Thus, multiplication originated when persons learned from experience what sums to expect following repeated additions of small numbers, and the actual addition process then became unnecessary. Perfection of the operation led to the knowledge that any two numbers, regardless of size, could be multiplied if one had memorized the products of all combinations of the digits 0–9. (The frequent occurrence in business situations of the number 12 makes knowledge of its multiples quite valuable also.)

MULTIPLICATION TABLE

The following table lists the products of the digits 2–9, as well as the numbers 10–12. The student should be able to recite instantly all products up through the multiples of 9. A knowledge of products through the multiples of 12 is also very useful.

	2	3	4	5	6	7	8	9	10	11	12
2	4	6	8	10	12	14	16	18	20	22	24
3	6	9	12	15	18	21	24	27	30	33	36
4	8	12	16	20	24	28	32	36	40	44	48
5	10	15	20	25	30	35	40	45	50	55	60
6	12	18	24	30	36	42	48	54	60	66	72
7	14	21	28	35	42	49	56	63	70	77	84
8	16	24	32	40	48	56	64	72	80	88	96
9	18	27	36	45	54	63	72	81	90	99	108
10	20	30	40	50	60	70	80	90	100	110	120
11	22	33	44	55	66	77	88	99	110	121	132
12	24	36	48	60	72	84	96	108	120	132	144

The numbers of an operation of multiplication have the following names:

Multiplicand (or Factor)	18
Multiplier (or Factor)	×4
Product	72

There are three properties affecting the operation of multiplication: (1) the commutative property of multiplication, (2) the associative property of multiplication, and (3) the distributive property.

The **commutative property of multiplication,** like the commutative property of addition, applies to the *order* in which *two* numbers are taken. The commutative property asserts that either factor can be written first, and the product will be the same. In general terms, the commutative property of multiplication is written

$$\text{CPM:} \qquad a \cdot b = b \cdot a$$

It can be illustrated using the factors 4 and 7:

$$4 \cdot 7 \overset{?}{=} 7 \cdot 4$$
$$28 = 28$$

The **associative property of multiplication** is similar to the associative property of addition in that it applies to the *grouping* of any *three* numbers. That is, if three numbers are to be multiplied, the product will be the same regardless of which two are multiplied first. The associative property of multiplication is expressed in general terms as

$$\text{APM:} \qquad (a \cdot b)c = a(b \cdot c)$$

Using the numbers 2, 5, and 3, the associative property is verified as follows:

$$(2 \cdot 5)3 \overset{?}{=} 2(5 \cdot 3)$$
$$(10)3 \overset{?}{=} 2(15)$$
$$30 = 30$$

The third property applies to the combination of multiplication and addition. It is the **distributive property,** sometimes called the **distributive property of multiplication over addition.** This property means that the product of the sum of two numbers equals the sum of the individual products. Stated differently, this means that if two numbers are added and their sum is multiplied by some other number, the final total is the same as if the two numbers were first separately multiplied by the third number and the products then added. The distributive property is expressed for all numbers as

$$\text{DP:} \qquad a(b+c) = ab + ac$$

Using 2 for the multiplier and the numbers 3 and 5 for the addends, the distributive property can be verified as follows:

$$2(3+5) \overset{?}{=} 2 \cdot 3 \ + \ 2 \cdot 5$$
$$2(8) \overset{?}{=} \ \ 6 \ \ + \ \ 10$$
$$16 = 16$$

NOTE: The distributive property has frequent application in business. One of the best examples is sales tax. When several items are purchased, the sales tax is found by adding all the prices and then multiplying only once by the applicable sales tax per cent. This is much simpler than multiplying the tax rate by the price of each separate item and then adding to find the total sales tax, although the total would be the same by either method.

While other methods are sometimes used, the easiest, quickest, and most reliable check of a multiplication problem is simply to repeat the multiplication. (If convenient, the factors may be reversed for the checking operation.)

Students often waste time and do much unnecessary work when *multiplying by numbers that contain zeros.* When multiplying by 10, 100, 1,000, etc., the product should be written immediately simply by affixing to the original factor the same number of zeros as contained in the multiplier. Thus,

$$54 \times 10 = 540; \quad 2{,}173 \times 100 = 217{,}300; \quad \text{and} \quad 145 \times 1{,}000 = 145{,}000.$$

When multiplying numbers ending in zeros, the factors should be written with the zeros to the right of the problem as it will actually be performed. After multiplication with the other digits has been completed, affix the zeros to the basic product, as in Example One.

Example One (a) 148×60

$$
\begin{array}{r}
148 \\
\times 6\,|\,0 \\
\hline
8,88\,|\,0
\end{array}
$$

(b) $6,700 \times 52$

$$
\begin{array}{r}
52 \\
\times 67\,|\,00 \\
\hline
364 \\
312 \\
\hline
348,4\,|\,00
\end{array}
$$

(c) $130 \times 1,500$

$$
\begin{array}{r}
13\,|\,0 \\
15\,|\,00 \\
\hline
65 \\
13 \\
\hline
195,\!000
\end{array}
$$

Note here that all three zeros are affixed to the product.

When a multiplier contains zeros within the number, many people write whole rows of useless zeros in order to be certain that the significant digits remain properly aligned. These unnecessary zeros should be omitted; the other digits will still be in correct order if the student practices this basic rule of multiplication: On each line of multiplication, the first digit to be written down is placed directly beneath the digit in the multiplier (second factor) being multiplied at the time.

Example Two (a) 671×305.

RIGHT

$$
\begin{array}{r}
671 \\
\times 305 \\
\hline
3355 \\
2013 \\
\hline
204,655
\end{array}
$$
(because $300 \times 1 = 300$)

INEFFICIENT

$$
\begin{array}{r}
671 \\
\times 305 \\
\hline
3355 \\
000 \\
2013 \\
\hline
204,655
\end{array}
$$

(b) $4,382 \times 3,004$.

$$
\begin{array}{r}
4,382 \\
\times 3,004 \\
\hline
17\,528 \\
13\,146 \\
\hline
13,163,528
\end{array}
$$
(because $3,000 \times 2 = 6,000$)

Division

This operation is the reverse of multiplication. The numbers in an operation of division are identified as follows:

$$\begin{array}{r} 4 \quad \text{Quotient} \\ \text{Divisor} \quad 18\overline{)77} \quad \text{Dividend} \\ \underline{72} \\ 5 \quad \text{Remainder} \end{array}$$

That is,

$$\begin{array}{l} \text{Quotient} \\ \text{Divisor}\,\overline{)\text{Dividend}} \qquad \text{or} \qquad \text{Dividend} \div \text{Divisor} = \text{Quotient} \end{array}$$

Division is neither commutative, associative, nor distributive, as can be determined by brief experiments. Obviously, $4\overline{)16}$ yields quite a different quotient from $16\overline{)4}$. An example to test the associative property reveals different quotients:

$$(36 \div 6) \div 3 \overset{?}{=} 36 \div (6 \div 3)$$
$$6 \quad \div 3 \overset{?}{=} 36 \div \quad 2$$
$$2 \neq 18$$

Similarly, a test of the distributive property reveals that it does not apply either:

$$60 \div (4 + 6) \overset{?}{=} 60 \div 4 + 60 \div 6$$
$$60 \div \quad 10 \quad \overset{?}{=} \quad 15 \; + \quad 10$$
$$6 \neq 25$$

Division by one-digit divisors should be carried out mentally and the quotient written directly; this method is commonly called *short division*. The student may find it helpful to write each remainder in front of the next number as the operation progresses. For example,

$$7\overline{)9422} \qquad \text{written} \qquad 7\overline{)9^2 4^3 2^4 2} \quad {}^{1\;3\;4\;6}$$

Division involving divisors of two or more digits is usually performed by writing each step completely. Division performed in this manner is known as *long division*. The following general rules apply to both long and short division and cover aspects of division where mistakes are often made:

1. The first digit of the quotient should be written directly above the last digit of the partial dividend which the divisor divides into. For example, when dividing $25\,\overline{\smash{\big)}\,17628}$, the first digit of the quotient should be written above the 6:

$$
\begin{array}{r}
7 \\
25\,\overline{\smash{\big)}\,17628} \\
175 \\
\end{array}
$$

2. The amount remaining after each succeeding step in division must always be smaller than the divisor. Otherwise, the divisor would have divided into the dividend at least one more time. (If a remainder is larger than the divisor, the previous step should be repeated to correct the corresponding digit in the quotient.) For example, if the first step had been

$$
\begin{array}{r}
6 \\
25\,\overline{\smash{\big)}\,17{,}628} \\
15\ 0 \\
\hline
2\ 6 \\
\end{array}
$$

         ←——remainder is
more than 25

the quotient should be corrected:

$$
\begin{array}{r}
7 \\
25\,\overline{\smash{\big)}\,17{,}628} \\
17\ 5 \\
\hline
1 \\
\end{array}
$$

        ←——remainder is
less than 25

3. Succeeding digits of the dividend should be brought down one at a time. For example,

$$
\begin{array}{r}
7 \\
25\,\overline{\smash{\big)}\,17{,}628} \\
17\ 5\downarrow \\
\hline
12 \\
\end{array}
$$

4. Each time a digit is brought down, a new digit must be affixed to the quotient directly over the digit that was just brought down. Thus, a

zero is affixed to the quotient when a brought-down digit does not create a number large enough for the divisor to divide into at least one whole time. For example,

$$
\begin{array}{r}
70 \\
25\overline{\smash{\big)}17{,}628} \\
\underline{17\ 5} \\
12
\end{array}
$$

The next digit is then brought down and the division process continued as follows:

$$
\begin{array}{r}
705 \\
25\overline{\smash{\big)}17{,}628} \\
\underline{17\ 5} \\
128 \\
\underline{125} \\
3
\end{array}
$$

5. The final remainder may be written directly after the quotient as follows:

$$
\begin{array}{r}
705\ \ \text{R3} \\
25\overline{\smash{\big)}17{,}628} \\
\underline{17\ 5} \\
128 \\
\underline{125} \\
3
\end{array}
$$

Division problems can be checked by multiplying the divisor by the quotient and adding the remainder (if any). This result should equal the original dividend. For example, for the above division problem,

$$
\begin{array}{r}
705 \\
\times\ \ 25 \\
\hline
17{,}625 \\
+3 \\
\hline
17{,}628
\end{array}
$$

SECTION 2 *Problems*

1. (a) Express the commutative property of addition, using the letter symbols k and l.

(b) Write and then verify the commutative property of addition, using 45 and 18.

(c) Express the associative property of addition, using *r, s,* and *t*.

(d) Write and verify the associative property of addition, using 9, 6, and 13.

(e) Express the commutative property of multiplication, using *v* and *w*.

(f) Write and then verify the commutative property of multiplication, using 12 and 26.

(g) Express the associative property of multiplication, using *p, q,* and *r*.

(h) Write and then verify the associative property of multiplication, using 4, 9, and 3.

(i) Express the distributive property, using *x, y,* and *z*.

(j) Write and then verify the distributive property, using 8, 2, and 5.

2. (a) Express the commutative property of addition, using *s* and *t*.

(b) Write and then verify the commutative property of addition, using 28 and 57.

(c) Express the associative property of addition, using *x, y,* and *z*.

(d) Write and then verify the associative property of addition, using 15, 19, and 6.

(e) Express the commutative property of multiplication, using *c* and *d*.

(f) Write and then verify the commutative property of multiplication, using 18 and 15.

(g) Express the associative property of multiplication, using *g, h,* and *k*.

(h) Write and verify the associative property of multiplication, using 8, 2, and 6.

(i) Express the distributive property, using *d, e,* and *f*.

(j) Write and then verify the distributive property, using 9, 6, and 3.

The following problems were especially designed to provide practice in adding by combinations which total 10.

3. (a) 9
2
1
8
———

(b) 8
7
3
5
———

(c) 4
6
8
5
2
———

(d) 7
5
9
5
1
———

(e) 2
9
8
3
7
———

(f) 8
8
1
2
9
4
———

(g) 6
9
4
9
6
1
———

(h) 44
43
86
69
21
———
163

(i) 67
35
28
75
52
———
257

4. (a) 7
4
3
6
———

(b) 6
5
8
5
———

(c) 1
9
7
8
2
———

(d) 5
3
4
7
6
———

(e) 9
7
1
6
4
———

(f) 6	(g) 4	(h) 46	(i) 52
2	3	45	96
5	6	27	38
8	1	35	16
3	5	83	64
7	9		

Add the following, using time-saving techniques where possible. Check your answers.

5.

(a) 9	(b) 4	(c) 8	(d) 5	(e) 36
3	7	7	9	78
5	1	6	3	45
2	3	5	7	66
6	8	4	8	53
		7	4	

(f) 71	(g) 65	(h) 48	(i) 56
84	27	73	49
49	89	68	25
58	34	68	71
63	57	58	68
		37	63

6.

(a) 243	(b) 308	(c) 418	(d) 4,272	(e) 4,616
658	475	37	3,060	3,872
291	632	295	7,355	9,524
445	487	646	9,298	6,636
	729	95		2,518

(f) 285	(g) 58,036	(h) 63,316	(i) $4,391.54
3,656	21,845	37,845	29.18
125	37,544	20,437	105.15
47	83,621	78,055	2,436.77
7,389		48,672	7.05
			455.93

7. (a) $65 + 82 + 27 + 77 + 54 = $ _____

(b) $58 + 71 + 66 + 49 + 24 = $ _____

(c) $799 + 482 + 345 + 651 + 575 = $ _____

(d) $585 + 872 + 604 + 519 + 368 = $ _____

(e) $8,491 + 5,767 + 2,390 + 7,542 + 6,684 = $ _____

(f) $37,845 + 701 + 5,639 + 22,088 + 16,642 = $ _____

8. Subtract in each of the following. Check by adding.

(a) 465
     382

(b) 954
     688

(c) 809
     538

(d) 2,537
     1,698

(e) 4,086
     2,918

(f) 7,545
     4,763

(g) 25,400
      9,396

(h) 75,811
     37,609

(i) 450,933
     378,416

9. Multiply.

(a) 356×10

(b) $1,000 \times 73$

(c) 582×100

(d) 56×170

(e) $1,300 \times 267$

(f) $36,000 \times 425$

(g) $7,600 \times 350$

(h) $1,720 \times 6,500$

(i) 641×407

(j) $9,216 \times 804$

(k) $8,363 \times 3,008$

(l) $142,053 \times 20,506$

10. Multiply.

(a) 48
     52

(b) 546
      27

(c) 717
      83

(d) 2,506
      317

(e) 8,693
      274

(f) 9,325
     7,109

(g) 28,069
      2,635

(h) 531,728
       3,057

(i) 7,328,619
         2,745

Divide. Check, using multiplication.

11. (a) $7\overline{)3,346}$

(b) $4\overline{)2,656}$

(c) $3\overline{)17,118}$

(d) $8\overline{)64,048}$

(e) $9\overline{)31,335}$

(f) $6\overline{)29,745}$

12. (a) $36\overline{)3,420}$

(b) $72\overline{)24,912}$

(c) $537\overline{)13,425}$

(d) $806\overline{)51,584}$

(e) $627\overline{)183,711}$

(f) $248\overline{)153,512}$

(g) $3,518\overline{)207,562}$

(h) $157\overline{)468,500}$

(i) $4,785\overline{)29,108,110}$

(j) $78,362\overline{)9,804,530}$

13. The following table shows the sales made by various departments of a drug store during 1 week. Find the total sales of the store for each day and the total sales of each department for the entire week. (This final total serves as a check of your addition: The sum of the weekly totals for each register must equal the sum of the daily totals for the entire store. That is, the sum of the totals in the right-hand column must equal the sum of the totals across the bottom.)

THE MEDICINE CHEST

Sales for Week of September 6

Dept.	Monday	Tuesday	Wednesday	Thursday	Friday	Saturday	Department Totals
1	$453.81	$380.25	$363.18	$465.97	$436.39	$479.92	$
2	328.91	267.43	281.27	310.52	321.47	344.68	
3	374.46	295.50	305.76	338.74	355.16	380.80	
4	295.77	261.29	289.80	307.53	298.89	315.12	
5	486.09	399.94	418.15	426.01	437.62	479.85	
6	119.38	100.78	125.69	133.47	151.75	162.77	
Daily Totals	$	$	$	$	$	$	$

14. Complete the following check record, which shows the checks written and deposits made in a personal checking account. Add the deposits to the balance in account and subtract the checks from this balance. Check as follows:

Original balance	$
Add: total deposits	+
	$
Subtract: total checks	−
Final balance	$

CHECK RECORD

CHECK NO.	DATE	CHECK ISSUED TO	AMOUNT OF CHECK		✓	AMOUNT OF DEPOSIT		BALANCE 215	69
144	11/18	Food Fair	37	27					
145	11/18	Thrifty Cleaners	8	45					
—	11/20	DEPOSIT				155	78		
146	11/23	Kendall Drug Co.	12	65					
147	11/25	Food Fair	26	19					
148	11/27	General Telephone	9	53					
149	11/29	Fidelity Insurance Co.	48	17					
—	12/1	DEPOSIT				786	29		
150	12/2	Cansler Realty	195	00					
151	12/2	Dept. of Water & Power	12	37					
152	12/2	Dr. Mason	28	00					
153	12/2	Food Fair	27	49					
154	12/4	Eastover Dept. Store	78	28					
155	12/6	Williams Furniture Co.	174	19					

15. Complete the following sales invoice. Multiply the cost of each item by the number of items purchased. Add to find the total cost of the purchase.

No. Purchased	Description	Cost per Item	Total
	ELECTRICAL DISTRIBUTORS Invoice		
18	Rolls, #3 gauge wire	$ 5.19	
15	Rolls, #5 gauge wire	6.43	
24	Rolls, #7 gauge wire	7.26	
175	Single switch plates, white	.59	
125	Single switch plates, brown	.57	
64	Double switch plates, white	.78	
48	Double switch plates, brown	.75	
6	Single switch plates, gold pl.	4.69	
72	CW-40 flourescent tubes	.85	
36	CW-80 flourescent tubes	1.54	
8	Cases, 50/100/150 bulbs	12.20	
5	Cases, 100/150/250 bulbs	18.76	
3	F37 ceiling fixtures	25.17	
6	D115 wall fixtures	40.98	
2	R72 chandeliers	136.45	_____
			$

16. Using the following breakdown, find the average amount of life insurance sold to clients in various states. (That is, divide the value of insurance sold in each state by the number of policies written.) Add to find the total value of all policies sold and the total number of policies; then find the average value per policy sold by the company (to the nearest dollar.)

STATE	TOTAL VALUE OF POLICIES SOLD	NO. OF POLICIES	AVERAGE VALUE PER POLICY
	THE ATLANTIC INSURANCE CO. Average Value of Policy by State		
Connecticut	$ 72,816,000	3,552	
Delaware	22,388,000	965	
Florida	108,480,000	8,475	
Georgia	100,011,000	6,290	
New Jersey	171,236,000	9,256	
New York	428,856,000	25,680	
North Carolina	94,461,000	6,845	
Pennsylvania	252,396,000	14,760	
South Carolina	51,794,000	3,572	
Virginia	89,333,000	5,690	
Total	$		$

SECTION 3
Common Fractions

The system of fractions was developed to meet the need for measuring quantities which are not whole amounts. The parts of a fraction are identified by the following terms:

numerator
denominator

$\dfrac{3}{5}$

A **common fraction** is an indicated division—a short method of writing a division problem. That is, if $3 is to be divided among five persons, each person's share is indicated

$$\$3 \div 5 \qquad \text{or} \qquad \$\tfrac{3}{5}$$

Thus, the fraction line indicates division (the numerator is to be divided by the denominator), and the entire fraction represents each person's share. We now see why common fractions are often known as "rational numbers." A **rational number** is any number which can be expressed as the quotient of two integers. The fraction $\tfrac{3}{5}$ is a rational number because it is expressed as the quotient of the integers (whole numbers) 3 and 5. The entire fraction represents the quotient—the value of 3 divided by 5.

A common fraction is called a **proper fraction** if its numerator is smaller than the denominator (for example, $\tfrac{4}{7}$) and if the indicated division would result in a value less than 1. The numerator of an **improper fraction** is equal to or greater than the denominator (for example, $\tfrac{7}{7}$ or $\tfrac{15}{7}$) and thus has a value equal to or greater than 1.

Reducing Fractions

Two fractions are equal if they represent the same quantity. When writing fractions, however, it is customary to use the smallest possible numbers. Thus, it is often necessary to *reduce* a fraction—to change it to a fraction of equal value but written with smaller numbers.

The fraction $\tfrac{3}{3}$ represents $3 \div 3$ or 1. Obviously, any number written over itself as a fraction equals 1 $\left(\dfrac{x}{x} = 1\right)$. We also know from multiplication that 1 times any number equals that same number $(1 \cdot x = x)$. These facts are the mathematical basis for reducing fractions. A fraction can be reduced if the same number is a factor of both the numerator and the denominator. For example,

$$\frac{6}{15} = \frac{2\times3}{5\times3} \quad \text{(the factors of 6 are 2 and 3)} \\ \text{(the factors of 15 are 5 and 3)}$$

But since $\frac{3}{3} = 1$, then

$$\frac{6}{15} = \frac{2\times3}{5\times3} = \frac{2}{5}\times\frac{3}{3} = \frac{2}{5}\times1 = \frac{2}{5}$$

Hence, $\frac{2}{5}$ represents the same quantity as $\frac{6}{15}$.

In actual practice, one reduces a fraction by testing mentally the numerator and denominator to determine the *greatest* factor which they have in common (that is, to determine the largest number which will divide into both evenly). The reduced fraction is then indicated by writing these quotients in fraction form:

$$\frac{20}{15} \quad \text{(think: 5 divides into 20 \textit{four} times and into 15 \textit{three} times)} \qquad \text{Write: } \frac{20}{15} = \frac{4}{3}$$

Sometimes, however, the greatest common factor may not be immediately obvious. When the greatest common factor is not apparent, a fraction may be reduced to its lowest terms by performing a series of reductions:

$$\frac{60}{84} = \frac{2}{2}\times\frac{30}{42} = \frac{30}{42} = \frac{2}{2}\times\frac{15}{21} = \frac{15}{21} = \frac{3}{3}\times\frac{5}{7} = 1\times\frac{5}{7} = \frac{5}{7}$$

The end result will be the same whether the reduction is performed in one step or in several steps. It should be noted that if a series of reductions is used, the product of these several common factors equals the number which would have been the greatest single common factor. For example, the fraction $\frac{60}{84}$ was reduced above by 2, 2, and 3; The product of these factors is 12, which is the greatest common factor:

$$\frac{60}{84} = \frac{2}{2}\times\frac{2}{2}\times\frac{3}{3}\times\frac{5}{7} = 1\times1\times1\times\frac{5}{7} = \frac{5}{7} \quad \text{or} \quad \frac{60}{84} = \frac{12}{12}\times\frac{5}{7} = 1\times\frac{5}{7} = \frac{5}{7}$$

Therefore, the student should divide by the largest number that he recognizes as a factor of both the numerator and denominator. However, one should always examine the result to determine whether it still contains another common factor.

Changing to Suppose that we wish to know whether $\frac{5}{6}$ or $\frac{7}{9}$ is
Higher Terms larger. In order to compare the size of fractions, as
a practical matter one should rewrite them using the
same denominator. The process of rewriting fractions so that they have a
common denominator (which is usually larger than either original denominator) is called *changing to higher terms.*

The product of the various denominators will provide a common denominator. However, it is customary to use the **least common denominator,** which is the smallest number which all the denominators will divide into evenly. Thus, the least (or lowest) common denominator is often a number which is smaller than the product of all the denominators. In fact, one of the given denominators may be the least common de-nominator.

When finding the least common denominator, the student should first consider the multiples of the largest given denominator. If this method does not reveal the least common denominator quickly, the student should find the product of the denominators. Before using this product as the common denominator, though, he should first consider $\frac{1}{2}$, $\frac{1}{3}$, or even $\frac{1}{4}$ of this product to determine if that might be the lowest common de-nominator. If not, then the product itself probably represents the lowest common denominator.

Consider the fractions $\frac{2}{3}$, $\frac{1}{6}$, and $\frac{3}{8}$. In order to find the least common denominator, examine the multiples of 8 (the largest denominator). The multiples of 8 are 8, 16, 24, 32, 40, etc. Neither 8 nor 16 is divisible by 3 or 6. However, 24 is divisible by both 3 and 6 (and, of course, by 8). Hence, 24 is the least common denominator of $\frac{2}{3}$, $\frac{1}{6}$, and $\frac{3}{8}$.

Next, consider the fractions $\frac{5}{6}$, $\frac{3}{7}$, and $\frac{5}{8}$. The product of the de-nominators is $6 \times 7 \times 8$, or 336. However, $\frac{1}{2}$ of 336, or 168 represents the smallest number which 6, 7, and 8 will all divide into evenly. Thus, 168 is the least common denominator. Also consider the fractions $\frac{1}{6}$, $\frac{2}{7}$, and $\frac{2}{9}$. The product of these denominators is $6 \times 7 \times 9$, or 378. One-half of 378 is 189, which is not divisible by 6. However, $\frac{1}{3}$ of 378 is 126, which is divisible by 6, 7, and 9 all. Hence, 126 is the least common denominator.

Changing to higher terms is based on the same principles as reducing fractions, but applied in reverse order. That is, the procedure is based on the facts that any number over itself equals 1 $\left(\dfrac{x}{x} = 1 \right)$, and that any number multiplied by 1 equals that same number ($x \cdot 1 = x$). Thus, once the least common denominator has been determined, one must then find how many times the given denominator divides into the common denominator. This result (written as a fraction equal to 1) is used to convert the fraction to higher terms. For example, suppose that we have already determined that 12 is the lowest common denominator for $\frac{3}{4}$ and $\frac{1}{6}$. To convert $\frac{3}{4}$ to higher terms, think, "4 divides into 12 *three* times." Thus, $\frac{3}{3}$ is used to change $\frac{3}{4}$ to higher terms:

$$\frac{3}{4} = \frac{3}{4} \times 1 = \frac{3}{4} \times \frac{3}{3} = \frac{3 \times 3}{4 \times 3} = \frac{9}{12}$$

We have multiplied $\frac{3}{4}$ by a value, $\frac{3}{3}$, equal to 1. Therefore, we know that the value of the fraction remains unchanged and that $\frac{3}{4} = \frac{9}{12}$. Similarly, 6 divides into 12 *two* times. Thus,

$$\frac{1}{6} = \frac{1}{6} \times 1 = \frac{1}{6} \times \frac{2}{2} = \frac{1 \times 2}{6 \times 2} = \frac{2}{12}$$

Hence, $\frac{1}{6} = \frac{2}{12}$.

In actual practice, it is unnecessary to write out this entire process. Rather, one mentally divides the denominator into the lowest common denominator and multiplies that quotient times the numerator to obtain the numerator of the converted fraction. Therefore, to change $\frac{3}{4}$ to twelfths, think: "4 divides into 12 *three* times; that *three* times the numerator 3 equals 9; thus $\frac{3}{4} = \frac{9}{12}$." Or, when changing $\frac{1}{6}$ to twelfths, think: "6 divides into 12 *two* times; *two* times 1 equals 2; therefore, $\frac{1}{6} = \frac{2}{12}$."

Now let us compare $\frac{5}{6}$ and $\frac{7}{9}$ to determine which is larger.

$$\frac{5}{6} = \frac{15}{18} \qquad \text{and} \qquad \frac{7}{9} = \frac{14}{18}$$

Thus, comparing the fractions on the same terms, $\frac{15}{18}$ is larger than $\frac{14}{18}$. Hence, $\frac{5}{6}$ is larger than $\frac{7}{9}$.

Addition and Subtraction

The same terminology and properties of operation that apply to integers apply to common fractions as well. Thus, the parts of each operation have the following names:

Addend	$\frac{3}{7}$	Minuend	$\frac{3}{7}$
Addend	$+\frac{2}{7}$	Subtrahend	$-\frac{2}{7}$
Sum	$\frac{5}{7}$	Difference or remainder	$\frac{1}{7}$

The commutative property of addition and the associative property of addition also apply to common fractions:

$$\text{CPA:} \qquad a + b = b + a$$

$$\tfrac{3}{7} + \tfrac{2}{7} \overset{?}{=} \tfrac{2}{7} + \tfrac{3}{7}$$

$$\tfrac{5}{7} = \tfrac{5}{7}$$

$$\text{APA:} \qquad (a + b) + c = a + (b + c)$$

$$(\tfrac{3}{7} + \tfrac{2}{7}) + \tfrac{1}{7} \overset{?}{=} \tfrac{3}{7} + (\tfrac{2}{7} + \tfrac{1}{7})$$

$$\tfrac{5}{7} + \tfrac{1}{7} \overset{?}{=} \tfrac{3}{7} + \tfrac{3}{7}$$

$$\tfrac{6}{7} = \tfrac{6}{7}$$

As in the case of whole numbers, neither of the properties above applies for subtraction.

Before common fractions can be either added or subtracted, the fractions must first be written with a common denominator. The numerators are then added or subtracted (whichever is indicated). The result is then written over the *same* common denominator. (The student should be certain this fact is firmly impressed in his mind, for mistakes are frequently made in this operation.) The answer should then be reduced, if possible. Consider the following examples.

Example One

(a)
$$\begin{aligned} \tfrac{3}{5} &= \tfrac{9}{15} \\ +\tfrac{2}{3} &= \tfrac{10}{15} \\ \hline &\quad \tfrac{19}{15} \end{aligned}$$

(b)
$$\begin{aligned} \tfrac{3}{4} &= \tfrac{9}{12} \\ \tfrac{2}{3} &= \tfrac{8}{12} \\ +\tfrac{5}{6} &= \tfrac{10}{12} \\ \hline &\quad \tfrac{27}{12} = \tfrac{9}{4} \end{aligned}$$

(c)
$$\tfrac{1}{4} + \tfrac{3}{8} + \tfrac{1}{6} = \tfrac{6}{24} + \tfrac{9}{24} + \tfrac{4}{24}$$
$$= \tfrac{6+9+4}{24}$$
$$\tfrac{1}{4} + \tfrac{3}{8} + \tfrac{1}{6} = \tfrac{19}{24}$$

(d)
$$\begin{aligned} \tfrac{9}{16} &= \tfrac{9}{16} \\ -\tfrac{3}{8} &= -\tfrac{6}{16} \\ \hline &\quad \tfrac{3}{16} \end{aligned}$$

(e)
$$\begin{aligned} \tfrac{5}{7} &= \tfrac{15}{21} \\ -\tfrac{1}{3} &= -\tfrac{7}{21} \\ \hline &\quad \tfrac{8}{21} \end{aligned}$$

(f)
$$\tfrac{1}{2} - \tfrac{1}{6} = \tfrac{3}{6} - \tfrac{1}{6}$$
$$= \tfrac{3-1}{6}$$
$$= \tfrac{2}{6}$$
$$\tfrac{1}{2} - \tfrac{1}{6} = \tfrac{1}{3}$$

Multiplication and Division

As would be expected, the terms previously used to identify the parts of multiplication and division with whole numbers also apply to those operations with fractions.

The commutative and associative properties of multiplication apply to fractions as they did to integers; and the distributive property of multiplication over addition holds for fractions as it did for whole numbers. (As before, none of these properties is true for division.)

$$\text{CPM:} \qquad a \times b = b \times a$$

$$\tfrac{1}{2} \times \tfrac{3}{5} \overset{?}{=} \tfrac{3}{5} \times \tfrac{1}{2}$$

$$\tfrac{3}{10} = \tfrac{3}{10}$$

$$\text{APM:} \qquad (a \times b)c = a(b \times c)$$

$$(\tfrac{1}{4} \times \tfrac{3}{5}) \times \tfrac{1}{2} = \tfrac{1}{4} \times (\tfrac{3}{5} \times \tfrac{1}{2})$$

$$\tfrac{3}{20} \times \tfrac{1}{2} = \tfrac{1}{4} \times \tfrac{3}{10}$$

$$\tfrac{3}{40} = \tfrac{3}{40}$$

$$\text{DP:} \qquad a(b + c) = ab + ac$$

$$\tfrac{1}{3}(\tfrac{1}{4} + \tfrac{2}{5}) \overset{?}{=} \tfrac{1}{3} \times \tfrac{1}{4} + \tfrac{1}{3} \times \tfrac{2}{5}$$

$$\tfrac{1}{3}(\tfrac{5}{20} + \tfrac{8}{20}) \overset{?}{=} \tfrac{1}{12} \quad + \tfrac{2}{15}$$

$$\tfrac{1}{3}(\tfrac{13}{20}) \overset{?}{=} \tfrac{5}{60} \quad + \tfrac{8}{60}$$

$$\tfrac{13}{60} = \tfrac{13}{60}$$

When multiplying fractions, we multiply the various numerators together to obtain the numerator of the product, and then multiply the denominators to obtain the denominator of the product. Where possible, the product should be reduced.

$$\tfrac{2}{5} \times \tfrac{2}{3} = \tfrac{2}{5} \times \tfrac{2}{3} = \tfrac{2 \times 2}{5 \times 3} = \tfrac{4}{15}$$

When one fraction is to be divided into another, the divisor (second fraction) must first be inverted (that is, the numerator and denominator must be interchanged). Then, proceed as in multiplication. When a fraction is inverted, the new fraction is called the **reciprocal** of the original fraction. Hence, the reciprocal of $\frac{3}{5}$ is $\frac{5}{3}$. Thus, it is often said that one divides by "multiplying by the reciprocal."

$$\frac{3}{4} \div \frac{2}{3} = \frac{3}{4} \times \frac{3}{2} = \frac{3 \times 3}{4 \times 2} = \frac{9}{8}$$

(To divide by $\frac{2}{3}$, *multiply* by the *reciprocal* $\frac{3}{2}$)

The student may be accustomed to "canceling" when multiplying or dividing fractions. When one uses cancellation, he is actually just reducing the problem rather than waiting and reducing the answer. We know that the value of a fraction remains unchanged when it is reduced. Thus, cancellation is permissible because it is a reduction process and does not change the value of the answer.

Consider the problem $\frac{3}{4} \times \frac{1}{3}$. If multiplied in the standard manner, the product would be $\frac{3}{12}$, which reduces to $\frac{1}{4}$. The following operations illustrate how the problem itself may be reduced before the answer is obtained:

$$\frac{3}{4} \times \frac{1}{3} = \frac{3 \times 1}{4 \times 3}$$

Since multiplication is commutative, we can reverse the order of the numbers:

$$\frac{3 \times 1}{4 \times 3} = \frac{1 \times 3}{4 \times 3}$$

$$= \frac{1}{4} \times \frac{3}{3}$$

$$= \frac{1}{4} \times 1$$

$$\frac{3 \times 1}{4 \times 3} = \frac{1}{4}$$

Thus, $\frac{3}{4} \times \frac{1}{3} = \frac{1}{4}$. However, one would not usually reduce by rewriting the problem to make the 3's form the fraction $\frac{3}{3}$ and thereby reduce to 1. Rather, seeing that there is one 3 in the numerator and another in the denominator, one would cancel the 3's (or reduce $\frac{3}{3}$ to 1) as follows:

$$\frac{3}{4} \times \frac{1}{3} = \frac{\overset{1}{\cancel{3}}}{4} \times \frac{1}{\underset{1}{\cancel{3}}} = \frac{1}{4}$$

Two numbers may be reduced even though they are widely separated in the problem, provided that one is in the numerator and the other in the denominator:

$$\tfrac{4}{5} \times \tfrac{3}{5} \times \tfrac{7}{8} = \tfrac{\overset{1}{4}}{5} \times \tfrac{3}{5} \times \tfrac{7}{\underset{2}{8}} = \tfrac{1}{5} \times \tfrac{3}{5} \times \tfrac{7}{2} = \tfrac{21}{50}$$

Now consider the division problem $\tfrac{4}{5} \div \tfrac{8}{15}$. If this problem were divided before it is reduced, the operation would be as follows:

$$\tfrac{4}{5} \div \tfrac{8}{15} = \tfrac{4}{5} \times \tfrac{15}{8}$$
$$= \tfrac{60}{40}$$
$$\tfrac{4}{5} \div \tfrac{8}{15} = \tfrac{3}{2}$$

The problem could also be reduced prior to the actual division:

$$\tfrac{4}{5} \div \tfrac{8}{15} = \tfrac{4}{5} \times \tfrac{15}{8}$$
$$= \tfrac{4}{5} \times \tfrac{5 \times 3}{4 \times 2}$$
$$\tfrac{4}{5} \div \tfrac{8}{15} = \tfrac{4 \times 5 \times 3}{5 \times 4 \times 2}$$

Because multiplication is commutative and associative, we may rearrange the numbers:

$$\tfrac{4 \times 5 \times 3}{5 \times 4 \times 2} = \tfrac{5 \times 4 \times 3}{5 \times 4 \times 2}$$
$$= \tfrac{5}{5} \times \tfrac{4}{4} \times \tfrac{3}{2}$$
$$= 1 \times 1 \times \tfrac{3}{2}$$
$$\tfrac{4 \times 5 \times 3}{5 \times 4 \times 2} = \tfrac{3}{2}$$

Hence, $\tfrac{4}{5} \div \tfrac{8}{15} = \tfrac{3}{2}$ by either method. In actual practice, however, neither method is normally used. Rather, after the divisor has been inverted, cancellation would be used to reduce the fractions. That is, the fraction $\tfrac{4}{8}$ would be reduced to $\tfrac{1}{2}$, and $\tfrac{15}{5}$ would be reduced to $\tfrac{3}{1}$ as follows:

$$\tfrac{4}{5} \div \tfrac{8}{15} = \tfrac{4}{5} \times \tfrac{15}{8}$$
$$= \tfrac{\overset{1}{4}}{\underset{1}{8}} \times \tfrac{\overset{3}{15}}{\underset{2}{8}}$$
$$= \tfrac{1}{1} \times \tfrac{3}{2}$$
$$\tfrac{4}{5} \div \tfrac{8}{15} = \tfrac{3}{2}$$

Thus, we see that cancellation is a method of reducing fractions and therefore produces the same answers as ordinary reduction. However, cancellation may be used only under the following conditions. Cancellation may be performed only in a multiplication problem, or in a division problem *after* the divisor has been inverted; and a number in the **numerator** and another number in the **denominator** must contain a common factor (that is, must comprise a fraction which can be reduced). The numbers being reduced are slashed with a diagonal mark; the quotient obtained when dividing by the common factor is written above the number in the numerator and below the number in the denominator. These reduced values are then used in performing the multiplication.

Mixed Numbers   A number composed of both a whole number and a fraction is known as a **mixed number** (for example, $3\frac{1}{2}$). Multiplication and division involving mixed numbers is easier if the mixed number is first converted to a common fraction.

Mixed numbers may be converted to fractions by applying the same basic principles that we have used to reduce fractions or to change to higher terms—namely, that any number over itself equals 1 $\left(\dfrac{x}{x} = 1\right)$ and that multiplying any number by 1 equals that same number ($x \cdot 1 = x$). The student will recall that a whole number may be written in fraction form using a denominator of 1. (That is, $5 = \frac{5}{1}$. This is correct because $\frac{5}{1}$ means $5 \div 1$, which equals the original 5.) Now consider the mixed number $3\frac{1}{2}$:

$$3\tfrac{1}{2} = 3 + \tfrac{1}{2}$$
$$= 3 \times 1 + \tfrac{1}{2}$$
$$= 3 \times \tfrac{2}{2} + \tfrac{1}{2}$$
$$= \tfrac{3}{1} \times \tfrac{2}{2} + \tfrac{1}{2}$$
$$= \tfrac{6}{2} + \tfrac{1}{2}$$
$$3\tfrac{1}{2} = \tfrac{7}{2}$$

Thus, we see that $3\frac{1}{2}$ may be converted to the common fraction $\frac{7}{2}$ by multiplying the whole-number part by a fraction equal to 1 and then adding the fraction from the mixed number. (The "fraction equal to 1" is always composed of the denominator from the fraction in the mixed number over itself—in this case, $\frac{2}{2}$. Thus, the mixed number $4\frac{2}{5}$ would be converted by substituting $\frac{5}{5}$ for 1.) Any mixed number always equals an improper fraction.

The familiar procedure used to convert a mixed number to a common fraction is to "multiply the denominator times the whole number and add the numerator." This total over the original denominator (in the fraction part) is the value of the common fraction equivalent to the mixed number. Thus,

$$3\tfrac{1}{2} = 3 \begin{smallmatrix} + \\ \longrightarrow 1 \\ \times \longleftarrow 2 \end{smallmatrix} = \begin{array}{r} 3 \\ \times 2 \text{ halves} \\ \hline 6 \text{ halves} + 1 \text{ half} = \tfrac{7}{2} \end{array}$$

If the whole number is so large that the product is not immediately obvious, the multiplication can be performed digit by digit and the numerator added in the same way as are numbers which have been "carried." For example,

$$16\tfrac{3}{8} = \frac{?}{8} \qquad \text{Think: "} 8 \times 6 \text{ is 48 plus 3 is 51"} —$$

$$\text{Write 1 and carry the 5} \left(16\tfrac{3}{8} = \frac{\cdots 1}{8} \right).$$

$$\text{Then, "} 8 \times 1 \text{ is 8 plus 5 is 13." So}$$

$$16\tfrac{3}{8} = \tfrac{131}{8}$$

Example Two demonstrates how mixed numbers are handled in multiplication and division problems.

Example Two

(a) $\quad 4\tfrac{1}{2} \times 3\tfrac{1}{3} = \tfrac{9}{2} \times \tfrac{10}{3}$

$\qquad\qquad = \dfrac{\overset{3}{\cancel{9}}}{\underset{1}{\cancel{2}}} \times \dfrac{\overset{5}{\cancel{10}}}{\underset{1}{\cancel{3}}}$

$\qquad\qquad = \tfrac{3}{1} \times \tfrac{5}{1}$

$\qquad\qquad = \tfrac{15}{1}$

$\quad 4\tfrac{1}{2} \times 3\tfrac{1}{3} = 15$

(b) $\quad 5\tfrac{2}{5} \div 3\tfrac{3}{5} = \tfrac{27}{5} \div \tfrac{18}{5}$

$\qquad\qquad = \tfrac{27}{5} \times \tfrac{5}{18}$

$\qquad\qquad = \dfrac{\overset{3}{\cancel{27}}}{\underset{1}{\cancel{5}}} \times \dfrac{\overset{1}{\cancel{5}}}{\underset{2}{\cancel{18}}}$

$\qquad\qquad = \tfrac{3}{1} \times \tfrac{1}{2}$

$\quad 5\tfrac{2}{5} \div 3\tfrac{3}{5} = \tfrac{3}{2}$

(c) $\quad 4\tfrac{7}{8} \div 1\tfrac{11}{16} = \tfrac{39}{8} \div \tfrac{27}{16}$

$\qquad\qquad = \tfrac{39}{8} \times \tfrac{16}{27}$

$\qquad\qquad = \dfrac{\overset{13}{\cancel{39}}}{\underset{1}{\cancel{8}}} \times \dfrac{\overset{2}{\cancel{16}}}{\underset{9}{\cancel{27}}}$

$\qquad\qquad = \tfrac{13}{1} \times \tfrac{2}{9}$

$\quad 4\tfrac{7}{8} \div 1\tfrac{11}{16} = \tfrac{26}{9}$

Notice in division that a mixed-number divisor should be converted to an improper fraction before the divisor is inverted.

In certain instances, it is necessary to change an improper fraction to a mixed number. This operation simply reverses the former procedure. Suppose that $\frac{19}{8}$ is to be converted to a mixed number. The numerator may first be broken down into a multiple of the denominator plus a remainder. The familiar properties of $1\left(\frac{x}{x}=1 \text{ and } x(1)=x\right)$ may then be applied as before:

$$\frac{19}{8} = \frac{2(8)+3}{8}$$

$$= \frac{2(8)}{8} + \frac{3}{8}$$

$$= \frac{2}{1} \times \frac{8}{8} + \frac{3}{8}$$

$$= \frac{2}{1} \times 1 + \frac{3}{8} = 2 + \frac{3}{8}$$

$$\frac{19}{8} = 2\frac{3}{8}$$

Thus, $\frac{19}{8} = 2\frac{3}{8}$. In actual practice, however, the procedure used to convert improper fractions to mixed numbers applies the fact that a fraction is an indicated division. That is, $\frac{19}{8}$ means $19 \div 8$, which equals 2 with a remainder of $\frac{3}{8}$. Hence, $\frac{19}{8} = 2\frac{3}{8}$.

Addition may be performed using mixed numbers (without changing them to improper fractions). Although it is generally considered acceptable to leave answers as improper fractions, it is not correct to leave a mixed number which includes an improper fraction. The improper fraction should be changed to a mixed number and this amount added to the whole number to obtain a mixed number which includes a proper fraction (reduced to lowest terms). Thus, if the sum of an addition problem is $7\frac{14}{6}$, this result must be converted as follows:

$$7\frac{14}{6} = 7 + \frac{14}{6}$$

$$= 7 + 2\frac{2}{6} = 9\frac{2}{6}$$

$$7\frac{14}{6} = 9\frac{1}{3}$$

Example Three shows cases of addition with mixed numbers.

Example Three

(a) $\begin{array}{r} 7\frac{5}{9} \\ +3\frac{1}{9} \\ \hline 10\frac{6}{9} = 10\frac{2}{3} \end{array}$

(b) $\begin{array}{r} 6\frac{5}{8} = 6\frac{15}{24} \\ +9\frac{2}{3} = 9\frac{16}{24} \\ \hline 15\frac{31}{24} = 16\frac{7}{24} \end{array}$

(c) $\begin{array}{r} 16\frac{2}{3} = 16\frac{4}{6} \\ +17\frac{5}{6} = 17\frac{5}{6} \\ \hline 33\frac{9}{6} = 34\frac{3}{6} = 34\frac{1}{2} \end{array}$

Subtraction may also be performed using mixed numbers. The student will recall that subtraction usually requires regrouping (or borrowing). This procedure, when applied to fractions, means that improper fractions must often be created where they did not exist.

Consider the problem $7\frac{3}{8} - 4\frac{7}{8}$. Although the mixed number $4\frac{7}{8}$ is smaller than $7\frac{3}{8}$, the fraction $\frac{7}{8}$ cannot be subtracted from $\frac{3}{8}$. In order to perform the operation, one must regroup the $7\frac{3}{8}$. Mixed numbers are regrouped by borrowing one unit from the whole number, converting this unit to a fraction (the common denominator over itself), and adding this fractional "1" to the fraction from the mixed number. Using this procedure, we regroup $7\frac{3}{8}$ as follows:

$$7\frac{3}{8} = \; 7 \; + \frac{3}{8}$$
$$= 6 + 1 + \frac{3}{8}$$
$$= 6 + \frac{8}{8} + \frac{3}{8}$$
$$= 6 + \; \frac{11}{8}$$
$$7\frac{3}{8} = 6\frac{11}{8}$$

Thus, $7\frac{3}{8}$ equals $6\frac{11}{8}$. In actual practice, the procedure of borrowing 1 and adding it to the existing fraction may be done mentally, with only the result being written. The subtraction problem above and other problems are illustrated in Example Four.

Example Four

(a) $\begin{array}{r} 5\frac{5}{6} \\ -1\frac{1}{6} \\ \hline 4\frac{4}{6} = 4\frac{2}{3} \end{array}$

(b) $\begin{array}{r} 7\frac{3}{8} = \; 6\frac{11}{8} \\ -4\frac{7}{8} = -4\frac{7}{8} \\ \hline 2\frac{4}{8} = 2\frac{1}{2} \end{array}$

(c) $\begin{array}{r} 15\frac{1}{3} = \; 15\frac{4}{12} = \; 14\frac{16}{12} \\ -8\frac{3}{4} = -8\frac{9}{12} = -8\frac{9}{12} \\ \hline 6\frac{7}{12} \end{array}$

Notice that the fractions in mixed numbers are first changed to fractions with a common denominator before regrouping for subtraction (c).

Express each of the properties requested, using the variables or numbers indicated.
Verify the properties when numbers are used.

1. (a) Commutative property of addition, using g and h.
  (b) Commutative property of addition, using $\frac{2}{9}$ and $\frac{1}{6}$.
  (c) Associative property of addition, using l, m, and n.
  (d) Associative property of addition, using $\frac{1}{4}$, $\frac{5}{6}$, and $\frac{2}{3}$.
  (e) Commutative property of multiplication, using h and k.
  (f) Commutative property of multiplication, using $3\frac{1}{5}$ and $4\frac{3}{8}$.
  (g) Associative property of multiplication, using x, y, and z.
  (h) Associative property of multiplication, using $\frac{5}{7}$, $\frac{3}{5}$, and $\frac{1}{6}$.
  (i) Distributive property, using t, u, and v.
  (j) Distributive property, using $\frac{1}{3}$, $\frac{6}{7}$, and $\frac{3}{5}$.

2. (a) Commutative property of addition, using j and k.
  (b) Commutative property of addition, using $4\frac{3}{8}$ and $3\frac{1}{4}$.
  (c) Associative property of addition, using s, t, and v.
  (d) Associative property of addition, using $\frac{1}{2}$, $\frac{2}{3}$, and $\frac{3}{4}$.
  (e) Commutative property of multiplication, using f and g.
  (f) Commutative property of multiplication, using $2\frac{1}{4}$ and $5\frac{1}{3}$.
  (g) Associative property of multiplication, using p, q, and r.
  (h) Associative property of multiplication, using $\frac{5}{7}$, $\frac{4}{5}$, and $\frac{7}{8}$.
  (i) Distributive property, using w, x, and y.
  (j) Distributive property, using $\frac{3}{4}$, $\frac{4}{5}$, and $\frac{8}{7}$.

3. Reduce the following fractions to lowest terms (that is, reduce as much as possible).

  (a) $\frac{16}{24}$ (b) $\frac{14}{6}$ (c) $\frac{28}{36}$ (d) $\frac{48}{84}$ (e) $\frac{34}{51}$
  (f) $\frac{75}{45}$ (g) $\frac{57}{76}$ (h) $\frac{108}{90}$ (i) $\frac{189}{231}$ (j) $\frac{168}{288}$

4. Convert the following fractions to fractions with least common denominators.

  (a) $\frac{1}{2}$ and $\frac{2}{5}$ (b) $\frac{2}{3}$ and $\frac{5}{7}$ (c) $\frac{3}{8}$ and $\frac{1}{4}$
  (d) $\frac{5}{12}$ and $\frac{3}{8}$ (e) $\frac{7}{9}$ and $\frac{3}{5}$ (f) $\frac{1}{4}$, $\frac{2}{3}$, and $\frac{5}{8}$
  (g) $\frac{5}{6}$, $\frac{5}{12}$, and $\frac{4}{9}$ (h) $\frac{3}{8}$, $\frac{5}{9}$, and $\frac{1}{6}$ (i) $\frac{4}{5}$, $\frac{3}{4}$, and $\frac{2}{3}$
  (j) $\frac{7}{16}$, $\frac{5}{6}$, and $\frac{3}{8}$ (k) $\frac{3}{4}$, $\frac{4}{5}$, and $\frac{5}{6}$ (l) $\frac{3}{5}$, $\frac{1}{6}$, and $\frac{4}{9}$

5. Compare the following fractions by converting to a common denominator. Then arrange the original fractions in order of size, starting with the smallest.

  (a) $\frac{3}{4}$, $\frac{5}{6}$, $\frac{7}{12}$, $\frac{2}{3}$, $\frac{3}{8}$, $\frac{5}{16}$
  (b) $\frac{5}{12}$, $\frac{1}{3}$, $\frac{3}{10}$, $\frac{5}{6}$, $\frac{7}{15}$, $\frac{2}{5}$

6. Change the following mixed numbers to improper fractions.

(a) $7\frac{1}{2}$ (b) $8\frac{3}{5}$ (c) $3\frac{4}{9}$ (d) $5\frac{5}{6}$ (e) $12\frac{4}{5}$

(f) $6\frac{5}{11}$ (g) $8\frac{2}{7}$ (h) $18\frac{5}{9}$ (i) $26\frac{4}{7}$ (j) $37\frac{7}{8}$

7. Convert the following improper fractions (and improper mixed numbers) to mixed numbers. Reduce if possible.

(a) $\frac{28}{8}$ (b) $\frac{32}{6}$ (c) $\frac{57}{12}$ (d) $\frac{61}{7}$ (e) $\frac{84}{16}$

(f) $\frac{82}{18}$ (g) $\frac{109}{13}$ (h) $\frac{92}{24}$ (i) $\frac{75}{11}$ (j) $7\frac{11}{3}$

(k) $5\frac{10}{4}$ (l) $12\frac{18}{8}$

8. Find the sums of the following addition problems, reducing where possible.

(a) $\frac{3}{4}$ $\frac{1}{2}$

(b) $\frac{7}{8}$ $\frac{2}{3}$

(c) $\frac{2}{5}$ $\frac{1}{3}$ $\frac{3}{10}$

(d) $\frac{3}{4}$ $\frac{2}{3}$ $\frac{1}{6}$

(e) $\frac{5}{7}$ $\frac{3}{5}$ $\frac{1}{2}$

(f) $\frac{5}{12}$ $\frac{2}{9}$ $\frac{3}{4}$ $\frac{1}{6}$

(g) $\frac{1}{4}$ $\frac{1}{8}$ $\frac{5}{6}$ $\frac{2}{3}$

(h) $\frac{1}{6}$ $\frac{7}{8}$ $\frac{11}{24}$ $\frac{5}{9}$

(i) $\frac{8}{15}$ $\frac{2}{5}$ $\frac{1}{4}$ $\frac{1}{3}$

(j) $\frac{5}{6}$ $\frac{2}{3}$ $\frac{7}{10}$ $\frac{3}{5}$

(k) $5\frac{1}{3}$ $7\frac{3}{4}$

(l) $3\frac{5}{6}$ $9\frac{1}{2}$

(m) $9\frac{1}{4}$ $6\frac{7}{9}$

(n) $2\frac{1}{2}$ $5\frac{3}{8}$

(o) $7\frac{1}{2}$ $8\frac{2}{3}$

(p) $6\frac{3}{8}$ $4\frac{5}{16}$ $3\frac{1}{4}$

(q) $7\frac{2}{3}$ $5\frac{3}{8}$ $2\frac{1}{6}$

(r) $4\frac{5}{6}$ $3\frac{1}{2}$ $8\frac{1}{3}$ $1\frac{2}{7}$

(s) $6\frac{3}{7}$ $\frac{1}{2}$ $8\frac{1}{4}$ $4\frac{3}{4}$

(t) $2\frac{3}{5}$ $7\frac{1}{4}$ $\frac{5}{8}$ $5\frac{1}{2}$

9. Subtract in each of the following, reducing where possible.

(a) $\frac{2}{3}$ $\frac{5}{12}$

(b) $\frac{7}{16}$ $\frac{1}{4}$

(c) $\frac{4}{5}$ $\frac{3}{8}$

(d) $\frac{5}{6}$ $\frac{2}{7}$

(e) $\frac{3}{4}$ $\frac{2}{5}$

(f) $8\frac{7}{8}$ $3\frac{2}{3}$

(g) $13\frac{3}{4}$ $7\frac{1}{6}$

(h) $24\frac{6}{7}$ $17\frac{2}{3}$

(i) $26\frac{1}{2}$ $19\frac{4}{5}$

(j) $35\frac{1}{4}$ $28\frac{5}{7}$

(k) $22\frac{2}{5}$ $12\frac{5}{6}$

(l) $35\frac{7}{2}$ $13\frac{3}{7}$

(m) $33\frac{4}{9}$ $18\frac{5}{6}$

(n) $46\frac{2}{5}$ $24\frac{2}{3}$

(o) $41\frac{3}{7}$ $27\frac{3}{4}$

10. Multiply, reducing wherever possible.

(a) $\frac{3}{4}\times\frac{7}{9}$ (b) $\frac{6}{7}\times\frac{2}{3}$ (c) $\frac{2}{5}\times\frac{5}{6}$ (d) $\frac{9}{16}\times\frac{4}{15}$ (e) $\frac{5}{12}\times\frac{8}{15}$

(f) $\frac{7}{8}\times5\frac{1}{3}$ (g) $\frac{5}{6}\times2\frac{2}{5}$ (h) $3\frac{1}{8}\times\frac{8}{15}$ (i) $4\frac{1}{2}\times\frac{10}{21}$ (j) $3\frac{1}{16}\times\frac{2}{7}$

(k) $6\times1\frac{2}{3}$ (l) $5\frac{1}{4}\times2\frac{2}{7}$ (m) $2\frac{1}{2}\times3\frac{1}{3}$ (n) $7\frac{1}{5}\times3\frac{1}{8}$ (o) $6\frac{2}{5}\times2\frac{1}{12}$

11. Multiply, reducing where possible.

(a) $\frac{6}{7}\times\frac{5}{8}\times\frac{3}{10}$ (b) $2\frac{4}{5}\times\frac{3}{7}\times3\frac{3}{4}$

(c) $3\frac{1}{7}\times\frac{3}{8}\times3\frac{1}{2}\times1\frac{5}{11}$ (d) $3\frac{1}{5}\times\frac{1}{18}\times\frac{3}{4}\times5\frac{5}{6}$

12. Divide, reducing to lowest terms.

(a) $\frac{1}{4}\div\frac{5}{8}$ (b) $\frac{3}{8}\div\frac{1}{2}$ (c) $\frac{5}{6}\div\frac{2}{3}$ (d) $\frac{2}{3}\div\frac{5}{6}$ (e) $\frac{7}{12}\div\frac{7}{8}$

(f) $18\div4\frac{1}{2}$ (g) $2\frac{4}{5}\div7$ (h) $4\frac{3}{8}\div15$ (i) $3\frac{3}{4}\div\frac{5}{16}$ (j) $\frac{3}{8}\div4\frac{1}{2}$

(k) $3\frac{1}{5}\div1\frac{3}{5}$ (l) $4\frac{2}{3}\div2\frac{1}{4}$ (m) $2\frac{2}{5}\div7\frac{1}{2}$ (n) $6\frac{3}{8}\div2\frac{5}{6}$ (o) $3\frac{3}{14}\div8\frac{4}{7}$

SECTION 4
Decimal Fractions

As the developing number system became more sophisticated, a method was devised for expressing parts of a whole without writing a complete common fraction; this is the system of **decimal notation**. Decimal values are actually abbreviated fractions. That is, the written number is only the numerator of an indicated fraction. The denominator of the indicated fraction is some power of 10. This denominator is not written, but is indicated by the location of the decimal point. For example, 0.7 indicates $\frac{7}{10}$, or 0.43 indicates $\frac{43}{100}$, without the 10 or 100 being written. Thus, since decimal values represent fractional parts of a whole, they are known as **decimal fractions**.

Decimal fractions are an extension of our whole number (and integer) system, both because they are based on powers of 10 and also because the value of any digit is determined by the position it holds in the number. Figure 56 shows the value and power of 10 that is associated with each place in a decimal number. (Some whole-number places are included to show that decimal values are an extension of whole-number place values.) Notice that the names for decimal place values repeat, in reverse order, the names of integer place values—except that the letters "-ths" are added to indicate that these are decimal–place values.

A decimal point (or period) is used in a number to show where the whole amount ends and the fractional portion begins. A whole number is usually written without a decimal point, but every integer is understood to have a decimal point after the units place. Thus, 15 could be written "15." (or "15.0," or "15.00," etc.) and would be just as correct.

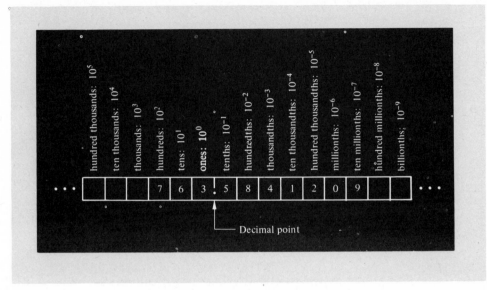

FIGURE 56: *Place Values for Decimals.*

The student will recall from our study of integers that 10^2 represents 100 and the digit 7 in Figure 56 thus has the value 7×100, or 700. Similarly, 10^{-2} represents $\frac{1}{100}$, and the digit 8 has the value $8 \times \frac{1}{100}$, or $\frac{8}{100}$. In the same manner, the digit 5 represents "5 tenths," or $\frac{5}{10}$; the digit 4 represents "4 thousandths," or $\frac{4}{1000}$. Hence, any digit in the first place following a decimal represents that number divided by 10 $\left(\frac{x}{10}\right)$; any number in the second place represents that number over 100 $\left(\frac{y}{100}\right)$; any number in the third decimal place represents that number over 1,000 $\left(\frac{z}{1000}\right)$; and so on.

As pointed out previously, a decimal is actually an abbreviated fraction. Thus, the decimal fraction 0.475 (the zero is placed before the decimal point purely for clarity) represents a common fraction with a numerator of 475 and (since the decimal contains three digits to the right of the decimal point) a denominator of 1,000. Therefore, the decimal fraction 0.475 could be written $\frac{475}{1000}$. This illustrates why decimal fractions, like common fractions, are known as **rational numbers**, since they can be expressed as the quotient of two integers.

Decimal fractions are written (or spoken) by writing the digits as if they represented a whole number and then writing the place-value associated with the farthest place to the right of the decimal point. Thus,

Number	Written (or Spoken) Form
0.9	"nine *tenths*"
0.14	"fourteen *hundredths*"
0.007	"seven *thousandths*"
0.3024	"three thousand twenty-four *ten-thousandths*"
0.00508	"five hundred eight *hundred-thousandths*"
25.6	"twenty-five and six *tenths*"
2.03	"two and three *hundredths*"
4,070.035	"four thousand seventy and thirty-five *thousandths*"

Notice that zeros between the decimal point and the first significant digit do not affect the written form. (For example, 0.007 is written "*seven thousandths*.") Also, the word "and" is written (or spoken) solely to indicate the location of the decimal point. (Thus, 2.03 is pronounced "two *and* three hundredths.") Zeros to the right of a decimal fraction (with no other digits following) do not affect its value. (Thus, 0.4, 0.40, 0.400, and 0.4000 are equal in value, because $\frac{4}{10} = \frac{40}{100} = \frac{400}{1000} = \frac{4,000}{10,000}$.)

Converting Common Fractions to Decimal Fractions

Manual computation can often be accomplished efficiently using common fractions, although at times common fractions become cumbersome. Most computation in modern offices, however, is done on electric machines, which are equipped to handle decimal values rather than common fractions. Thus, business efficiency requires a knowledge not only of common fractions and decimal fractions separately but also of how to convert each form to the other.

The student will recall that a common fraction is an indicated division. Hence, $\frac{2}{5}$ means $2 \div 5$. This principle is the basis for converting common fractions to decimal fractions. That is, a common fraction is converted to a decimal fraction by dividing the denominator into the numerator:

$$\frac{n}{d} = n \div d = d \overline{\smash{)}n}$$

This procedure applies to improper as well as to proper fractions. If a mixed number is to be converted to a decimal number, the fractional part of the mixed number is converted in this same manner, and the decimal equivalent is then affixed to the whole number of the mixed number. Example One illustrates these procedures.

Example One

(a)
$$\frac{2}{5} = 5\overline{\smash{\big)}\,2.0} \quad \frac{.4 = 0.4}{2.0}$$

(c)
$$\frac{9}{8} = 8\overline{\smash{\big)}\,9.000} \quad 1.125 = 1.125$$

(b)
$$\frac{3}{40} = 40\overline{\smash{\big)}\,3.000} \quad \frac{.075 = 0.075}{\begin{array}{l}2\,80\\ \hline 200\\ 200\end{array}}$$

(d)
$$2\frac{8}{25}: \quad \frac{8}{25} = 25\overline{\smash{\big)}\,8.00} \quad .32 = 0.32$$
$$\text{so} \quad 2\frac{8}{25} = 2.32$$

The student is no doubt aware that many fractions do not have an exact decimal equivalent. This will always be the case (unless the fraction represents a whole number) if the denominator is 3 or is divisible by 3, or if the denominator is a prime number larger than five. (A **prime number** is any number that is divisible by no numbers except itself and 1—for example, 7, 11, 17, 23, 31, to name but a few.)

The student may not always recognize whether a fraction has an exact decimal equivalent. The *recommended procedure for converting fractions* is first to divide to the hundredths place (two decimal places). If further inspection reveals that the quotient will come out to an exact digit after one more division, then include the third decimal place. If it is obvious that the quotient would not be exact even with three decimal places, then stop dividing after two decimal places and express the remainder as a fraction. (Students using calculators may round quotients to the nearest thousandth, or third decimal place. Rounding is reviewed in Chapter 1.) Consider the following examples.

Example One (cont.)

(e)
$$\frac{3}{8} = 8\overline{\smash{\big)}\,3.000} \quad .375 = 0.375$$

(f)
$$\frac{13}{200} = 200\overline{\smash{\big)}\,13.000} \quad .065 = 0.065$$

Example One (*cont.*)

(g) $\frac{3}{7} = 7\overline{)3.00}$ $.42\frac{6}{7} = 0.42\frac{6}{7}$ (or 0.429)

(h) $\frac{16}{29} = 29\overline{)16.00}$ $.55\frac{5}{29} = 0.55\frac{5}{29}$ (or 0.552)

Converting Decimal Fractions to Common Fractions

The standard procedure for converting a decimal fraction to a common fraction is to pronounce the value of the decimal, write this value in fraction form, and then reduce this fraction. This is shown in Example Two, parts (a)–(d).

Example Two

(a) 0.2 $=$ 2 tenths $= \frac{2}{10}$ $= \frac{1}{5}$

(b) 0.12 $=$ 12 hundredths $= \frac{12}{100}$ $= \frac{3}{25}$

(c) 0.336 $= 336$ thousandths $= \frac{336}{1,000}$ $= \frac{42}{125}$

(d) $0.0045 =$ 45 ten-thousandths $= \frac{45}{10,000} = \frac{9}{2,000}$

If a decimal fraction also contains a common fraction, the conversion process begins in a similar manner but requires additional steps. After the given decimal is rewritten as a fraction, we multiply by a fraction equal to one $\left(\frac{x}{x} = 1\right)$, and then reduce. Parts (e) and (f) below show how $0.83\frac{1}{3}$ and $0.31\frac{1}{4}$ are converted to fractions.

Example Two (*cont.*)

(e) $0.83\frac{1}{3} = \dfrac{83\frac{1}{3}}{100}$

$= \dfrac{83\frac{1}{3}}{100} \times \dfrac{3}{3}$

$= \dfrac{\frac{250}{\cancel{3}}}{100} \times \dfrac{\cancel{3}}{3}$

$= \dfrac{250}{300}$

$0.83\frac{1}{3} = \frac{5}{6}$

(f) $0.31\frac{1}{4} = \dfrac{31\frac{1}{4}}{100}$

$= \dfrac{31\frac{1}{4}}{100} \times \dfrac{4}{4}$

$= \dfrac{\frac{125}{4}}{100} \times \dfrac{4}{4}$

$= \dfrac{125}{400}$

$0.31\frac{1}{4} = \frac{5}{16}$

As noted previously, many computations can be done more easily by using fractional equivalents for decimal numbers, especially if the decimals are as complicated as those above. In order to save time, however, the student should be able to recognize when a decimal is the equivalent of one of the common fractions most often used—without having actually to convert it. These equivalents are listed on page 58, and the student should memorize all that he or she does not already know.

Addition and Subtraction

Addition and subtraction with decimals are very similar to addition and subtraction with integers. The same names apply to the parts of each problem:

Addend	0.36	Minuend	0.73
Addend	+0.58	Subtrahend	−0.46
Sum	0.94	Difference or Remainder	0.27

The basic properties of addition (the commutative and associative properties of addition) also apply when decimal fractions are used:

CPA:
$$a + b = b + a$$
$$0.3 + 0.5 \stackrel{?}{=} 0.5 + 0.3$$
$$0.8 = 0.8$$

APA:
$$(a + b) + c = a + (b + c)$$
$$(0.3 + 0.4) + 0.2 \stackrel{?}{=} 0.3 + (0.4 + 0.2)$$
$$0.7 + 0.2 \stackrel{?}{=} 0.3 + 0.6$$
$$0.9 = 0.9$$

As for addition and subtraction with whole numbers, decimal numbers must also be arranged so that all the digits of the same place are in the same column. That is, all the tenths' places must be in a vertical line, all the hundredths' places in one column, and so forth. In so arranging decimal numbers, the decimal points will always fall in a straight line. Therefore, in actual practice, we arrange the numbers by aligning the decimal points.

The actual addition or subtraction of decimal fractions is performed in exactly the same way as with integers; the decimal points have no effect on the operations. The decimal point in the answer is located directly under the decimal points of the problem.

It was pointed out earlier that appending zeros to the right of a decimal number does not alter its value. (That is, $3.7 = 3.70 = 3.700$, etc.). Thus, if the numbers of a problem contain different numbers of decimal places, the student may wish to add zeros so that all will contain the same number of decimal places. This is particularly helpful in subtraction problems where the subtrahend contains more decimal places than the minuend.

Example Three   (a) Add: $0.306 + 9.8 + 14.65 + 6.775 + 24 + 0.09$.
(b) Subtract: $18.6 - 5.897$.

Solution   (a)   0.306   (b)   18.600
                     9.8 -5.897
                     14.65   ‾‾‾‾‾‾
                     6.775   12.703
                     24.
                     0.09
                     ‾‾‾‾‾‾
                     55.621

Notice that zeros were inserted in the minuend to facilitate the subtraction.

Multiplication   The standard terminology is used to identify decimal numbers in a multiplication problem:

Multiplicand or factor   0.3
Multiplier or factor $\times 0.4$
                            ‾‾‾‾‾
Product   0.12

The commutative and associative properties of multiplication and the distributive property of multiplication over addition also hold for decimal fractions:

CPM: $a \times b = b \times a$

$0.7 \times 0.4 \stackrel{?}{=} 0.4 \times 0.7$

$0.28 = 0.28$

APM: $(a \times b)c \qquad = \qquad a(b \times c)$

$(0.7 \times 0.3) \times 0.5 \overset{?}{=} 0.7 \times (0.3 \times 0.5)$

$0.21 \times 0.5 \overset{?}{=} 0.7 \times 0.15$

$0.105 = 0.105$

DP: $\qquad\qquad a(b + c) = \qquad ab \quad + \quad ac$

$0.3(0.4 + 0.5) \overset{?}{=} 0.3 \times 0.4 + 0.3 \times 0.5$

$0.3(0.9) \overset{?}{=} 0.12 + 0.15$

$0.27 = 0.27$

Decimal numbers are written down for multiplication in the same arrangement that would be used if there were no decimal points. The actual multiplication of digits is also performed in the same way as for integers. The only variation comes in the placing of a decimal point in the product. In order to determine how this is done, consider the problem 12.4×3.13:

12.4
× 3.13
———
372
124
372
———
38812

Observe that this multiplication problem is approximately 12×3; therefore, the product must be approximately 36. This indicates that the decimal point must be located between the 8's. Thus,

12.4
× 3.13
———
372
124
372
———
38.812

The correct position of the decimal point in every multiplication product could thus be determined by approximating the answer and locating the decimal point accordingly. However, the product would invariably contain the same number of decimal places as the total number of decimal places in the factors. Therefore, as a time-saving device, it is customary to count the total number of decimal places in the factors and place the decimal point accordingly, rather than to estimate the product. (In the preceding problem, 12.4 contained one decimal place and 3.13 contained two decimal places; thus, the product contained three decimal places—38.812.) This example can also be explained as $\frac{124}{10} \times \frac{313}{100} = \frac{38,812}{1,000}$. Observe that the denominator of 1,000 indicates three decimal places.

Sometimes basic multiplication produces a number containing fewer digits than the total number of decimal places required for the product. In this case, the student must insert a zero or zeros between the decimal point and the first significant digit so that the product will contain the correct number of decimal places. Consider the example, 0.04×0.2:

$$\begin{array}{r} 0.04 \\ \times 0.2 \\ \hline 8 \end{array}$$

The factors require a three-digit product. Thus, two zeros must be inserted after the decimal point:

$$\begin{array}{r} 0.04 \\ \times 0.2 \\ \hline 0.008 \end{array}$$

The student can readily understand that 0.008 is the correct answer, because 0.04×0.2 is equal to $\frac{4}{100} \times \frac{2}{10} = \frac{8}{1,000}$.

Some additional examples are given below.

Example Four

(a)
$$\begin{array}{r} 41.8173 \\ \times 2.36 \\ \hline 2509038 \\ 1254519 \\ 836346 \\ \hline 98.688828 \end{array}$$

(b)
$$\begin{array}{r} 0.0547 \\ \times 3.6 \\ \hline 3282 \\ 1641 \\ \hline 0.19692 \end{array}$$

(c)
$$\begin{array}{r} 7.38 \\ \times 0.004 \\ \hline 0.02952 \end{array}$$

(d)
$$\begin{array}{r} 0.24 \\ \times 0.03 \\ \hline 0.0072 \end{array}$$

Multiplication by powers of 10 presents a special case. Study the operations in Example Five.

Example Five

(a)
$$\begin{array}{r} 25.13 \\ \times 10 \\ \hline 251.30 \end{array}$$

(b)
$$\begin{array}{r} 65.8 \\ \times 100 \\ \hline 6,580.0 \end{array}$$

(c)
$$\begin{array}{r} 78 \\ \times 100 \\ \hline 7,800 \end{array}$$

(d)
$$\begin{array}{r} 3.9471 \\ \times \ 1,000 \\ \hline 3,947.1000 \end{array}$$

Observe that each product contains the same digits as the multiplicand (along with some zeros appended) and that each decimal point has been moved to the right the same number of places as there were zeros in the power of 10. By applying this information, students should never actually have to multiply by a power of 10. Instead they should obtain the product simply by moving the decimal point as many places to the right as there are zeros in the power of 10. This is shown in Example Six.

Example Six

(a) $25.13 \times 10 = 25{\times}1.3$

$25.13 \times 10 = 251.3$

(b) $65.8 \times 100 = 65{\times}80.$

$65.8 \times 100 = 6,580$

(c) $78 \times 100 = 78{\times}00.$

$78 \times 100 = 7,800$

(d) $3.9471 \times 1,000 = 3{\times}947.1$

$3.9471 \times 1,000 = 3,947.1$

Division

Decimal numbers in a division problem are identified by the terms previously learned:

$$\text{Divisor} \quad 1.5 \overline{)7.95} \quad \begin{array}{l}5.3 \quad \text{Quotient}\\ \text{Dividend}\end{array}$$

The basic operation of division is performed in the same manner for decimal numbers as for whole numbers. The decimal points do not affect the division process itself, but only the location of the decimal point in the quotient. In order to understand how the decimal points are handled, consider the following example:

$$
\begin{array}{r}
51 \\
3.02 \overline{)15.402} \\
15\ 10 \\
\hline
302 \\
302 \\
\hline
\end{array}
$$

Notice that this division is approximately $3\overline{)15}$; therefore, the quotient must be approximately 5. This indicates the decimal point in the quotient must be located after the 5.

$$
\begin{array}{r}
5.1 \\
3.02 \overline{)15.402} \\
15\ 10 \\
\hline
302 \\
302 \\
\hline
\end{array}
$$

It would be possible to position the decimal point in every quotient by first estimating the result and then placing the decimal point accordingly. However, this requires additional time and effort; hence, some quick, easy method for determining the correct location of the quotient decimal is necessary. The student is no doubt familiar with the method commonly used to position the decimal quickly; that is, to "move the decimal point to the end of the divisor and move the decimal in the dividend the same number of places." Let us see why this procedure is permissible.

It was observed that the decimal point of the quotient is always located directly above the decimal point of the dividend if the divisor is a whole number. For example,

```
     2 13
12 | 25.56
    24
    ——
    15
    12
    ——
    36
    36
    ——
```

Since this problem is approximately $12\overline{)25}$, the result must be approximately 2. Thus, the decimal point of the quotient should be located directly above the decimal point in the operation:

```
       2.13
12 | 25.56
    24
    ——
    15
    12
    ——
    36
    36
    ——
```

Thus, the student knows exactly where the decimal point belongs if the divisor is a whole number. With this in mind, let us apply three familiar principles—namely, that a fraction is an indicated division; that any number over itself equals 1 $\left(\dfrac{x}{x}=1\right)$; and that multiplying any number by 1 equals that same number $(x \cdot 1 = x)$. Now suppose that we have the division problem $3.2\overline{)9.28}$. This is the division indicated by the fraction $\frac{9.28}{3.2}$. Then,

$$\frac{9.28}{3.2} = \frac{9.28}{3.2} \times 1$$

$$= \frac{9.28}{3.2} \times \frac{10}{10}$$

$$\frac{9.28}{3.2} = \frac{92.8}{32}$$

Thus the divisions indicated by each fraction are equal; or

$$3.2\overline{)9.28} = 32\overline{)92.8}$$

But we know the correct location for the decimal point when dividing by a whole number:

$$= 32 \overline{\smash{\big)}\, 92.8} \atop \begin{array}{r} 2.9 \\ \hline \end{array}$$

$$
\begin{array}{r}
2.9 \\
32 \overline{\smash{)}92.8} \\
\underline{64} \\
28\ 8 \\
\underline{28\ 8}
\end{array}
$$

Therefore, the other quotient must also be 2.9:

$$
\begin{array}{r}
2.9 \\
3.2 \overline{\smash{)}9.28}
\end{array}
=
\begin{array}{r}
2.9 \\
32 \overline{\smash{)}92.8}
\end{array}
$$

$$
\begin{array}{r}
6\ 4 \\
\hline
2\ 88 \\
2\ 88
\end{array}
$$

Thus, we can always position the decimal easily by "making the divisor a whole number," so to speak. But when we "move the decimal point to the end of the divisor and move the decimal point in the dividend a corresponding number of places," we are, in effect, multiplying by 1, which does not change the value. Stated differently, moving both decimals one place to the right is the same as multiplying a fraction by $\frac{10}{10}$; moving the decimals two places is equivalent to multiplying by $\frac{100}{100}$; moving the decimals three digits is equivalent to multiplying by $\frac{1,000}{1,000}$; and so forth.

Having determined why it is permissible to "move the decimal points," let us now consider some special cases. The decimal point in a dividend must often be moved more places to the right than there are digits. In this case, the student must append zeros to the dividend in order to fill in the required number of places. (Suppose that the decimal point in the number 14.3 must be moved three places. This is the same as multiplying 14.3 times 1,000; so, $14.3\underset{\smile}{}. = 14,300$.) If the dividend is a whole number, the student obviously must first insert a decimal point before moving it to the right. (For example, if a divisor must be multiplied by 10 to become a whole number and the dividend is 17, then 17 must also be multiplied by 10. That is, the decimal point must be moved one place to the right: $17 \times 10 = 17. \times 10 = 17.\underset{\smile}{}= 170$.)

It has been pointed out that appending zeros to the right of a decimal fraction does not change its value. (That is, $0.52 = 0.520 = 0.5200 = 0.52000$, etc.) When a division problem does not terminate (or end) within the number of digits contained in the dividend, the operation may be continued by appending zeros to the dividend. The process may be continued until the quotient terminates or until it contains as many decimal places as required.

Once the decimal point has been located in the quotient, each succeeding place must contain a digit. If normal division skips some of the first decimal places, these places must be held by zeros. (This procedure is similar to that in multiplication, when zeros must be inserted after the decimal point in order to complete the required number of decimal places.)

Example Seven shows how these procedures apply.

Example Seven

(a) $3.02 \overline{\smash{\big)}15.402.}$

$$
\begin{array}{r}
5.1 \\
3.02\,\overline{\smash{\big)}15.40\,2} \\
15\ 10 \\
\hline
30\ 2 \\
30\ 2 \\
\hline
\end{array}
$$

(b) $4.725 \overline{\smash{\big)}37.8.}$

$$
\begin{array}{r}
8. = 8 \\
4.725\,\overline{\smash{\big)}37.800.} \\
37\ 800 \\
\hline
\end{array}
$$

(c) $0.72 \overline{\smash{\big)}36.}$

$$
\begin{array}{r}
50 \\
0.72\,\overline{\smash{\big)}36.00} \\
36\ 0 \\
\hline
0 \\
0 \\
\hline
\end{array}
$$

(d) $6.4 \overline{\smash{\big)}0.3968.}$

$$
\begin{array}{r}
.062 \\
6.4\,\overline{\smash{\big)}0.3.968} \\
3\ 84 \\
\hline
128 \\
128 \\
\hline
\end{array}
$$

A special case develops when the divisor of a problem is a power of 10 (Example Eight).

Example Eight

(a) $10 \overline{\smash{\big)}13.6.}$

$$
\begin{array}{r}
1.36 \\
10\,\overline{\smash{\big)}13.60} \\
10 \\
\hline
3\ 6 \\
3\ 0 \\
\hline
60 \\
60 \\
\hline
\end{array}
$$

(b) $100 \overline{\smash{\big)}245.3}$

$$
\begin{array}{r}
2.453 \\
100\,\overline{\smash{\big)}245.300} \\
200 \\
\hline
45\ 3 \\
40\ 0 \\
\hline
5\ 30 \\
5\ 00 \\
\hline
300 \\
300 \\
\hline
\end{array}
$$

(c) $100\,\overline{)7.31}$

$$
\begin{array}{r}
.0731 \\
100\,\overline{)7.3100} \\
7\ 00 \\
\hline
310 \\
300 \\
\hline
100 \\
100 \\
\hline
\end{array}
$$

(d) $1{,}000\,\overline{)629.}$

$$
\begin{array}{r}
.629 \\
1{,}000\,\overline{)629.000} \\
600\ 0 \\
\hline
29\ 00 \\
20\ 00 \\
\hline
9\ 000 \\
9\ 000 \\
\hline
\end{array}
$$

In each operation directly above, the quotient contains the same digits as the dividend, but the decimal point is moved to the left the same number of places as there were zeros in the divisor. Knowing this, students should never actually have to perform a division by a power of 10. Rather, they should obtain the answer simply by moving the decimal point to the left. This is shown in Example Nine.

Example Nine

(a) $13.6 \div 10 = 1.3{\times}6$

$13.6 \div 10 = 1.36$

(b) $245.3 \div 100 = 2.45{\times}3$

$245.3 \div 100 = 2.453$

(c) $7.31 \div 100 = .{\_}7{\times}31$

$7.31 \div 100 = 0.0731$

(d) $629 \div 1{,}000 = .629$

$629 \div 1{,}000 = 0.629$

NOTE: Students often confuse multiplication and division by powers of 10 and forget which way to move the decimal point. If this happens, the student can quickly determine the correct direction by making up an example using small numbers. For example, $4 \times 10 = 40$ (that is, $4.0 \times 10 = 40$). The decimal point of the 4 moved to the right; therefore, the decimal point moves toward the right for all multiplication by powers of 10. Hence, the decimal point obviously moves to the left for division.

SECTION 4 *Problems*

Express each of the properties requested, using the variables or numbers indicated. Verify the properties when numbers are used.

1. (a) Commutative property of addition, using v and w.
   (b) Commutative property of addition, using 8.73 and 9.48.
   (c) Associative property of addition, using f, g, and h.

(d) Associative property of addition, using 0.27, 0.55, and 0.84.

(e) Commutative property of multiplication, using s and t.

(f) Commutative property of multiplication, using 0.7 and 0.8.

(g) Associative property of multiplication, using p, q, and r.

(h) Associative property of multiplication, using 0.4, 0.7, and 0.2.

(i) Distributive property, using k, l, and m.

(j) Distributive property, using 0.3, 0.5, and 0.7.

2. (a) Commutative property of addition, using m and n.

(b) Commutative property of addition, using 3.75 and 4.18.

(c) Associative property of addition, using g, h, and k.

(d) Associative property of addition, using 2.7, 0.4, and 1.5.

(e) Commutative property of multiplication, using u and v.

(f) Commutative property of multiplication, using 0.6 and 0.3.

(g) Associative property of multiplication, using d, e, and f.

(h) Associative property of multiplication, using 0.9, 0.4, and 0.2.

(i) Distributive property, using x, y, and z.

(j) Distributive property, using 0.2, 0.5, and 0.8.

3. In the number 2,738.14596, identify the place value associated with each of the following digits.

(a) 1   (b) 2   (c) 3

(d) 4   (e) 5   (f) 6

(g) 7   (h) 8   (i) 9

4. Write in words the values of the following numbers.

(a) 0.368   (b) 0.08   (c) 0.075

(d) 0.2066   (e) 18.8   (f) 76.63

(g) 300.708   (h) 4.0016

5. Convert the following common fractions (and mixed numbers) to their decimal fraction equivalents.

(a) $\frac{4}{5}$ (b) $\frac{3}{4}$ (c) $\frac{12}{25}$ (d) $\frac{13}{20}$ (e) $\frac{27}{40}$

(f) $\frac{39}{250}$ (g) $\frac{7}{8}$ (h) $\frac{4}{7}$ (i) $\frac{11}{16}$ (j) $\frac{7}{12}$

(k) $\frac{5}{18}$ (l) $\frac{19}{24}$ (m) $\frac{13}{8}$ (n) $\frac{153}{25}$ (o) $\frac{29}{6}$

(p) $6\frac{5}{9}$ (q) $18\frac{4}{11}$ (r) $3\frac{103}{125}$

6. Find the common fraction equivalent to each of the following decimals.

(a) 0.72   (b) 0.4   (c) 0.375   (d) 0.35   (e) 0.424

(f) 0.06   (g) 0.2575   (h) $0.14\frac{2}{7}$ (i) $0.63\frac{7}{11}$ (j) $0.08\frac{1}{3}$

(k) $0.27\frac{7}{9}$ (l) $0.45\frac{5}{6}$

7. Multiply or divide, as indicated, by moving the decimal points.

(a) $153.8 \div 10$ (b) 2.479×100 (c) $366.52 \div 1{,}000$

(d) $403.81 \div 100$ (e) $0.7116 \times 1{,}000$ (f) $43 \div 10$

(g) 10.45×10 (h) $6.913 \div 100$ (i) 1.4×100

(j) $7.206 \div 1,000$ (k) $216 \times 1,000$ (l) $0.822 \div 100$

(m) $67.8 \times 10,000$ (n) $0.02 \div 100$ (o) $42.5 \div 10,000$

8. Add. [Arrange problems (j)–(m) in columns before adding.]

(a)	(b)	(c)	(d)	(e)
3.85	0.455	0.2676	12.371	475.821
7.09	0.937	0.4395	17.859	795.044
5.53	0.246	0.8479	23.076	608.149
8.76	0.118	0.6071	38.944	597.624

(f)	(g)	(h)	(i)
17.931	0.92	5.6	15.79
4.09	59.6	128	139.9
124.8	7.483	7.79	46.432
0.796	385.2	13.855	5.91
38.5	16.793	0.738	347.8
0.005	154.87	358.68	269.917

(j) $127.9 + 0.485 + 16.76 + 145.269 + 7.382 + 119.65$

(k) $45.18 + 7.934 + 318.6 + 275 + 8.55 + 139.7$

(l) $6.791 + 403.84 + 25.633 + 381.069 + 0.648 + 57.29$

(m) $93.711 + 253 + 7.09 + 76.6 + 125.27 + 208.719$

9. Subtract. [Arrange problems (n)–(q) in columns before subtracting.]

(a)	(b)	(c)	(d)	(e)
238.85	6.242	26.377	538.402	78.1164
72.96	3.487	9.493	246.684	49.3208

(f)	(g)	(h)	(i)	(j)
36.008	540.703	17.459	62.5008	156.76
21.129	78.428	13.78	3.091	87.081

(k)	(l)	(m)
207.4	345.6	85
33.62	87.244	26.407

(n) $36.4 - 8.59$ (o) $238 - 43.45$

(p) $501.4 - 70.604$ (q) $6.3 - 0.7115$

10. Multiply.

(a)	(b)	(c)	(d)	(e)
4.73	15.8	7.64	324.9	0.563
7.6	6.4	0.82	0.075	5.41

(f)	(g)	(h)	(i)	(j)
0.324	0.148	0.0316	0.078	0.0138
0.26	0.62	2.47	0.016	0.43

11. Divide. (When quotients are not exact whole numbers, follow the procedure recommended in this section for changing fractions to decimals.)

(a) $6.45\overline{)83.85}$ (b) $14.6\overline{)68.62}$ (c) $0.378\overline{)5.9346}$

(d) $0.962\overline{)0.51948}$ (e) $5.83\overline{)0.41976}$ (f) $0.349\overline{)0.09423}$

(g) $17.2\overline{)0.9976}$ (h) $0.4678\overline{)0.0014034}$ (i) $7.125\overline{)342}$

(j) $3.925\overline{)62.8}$ (k) $36.56\overline{)45.7}$ (l) $0.0625\overline{)23.5}$

(m) $71.4\overline{)358.785}$ (n) $6.24\overline{)14.84}$ (o) $0.838\overline{)28.52}$

(p) $3.741\overline{)16.8}$

APPENDIX A *Glossary*

Addend. Any of the numbers being combined in addition. (Example: If $2+3=5$, then 2 and 3 are addends.)

Associative property. Pertains to the grouping of three numbers for addition or multiplication; states that the result will be the same regardless of which two numbers are added (or multiplied) first. [Examples: $(a+b)+c = a+(b+c)$ for addition; $(a \cdot b)c = a(b \cdot c)$ for multiplication.]

Common fraction. An indicated division, using a horizontal line. (Examples: $\frac{3}{5}$ or $\frac{7}{4}$.)

Commutative property. Pertains to the order of two numbers for addition or multiplication; states that the result will be the same regardless of which number is taken first. (Examples: $a+b = b+a$ for addition; $a \cdot b = b \cdot a$ for multiplication.)

Counting numbers. (See "Natural numbers.")

Decimal fraction. An abbreviated fraction whose denominator is a certain power of 10 indicated by the location of a dot called the decimal point. (Example: 0.37 means $\frac{37}{100}$.)

Decimal notation. The system used to denote decimal fractions.

Denominator. The number below the division line of a common fraction. (Example: The denominator of $\frac{3}{5}$ is 5.)

Difference. The result in a subtraction operation.

Digit. Any of the 10 characters 0–9 with which decimal (or base 10) numbers are formed.

Distributive property. States that the product of the sum of two numbers equals the sum of the individual products; that is, $a(b+c) = ab + ac$.

Dividend. In a division operation, the number that is being divided: Dividend ÷ Divisor = Quotient.

Divisor. In a division operation, the number that divides into another. (Example: In $4\overline{)12}$ with quotient 3, the divisor is 4.)

Exponent. A superscript that indicates how many times another number, called the base, should be written for repeated multiplication times itself. (Example: The exponent 4 denotes that $10^4 = 10 \cdot 10 \cdot 10 \cdot 10 = 10,000$.)

Factor. Any number (multiplicand or multiplier) used in multiplication.

Fraction. (See "Common fraction.")

Higher terms. An equivalent fraction with a larger denominator. (Example: $\frac{3}{5}$ may be expressed in higher terms as $\frac{9}{15}$.)

Improper fraction. A common fraction whose numerator is equal to or larger than the denominator. (Examples: $\frac{7}{7}$ or $\frac{15}{8}$.)

Integer. Any number, positive or negative, that can be expressed without a decimal or fraction. (Example: Any number from the set $\{..., -3, -2, -1, 0, 1, 2, 3, ...\}$.)

Least common denominator. The smallest number (denominator) into which any given denominators will all divide.

Minuend. In a subtraction operation, the number from which another number is subtracted. (Example: Minuend − Subtrahend = Difference.)

Mixed number. A number composed of a whole number and a fraction. (Example: $12\frac{3}{7}$.)

Multiplicand. The first (or top) factor in a multiplication operation. (For Example: Multiplicand × Multiplier = Product.)

Multiplier. The second (or bottom) factor in a multiplication operation. (Example: In 8×5, the multiplier is 5.)

Natural (or counting) number. Any number that may be used in counting objects. (Example: Any number from the set $\{1, 2, 3, 4, \ldots\}$.)

Numerator. The number above the division line of a common fraction. (Example: The numerator of $\dfrac{4}{9}$ is 4.)

Operation. Any of the arithmetic processes of addition, subtraction, multiplication, or division.

Place value. The value associated with a digit because of its position in a whole number or decimal number.

Prime number. A number (larger than 1) that can be evenly divided only by itself and 1.

Product. The result in a multiplication operation.

Proper fraction. A fraction whose numerator is smaller than the denominator. (Example: $\frac{4}{5}$.)

Quotient. The result in a division operation.

Rational number. Any number that can be expressed as a common fraction (the quotient of two integers).

Reciprocal (of a fraction). A fraction formed by interchanging the original numerator and denominator. (Example: The reciprocal of $\frac{5}{8}$ is $\frac{8}{5}$.)

Subtrahend. In a subtraction operation, the number being subtracted from another. (Example: In $10 - 7 = 3$, the subtrahend is 7.)

Sum. The result in an addition operation.

Whole number. Any number zero or larger which can be expressed without a decimal or fraction. (Example: Any number from the set $\{0, 1, 2, 3, 4, \ldots\}$.)

APPENDIX B

The Metric System

APPENDIX B OBJECTIVES

Upon completing Appendix B, the student will be able to:

1. Define and use correctly the terminology in each topic.

2. Given any multiple of a metric unit,
   a. Name its single equivalent metric unit; or
   b. Convert the given measurement to its equivalent measurement in another given metric unit. *(Example 1; Problems 1–4)*

3. Given a metric measurement, find its equivalent in a given U.S. unit. *(Example 2; Problems 5, 6, 9, 10, 15, 16)*

4. Given a U.S. measurement, determine its equivalent in a given metric unit. *(Example 3; Problems 7–14)*

B

Its development begun in 1790 by the French Academy of Sciences, the **metric system** has now been adopted by all major nations except the U.S., and adoption here is anticipated in the near future. Already, the metric system has long been standard in U.S. scientific and engineering fields. The basic unit of the system—the meter— was derived by calculation (erroneously, it was later discovered) to be $\frac{1}{10,000,000}$ of the distance from the North Pole to the equator. The superior advantage of this system is that each unit is 10 times the size of the next smaller unit, thus greatly simplifying conversions from one unit to another.

The metric system was established with the **meter** as the basic unit for length, the **gram** as the basic unit for weight, and the **liter** as the basic unit for liquid volume or capacity. Prefixes before each basic unit are used to name the other units of the system and to identify its multiple of the basic unit. The principal prefixes and indicated multiples of the basic unit are as follows:

Metric Prefix	Multiple of Basic Unit	Metric Prefix	Multiple of Basic Unit
deca	10	**deci**	$\frac{1}{10}$ or 0.1
hecto	100	**centi**	$\frac{1}{100}$ or 0.01
kilo	1000	**milli**	$\frac{1}{1000}$ or 0.001
mega	1 000 000	**micro**	$\frac{1}{1\,000\,000}$ or 0.000001

Using the information in the table, we see that

$$1 \; kilo\text{meter} = 1000 \text{ meters}$$

$$1 \; deca\text{liter} = 10 \text{ liters}$$

$$1 \; centi\text{gram} = 0.01 \text{ gram}$$

and so on. Figure 57, which is similar to a place-value table for numbers, will help identify the power of 10 associated with each prefix.

FIGURE 57

For example,   (a)   1 decameter   = 10 meters;

similarly,   (b)   1 gram   = 100 centigrams;

or   (c)   1 hectoliter   = 1000 deciliters.

Conversely,   (a)   1 liter   = 0.1 decaliter;

similarly,   (b)   1 centimeter   = 0.01 meter;

or   (c)   1 decigram   = 0.001 hectogram.

Example One   Identify the unit name or convert the given metric measurements as indicated.
(a) 1000 meters = 1 ____   (b) 0.1 liter = 1 ____
(c) 1 hectogram = ? grams   (d) 1 centigram = ? gram
(e) 12.5 decaliters = ? liters

Solution   Using the basic units and prefix definitions given above:
(a) 1000 meters = 1 kilometer   (b) 0.1 liter = 1 deciliter
(c) 1 hectogram = 100 grams   (d) 1 centigram = 0.01 gram

Conversions are best performed by first identifying the units' relationship and then multiplying by the given number of units.

(e)   1 decaliter =   10 liters
     ×12.5   ×12.5
     ————————   ————————
    12.5 decaliters =   125 liters

After you have used the metric system for a while, conversions such as those above can be done mentally. Not all the metric units will be used equally; certain units will be more convenient for certain types of measurements and will therefore be used more. Most conversions will simply be to change a measurement to the basic unit or to a smaller number, as in our example. Actually measuring things with a metric instrument will be no more difficult than measuring with any ordinary instrument.

The principal obstacle when the metric system is first adopted is to develop a mental picture of the quantities that metric measures represent. By rough approximation, 1 meter is slightly longer than 1 yard; 1 liter is nearly equivalent to 1 quart. The gram is so small that it is used to weigh only small amounts, such as food items. Larger amounts are weighed using the kilogram, which is somewhat more than 2 pounds. Distances are expressed in kilometers, each of which is about $\frac{5}{8}$ mile.

Example Two Convert the following metric measurements to their U.S. equivalents, using the equivalents given in Table B-1.
(a) 10 meters = ? feet
(b) 5 liters = ? quarts
(c) 200 grams = ? ounces
(d) 500 kilograms = ? pounds

Solution

(a)
$$1 \text{ meter} = 3.28 \text{ feet}$$
$$\underline{\times 10 \qquad\qquad \times 10}$$
$$10 \text{ meters} = 32.8 \text{ feet}$$

(b)
$$1 \text{ liter} = 1.06 \text{ quarts}$$
$$\underline{\times 5 \qquad\qquad \times 5}$$
$$5 \text{ liters} = 5.3 \text{ quarts}$$

(c)
$$1 \text{ gram} = 0.035 \text{ ounce}$$
$$\underline{\times 200 \qquad\quad \times 200}$$
$$200 \text{ grams} = 7.0 \text{ ounces}$$

(d)
$$1 \text{ kilogram} = 2.20 \text{ pounds}$$
$$\underline{\times 500 \qquad\qquad \times 500}$$
$$500 \text{ kilograms} = 1,100 \text{ pounds}$$

TABLE B-1: METRIC MEASURES WITH U.S. EQUIVALENTS

Length	Weight	Liquid Capacity
1 millimeter = 0.039 inch	1 gram[a] = 0.035 ounce	1 liter[a] = 33.8 ounces
1 centimeter = 0.394 inch	1 kilogram = 2.20 pounds	= 2.11 pints
1 decimeter = 3.94 inches		= 1.06 quarts
1 meter = 39.37 inches		= 0.264 gallon
= 3.28 feet		
= 1.09 yards		
1 kilometer = 0.621 mile		

[a] One gram is defined as the weight of 1 cubic centimeter of pure water at 4° Celsius. One liter is defined as the capacity of a cube that is 1 decimeter long on each edge.

Example Three Use the equivalents given in Table B-2 to find the metric equivalents of the following U.S. measurements.
(a) 50 yards = ? meters
(b) 4 gallons = ? liters
(c) 6 inches = ? centimeters
(d) 150 pounds = ? kilograms

Solution

(a)
$$1 \text{ yard } = 0.914 \text{ meter}$$
$$\times 50 \qquad \times 50$$
$$50 \text{ yards} = 45.7 \text{ meters}$$

(b)
$$1 \text{ gallon } = 3.79 \text{ liters}$$
$$\times 4 \qquad \times 4$$
$$4 \text{ gallons} = 15.2 \text{ liters}$$

(c)
$$1 \text{ inch } = 2.54 \text{ centimeters}$$
$$\times 6 \qquad \times 6$$
$$6 \text{ inches} = 15.2 \text{ centimeters}$$

(d)
$$1 \text{ pound} = 0.454$$
$$\times 150 \qquad \times 150$$
$$150 \text{ pounds} = 68.1 \text{ kilograms}$$

TABLE B-2: U.S. MEASURES WITH METRIC EQUIVALENTS

Length	Weight	Liquid Capacity
1 inch = 2.54 centimeters	1 ounce = 28.4 grams	1 ounce = 0.030 liter
1 foot = 0.305 meter	1 pound = 454 grams	1 pint = 0.473 liter
1 yard = 0.914 meter	= 0.454 kilogram	1 quart = 0.946 liter
1 mile = 1.61 kilometers		1 gallon = 3.79 liters

Metric quantities will develop meaning to you as you use them, including the **Celsius** (or **centigrade**) temperature scale. You will learn, for example, that 10° C is a cool day, that 20°–25° C is the comfortable indoor range, and that 35° C is a hot summer day, as shown below:

$$32° \text{F} = 0°\text{C} \qquad 68° \text{F} = 20° \text{C} \qquad 95° \text{F} = 35° \text{C}$$
$$50° \text{F} = 10° \text{C} \qquad 77° \text{F} = 25° \text{C} \qquad 212° \text{F} = 100° \text{C}$$

Once you are accustomed to the metric system, the present U.S. system of weights and measures will seem as inefficient as any foreign monetary system that is not based on dollars and 100 cents.

APPENDIX B *Problems*

Name each metric unit or indicate the multiple of each given unit.

1. (a) 1 kilogram = ? grams
   (b) 10 meters = 1 __?__
   (c) 0.01 liter = 1 __?__
   (d) 1 millimeter = ? meter
   (e) 1 meter = ? kilometer
   (f) 0.01 hectoliter = 1 __?__
   (g) 10 decigrams = 1 __?__
   (h) 1 liter = ? centiliters
   (i) 1 hectometer = ? decameters

(j) 1000 centigrams = 1 ___?___
(k) 0.01 deciliter = 1 ___?___
(l) 1 hectoliter = ? kiloliters

2. (a) 100 liters = 1 ___?___
    (b) 1 kilometer = ? meters
    (c) 1 deciliter = ? liters
    (d) 0.001 gram = 1 ___?___
    (e) 0.01 hectometer = 1 ___?___
    (f) 1 gram = ? decagrams
    (g) 1 liter = ? deciliters
    (h) 1000 milligrams = 1 ___?___
    (i) 0.001 hectometer = 1 ___?___
    (j) 1 deciliter = ? centiliters
    (k) 1 millimeter = ? centimeters
    (l) 100 decagrams = 1 ___?___

Convert the following metric measurements as indicated.

3. (a) 1.5 hectometers = ? meters
    (b) 125 centimeters = ? meters
    (c) 36 decagrams = ? grams
    (d) 2137 milliliters = ? liters
    (e) 1475 grams = ? kilograms
    (f) 17.4 grams = ? centigrams
    (g) 24 liters = ? decaliters
    (h) 50 meters = ? millimeters
    (i) 75 hectometers = ? kilometers
    (j) 362 grams = ? kilograms

4. (a) 52 kiloliters = ? liters
    (b) 48 decimeters = ? meters
    (c) 6.8 hectograms = ? grams
    (d) 312 centigrams = ? grams
    (e) 12 meters = ? decameters
    (f) 2.5 liters = ? milliliters
    (g) 2600 grams = ? hectograms
    (h) 60 meters = ? decimeters
    (i) 58 millimeters = ? centimeters
    (j) 472 grams = ? kilograms

Determine the U.S. equivalent of the following metric measurements. (Note: *Recall*

that a product cannot have more significant digits than do the factors used. Assume that the whole numbers given are correct for four significant digits.)

5. (a) 10 centimeters = ? inches
    (b) 3 meters = ? inches
    (c) 4 kilograms = ? pounds
    (d) 6 liters = ? ounces
    (e) 20 meters = ? yards
    (f) 5 decimeters = ? inches
    (g) 8 liters = ? quarts
    (h) 50 kilometers = ? miles

6. (a) 600 grams = ? ounces
    (b) 80 millimeters = ? inches
    (c) 50 meters = ? feet
    (d) 7 liters = ? pints
    (e) 40 kilometers = ? miles
    (f) 10 meters = ? yards
    (g) 5 centimeters = ? inches
    (h) 3 liters = ? quarts

Find the metric equivalent of the following U.S. measurements. (Assume that the whole numbers given contain three significant digits, and write products in correct number of significant digits.)

7. (a) 8 inches = ? centimeters
    (b) 10 miles = ? kilometers
    (c) 8 ounces = ? grams
    (d) 6 quarts = ? liters
    (e) 3 pounds = ? grams
    (f) 20 ounces = ? liters
    (g) 6 feet = ? meters
    (h) 50 gallons = ? liters

8. (a) 50 yards = ? meters
    (b) 90 pounds = ? kilograms
    (c) 30 inches = ? centimeters
    (d) 10 quarts = ? liters
    (e) 200 miles = ? kilometers
    (f) 4 ounces = ? grams

(g) 4 gallons = ? liters

(h) 6 pints = ? liters

Find each measurement below as indicated.

9. Track sprinters run the 100-yard dash, while swimmers compete in 100-meter races. (a) How many meters is 100 yards? (b) How many yards is 100 meters? (c) Which race is longer and by how many meters?

10. An American-made car has a 120-inch wheel base, and a European car has a 250-centimeter wheel base. (a) How many centimeters is the wheel base of the American car? (b) How many inches is the European car? (c) Which wheel base is longer and by how many centimeters?

11. Bill Gray is 5 feet 10 inches tall and weighs 170 pounds. Express his (a) height in centimeters and (b) weight in kilograms. (*Hint*: First convert his height to inches.)

12. Kathy Ramsey is 5 feet 4 inches tall and weighs 100 pounds. Express her (a) height in centimeters and (b) weight in kilograms.

13. The United States is approximately 3,000 miles wide. The earth is approximately 25,000 miles in circumference. Express each distance in kilometers.

14. Tasty Food Processors market a pancake mix with a net weight of 40 ounces and a pancake syrup that contains 30 fluid (liquid) ounces. What metric equivalents should the labels contain for (a) the mix in grams and (b) the syrup in liters?

15. The Corner Delicatessen sells a Danish ham weighing 1.5 kilograms and a package of imported cheese weighing 400 grams. What is the U.S. equivalent of (a) the ham in pounds and (b) the cheese in ounces?

16. The gas tank of a European car holds 50 liters, and 4 liters of oil are required in the motor. What is the U.S. equivalent of (a) the gas tank capacity in gallons and (b) the oil in quarts?

APPENDIX B *Glossary*

Celsius (centigrade). Metric temperature scale using 100° for the range from the freezing point of water (0° C) to the boiling point (100° C).

Centi. Prefix indicating 0.01 of a basic metric unit. (Example: 1 centimeter = 0.01 meter.)

Centigrade. (See "Celsius.")

Deca. Prefix indicating 10 times a basic metric unit. (Example: 1 decaliter = 10 liters.)

Deci. Prefix indicating 0.1 of a basic metric unit. (Example: 1 decigram = 0.1 gram.)

Gram. Basic metric unit of weight; defined as the weight of 1 cubic centimeter of pure water at 4° C.

Hecto. Prefix indicating 100 times a basic metric unit. (Example: 1 hectometer = 100 meters.)

Kilo. Prefix indicating 1000 times a basic metric unit. (Example: 1 kilogram = 1000 grams.)

Liter. Basic metric unit of liquid volume (or capacity); defined as the capacity of a cube that is 1 decimeter long on each edge.

Mega. Prefix indicating 1 million times a basic metric unit.

Meter. Basic metric unit of length; originally defined (erroneously) as 1 ten-millionth of a quadrant ($\frac{1}{4}$) of the earth's circumference; now officially defined as a multiple of a certain wavelength of krypton 86, a rare gas.

Metric system. Decimal system of weights and

measures, where each unit is 10 times the size of the next smaller unit. Its basic units are the meter (length), the gram (weight), and the liter (capacity).

Micro. Prefix indicating 1 millionth of a basic metric unit.

Milli. Prefix indicating 0.001 of a basic metric unit. (Example: 1 milliliter = 0.001 liter.)

Metric Talk

When the United States goes to the metric system, perhaps some of our favorite sayings will have to be changed thus:

- Traffic was *2.54 centimetering* along the freeway.

- If hit me like *907 kilograms* of bricks.

- Cried *3.79 liters* of tears.

- A miss is as good as *1.61 kilometers*.

- A *decigram* of salt.

- Beat him within *2.54 centimeters* of his life.

- All wool and *91.4 centimeters* wide.

- Give him *2.54 centimeters* and he takes *1.61 kilometers*.

- Give him *454 grams* of flesh.

- Missed it by *1.61 country kilometers*.

APPENDIX C

Tables

LIST OF TABLES

TABLE I: SALES TAX INTERVALS

SALES MADE WITHIN STATE		SALES MADE WITHIN CITY	
Amount of Sale or Interval	Tax	Amount of Sale or Interval	Tax
Per whole dollar	3¢	Per whole dollar	4¢
Additional cents:		Additional cents:	
$.00–$.09	0	$.00–$.09	0
.10– .39	1¢	.10– .39	1¢
.40– .69	2¢	.40– .49	2¢
.70– .99	3¢	.50– .69	3¢
		.70– .99	4¢

TABLE II: ANNUAL FIRE INSURANCE PREMIUMS FOR DWELLINGS

Amount of Insurance	STRUCTURE CLASS				CONTENTS CLASS			
	A	B	C	D	A	B	C	D
$ 5,000	$12	$18	$25	$30	$15	$17	$29	$31
10,000	15	21	29	36	18	25	32	40
15,000	20	32	45	50	24	35	48	54
20,000	24	37	49	55	29	38	55	60
25,000	28	40	52	58	32	43	57	64

ANNUAL FIRE INSURANCE RATES FOR BUILDINGS PER $100 OF COVERAGE

Type of Construction	CLASS			
	A	B	C	D
Brick	$.15	$ .25	$ .325	$ .40
Frame	.875	1.15	1.40	1.625

TABLE III: SHORT-TERM AND CANCELLATION RATES

SHORT-TERM RATES
(INCLUDING CANCELLATIONS BY THE INSURED)

Months of Coverage	Per Cent of Annual Premium Charged	Months of Coverage	Per Cent of Annual Premium Charged
1	20%	7	75%
2	30	8	80
3	40	9	85
4	50	10	90
5	60	11	95
6	70	12	100

TABLE IV: DRIVER CLASSIFICATIONS
Multiples of Base Annual Automobile Insurance Premiums

			Pleasure; Less than 3 Miles To Work Each Way	Drives to Work, 3 to 10 Miles Each Way	Drives to Work, 10 Miles or More Each Way	Used in Business
No young operators	Only operator is female, age 30–64		.90	1.00	1.30	1.40
	One or more operators aged 65 or over		1.00	1.10	1.40	1.50
	All others		1.00	1.10	1.40	1.50
Young females	Age 16	DT[a]	1.40	1.50	1.80	1.90
		No DT	1.55	1.65	1.95	2.05
	Age 20	DT	1.05	1.15	1.45	1.55
		No DT	1.10	1.20	1.50	1.60
Young males (married)	Age 16	DT	1.60	1.70	2.00	2.10
		No DT	1.80	1.90	2.20	2.30
	Age 20	DT	1.45	1.55	1.85	1.95
		No DT	1.50	1.60	1.90	2.00
	Age 21		1.40	1.50	1.80	1.90
	Age 24		1.10	1.20	1.50	1.60
Young unmarried males (not principal operator)	Age 16	DT	2.05	2.15	2.45	2.55
		No DT	2.30	2.40	2.70	2.80
	Age 20	DT	1.60	1.70	2.00	2.10
		No DT	1.70	1.80	2.10	2.20
	Age 21		1.55	1.65	1.95	2.05
	Age 24		1.10	1.20	1.50	1.60
Young unmarried males (owner or principal operator)	Age 16	DT	2.70	2.80	3.10	3.20
		No DT	3.30	3.40	3.70	3.80
	Age 20	DT	2.55	2.65	2.95	3.05
		No DT	2.70	2.80	3.10	3.20
	Age 21		2.50	2.60	2.90	3.00
	Age 24		1.90	2.00	2.30	2.40
	Age 26		1.50	1.60	1.90	2.00
	Age 29		1.10	1.20	1.50	1.60

[a] "DT" indicates completion of a certified driver training course.

TABLE V: AUTOMOBILE LIABILITY INSURANCE AND MEDICAL PAYMENT INSURANCE
Base Annual Premiums

	BODILY INJURY				PROPERTY DAMAGE		
Coverage	*Territory* 1	*Territory* 2	*Territory* 3	*Coverage*	*Territory* 1	*Territory* 2	*Territory* 3
				$ 5,000	$33	$45	$50
10/20	$28	$37	$55	10,000	35	47	53
15/30	31	41	62	25,000	36	49	54
25/25	33	44	65	50,000	37	51	57
25/50	36	47	70	100,000	40	53	59
50/50	38	51	75				
50/100	40	53	79		MEDICAL PAYMENT		
100/100	41	54	81				
100/200	44	58	86	$1,000	$12	$13	$14
100/300	45	60	89	2,500	15	16	17
200/300	48	62	91	5,000	17	18	19
300/300	50	65	94				

TABLE VI: COMPREHENSIVE AND COLLISION INSURANCE
Base Annual Premiums

		TERRITORY 1			TERRITORY 2			TERRITORY 3		
		COMPREHENSIVE	COLLISION		COMPREHENSIVE	COLLISION		COMPREHENSIVE	COLLISION	
Model Class	*Age Group*	*Comprehensive*	*$50 Deductible*	*$100 Deductible*	*Comprehensive*	*$50 Deductible*	*$100 Deductible*	*Comprehensive*	*$50 Deductible*	*$100 Deductible*
(1)	1	$15	$ 42	$36	$19	$ 52	$40	$23	$ 60	$ 51
A–G	2, 3	12	37	33	16	46	36	18	54	45
	4	9	31	27	11	39	30	14	45	38
(3)	1	23	71	61	29	88	68	35	101	87
J–K	2, 3	19	63	55	24	78	61	28	91	78
	4	14	53	46	17	66	51	21	76	65
(4)	1	28	83	72	36	103	80	43	119	102
L–M	2, 3	24	75	64	30	93	72	35	107	92
	4	17	62	54	22	77	60	26	89	77
(5)	1	37	100	86	46	124	96	55	143	122
N–O	2, 3	30	90	77	37	111	86	45	128	110
	4	22	75	65	28	93	72	33	107	92

TABLE VII: ANNUAL LIFE INSURANCE PREMIUMS
Per $1,000 of Face Value For Male Applicants

Age Issued	Term 10-Year	Whole Life	Limited Payment 20-Year	Endowment 20-Year	Age Issued	Term 10-Year	Whole Life	Limited Payment 20-Year	Endowment 20-Year
18	$ 6.81	$14.77	$24.69	$43.82	30	7.59	19.73	31.12	51.88
20	6.88	15.46	25.59	44.95	35	8.68	23.99	35.80	56.06
22	6.95	16.12	26.53	46.16	40	10.64	28.26	40.34	61.40
24	7.05	16.82	27.53	47.44	45	14.52	33.79	46.01	68.28
25	7.10	17.22	28.06	48.10	50	22.18	40.77	53.24	76.12
26	7.18	17.67	28.63	48.80	55	32.93	51.38	64.77	—
28	7.35	18.64	29.84	50.29	60	—	59.32	70.86	—

TABLE VIII: NONFORFEITURE OPTIONS[a] ON TYPICAL LIFE INSURANCE POLICIES
Issued at Age 25

Years in Force	WHOLE LIFE				20-PAYMENT LIFE				20-YEAR ENDOWMENT			
	Cash Value	Paid-up Insurance	Ext. Term Years	Ext. Term Days	Cash Value	Paid-up Insurance	Ext. Term Years	Ext. Term Days	Cash Value	Paid-up Insurance	Ext. Term Years	Ext. Term Days
3	$ 4	$ 14	1	174	$ 27	$ 89	10	84	$ 39	$ 104	14	42
5	26	82	9	71	69	213	19	184	90	227	23	126
10	88	243	18	46	182	502	28	186	316	515	30	131
15	157	382	20	148	314	763	32	164	590	772	35	290
20	246	530	21	137	465	1,000	Life		590	1,000	Life	
40	571	822	—	—	696				1,000			

[a] The "cash value" and "paid-up insurance" nonforfeiture values are per $1,000 of life insurance coverage. The time period for "extended term insurance" applies as shown to all policies, regardless of face value.

TABLE IX: INTEREST ADJUSTMENT FACTORS FOR INTEREST[a] ADJUSTED NET COST

Years in Force	Factor
5	0.88763
10	0.80087
20	0.64580

[a] Interest at 4% compounded annually.

TABLE X: SETTLEMENT OPTIONS

Monthly Installments per $1,000 of Face Value

FIXED AMOUNT OR FIXED NUMBER OF YEARS		INCOME FOR LIFE				
		AGE WHEN ANNUITY BEGINS		Life Annuity	With 10 Years Certain	With 20 Years Certain
Years	Amount	Male	Female			
10	$9.41	40	45	$3.80	$3.76	$3.64
12	8.03	45	50	4.15	4.09	3.90
14	7.05	50	55	4.58	4.50	4.18
15	6.65	55	60	5.14	5.01	4.47
16	6.31	60	65	5.86	5.61	4.75
18	5.74	65	70	6.82	6.30	4.98
20	5.29					

TABLE XI: SOCIAL SECURITY EMPLOYEE TAX TABLE

5.85 percent employee tax deductions

Wages At least	But less than	Tax to be withheld	Wages At least	But less than	Tax to be withheld	Wages At least	But less than	Tax to be withheld	Wages At least	But less than	Tax to be withheld
$88.81	$88.98	$5.20	$99.92	$100.09	$5.85	$111.03	$111.20	$6.50	$122.14	$122.31	$7.15
88.98	89.15	5.21	100.09	100.26	5.86	111.20	111.37	6.51	122.31	122.48	7.16
89.15	89.32	5.22	100.26	100.43	5.87	111.37	111.54	6.52	122.48	122.65	7.17
89.32	89.49	5.23	100.43	100.60	5.88	111.54	111.71	6.53	122.65	122.83	7.18
89.49	89.66	5.24	100.60	100.77	5.89	111.71	111.89	6.54	122.83	123.00	7.19
89.66	89.83	5.25	100.77	100.95	5.90	111.89	112.06	6.55	123.00	123.17	7.20
89.83	90.00	5.26	100.95	101.12	5.91	112.06	112.23	6.56	123.17	123.34	7.21
90.00	90.18	5.27	101.12	101.29	5.92	112.23	112.40	6.57	123.34	123.51	7.22
90.18	90.35	5.28	101.29	101.46	5.93	112.40	112.57	6.58	123.51	123.68	7.23
90.35	90.52	5.29	101.46	101.63	5.94	112.57	112.74	6.59	123.68	123.85	7.24
90.52	90.69	5.30	101.63	101.80	5.95	112.74	112.91	6.60	123.85	124.02	7.25
90.69	90.86	5.31	101.80	101.97	5.96	112.91	113.08	6.61	124.02	124.19	7.26
90.86	91.03	5.32	101.97	102.14	5.97	113.08	113.25	6.62	124.19	124.36	7.27
91.03	91.20	5.33	102.14	102.31	5.98	113.25	113.42	6.63	124.36	124.53	7.28
91.20	91.37	5.34	102.31	102.48	5.99	113.42	113.59	6.64	124.53	124.71	7.29
91.37	91.54	5.35	102.48	102.65	6.00	113.59	113.77	6.65	124.71	124.88	7.30
91.54	91.71	5.36	102.65	102.83	6.01	113.77	113.94	6.66	124.88	125.05	7.31
91.71	91.89	5.37	102.83	103.00	6.02	113.94	114.11	6.67	125.05	125.22	7.32
91.89	92.06	5.38	103.00	103.17	6.03	114.11	114.28	6.68	125.22	125.39	7.33
92.06	92.23	5.39	103.17	103.34	6.04	114.28	114.45	6.69	125.39	125.56	7.34
92.23	92.40	5.40	103.34	103.51	6.05	114.45	114.62	6.70	125.56	125.73	7.35
92.40	92.57	5.41	103.51	103.68	6.06	114.62	114.79	6.71	125.73	125.90	7.36
92.57	92.74	5.42	103.68	103.85	6.07	114.79	114.96	6.72	125.90	126.07	7.37
92.74	92.91	5.43	103.85	104.02	6.08	114.96	115.13	6.73	126.07	126.24	7.38
92.91	93.08	5.44	104.02	104.19	6.09	115.13	115.30	6.74	126.24	126.42	7.39
93.08	93.25	5.45	104.19	104.36	6.10	115.30	115.48	6.75	126.42	126.59	7.40
93.25	93.42	5.46	104.36	104.53	6.11	115.48	115.65	6.76	126.59	126.76	7.41
93.42	93.59	5.47	104.53	104.71	6.12	115.65	115.82	6.77	126.76	126.93	7.42
93.59	93.77	5.48	104.71	104.88	6.13	115.82	115.99	6.78	126.93	127.10	7.43
93.77	93.94	5.49	104.88	105.05	6.14	115.99	116.16	6.79	127.10	127.27	7.44
93.94	94.11	5.50	105.05	105.22	6.15	116.16	116.33	6.80	127.27	127.44	7.45
94.11	94.28	5.51	105.22	105.39	6.16	116.33	116.50	6.81	127.44	127.61	7.46
94.28	94.45	5.52	105.39	105.56	6.17	116.50	116.67	6.82	127.61	127.78	7.47
94.45	94.62	5.53	105.56	105.73	6.18	116.67	116.84	6.83	127.78	127.95	7.48
94.62	94.79	5.54	105.73	105.90	6.19	116.84	117.01	6.84	127.95	128.12	7.49
94.79	94.96	5.55	105.90	106.07	6.20	117.01	117.18	6.85	128.12	128.30	7.50
94.96	95.13	5.56	106.07	106.24	6.21	117.18	117.36	6.86	128.30	128.47	7.51
95.13	95.30	5.57	106.24	106.42	6.22	117.36	117.53	6.87	128.47	128.64	7.52
95.30	95.48	5.58	106.42	106.59	6.23	117.53	117.70	6.88	128.64	128.81	7.53
95.48	95.65	5.59	106.59	106.76	6.24	117.70	117.87	6.89	128.81	128.98	7.54
95.65	95.82	5.60	106.76	106.93	6.25	117.87	118.04	6.90	128.98	129.15	7.55
95.82	95.99	5.61	106.93	107.10	6.26	118.04	118.21	6.91	129.15	129.32	7.56
95.99	96.16	5.62	107.10	107.27	6.27	118.21	118.38	6.92	129.32	129.49	7.57
96.16	96.33	5.63	107.27	107.44	6.28	118.38	118.55	6.93	129.49	129.66	7.58
96.33	96.50	5.64	107.44	107.61	6.29	118.55	118.72	6.94	129.66	129.83	7.59
96.50	96.67	5.65	107.61	107.78	6.30	118.72	118.89	6.95	129.83	130.00	7.60
96.67	96.84	5.66	107.78	107.95	6.31	118.89	119.06	6.96	130.00	130.18	7.61
96.84	97.01	5.67	107.95	108.12	6.32	119.06	119.24	6.97	130.18	130.35	7.62
97.01	97.18	5.68	108.12	108.30	6.33	119.24	119.41	6.98	130.35	130.52	7.63
97.18	97.36	5.69	108.30	108.47	6.34	119.41	119.58	6.99	130.52	130.69	7.64
97.36	97.53	5.70	108.47	108.64	6.35	119.58	119.75	7.00	130.69	130.86	7.65
97.53	97.70	5.71	108.64	108.81	6.36	119.75	119.92	7.01	130.86	131.03	7.66
97.70	97.87	5.72	108.81	108.98	6.37	119.92	120.09	7.02	131.03	131.20	7.67
97.87	98.04	5.73	108.98	109.15	6.38	120.09	120.26	7.03	131.20	131.37	7.68
98.04	98.21	5.74	109.15	109.32	6.39	120.26	120.43	7.04	131.37	131.54	7.69
98.21	98.38	5.75	109.32	109.49	6.40	120.43	120.60	7.05	131.54	131.71	7.70
98.38	98.55	5.76	109.49	109.66	6.41	120.60	120.77	7.06	131.71	131.89	7.71
98.55	98.72	5.77	109.66	109.83	6.42	120.77	120.95	7.07	131.89	132.06	7.72
98.72	98.89	5.78	109.83	110.00	6.43	120.95	121.12	7.08	132.06	132.23	7.73
98.89	99.06	5.79	110.00	110.18	6.44	121.12	121.29	7.09	132.23	132.40	7.74
99.06	99.24	5.80	110.18	110.35	6.45	121.29	121.46	7.10	132.40	132.57	7.75
99.24	99.41	5.81	110.35	110.52	6.46	121.46	121.63	7.11	132.57	132.74	7.76
99.41	99.58	5.82	110.52	110.69	6.47	121.63	121.80	7.12	132.74	132.91	7.77
99.58	99.75	5.83	110.69	110.86	6.48	121.80	121.97	7.13	132.91	133.08	7.78
99.75	99.92	5.84	110.86	111.03	6.49	121.97	122.14	7.14	133.08	133.25	7.79

TABLE XI: SOCIAL SECURITY EMPLOYEE TAX TABLE (CONTINUED)

5.85 percent employee tax deductions

Wages		Tax to be withheld	Wages		Tax to be withheld	Wages		Tax to be withheld	Wages		Tax to be withheld
At least	But less than		At least	But less than		At least	But less than		At least	But less than	
$133.25	$133.42	$7.80	$144.36	$144.53	$8.45	$155.48	$155.65	$9.10	$166.59	$166.76	$9.75
133.42	133.59	7.81	144.53	144.71	8.46	155.65	155.82	9.11	166.76	166.93	9.76
133.59	133.77	7.82	144.71	144.88	8.47	155.82	155.99	9.12	166.93	167.10	9.77
133.77	133.94	7.83	144.88	145.05	8.48	155.99	156.16	9.13	167.10	167.27	9.78
133.94	134.11	7.84	145.05	145.22	8.49	156.16	156.33	9.14	167.27	167.44	9.79
134.11	134.28	7.85	145.22	145.39	8.50	156.33	156.50	9.15	167.44	167.61	9.80
134.28	134.45	7.86	145.39	145.56	8.51	156.50	156.67	9.16	167.61	167.78	9.81
134.45	134.62	7.87	145.56	145.73	8.52	156.67	156.84	9.17	167.78	167.95	9.82
134.62	134.79	7.88	145.73	145.90	8.53	156.84	157.01	9.18	167.95	168.12	9.83
134.79	134.96	7.89	145.90	146.07	8.54	157.01	157.18	9.19	168.12	168.30	9.84
134.96	135.13	7.90	146.07	146.24	8.55	157.18	157.36	9.20	168.30	168.47	9.85
135.13	135.30	7.91	146.24	146.42	8.56	157.36	157.53	9.21	168.47	168.64	9.86
135.30	135.48	7.92	146.42	146.59	8.57	157.53	157.70	9.22	168.64	168.81	9.87
135.48	135.65	7.93	146.59	146.76	8.58	157.70	157.87	9.23	168.81	168.98	9.88
135.65	135.82	7.94	146.76	146.93	8.59	157.87	158.04	9.24	168.98	169.15	9.89
135.82	135.99	7.95	146.93	147.10	8.60	158.04	158.21	9.25	169.15	169.32	9.90
135.99	136.16	7.96	147.10	147.27	8.61	158.21	158.38	9.26	169.32	169.49	9.91
136.16	136.33	7.97	147.27	147.44	8.62	158.38	158.55	9.27	169.49	169.66	9.92
136.33	136.50	7.98	147.44	147.61	8.63	158.55	158.72	9.28	169.66	169.83	9.93
136.50	136.67	7.99	147.61	147.78	8.64	158.72	158.89	9.29	169.83	170.00	9.94
136.67	136.84	8.00	147.78	147.95	8.65	158.89	159.06	9.30	170.00	170.18	9.95
136.84	137.01	8.01	147.95	148.12	8.66	159.06	159.24	9.31	170.18	170.35	9.96
137.01	137.18	8.02	148.12	148.30	8.67	159.24	159.41	9.32	170.35	170.52	9.97
137.18	137.36	8.03	148.30	148.47	8.68	159.41	159.58	9.33	170.52	170.69	9.98
137.36	137.53	8.04	148.47	148.64	8.69	159.58	159.75	9.34	170.69	170.86	9.99
137.53	137.70	8.05	148.64	148.81	8.70	159.75	159.92	9.35	170.86	171.03	10.00
137.70	137.87	8.06	148.81	148.98	8.71	159.92	160.09	9.36	171.03	171.20	10.01
137.87	138.04	8.07	148.98	149.15	8.72	160.09	160.26	9.37	171.20	171.37	10.02
138.04	138.21	8.08	149.15	149.32	8.73	160.26	160.43	9.38	171.37	171.54	10.03
138.21	138.38	8.09	149.32	149.49	8.74	160.43	160.60	9.39	171.54	171.71	10.04
138.38	138.55	8.10	149.49	149.66	8.75	160.60	160.77	9.40	171.71	171.89	10.05
138.55	138.72	8.11	149.66	149.83	8.76	160.77	160.95	9.41	171.89	172.06	10.06
138.72	138.89	8.12	149.83	150.00	8.77	160.95	161.12	9.42	172.06	172.23	10.07
138.89	139.06	8.13	150.00	150.18	8.78	161.12	161.29	9.43	172.23	172.40	10.08
139.06	139.24	8.14	150.18	150.35	8.79	161.29	161.46	9.44	172.40	172.57	10.09
139.24	139.41	8.15	150.35	150.52	8.80	161.46	161.63	9.45	172.57	172.74	10.10
139.41	139.58	8.16	150.52	150.69	8.81	161.63	161.80	9.46	172.74	172.91	10.11
139.58	139.75	8.17	150.69	150.86	8.82	161.80	161.97	9.47	172.91	173.08	10.12
139.75	139.92	8.18	150.86	151.03	8.83	161.97	162.14	9.48	173.08	173.25	10.13
139.92	140.09	8.19	151.03	151.20	8.84	162.14	162.31	9.49	173.25	173.42	10.14
140.09	140.26	8.20	151.20	151.37	8.85	162.31	162.48	9.50	173.42	173.59	10.15
140.26	140.43	8.21	151.37	151.54	8.86	162.48	162.65	9.51	173.59	173.77	10.16
140.43	140.60	8.22	151.54	151.71	8.87	162.65	162.83	9.52	173.77	173.94	10.17
140.60	140.77	8.23	151.71	151.89	8.88	162.83	163.00	9.53	173.94	174.11	10.18
140.77	140.95	8.24	151.89	152.06	8.89	163.00	163.17	9.54	174.11	174.28	10.19
140.95	141.12	8.25	152.06	152.23	8.90	163.17	163.34	9.55	174.28	174.45	10.20
141.12	141.29	8.26	152.23	152.40	8.91	163.34	163.51	9.56	174.45	174.62	10.21
141.29	141.46	8.27	152.40	152.57	8.92	163.51	163.68	9.57	174.62	174.79	10.22
141.46	141.63	8.28	152.57	152.74	8.93	163.68	163.85	9.58	174.79	174.96	10.23
141.63	141.80	8.29	152.74	152.91	8.94	163.85	164.02	9.59	174.96	175.13	10.24
141.80	141.97	8.30	152.91	153.08	8.95	164.02	164.19	9.60	175.13	175.30	10.25
141.97	142.14	8.31	153.08	153.25	8.96	164.19	164.36	9.61	175.30	175.48	10.26
142.14	142.31	8.32	153.25	153.42	8.97	164.36	164.53	9.62	175.48	175.65	10.27
142.31	142.48	8.33	153.42	153.59	8.98	164.53	164.71	9.63	175.65	175.82	10.28
142.48	142.65	8.34	153.59	153.77	8.99	164.71	164.88	9.64	175.82	175.99	10.29
142.65	142.83	8.35	153.77	153.94	9.00	164.88	165.05	9.65	175.99	176.16	10.30
142.83	143.00	8.36	153.94	154.11	9.01	165.05	165.22	9.66	176.16	176.33	10.31
143.00	143.17	8.37	154.11	154.28	9.02	165.22	165.39	9.67	176.33	176.50	10.32
143.17	143.34	8.38	154.28	154.45	9.03	165.39	165.56	9.68	176.50	176.67	10.33
143.34	143.51	8.39	154.45	154.62	9.04	165.56	165.73	9.69	176.67	176.84	10.34
143.51	143.68	8.40	154.62	154.79	9.05	165.73	165.90	9.70	176.84	177.01	10.35
143.68	143.85	8.41	154.79	154.96	9.06	165.90	166.07	9.71	177.01	177.18	10.36
143.85	144.02	8.42	154.96	155.13	9.07	166.07	166.24	9.72	177.18	177.36	10.37
144.02	144.19	8.43	155.13	155.30	9.08	166.24	166.42	9.73	177.36	177.53	10.38
144.19	144.36	8.44	155.30	155.48	9.09	166.42	166.59	9.74	177.53	177.70	10.39

TABLE XI: SOCIAL SECURITY EMPLOYEE TAX TABLE (CONTINUED)

5.85 percent employee tax deductions

At least	But less than	Tax to be withheld	At least	But less than	Tax to be withheld	At least	But less than	Tax to be withheld	At least	But less than	Tax to be withheld
$177.70	$177.87	$10.40	$188.81	$188.98	$11.05	$199.92	$200.09	$11.70	$211.03	$211.20	$12.35
177.87	178.04	10.41	188.98	189.15	11.06	200.09	200.26	11.71	211.20	211.37	12.36
178.04	178.21	10.42	189.15	189.32	11.07	200.26	200.43	11.72	211.37	211.54	12.37
178.21	178.38	10.43	189.32	189.49	11.08	200.43	200.60	11.73	211.54	211.71	12.38
178.38	178.55	10.44	189.49	189.66	11.09	200.60	200.77	11.74	211.71	211.89	12.39
178.55	178.72	10.45	189.66	189.83	11.10	200.77	200.95	11.75	211.89	212.06	12.40
178.72	178.89	10.46	189.83	190.00	11.11	200.95	201.12	11.76	212.06	212.23	12.41
178.89	179.06	10.47	190.00	190.18	11.12	201.12	201.29	11.77	212.23	212.40	12.42
179.06	179.24	10.48	190.18	190.35	11.13	201.29	201.46	11.78	212.40	212.57	12.43
179.24	179.41	10.49	190.35	190.52	11.14	201.46	201.63	11.79	212.57	212.74	12.44
179.41	179.58	10.50	190.52	190.69	11.15	201.63	201.80	11.80	212.74	212.91	12.45
179.58	179.75	10.51	190.69	190.86	11.16	201.80	201.97	11.81	212.91	213.08	12.46
179.75	179.92	10.52	190.86	191.03	11.17	201.97	202.14	11.82	213.08	213.25	12.47
179.92	180.09	10.53	191.03	191.20	11.18	202.14	202.31	11.83	213.25	213.42	12.48
180.09	180.26	10.54	191.20	191.37	11.19	202.31	202.48	11.84	213.42	213.59	12.49
180.26	180.43	10.55	191.37	191.54	11.20	202.48	202.65	11.85	213.59	213.77	12.50
180.43	180.60	10.56	191.54	191.71	11.21	202.65	202.83	11.86	213.77	213.94	12.51
180.60	180.77	10.57	191.71	191.89	11.22	202.83	203.00	11.87	213.94	214.11	12.52
180.77	180.95	10.58	191.89	192.06	11.23	203.00	203.17	11.88	214.11	214.28	12.53
180.95	181.12	10.59	192.06	192.23	11.24	203.17	203.34	11.89	214.28	214.45	12.54
181.12	181.29	10.60	192.23	192.40	11.25	203.34	203.51	11.90	214.45	214.62	12.55
181.29	181.46	10.61	192.40	192.57	11.26	203.51	203.68	11.91	214.62	214.79	12.56
181.46	181.63	10.62	192.57	192.74	11.27	203.68	203.85	11.92	214.79	214.96	12.57
181.63	181.80	10.63	192.74	192.91	11.28	203.85	204.02	11.93	214.96	215.13	12.58
181.80	181.97	10.64	192.91	193.08	11.29	204.02	204.19	11.94	215.13	215.30	12.59
181.97	182.14	10.65	193.08	193.25	11.30	204.19	204.36	11.95	215.30	215.48	12.60
182.14	182.31	10.66	193.25	193.42	11.31	204.36	204.53	11.96	215.48	215.65	12.61
182.31	182.48	10.67	193.42	193.59	11.32	204.53	204.71	11.97	215.65	215.82	12.62
182.48	182.65	10.68	193.59	193.77	11.33	204.71	204.88	11.98	215.82	215.99	12.63
182.65	182.83	10.69	193.77	193.94	11.34	204.88	205.05	11.99	215.99	216.16	12.64
182.83	183.00	10.70	193.94	194.11	11.35	205.05	205.22	12.00	216.16	216.33	12.65
183.00	183.17	10.71	194.11	194.28	11.36	205.22	205.39	12.01	216.33	216.50	12.66
183.17	183.34	10.72	194.28	194.45	11.37	205.39	205.56	12.02	216.50	216.67	12.67
183.34	183.51	10.73	194.45	194.62	11.38	205.56	205.73	12.03	216.67	216.84	12.68
183.51	183.68	10.74	194.62	194.79	11.39	205.73	205.90	12.04	216.84	217.01	12.69
183.68	183.85	10.75	194.79	194.96	11.40	205.90	206.07	12.05	217.01	217.18	12.70
183.85	184.02	10.76	194.96	195.13	11.41	206.07	206.24	12.06	217.18	217.36	12.71
184.02	184.19	10.77	195.13	195.30	11.42	206.24	206.42	12.07	217.36	217.53	12.72
184.19	184.36	10.78	195.30	195.48	11.43	206.42	206.59	12.08	217.53	217.70	12.73
184.36	184.53	10.79	195.48	195.65	11.44	206.59	206.76	12.09	217.70	217.87	12.74
184.53	184.71	10.80	195.65	195.82	11.45	206.76	206.93	12.10	217.87	218.04	12.75
184.71	184.88	10.81	195.82	195.99	11.46	206.93	207.10	12.11	218.04	218.21	12.76
184.88	185.05	10.82	195.99	196.16	11.47	207.10	207.27	12.12	218.21	218.38	12.77
185.05	185.22	10.83	196.16	196.33	11.48	207.27	207.44	12.13	218.38	218.55	12.78
185.22	185.39	10.84	196.33	196.50	11.49	207.44	207.61	12.14	218.55	218.72	12.79
185.39	185.56	10.85	196.50	196.67	11.50	207.61	207.78	12.15	218.72	218.89	12.80
185.56	185.73	10.86	196.67	196.84	11.51	207.78	207.95	12.16	218.89	219.06	12.81
185.73	185.90	10.87	196.84	197.01	11.52	207.95	208.12	12.17	219.06	219.24	12.82
185.90	186.07	10.88	197.01	197.18	11.53	208.12	208.30	12.18	219.24	219.41	12.83
186.07	186.24	10.89	197.18	197.36	11.54	208.30	208.47	12.19	219.41	219.58	12.84
186.24	186.42	10.90	197.36	197.53	11.55	208.47	208.64	12.20	219.58	219.75	12.85
186.42	186.59	10.91	197.53	197.70	11.56	208.64	208.81	12.21	219.75	219.92	12.86
186.59	186.76	10.92	197.70	197.87	11.57	208.81	208.98	12.22	219.92	220.09	12.87
186.76	186.93	10.93	197.87	198.04	11.58	208.98	209.15	12.23	220.09	220.26	12.88
186.93	187.10	10.94	198.04	198.21	11.59	209.15	209.32	12.24	220.26	220.43	12.89
187.10	187.27	10.95	198.21	198.38	11.60	209.32	209.49	12.25	220.43	220.60	12.90
187.27	187.44	10.96	198.38	198.55	11.61	209.49	209.66	12.26	220.60	220.77	12.91
187.44	187.61	10.97	198.55	198.72	11.62	209.66	209.83	12.27	220.77	220.95	12.92
187.61	187.78	10.98	198.72	198.89	11.63	209.83	210.00	12.28	220.95	221.12	12.93
187.78	187.95	10.99	198.89	199.06	11.64	210.00	210.18	12.29	221.12	221.29	12.94
187.95	188.12	11.00	199.06	199.24	11.65	210.18	210.35	12.30	221.29	221.46	12.95
188.12	188.30	11.01	199.24	199.41	11.66	210.35	210.52	12.31	221.46	221.63	12.96
188.30	188.47	11.02	199.41	199.58	11.67	210.52	210.69	12.32	221.63	221.80	12.97
188.47	188.64	11.03	199.58	199.75	11.68	210.69	210.86	12.33	221.80	221.97	12.98
188.64	188.81	11.04	199.75	199.92	11.69	210.86	211.03	12.34	221.97	222.14	12.99

TABLE XI: SOCIAL SECURITY EMPLOYEE TAX TABLE (CONTINUED)

5.85 percent employee tax deductions

Wages		Tax to be withheld	Wages		Tax to be withheld	Wages		Tax to be withheld	Wages		Tax to be withheld
At least	But less than		At least	But less than		At least	But less than		At least	But less than	
$222.14	$222.31	$13.00	$233.25	$233.42	$13.65	$244.36	$244.53	$14.30	$255.48	$255.65	$14.95
222.31	222.48	13.01	233.42	233.59	13.66	244.53	244.71	14.31	255.65	255.82	14.96
222.48	222.65	13.02	233.59	233.77	13.67	244.71	244.88	14.32	255.82	255.99	14.97
222.65	222.83	13.03	233.77	233.94	13.68	244.88	245.05	14.33	255.99	256.16	14.98
222.83	223.00	13.04	233.94	234.11	13.69	245.05	245.22	14.34	256.16	256.33	14.99
223.00	223.17	13.05	234.11	234.28	13.70	245.22	245.39	14.35	256.33	256.50	15.00
223.17	223.34	13.06	234.28	234.45	13.71	245.39	245.56	14.36	256.50	256.67	15.01
223.34	223.51	13.07	234.45	234.62	13.72	245.56	245.73	14.37	256.67	256.84	15.02
223.51	223.68	13.08	234.62	234.79	13.73	245.73	245.90	14.38	256.84	257.01	15.03
223.68	223.85	13.09	234.79	234.96	13.74	245.90	246.07	14.39	257.01	257.18	15.04
223.85	224.02	13.10	234.96	235.13	13.75	246.07	246.24	14.40	257.18	257.36	15.05
224.02	224.19	13.11	235.13	235.30	13.76	246.24	246.42	14.41	257.36	257.53	15.06
224.19	224.36	13.12	235.30	235.48	13.77	246.42	246.59	14.42	257.53	257.70	15.07
224.36	224.53	13.13	235.48	235.65	13.78	246.59	246.76	14.43	257.70	257.87	15.08
224.53	224.71	13.14	235.65	235.82	13.79	246.76	246.93	14.44	257.87	258.04	15.09
224.71	224.88	13.15	235.82	235.99	13.80	246.93	247.10	14.45	258.04	258.21	15.10
224.88	225.05	13.16	235.99	236.16	13.81	247.10	247.27	14.46	258.21	258.38	15.11
225.05	225.22	13.17	236.16	236.33	13.82	247.27	247.44	14.47	258.38	258.55	15.12
225.22	225.39	13.18	236.33	236.50	13.83	247.44	247.61	14.48	258.55	258.72	15.13
225.39	225.56	13.19	236.50	236.67	13.84	247.61	247.78	14.49	258.72	258.89	15.14
225.56	225.73	13.20	236.67	236.84	13.85	247.78	247.95	14.50	258.89	259.06	15.15
225.73	225.90	13.21	236.84	237.01	13.86	247.95	248.12	14.51	259.06	259.24	15.16
225.90	226.07	13.22	237.01	237.18	13.87	248.12	248.30	14.52	259.24	259.41	15.17
226.07	226.24	13.23	237.18	237.36	13.88	248.30	248.47	14.53	259.41	259.58	15.18
226.24	226.42	13.24	237.36	237.53	13.89	248.47	248.64	14.54	259.58	259.75	15.19
226.42	226.59	13.25	237.53	237.70	13.90	248.64	248.81	14.55	259.75	259.92	15.20
226.59	226.76	13.26	237.70	237.87	13.91	248.81	248.98	14.56	259.92	260.09	15.21
226.76	226.93	13.27	237.87	238.04	13.92	248.98	249.15	14.57	260.09	260.26	15.22
226.93	227.10	13.28	238.04	238.21	13.93	249.15	249.32	14.58	260.26	260.43	15.23
227.10	227.27	13.29	238.21	238.38	13.94	249.32	249.49	14.59	260.43	260.60	15.24
227.27	227.44	13.30	238.38	238.55	13.95	249.49	249.66	14.60	260.60	260.77	15.25
227.44	227.61	13.31	238.55	238.72	13.96	249.66	249.83	14.61	260.77	260.95	15.26
227.61	227.78	13.32	238.72	238.89	13.97	249.83	250.00	14.62	260.95	261.12	15.27
227.78	227.95	13.33	238.89	239.06	13.98	250.00	250.18	14.63	261.12	261.29	15.28
227.95	228.12	13.34	239.06	239.24	13.99	250.18	250.35	14.64	261.29	261.46	15.29
228.12	228.30	13.35	239.24	239.41	14.00	250.35	250.52	14.65	261.46	261.63	15.30
228.30	228.47	13.36	239.41	239.58	14.01	250.52	250.69	14.66	261.63	261.80	15.31
228.47	228.64	13.37	239.58	239.75	14.02	250.69	250.86	14.67	261.80	261.97	15.32
228.64	228.81	13.38	239.75	239.92	14.03	250.86	251.03	14.68	261.97	262.14	15.33
228.81	228.98	13.39	239.92	240.09	14.04	251.03	251.20	14.69	262.14	262.31	15.34
228.98	229.15	13.40	240.09	240.26	14.05	251.20	251.37	14.70	262.31	262.48	15.35
229.15	229.32	13.41	240.26	240.43	14.06	251.37	251.54	14.71	262.48	262.65	15.36
229.32	229.49	13.42	240.43	240.60	14.07	251.54	251.71	14.72	262.65	262.83	15.37
229.49	229.66	13.43	240.60	240.77	14.08	251.71	251.89	14.73	262.83	263.00	15.38
229.66	229.83	13.44	240.77	240.95	14.09	251.89	252.06	14.74	263.00	263.17	15.39
229.83	230.00	13.45	240.95	241.12	14.10	252.06	252.23	14.75	263.17	263.34	15.40
230.00	230.18	13.46	241.12	241.29	14.11	252.23	252.40	14.76	263.34	263.51	15.41
230.18	230.35	13.47	241.29	241.46	14.12	252.40	252.57	14.77	263.51	263.68	15.42
230.35	230.52	13.48	241.46	241.63	14.13	252.57	252.74	14.78	263.68	263.85	15.43
230.52	230.69	13.49	241.63	241.80	14.14	252.74	252.91	14.79	263.85	264.02	15.44
230.69	230.86	13.50	241.80	241.97	14.15	252.91	253.08	14.80	264.02	264.19	15.45
230.86	231.03	13.51	241.97	242.14	14.16	253.08	253.25	14.81	264.19	264.36	15.46
231.03	231.20	13.52	242.14	242.31	14.17	253.25	253.42	14.82	264.36	264.53	15.47
231.20	231.37	13.53	242.31	242.48	14.18	253.42	253.59	14.83	264.53	264.71	15.48
231.37	231.54	13.54	242.48	242.65	14.19	253.59	253.77	14.84	264.71	264.88	15.49
231.54	231.71	13.55	242.65	242.83	14.20	253.77	253.94	14.85	264.88	265.05	15.50
231.71	231.89	13.56	242.83	243.00	14.21	253.94	254.11	14.86	265.05	265.22	15.51
231.89	232.06	13.57	243.00	243.17	14.22	254.11	254.28	14.87	265.22	265.39	15.52
232.06	232.23	13.58	243.17	243.34	14.23	254.28	254.45	14.88	265.39	265.56	15.53
232.23	232.40	13.59	243.34	243.51	14.24	254.45	254.62	14.89	265.56	265.73	15.54
232.40	232.57	13.60	243.51	243.68	14.25	254.62	254.79	14.90	265.73	265.90	15.55
232.57	232.74	13.61	243.68	243.85	14.26	254.79	254.96	14.91	265.90	266.07	15.56
232.74	232.91	13.62	243.85	244.02	14.27	254.96	255.13	14.92	266.07	266.24	15.57
232.91	233.08	13.63	244.02	244.19	14.28	255.13	255.30	14.93	266.24	266.42	15.58
233.08	233.25	13.64	244.19	244.36	14.29	255.30	255.48	14.94	266.42	266.59	15.59

TABLE XII: FEDERAL INCOME TAX WITHHOLDING TABLE

SINGLE persons — Weekly payroll period

And the wages are—		And the number of withholding allowances claimed is—										
At least	But less than	0	1	2	3	4	5	6	7	8	9	10 or more
		The amount of income tax to be withheld shall be—										
$0	$25	$0	$0	$0	$0	$0	$0	$0	$0	$0	$0	$0
25	26	.10	0	0	0	0	0	0	0	0	0	0
26	27	.20	0	0	0	0	0	0	0	0	0	0
27	28	.40	0	0	0	0	0	0	0	0	0	0
28	29	.60	0	0	0	0	0	0	0	0	0	0
29	30	.70	0	0	0	0	0	0	0	0	0	0
30	31	.90	0	0	0	0	0	0	0	0	0	0
31	32	1.00	0	0	0	0	0	0	0	0	0	0
32	33	1.20	0	0	0	0	0	0	0	0	0	0
33	34	1.40	0	0	0	0	0	0	0	0	0	0
34	35	1.50	0	0	0	0	0	0	0	0	0	0
35	36	1.70	0	0	0	0	0	0	0	0	0	0
36	37	1.80	0	0	0	0	0	0	0	0	0	0
37	38	2.00	0	0	0	0	0	0	0	0	0	0
38	39	2.20	0	0	0	0	0	0	0	0	0	0
39	40	2.30	0	0	0	0	0	0	0	0	0	0
40	41	2.50	.20	0	0	0	0	0	0	0	0	0
41	42	2.60	.30	0	0	0	0	0	0	0	0	0
42	43	2.80	.50	0	0	0	0	0	0	0	0	0
43	44	3.00	.70	0	0	0	0	0	0	0	0	0
44	45	3.10	.80	0	0	0	0	0	0	0	0	0
45	46	3.30	1.00	0	0	0	0	0	0	0	0	0
46	47	3.40	1.10	0	0	0	0	0	0	0	0	0
47	48	3.60	1.30	0	0	0	0	0	0	0	0	0
48	49	3.80	1.50	0	0	0	0	0	0	0	0	0
49	50	3.90	1.60	0	0	0	0	0	0	0	0	0
50	51	4.10	1.80	0	0	0	0	0	0	0	0	0
51	52	4.20	1.90	0	0	0	0	0	0	0	0	0
52	53	4.40	2.10	0	0	0	0	0	0	0	0	0
53	54	4.60	2.30	0	0	0	0	0	0	0	0	0
54	55	4.70	2.40	.10	0	0	0	0	0	0	0	0
55	56	4.90	2.60	.30	0	0	0	0	0	0	0	0
56	57	5.00	2.70	.40	0	0	0	0	0	0	0	0
57	58	5.20	2.90	.60	0	0	0	0	0	0	0	0
58	59	5.40	3.10	.70	0	0	0	0	0	0	0	0
59	60	5.50	3.20	.90	0	0	0	0	0	0	0	0
60	62	5.80	3.50	1.10	0	0	0	0	0	0	0	0
62	64	6.10	3.80	1.50	0	0	0	0	0	0	0	0
64	66	6.40	4.10	1.80	0	0	0	0	0	0	0	0
66	68	6.70	4.40	2.10	0	0	0	0	0	0	0	0
68	70	7.10	4.70	2.40	.10	0	0	0	0	0	0	0
70	72	7.50	5.10	2.70	.40	0	0	0	0	0	0	0
72	74	7.90	5.40	3.10	.80	0	0	0	0	0	0	0
74	76	8.30	5.70	3.40	1.10	0	0	0	0	0	0	0
76	78	8.70	6.00	3.70	1.40	0	0	0	0	0	0	0
78	80	9.10	6.30	4.00	1.70	0	0	0	0	0	0	0
80	82	9.50	6.70	4.30	2.00	0	0	0	0	0	0	0
82	84	9.90	7.00	4.70	2.40	0	0	0	0	0	0	0
84	86	10.30	7.40	5.00	2.70	.40	0	0	0	0	0	0
86	88	10.70	7.80	5.30	3.00	.70	0	0	0	0	0	0
88	90	11.10	8.20	5.60	3.30	1.00	0	0	0	0	0	0
90	92	11.50	8.60	5.90	3.60	1.30	0	0	0	0	0	0
92	94	11.90	9.00	6.30	4.00	1.60	0	0	0	0	0	0
94	96	12.30	9.40	6.60	4.30	2.00	0	0	0	0	0	0
96	98	12.70	9.80	6.90	4.60	2.30	0	0	0	0	0	0
98	100	13.10	10.20	7.30	4.90	2.60	.30	0	0	0	0	0
100	105	13.80	10.90	8.00	5.50	3.20	.90	0	0	0	0	0
105	110	14.80	11.90	9.00	6.30	4.00	1.70	0	0	0	0	0
110	115	15.80	12.90	10.00	7.20	4.80	2.50	.20	0	0	0	0
115	120	16.90	13.90	11.00	8.20	5.60	3.30	1.00	0	0	0	0

TABLE XII: FEDERAL INCOME TAX WITHHOLDING TABLE (CONTINUED)

SINGLE persons — Weekly payroll period

And the wages are—		\multicolumn{11}{c}{And the number of withholding allowances claimed is—}
At least	But less than	0	1	2	3	4	5	6	7	8	9	10 or more
		\multicolumn{11}{c}{The amount of income tax to be withheld shall be—}
$120	$125	$18.00	$14.90	$12.00	$9.20	$6.40	$4.10	$1.80	$0	$0	$0	$0
125	130	19.20	15.90	13.00	10.20	7.30	4.90	2.60	.20	0	0	0
130	135	20.30	17.00	14.00	11.20	8.30	5.70	3.40	1.00	0	0	0
135	140	21.50	18.20	15.00	12.20	9.30	6.50	4.20	1.80	0	0	0
140	145	22.60	19.30	16.00	13.20	10.30	7.40	5.00	2.60	.30	0	0
145	150	23.80	20.50	17.10	14.20	11.30	8.40	5.80	3.40	1.10	0	0
150	160	25.50	22.20	18.90	15.70	12.80	9.90	7.00	4.60	2.30	0	0
160	170	27.80	24.50	21.20	17.80	14.80	11.90	9.00	6.20	3.90	1.60	0
170	180	30.10	26.80	23.50	20.10	16.80	13.90	11.00	8.10	5.50	3.20	.90
180	190	32.40	29.10	25.80	22.40	19.10	15.90	13.00	10.10	7.20	4.80	2.50
190	200	34.50	31.40	28.10	24.70	21.40	18.10	15.00	12.10	9.20	6.40	4.10
200	210	36.60	33.50	30.40	27.00	23.70	20.40	17.10	14.10	11.20	8.30	5.70
210	220	38.70	35.60	32.60	29.30	26.00	22.70	19.40	16.10	13.20	10.30	7.50
220	230	40.80	37.70	34.70	31.60	28.30	25.00	21.70	18.40	15.20	12.30	9.50
230	240	42.90	39.80	36.80	33.80	30.60	27.30	24.00	20.70	17.40	14.30	11.50
240	250	45.20	41.90	38.90	35.90	32.80	29.60	26.30	23.00	19.70	16.30	13.50
250	260	47.80	44.00	41.00	38.00	34.90	31.90	28.60	25.30	22.00	18.60	15.50
260	270	50.40	46.60	43.10	40.10	37.00	34.00	30.90	27.60	24.30	20.90	17.60
270	280	53.00	49.20	45.50	42.20	39.10	36.10	33.10	29.90	26.60	23.20	19.90
280	290	55.80	51.80	48.10	44.30	41.20	38.20	35.20	32.10	28.90	25.50	22.20
290	300	58.80	54.50	50.70	46.90	43.30	40.30	37.30	34.20	31.20	27.80	24.50
300	310	61.80	57.50	53.30	49.50	45.80	42.40	39.40	36.30	33.30	30.10	26.80
310	320	64.80	60.50	56.20	52.10	48.40	44.60	41.50	38.40	35.40	32.40	29.10
320	330	67.80	63.50	59.20	54.80	51.00	47.20	43.60	40.50	37.50	34.50	31.40
330	340	70.80	66.50	62.20	57.80	53.60	49.80	46.10	42.60	39.60	36.60	33.60
340	350	73.80	69.50	65.20	60.80	56.50	52.40	48.70	44.90	41.70	38.70	35.70
350	360	77.40	72.50	68.20	63.80	59.50	55.20	51.30	47.50	43.80	40.80	37.80
360	370	81.00	75.80	71.20	66.80	62.50	58.20	53.90	50.10	46.40	42.90	39.90
370	380	84.60	79.40	74.20	69.80	65.50	61.20	56.90	52.70	49.00	45.20	42.00
380	390	88.20	83.00	77.80	72.80	68.50	64.20	59.90	55.50	51.60	47.80	44.10
390	400	91.80	86.60	81.40	76.20	71.50	67.20	62.90	58.50	54.20	50.40	46.70
400	410	95.40	90.20	85.00	79.80	74.60	70.20	65.90	61.50	57.20	53.00	49.30
410	420	99.00	93.80	88.60	83.40	78.20	73.20	68.90	64.50	60.20	55.90	51.90
420	430	102.60	97.40	92.20	87.00	81.80	76.60	71.90	67.50	63.20	58.90	54.60
430	440	106.20	101.00	95.80	90.60	85.40	80.20	75.00	70.50	66.20	61.90	57.60
440	450	109.80	104.60	99.40	94.20	89.00	83.80	78.60	73.50	69.20	64.90	60.60
450	460	113.40	108.20	103.00	97.80	92.60	87.40	82.20	77.00	72.20	67.90	63.60
460	470	117.00	111.80	106.60	101.40	96.20	91.00	85.80	80.60	75.40	70.90	66.60
470	480	120.60	115.40	110.20	105.00	99.80	94.60	89.40	84.20	79.00	73.90	69.60
480	490	124.20	119.00	113.80	108.60	103.40	98.20	93.00	87.80	82.60	77.40	72.60
490	500	127.80	122.60	117.40	112.20	107.00	101.80	96.60	91.40	86.20	81.00	75.80
500	510	131.40	126.20	121.00	115.80	110.60	105.40	100.20	95.00	89.80	84.60	79.40
510	520	135.00	129.80	124.60	119.40	114.20	109.00	103.80	98.60	93.40	88.20	83.00
520	530	138.60	133.40	128.20	123.00	117.80	112.60	107.40	102.20	97.00	91.80	86.60
530	540	142.20	137.00	131.80	126.60	121.40	116.20	111.00	105.80	100.60	95.40	90.20
540	550	145.80	140.60	135.40	130.20	125.00	119.80	114.60	109.40	104.20	99.00	93.80
550	560	149.40	144.20	139.00	133.80	128.60	123.40	118.20	113.00	107.80	102.60	97.40
560	570	153.00	147.80	142.60	137.40	132.20	127.00	121.80	116.60	111.40	106.20	101.00
570	580	156.60	151.40	146.20	141.00	135.80	130.60	125.40	120.20	115.00	109.80	104.60
580	590	160.20	155.00	149.80	144.60	139.40	134.20	129.00	123.80	118.60	113.40	108.20
590	600	163.80	158.60	153.40	148.20	143.00	137.80	132.60	127.40	122.20	117.00	111.80
600	610	167.40	162.20	157.00	151.80	146.60	141.40	136.20	131.00	125.80	120.60	115.40
610	620	171.00	165.80	160.60	155.40	150.20	145.00	139.80	134.60	129.40	124.20	119.00
620	630	174.60	169.40	164.20	159.00	153.80	148.60	143.40	138.20	133.00	127.80	122.60
630	640	178.20	173.00	167.80	162.60	157.40	152.20	147.00	141.80	136.60	131.40	126.20
		\multicolumn{11}{c}{36 percent of the excess over $640 plus—}
$640 and over		180.00	174.80	169.60	164.40	159.20	154.00	148.80	143.60	138.40	133.20	128.00

TABLE XII: FEDERAL INCOME TAX WITHHOLDING TABLE (CONTINUED)

MARRIED persons — Weekly payroll period

And the wages are—		And the number of withholding allowances claimed is—										
At least	But less than	0	1	2	3	4	5	6	7	8	9	10 or more
		The amount of income tax to be withheld shall be—										
$0	$48	$0	$0	$0	$0	$0	$0	$0	$0	$0	$0	$0
48	49	.10	0	0	0	0	0	0	0	0	0	0
49	50	.20	0	0	0	0	0	0	0	0	0	0
50	51	.40	0	0	0	0	0	0	0	0	0	0
51	52	.60	0	0	0	0	0	0	0	0	0	0
52	53	.80	0	0	0	0	0	0	0	0	0	0
53	54	.90	0	0	0	0	0	0	0	0	0	0
54	55	1.10	0	0	0	0	0	0	0	0	0	0
55	56	1.30	0	0	0	0	0	0	0	0	0	0
56	57	1.40	0	0	0	0	0	0	0	0	0	0
57	58	1.60	0	0	0	0	0	0	0	0	0	0
58	59	1.80	0	0	0	0	0	0	0	0	0	0
59	60	1.90	0	0	0	0	0	0	0	0	0	0
60	62	2.20	0	0	0	0	0	0	0	0	0	0
62	64	2.50	.10	0	0	0	0	0	0	0	0	0
64	66	2.90	.40	0	0	0	0	0	0	0	0	0
66	68	3.20	.80	0	0	0	0	0	0	0	0	0
68	70	3.60	1.10	0	0	0	0	0	0	0	0	0
70	72	3.90	1.40	0	0	0	0	0	0	0	0	0
72	74	4.20	1.80	0	0	0	0	0	0	0	0	0
74	76	4.60	2.10	0	0	0	0	0	0	0	0	0
76	78	4.90	2.50	0	0	0	0	0	0	0	0	0
78	80	5.30	2.80	.40	0	0	0	0	0	0	0	0
80	82	5.60	3.10	.70	0	0	0	0	0	0	0	0
82	84	5.90	3.50	1.00	0	0	0	0	0	0	0	0
84	86	6.30	3.80	1.40	0	0	0	0	0	0	0	0
86	88	6.60	4.20	1.70	0	0	0	0	0	0	0	0
88	90	7.00	4.50	2.10	0	0	0	0	0	0	0	0
90	92	7.30	4.80	2.40	0	0	0	0	0	0	0	0
92	94	7.60	5.20	2.70	.30	0	0	0	0	0	0	0
94	96	8.00	5.50	3.10	.60	0	0	0	0	0	0	0
96	98	8.30	5.90	3.40	1.00	0	0	0	0	0	0	0
98	100	8.70	6.20	3.80	1.30	0	0	0	0	0	0	0
100	105	9.40	6.80	4.30	1.90	0	0	0	0	0	0	0
105	110	10.40	7.70	5.20	2.70	.30	0	0	0	0	0	0
110	115	11.40	8.60	6.00	3.60	1.10	0	0	0	0	0	0
115	120	12.40	9.60	6.90	4.40	2.00	0	0	0	0	0	0
120	125	13.40	10.60	7.70	5.30	2.80	.40	0	0	0	0	0
125	130	14.40	11.60	8.70	6.10	3.70	1.20	0	0	0	0	0
130	135	15.40	12.60	9.70	7.00	4.50	2.10	0	0	0	0	0
135	140	16.40	13.60	10.70	7.80	5.40	2.90	.50	0	0	0	0
140	145	17.40	14.60	11.70	8.80	6.20	3.80	1.30	0	0	0	0
145	150	18.40	15.60	12.70	9.80	7.10	4.60	2.20	0	0	0	0
150	160	19.90	17.10	14.20	11.30	8.40	5.90	3.50	1.00	0	0	0
160	170	21.90	19.10	16.20	13.30	10.40	7.60	5.20	2.70	.30	0	0
170	180	23.90	21.10	18.20	15.30	12.40	9.50	6.90	4.40	2.00	0	0
180	190	25.60	23.10	20.20	17.30	14.40	11.50	8.60	6.10	3.70	1.20	0
190	200	27.30	24.80	22.20	19.30	16.40	13.50	10.60	7.80	5.40	2.90	.50
200	210	29.00	26.50	24.10	21.30	18.40	15.50	12.60	9.80	7.10	4.60	2.20
210	220	30.70	28.20	25.80	23.30	20.40	17.50	14.60	11.80	8.90	6.30	3.90
220	230	32.40	29.90	27.50	25.00	22.40	19.50	16.60	13.80	10.90	8.00	5.60
230	240	34.10	31.60	29.20	26.70	24.30	21.50	18.60	15.80	12.90	10.00	7.30
240	250	35.80	33.30	30.90	28.40	26.00	23.50	20.60	17.80	14.90	12.00	9.10
250	260	37.50	35.00	32.60	30.10	27.70	25.20	22.60	19.80	16.90	14.00	11.10
260	270	39.20	36.70	34.30	31.80	29.40	26.90	24.50	21.80	18.90	16.00	13.10
270	280	41.70	38.40	36.00	33.50	31.10	28.60	26.20	23.70	20.90	18.00	15.10
280	290	44.20	40.60	37.70	35.20	32.80	30.30	27.90	25.40	22.90	20.00	17.10
290	300	46.70	43.10	39.50	36.90	34.50	32.00	29.60	27.10	24.70	22.00	19.10
300	310	49.20	45.60	42.00	38.60	36.20	33.70	31.30	28.80	26.40	23.90	21.10
310	320	51.70	48.10	44.50	40.90	37.90	35.40	33.00	30.50	28.10	25.60	23.10

TABLE XIII: THE NUMBER OF EACH DAY OF THE YEAR

Day of Month	Jan.	Feb.	Mar.	Apr.	May	June	July	Aug.	Sept.	Oct.	Nov.	Dec.	Day of Month
1	1	32	60	91	121	152	182	213	244	274	305	335	1
2	2	33	61	92	122	153	183	214	245	275	306	336	2
3	3	34	62	93	123	154	184	215	246	276	307	337	3
4	4	35	63	94	124	155	185	216	247	277	308	338	4
5	5	36	64	95	125	156	186	217	248	278	309	339	5
6	6	37	65	96	126	157	187	218	249	279	310	340	6
7	7	38	66	97	127	158	188	219	250	280	311	341	7
8	8	39	67	98	128	159	189	220	251	281	312	342	8
9	9	40	68	99	129	160	190	221	252	282	313	343	9
10	10	41	69	100	130	161	191	222	253	283	314	344	10
11	11	42	70	101	131	162	192	223	254	284	315	345	11
12	12	43	71	102	132	163	193	224	255	285	316	346	12
13	13	44	72	103	133	164	194	225	256	286	317	347	13
14	14	45	73	104	134	165	195	226	257	287	318	348	14
15	15	46	74	105	135	166	196	227	258	288	319	349	15
16	16	47	75	106	136	167	197	228	259	289	320	350	16
17	17	48	76	107	137	168	198	229	260	290	321	351	17
18	18	49	77	108	138	169	199	230	261	291	322	352	18
19	19	50	78	109	139	170	200	231	262	292	323	353	19
20	20	51	79	110	140	171	201	232	263	293	324	354	20
21	21	52	80	111	141	172	202	233	264	294	325	355	21
22	22	53	81	112	142	173	203	234	265	295	326	356	22
23	23	54	82	113	143	174	204	235	266	296	327	357	23
24	24	55	83	114	144	175	205	236	267	297	328	358	24
25	25	56	84	115	145	176	206	237	268	298	329	359	25
26	26	57	85	116	146	177	207	238	269	299	330	360	26
27	27	58	86	117	147	178	208	239	270	300	331	361	27
28	28	59	87	118	148	179	209	240	271	301	332	362	28
29	29		88	119	149	180	210	241	272	302	333	363	29
30	30		89	120	150	181	211	242	273	303	334	364	30
31	31		90		151		212	243		304		365	31

NOTE: In leap years, after February 28, add 1 to the tabular number.

		XIV COMPOUND AMOUNT	XV AMOUNT OF ANNUITY	XVI SINKING FUND	XVII PRESENT VALUE	XVIII PRESENT VALUE OF ANNUITY	XIX AMORTIZATION	
RATE 5/12%	PERIODS	AMOUNT OF 1 — How $1 left at compound interest will grow.	AMOUNT OF 1 PER PERIOD — How $1 deposited periodically will grow.	SINKING FUND — Periodic deposit that will grow to $1 at future date.	PRESENT WORTH OF 1 — What $1 due in the future is worth today.	PRESENT WORTH OF 1 PER PERIOD — What $1 payable periodically is worth today.	PARTIAL PAYMENT — Annuity worth $1 today. Periodic payment necessary to pay off a loan of $1.	PERIODS
	1	1.004 166 6667	1.000 000 0000	1.000 000 0000	.995 850 6224	.995 850 6224	1.004 166 6667	1
	2	1.008 350 6944	2.004 166 6667	.498 960 4990	.991 718 4621	1.987 569 0846	.503 127 1656	2
	3	1.012 552 1557	3.012 517 3611	.331 948 2944	.987 603 4478	2.975 172 5323	.336 114 9611	3
	4	1.016 771 1230	4.025 069 5168	.248 442 9140	.983 505 5082	3.958 678 0405	.252 609 5807	4
	5	1.021 007 6693	5.041 840 6398	.198 340 2633	.979 424 5724	4.938 102 6129	.202 506 9300	5
	6	1.025 261 8680	6.062 848 3091	.164 938 9774	.975 360 5701	5.913 463 1830	.169 105 6440	6
	7	1.029 533 7924	7.088 110 1771	.141 081 3285	.971 313 4308	6.884 776 6138	.145 247 9951	7
	8	1.033 823 5165	8.117 643 9695	.123 188 4527	.967 283 0846	7.852 059 6984	.127 355 1193	8
	9	1.038 131 1145	9.151 467 4860	.109 272 0923	.963 269 4618	8.815 329 1602	.113 438 7590	9
	10	1.042 456 6608	10.189 598 6005	.098 139 2927	.959 272 4931	9.774 601 6533	.102 305 9594	10
	11	1.046 800 2303	11.232 055 2614	.089 030 9010	.955 292 1093	10.729 893 7626	.093 197 5677	11
	12	1.051 161 8979	12.278 855 4916	.081 440 8151	.951 328 2416	11.681 222 0043	.085 607 4818	12
	13	1.055 541 7391	13.330 017 3895	.075 018 6568	.947 380 8216	12.628 602 8259	.079 185 3235	13
	14	1.059 939 8297	14.385 559 1286	.069 514 1559	.943 449 7808	13.572 052 6067	.073 680 8226	14
	15	1.064 356 2457	15.445 498 9583	.064 743 7809	.939 535 0514	14.511 587 6581	.068 910 4475	15
	16	1.068 791 0633	16.509 855 2040	.060 569 8831	.935 636 5657	15.447 224 2238	.064 736 5498	16
	17	1.073 244 3594	17.578 646 2673	.056 887 2019	.931 754 2563	16.378 978 4802	.061 053 8686	17
	18	1.077 716 2109	18.651 890 6268	.053 613 8679	.927 888 0561	17.306 866 5363	.057 780 5346	18
	19	1.082 206 6952	19.729 606 8377	.050 685 2472	.924 037 8982	18.230 904 4344	.054 851 9139	19
	20	1.086 715 8897	20.811 813 5329	.048 049 6329	.920 203 7160	19.151 108 1505	.052 216 2996	20
	21	1.091 243 8726	21.898 529 4226	.045 665 1669	.916 385 4434	20.067 493 5938	.049 831 8335	21
	22	1.095 790 7221	22.989 773 2952	.043 497 6016	.912 583 0141	20.980 076 6080	.047 664 2683	22
	23	1.100 356 5167	24.085 564 0173	.041 518 6457	.908 796 3626	21.888 872 9706	.045 685 3124	23
	24	1.104 941 3356	25.185 920 5340	.039 704 7231	.905 025 4234	22.793 898 3940	.043 871 3897	24
	25	1.109 545 2578	26.290 861 8696	.038 030 0296	.901 270 1311	23.695 168 5251	.042 202 6963	25
	26	1.114 168 3630	27.400 407 1273	.036 495 8081	.897 530 4211	24.592 698 9462	.040 662 4748	26
	27	1.118 810 7312	28.514 575 4904	.035 069 7839	.893 806 2284	25.486 505 1746	.039 236 4506	27
	28	1.123 472 4426	29.633 386 2216	.033 745 7215	.890 097 4889	26.376 602 6635	.037 912 3882	28
	29	1.128 153 5778	30.756 858 6642	.032 513 0733	.886 404 1383	27.263 006 8018	.036 679 7400	29
	30	1.132 854 2177	31.885 012 2419	.031 362 6977	.882 726 1129	28.145 732 9147	.035 529 3644	30
	31	1.137 574 4436	33.017 866 4596	.030 286 6329	.879 063 3489	29.024 796 2636	.034 453 2995	31
	32	1.142 314 3371	34.155 440 9032	.029 277 9122	.875 415 7831	29.900 212 0467	.033 444 5789	32
	33	1.147 073 9802	35.297 755 2403	.028 330 4135	.871 783 3525	30.771 995 3992	.032 497 0801	33
	34	1.151 853 4551	36.444 829 2205	.027 438 7347	.868 165 9942	31.640 161 3934	.031 605 4014	34
	35	1.156 652 8445	37.596 682 6756	.026 598 0913	.864 563 6457	32.504 725 0391	.030 764 7580	35
	36	1.161 472 2313	38.753 335 5200	.025 804 2304	.860 976 2447	33.365 701 2837	.029 970 8971	36
	37	1.166 311 6990	39.914 807 7514	.025 053 3588	.857 403 7291	34.223 105 0129	.029 220 0255	37
	38	1.171 171 3310	41.081 119 4503	.024 342 0825	.853 846 0373	35.076 951 0501	.028 508 7492	38
	39	1.176 051 2116	42.252 290 7814	.023 667 3558	.850 303 1077	35.927 254 1578	.027 834 0225	39
	40	1.180 951 4250	43.428 341 9930	.023 026 4374	.846 774 8790	36.774 029 0368	.027 193 1041	40
	41	1.185 872 0559	44.609 293 4179	.022 416 8536	.843 261 2903	37.617 290 3271	.026 583 5203	41
	42	1.190 813 1895	45.795 165 4738	.021 836 3661	.839 762 2808	38.457 052 6079	.026 003 0328	42
	43	1.195 774 9111	46.985 978 6633	.021 282 9450	.836 277 7900	39.293 330 3979	.025 449 6117	43
	44	1.200 757 3066	48.181 753 5744	.020 754 7448	.832 807 7577	40.126 138 1556	.024 921 4115	44
	45	1.205 760 4620	49.382 510 8810	.020 250 0841	.829 352 1238	40.955 490 2795	.024 416 7508	45
	46	1.210 784 4639	50.588 271 3430	.019 767 4278	.825 910 8287	41.781 401 1082	.023 934 0944	46
	47	1.215 829 3992	51.799 055 8069	.019 305 3712	.822 483 8128	42.603 884 9210	.023 472 0379	47
	48	1.220 895 3550	53.014 885 2061	.018 862 6269	.819 071 0169	43.422 955 9379	.023 029 2936	48
	49	1.225 982 4190	54.235 780 5611	.018 438 0125	.815 672 3820	44.238 628 3199	.022 604 6792	49
	50	1.231 090 6791	55.461 762 9801	.018 030 4402	.812 287 8493	45.050 916 1692	.022 197 1069	50
	51	1.236 220 2236	56.692 853 6592	.017 638 9075	.808 917 3603	45.859 833 5295	.021 805 5741	51
	52	1.241 371 1412	57.929 073 8828	.017 262 4890	.805 560 8567	46.665 394 3862	.021 429 1557	52
	53	1.246 543 5209	59.170 445 0240	.016 900 3292	.802 218 2806	47.467 612 6668	.021 066 9959	53
	54	1.251 737 4523	60.416 988 5449	.016 551 6360	.798 889 5740	48.266 502 2408	.020 718 3026	54
	55	1.256 953 0250	61.668 725 9972	.016 215 6747	.795 574 6795	49.062 076 9203	.020 382 3414	55
	56	1.262 190 3293	62.925 679 0222	.015 891 7634	.792 273 5397	49.854 350 4600	.020 058 4300	56
	57	1.267 449 4556	64.187 869 3514	.015 579 2677	.788 986 0977	50.643 336 5577	.019 745 9344	57
	58	1.272 730 4950	65.455 318 8071	.015 277 5973	.785 712 2964	51.429 048 8542	.019 444 2639	58
	59	1.278 033 5388	66.728 049 3021	.014 986 2016	.782 452 0794	52.211 500 9336	.019 152 8683	59
	60	1.283 358 6785	68.006 082 8408	.014 704 5670	.779 205 3903	52.990 706 3239	.018 871 2336	60
	61	1.288 706 0063	69.289 441 5193	.014 432 2133	.775 972 1729	53.766 678 4969	.018 598 8800	61
	62	1.294 075 6147	70.578 147 5257	.014 168 6915	.772 752 3714	54.539 430 8682	.018 335 3582	62
	63	1.299 467 5964	71.872 223 1404	.013 913 5810	.769 545 9300	55.308 976 7982	.018 080 2477	63
	64	1.304 882 0447	73.171 690 7368	.013 666 4875	.766 352 7934	56.075 329 5916	.017 833 1542	64
	65	1.310 319 0533	74.476 572 7815	.013 427 0410	.763 172 9063	56.838 502 4979	.017 593 7077	65
	66	1.315 778 7160	75.786 891 8348	.013 194 8939	.760 006 2137	57.598 508 7116	.017 361 5606	66
	67	1.321 261 1273	77.102 670 5508	.012 969 7194	.756 852 6609	58.355 361 3725	.017 136 3860	67
	68	1.326 766 3820	78.423 931 6781	.012 751 2097	.753 712 1935	59.109 073 5660	.016 917 8764	68
	69	1.332 294 5753	79.750 698 0600	.012 539 0752	.750 584 7570	59.859 658 3230	.016 705 7419	69
	70	1.337 845 8026	81.082 992 6353	.012 333 0426	.747 470 2974	60.607 128 6204	.016 499 7092	70
	71	1.343 420 1602	82.420 838 4379	.012 132 8540	.744 368 7609	61.351 497 3813	.016 299 5207	71
	72	1.349 017 7442	83.764 258 5981	.011 938 2660	.741 280 0939	62.092 777 4752	.016 104 9327	72
	73	1.354 638 6514	85.113 276 3423	.011 749 0484	.738 204 2428	62.830 981 7180	.015 915 7150	73
	74	1.360 282 9791	86.467 914 9937	.011 564 9834	.735 141 1547	63.566 122 8727	.015 731 6500	74
	75	1.365 950 8249	87.828 197 9728	.011 385 8649	.732 090 7765	64.298 213 6492	.015 552 5316	75
	76	1.371 642 2867	89.194 148 7977	.011 211 4978	.729 053 0554	65.027 266 7046	.015 378 1644	76
	77	1.377 357 4629	90.565 791 0844	.011 041 6967	.726 027 9390	65.753 294 6435	.015 208 3634	77
	78	1.383 096 4523	91.943 148 5472	.010 876 2862	.723 015 3749	66.476 310 0185	.015 042 9529	78
	79	1.388 859 3542	93.326 244 9995	.010 715 0995	.720 015 3111	67.196 325 3296	.014 881 7662	79
	80	1.394 646 2681	94.715 104 3537	.010 557 9781	.717 027 6957	67.913 353 0253	.014 724 6448	80
	81	1.400 457 2943	96.109 750 6218	.010 404 7716	.714 052 4771	68.627 405 5024	.014 571 4382	81
	82	1.406 292 5330	97.510 207 9161	.010 255 3366	.711 089 6037	69.338 495 1061	.014 422 0032	82
	83	1.412 152 0852	98.916 500 4490	.010 109 5368	.708 139 0245	70.046 634 1306	.014 276 2035	83
	84	1.418 036 0522	100.328 652 5342	.009 967 2424	.705 200 6883	70.751 834 8188	.014 133 9091	84
	85	1.423 944 5358	101.746 688 5865	.009 828 3297	.702 274 5443	71.454 109 3632	.013 994 9964	85
	86	1.429 877 6380	103.170 633 1223	.009 692 6807	.699 360 5421	72.153 469 9052	.013 859 3473	86
	87	1.435 835 4615	104.600 510 7603	.009 560 1828	.696 458 6311	72.849 928 5363	.013 726 8494	87
	88	1.441 818 1093	106.036 346 2218	.009 430 7286	.693 568 7613	73.543 497 2976	.013 597 3952	88
	89	1.447 825 6847	107.478 164 3310	.009 304 2155	.690 690 8826	74.234 188 1802	.013 470 8821	89
	90	1.453 858 2917	108.925 990 0157	.009 180 5454	.687 824 9453	74.922 013 1255	.013 347 2121	90
	91	1.459 916 0346	110.379 848 3075	.009 059 6247	.684 970 8999	75.606 984 0254	.013 226 2914	91
	92	1.465 999 0181	111.839 764 3421	.008 941 3636	.682 128 6970	76.289 112 7224	.013 108 0303	92
	93	1.472 107 3473	113.305 763 3602	.008 825 6764	.679 298 2875	76.968 411 0098	.012 992 3431	93
	94	1.478 241 1279	114.777 870 7075	.008 712 4808	.676 479 6224	77.644 890 6322	.012 879 1475	94
	95	1.484 400 4660	116.256 111 8355	.008 601 6983	.673 672 6530	78.318 563 2852	.012 768 3650	95
	96	1.490 585 4679	117.740 512 3014	.008 493 2533	.670 877 3308	78.989 440 6159	.012 659 9200	96
	97	1.496 796 2407	119.231 097 7694	.008 387 0737	.668 093 6074	79.657 534 2233	.012 553 7403	97
	98	1.503 032 8917	120.727 894 0101	.008 283 0899	.665 321 4348	80.322 855 6581	.012 449 7566	98
	99	1.509 295 5288	122.230 926 9018	.008 181 2355	.662 560 7649	80.985 416 4230	.012 347 9022	99
	100	1.515 584 2601	123.740 222 4305	.008 081 4466	.659 811 5501	81.645 227 9731	.012 248 1133	100

RATE 1/2%	PERIODS	XIV COMPOUND AMOUNT — AMOUNT OF 1 — How $1 left at compound interest will grow.	XV AMOUNT OF ANNUITY — AMOUNT OF 1 PER PERIOD — How $1 deposited periodically will grow.	XVI SINKING FUND — SINKING FUND — Periodic deposit that will grow to $1 at future date.	XVII PRESENT VALUE — PRESENT WORTH OF 1 — What $1 due in the future is worth today.	XVIII PRESENT VALUE OF ANNUITY — PRESENT WORTH OF 1 PER PERIOD — What $1 payable periodically is worth today.=	XIX AMORTIZATION — PARTIAL PAYMENT — Annuity worth $1 today. Periodic payment necessary to pay off a loan of $1.	PERIODS
	1	1.005 000 0000	1.000 000 0000	1.000 000 0000	.995 024 8756	.995 024 8756	1.005 000 0000	1
	2	1.010 025 0000	2.005 000 0000	.498 753 1172	.990 074 5031	1.985 099 3787	.503 753 1172	2
	3	1.015 075 1250	3.015 025 0000	.331 672 2084	.985 148 7593	2.970 248 1380	.336 672 2084	3
	4	1.020 150 5006	4.030 100 1250	.248 132 7930	.980 247 5217	3.950 495 6597	.253 132 7930	4
	5	1.025 251 2531	5.050 250 6256	.198 009 9750	.975 370 6684	4.925 866 3281	.203 009 9750	5
	6	1.030 377 5094	6.075 501 8788	.164 595 4556	.970 518 0780	5.896 384 4061	.169 595 4556	6
	7	1.035 529 3969	7.105 879 3881	.140 728 5355	.965 689 6298	6.862 074 0359	.145 728 5355	7
	8	1.040 707 0439	8.141 408 7851	.122 828 8649	.960 885 2038	7.822 959 2397	.127 828 8649	8
	9	1.045 910 5791	9.182 115 8290	.108 907 3606	.956 104 6804	8.779 063 9201	.113 907 3606	9
	10	1.051 140 1320	10.228 026 4082	.097 770 5727	.951 347 9407	9.730 411 8608	.102 770 5727	10
	11	1.056 395 8327	11.279 166 5402	.088 659 0331	.946 614 8664	10.677 026 7272	.093 659 0331	11
	12	1.061 677 8119	12.335 562 3729	.081 066 4297	.941 905 3397	11.618 932 0668	.086 066 4297	12
	13	1.066 986 2009	13.397 240 1848	.074 642 2387	.937 219 2434	12.556 151 3103	.079 642 2387	13
	14	1.072 321 1319	14.464 226 3857	.069 136 0860	.932 556 4611	13.488 707 7714	.074 136 0860	14
	15	1.077 682 7376	15.536 547 5176	.064 364 3640	.927 916 8768	14.416 624 6482	.069 364 3640	15
	16	1.083 071 1513	16.614 230 2552	.060 189 3669	.923 300 3749	15.339 925 0231	.065 189 3669	16
	17	1.088 486 5070	17.697 301 4065	.056 505 7902	.918 706 8407	16.258 631 8637	.061 505 7902	17
	18	1.093 928 9396	18.785 787 9135	.053 231 7305	.914 136 1599	17.172 768 0236	.058 231 7305	18
	19	1.099 398 5843	19.879 716 8531	.050 302 5273	.909 588 2188	18.082 356 2424	.055 302 5273	19
	20	1.104 895 5772	20.979 115 4373	.047 666 4520	.905 062 9043	18.987 419 1467	.052 666 4520	20
	21	1.110 420 0551	22.084 011 0145	.045 281 6293	.900 560 1037	19.887 979 2504	.050 281 6293	21
	22	1.115 972 1553	23.194 431 0696	.043 113 7973	.896 079 7052	20.784 058 9556	.048 113 7973	22
	23	1.121 552 0161	24.310 403 2250	.041 134 6530	.891 621 5972	21.675 680 5529	.046 134 6530	23
	24	1.127 159 7762	25.431 955 2411	.039 320 6103	.887 185 6689	22.562 866 2218	.044 320 6103	24
	25	1.132 795 5751	26.559 115 0173	.037 651 8570	.882 771 8098	23.445 638 0316	.042 651 8570	25
	26	1.138 459 5530	27.691 910 5924	.036 111 6289	.878 379 9103	24.324 017 9419	.041 111 6289	26
	27	1.144 151 8507	28.830 370 1453	.034 685 6456	.874 009 8610	25.198 027 8029	.039 685 6456	27
	28	1.149 872 6100	29.974 521 9961	.033 361 6663	.869 661 5532	26.067 689 3561	.038 361 6663	28
	29	1.155 621 9730	31.124 394 6060	.032 129 1390	.865 334 8788	26.933 024 2349	.037 129 1390	29
	30	1.161 400 0829	32.280 016 5791	.030 978 9184	.861 029 7302	27.794 053 9651	.035 978 9184	30
	31	1.167 207 0833	33.441 416 6620	.029 903 0394	.856 746 0002	28.650 799 9653	.034 903 0394	31
	32	1.173 043 1187	34.608 623 7453	.028 894 5324	.852 483 5823	29.503 283 5475	.033 894 5324	32
	33	1.178 908 3343	35.781 666 8640	.027 947 2727	.848 242 3704	30.351 525 9179	.032 947 2727	33
	34	1.184 802 8760	36.960 575 1983	.027 055 8560	.844 022 2591	31.195 548 1771	.032 055 8560	34
	35	1.190 726 8904	38.145 378 0743	.026 215 4958	.839 823 1434	32.035 371 3205	.031 215 4958	35
	36	1.196 680 5248	39.336 104 9647	.025 421 9375	.835 644 9188	32.871 016 2393	.030 421 9375	36
	37	1.202 663 9274	40.532 785 4895	.024 671 3861	.831 487 4814	33.702 503 7207	.029 671 3861	37
	38	1.208 677 2471	41.735 449 4170	.023 960 4464	.827 350 7278	34.529 854 4484	.028 960 4464	38
	39	1.214 720 6333	42.944 126 6640	.023 286 0714	.823 234 5550	35.353 089 0034	.028 286 0714	39
	40	1.220 794 2365	44.158 847 2974	.022 645 5186	.819 138 8607	36.172 227 8641	.027 645 5186	40
	41	1.226 898 2077	45.379 641 5338	.022 036 3133	.815 063 5430	36.987 291 4070	.027 036 3133	41
	42	1.233 032 6987	46.606 539 7415	.021 456 2163	.811 008 5005	37.798 299 9075	.026 456 2163	42
	43	1.239 197 8622	47.839 572 4402	.020 903 1969	.806 973 6323	38.605 273 5398	.025 903 1969	43
	44	1.245 393 8515	49.078 770 3024	.020 375 4086	.802 958 8381	39.408 232 3779	.025 375 4086	44
	45	1.251 620 8208	50.324 164 1539	.019 871 1696	.798 964 0180	40.207 196 3959	.024 871 1696	45
	46	1.257 878 9249	51.575 784 9747	.019 388 9439	.794 989 0727	41.002 185 4686	.024 388 9439	46
	47	1.264 168 3195	52.833 663 8996	.018 927 3264	.791 033 9031	41.793 219 3717	.023 927 3264	47
	48	1.270 489 1611	54.097 832 2191	.018 485 0290	.787 098 4111	42.580 317 7828	.023 485 0290	48
	49	1.276 841 6069	55.368 321 3802	.018 060 8690	.783 182 4986	43.363 500 2814	.023 060 8690	49
	50	1.283 225 8149	56.645 162 9871	.017 653 7580	.779 286 0683	44.142 786 3497	.022 653 7580	50
	51	1.289 641 9440	57.928 388 8020	.017 262 6931	.775 409 0231	44.918 195 3728	.022 262 6931	51
	52	1.296 090 1537	59.218 030 7460	.016 886 7486	.771 551 2668	45.689 746 6396	.021 886 7486	52
	53	1.302 570 6045	60.514 120 8997	.016 525 0686	.767 712 7033	46.457 459 3429	.021 525 0686	53
	54	1.309 083 4575	61.816 691 5042	.016 176 8606	.763 893 2371	47.221 352 5800	.021 176 8606	54
	55	1.315 628 8748	63.125 774 9618	.015 841 3897	.760 092 7732	47.981 445 3532	.020 841 3897	55
	56	1.322 207 0192	64.441 403 8366	.015 517 9735	.756 311 2171	48.737 756 5704	.020 517 9735	56
	57	1.328 818 0543	65.763 610 8558	.015 205 9777	.752 548 4748	49.490 305 0452	.020 205 9777	57
	58	1.335 462 1446	67.092 428 9100	.014 904 8114	.748 804 4525	50.239 109 4977	.019 904 8114	58
	59	1.342 139 4553	68.427 891 0546	.014 613 9240	.745 079 0572	50.984 188 5549	.019 613 9240	59
	60	1.348 850 1525	69.770 030 5099	.014 332 8015	.741 372 1962	51.725 560 7511	.019 332 8015	60
	61	1.355 594 4033	71.118 880 6624	.014 060 9637	.737 683 7774	52.463 244 5285	.019 060 9637	61
	62	1.362 372 3753	72.474 475 0657	.013 797 9613	.734 013 7088	53.197 258 2373	.018 797 9613	62
	63	1.369 184 2372	73.836 847 4411	.013 543 3735	.730 361 8993	53.927 620 1366	.018 543 3735	63
	64	1.376 030 1584	75.206 031 6783	.013 296 8058	.726 728 2580	54.654 348 3946	.018 296 8058	64
	65	1.382 910 3092	76.582 061 8366	.013 057 8882	.723 112 6946	55.377 461 0892	.018 057 8882	65
	66	1.389 824 8607	77.964 972 1458	.012 826 2728	.719 515 1190	56.096 976 2082	.017 826 2728	66
	67	1.396 773 9850	79.354 797 0066	.012 601 6326	.715 935 4418	56.812 911 6499	.017 601 6326	67
	68	1.403 757 8550	80.751 570 9916	.012 383 6600	.712 373 5739	57.525 285 2238	.017 383 6600	68
	69	1.410 776 6442	82.155 328 8466	.012 172 0650	.708 829 4267	58.234 114 6505	.017 172 0650	69
	70	1.417 830 5275	83.566 105 4908	.011 966 5742	.705 302 9122	58.939 417 5627	.016 966 5742	70
	71	1.424 919 6801	84.983 936 0182	.011 766 9297	.701 793 9425	59.641 211 5052	.016 766 9297	71
	72	1.432 044 2785	86.408 855 6983	.011 572 8879	.698 302 4303	60.339 513 9355	.016 572 8879	72
	73	1.439 204 4999	87.840 899 9768	.011 384 2185	.694 828 2889	61.034 342 2244	.016 384 2185	73
	74	1.446 400 5224	89.280 104 4767	.011 200 7037	.691 371 4317	61.725 713 6561	.016 200 7037	74
	75	1.453 632 5250	90.726 504 9991	.011 022 1374	.687 931 7729	62.413 645 4290	.016 022 1374	75
	76	1.460 900 6876	92.180 137 5241	.010 848 3240	.684 509 2267	63.098 154 6557	.015 848 3240	76
	77	1.468 205 1911	93.641 038 2117	.010 679 0785	.681 103 7082	63.779 258 3639	.015 679 0785	77
	78	1.475 546 2170	95.109 243 4028	.010 514 2252	.677 715 1325	64.456 973 4964	.015 514 2252	78
	79	1.482 923 9481	96.584 789 6198	.010 353 5971	.674 343 4154	65.131 316 9118	.015 353 5971	79
	80	1.490 338 5678	98.067 713 5679	.010 197 0359	.670 988 4731	65.802 305 3849	.015 197 0359	80
	81	1.497 790 2607	99.558 052 1357	.010 044 3910	.667 650 2220	66.469 955 6069	.015 044 3910	81
	82	1.505 279 2120	101.055 842 3964	.009 895 5189	.664 328 5791	67.134 284 1859	.014 895 5189	82
	83	1.512 805 6080	102.561 121 6084	.009 750 2834	.661 023 4618	67.795 307 6477	.014 750 2834	83
	84	1.520 369 6361	104.073 927 2164	.009 608 5545	.657 734 7878	68.453 042 4355	.014 608 5545	84
	85	1.527 971 4843	105.594 296 8525	.009 470 2084	.654 462 4754	69.107 504 9110	.014 470 2084	85
	86	1.535 611 3417	107.122 268 3368	.009 335 1272	.651 206 4432	69.758 711 3542	.014 335 1272	86
	87	1.543 289 3984	108.657 879 6784	.009 203 1982	.647 966 6102	70.406 677 9644	.014 203 1982	87
	88	1.551 005 8454	110.201 169 0768	.009 074 3139	.644 742 8957	71.051 420 8601	.014 074 3139	88
	89	1.558 760 8746	111.752 174 9222	.008 948 3717	.641 535 2196	71.692 956 0797	.013 948 3717	89
	90	1.566 554 6790	113.310 935 7968	.008 825 2735	.638 343 5021	72.331 299 5818	.013 825 2735	90
	91	1.574 387 4524	114.877 490 4758	.008 704 9255	.635 167 6638	72.966 467 2455	.013 704 9255	91
	92	1.582 259 3896	116.451 877 9282	.008 587 2381	.632 007 6256	73.598 474 8712	.013 587 2381	92
	93	1.590 170 6866	118.034 137 3178	.008 472 1253	.628 863 3091	74.227 338 1803	.013 472 1253	93
	94	1.598 121 5400	119.624 308 0044	.008 359 5050	.625 734 6359	74.853 072 8162	.013 359 5050	94
	95	1.606 112 1477	121.222 429 5445	.008 249 2984	.622 621 5283	75.475 694 3445	.013 249 2984	95
	96	1.614 142 7085	122.828 541 6922	.008 141 4302	.619 523 9087	76.095 218 2532	.013 141 4302	96
	97	1.622 213 4220	124.442 684 4006	.008 035 8279	.616 441 7002	76.711 659 9535	.013 035 8279	97
	98	1.630 324 4891	126.064 897 8226	.007 932 4222	.613 374 8261	77.325 034 7796	.012 932 4222	98
	99	1.638 476 1116	127.695 222 3118	.007 831 1466	.610 323 2101	77.935 357 9896	.012 831 1466	99
	100	1.646 668 4921	129.333 698 4233	.007 731 9369	.607 286 7762	78.542 644 7658	.012 731 9369	100

		XIV COMPOUND AMOUNT	XV AMOUNT OF ANNUITY	XVI SINKING FUND	XVII PRESENT VALUE	XVIII PRESENT VALUE OF ANNUITY	XIX AMORTIZATION	
RATE **7/12%**	P E R I O D S	AMOUNT OF 1 *How $1 left at compound interest will grow.*	AMOUNT OF 1 PER PERIOD *How $1 deposited periodically will grow.*	SINKING FUND *Periodic deposit that will grow to $1 at future date.*	PRESENT WORTH OF 1 *What $1 due in the future is worth today.*	PRESENT WORTH OF 1 PER PERIOD *What $1 payable periodically is worth today.*	PARTIAL PAYMENT *Annuity worth $1 today. Periodic payment necessary to pay off a loan of $1.*	P E R I O D S
	1	1.005 833 3333	1.000 000 0000	1.000 000 0000	.994 200 4971	.994 200 4971	1.005 833 3333	1
	2	1.011 700 6944	2.005 833 3333	.498 545 9078	.988 434 6284	1.982 635 1255	.504 379 2411	2
	3	1.017 602 2818	3.017 534 0278	.331 396 4286	.982 702 1989	2.965 337 3245	.337 229 7619	3
	4	1.023 538 2951	4.035 136 3096	.247 823 1027	.977 003 0147	3.942 340 3392	.253 656 4360	4
	5	1.029 508 9352	5.058 674 6047	.197 680 2380	.971 336 8829	4.913 677 2220	.203 513 5714	5
	6	1.035 514 4040	6.088 183 5399	.164 252 6040	.965 703 6118	5.879 380 8338	.170 085 9373	6
	7	1.041 554 9047	7.123 697 9439	.140 376 5303	.960 103 0109	6.839 483 8447	.146 209 8636	7
	8	1.047 630 6416	8.165 252 8486	.122 470 1817	.954 534 8907	7.794 018 7355	.128 303 5150	8
	9	1.053 741 8204	9.212 883 4902	.108 543 6499	.948 999 0628	8.743 017 7983	.114 376 9832	9
	10	1.059 888 6476	10.266 625 3106	.097 402 9898	.943 495 3400	9.686 513 1383	.103 236 3233	10
	11	1.066 071 3314	11.326 513 9582	.088 288 4181	.938 023 5361	10.624 536 6744	.094 121 7514	11
	12	1.072 290 0809	12.392 585 2896	.080 693 4128	.932 583 4658	11.557 120 1402	.086 526 7461	12
	13	1.078 545 1063	13.464 875 3705	.074 267 3046	.927 174 9453	12.484 295 0856	.080 100 6379	13
	14	1.084 836 6194	14.543 420 4768	.068 759 6155	.921 797 7916	13.406 092 8771	.074 592 9488	14
	15	1.091 164 8331	15.628 257 0963	.063 986 6617	.916 451 8226	14.322 544 6997	.069 819 9950	15
	16	1.097 529 9613	16.719 421 9293	.059 810 6803	.911 136 8576	15.233 681 5573	.065 644 0136	16
	17	1.103 932 2194	17.816 951 8906	.056 126 3232	.905 852 7167	16.139 534 2740	.061 959 6565	17
	18	1.110 371 8240	18.920 884 1100	.052 851 6529	.900 599 2213	17.040 133 4953	.058 684 9863	18
	19	1.116 848 9929	20.031 255 9339	.049 921 9821	.895 376 1935	17.935 509 6888	.055 755 3154	19
	20	1.123 363 9454	21.148 104 9269	.047 285 5607	.890 183 4567	18.825 693 1454	.053 118 8941	20
	21	1.129 916 9018	22.271 468 8723	.044 900 4960	.885 020 8351	19.710 713 9805	.050 733 8294	21
	22	1.136 508 0837	23.401 385 7740	.042 732 5121	.879 888 1542	20.590 602 1348	.048 565 8454	22
	23	1.143 137 7142	24.537 893 8577	.040 753 2939	.874 785 2403	21.465 387 3751	.046 586 6272	23
	24	1.149 806 0175	25.681 031 5719	.038 939 2458	.869 711 9208	22.335 099 2958	.044 772 5791	24
	25	1.156 513 2193	26.830 837 5894	.037 270 5472	.864 668 0240	23.199 767 3198	.043 103 8806	25
	26	1.163 259 5464	27.987 350 8087	.035 730 4272	.859 653 3793	24.059 420 6991	.041 563 7605	26
	27	1.170 045 2271	29.150 610 3550	.034 304 5990	.854 667 8170	24.914 088 5161	.040 137 9324	27
	28	1.176 870 4909	30.320 655 5821	.032 980 8172	.849 711 1685	25.763 799 6846	.038 814 1506	28
	29	1.183 735 5688	31.497 526 0730	.031 748 5252	.844 783 2661	26.608 582 9507	.037 581 8585	29
	30	1.190 640 6929	32.681 261 6418	.030 598 5739	.839 883 9431	27.448 466 8938	.036 431 9072	30
	31	1.197 586 0970	33.871 902 3347	.029 522 9949	.835 013 0338	28.283 479 9276	.035 356 3282	31
	32	1.204 572 0159	35.069 488 4316	.028 514 8157	.830 170 3732	29.113 650 3008	.034 348 1491	32
	33	1.211 598 6859	36.274 060 4475	.027 567 9091	.825 355 7978	29.939 006 0986	.033 401 2424	33
	34	1.218 666 3449	37.485 659 1334	.026 676 8685	.820 569 1444	30.759 575 2430	.032 510 2019	34
	35	1.225 775 2320	38.704 325 4784	.025 836 9055	.815 810 2513	31.575 385 4943	.031 670 2388	35
	36	1.232 925 5875	39.930 100 7103	.025 043 7635	.811 078 9574	32.386 464 4516	.030 877 0969	36
	37	1.240 117 6534	41.163 026 2978	.024 293 6463	.806 375 1026	33.192 839 5542	.030 126 9796	37
	38	1.247 351 6730	42.403 143 9512	.023 583 1570	.801 698 5279	33.994 538 0821	.029 416 4903	38
	39	1.254 627 8911	43.650 495 6243	.022 909 2473	.797 049 0749	34.791 587 1570	.028 742 5807	39
	40	1.261 946 5538	44.905 123 5154	.022 269 1738	.792 426 5865	35.584 013 7435	.028 102 5071	40
	41	1.269 307 9087	46.167 070 0692	.021 660 4606	.787 830 9062	36.371 844 6497	.027 493 7939	41
	42	1.276 712 2049	47.436 377 9780	.021 080 8675	.783 261 8786	37.155 106 5283	.026 914 2009	42
	43	1.284 159 6927	48.713 090 1829	.020 528 3630	.778 719 3490	37.933 825 8773	.026 361 6964	43
	44	1.291 650 6243	49.997 249 8756	.020 001 1001	.774 203 1639	38.708 029 0413	.025 834 4334	44
	45	1.299 185 2529	51.288 900 4999	.019 497 3959	.769 713 1704	39.477 742 2117	.025 330 7293	45
	46	1.306 763 8336	52.588 085 7528	.019 015 7140	.765 249 2167	40.242 991 4284	.024 849 0474	46
	47	1.314 386 6226	53.894 849 5863	.018 554 6487	.760 811 1516	41.003 802 5800	.024 387 9820	47
	48	1.322 053 8779	55.209 236 2089	.018 112 9113	.756 398 8251	41.760 201 4051	.023 946 2447	48
	49	1.329 765 8588	56.531 290 0868	.017 689 3186	.752 012 0880	42.512 213 4931	.023 522 6519	49
	50	1.337 522 8263	57.861 055 9456	.017 282 7817	.747 650 7917	43.259 864 2848	.023 116 1151	50
	51	1.345 325 0428	59.198 578 7720	.016 892 2974	.743 314 7887	44.003 179 0735	.022 725 6308	51
	52	1.353 172 7723	60.543 903 8148	.016 516 9396	.739 003 9325	44.742 183 0060	.022 350 2729	52
	53	1.361 066 2801	61.897 076 5871	.016 155 8519	.734 718 0770	45.476 901 0830	.021 989 1852	53
	54	1.369 005 8334	63.258 142 8672	.015 808 2415	.730 457 0774	46.207 358 1604	.021 641 5748	54
	55	1.376 991 7008	64.627 148 7006	.015 473 3733	.726 220 7895	46.933 578 9498	.021 306 7067	55
	56	1.385 024 1523	66.004 140 4013	.015 150 5647	.722 009 0699	47.655 588 0197	.020 983 8980	56
	57	1.393 103 4599	67.389 164 5537	.014 839 1808	.717 821 7762	48.373 409 7959	.020 672 5142	57
	58	1.401 229 8967	68.782 268 0136	.014 538 6308	.713 658 7667	49.087 068 5626	.020 371 9641	58
	59	1.409 403 7378	70.183 497 9103	.014 248 3636	.709 519 9006	49.796 588 4633	.020 081 6970	59
	60	1.417 625 2596	71.592 901 6481	.013 967 8652	.705 405 0379	50.501 993 5012	.019 801 1985	60
	61	1.425 894 7403	73.010 526 9077	.013 696 6550	.701 314 0393	51.203 307 5405	.019 529 9884	61
	62	1.434 212 4596	74.436 421 6480	.013 434 2836	.697 246 7665	51.900 554 3071	.019 267 6170	62
	63	1.442 578 6990	75.870 634 1076	.013 180 3301	.693 203 0819	52.593 757 3890	.019 013 6634	63
	64	1.450 993 7414	77.313 212 8066	.012 934 3997	.689 182 8486	53.282 940 2376	.018 767 7331	64
	65	1.459 457 8715	78.764 206 5480	.012 696 1223	.685 185 9307	53.968 126 1683	.018 529 4556	65
	66	1.467 971 3758	80.223 664 4195	.012 465 1499	.681 212 1929	54.649 338 3611	.018 298 4832	66
	67	1.476 534 5421	81.691 635 7953	.012 241 1553	.677 261 5008	55.326 599 8619	.018 074 4886	67
	68	1.485 147 6603	83.168 170 3374	.012 023 8307	.673 333 7208	55.999 933 5827	.017 857 1640	68
	69	1.493 811 0217	84.653 317 9977	.011 812 8861	.669 428 7199	56.669 362 3026	.017 646 2194	69
	70	1.502 524 9193	86.147 129 0194	.011 608 0479	.665 546 3661	57.334 908 6687	.017 441 3812	70
	71	1.511 289 6480	87.649 653 9387	.011 409 0582	.661 686 5280	57.996 595 1967	.017 242 3915	71
	72	1.520 105 5043	89.160 943 5866	.011 215 6721	.657 849 0751	58.654 444 2718	.017 049 0065	72
	73	1.528 972 7864	90.681 049 0909	.011 027 6625	.654 033 8775	59.308 478 1493	.016 860 9958	73
	74	1.537 891 7943	92.210 021 8772	.010 844 8082	.650 240 8061	59.958 718 9554	.016 678 1415	74
	75	1.546 862 8298	93.747 913 6715	.010 666 9040	.646 469 7327	60.605 188 6880	.016 500 2374	75
	76	1.555 886 1963	95.294 776 5013	.010 493 7546	.642 720 5296	61.247 909 2176	.016 327 0879	76
	77	1.564 962 1991	96.850 662 6975	.010 325 1746	.638 993 0700	61.886 902 2876	.016 158 5079	77
	78	1.574 091 1452	98.415 624 8966	.010 160 9882	.635 287 2278	62.522 189 5154	.015 994 3215	78
	79	1.583 273 3436	99.989 716 0418	.010 001 0285	.631 602 8777	63.153 792 3931	.015 834 3618	79
	80	1.592 509 1047	101.572 989 3854	.009 845 1370	.627 939 8950	63.781 732 2881	.015 678 4704	80
	81	1.601 798 7412	103.165 498 4902	.009 693 1631	.624 298 1557	64.406 030 4438	.015 526 4964	81
	82	1.611 142 5672	104.767 297 2314	.009 544 9632	.620 677 5368	65.026 707 9806	.015 378 2966	82
	83	1.620 540 8988	106.378 439 7985	.009 400 4011	.617 077 9156	65.643 785 8962	.015 233 7344	83
	84	1.629 994 0541	107.998 980 6974	.009 259 3466	.613 499 1704	66.257 285 0667	.015 092 6800	84
	85	1.639 502 3527	109.628 974 7514	.009 121 6761	.609 941 1802	66.867 226 2469	.014 955 0094	85
	86	1.649 066 1164	111.268 477 1041	.008 987 2714	.606 403 8246	67.473 630 0715	.014 820 6047	86
	87	1.658 685 6688	112.917 543 2206	.008 856 0198	.602 886 9838	68.076 517 0553	.014 689 3531	87
	88	1.668 361 3352	114.576 228 8894	.008 727 8139	.599 390 5390	68.675 907 5944	.014 561 1472	88
	89	1.678 093 4430	116.244 590 2246	.008 602 5509	.595 914 3719	69.271 821 9662	.014 435 8842	89
	90	1.687 882 3214	117.922 683 6675	.008 480 1327	.592 458 3647	69.864 280 3310	.014 313 4660	90
	91	1.697 728 3016	119.610 565 9889	.008 360 4654	.589 022 4007	70.453 302 7317	.014 193 7987	91
	92	1.707 631 7167	121.308 294 2905	.008 243 4594	.585 606 3636	71.038 909 0953	.014 076 7927	92
	93	1.717 592 9017	123.015 926 0072	.008 129 0288	.582 210 1378	71.621 119 2331	.013 962 3621	93
	94	1.727 612 1936	124.733 518 9089	.008 017 0912	.578 833 6084	72.199 952 8415	.013 850 4246	94
	95	1.737 689 9314	126.461 131 1026	.007 907 5681	.575 476 6612	72.775 429 5028	.013 740 9014	95
	96	1.747 826 4560	128.198 821 0340	.007 800 3837	.572 139 1827	73.347 568 6854	.013 633 7171	96
	97	1.758 022 1104	129.946 647 4900	.007 695 4659	.568 821 0598	73.916 389 7453	.013 528 7993	97
	98	1.768 277 2393	131.704 669 6004	.007 592 7452	.565 522 1804	74.481 911 9257	.013 426 0785	98
	99	1.778 592 1899	133.472 946 8397	.007 492 1550	.562 242 4329	75.044 154 3586	.013 325 4883	99
	100	1.788 967 3110	135.251 539 0296	.007 393 6312	.558 981 7063	75.603 136 0649	.013 226 9645	100

		XIV COMPOUND AMOUNT	XV AMOUNT OF ANNUITY	XVI SINKING FUND	XVII PRESENT VALUE	XVIII PRESENT VALUE OF ANNUITY	XIX AMORTIZATION	
RATE 2/3%	P E R I O D S	AMOUNT OF 1 *How $1 left at compound interest will grow.*	AMOUNT OF 1 PER PERIOD *How $1 deposited periodically will grow.*	SINKING FUND *Periodic deposit that will grow to $1 at future date.*	PRESENT WORTH OF 1 *What $1 due in the future is worth today.*	PRESENT WORTH OF 1 PER PERIOD *What $1 payable periodically is worth today.*	PARTIAL PAYMENT *Annuity worth $1 today. Periodic payment necessary to pay off a loan of $1.*	P E R I O D S
	1	1.006 666 6667	1.000 000 0000	1.000 000 0000	.993 377 4834	.993 377 4834	1.006 666 6667	1
	2	1.013 377 7778	2.006 666 6667	.498 338 8704	.986 798 8246	1.980 176 3081	.505 005 5371	2
	3	1.020 133 6296	3.020 044 4444	.331 120 9548	.980 263 7331	2.960 440 0411	.337 787 6215	3
	4	1.026 934 5205	4.040 178 0741	.247 513 8426	.973 771 9203	3.934 211 9614	.254 180 5093	4
	5	1.033 780 7506	5.067 112 5946	.197 351 0518	.967 323 0996	4.901 535 0610	.204 017 7184	5
	6	1.040 672 6223	6.100 893 3452	.163 910 4215	.960 916 9864	5.862 452 0473	.170 577 0882	6
	7	1.047 610 4398	7.141 565 9675	.140 025 3116	.954 553 2977	6.817 005 3450	.146 691 9783	7
	8	1.054 594 5094	8.189 176 4073	.122 112 4018	.948 231 7527	7.765 237 0977	.128 779 0685	8
	9	1.061 625 1394	9.243 770 9167	.108 180 9587	.941 952 0722	8.707 189 1699	.114 847 6254	9
	10	1.068 702 6404	10.305 396 0561	.097 036 5423	.935 713 9790	9.642 903 1489	.103 703 2089	10
	11	1.075 827 3246	11.374 098 6965	.087 919 0542	.929 517 1977	10.572 420 3466	.094 585 7209	11
	12	1.082 999 5068	12.449 926 0211	.080 321 7624	.923 361 4547	11.495 781 8013	.086 988 4291	12
	13	1.090 219 5035	13.532 925 5279	.073 893 8523	.917 246 4781	12.413 028 2794	.080 560 5190	13
	14	1.097 487 6335	14.623 145 0315	.068 384 7420	.911 171 9981	13.324 200 2775	.075 051 4087	14
	15	1.104 804 2178	15.720 632 6650	.063 610 6715	.905 137 7465	14.229 338 0240	.070 277 3382	15
	16	1.112 169 5792	16.825 436 8828	.059 433 8208	.899 143 4568	15.128 481 4808	.066 100 4874	16
	17	1.119 584 0431	17.937 606 4620	.055 748 7980	.893 188 8644	16.021 670 3452	.062 415 4647	17
	18	1.127 047 9367	19.057 190 5051	.052 473 6319	.887 273 7063	16.908 944 0515	.059 140 2986	18
	19	1.134 561 5896	20.184 238 4418	.049 543 6081	.881 397 7215	17.790 341 7730	.056 210 2748	19
	20	1.142 125 3335	21.318 800 0314	.046 906 9553	.875 560 6505	18.665 902 4236	.053 573 6220	20
	21	1.149 739 5024	22.460 925 3649	.044 521 7632	.869 762 2356	19.535 664 6592	.051 188 4299	21
	22	1.157 404 4324	23.610 664 8673	.042 353 7417	.864 002 2208	20.399 666 8800	.049 020 4083	22
	23	1.165 120 4620	24.768 069 2998	.040 374 5640	.858 280 3518	21.257 947 2317	.047 041 2307	23
	24	1.172 887 9317	25.933 189 7618	.038 560 6248	.852 596 3759	22.110 543 6077	.045 227 2915	24
	25	1.180 707 1846	27.106 077 6935	.036 892 0952	.846 950 0423	22.957 493 6500	.043 558 7619	25
	26	1.188 578 5659	28.286 784 8782	.035 352 1973	.841 341 1017	23.798 834 7517	.042 018 8640	26
	27	1.196 502 4230	29.475 363 4440	.033 926 6385	.835 769 3063	24.634 604 0580	.040 593 3052	27
	28	1.204 479 1058	30.671 865 8670	.032 603 1681	.830 234 4102	25.464 838 4682	.039 269 8348	28
	29	1.212 508 9665	31.876 344 9728	.031 371 2253	.824 736 1691	26.289 574 6373	.038 037 8920	29
	30	1.220 592 3596	33.088 853 9392	.030 221 6572	.819 274 3402	27.108 848 9774	.036 888 3238	30
	31	1.228 729 6420	34.309 446 2988	.029 146 4919	.813 848 6823	27.922 697 6597	.035 813 1586	31
	32	1.236 921 1729	35.538 175 9408	.028 138 7543	.808 458 9559	28.731 156 6156	.034 805 4209	32
	33	1.245 167 3141	36.775 097 1138	.027 192 3143	.803 104 9231	29.534 261 5387	.033 858 9810	33
	34	1.253 468 4295	38.020 264 4279	.026 301 7634	.797 786 3474	30.332 047 8861	.032 968 4301	34
	35	1.261 824 8857	39.273 732 8574	.025 462 3110	.792 502 9941	31.124 550 8802	.032 128 9777	35
	36	1.270 237 0516	40.535 557 7431	.024 669 6988	.787 254 6299	31.911 805 5101	.031 336 3655	36
	37	1.278 705 2986	41.805 794 7947	.023 920 1289	.782 041 0231	32.693 846 5333	.030 586 7956	37
	38	1.287 230 0006	43.084 500 0934	.023 210 2032	.776 861 9435	33.470 708 4767	.029 876 8698	38
	39	1.295 811 5340	44.371 730 0940	.022 536 8720	.771 717 1624	34.242 425 6392	.029 203 5386	39
	40	1.304 450 2775	45.667 541 6279	.021 897 3907	.766 606 4527	35.009 032 0919	.028 564 0573	40
	41	1.313 146 6127	46.971 991 9055	.021 289 2824	.761 529 5888	35.770 561 6807	.027 955 9491	41
	42	1.321 900 9235	48.285 138 5182	.020 710 3061	.756 486 3465	36.527 048 0272	.027 376 9728	42
	43	1.330 713 5963	49.607 039 4416	.020 158 4294	.751 476 5031	37.278 524 5303	.026 825 0960	43
	44	1.339 585 0203	50.937 753 0379	.019 631 8043	.746 499 8375	38.025 024 3678	.026 298 4710	44
	45	1.348 515 5871	52.277 338 0581	.019 128 7475	.741 556 1300	38.766 580 4978	.025 795 4142	45
	46	1.357 505 6910	53.625 853 6452	.018 647 7218	.736 645 1623	39.503 225 6601	.025 314 3885	46
	47	1.366 555 7289	54.983 359 3362	.018 187 3209	.731 766 7175	40.234 992 3776	.024 853 9876	47
	48	1.375 666 1004	56.349 915 0651	.017 746 2557	.726 920 5803	40.961 912 9579	.024 412 9223	48
	49	1.384 837 2078	57.725 581 1655	.017 323 3423	.722 106 5367	41.684 019 4946	.023 990 0089	49
	50	1.394 069 4558	59.110 418 3733	.016 917 4915	.717 324 3742	42.401 343 8688	.023 584 1582	50
	51	1.403 363 2522	60.504 487 8291	.016 527 6996	.712 573 8817	43.113 917 7505	.023 194 3663	51
	52	1.412 719 0072	61.907 851 0813	.016 153 0401	.707 854 8493	43.821 772 5998	.022 819 7068	52
	53	1.422 137 1339	63.320 570 0885	.015 792 6563	.703 167 0689	44.524 939 6687	.022 459 3230	53
	54	1.431 618 0481	64.742 707 2224	.015 445 7551	.698 510 3333	45.223 450 0020	.022 112 4218	54
	55	1.441 162 1685	66.174 325 2706	.015 111 6010	.693 884 4371	45.917 334 4391	.021 778 2677	55
	56	1.450 769 9163	67.615 487 4390	.014 789 5111	.689 289 1759	46.606 623 6150	.021 456 1777	56
	57	1.460 441 7157	69.066 257 3553	.014 478 8503	.684 724 3469	47.291 347 9619	.021 145 5170	57
	58	1.470 177 9938	70.526 699 0710	.014 179 0274	.680 189 7486	47.971 537 7105	.020 845 6941	58
	59	1.479 979 1804	71.996 877 0648	.013 889 4913	.675 685 1807	48.647 222 8912	.020 556 1580	59
	60	1.489 845 7083	73.476 856 2452	.013 609 7276	.671 210 4444	49.318 433 3356	.020 276 3943	60
	61	1.499 778 0130	74.966 701 9535	.013 339 2556	.666 765 3421	49.985 198 6778	.020 005 9223	61
	62	1.509 776 5331	76.466 479 9666	.013 077 6257	.662 349 6776	50.647 548 3554	.019 744 2923	62
	63	1.519 841 7100	77.976 256 4997	.012 824 4166	.657 963 2559	51.305 511 6113	.019 491 0833	63
	64	1.529 973 9881	79.496 098 2097	.012 579 2337	.653 605 8834	51.959 117 4947	.019 245 9004	64
	65	1.540 173 8147	81.026 072 1977	.012 341 7065	.649 277 3676	52.608 394 8623	.019 008 3731	65
	66	1.550 441 6401	82.566 246 0124	.012 111 4868	.644 977 5175	53.253 372 3798	.018 778 1535	66
	67	1.560 777 9177	84.116 687 6525	.011 888 2475	.640 706 1432	53.894 078 5229	.018 554 9141	67
	68	1.571 183 1038	85.677 465 5702	.011 671 6805	.636 463 0561	54.530 541 5791	.018 338 3471	68
	69	1.581 657 6578	87.248 648 6740	.011 461 4956	.632 248 0690	55.162 789 6481	.018 128 1622	69
	70	1.592 202 0422	88.830 306 3318	.011 257 4192	.628 060 9907	55.790 850 6438	.017 924 0859	70
	71	1.602 816 7225	90.422 508 3740	.011 059 1933	.623 901 6514	56.414 752 2952	.017 725 8600	71
	72	1.613 502 1673	92.025 325 0965	.010 866 5739	.619 769 8523	57.034 522 1475	.017 533 2406	72
	73	1.624 258 8484	93.638 827 2638	.010 679 3307	.615 665 4162	57.650 187 5637	.017 345 9973	73
	74	1.635 087 2407	95.263 086 1122	.010 497 2455	.611 588 1618	58.261 775 7256	.017 163 9121	74
	75	1.645 987 8224	96.898 173 3530	.010 320 1120	.607 537 9091	58.869 313 6347	.016 986 7787	75
	76	1.656 961 0745	98.544 161 1753	.010 147 7347	.603 514 4792	59.472 828 1139	.016 814 4013	76
	77	1.668 007 4817	100.201 122 2498	.009 979 9281	.599 517 6946	60.072 345 8085	.016 646 5948	77
	78	1.679 127 5315	101.869 129 7315	.009 816 5166	.595 547 3788	60.667 893 1873	.016 483 1832	78
	79	1.690 321 7151	103.548 257 2630	.009 657 3330	.591 603 3564	61.259 496 5437	.016 323 9996	79
	80	1.701 590 5265	105.238 578 9781	.009 502 2188	.587 685 4534	61.847 181 9970	.016 168 8854	80
	81	1.712 934 4634	106.940 169 5046	.009 351 0231	.583 793 4967	62.430 975 4937	.016 017 6898	81
	82	1.724 354 0265	108.653 103 9680	.009 203 6027	.579 927 3146	63.010 902 8083	.015 870 2694	82
	83	1.735 849 7200	110.377 457 9945	.009 059 8209	.576 086 7364	63.586 989 5447	.015 726 4876	83
	84	1.747 422 0514	112.113 307 7144	.008 919 5477	.572 271 5924	64.159 261 1371	.015 586 2144	84
	85	1.759 071 5318	113.860 729 7659	.008 782 6593	.568 481 7143	64.727 742 8514	.015 449 3260	85
	86	1.770 798 6753	115.619 801 2976	.008 649 0375	.564 716 9348	65.292 459 7862	.015 315 7042	86
	87	1.782 603 9998	117.390 599 9729	.008 518 5696	.560 977 0875	65.853 436 8737	.015 185 2363	87
	88	1.794 488 0265	119.173 203 9728	.008 391 1481	.557 262 0075	66.410 698 8812	.015 057 8147	88
	89	1.806 451 2800	120.967 691 9992	.008 266 6701	.553 571 5306	66.964 270 4118	.014 933 3367	89
	90	1.818 494 2885	122.774 143 2792	.008 145 0375	.549 905 4940	67.514 175 9057	.014 811 7042	90
	91	1.830 617 5838	124.592 637 5678	.008 026 1564	.546 263 7357	68.060 439 6414	.014 692 8231	91
	92	1.842 821 7010	126.423 255 1516	.007 909 9371	.542 646 0951	68.603 085 7365	.014 576 6038	92
	93	1.855 107 1790	128.266 076 8526	.007 796 2936	.539 052 4123	69.142 138 1489	.014 462 9603	93
	94	1.867 474 5602	130.121 184 0316	.007 685 1437	.535 482 5288	69.677 620 6777	.014 351 8104	94
	95	1.879 924 3906	131.988 658 5918	.007 576 4085	.531 936 2869	70.209 556 9646	.014 243 0752	95
	96	1.892 457 2199	133.868 582 9824	.007 470 0126	.528 413 5300	70.737 970 4946	.014 136 6793	96
	97	1.905 073 6013	135.761 040 2023	.007 365 8835	.524 914 1027	71.262 884 5973	.014 032 5501	97
	98	1.917 774 0920	137.666 113 8036	.007 263 9517	.521 437 8503	71.784 322 4477	.013 930 6184	98
	99	1.930 559 2526	139.583 887 8957	.007 164 1506	.517 984 6196	72.302 307 0672	.013 830 8173	99
	100	1.943 429 6477	141.514 447 1483	.007 066 4163	.514 554 2578	72.816 861 3250	.013 733 0830	100

	XIV COMPOUND AMOUNT	XV AMOUNT OF ANNUITY	XVI SINKING FUND	XVII PRESENT VALUE	XVIII PRESENT VALUE OF ANNUITY	XIX AMORTIZATION	
RATE 3/4% PERIODS	AMOUNT OF 1 — How $1 left at compound interest will grow.	AMOUNT OF 1 PER PERIOD — How $1 deposited periodically will grow.	SINKING FUND — Periodic deposit that will grow to $1 at future date.	PRESENT WORTH OF 1 — What $1 due in the future is worth today.	PRESENT WORTH OF 1 PER PERIOD — What $1 payable periodically is worth today.	PARTIAL PAYMENT — Annuity worth $1 today. Periodic payment necessary to pay off a loan of $1.	PERIODS
1	1.007 500 0000	1.000 000 0000	1.000 000 0000	.992 555 8313	.992 555 8313	1.007 500 0000	1
2	1.015 056 2500	2.007 500 0000	.498 132 0050	.985 167 0782	1.977 722 9094	.505 632 0050	2
3	1.022 669 1719	3.022 556 2500	.330 845 7866	.977 833 3282	2.955 556 2377	.338 345 7866	3
4	1.030 339 1907	4.045 225 4219	.247 205 0123	.970 554 1719	3.926 110 4096	.254 705 0123	4
5	1.038 066 7346	5.075 564 6125	.197 022 4155	.963 329 2029	4.889 439 6125	.204 522 4155	5
6	1.045 852 2351	6.113 631 3471	.163 568 9074	.956 158 0178	5.845 597 6303	.171 068 9074	6
7	1.053 696 1269	7.159 483 5822	.139 674 8786	.949 040 2162	6.794 637 8464	.147 174 8786	7
8	1.061 598 8478	8.213 179 7091	.121 755 5241	.941 975 4006	7.736 613 2471	.129 255 5241	8
9	1.069 560 8392	9.274 778 5569	.107 819 2858	.934 963 1768	8.671 576 4239	.115 319 2858	9
10	1.077 582 5455	10.344 339 3961	.096 671 2287	.928 003 1532	9.599 579 5771	.104 171 2287	10
11	1.085 664 4146	11.421 921 9416	.087 550 9398	.921 094 9411	10.520 674 5182	.095 050 9398	11
12	1.093 806 8977	12.507 586 3561	.079 951 4768	.914 238 1550	11.434 912 6731	.087 451 4768	12
13	1.102 010 4494	13.601 393 2538	.073 521 8798	.907 432 4119	12.342 345 0850	.081 021 8798	13
14	1.110 275 5278	14.703 403 7032	.068 011 4632	.900 677 3319	13.243 022 4169	.075 511 4632	14
15	1.118 602 5942	15.813 679 2310	.063 236 3908	.893 972 5378	14.136 994 9547	.070 736 3908	15
16	1.126 992 1137	16.932 281 8252	.059 058 7855	.887 317 6554	15.024 312 6101	.066 558 7855	16
17	1.135 444 5545	18.059 273 9389	.055 373 2118	.880 712 3131	15.905 024 9232	.062 873 2118	17
18	1.143 960 3887	19.194 718 4934	.052 097 6643	.874 156 1420	16.779 181 0652	.059 597 6643	18
19	1.152 540 0916	20.338 678 8821	.049 167 4020	.867 648 7762	17.646 829 8414	.056 667 4020	19
20	1.161 184 1423	21.491 218 9738	.046 530 6319	.861 189 8523	18.508 019 6937	.054 030 6319	20
21	1.169 893 0234	22.652 403 1161	.044 145 4266	.854 779 0097	19.362 798 7034	.051 645 4266	21
22	1.178 667 2210	23.822 296 1394	.041 977 4817	.848 415 8905	20.211 214 5940	.049 477 4817	22
23	1.187 507 2252	25.000 963 3605	.039 998 4587	.842 100 1395	21.053 314 7335	.047 498 4587	23
24	1.196 413 5294	26.188 470 5857	.038 184 7423	.835 831 4040	21.889 146 1374	.045 684 7423	24
25	1.205 386 6309	27.384 884 1151	.036 516 4956	.829 609 3340	22.718 755 4714	.044 016 4956	25
26	1.214 427 0306	28.590 270 7459	.034 976 9335	.823 433 5821	23.542 189 0535	.042 476 9335	26
27	1.223 535 2333	29.804 697 7765	.033 551 7578	.817 303 8036	24.359 492 8571	.041 051 7578	27
28	1.232 711 7476	31.028 233 0099	.032 228 7125	.811 219 6562	25.170 712 5132	.039 728 7125	28
29	1.241 957 0857	32.260 944 7574	.030 997 2323	.805 180 8001	25.975 893 3134	.038 497 2323	29
30	1.251 271 7638	33.502 901 8431	.029 848 1608	.799 186 8984	26.775 080 2118	.037 348 1608	30
31	1.260 656 3021	34.754 173 6069	.028 773 5226	.793 237 6163	27.568 317 8281	.036 273 5226	31
32	1.270 111 2243	36.014 829 9090	.027 766 3397	.787 332 6216	28.355 650 4497	.035 266 3397	32
33	1.279 637 0585	37.284 941 1333	.026 820 4795	.781 471 5847	29.137 122 0344	.034 320 4795	33
34	1.289 234 3364	38.564 578 1918	.025 930 5313	.775 654 1784	29.912 776 2128	.033 430 5313	34
35	1.298 903 5940	39.853 812 5282	.025 091 7023	.769 880 0778	30.682 656 2907	.032 591 7023	35
36	1.308 645 3709	41.152 716 1222	.024 299 7327	.764 148 9606	31.446 805 2513	.031 799 7327	36
37	1.318 460 2112	42.461 361 4931	.023 550 8228	.758 460 5068	32.205 265 7581	.031 050 8228	37
38	1.328 348 6628	43.779 821 7043	.022 841 5732	.752 814 3988	32.958 080 1569	.030 341 5732	38
39	1.338 311 2778	45.108 170 3671	.022 168 9329	.747 210 3214	33.705 290 4783	.029 668 9329	39
40	1.348 348 6123	46.446 481 6449	.021 530 1561	.741 647 9617	34.446 938 4400	.029 030 1561	40
41	1.358 461 2269	47.794 830 2572	.020 922 7650	.736 127 0091	35.183 065 4492	.028 422 7650	41
42	1.368 649 6861	49.153 291 4841	.020 344 5175	.730 647 1555	35.913 712 6046	.027 844 5175	42
43	1.378 914 5688	50.521 941 1703	.019 793 3804	.725 208 0948	36.638 920 6994	.027 293 3804	43
44	1.389 256 4180	51.900 855 7290	.019 267 5051	.719 809 5233	37.358 730 2227	.026 767 5051	44
45	1.399 675 8411	53.290 112 1470	.018 765 2073	.714 451 1398	38.073 181 3625	.026 265 2073	45
46	1.410 173 4099	54.689 787 9881	.018 284 9493	.709 132 6449	38.782 314 0074	.025 784 9493	46
47	1.420 749 7105	56.099 961 3980	.017 825 3242	.703 853 7419	39.486 167 7493	.025 325 3242	47
48	1.431 405 3333	57.520 711 1085	.017 385 0424	.698 614 1359	40.184 781 8852	.024 885 0424	48
49	1.442 140 8733	58.952 116 4418	.016 962 9194	.693 413 5344	40.878 195 4195	.024 462 9194	49
50	1.452 956 9299	60.394 257 3151	.016 557 8657	.688 251 6470	41.566 447 0665	.024 057 8657	50
51	1.463 854 1068	61.847 214 2450	.016 168 8770	.683 128 1856	42.249 575 2521	.023 668 8770	51
52	1.474 833 0126	63.311 068 3518	.015 795 0265	.678 042 8641	42.927 618 1163	.023 295 0265	52
53	1.485 894 2602	64.785 901 3645	.015 435 4571	.672 995 3986	43.600 613 5149	.022 935 4571	53
54	1.497 038 4672	66.271 795 6247	.015 089 3754	.667 985 5073	44.268 599 0222	.022 589 3754	54
55	1.508 266 2557	67.768 834 0919	.014 756 0455	.663 012 9105	44.931 611 9327	.022 256 0455	55
56	1.519 578 2526	69.277 100 3476	.014 434 7843	.658 077 3305	45.589 689 2633	.021 934 7843	56
57	1.530 975 0895	70.796 678 6002	.014 124 9564	.653 178 4918	46.242 867 7551	.021 624 9564	57
58	1.542 457 4027	72.327 653 6897	.013 825 9704	.648 316 1209	46.891 183 8760	.021 325 9704	58
59	1.554 025 8332	73.870 111 0923	.013 537 2749	.643 489 9463	47.534 673 8224	.021 037 2749	59
60	1.565 681 0269	75.424 136 9255	.013 258 3552	.638 699 6986	48.173 373 5210	.020 758 3552	60
61	1.577 423 6346	76.989 817 9525	.012 988 7305	.633 945 1103	48.807 318 6312	.020 488 7305	61
62	1.589 254 3119	78.567 241 5871	.012 727 9510	.629 225 9159	49.436 544 5471	.020 227 9510	62
63	1.601 173 7192	80.156 495 8990	.012 475 5953	.624 541 8520	50.061 086 3991	.019 975 5953	63
64	1.613 182 5221	81.757 669 6183	.012 231 2684	.619 892 6571	50.680 979 0562	.019 731 2684	64
65	1.625 281 3911	83.370 852 1404	.011 994 5997	.615 278 0715	51.296 257 1278	.019 494 5997	65
66	1.637 471 0015	84.996 133 5315	.011 765 2411	.610 697 8387	51.906 954 9655	.019 265 2411	66
67	1.649 752 0340	86.633 604 5329	.011 542 8650	.606 151 7000	52.513 106 6655	.019 042 8650	67
68	1.662 125 1743	88.283 356 5669	.011 327 1633	.601 639 4045	53.114 746 0700	.018 827 1633	68
69	1.674 591 1131	89.945 481 7412	.011 117 8458	.597 160 6992	53.711 906 7692	.018 617 8458	69
70	1.687 150 5464	91.620 072 8543	.010 914 6388	.592 715 3342	54.304 622 1035	.018 414 6388	70
71	1.699 804 1755	93.307 223 4007	.010 717 2839	.588 303 0613	54.892 925 1647	.018 217 2839	71
72	1.712 552 7068	95.007 027 5762	.010 525 5372	.583 923 6340	55.476 848 7987	.018 025 5372	72
73	1.725 396 8521	96.719 580 2830	.010 339 1681	.579 576 8079	56.056 425 6067	.017 839 1681	73
74	1.738 337 3285	98.444 977 1351	.010 157 9586	.575 262 3404	56.631 687 9471	.017 657 9586	74
75	1.751 374 8585	100.183 314 4636	.009 981 7021	.570 979 9905	57.202 667 9375	.017 481 7021	75
76	1.764 510 1699	101.934 689 3221	.009 810 2030	.566 729 5191	57.769 397 4566	.017 310 2030	76
77	1.777 743 9962	103.699 199 4920	.009 643 2760	.562 510 6889	58.331 908 1455	.017 143 2760	77
78	1.791 077 0762	105.476 943 4882	.009 480 7450	.558 323 2644	58.890 231 4099	.016 980 7450	78
79	1.804 510 1542	107.268 020 5644	.009 322 4429	.554 167 0118	59.444 398 4218	.016 822 4429	79
80	1.818 043 9804	109.072 530 7186	.009 168 2112	.550 041 6991	59.994 440 1209	.016 668 2112	80
81	1.831 679 3102	110.890 574 6990	.009 017 8990	.545 947 0959	60.540 387 2168	.016 517 8990	81
82	1.845 416 9051	112.722 254 0093	.008 871 3627	.541 882 9736	61.082 270 1903	.016 371 3627	82
83	1.859 257 5319	114.567 670 9143	.008 728 4658	.537 849 1053	61.620 119 2956	.016 228 4658	83
84	1.873 201 9633	116.426 928 4462	.008 589 0783	.533 845 2658	62.153 964 5614	.016 089 0783	84
85	1.887 250 9781	118.300 130 4095	.008 453 0761	.529 871 2316	62.683 835 7930	.015 953 0761	85
86	1.901 405 3604	120.187 381 3876	.008 320 3410	.525 926 7807	63.209 762 5736	.015 820 3410	86
87	1.915 665 9006	122.088 786 7480	.008 190 7604	.522 011 6930	63.731 774 2666	.015 690 7604	87
88	1.930 033 3949	124.004 452 6486	.008 064 2266	.518 125 7499	64.249 900 0165	.015 564 2266	88
89	1.944 508 6453	125.934 486 0435	.007 940 6367	.514 268 7344	64.764 168 7509	.015 440 6367	89
90	1.959 092 4602	127.878 994 6888	.007 819 8926	.510 440 4311	65.274 609 1820	.015 319 8926	90
91	1.973 785 6536	129.838 087 1490	.007 701 9003	.506 640 6264	65.781 249 8085	.015 201 9003	91
92	1.988 589 0460	131.811 872 8026	.007 586 5700	.502 869 1081	66.284 118 9166	.015 086 5700	92
93	2.003 503 4639	133.800 461 8486	.007 473 8158	.499 125 6656	66.783 244 5822	.014 973 8158	93
94	2.018 529 7398	135.803 965 3125	.007 363 5552	.495 410 0900	67.278 654 6722	.014 863 5552	94
95	2.033 668 7129	137.822 495 0523	.007 255 7096	.491 722 1737	67.770 376 8458	.014 755 7096	95
96	2.048 921 2282	139.856 163 7652	.007 150 2033	.488 061 7108	68.258 438 5567	.014 650 2033	96
97	2.064 288 1375	141.905 084 9934	.007 046 9638	.484 428 4971	68.742 867 0538	.014 546 9638	97
98	2.079 770 2985	143.969 373 1309	.006 945 9217	.480 822 3296	69.223 689 3834	.014 445 9217	98
99	2.095 368 5757	146.049 143 4294	.006 847 0104	.477 243 0071	69.700 932 3905	.014 347 0104	99
100	2.111 083 8400	148.144 512 0051	.006 750 1657	.473 690 3296	70.174 622 7201	.014 250 1657	100

P E R I O D S	XIII COMPOUND AMOUNT — AMOUNT OF 1 (How $1 left at compound interest will grow.)	XIV AMOUNT OF ANNUITY — AMOUNT OF 1 PER PERIOD (How $1 deposited periodically will grow.)	XV SINKING FUND (Periodic deposit that will grow to $1 at future date.)	XVI PRESENT VALUE — PRESENT WORTH OF 1 (What $1 due in the future is worth today.)	XVII PRESENT VALUE OF ANNUITY — PRESENT WORTH OF 1 PER PERIOD (What $1 payable periodically is worth today.)	XVIII AMORTIZATION — PARTIAL PAYMENT (Annuity worth $1 today. Periodic payment necessary to pay off a loan of $1.)	P E R I O D S	RATE 1%
1	1.010 000 0000	1.000 000 0000	1.000 000 0000	.990 099 0099	.990 099 0099	1.010 000 0000	1	
2	1.020 100 0000	2.010 000 0000	.497 512 4378	.980 296 0494	1.970 395 0593	.507 512 4378	2	
3	1.030 301 0000	3.030 100 0000	.330 022 1115	.970 590 1479	2.940 985 2072	.340 022 1115	3	
4	1.040 604 0100	4.060 401 0000	.246 281 0939	.960 980 3445	3.901 965 5517	.256 281 0939	4	
5	1.051 010 0501	5.101 005 0100	.196 039 7996	.951 465 6876	4.853 431 2393	.206 039 7996	5	
6	1.061 520 1506	6.152 015 0601	.162 548 3667	.942 045 2353	5.795 476 4746	.172 548 3667	6	
7	1.072 135 3521	7.213 535 2107	.138 628 2829	.932 718 0547	6.728 194 5293	.148 628 2829	7	
8	1.082 856 7056	8.285 670 5628	.120 690 2920	.923 483 2225	7.651 677 7518	.130 690 2920	8	
9	1.093 685 2727	9.368 527 2684	.106 740 3628	.914 339 8242	8.566 017 5760	.116 740 3628	9	
10	1.104 622 1254	10.462 212 5411	.095 582 0766	.905 286 9547	9.471 304 5307	.105 582 0766	10	
11	1.115 668 3467	11.566 834 6665	.086 454 0757	.896 323 7175	10.367 628 2482	.096 454 0757	11	
12	1.126 825 0301	12.682 503 0132	.078 848 7887	.887 449 2253	11.255 077 4735	.088 848 7887	12	
13	1.138 093 2804	13.809 328 0433	.072 414 8197	.878 662 5993	12.133 740 0728	.082 414 8197	13	
14	1.149 474 2132	14.947 421 3238	.066 901 1717	.869 962 9696	13.003 703 0423	.076 901 1717	14	
15	1.160 968 9554	16.096 895 5370	.062 123 7802	.861 349 4748	13.865 052 5172	.072 123 7802	15	
16	1.172 578 6449	17.257 864 4924	.057 944 5968	.852 821 2622	14.717 873 7794	.067 944 5968	16	
17	1.184 304 4314	18.430 443 1373	.054 258 0551	.844 377 4873	15.562 251 2667	.064 258 0551	17	
18	1.196 147 4757	19.614 747 5687	.050 982 0479	.836 017 3142	16.398 268 5809	.060 982 0479	18	
19	1.208 108 9504	20.810 895 0444	.048 051 7536	.827 739 9150	17.226 008 4959	.058 051 7536	19	
20	1.220 190 0399	22.019 003 9948	.045 415 3149	.819 544 4703	18.045 552 9663	.055 415 3149	20	
21	1.232 391 9403	23.239 194 0347	.043 030 7522	.811 430 1687	18.856 983 1349	.053 030 7522	21	
22	1.244 715 8598	24.471 585 9751	.040 863 7185	.803 396 2066	19.660 379 3415	.050 863 7185	22	
23	1.257 163 0183	25.716 301 8348	.038 885 8401	.795 441 7887	20.455 821 1302	.048 885 8401	23	
24	1.269 734 6485	26.973 464 8532	.037 073 4722	.787 566 1274	21.243 387 2576	.047 073 4722	24	
25	1.282 431 9950	28.243 199 5017	.035 406 7534	.779 768 4430	22.023 155 7006	.045 406 7534	25	
26	1.295 256 3150	29.525 631 4967	.033 868 8776	.772 047 9634	22.795 203 6640	.043 868 8776	26	
27	1.308 208 8781	30.820 887 8117	.032 445 5287	.764 403 9241	23.559 607 5881	.042 445 5287	27	
28	1.321 290 9669	32.129 096 6898	.031 124 4356	.756 835 5684	24.316 443 1565	.041 124 4356	28	
29	1.334 503 8766	33.450 387 6567	.029 895 0198	.749 342 1470	25.065 785 3035	.039 895 0198	29	
30	1.347 848 9153	34.784 891 5333	.028 748 1132	.741 922 9178	25.807 708 2213	.038 748 1132	30	
31	1.361 327 4045	36.132 740 4486	.027 675 7309	.734 577 1463	26.542 285 3676	.037 675 7309	31	
32	1.374 940 6785	37.494 067 8531	.026 670 8857	.727 304 1053	27.269 589 4729	.036 670 8857	32	
33	1.388 690 0853	38.869 008 5316	.025 727 4378	.720 103 0745	27.989 692 5474	.035 727 4378	33	
34	1.402 576 9862	40.257 698 6170	.024 839 9694	.712 973 3411	28.702 665 8885	.034 839 9694	34	
35	1.416 602 7560	41.660 275 6031	.024 003 6818	.705 914 1991	29.408 580 0876	.034 003 6818	35	
36	1.430 768 7836	43.076 878 3592	.023 214 3098	.698 924 9496	30.107 505 0373	.033 214 3098	36	
37	1.445 076 4714	44.507 647 1427	.022 468 0491	.692 004 9006	30.799 509 9379	.032 468 0491	37	
38	1.459 527 2361	45.952 723 6142	.021 761 4958	.685 153 3670	31.484 663 3048	.031 761 4958	38	
39	1.474 122 5085	47.412 250 8503	.021 091 5951	.678 369 6702	32.163 032 9751	.031 091 5951	39	
40	1.488 863 7336	48.886 373 3588	.020 455 5980	.671 653 1389	32.834 686 1140	.030 455 5980	40	
41	1.503 752 3709	50.375 237 0924	.019 851 0232	.665 003 1078	33.499 689 2217	.029 851 0232	41	
42	1.518 789 8946	51.878 989 4633	.019 275 6260	.658 418 9186	34.158 108 1403	.029 275 6260	42	
43	1.533 977 7936	53.397 779 3580	.018 727 3705	.651 899 9194	34.810 008 0597	.028 727 3705	43	
44	1.549 317 5715	54.931 757 1515	.018 204 4058	.645 445 4648	35.455 453 5245	.028 204 4058	44	
45	1.564 810 7472	56.481 074 7231	.017 705 0455	.639 054 9156	36.094 508 4401	.027 705 0455	45	
46	1.580 458 8547	58.045 885 4703	.017 227 7499	.632 727 6392	36.727 236 0793	.027 227 7499	46	
47	1.596 263 4432	59.626 344 3250	.016 771 1103	.626 463 0091	37.353 699 0884	.026 771 1103	47	
48	1.612 226 0777	61.222 607 7682	.016 333 8354	.620 260 4051	37.973 959 4935	.026 333 8354	48	
49	1.628 348 3385	62.834 833 8459	.015 914 7393	.614 119 2129	38.588 078 7064	.025 914 7393	49	
50	1.644 631 8218	64.463 182 1844	.015 512 7309	.608 038 8247	39.196 117 5311	.025 512 7309	50	
51	1.661 078 1401	66.107 814 0062	.015 126 8048	.602 018 6383	39.798 136 1694	.025 126 8048	51	
52	1.677 688 9215	67.768 892 1463	.014 756 0329	.596 058 0577	40.394 194 2271	.024 756 0329	52	
53	1.694 465 8107	69.446 581 0678	.014 399 5570	.590 156 4928	40.984 350 7199	.024 399 5570	53	
54	1.711 410 4688	71.141 046 8784	.014 056 5826	.584 313 3592	41.568 664 0791	.024 056 5826	54	
55	1.728 524 5735	72.852 457 3472	.013 726 3730	.578 528 0784	42.147 192 1576	.023 726 3730	55	
56	1.745 809 8192	74.580 981 9207	.013 408 2440	.572 800 0776	42.719 992 2352	.023 408 2440	56	
57	1.763 267 9174	76.326 791 7399	.013 101 5595	.567 128 7898	43.287 121 0250	.023 101 5595	57	
58	1.780 900 5966	78.090 059 6573	.012 805 7272	.561 513 6532	43.848 634 6782	.022 805 7272	58	
59	1.798 709 6025	79.870 960 2539	.012 520 1950	.555 954 1121	44.404 588 7903	.022 520 1950	59	
60	1.816 696 6986	81.669 669 8564	.012 244 4477	.550 449 6159	44.955 038 4062	.022 244 4477	60	
61	1.834 863 6655	83.486 366 5550	.011 978 0036	.544 999 6197	45.500 038 0260	.021 978 0036	61	
62	1.853 212 3022	85.321 230 2205	.011 720 4123	.539 603 5839	46.039 641 6099	.021 720 4123	62	
63	1.871 744 4252	87.174 442 5227	.011 471 2520	.534 260 9742	46.573 902 5840	.021 471 2520	63	
64	1.890 461 8695	89.046 186 9480	.011 230 1271	.528 971 2615	47.102 873 8456	.021 230 1271	64	
65	1.909 366 4882	90.936 648 8174	.010 996 6665	.523 733 9223	47.626 607 7679	.020 996 6665	65	
66	1.928 460 1531	92.846 015 3056	.010 770 5215	.518 548 4379	48.145 156 2058	.020 770 5215	66	
67	1.947 744 7546	94.774 475 4587	.010 551 3641	.513 414 2950	48.658 570 5008	.020 551 3641	67	
68	1.967 222 2021	96.722 220 2133	.010 338 8859	.508 330 9851	49.166 901 4860	.020 338 8859	68	
69	1.986 894 4242	98.689 442 4154	.010 132 7961	.503 298 0051	49.670 199 4911	.020 132 7961	69	
70	2.006 763 3684	100.676 336 8395	.009 932 8207	.498 314 8565	50.168 514 3476	.019 932 8207	70	
71	2.026 831 0021	102.683 100 2079	.009 738 7009	.493 381 0461	50.661 895 3936	.019 738 7009	71	
72	2.047 099 3121	104.709 931 2100	.009 550 1925	.488 496 0852	51.150 391 4789	.019 550 1925	72	
73	2.067 570 3052	106.757 030 5221	.009 367 0646	.483 659 4903	51.634 050 9692	.019 367 0646	73	
74	2.088 246 0083	108.824 600 8273	.009 189 0987	.478 870 7825	52.112 921 7516	.019 189 0987	74	
75	2.109 128 4684	110.912 846 8356	.009 016 0881	.475 129 4876	52.587 051 2393	.019 016 0881	75	
76	2.130 219 7530	113.021 975 3040	.008 847 8369	.469 435 1362	53.056 486 3755	.018 847 8369	76	
77	2.151 521 9506	115.152 195 0570	.008 684 1593	.464 787 2636	53.521 273 6391	.018 684 1593	77	
78	2.173 037 1701	117.303 717 0076	.008 524 8791	.460 185 4095	53.981 459 0486	.018 524 8791	78	
79	2.194 767 5418	119.476 754 1776	.008 369 8290	.455 629 1183	54.437 088 1670	.018 369 8290	79	
80	2.216 715 2172	121.671 521 7194	.008 218 8501	.451 117 9389	54.888 206 1059	.018 218 8501	80	
81	2.238 882 3694	123.888 236 9366	.008 071 7914	.446 651 4247	55.334 857 5306	.018 071 7914	81	
82	2.261 271 1931	126.127 119 3060	.007 928 5090	.442 229 1334	55.777 086 6639	.017 928 5090	82	
83	2.283 883 9050	128.388 390 4990	.007 788 8662	.437 850 6271	56.214 937 2910	.017 788 8662	83	
84	2.306 722 7440	130.672 274 4040	.007 652 7328	.433 515 4724	56.648 452 7634	.017 652 7328	84	
85	2.329 789 9715	132.978 997 1481	.007 519 9845	.429 223 2400	57.077 676 0034	.017 519 9845	85	
86	2.353 087 8712	135.308 787 1196	.007 390 5030	.424 973 5049	57.502 649 5083	.017 390 5030	86	
87	2.376 618 7499	137.661 874 9908	.007 264 1754	.420 765 8465	57.923 415 3547	.017 264 1754	87	
88	2.400 384 9374	140.038 493 7407	.007 140 8937	.416 599 8480	58.340 015 2027	.017 140 8937	88	
89	2.424 388 7868	142.438 878 6781	.007 020 5551	.412 475 0970	58.752 490 2997	.017 020 5551	89	
90	2.448 632 6746	144.863 267 4648	.006 903 0612	.408 391 1852	59.160 881 4849	.016 903 0612	90	
91	2.473 119 0014	147.311 900 1395	.006 788 3178	.404 347 7081	59.565 229 1929	.016 788 3178	91	
92	2.497 850 1914	149.785 019 1409	.006 676 2351	.400 344 2654	59.965 573 4584	.016 676 2351	92	
93	2.522 828 6933	152.282 869 3323	.006 566 7268	.396 380 4608	60.361 953 9192	.016 566 7268	93	
94	2.548 056 9803	154.805 698 0256	.006 459 7105	.392 455 9018	60.754 409 8210	.016 459 7105	94	
95	2.573 537 5501	157.353 755 0059	.006 355 1073	.388 570 1998	61.142 980 0207	.016 355 1073	95	
96	2.599 272 9256	159.927 292 5559	.006 252 8414	.384 722 9701	61.527 702 9908	.016 252 8414	96	
97	2.625 265 6548	162.526 565 4815	.006 152 8403	.380 913 8318	61.908 616 8226	.016 152 8403	97	
98	2.651 518 3114	165.151 831 1363	.006 055 0343	.377 142 4077	62.285 759 2303	.016 055 0343	98	
99	2.678 033 4945	167.803 349 4477	.005 959 3566	.373 408 3245	62.659 167 5548	.015 959 3566	99	
100	2.704 813 8294	170.481 382 9422	.005 865 7431	.369 711 2123	63.028 878 7671	.015 856 7431	100	

RATE 1 1/4%

PERIODS	XIV COMPOUND AMOUNT — AMOUNT OF 1 — How $1 left at compound interest will grow.	XV AMOUNT OF ANNUITY — AMOUNT OF 1 PER PERIOD — How $1 deposited periodically will grow.	XVI SINKING FUND — SINKING FUND — Periodic deposit that will grow to $1 at future date.	XVII PRESENT VALUE — PRESENT WORTH OF 1 — What $1 due in the future is worth today.	XVIII PRESENT VALUE OF ANNUITY — PRESENT WORTH OF 1 PER PERIOD — What $1 payable periodically is worth today.	XIX AMORTIZATION — PARTIAL PAYMENT — Annuity worth $1 today. Periodic payment necessary to pay off a loan of $1.	PERIODS
1	1.012 500 0000	1.000 000 0000	1.000 000 0000	.987 654 3210	.987 654 3210	1.012 500 0000	1
2	1.025 156 2500	2.012 500 0000	.496 894 4099	.975 461 0578	1.963 115 3788	.509 394 4099	2
3	1.037 970 7031	3.037 656 2500	.329 201 1728	.963 418 3287	2.926 533 7074	.341 701 1728	3
4	1.050 945 3369	4.075 626 9531	.245 361 0233	.951 524 2752	3.878 057 9826	.257 861 0233	4
5	1.064 082 1536	5.126 572 2900	.195 062 1084	.939 777 0619	4.817 835 0446	.207 562 1084	5
6	1.077 383 1805	6.190 654 4437	.161 533 8102	.928 174 8760	5.746 009 9206	.174 033 8102	6
7	1.090 850 4703	7.268 037 6242	.137 588 7209	.916 715 9269	6.662 725 8475	.150 088 7209	7
8	1.104 486 1012	8.358 888 0945	.119 633 1365	.905 398 4463	7.568 124 2938	.132 133 1365	8
9	1.118 292 1774	9.463 374 1957	.105 670 5546	.894 220 6877	8.462 344 9815	.118 170 5546	9
10	1.132 270 8297	10.581 666 3731	.094 503 0740	.883 180 9262	9.345 525 9077	.107 003 0740	10
11	1.146 424 2150	11.713 937 2028	.085 368 3935	.872 277 4579	10.217 803 3656	.097 868 3935	11
12	1.160 754 5177	12.860 361 4178	.077 758 3123	.861 508 6004	11.079 311 9660	.090 258 3123	12
13	1.175 263 9492	14.021 115 9356	.071 320 9993	.850 872 6918	11.930 184 6578	.083 820 9993	13
14	1.189 954 7486	15.196 379 8848	.065 805 1462	.840 368 0906	12.770 552 7485	.078 305 1462	14
15	1.204 829 1829	16.386 334 6333	.061 026 4603	.829 993 1759	13.600 545 9244	.073 526 4603	15
16	1.219 889 5477	17.591 163 8162	.056 846 7221	.819 746 3466	14.420 292 2710	.069 346 7221	16
17	1.235 138 1670	18.811 053 3639	.053 160 2341	.809 626 0213	15.229 918 2924	.065 660 2341	17
18	1.250 577 3941	20.046 191 5310	.049 884 7873	.799 630 6384	16.029 548 9307	.062 384 7873	18
19	1.266 209 6116	21.296 768 9251	.046 955 4797	.789 758 6552	16.819 307 5859	.059 455 4797	19
20	1.282 037 2317	22.562 978 5367	.044 320 3896	.780 008 5483	17.599 316 1342	.056 820 3896	20
21	1.298 062 6971	23.845 015 7684	.041 937 4854	.770 378 8132	18.369 694 9474	.054 437 4854	21
22	1.314 288 4808	25.143 078 4655	.039 772 3772	.760 867 9636	19.130 562 9110	.052 272 3772	22
23	1.330 717 0868	26.457 366 9463	.037 796 6561	.751 474 5320	19.882 037 4430	.050 296 6561	23
24	1.347 351 0504	27.788 084 0331	.035 986 6480	.742 197 0686	20.624 234 5116	.048 486 6480	24
25	1.364 192 9385	29.135 435 0836	.034 322 4667	.733 034 1418	21.357 268 6534	.046 822 4667	25
26	1.381 245 3503	30.499 628 0221	.032 787 2851	.723 984 3376	22.081 252 9910	.045 287 2851	26
27	1.398 510 9172	31.880 873 3724	.031 366 7693	.715 046 2594	22.796 299 2504	.043 866 7693	27
28	1.415 992 3036	33.279 384 2895	.030 048 6329	.706 218 5278	23.502 517 7784	.042 548 6329	28
29	1.433 692 2074	34.695 376 5932	.028 822 2841	.697 499 7805	24.200 017 5587	.041 322 2841	29
30	1.451 613 3600	36.129 068 8006	.027 678 5434	.688 888 6721	24.888 906 2308	.040 178 5434	30
31	1.469 758 5270	37.580 682 1606	.026 609 4159	.680 383 8737	25.569 290 1045	.039 109 4159	31
32	1.488 130 5086	39.050 440 6876	.025 607 9056	.671 984 0728	26.241 274 1773	.038 107 9056	32
33	1.506 732 1400	40.538 571 1962	.024 667 8650	.663 687 9731	26.904 962 1504	.037 167 8650	33
34	1.525 566 2917	42.045 303 3361	.023 783 8693	.655 494 2944	27.560 456 4448	.036 283 8693	34
35	1.544 635 8703	43.570 869 6278	.022 951 1141	.647 401 7723	28.207 858 2171	.035 451 1141	35
36	1.563 943 8187	45.115 505 4982	.022 165 3285	.639 409 1578	28.847 267 3749	.034 665 3285	36
37	1.583 493 1165	46.679 449 3169	.021 422 7035	.631 515 2176	29.478 782 5925	.033 922 7035	37
38	1.603 286 7804	48.262 942 4334	.020 719 8308	.623 718 7334	30.102 501 3259	.033 219 8308	38
39	1.623 327 8652	49.866 229 2138	.020 053 6519	.616 018 5021	30.718 519 8281	.032 553 6519	39
40	1.643 619 4635	51.489 557 0790	.019 421 4139	.608 413 3355	31.326 933 1635	.031 921 4139	40
41	1.664 164 7068	53.133 176 5424	.018 820 6327	.600 902 0597	31.927 835 2233	.031 320 6327	41
42	1.684 966 7656	54.797 341 2492	.018 249 0606	.593 483 5158	32.521 318 7390	.030 749 0606	42
43	1.706 028 8502	56.482 308 0148	.017 704 6589	.586 156 5588	33.107 475 2978	.030 204 6589	43
44	1.727 354 2108	58.188 336 8650	.017 185 5745	.578 920 0581	33.686 395 3558	.029 685 5745	44
45	1.748 946 1384	59.915 691 0758	.016 690 1188	.571 772 8968	34.258 168 2527	.029 190 1188	45
46	1.770 807 9652	61.664 637 2143	.016 216 7499	.564 713 9722	34.822 882 2249	.028 716 7499	46
47	1.792 943 0647	63.435 445 1795	.015 764 0574	.557 742 1948	35.380 624 4196	.028 264 0574	47
48	1.815 354 8531	65.228 388 2442	.015 330 7483	.550 856 4886	35.931 480 9083	.027 830 7483	48
49	1.838 046 7887	67.043 743 0973	.014 915 6350	.544 055 7913	36.475 536 6995	.027 415 6350	49
50	1.861 022 3736	68.881 789 8860	.014 517 6251	.537 339 0531	37.012 875 7526	.027 017 6251	50
51	1.884 285 1532	70.742 812 2596	.014 135 7117	.530 705 2376	37.543 580 9902	.026 635 7117	51
52	1.907 838 7177	72.627 097 4128	.013 768 9655	.524 153 3211	38.067 734 3114	.026 268 9655	52
53	1.931 686 7016	74.534 936 1305	.013 416 5272	.517 682 2925	38.585 416 6038	.025 916 5272	53
54	1.955 832 7854	76.466 622 8321	.013 077 6012	.511 291 1530	39.096 707 7568	.025 577 6012	54
55	1.980 280 6952	78.422 455 6175	.012 751 4497	.504 978 9166	39.601 686 6734	.025 251 4497	55
56	2.005 034 2039	80.402 736 3127	.012 437 3877	.498 744 6090	40.100 431 2824	.024 937 3877	56
57	2.030 097 1315	82.407 770 5166	.012 134 7780	.492 587 2681	40.593 018 5505	.024 634 7780	57
58	2.055 473 3456	84.437 867 6481	.011 843 0276	.486 505 9438	41.079 524 4943	.024 343 0276	58
59	2.081 166 7624	86.493 340 9937	.011 561 5837	.480 499 6976	41.560 024 1919	.024 061 5837	59
60	2.107 181 3470	88.574 507 7561	.011 289 9301	.474 567 6026	42.034 591 7945	.023 789 9301	60
61	2.133 521 1138	90.681 689 1031	.011 027 5846	.468 708 7433	42.503 300 5378	.023 527 5846	61
62	2.160 190 1277	92.815 210 2168	.010 774 0962	.462 922 2156	42.966 222 7534	.023 274 0962	62
63	2.187 192 5043	94.975 400 3445	.010 529 0422	.457 207 1265	43.423 429 8799	.023 029 0422	63
64	2.214 532 4106	97.162 592 8489	.010 292 0267	.451 562 5941	43.874 992 4739	.022 792 0267	64
65	2.242 214 0657	99.377 125 2595	.010 062 6779	.445 987 7472	44.320 980 2212	.022 562 6779	65
66	2.270 241 7416	101.619 339 3252	.009 840 6465	.440 481 7257	44.761 461 9468	.022 340 6465	66
67	2.298 619 7633	103.889 581 0668	.009 625 6043	.435 043 6797	45.196 505 6265	.022 125 6043	67
68	2.327 352 5104	106.188 200 8301	.009 417 2421	.429 672 7700	45.626 178 3966	.021 917 2421	68
69	2.356 444 4168	108.515 553 3405	.009 215 2689	.424 368 1679	46.050 546 5645	.021 715 2689	69
70	2.385 899 9720	110.871 997 7572	.009 019 4100	.419 129 0548	46.469 675 6193	.021 519 4100	70
71	2.415 723 7216	113.257 897 7292	.008 829 4063	.413 954 6220	46.883 630 2412	.021 329 4063	71
72	2.445 920 2681	115.673 621 4508	.008 645 0133	.408 844 0711	47.292 474 3123	.021 145 0133	72
73	2.476 494 2715	118.119 541 7190	.008 456 9997	.403 796 6134	47.696 270 9258	.020 965 9997	73
74	2.507 450 4499	120.596 035 9904	.008 292 1465	.398 811 4701	48.095 082 3958	.020 792 1465	74
75	2.538 793 5805	123.103 486 4403	.008 123 2468	.393 887 8717	48.488 970 2675	.020 623 2468	75
76	2.570 528 5003	125.642 280 0208	.007 959 1042	.389 025 0584	48.877 995 3259	.020 459 1042	76
77	2.602 660 1065	128.212 808 5211	.007 799 5328	.384 222 2799	49.262 217 6058	.020 299 5328	77
78	2.635 193 3578	130.815 468 6276	.007 644 3559	.379 478 7950	49.641 696 4008	.020 144 3559	78
79	2.668 133 2748	133.450 661 9854	.007 493 4061	.374 793 8716	50.016 490 2724	.019 993 4061	79
80	2.701 484 9408	136.118 795 2603	.007 346 5240	.370 166 7868	50.386 657 0592	.019 846 5240	80
81	2.735 253 5025	138.820 280 2010	.007 203 5584	.365 596 8264	50.752 253 8856	.019 703 5584	81
82	2.769 444 1713	141.555 533 7035	.007 064 3653	.361 083 2854	51.113 337 1710	.019 564 3653	82
83	2.804 062 2234	144.324 977 8748	.006 928 8076	.356 625 4670	51.469 962 6380	.019 428 8076	83
84	2.839 113 0012	147.129 040 0983	.006 796 7547	.352 222 6835	51.822 185 3215	.019 296 7547	84
85	2.874 601 9137	149.968 153 0995	.006 668 0824	.347 874 2553	52.170 059 5768	.019 168 0824	85
86	2.910 534 4377	152.842 755 0132	.006 542 6719	.343 579 5114	52.513 639 0882	.019 042 6719	86
87	2.946 916 1181	155.753 289 4509	.006 420 4101	.339 337 7890	52.852 976 8772	.018 920 4101	87
88	2.983 752 5696	158.700 205 5690	.006 301 1891	.335 148 4336	53.188 125 3108	.018 801 1891	88
89	3.021 049 4767	161.683 958 1386	.006 184 9055	.331 010 7986	53.519 136 1094	.018 684 9055	89
90	3.058 812 5952	164.705 007 6154	.006 071 4608	.326 924 2446	53.846 060 3550	.018 571 4608	90
91	3.097 047 7526	167.763 820 2106	.005 960 7608	.322 888 1438	54.168 948 4988	.018 460 7608	91
92	3.135 760 8495	170.860 867 9632	.005 852 7152	.318 901 8704	54.487 850 3692	.018 352 7152	92
93	3.174 957 8602	173.996 628 8127	.005 747 2378	.314 964 8103	54.802 815 1794	.018 247 2378	93
94	3.214 644 8334	177.171 586 6729	.005 644 2459	.311 076 3558	55.113 891 5352	.018 144 2459	94
95	3.254 827 8938	180.386 231 5063	.005 543 6604	.307 235 9070	55.421 127 4422	.018 043 6604	95
96	3.295 513 2425	183.641 059 4001	.005 445 4053	.303 442 8711	55.724 570 3133	.017 945 4053	96
97	3.336 707 1580	186.936 572 6426	.005 349 4080	.299 696 6628	56.024 266 9761	.017 849 4080	97
98	3.378 415 9975	190.273 279 8007	.005 255 5987	.295 996 7040	56.320 263 6801	.017 755 5987	98
99	3.420 646 1975	193.651 695 7982	.005 163 9104	.292 342 4237	56.612 606 1038	.017 663 9104	99
100	3.463 404 2749	197.072 341 9957	.005 074 2788	.288 733 2580	56.901 339 3618	.017 574 2788	100

	XIV COMPOUND AMOUNT	XV AMOUNT OF ANNUITY	XVI SINKING FUND	XVII PRESENT VALUE	XVIII PRESENT VALUE OF ANNUITY	XIX AMORTIZATION	
RATE 1 1/2% PERIODS	AMOUNT OF 1 How $1 left at compound interest will grow.	AMOUNT OF 1 PER PERIOD How $1 deposited periodically will grow.	SINKING FUND Periodic deposit that will grow to $1 at future date.	PRESENT WORTH OF 1 What $1 due in the future is worth today.	PRESENT WORTH OF 1 PER PERIOD What $1 payable periodically is worth today.	PARTIAL PAYMENT Annuity worth $1 today. Periodic payment necessary to pay off a loan of $1.	PERIODS
1	1.015 000 0000	1.000 000 0000	1.000 000 0000	.985 221 6749	.985 221 6749	1.015 000 0000	1
2	1.030 225 0000	2.015 000 0000	.496 277 9156	.970 661 7486	1.955 883 4235	.511 277 9156	2
3	1.045 678 3750	3.045 225 0000	.328 382 9602	.956 316 9937	2.912 200 4173	.343 382 9602	3
4	1.061 363 5506	4.090 903 3750	.244 444 7860	.942 184 2303	3.854 384 6476	.259 444 7860	4
5	1.077 284 0039	5.152 266 9256	.194 089 3231	.928 260 3254	4.782 644 9730	.209 089 3131	5
6	1.093 443 2639	6.229 550 9295	.160 525 2146	.914 542 1925	5.697 187 1655	.175 525 2146	6
7	1.109 844 9129	7.322 994 1935	.136 556 1645	.901 026 7907	6.598 213 9561	.151 556 1645	7
8	1.126 492 5866	8.432 839 1064	.118 584 0246	.887 711 1238	7.485 925 0799	.133 584 0246	8
9	1.143 389 9754	9.559 331 6929	.104 609 8234	.874 592 2402	8.360 517 3201	.119 609 8234	9
10	1.160 540 8250	10.702 721 6683	.093 434 1779	.861 667 2317	9.222 184 5519	.108 434 1779	10
11	1.177 948 9374	11.863 262 4934	.084 293 8442	.848 933 2332	10.071 117 7851	.099 293 8442	11
12	1.195 618 1715	13.041 211 4308	.076 679 9929	.836 387 4219	10.907 505 2070	.091 679 9929	12
13	1.213 552 4440	14.236 829 6022	.070 240 3574	.824 027 0166	11.731 532 2236	.085 240 3574	13
14	1.231 755 7307	15.450 382 0463	.064 723 3186	.811 849 2775	12.543 381 5011	.079 723 3186	14
15	1.250 232 0667	16.682 137 7770	.059 944 3557	.799 851 5049	13.343 233 0060	.074 944 3557	15
16	1.268 985 5477	17.932 369 8436	.055 765 0778	.788 031 0393	14.131 264 0453	.070 765 0778	16
17	1.288 020 3309	19.201 355 3913	.052 079 6569	.776 385 2604	14.907 649 3057	.067 079 6569	17
18	1.307 340 6358	20.489 375 7221	.048 805 7818	.764 911 5866	15.672 560 8924	.063 805 7818	18
19	1.326 950 7454	21.796 716 3580	.045 878 4701	.753 607 4745	16.426 168 3669	.060 878 4701	19
20	1.346 855 0066	23.123 667 1033	.043 245 7359	.742 470 4182	17.168 638 7851	.058 245 7359	20
21	1.367 057 8316	24.470 522 1099	.040 865 4950	.731 497 9490	17.900 136 7341	.055 865 4950	21
22	1.387 563 6991	25.837 579 9415	.038 703 3152	.720 687 6345	18.620 824 3685	.053 703 3152	22
23	1.408 377 1546	27.225 143 6407	.036 730 7520	.710 037 0783	19.330 861 4468	.051 730 7520	23
24	1.429 502 8119	28.633 520 7953	.034 924 1020	.699 543 9195	20.030 405 3663	.049 924 1020	24
25	1.450 945 3541	30.063 023 6072	.033 263 4539	.689 205 8320	20.719 611 1984	.048 263 4539	25
26	1.472 709 5344	31.513 968 9613	.031 731 9599	.679 020 5242	21.398 631 7225	.046 731 9599	26
27	1.494 800 1774	32.986 678 4957	.030 315 2680	.668 985 7381	22.067 617 4606	.045 315 2680	27
28	1.517 222 1801	34.481 478 6732	.029 001 0765	.659 099 2494	22.726 716 7100	.044 001 0765	28
29	1.539 980 5128	35.998 700 8533	.027 778 7802	.649 358 8664	23.376 075 5763	.042 778 7802	29
30	1.563 080 2205	37.538 681 3661	.026 639 1883	.639 762 4299	24.015 838 0062	.041 639 1883	30
31	1.586 526 4238	39.101 761 5865	.025 574 2954	.630 307 8127	24.646 145 8189	.040 574 2954	31
32	1.610 324 3202	40.688 288 0103	.024 577 0970	.620 992 9189	25.267 138 7379	.039 577 0970	32
33	1.634 479 1850	42.298 612 3305	.023 641 4375	.611 815 6837	25.878 954 4216	.038 641 4375	33
34	1.658 996 3727	43.933 091 5155	.022 761 8855	.602 774 0726	26.481 728 4941	.037 761 8855	34
35	1.683 881 3183	45.592 087 8882	.021 933 6303	.593 866 0814	27.075 594 5755	.036 933 6303	35
36	1.709 139 5381	47.275 969 2065	.021 152 3955	.585 089 7353	27.660 684 3109	.036 152 3955	36
37	1.734 776 6312	48.985 108 7446	.020 414 3673	.576 443 0890	28.237 127 3999	.035 414 3673	37
38	1.760 798 2806	50.719 885 3758	.019 716 1329	.567 924 2256	28.805 051 6255	.034 716 1329	38
39	1.787 210 2548	52.480 683 6564	.019 054 6298	.559 531 2568	29.364 582 8822	.034 054 6298	39
40	1.814 018 4087	54.267 893 9113	.018 427 1017	.551 262 3219	29.915 845 2042	.033 427 1017	40
41	1.841 228 6848	56.081 912 3199	.017 831 0610	.543 115 5881	30.458 960 7923	.032 831 0610	41
42	1.868 847 1151	57.923 141 0047	.017 264 2571	.535 089 2494	30.994 050 0417	.032 264 2571	42
43	1.896 879 8218	59.791 988 1198	.016 724 6488	.527 181 5265	31.521 231 5681	.031 724 6488	43
44	1.925 333 0191	61.688 867 9416	.016 210 3801	.519 390 6665	32.040 622 2346	.031 210 3804	44
45	1.954 213 0144	63.614 200 9607	.015 719 7604	.511 714 9423	32.552 337 1770	.030 719 7604	45
46	1.983 526 2096	65.568 413 9751	.015 251 2458	.504 152 6526	33.056 489 8295	.030 251 2458	46
47	2.013 279 1028	67.551 940 1848	.014 803 4238	.496 702 1207	33.553 191 9503	.029 803 4238	47
48	2.043 478 2893	69.565 219 2875	.014 374 9996	.489 361 6953	34.042 553 6456	.029 374 9996	48
49	2.074 130 4637	71.608 697 5768	.013 964 7841	.482 129 7491	34.524 683 3947	.028 964 7841	49
50	2.105 242 4206	73.682 828 0405	.013 571 6832	.475 004 6789	34.999 688 0736	.028 571 6832	50
51	2.136 821 0569	75.788 070 4611	.013 194 6887	.467 984 9053	35.467 672 9789	.028 194 6887	51
52	2.168 873 3728	77.924 891 5180	.012 832 8700	.461 068 8722	35.928 741 8511	.027 832 8700	52
53	2.201 406 4734	80.093 764 8908	.012 485 3664	.454 255 0465	36.382 996 8977	.027 485 3664	53
54	2.234 427 5705	82.295 171 3642	.012 151 3812	.447 541 9178	36.830 538 8154	.027 151 3812	54
55	2.267 943 9840	84.529 598 9346	.011 830 1756	.440 927 9978	37.271 466 8132	.026 830 1756	55
56	2.301 963 1438	86.797 542 9186	.011 521 0635	.434 411 8205	37.705 878 6337	.026 521 0635	56
57	2.336 492 5909	89.099 506 0624	.011 223 4068	.427 991 9414	38.133 870 5751	.026 223 4068	57
58	2.371 539 9798	91.435 998 6534	.010 936 6116	.421 666 9373	38.555 537 5124	.025 936 6116	58
59	2.407 113 0795	93.807 538 6332	.010 660 1241	.415 435 4062	38.970 972 9186	.025 660 1241	59
60	2.443 219 7757	96.214 651 7126	.010 393 4274	.409 295 9667	39.380 268 8853	.025 393 4274	60
61	2.479 868 0723	98.657 871 4883	.010 136 0387	.403 247 2579	39.783 516 1432	.025 136 0387	61
62	2.517 066 0934	101.137 739 5607	.009 887 5059	.397 287 9388	40.180 804 0820	.024 887 5059	62
63	2.554 822 0848	103.654 805 6541	.009 647 4061	.391 416 6884	40.572 220 7704	.024 647 4061	63
64	2.593 144 4161	106.209 627 7389	.009 415 3423	.385 632 2054	40.957 852 9758	.024 415 3423	64
65	2.632 041 5823	108.802 772 1550	.009 190 9423	.379 933 2073	41.337 786 1830	.024 190 9423	65
66	2.671 522 2061	111.434 813 7373	.008 973 8563	.374 318 4308	41.712 104 6138	.023 973 8563	66
67	2.711 595 0392	114.106 335 9434	.008 763 7552	.368 786 6313	42.080 891 2451	.023 763 7552	67
68	2.752 268 9647	116.817 930 9825	.008 560 3297	.363 336 5826	42.444 227 8277	.023 560 3297	68
69	2.793 552 9992	119.570 199 9472	.008 363 2878	.357 967 0764	42.802 194 9042	.023 363 2878	69
70	2.835 456 2942	122.363 752 9464	.008 172 3548	.352 676 9226	43.154 871 8268	.023 172 3548	70
71	2.877 988 1386	125.199 209 2406	.007 987 2709	.347 464 9484	43.502 336 7751	.022 987 2709	71
72	2.921 157 9607	128.077 197 3793	.007 807 7911	.342 329 9984	43.844 666 7735	.022 807 7911	72
73	2.964 975 3301	130.998 355 3399	.007 633 6836	.337 270 9344	44.181 937 7079	.022 633 6836	73
74	3.009 449 9601	133.963 330 6700	.007 464 7293	.332 286 6349	44.514 224 3428	.022 464 7293	74
75	3.054 591 7095	136.972 780 6301	.007 300 7206	.327 375 9949	44.841 600 3377	.022 300 7206	75
76	3.100 410 5851	140.027 372 3395	.007 141 4609	.322 537 9260	45.164 138 2638	.022 141 4609	76
77	3.146 916 7439	143.127 782 9246	.006 986 7637	.317 771 3557	45.481 909 6195	.021 986 7637	77
78	3.194 120 4950	146.274 699 6685	.006 836 4523	.313 075 2273	45.794 984 8468	.021 836 4523	78
79	3.242 032 3025	149.468 820 1635	.006 690 3586	.308 448 4998	46.103 433 3466	.021 690 3586	79
80	3.290 662 7870	152.710 852 4660	.006 548 3231	.303 890 1476	46.407 323 4941	.021 548 3231	80
81	3.340 022 7288	156.001 515 2530	.006 410 1941	.299 399 1602	46.706 722 6543	.021 410 1941	81
82	3.390 123 0697	159.341 537 9818	.006 275 8275	.294 974 5421	47.001 697 1964	.021 275 8275	82
83	3.440 974 9158	162.731 661 0515	.006 145 0857	.290 615 3124	47.292 312 5088	.021 145 0857	83
84	3.492 589 5395	166.172 635 9673	.006 017 8380	.286 320 5048	47.578 633 0136	.021 017 8380	84
85	3.544 978 3826	169.665 225 5068	.005 893 9597	.282 089 1673	47.860 722 1808	.020 893 9597	85
86	3.598 153 0583	173.210 203 8894	.005 773 3319	.277 920 3619	48.138 642 5427	.020 773 3319	86
87	3.652 125 3542	176.808 356 9477	.005 655 8413	.273 813 1644	48.412 455 7071	.020 655 8413	87
88	3.706 907 2345	180.460 482 3019	.005 541 3795	.269 766 6644	48.682 222 3715	.020 541 3794	88
89	3.762 510 8430	184.167 389 5365	.005 429 8429	.265 779 9650	48.948 002 3365	.020 429 8429	89
90	3.818 948 5057	187.929 900 3795	.005 321 1330	.261 852 1822	49.209 854 5187	.020 321 1330	90
91	3.876 232 7333	191.748 848 8852	.005 215 1552	.257 982 4455	49.467 836 9642	.020 215 1552	91
92	3.934 376 2243	195.625 081 6185	.005 111 8190	.254 169 8971	49.722 006 8613	.020 111 8190	92
93	3.993 391 8676	199.559 457 8428	.005 011 0379	.250 413 6917	49.972 420 5530	.020 011 0379	93
94	4.053 292 7457	203.552 849 7104	.004 912 7291	.246 712 9968	50.219 133 5498	.019 912 7291	94
95	4.114 092 1368	207.606 142 4561	.004 816 8132	.243 066 9919	50.462 200 5416	.019 816 8132	95
96	4.175 803 5189	211.720 234 5929	.004 723 2141	.239 474 8688	50.701 675 4105	.019 723 2142	96
97	4.238 440 5717	215.896 038 1118	.004 631 8590	.235 935 8314	50.937 611 2419	.019 631 8590	97
98	4.302 017 1803	220.134 478 6835	.004 542 6778	.232 449 0949	51.170 060 3368	.019 542 6778	98
99	4.366 547 4380	224.436 495 8637	.004 455 6033	.229 013 8866	51.399 074 2235	.019 455 6033	99
100	4.432 045 6495	228.803 043 3017	.004 370 5712	.225 629 4450	51.624 703 6684	.019 370 5712	100

		XIV COMPOUND AMOUNT	XV AMOUNT OF ANNUITY	XVI SINKING FUND	XVII PRESENT VALUE	XVIII PRESENT VALUE OF ANNUITY	XIX AMORTIZATION	
RATE 1 3/4%	P E R I O D S	AMOUNT OF 1 How $1 left at compound interest will grow.	AMOUNT OF 1 PER PERIOD How $1 deposited periodically will grow.	SINKING FUND Periodic deposit that will grow to $1 at future date.	PRESENT WORTH OF 1 What $1 due in the future is worth today.	PRESENT WORTH OF 1 PER PERIOD What $1 payable periodically is worth today.	PARTIAL PAYMENT Annuity worth $1 today. Periodic payment necessary to pay off a loan of $1.	P E R I O D S
	1	1.017 500 0000	1.000 000 0000	1.000 000 0000	.982 800 9828	.982 800 9828	1.017 500 0000	1
	2	1.035 306 2500	2.017 500 0000	.495 662 9492	.965 897 7718	1.948 698 7546	.513 162 9492	2
	3	1.053 424 1094	3.052 806 2500	.327 567 4635	.949 285 2794	2.897 984 0340	.345 067 4635	3
	4	1.071 859 0313	4.106 230 3594	.243 532 3673	.932 958 5056	3.830 942 5396	.261 032 3673	4
	5	1.090 616 5643	5.178 089 3907	.193 121 4246	.916 912 5362	4.747 855 0757	.210 621 4246	5
	6	1.109 702 3542	6.268 705 9550	.159 522 5565	.901 142 5417	5.648 997 6174	.177 022 5565	6
	7	1.129 122 1454	7.378 408 3092	.135 530 5857	.885 643 7756	6.534 641 3930	.153 030 5857	7
	8	1.148 881 7830	8.507 530 4546	.117 542 9233	.870 411 5731	7.405 052 9661	.135 042 9233	8
	9	1.168 987 2142	9.656 412 2376	.103 558 1306	.855 441 3495	8.260 494 3156	.121 058 1306	9
	10	1.189 444 4904	10.825 399 4517	.092 375 3442	.840 728 5990	9.101 222 9146	.109 875 3442	10
	11	1.210 259 7690	12.014 843 9421	.083 230 3778	.826 268 8934	9.927 491 8080	.100 730 3778	11
	12	1.231 439 3149	13.225 103 7111	.075 613 7738	.812 057 8805	10.739 549 6884	.095 113 7738	12
	13	1.252 989 5030	14.456 543 0261	.069 172 8305	.798 091 2830	11.537 640 9714	.086 672 8305	13
	14	1.274 916 8193	15.709 532 5290	.063 655 6179	.784 364 8973	12.322 005 8687	.081 155 6179	14
	15	1.297 227 8636	16.984 449 3483	.058 877 3872	.770 874 5919	13.092 880 4607	.076 377 3872	15
	16	1.319 929 3512	18.281 677 2119	.054 699 5764	.757 616 3066	13.850 496 7672	.072 199 5764	16
	17	1.343 028 1149	19.601 606 5631	.051 016 2265	.744 586 0507	14.595 082 8179	.068 516 2265	17
	18	1.366 531 1069	20.944 634 6779	.047 744 9244	.731 779 9024	15.326 862 7203	.065 244 9244	18
	19	1.390 445 4012	22.311 165 7848	.044 820 6073	.719 194 0073	16.046 056 7276	.062 320 6073	19
	20	1.414 778 1958	23.701 611 1860	.042 191 2246	.706 824 5772	16.752 881 3048	.059 691 2246	20
	21	1.439 536 8142	25.116 389 3818	.039 814 6399	.694 667 8891	17.447 549 1939	.057 314 6399	21
	22	1.464 728 7084	26.555 926 1960	.037 656 3782	.682 720 2841	18.130 269 4780	.055 156 3782	22
	23	1.490 361 4608	28.020 654 9044	.035 687 9596	.670 978 1662	18.801 247 6442	.053 187 9596	23
	24	1.516 442 7864	29.511 016 3652	.033 885 6510	.659 438 0012	19.460 685 6454	.051 385 6510	24
	25	1.542 980 5352	31.027 459 5163	.032 229 5163	.648 096 3157	20.108 781 9611	.049 729 5163	25
	26	1.569 982 6945	32.570 439 6868	.030 702 6865	.636 949 6960	20.745 731 6571	.048 202 6865	26
	27	1.597 457 3917	34.140 422 3813	.029 290 7917	.625 994 7872	21.371 726 4443	.046 790 7917	27
	28	1.625 412 8960	35.737 879 7730	.027 981 5145	.615 228 2921	21.986 954 7364	.045 481 5145	28
	29	1.653 857 6217	37.363 292 6690	.026 764 2365	.604 646 9701	22.591 601 7066	.044 264 2365	29
	30	1.682 800 1301	39.017 150 2907	.025 629 7549	.594 247 6365	23.185 849 3431	.043 129 7549	30
	31	1.712 249 1324	40.699 950 4208	.024 570 0545	.584 027 1612	23.769 876 5042	.042 070 0545	31
	32	1.742 213 4922	42.412 199 5532	.023 578 1216	.573 982 4680	24.343 858 9722	.041 078 1216	32
	33	1.772 702 2283	44.154 413 0453	.022 647 7928	.564 110 5336	24.907 969 5059	.040 147 7928	33
	34	1.803 724 5173	45.927 115 2736	.021 773 6297	.554 408 3869	25.462 377 8928	.039 273 6297	34
	35	1.835 289 6963	47.730 839 7909	.020 950 8151	.544 873 1075	26.007 251 0003	.038 450 8151	35
	36	1.867 407 2660	49.566 129 4873	.020 175 0673	.535 501 8255	26.542 752 8258	.037 675 0673	36
	37	1.900 086 8932	51.433 536 7533	.019 442 5673	.526 291 7204	27.069 044 5462	.036 942 5673	37
	38	1.933 338 4138	53.333 623 6465	.018 749 8979	.517 240 0201	27.586 284 5663	.036 249 8979	38
	39	1.967 171 8361	55.266 962 0603	.018 093 9926	.508 344 0001	28.094 628 5664	.035 593 9926	39
	40	2.001 597 3432	57.234 133 8963	.017 472 0911	.499 600 9829	28.594 229 5493	.034 972 0911	40
	41	2.036 625 2967	59.235 731 2395	.016 881 7026	.491 008 3370	29.085 237 8863	.034 381 7026	41
	42	2.072 266 2394	61.272 356 5362	.016 320 5735	.482 563 4762	29.567 801 3625	.033 820 5735	42
	43	2.108 530 8986	63.344 622 7756	.015 786 6596	.474 263 8586	30.042 065 2211	.033 286 6596	43
	44	2.145 430 1893	65.453 153 6742	.015 278 1026	.466 106 9864	30.508 172 2075	.032 778 1026	44
	45	2.182 975 2176	67.598 583 8635	.014 793 2093	.458 090 4043	30.966 262 6117	.032 293 2093	45
	46	2.221 177 2839	69.781 559 0811	.014 330 4336	.450 211 6996	31.416 474 3113	.031 830 4336	46
	47	2.260 047 8864	72.002 736 3650	.013 888 3611	.442 468 5008	31.858 942 8121	.031 388 3611	47
	48	2.299 598 7244	74.262 784 2514	.013 465 6950	.434 858 4774	32.293 801 2895	.030 965 6950	48
	49	2.339 841 7021	76.562 382 9758	.013 061 2445	.427 379 3390	32.721 180 6285	.030 561 2445	49
	50	2.380 788 9319	78.902 224 6779	.012 673 9139	.420 028 8344	33.141 209 4629	.030 173 9139	50
	51	2.422 452 7382	81.283 013 6097	.012 302 6935	.412 804 7513	33.554 014 2142	.029 802 6935	51
	52	2.464 845 6611	83.705 466 3479	.011 946 6511	.405 704 9152	33.959 719 1294	.029 446 6511	52
	53	2.507 980 4602	86.170 312 0090	.011 604 9249	.398 727 1894	34.358 446 3188	.029 104 9249	53
	54	2.551 870 1182	88.678 292 4691	.011 276 7169	.391 869 4736	34.750 315 7925	.028 776 7169	54
	55	2.596 527 8453	91.230 162 5874	.010 961 2871	.385 129 7033	35.135 445 4963	.028 461 2871	55
	56	2.641 967 0826	93.826 690 4326	.010 657 9481	.378 505 8514	35.513 951 3477	.028 157 9481	56
	57	2.688 201 5065	96.468 657 5152	.010 366 0611	.371 995 9228	35.885 947 2705	.027 866 0611	57
	58	2.735 245 0329	99.156 859 0217	.010 085 0310	.365 597 9585	36.251 545 2290	.027 585 0310	58
	59	2.783 111 8210	101.892 104 0546	.009 814 3032	.359 310 0329	36.610 855 2619	.027 314 3032	59
	60	2.831 816 2778	104.675 215 8756	.009 553 3598	.353 130 2535	36.963 985 5154	.027 053 3598	60
	61	2.881 373 0627	107.507 032 1534	.009 301 7171	.347 056 7602	37.311 042 2755	.026 801 7171	61
	62	2.931 797 0913	110.388 405 2161	.009 058 9224	.341 087 7250	37.652 130 0005	.026 558 9224	62
	63	2.983 103 5404	113.320 202 3073	.008 824 5518	.335 221 3513	37.987 351 3519	.026 324 5518	63
	64	3.035 307 8523	116.303 305 8477	.008 598 2079	.329 455 8736	38.316 807 2254	.026 098 2079	64
	65	3.088 425 7398	119.338 613 7001	.008 379 5175	.323 789 5563	38.640 596 7817	.025 879 5175	65
	66	3.142 473 1902	122.427 039 4398	.008 168 1302	.318 220 6942	38.958 817 4759	.025 668 1302	66
	67	3.197 466 4710	125.569 512 6300	.007 963 7165	.312 747 6110	39.271 565 0869	.025 463 7165	67
	68	3.253 422 1343	128.766 979 1010	.007 765 9661	.307 368 6594	39.578 933 7463	.025 265 9661	68
	69	3.310 357 0216	132.020 401 2353	.007 574 5869	.302 082 2206	39.881 015 9669	.025 074 5869	69
	70	3.368 288 2695	135.330 758 2569	.007 389 3032	.296 886 7033	40.177 902 6702	.024 889 3032	70
	71	3.427 233 3142	138.699 046 5264	.007 209 8549	.291 780 5438	40.469 683 2139	.024 709 8549	71
	72	3.487 209 8972	142.126 279 8406	.007 035 9964	.286 762 2052	40.756 445 4191	.024 535 9964	72
	73	3.548 236 0704	145.613 489 7378	.006 867 4956	.281 830 1771	41.038 275 5962	.024 367 4956	73
	74	3.610 330 2016	149.161 725 8083	.006 704 1327	.276 982 9750	41.315 258 5712	.024 204 1327	74
	75	3.673 510 9802	152.772 056 0099	.006 545 6997	.272 219 1401	41.587 477 7112	.024 045 6997	75
	76	3.737 797 4223	156.445 566 9901	.006 391 9996	.267 537 2384	41.855 014 9496	.023 891 9996	76
	77	3.803 208 8772	160.183 364 4124	.006 242 8455	.262 935 8608	42.117 950 8104	.023 742 8455	77
	78	3.869 765 0326	163.986 573 2896	.006 098 0602	.258 413 6224	42.376 364 4329	.023 598 0602	78
	79	3.937 485 9206	167.856 338 3222	.005 957 4754	.253 969 1621	42.630 333 5949	.023 457 4754	79
	80	4.006 391 9242	171.793 824 2428	.005 820 9310	.249 601 1421	42.879 934 7370	.023 320 9310	80
	81	4.076 503 7829	175.800 216 1671	.005 688 2751	.245 308 2478	43.125 242 9848	.023 188 2751	81
	82	4.147 842 5991	179.876 719 9500	.005 559 3631	.241 089 1870	43.366 332 1718	.023 059 3631	82
	83	4.220 429 8446	184.024 562 5491	.005 434 0572	.236 942 6899	43.603 274 8617	.022 934 0572	83
	84	4.294 287 3669	188.244 992 3937	.005 312 2263	.232 867 5085	43.836 142 3702	.022 812 2263	84
	85	4.369 437 3958	192.539 279 7606	.005 193 7454	.228 862 4162	44.065 004 7865	.022 693 7454	85
	86	4.445 902 5502	196.908 717 1564	.005 078 4953	.224 926 2076	44.289 930 9941	.022 578 4953	86
	87	4.523 705 8449	201.354 619 7067	.004 966 3623	.221 057 6979	44.510 988 6920	.022 466 3623	87
	88	4.602 870 6972	205.878 325 5515	.004 857 2379	.217 255 7227	44.728 244 4147	.022 357 2379	88
	89	4.683 420 9344	210.481 196 2487	.004 751 0182	.213 519 1378	44.941 763 5525	.022 251 0182	89
	90	4.765 380 8007	215.164 617 1830	.004 647 6043	.209 846 8185	45.151 610 3711	.022 147 6043	90
	91	4.848 774 9647	219.929 997 9837	.004 546 9013	.206 237 6595	45.357 848 0305	.022 046 9013	91
	92	4.933 628 5266	224.778 772 9485	.004 448 8187	.202 690 5744	45.560 538 6049	.021 948 8187	92
	93	5.019 967 0258	229.712 401 4751	.004 353 2695	.199 204 4957	45.759 743 1007	.021 853 2695	93
	94	5.107 816 4488	234.732 368 5009	.004 260 1709	.195 778 3742	45.955 521 4749	.021 760 1709	94
	95	5.197 203 2366	239.840 184 9496	.004 169 4431	.192 411 1786	46.147 932 6534	.021 669 4431	95
	96	5.288 154 2933	245.037 388 1863	.004 081 0099	.189 101 8954	46.337 034 5488	.021 581 0099	96
	97	5.380 696 9934	250.325 542 4795	.003 994 7981	.185 849 5286	46.522 884 0775	.021 494 7981	97
	98	5.474 859 1908	255.706 239 4729	.003 910 7376	.182 653 0994	46.705 537 1769	.021 410 7376	98
	99	5.570 669 2266	261.181 098 6637	.003 828 7610	.179 511 6456	46.885 048 8225	.021 328 7610	99
	100	5.668 155 9381	266.751 767 8903	.003 748 8036	.176 424 2217	47.061 473 0442	.021 248 8036	100

		XIV COMPOUND AMOUNT	XV AMOUNT OF ANNUITY	XVI SINKING FUND	XVII PRESENT VALUE	XVIII PRESENT VALUE OF ANNUITY	XIX AMORTIZATION	
RATE 2%	PERIODS	AMOUNT OF 1	AMOUNT OF 1 PER PERIOD	SINKING FUND	PRESENT WORTH OF 1	PRESENT WORTH OF 1 PER PERIOD	PARTIAL PAYMENT	PERIODS
		How $1 left at compound interest will grow	How $1 deposited periodically will grow.	Periodic deposit that will grow to $1 at future date.	What $1 due in the future is worth today.	What $1 payable periodically is worth today.	Annuity worth $1 today Periodic payment necessary to pay off a loan of $1	
	1	1.020 000 0000	1.000 000 0000	1.000 000 0000	.980 392 1569	.980 392 1569	1.020 000 0000	1
	2	1.040 400 0000	2.020 000 0000	.495 049 5050	.961 168 7812	1.941 560 9381	.515 049 5050	2
	3	1.061 208 0000	3.060 400 0000	.326 754 6726	.942 322 3345	2.883 883 2726	.346 754 6726	3
	4	1.082 432 1600	4.121 608 0000	.242 623 7527	.923 845 4260	3.807 728 6987	.262 623 7527	4
	5	1.104 080 8032	5.204 040 1600	.192 158 3941	.905 730 8098	4.713 459 5085	.212 158 3941	5
	6	1.126 162 4193	6.308 120 9632	.158 525 8123	.887 971 3822	5.601 430 8907	.178 525 8123	6
	7	1.148 685 6676	7.434 283 3825	.134 511 9561	.870 560 1786	6.471 991 0693	.154 511 9561	7
	8	1.171 659 3810	8.582 969 0501	.116 509 7991	.853 490 3712	7.325 481 4405	.136 509 7991	8
	9	1.195 092 5686	9.754 628 4311	.102 515 4374	.836 755 2659	8.162 236 7064	.122 515 4374	9
	10	1.218 994 4200	10.949 720 9997	.091 326 5279	.820 348 2999	8.982 585 0062	.111 326 5279	10
	11	1.243 374 3084	12.168 715 4197	.082 177 9428	.804 263 0391	9.786 848 0453	.102 177 9428	11
	12	1.268 241 7946	13.412 089 7281	.074 559 5966	.788 493 1756	10.575 341 2209	.094 559 5966	12
	13	1.293 606 6305	14.680 331 5227	.068 118 3527	.773 032 5251	11.348 373 7460	.088 118 3527	13
	15	1.319 478 7631	15.973 938 1531	.062 601 9702	.757 875 0246	12.106 248 7706	.082 601 9702	14
	15	1.345 868 3383	17.293 416 9162	.057 825 4723	.743 014 7300	12.849 263 5006	.077 825 4723	15
	16	1.372 785 7051	18.639 285 2545	.053 650 1259	.728 445 8137	13.577 709 3143	.073 650 1259	16
	17	1.400 241 4192	20.012 070 9596	.049 969 8408	.714 162 5625	14.291 871 8768	.069 969 8408	17
	18	1.428 246 2476	21.412 312 3788	.046 702 1022	.700 159 3750	14.992 031 2517	.066 702 1022	18
	19	1.456 811 1725	22.840 558 6264	.043 781 7663	.686 430 7598	15.678 462 0115	.063 781 7663	19
	20	1.485 947 3960	24.297 369 7989	.041 156 7181	.672 971 3331	16.351 433 3446	.061 156 7181	20
	21	1.515 666 3439	25.783 317 1949	.038 784 7689	.659 775 8168	17.011 209 1614	.058 784 7689	21
	22	1.545 979 6708	27.298 983 5388	.036 631 4005	.646 839 0361	17.658 048 1974	.056 631 4005	22
	23	1.576 899 2642	28.844 963 2096	.034 668 0976	.634 155 9177	18.292 204 1151	.054 668 0976	23
	24	1.608 437 2495	30.421 862 4738	.032 871 0973	.621 721 4879	18.913 925 6031	.052 871 0973	24
	25	1.640 605 9945	32.030 299 7232	.031 220 4384	.609 530 8705	19.523 456 4736	.051 220 4384	25
	26	1.673 418 1144	33.670 905 7177	.029 699 2308	.597 579 2848	20.121 035 7584	.049 699 2308	26
	27	1.706 886 4766	35.344 323 8321	.028 293 0862	.585 862 0440	20.706 897 8024	.048 293 0862	27
	28	1.741 024 2062	37.051 210 3087	.026 989 6716	.574 374 5529	21.281 272 3553	.046 989 6716	28
	29	1.775 844 6903	38.792 234 5149	.025 778 3552	.563 112 3068	21.844 384 6620	.045 778 3552	29
	30	1.811 361 5841	40.568 079 2052	.024 649 9223	.552 070 8890	22.396 455 5510	.044 649 9223	30
	31	1.847 588 8158	42.379 440 7893	.023 596 3472	.541 245 9696	22.937 701 5206	.043 596 3472	31
	32	1.884 540 5921	44.227 029 6051	.022 610 6073	.530 633 3035	23.468 334 8241	.042 610 6073	32
	33	1.922 231 4039	46.111 570 1972	.021 686 5311	.520 228 7289	23.988 563 5530	.041 686 5311	33
	34	1.960 676 0320	48.033 801 6011	.020 818 6728	.510 028 1656	24.498 591 7187	.040 818 6728	34
	35	1.999 889 5527	49.994 477 6331	.020 002 2092	.500 027 6134	24.998 619 3320	.040 002 2092	35
	36	2.039 887 3437	51.994 367 1858	.019 232 8526	.490 223 1504	25.488 842 4824	.039 232 8526	36
	37	2.080 685 0906	54.034 254 5295	.018 506 7789	.480 610 9317	25.969 453 4141	.038 506 7789	37
	38	2.122 298 7924	56.114 939 6201	.017 820 5663	.471 187 1880	26.440 640 6021	.037 820 5663	38
	39	2.164 744 7682	58.237 238 4125	.017 171 1439	.461 948 2235	26.902 588 8256	.037 171 1439	39
	40	2.208 039 6636	60.401 983 1807	.016 555 7478	.452 890 4152	27.355 479 2407	.036 555 7478	40
	41	2.252 200 4569	62.610 022 8444	.015 971 8836	.444 010 2110	27.799 489 4517	.035 971 8836	41
	42	2.297 244 4660	64.862 223 3012	.015 417 2945	.435 304 1284	28.234 793 5801	.035 417 2945	42
	43	2.343 189 3553	67.159 467 7673	.014 889 9334	.426 768 7533	28.661 562 3334	.034 889 9334	43
	44	2.390 053 1425	69.502 657 1226	.014 387 9391	.418 400 7386	29.079 963 0720	.034 387 9391	44
	45	2.437 854 2053	71.892 710 2651	.013 909 6161	.410 196 8025	29.490 159 8745	.033 909 6161	45
	46	2.486 611 2894	74.330 564 4704	.013 453 4159	.402 153 7280	29.892 313 6025	.033 453 4159	46
	47	2.536 343 5152	76.817 175 7598	.013 017 9220	.394 268 3607	30.286 581 9632	.033 017 9220	47
	48	2.587 070 3855	79.353 519 2750	.012 601 8355	.386 537 6086	30.673 119 5718	.032 601 8355	48
	49	2.638 811 7932	81.940 589 6605	.012 203 9639	.378 958 4398	31.052 078 0115	.032 203 9639	49
	50	2.691 588 0291	84.579 401 4537	.011 823 2097	.371 527 8821	31.423 605 8937	.031 823 2097	50
	51	2.745 419 7897	87.270 989 4828	.011 458 5615	.364 243 0217	31.787 848 9153	.031 458 5615	51
	52	2.800 328 1854	90.016 409 2724	.011 109 0856	.357 101 0017	32.144 949 9170	.031 109 0856	52
	53	2.856 334 7492	92.816 737 4579	.010 773 9189	.350 099 0212	32.495 048 9382	.030 773 9189	53
	54	2.913 461 4441	95.673 072 2070	.010 452 2618	.343 234 3345	32.838 283 2728	.030 452 2618	54
	55	2.971 730 6730	98.586 533 6512	.010 143 3732	.336 504 2496	33.174 787 5223	.030 143 3732	55
	56	3.031 165 2865	101.558 264 3242	.009 846 5645	.329 906 1270	33.504 693 6494	.029 846 5645	56
	57	3.091 788 5922	104.589 429 6107	.009 561 1957	.323 437 3794	33.828 131 0288	.029 561 1957	57
	58	3.153 624 3641	107.681 218 2029	.009 286 6706	.317 095 4700	34.145 226 4988	.029 286 6706	58
	59	3.216 696 8513	110.834 842 5669	.009 022 4335	.310 877 9118	34.456 104 4106	.029 022 4335	59
	60	3.281 030 7884	114.051 539 4183	.008 767 9658	.304 782 2665	34.760 886 6770	.028 767 9658	60
	61	3.346 651 4041	117.332 570 2066	.008 522 7827	.298 806 1436	35.059 692 8206	.028 522 7827	61
	62	3.413 584 4322	120.679 221 6108	.008 286 4306	.292 947 1996	35.352 640 0202	.028 286 4306	62
	63	3.481 856 1209	124.092 806 0430	.008 058 4849	.287 203 1369	35.639 843 1571	.028 058 4849	63
	64	3.551 493 2433	127.574 662 1638	.007 838 5471	.281 571 7028	35.921 414 8599	.027 838 5471	64
	65	3.622 523 1081	131.126 155 4071	.007 626 2436	.276 050 6890	36.197 465 5489	.027 626 2436	65
	66	3.694 973 5703	134.748 678 5153	.007 421 2231	.270 637 9304	36.468 103 4793	.027 421 2231	66
	67	3.768 873 0417	138.443 652 0856	.007 223 1553	.265 331 3043	36.733 434 7837	.027 223 1553	67
	68	3.844 250 5025	142.212 525 1273	.007 031 7294	.260 128 7297	36.993 563 5134	.027 031 7294	68
	69	3.921 135 5126	146.056 775 6298	.006 846 6526	.255 028 1664	37.248 591 6798	.026 846 6526	69
	70	3.999 558 2228	149.977 911 1424	.006 667 6485	.250 027 6141	37.498 619 2939	.026 667 6485	70
	71	4.079 549 3873	153.977 469 3652	.006 494 4567	.245 125 1119	37.743 744 4058	.026 494 4567	71
	72	4.161 140 3751	158.057 018 7526	.006 326 8307	.240 318 7371	37.984 063 1429	.026 326 8307	72
	73	4.244 363 1826	162.218 159 1276	.006 164 5380	.235 606 6050	38.219 669 7480	.026 164 5380	73
	74	4.329 250 4462	166.462 522 3102	.006 007 3582	.230 986 8677	38.450 656 6157	.026 007 3582	74
	75	4.415 835 4551	170.791 772 7564	.005 855 0830	.226 457 7134	38.677 114 3291	.025 855 0830	75
	76	4.504 152 1642	175.207 608 2115	.005 707 5147	.222 017 3661	38.899 131 6952	.025 707 5147	76
	77	4.594 235 2075	179.711 760 3757	.005 564 4661	.217 664 0844	39.116 795 7796	.025 564 4661	77
	78	4.686 119 9117	184.305 995 5833	.005 425 7595	.213 396 1612	39.330 191 9408	.025 425 7595	78
	79	4.779 842 3099	188.992 115 4949	.005 291 2260	.209 211 9227	39.539 403 8635	.025 291 2260	79
	80	4.875 439 1561	193.771 957 8048	.055 160 7055	.205 109 7282	39.744 513 5917	.025 160 7055	80
	81	4.972 947 9392	198.647 396 9609	.005 034 0453	.201 087 9688	39.945 601 5605	.025 034 0453	81
	82	5.072 406 8980	203.620 344 9001	.004 911 1006	.197 145 0674	40.142 746 6279	.024 911 1006	82
	83	5.173 855 0360	208.692 751 7981	.004 791 7333	.193 279 4779	40.336 026 1058	.024 791 7333	83
	84	5.277 332 1367	213.866 606 8341	.004 675 8118	.189 489 6842	40.525 515 7900	.024 675 8118	84
	85	5.382 878 7794	219.143 938 9708	.004 563 2108	.185 774 2002	40.711 289 9902	.024 563 2108	85
	86	5.490 536 3550	224.526 817 7502	.004 453 8110	.182 131 5688	40.893 421 5590	.024 453 8110	86
	87	5.600 347 0821	230.017 354 1052	.004 347 4981	.178 560 3616	41.071 981 9206	.024 347 4981	87
	88	5.712 354 0237	235.617 701 1873	.004 244 1633	.175 059 1780	41.247 041 0986	.024 244 1633	88
	89	5.826 601 1042	241.330 055 2111	.004 143 7027	.171 626 6451	41.418 667 7437	.024 143 7027	89
	90	5.943 133 1263	247.156 656 3153	.004 046 0169	.168 261 4168	41.586 929 1605	.024 046 0169	90
	91	6.061 995 7888	253.099 789 4416	.003 951 0108	.164 962 1733	41.751 891 3339	.023 951 0108	91
	92	6.183 235 7046	259.161 785 2304	.003 858 5936	.161 727 6209	41.913 618 9548	.023 858 5936	92
	93	6.306 900 4187	265.345 020 9350	.003 768 6782	.158 556 4911	42.072 175 4458	.023 768 6782	93
	94	6.433 038 4271	271.651 921 3537	.003 681 1814	.155 447 5403	42.227 622 9861	.023 681 1814	94
	95	6.561 699 1956	278.084 959 7808	.003 596 0233	.152 399 5493	42.380 022 5354	.023 596 0233	95
	96	6.692 933 1795	284.646 658 9764	.003 513 1275	.149 411 3228	42.529 433 8582	.023 513 1275	96
	97	6.826 791 8431	291.339 592 1559	.003 432 4205	.146 481 6891	42.675 915 5473	.023 432 4205	97
	98	6.963 327 6800	298.166 383 9991	.003 353 8321	.143 609 4991	42.819 525 0464	.023 353 8321	98
	99	7.102 594 2336	305.129 711 6790	.003 277 2947	.140 793 6265	42.960 318 6729	.023 277 2947	99
	100	7.244 646 1183	312.232 305 9126	.003 202 7435	.138 032 9672	43.098 351 6401	.023 202 7435	100

RATE 2 1/4%							
PERIODS	XIV COMPOUND AMOUNT — AMOUNT OF 1 (How $1 left at compound interest will grow.)	XV AMOUNT OF ANNUITY — AMOUNT OF 1 PER PERIOD (How $1 deposited periodically will grow.)	XVI SINKING FUND — SINKING FUND (Periodic deposit that will grow to $1 at future date.)	XVII PRESENT VALUE — PRESENT WORTH OF 1 (What $1 due in the future is worth today.)	XVIII PRESENT VALUE OF ANNUITY — PRESENT WORTH OF 1 PER PERIOD (What $1 payable periodically is worth today.)	XIX AMORTIZATION — PARTIAL PAYMENT (Annuity worth $1 today. Periodic payment necessary to pay off a loan of $1.)	PERIODS
1	1.022 500 0000	1.000 000 0000	1.000 000 0000	.977 995 1100	.977 995 1100	1.022 500 0000	1
2	1.045 506 2500	2.022 500 2500	.494 437 5773	.956 474 4352	1.934 469 5453	.516 937 5773	2
3	1.069 030 1406	3.068 006 2500	.325 944 5772	.935 427 3205	2.869 896 8658	.348 444 5772	3
4	1.093 083 3188	4.137 036 3906	.241 718 9277	.914 843 3453	3.784 740 2110	.264 218 9277	4
5	1.117 677 6935	5.230 119 7094	.191 200 2125	.894 712 3181	4.679 452 5291	.213 700 2125	5
6	1.142 825 4416	6.347 797 4029	.157 534 9584	.875 024 2720	5.554 476 8011	.180 034 9584	6
7	1.168 539 0140	7.490 622 8444	.133 500 2470	.855 769 4591	6.410 246 2602	.156 000 2470	7
8	1.194 831 1418	8.659 161 8584	.115 484 6181	.836 938 3464	7.247 184 6066	.137 984 6181	8
9	1.221 714 8425	9.853 993 0003	.101 481 7039	.818 521 6101	8.065 706 2167	.123 981 7039	9
10	1.249 203 4265	11.075 707 8428	.090 287 6831	.800 510 1322	8.866 216 3489	.112 787 6831	10
11	1.277 310 5036	12.324 911 2692	.081 136 4868	.782 894 9948	9.649 111 3436	.103 636 4868	11
12	1.306 049 9889	13.602 221 7728	.073 517 4015	.765 667 4765	10.414 778 8202	.096 017 4015	12
13	1.335 436 1147	14.908 271 7627	.067 076 8561	.748 819 0480	11.163 597 8681	.089 576 8561	13
14	1.365 483 4272	16.243 707 8773	.061 562 2989	.732 341 3672	11.895 939 2354	.084 062 2989	14
15	1.396 206 8044	17.609 191 3046	.056 788 5250	.716 226 2760	12.612 165 5113	.079 288 5250	15
16	1.427 621 4575	19.005 398 1089	.052 616 6300	.700 465 7956	13.312 631 3069	.075 116 6300	16
17	1.459 742 9402	20.433 019 5664	.048 940 3926	.685 052 1228	13.997 683 4298	.071 440 3926	17
18	1.492 587 1564	21.892 762 5066	.045 677 1958	.669 977 6262	14.667 661 0560	.068 177 1958	18
19	1.526 170 3674	23.385 349 6630	.042 761 8152	.665 234 8423	15.322 895 8983	.065 261 8152	19
20	1.560 509 2007	24.911 520 0304	.040 142 0708	.640 816 4717	15.963 712 3700	.062 642 0708	20
21	1.595 620 6577	26.472 029 2311	.037 775 7214	.626 715 3757	16.590 427 7457	.060 275 7214	21
22	1.631 522 1225	28.067 649 8888	.035 628 2056	.612 924 5728	17.203 352 3185	.058 128 2056	22
23	1.668 231 3703	29.699 172 0113	.033 670 9724	.599 437 2350	17.802 789 5536	.056 170 9724	23
24	1.705 766 5761	31.367 403 3816	.031 880 2289	.586 246 6846	18.389 036 2382	.054 380 2289	24
25	1.744 146 3240	33.073 169 9577	.030 235 9889	.573 346 3908	18.962 382 6291	.052 735 9889	25
26	1.783 389 6163	34.817 316 2817	.028 721 3406	.560 729 9666	19.523 112 5957	.051 221 3406	26
27	1.823 515 8827	36.600 705 8980	.027 321 8774	.548 391 1654	20.071 503 7610	.049 821 8774	27
28	1.864 544 9901	38.424 221 7807	.026 025 2506	.536 323 8781	20.607 827 6392	.048 525 2506	28
29	1.906 497 2523	40.288 766 7708	.024 820 8143	.524 522 1302	21.132 349 7693	.047 320 8143	29
30	1.949 393 4405	42.195 264 0232	.023 699 3422	.512 980 0784	21.645 329 8478	.046 199 3422	30
31	1.993 254 7929	44.144 657 4637	.022 652 7978	.501 692 0082	22.147 021 8560	.045 152 7978	31
32	2.038 103 0258	46.137 912 2566	.021 674 1493	.490 652 3308	22.637 674 1868	.044 174 1493	32
33	2.083 960 3439	48.176 015 2824	.020 757 2169	.479 855 5802	23.117 529 7670	.043 257 2169	33
34	2.130 849 4516	50.259 975 6262	.019 896 5477	.469 296 4110	23.586 826 1780	.042 396 5477	34
35	2.178 793 5643	52.390 825 0778	.019 087 3115	.458 969 5951	24.045 795 7731	.041 587 3115	35
36	2.227 816 4194	54.569 618 6421	.018 325 2151	.448 870 0197	24.494 665 7928	.040 825 2151	36
37	2.277 942 2889	56.797 435 0615	.017 606 4289	.438 992 6843	24.933 658 4771	.040 106 4289	37
38	2.329 195 9904	59.075 377 3504	.016 927 5262	.429 332 6985	25.362 991 1756	.039 427 5262	38
39	2.381 602 9002	61.404 573 3408	.016 285 4319	.419 885 2798	25.782 876 4554	.038 785 4319	39
40	2.435 188 9654	63.786 176 2410	.015 677 3781	.410 645 7504	26.193 522 2057	.038 177 3781	40
41	2.489 980 7171	66.221 365 2064	.015 100 8666	.401 609 5358	26.595 131 7416	.037 600 8666	41
42	2.546 005 2833	68.711 345 9235	.014 553 6372	.392 772 1622	26.987 903 9037	.037 053 6372	42
43	2.603 290 4022	71.257 351 2068	.014 033 6398	.384 129 2540	27.372 033 1577	.036 533 6398	43
44	2.661 864 4362	73.860 641 6090	.013 539 0105	.375 676 5320	27.747 709 6897	.036 039 0105	44
45	2.721 756 3860	76.522 506 0452	.013 068 0508	.367 409 8112	28.115 119 5009	.035 568 0508	45
46	2.782 995 9047	79.244 262 4312	.012 619 2101	.359 324 9988	28.474 444 4997	.035 119 2101	46
47	2.845 613 2126	82.027 258 3359	.012 191 0694	.351 418 0917	28.825 862 5913	.034 691 0694	47
48	2.909 639 6121	84.872 871 6484	.011 782 3279	.343 685 1753	29.169 547 7666	.034 282 3279	48
49	2.975 106 5034	87.782 511 2605	.011 391 7908	.336 122 4208	29.505 670 1874	.033 891 7908	49
50	3.042 046 3997	90.757 617 7639	.011 018 3588	.328 726 0839	29.834 396 2713	.033 518 3588	50
51	3.110 492 4437	93.799 664 1636	.010 661 0190	.321 492 5026	30.155 888 7739	.033 161 0190	51
52	3.180 478 5237	96.910 156 6073	.010 318 8359	.314 418 0954	30.470 306 8693	.032 818 8359	52
53	3.252 039 2904	100.090 635 1309	.009 990 9447	.307 499 3598	30.777 806 2291	.032 490 9447	53
54	3.325 210 1745	103.342 674 4214	.009 676 5446	.300 732 8703	31.078 539 0994	.032 176 5446	54
55	3.400 027 4034	106.667 884 5958	.009 374 8930	.294 115 2765	31.372 654 3760	.031 874 8930	55
56	3.476 528 0200	110.067 911 9993	.009 085 3000	.287 643 3022	31.660 297 6782	.031 585 3000	56
57	3.554 749 9004	113.544 440 0192	.008 807 1243	.281 313 7430	31.941 611 4212	.031 307 1243	57
58	3.634 731 7732	117.099 189 9197	.008 539 7687	.275 123 4651	32.216 734 8863	.031 039 7687	58
59	3.716 513 2381	120.733 921 6929	.008 282 6764	.269 069 4035	32.485 804 2898	.030 782 6764	59
60	3.800 134 7859	124.450 434 9310	.008 035 3275	.263 148 5609	32.748 952 8506	.030 535 3275	60
61	3.885 637 8186	128.250 569 7169	.007 797 2363	.257 358 0057	33.006 310 8563	.030 297 2363	61
62	3.973 064 6695	132.136 207 5355	.007 567 9484	.251 694 8711	33.258 005 7275	.030 067 9484	62
63	4.062 458 6246	136.109 272 2051	.007 347 0380	.246 156 3532	33.504 162 0807	.029 847 0380	63
64	4.153 863 9437	140.171 730 8297	.007 134 1061	.240 739 7097	33.744 901 7904	.029 634 1061	64
65	4.247 325 8824	144.325 594 7734	.006 928 7780	.235 442 2589	33.980 344 0493	.029 428 7780	65
66	4.342 890 7148	148.572 920 6558	.006 730 7016	.230 261 3779	34.210 605 4272	.029 230 7016	66
67	4.440 605 7558	152.915 811 3705	.006 539 5461	.225 194 5016	34.435 799 9288	.029 039 5461	67
68	4.540 519 3853	157.356 417 1264	.006 354 9998	.220 239 1214	34.656 039 0501	.028 854 9998	68
69	4.642 681 0715	161.896 936 5117	.006 176 7691	.215 392 7837	34.871 431 8339	.028 676 7691	69
70	4.747 141 3956	166.539 617 5832	.006 004 5773	.210 653 0892	35.082 084 9231	.028 504 5773	70
71	4.853 952 0770	171.286 758 9788	.005 838 1629	.206 017 6912	35.288 102 6143	.028 338 1629	71
72	4.963 165 9988	176.140 711 0559	.005 677 2792	.201 484 2946	35.489 586 9088	.028 177 2792	72
73	5.074 837 2337	181.103 877 0546	.005 521 6929	.197 050 6548	35.686 637 5637	.028 021 6929	73
74	5.189 021 0715	186.178 714 2883	.005 371 1833	.192 714 5768	35.879 352 1405	.027 871 1833	74
75	5.305 774 0456	191.367 735 3598	.005 225 5413	.188 473 9138	36.067 826 0543	.027 725 5413	75
76	5.425 153 9616	196.673 509 4054	.005 084 5689	.184 326 5660	36.252 152 6203	.027 584 5689	76
77	5.547 219 9258	202.098 663 3670	.004 948 0782	.180 270 4802	36.432 423 1006	.027 448 0782	77
78	5.672 032 3741	207.645 883 2928	.004 815 8913	.176 303 6482	36.608 726 7487	.027 315 8913	78
79	5.799 653 1025	213.317 915 6669	.004 687 8388	.172 424 1058	36.781 150 8545	.027 187 8388	79
80	5.930 145 2973	219.117 568 7694	.004 563 7600	.168 629 9323	36.949 780 7868	.027 063 7600	80
81	6.063 573 5665	225.047 714 0667	.004 443 5021	.164 919 2492	37.114 700 0360	.026 943 5021	81
82	6.200 003 9717	231.111 287 6332	.004 326 9198	.161 290 2193	37.275 990 2552	.026 826 9198	82
83	6.339 504 0611	237.311 291 6050	.004 213 8745	.157 741 0457	37.433 731 3010	.026 713 8745	83
84	6.482 142 9025	243.650 795 6661	.004 104 2345	.154 269 9714	37.588 001 2723	.026 604 2345	84
85	6.627 991 1178	250.132 938 5686	.003 997 8741	.150 875 2776	37.738 876 5500	.026 497 8741	85
86	6.777 120 9179	256.760 929 6863	.003 894 6735	.147 555 2837	37.886 431 8337	.026 394 6735	86
87	6.929 606 1386	263.538 050 6043	.003 794 5185	.144 308 3460	38.030 740 1797	.026 294 5185	87
88	7.085 522 2767	270.467 656 7429	.003 697 2998	.141 132 8567	38.171 873 0363	.026 197 2998	88
89	7.244 946 5279	277.553 179 0196	.003 602 9132	.138 027 2437	38.309 900 2800	.026 102 9132	89
90	7.407 957 8248	284.798 125 5475	.003 511 2591	.134 989 9694	38.444 890 2494	.026 011 2591	90
91	7.574 636 8759	292.206 083 3724	.003 422 2422	.132 019 5300	38.576 909 7794	.025 922 2422	91
92	7.745 066 2056	299.780 720 2482	.003 335 7716	.129 114 4547	38.706 024 2341	.025 835 7716	92
93	7.919 330 1952	307.525 786 4538	.003 251 7598	.126 273 3054	38.832 297 5395	.025 751 7598	93
94	8.097 515 1246	315.445 116 6490	.003 170 1236	.123 494 6752	38.955 792 2147	.025 670 1236	94
95	8.279 709 2149	323.542 631 7736	.003 090 7828	.120 777 1884	39.076 569 4031	.025 590 7828	95
96	8.466 002 6722	331.822 340 9885	.003 013 6609	.118 119 4997	39.194 688 9028	.025 513 6609	96
97	8.656 487 7324	340.288 343 6608	.002 938 6843	.115 520 2931	39.310 209 1959	.025 438 6843	97
98	8.851 258 7063	348.944 831 3932	.002 865 7825	.112 978 2818	39.423 187 4776	.025 365 7825	98
99	9.050 412 0272	357.796 090 0995	.002 794 8880	.110 492 2071	39.533 679 6847	.025 294 8880	99
100	9.254 046 2979	366.846 502 1267	.002 725 9358	.108 060 8382	39.641 740 5229	.025 225 9358	100

	XIV COMPOUND AMOUNT	XV AMOUNT OF ANNUITY	XVI SINKING FUND	XVII PRESENT VALUE	XVIII PRESENT VALUE OF ANNUITY	XIX AMORTIZATION	
RATE 2 1/2% P E R I O D S	AMOUNT OF 1 How $1 left at compound interest will grow.	AMOUNT OF 1 PER PERIOD How $1 deposited periodically will grow.	SINKING FUND Periodic deposit that will grow to $1 at future date.	PRESENT WORTH OF 1 What $1 due in the future is worth today.	PRESENT WORTH OF 1 PER PERIOD What $1 payable periodically is worth today.	PARTIAL PAYMENT Annuity worth $1 today Periodic payment necessary to pay off a loan of $1.	P E R I O D S
1	1.025 000 0000	1.000 000 0000	1.000 000 0000	.975 609 7561	.975 609 7561	1.025 000 0000	1
2	1.050 625 0000	2.025 000 0000	.493 827 1605	.951 814 3962	1.927 424 1523	.518 827 1605	2
3	1.076 890 6250	3.075 625 0000	.325 137 1672	.928 599 4109	2.856 023 5632	.350 137 1672	3
4	1.103 812 8906	4.152 515 6250	.240 817 8777	.905 950 6448	3.761 974 2080	.265 817 8777	4
5	1.131 408 2129	5.256 328 5156	.190 246 8609	.883 854 2876	4.645 828 4956	.215 246 8609	5
6	1.159 693 4182	6.387 736 7285	.156 549 9711	.862 296 8660	5.508 125 3616	.181 549 9711	6
7	1.188 685 7537	7.547 430 1467	.132 495 4296	.841 265 2351	6.349 390 5967	.157 495 4296	7
8	1.218 402 8975	8.736 115 9004	.114 467 3458	.820 746 5708	7.170 137 1675	.139 467 3458	8
9	1.248 862 9699	9.954 518 7979	.100 456 8900	.800 728 3618	7.970 865 5292	.125 456 8900	9
10	1.280 084 5442	11.203 381 7679	.089 258 7632	.781 198 4017	8.752 063 9310	.114 258 7632	10
11	1.312 086 6578	12.483 466 3121	.080 105 9558	.762 144 7822	9.514 208 7131	.105 105 9558	11
12	1.344 888 8242	13.795 552 9699	.072 487 1270	.743 555 8850	10.257 764 5982	.097 487 1270	12
13	1.378 511 0449	15.140 441 7941	.066 048 2708	.725 420 3757	10.983 184 9738	.091 048 2708	13
14	1.412 973 8210	16.518 952 8390	.060 536 5249	.707 727 1958	11.690 912 1696	.085 536 5249	14
15	1.448 298 1665	17.931 926 6599	.055 766 4561	.690 465 5568	12.381 377 7264	.080 766 4561	15
16	1.484 505 6207	19.380 224 8264	.051 598 9886	.673 624 9335	13.055 002 6599	.076 598 9886	16
17	1.521 618 2612	20.864 730 4471	.047 927 7699	.657 195 0571	13.712 197 7170	.072 927 7699	17
18	1.559 658 7177	22.386 348 7083	.044 670 0805	.641 165 9093	14.353 363 6264	.069 670 0805	18
19	1.598 650 1856	23.946 007 4260	.041 760 6151	.625 527 7164	14.978 891 3428	.066 760 6151	19
20	1.638 616 4403	25.544 657 6116	.039 147 1287	.610 270 9429	15.589 162 2856	.064 147 1287	20
21	1.679 581 8513	27.183 274 0519	.036 787 3273	.595 386 2857	16.184 548 5714	.061 787 3273	21
22	1.721 571 3976	28.862 855 9032	.034 646 6061	.580 864 6690	16.765 413 2404	.059 646 6061	22
23	1.764 610 6825	30.584 427 3008	.032 696 3781	.566 697 2380	17.332 110 4784	.057 696 3781	23
24	1.808 725 9496	32.349 037 9833	.030 912 8204	.552 875 3542	17.884 985 8326	.055 912 8204	24
25	1.853 944 0983	34.157 763 9329	.029 275 9210	.539 390 5894	18.424 376 4220	.054 275 9210	25
26	1.900 292 7008	36.011 708 0312	.027 768 7467	.526 234 7214	18.950 611 1434	.052 768 7467	26
27	1.947 800 0183	37.912 000 7320	.026 376 8722	.513 399 7282	19.464 010 8717	.051 376 8722	27
28	1.996 495 0188	39.859 800 7503	.025 087 9327	.500 877 7836	19.964 888 6553	.050 087 9327	28
29	2.046 407 3942	41.856 295 7690	.023 891 2685	.488 661 2523	20.453 549 9076	.048 891 2685	29
30	2.097 567 5791	43.902 703 1633	.022 777 6407	.476 742 6852	20.930 292 5928	.047 777 6407	30
31	2.150 006 7686	46.000 270 7424	.021 739 0025	.465 114 8148	21.395 407 4076	.046 739 0025	31
32	2.203 756 9378	48.150 277 5109	.020 768 3123	.453 770 5510	21.849 177 9586	.045 768 3123	32
33	2.258 850 8612	50.354 034 4487	.019 859 3819	.442 702 9766	22.291 880 9352	.044 859 3819	33
34	2.315 322 1327	52.612 885 3099	.019 006 7508	.431 905 3430	22.723 786 2783	.044 006 7508	34
35	2.375 205 1861	54.928 207 4426	.018 205 5823	.421 371 0664	23.145 157 3447	.043 205 5823	35
36	2.432 535 3157	57.301 412 6287	.017 451 5767	.411 093 7233	23.556 251 0680	.042 451 5767	36
37	2.493 348 6986	59.733 947 9444	.016 740 8992	.401 067 0471	23.957 318 1151	.041 740 8992	37
38	2.555 682 4161	62.227 296 6430	.016 070 1180	.391 284 9240	24.348 603 0391	.041 070 1180	38
39	2.619 574 4765	64.782 979 0591	.015 436 1534	.381 741 3893	24.730 344 4284	.040 436 1534	39
40	2.685 063 8384	67.402 553 5356	.014 836 2332	.372 430 6237	25.102 775 0521	.039 836 2332	40
41	2.752 190 4343	70.087 617 3740	.014 267 8555	.363 346 9499	25.466 122 0020	.039 267 8555	41
42	2.820 995 1952	72.839 807 8083	.013 728 7567	.354 484 8292	25.820 606 8313	.038 728 7567	42
43	2.891 520 0751	75.660 803 0035	.013 216 8833	.345 838 8578	26.166 445 6890	.038 216 8833	43
44	2.963 808 0770	78.552 323 0786	.012 730 3683	.337 403 7637	26.503 849 4527	.037 730 3683	44
45	3.037 903 2789	81.516 131 1556	.012 267 5106	.329 174 4036	26.833 023 8563	.037 267 5106	45
46	3.113 850 8609	84.554 034 4345	.011 826 7568	.321 145 7596	27.154 169 6159	.036 826 7568	46
47	3.191 697 1324	87.667 885 2954	.011 406 6855	.313 312 9362	27.467 482 5521	.036 406 6855	47
48	3.271 489 5607	90.859 582 4277	.011 005 9938	.305 671 1573	27.773 153 7094	.036 005 9938	48
49	3.353 276 7997	94.131 071 9884	.010 623 4847	.298 215 7632	28.071 369 4726	.035 623 4847	49
50	3.437 108 7197	97.484 348 7881	.010 258 0569	.290 942 2080	28.362 311 6805	.035 258 0569	50
51	3.523 036 4377	100.921 457 5078	.009 908 6956	.283 846 0566	28.646 157 7371	.034 908 6956	51
52	3.611 112 3486	104.444 493 9455	.009 574 4635	.276 922 9820	28.923 080 7191	.034 574 4635	52
53	3.701 390 1574	108.055 606 2942	.009 254 4944	.270 168 7629	29.193 249 4821	.034 254 4944	53
54	3.793 924 9113	111.756 996 4515	.008 947 9856	.263 579 2809	29.456 828 7630	.033 947 9856	54
55	3.888 773 0341	115.550 921 3628	.008 654 1932	.257 150 5180	29.713 979 2810	.033 654 1932	55
56	3.985 992 3599	119.439 694 3969	.008 372 4260	.250 878 5541	29.964 857 8351	.033 372 4260	56
57	4.085 642 1689	123.425 686 7568	.008 102 0412	.244 759 5650	30.209 617 4001	.033 102 0412	57
58	4.187 783 2231	127.511 328 9257	.007 842 4404	.238 789 8195	30.448 407 2196	.032 842 4404	58
59	4.292 477 8037	131.699 112 1489	.007 593 0656	.232 965 6776	30.681 372 8972	.032 593 0656	59
60	4.399 789 7488	135.991 589 9526	.007 353 3959	.227 283 5879	30.908 656 4851	.032 353 3959	60
61	4.509 784 4925	140.391 379 7014	.007 122 9445	.221 740 0857	31.130 396 5708	.032 122 9445	61
62	4.622 529 1048	144.901 164 1940	.006 901 2558	.216 331 7910	31.346 728 3617	.031 901 2558	62
63	4.738 092 3325	149.523 693 2988	.006 687 9033	.211 055 4068	31.557 783 7676	.031 687 9033	63
64	4.856 544 6408	154.261 785 6313	.006 482 4869	.205 907 7130	31.763 691 4805	.031 482 4869	64
65	4.977 958 2568	159.118 330 2721	.006 284 6311	.200 885 5574	31.964 577 0542	.031 284 6311	65
66	5.102 407 2132	164.096 288 5289	.006 093 9830	.195 985 9255	32.160 562 9797	.031 093 9830	66
67	5.229 967 3936	169.198 695 7421	.005 910 2110	.191 205 7810	32.351 768 7607	.030 910 2110	67
68	5.360 716 5784	174.428 663 1356	.005 733 0027	.186 542 2253	32.538 310 9860	.030 733 0027	68
69	5.494 734 4929	179.789 379 7140	.005 562 0638	.181 992 4150	32.720 303 4010	.030 562 0638	69
70	5.632 102 8552	185.284 114 2069	.005 397 1168	.177 553 5756	32.897 856 9766	.030 397 1168	70
71	5.772 905 4266	190.916 217 0620	.005 237 8997	.173 223 0006	33.071 079 9772	.030 237 8997	71
72	5.917 228 0622	196.689 122 4886	.005 084 1652	.168 998 0493	33.240 078 0265	.030 084 1652	72
73	6.065 158 7638	202.606 350 5508	.004 935 6794	.164 876 1457	33.404 954 1722	.029 935 6794	73
74	6.216 787 7329	208.671 509 3146	.004 792 221	.160 854 7763	33.565 808 9485	.029 792 2211	74
75	6.372 207 4262	214.888 297 0474	.004 653 5806	.156 931 4891	33.722 740 4375	.029 653 5806	75
76	6.531 512 6118	221.260 504 4736	.004 519 5594	.153 103 8918	33.875 844 3293	.029 519 5594	76
77	6.694 800 4271	227.792 017 0855	.004 389 9695	.149 369 6505	34.025 213 9798	.029 389 9695	77
78	6.862 170 4378	234.486 817 5126	.004 264 6321	.145 726 4883	34.170 940 4681	.029 264 6321	78
79	7.033 724 6988	241.348 987 9504	.004 143 3776	.142 172 1837	34.313 112 6518	.029 143 3776	79
80	7.209 567 8162	248.382 712 6492	.004 026 0451	.138 704 5695	34.451 817 2213	.029 026 0451	80
81	7.389 807 0116	255.592 280 4654	.003 912 4812	.135 321 5328	34.587 138 7525	.028 912 4812	81
82	7.574 552 1869	262.982 087 4770	.003 802 5404	.132 021 0060	34.719 159 7585	.028 802 5404	82
83	7.763 915 9916	270.556 639 6640	.003 696 0838	.128 800 9815	34.847 960 7400	.028 696 0838	83
84	7.958 013 8914	278.320 555 6556	.003 592 9793	.125 659 4941	34.973 620 2342	.028 592 9793	84
85	8.156 964 2387	286.278 569 5470	.003 493 1011	.122 594 6284	35.096 214 8626	.028 493 1011	85
86	8.360 888 3446	294.435 533 7856	.003 396 3292	.119 604 5155	35.215 819 3781	.028 396 3292	86
87	8.569 910 5533	302.796 422 1303	.003 302 5489	.116 687 3322	35.332 506 7104	.028 302 5489	87
88	8.784 158 3171	311.366 332 6835	.003 211 6510	.113 841 2997	35.446 348 0101	.028 211 6510	88
89	9.003 762 2750	320.150 491 0006	.003 123 5311	.111 064 6827	35.557 412 6928	.028 123 5311	89
90	9.228 856 3319	329.154 253 2756	.003 038 0893	.108 355 7880	35.665 768 4808	.028 038 0893	90
91	9.459 577 7402	338.383 109 6075	.002 955 2302	.105 712 9639	35.771 481 4447	.027 955 2302	91
92	9.696 067 1837	347.842 687 3477	.002 874 8628	.103 134 5989	35.874 616 0436	.027 874 8628	92
93	9.938 468 8633	357.538 754 5314	.002 796 8996	.100 619 1209	35.975 235 1645	.027 796 8996	93
94	10.186 930 5849	367.477 223 3947	.002 721 2571	.098 164 9960	36.073 400 1605	.027 721 2571	94
95	10.441 603 8495	377.664 153 9796	.002 647 8552	.095 770 7278	36.169 170 8882	.027 647 8552	95
96	10.702 643 9457	388.105 757 8290	.002 576 6173	.093 434 8564	36.262 605 7446	.027 576 6173	96
97	10.970 210 0444	398.808 401 7748	.002 507 4697	.091 155 9574	36.353 761 7021	.027 507 4697	97
98	11.244 465 2955	409.778 611 8191	.002 440 3421	.088 932 6414	36.442 694 3435	.027 440 3421	98
99	11.525 576 9279	421.023 077 1146	.002 375 1667	.086 763 5526	36.529 457 8961	.027 375 1667	99
100	11.813 716 3511	432.548 654 0425	.002 311 8787	.084 647 3684	36.614 105 2645	.027 311 8787	100

	XIV COMPOUND AMOUNT	XV AMOUNT OF ANNUITY	XVI SINKING FUND	XVII PRESENT VALUE	XVIII PRESENT VALUE OF ANNUITY	XIX AMORTIZATION	
RATE 3% PERIODS	AMOUNT OF 1	AMOUNT OF 1 PER PERIOD	SINKING FUND	PRESENT WORTH OF 1	PRESENT WORTH OF 1 PER PERIOD	PARTIAL PAYMENT	PERIODS
	How $1 left at compound interest will grow.	How $1 deposited periodically will grow.	Periodic deposit that will grow to $1 at future date.	What $1 due in the future is worth today.	What $1 payable periodically is worth today.	Annuity worth $1 today. Periodic payment necessary to pay off a loan of $1	
1	1.030 000 0000	1.000 000 0000	1.000 000 0000	.970 873 7864	.970 873 7864	1.030 000 0000	1
2	1.060 900 0000	2.030 000 0000	.492 610 8374	.942 595 9091	1.913 469 6955	.522 610 8374	2
3	1.092 727 0000	3.090 900 0000	.323 530 3633	.915 141 6594	2.828 611 3549	.353 530 3633	3
4	1.125 508 8100	4.183 627 0000	.239 027 0452	.888 487 0479	3.717 098 4028	.269 027 0452	4
5	1.159 274 0743	5.309 135 8100	.188 354 5714	.862 608 7844	4.579 707 1872	.218 354 5714	5
6	1.194 052 2965	6.468 409 8843	.154 597 5005	.837 484 2567	5.417 191 4439	.184 597 5005	6
7	1.229 873 8654	7.662 462 1808	.130 506 3538	.813 091 5113	6.230 282 9552	.160 506 3538	7
8	1.266 770 0814	8.892 336 0463	.112 456 3888	.789 409 2343	7.019 692 1895	.142 456 3888	8
9	1.304 773 1838	10.159 106 1276	.098 433 8570	.766 416 7323	7.786 108 9219	.128 433 8570	9
10	1.343 916 3793	11.463 879 3115	.087 230 5066	.744 093 9149	8.530 202 8368	.117 230 5066	10
11	1.384 233 8707	12.807 795 6908	.078 077 4478	.722 421 2766	9.252 624 1134	.108 077 4478	11
12	1.425 760 8868	14.192 029 5615	.070 462 0855	.701 379 8802	9.954 004 9936	.100 462 0855	12
13	1.468 533 7135	15.617 790 4484	.064 029 5440	.680 951 3400	10.634 955 3336	.094 029 5440	13
14	1.512 589 7249	17.086 324 1618	.058 526 3390	.661 117 8058	11.296 073 1394	.088 526 3390	14
15	1.557 967 4166	18.598 913 8867	.053 766 5805	.641 861 9474	11.937 935 0868	.083 766 5805	15
16	1.604 706 4391	20.156 881 3033	.049 610 8493	.623 166 9392	12.561 102 0260	.079 610 8493	16
17	1.652 847 6323	21.761 587 7424	.045 952 5294	.605 016 4458	13.166 118 4718	.075 952 5294	17
18	1.702 433 0612	23.414 435 3747	.042 708 6959	.587 394 6076	13.753 513 0795	.072 708 6959	18
19	1.753 506 0531	25.116 868 4359	.039 813 8806	.570 286 0268	14.323 799 1063	.069 813 8806	19
20	1.806 111 2347	26.870 374 4890	.037 215 7076	.553 675 7542	14.877 474 8605	.067 215 7076	20
21	1.860 294 5717	28.676 485 7236	.034 871 7765	.537 549 2759	15.415 024 1364	.064 871 7765	21
22	1.916 103 4089	30.536 780 2954	.032 747 3948	.521 892 5009	15.936 916 6372	.062 747 3948	22
23	1.973 586 5111	32.452 883 7042	.030 813 9027	.506 691 7484	16.443 608 3857	.060 813 9027	23
24	2.032 794 1065	34.426 470 2153	.029 047 4159	.491 933 7363	16.935 542 1220	.059 047 4159	24
25	2.093 777 9297	36.459 264 3218	.027 427 8710	.477 605 5693	17.413 147 6913	.057 427 8710	25
26	2.156 591 2675	38.553 042 2515	.025 938 2903	.463 694 7274	17.876 842 4187	.055 938 2903	26
27	2.221 289 0056	40.709 633 5190	.024 564 2103	.450 189 0558	18.327 031 4745	.054 564 2103	27
28	2.287 927 6757	42.930 922 5246	.023 293 2334	.437 076 7532	18.764 108 2277	.053 293 2334	28
29	2.356 565 5060	45.218 850 2003	.022 114 6711	.424 346 3623	19.188 454 5900	.052 114 6711	29
30	2.427 262 4712	47.575 415 7063	.021 019 2593	.411 986 7595	19.600 441 3495	.051 019 2593	30
31	2.500 080 3453	50.002 678 1775	.019 998 9288	.399 987 1452	20.000 428 4946	.049 998 9288	31
32	2.575 082 7557	52.502 758 5228	.019 046 6183	.388 337 0341	20.388 765 5288	.049 046 6183	32
33	2.652 335 2384	55.077 841 2785	.018 156 1219	.377 026 2467	20.765 791 7755	.048 156 1219	33
34	2.731 905 2955	57.730 176 5169	.017 321 9633	.366 044 8997	21.131 836 6752	.047 321 9633	34
35	2.813 862 4544	60.462 081 8124	.016 539 2916	.355 383 3978	21.487 220 0731	.046 539 2916	35
36	2.898 278 3280	63.275 944 2668	.015 803 7942	.345 032 4251	21.832 252 4981	.045 803 7942	36
37	2.985 226 6778	66.174 222 5948	.015 111 6244	.334 982 9369	22.167 235 4351	.045 111 6244	37
38	3.074 783 4782	69.159 449 2726	.014 459 3401	.325 226 1524	22.492 461 5874	.044 459 3401	38
39	3.167 026 9825	72.234 232 7508	.013 843 8516	.315 753 5460	22.808 215 1334	.043 843 8516	39
40	3.262 037 7920	75.401 259 7333	.013 262 3779	.306 556 8408	23.114 771 9742	.043 262 3779	40
41	3.359 898 9258	78.663 297 5253	.012 712 4089	.297 628 0008	23.412 399 9750	.042 712 4089	41
42	3.460 695 8935	82.023 196 4511	.012 191 6731	.288 959 2240	23.701 359 1990	.042 191 6731	42
43	3.564 516 7703	85.483 892 3446	.011 698 1103	.280 542 9360	23.981 902 1349	.041 698 1103	43
44	3.671 452 2734	89.048 409 1149	.011 229 8469	.272 371 7825	24.254 273 9174	.041 229 8469	44
45	3.781 595 8417	92.719 861 3884	.010 785 1757	.264 438 6238	24.518 712 5412	.040 785 1757	45
46	3.895 043 7169	96.501 457 2300	.010 362 5378	.256 736 5279	24.775 449 0691	.040 362 5378	46
47	4.011 895 0284	100.396 500 9469	.009 960 5065	.249 258 7650	25.024 707 8341	.039 960 5065	47
48	4.132 251 8793	104.408 395 9753	.009 577 7738	.241 998 8009	25.266 706 6350	.039 577 7738	48
49	4.256 219 4356	108.540 647 8546	.009 213 1383	.234 950 2922	25.501 656 9272	.039 213 1383	49
50	4.383 906 0187	112.796 867 2902	.008 865 4944	.228 107 0798	25.729 764 0070	.038 865 4944	50
51	4.515 423 1993	117.180 773 3089	.008 533 8232	.221 463 1843	25.951 227 1913	.038 533 8232	51
52	4.650 885 8952	121.696 196 5082	.008 217 1837	.215 012 8003	26.166 239 9915	.038 217 1837	52
53	4.790 412 4721	126.347 082 4035	.007 914 7059	.208 750 2915	26.374 990 2830	.037 914 7059	53
54	4.934 124 8463	131.137 494 8756	.007 625 5841	.202 670 1859	26.577 660 4690	.037 625 5841	54
55	5.082 148 5917	136.071 619 7218	.007 349 0710	.196 767 1708	26.774 427 6398	.037 349 0710	55
56	5.234 613 0494	141.153 768 3135	.007 084 4726	.191 036 0882	26.965 463 7279	.037 084 4726	56
57	5.391 651 4409	146.388 381 3629	.006 831 1432	.185 471 9303	27.150 935 6582	.036 831 1432	57
58	5.553 400 9841	151.780 032 8038	.006 588 4819	.180 069 8352	27.331 005 4934	.036 588 4819	58
59	5.720 003 0136	157.333 433 7879	.006 355 9281	.174 825 0827	27.505 830 5761	.036 355 9281	59
60	5.891 603 1040	163.053 436 8015	.006 132 9587	.169 733 0900	27.675 563 6661	.036 132 9587	60
61	6.068 351 1972	168.945 039 9056	.005 919 0847	.164 789 4978	27.840 353 0739	.035 919 0847	61
62	6.250 401 7331	175.013 391 1027	.005 713 8485	.159 989 7163	28.000 342 7902	.035 713 8485	62
63	6.437 913 7851	181.263 792 8358	.005 516 8216	.155 329 8216	28.155 672 6118	.035 516 8216	63
64	6.631 051 1986	187.701 706 6209	.005 327 6021	.150 805 6521	28.306 478 2639	.035 327 6021	64
65	6.829 982 7346	194.332 757 8195	.005 145 8128	.146 413 2544	28.452 891 5184	.035 145 8128	65
66	7.034 882 2166	201.162 740 5541	.004 971 0995	.142 148 7907	28.595 040 3091	.034 971 0995	66
67	7.245 928 6831	208.197 622 7707	.004 803 1288	.138 008 5347	28.733 048 8438	.034 803 1288	67
68	7.463 306 5436	215.443 551 4539	.004 641 5871	.133 988 8686	28.867 037 7124	.034 641 5871	68
69	7.687 205 7399	222.906 857 9975	.004 486 1787	.130 086 2802	28.997 123 9926	.034 486 1787	69
70	7.917 821 9121	230.594 063 7374	.004 336 6251	.126 297 3594	29.123 421 3521	.034 336 6251	70
71	8.155 356 5695	238.511 885 6495	.004 192 6632	.122 618 7956	29.246 040 1476	.034 192 6632	71
72	8.400 017 2666	246.667 242 2190	.004 054 0446	.119 047 3743	29.365 087 5220	.034 054 0446	72
73	8.652 017 7846	255.067 259 4856	.003 920 5345	.115 579 9751	29.480 667 4971	.033 920 5345	73
74	8.911 578 3181	263.719 277 2701	.003 791 9109	.112 213 5680	29.592 881 0651	.033 791 9109	74
75	9.178 925 6676	272.630 855 5882	.003 667 9634	.108 945 2117	29.701 826 2768	.033 667 9634	75
76	9.454 293 4377	281.809 781 2559	.003 548 4929	.105 772 0502	29.807 598 3270	.033 548 4929	76
77	9.737 922 2408	291.264 074 6936	.003 433 3105	.102 691 3109	29.910 289 6379	.033 433 3105	77
78	10.030 059 9080	301.001 996 9344	.003 322 2371	.099 700 3018	30.009 989 9397	.033 322 2371	78
79	10.330 961 7053	311.032 056 8424	.003 215 1027	.096 796 4095	30.106 786 3492	.033 215 1027	79
80	10.640 890 5564	321.363 018 5477	.003 111 7457	.093 977 0966	30.200 763 4458	.033 111 7457	80
81	10.960 117 2731	332.003 909 1041	.003 012 0127	.091 239 8996	30.292 003 3455	.033 012 0127	81
82	11.288 920 7913	342.964 026 3772	.002 915 7577	.088 582 4268	30.380 585 7723	.032 915 7577	82
83	11.627 588 4151	354.252 947 1685	.002 822 8417	.086 002 3561	30.466 588 1284	.032 822 8417	83
84	11.976 416 0675	365.880 535 5836	.002 733 1325	.083 497 4332	30.550 085 5616	.032 733 1325	84
85	12.335 708 5495	377.856 951 6511	.002 646 5042	.081 065 4691	30.631 151 0307	.032 646 5042	85
86	12.705 779 8060	390.192 660 2006	.002 562 8365	.078 704 3389	30.709 855 3696	.032 562 8365	86
87	13.086 953 2002	402.898 440 0067	.002 482 0151	.076 411 9795	30.786 267 3491	.032 482 0151	87
88	13.479 561 7962	415.985 393 2069	.002 403 9306	.074 186 3879	30.860 453 7370	.032 403 9306	88
89	13.883 948 6501	429.464 955 0031	.002 328 4787	.072 025 6193	30.932 479 3563	.032 328 4787	89
90	14.300 467 1096	443.348 903 6532	.002 255 5599	.069 927 7857	31.002 407 1421	.032 255 5599	90
91	14.729 481 1229	457.649 370 7628	.002 185 0789	.067 891 0541	31.070 298 1962	.032 185 0789	91
92	15.171 365 5566	472.378 851 8856	.002 116 9449	.065 913 6448	31.136 211 8409	.032 116 9449	92
93	15.626 506 5233	487.550 217 4422	.002 051 0708	.063 993 8299	31.200 205 6708	.032 051 0708	93
94	16.095 301 7190	503.176 723 9655	.001 987 3733	.062 129 9319	31.262 335 6027	.031 987 3733	94
95	16.578 160 7705	519.272 025 6844	.001 925 7729	.060 320 3223	31.322 655 9250	.031 925 7729	95
96	17.075 505 5936	535.850 186 4550	.001 866 1932	.058 563 4197	31.381 219 3446	.031 866 1932	96
97	17.587 770 7615	552.925 692 0486	.001 808 5613	.056 857 6890	31.438 077 0336	.031 808 5613	97
98	18.115 403 8843	570.513 462 8101	.001 752 8070	.055 201 6398	31.493 278 6734	.031 752 8070	98
99	18.658 866 0008	588.628 866 6944	.001 698 8633	.053 593 8250	31.546 872 4985	.031 698 8633	99
100	19.218 631 9809	607.287 732 6952	.001 646 6659	.052 032 8399	31.598 905 3383	.031 646 6659	100

		XIV COMPOUND AMOUNT	XV AMOUNT OF ANNUITY	XVI SINKING FUND	XVII PRESENT VALUE	XVIII PRESENT VALUE OF ANNUITY	XIX AMORTIZATION		
RATE 3 1/2%	**P E R I O D S**	AMOUNT OF 1 *How $1 left at compound interest will grow.*	AMOUNT OF 1 PER PERIOD *How $1 deposited periodically will grow.*	SINKING FUND *Periodic deposit that will grow to $1 at future date.*	PRESENT WORTH OF 1 *What $1 due in the future is worth today.*	PRESENT WORTH OF 1 PER PERIOD *What $1 payable periodically is worth today.*	PARTIAL PAYMENT *Annuity worth $1 today. Periodic payment necessary to pay off a loan of $1.*	**P E R I O D S**
	1	1.035 000 0000	1.000 000 0000	1.000 000 0000	.966 183 5749	.966 183 5749	1.035 000 0000	1
	2	1.071 225 0000	2.035 000 0000	.491 400 4914	.933 510 7004	1.899 694 2752	.526 400 4914	2
	3	1.108 717 8750	3.106 225 0000	.321 934 1806	.901 942 7057	2.801 636 9809	.356 934 1806	3
	4	1.147 523 0006	4.214 942 8750	.237 251 1395	.871 442 2277	3.673 079 2086	.272 251 1395	4
	5	1.187 686 3056	5.362 465 8756	.186 481 3732	.841 973 1669	4.515 052 3755	.221 481 3732	5
	6	1.229 255 3263	6.550 152 1813	.152 668 2087	.813 500 6443	5.328 553 0198	.187 668 2087	6
	7	1.272 279 2628	7.779 407 5076	.128 544 4938	.785 990 9607	6.114 543 9805	.163 544 4938	7
	8	1.316 809 0370	9.051 686 7704	.110 476 6465	.759 411 5562	6.873 955 5367	.145 476 6465	8
	9	1.362 897 7533	10.368 495 8073	.096 446 0051	.733 730 9722	7.607 686 5089	.131 446 0051	9
	10	1.410 598 7606	11.731 393 1606	.085 241 3679	.708 918 8137	8.316 605 3226	.120 241 3679	10
	11	1.459 969 7172	13.141 991 9212	.076 091 9658	.684 945 7137	9.001 551 0363	.111 091 9658	11
	12	1.511 068 6573	14.601 961 6385	.068 483 9493	.661 783 2983	9.663 334 3346	.103 483 9493	12
	13	1.563 956 0604	16.113 030 2958	.062 061 5726	.639 404 1529	10.302 738 4875	.097 061 5726	13
	14	1.618 694 5225	17.676 986 3562	.056 570 7287	.617 781 7903	10.920 520 2778	.091 570 7287	14
	15	1.675 348 8308	19.295 680 8786	.051 825 0694	.596 890 6186	11.517 410 8964	.086 825 0694	15
	16	1.733 986 0398	20.971 029 7094	.047 684 8306	.576 705 9117	12.094 116 8081	.082 684 8306	16
	17	1.794 675 5512	22.705 015 7492	.044 043 1317	.557 203 7794	12.651 320 5876	.079 043 1317	17
	18	1.857 489 1955	24.499 691 3004	.040 816 8408	.538 361 1396	13.189 681 7271	.075 816 8408	18
	19	1.922 501 3174	26.357 180 4960	.037 940 3252	.520 155 6904	13.709 837 4175	.072 940 3252	19
	20	1.989 788 8635	28.279 681 8133	.035 361 0768	.502 565 8844	14.212 403 3020	.070 361 0768	20
	21	2.059 431 4737	30.269 470 6768	.033 036 5870	.485 570 9028	14.697 974 2048	.068 036 5870	21
	22	2.131 511 5753	32.328 902 1505	.030 932 0742	.469 150 6308	15.167 124 8355	.065 932 0742	22
	23	2.206 114 4804	34.460 413 7257	.029 018 8042	.453 285 6336	15.620 410 4691	.064 018 8042	23
	24	2.283 328 4872	36.666 528 2061	.027 272 8303	.437 957 1339	16.058 367 6030	.062 272 8303	24
	25	2.363 244 9843	38.949 856 6933	.025 674 0354	.423 146 9893	16.481 514 5923	.060 674 0354	25
	26	2.445 958 5587	41.313 101 6776	.024 205 3963	.408 837 6708	16.890 352 2631	.059 205 3963	26
	27	2.531 567 1083	43.759 060 2363	.022 852 4103	.395 012 2423	17.285 364 5054	.057 852 4103	27
	28	2.620 171 9571	46.290 627 3446	.021 602 6452	.381 654 3404	17.667 018 8458	.056 602 6452	28
	29	2.711 877 9756	48.910 799 3017	.020 445 3825	.368 748 1550	18.035 767 0008	.055 445 3825	29
	30	2.806 793 7047	51.622 677 2772	.019 371 3316	.356 278 4106	18.392 045 4114	.054 371 3316	30
	31	2.905 031 4844	54.429 470 9819	.018 372 3998	.344 230 3484	18.736 275 7598	.053 372 3998	31
	32	3.006 707 5863	57.334 502 4663	.017 441 5048	.332 589 7086	19.068 865 4684	.052 441 5048	32
	33	3.111 942 3518	60.341 210 0526	.016 572 4221	.321 342 7136	19.390 208 1820	.051 572 4221	33
	34	3.220 860 3342	63.453 152 4044	.015 759 6583	.310 476 0518	19.700 684 2338	.050 759 6583	34
	35	3.333 590 4459	66.674 012 7386	.014 998 3473	.299 976 8617	20.000 661 0955	.049 998 3473	35
	36	3.450 266 1115	70.007 603 1845	.014 284 1628	.289 832 7166	20.290 493 8121	.049 284 1628	36
	37	3.571 025 4254	73.457 869 2959	.013 613 2454	.280 031 6102	20.570 525 4223	.048 613 2454	37
	38	3.696 011 3152	77.028 894 7213	.012 982 1414	.270 561 9422	20.841 087 3645	.047 982 1414	38
	39	3.825 371 7113	80.724 906 0365	.012 387 7506	.261 412 5046	21.102 499 8691	.047 387 7506	39
	40	3.959 259 7212	84.550 277 7478	.011 827 2823	.252 572 4682	21.355 072 3373	.046 827 2823	40
	41	4.097 833 8114	88.509 537 4690	.011 298 2174	.244 031 3702	21.599 103 7075	.046 298 2174	41
	42	4.241 257 9948	92.607 371 2804	.010 798 2765	.235 779 1017	21.834 882 8092	.045 798 2765	42
	43	4.389 702 0246	96.848 629 2752	.010 325 3914	.227 805 8953	22.062 688 7046	.045 325 3914	43
	44	4.543 341 5955	101.238 331 2998	.009 877 6816	.220 102 3143	22.282 791 0189	.044 877 6816	44
	45	4.702 358 5513	105.781 672 8953	.009 453 4334	.212 659 2409	22.495 450 2598	.044 453 4334	45
	46	4.866 941 1006	110.484 031 4467	.009 051 0817	.205 467 8656	22.700 918 1254	.044 051 0817	46
	47	5.037 284 0392	115.350 972 5473	.008 669 1944	.198 519 6769	22.899 437 8023	.043 669 1944	47
	48	5.213 588 9805	120.388 256 5864	.008 306 4580	.191 806 4511	23.091 244 2535	.043 306 4580	48
	49	5.396 064 5948	125.601 845 5670	.007 961 6665	.185 320 2426	23.276 564 4961	.042 961 6665	49
	50	5.584 926 8557	130.997 910 1618	.007 633 7096	.179 053 3745	23.455 617 8706	.042 633 7096	50
	51	5.780 399 2956	136.582 837 0175	.007 321 5641	.172 998 4295	23.628 616 3001	.042 321 5641	51
	52	5.982 713 2710	142.363 236 3131	.007 024 2854	.167 148 2411	23.795 764 5412	.042 024 2854	52
	53	6.192 108 2354	148.345 949 5840	.006 740 9997	.161 495 8851	23.957 260 4263	.041 740 9997	53
	54	6.408 832 0237	154.538 057 8195	.006 470 8979	.156 034 6716	24.113 295 0978	.041 470 8979	54
	55	6.633 141 1445	160.946 889 8432	.006 213 2297	.150 758 1368	24.264 053 2346	.041 213 2297	55
	56	6.865 301 0846	167.580 030 9877	.005 967 2981	.145 660 0355	24.409 713 2702	.040 967 2981	56
	57	7.105 586 6225	174.445 332 0722	.005 732 4549	.140 734 3339	24.550 447 6040	.040 732 4549	57
	58	7.354 282 1543	181.550 918 6948	.005 508 0966	.135 975 2018	24.686 422 8058	.040 508 0966	58
	59	7.611 682 0297	188.905 200 8491	.005 293 6605	.131 377 0066	24.817 799 8124	.040 293 6605	59
	60	7.878 090 9008	196.516 882 8788	.005 088 6213	.126 934 3059	24.944 734 1182	.040 088 6213	60
	61	8.153 824 0823	204.394 973 7796	.004 892 4882	.122 641 8414	25.067 375 9597	.039 892 4882	61
	62	8.439 207 9252	212.548 797 8619	.004 704 8020	.118 494 5328	25.185 870 4924	.039 704 8020	62
	63	8.734 580 2025	220.988 005 7870	.004 525 1325	.114 487 4713	25.300 357 9637	.039 525 1325	63
	64	9.040 290 5096	229.722 585 9896	.004 353 0765	.110 615 9143	25.410 973 8780	.039 353 0765	64
	65	9.356 700 6775	238.762 876 4992	.004 188 2558	.106 875 2795	25.517 849 1575	.039 188 2558	65
	66	9.684 185 2012	248.119 577 1767	.004 030 3148	.103 261 1396	25.621 110 2971	.039 030 3148	66
	67	10.023 131 6832	257.803 762 3779	.003 878 9193	.099 769 2170	25.720 879 5141	.038 878 9193	67
	68	10.373 941 2921	267.826 894 0611	.003 733 7550	.096 396 3788	25.817 274 8928	.038 733 7550	68
	69	10.737 029 2374	278.200 835 3532	.003 594 5255	.093 135 6316	25.910 410 5245	.038 594 5255	69
	70	11.112 825 2607	288.937 864 5906	.003 460 9517	.089 986 1175	26.000 396 6420	.038 460 9517	70
	71	11.501 774 1448	300.050 689 8512	.003 332 7702	.086 943 1087	26.087 339 7507	.038 332 7702	71
	72	11.904 336 2399	311.552 463 9960	.003 209 7323	.084 003 0036	26.171 342 7543	.038 209 7323	72
	73	12.320 988 0083	323.456 800 2359	.003 091 6030	.081 162 3223	26.252 505 0766	.038 091 6030	73
	74	12.752 222 5885	335.777 788 2442	.002 978 1601	.078 417 7027	26.330 922 7794	.037 978 1601	74
	75	13.198 550 3791	348.530 010 8327	.002 869 1934	.075 765 8964	26.406 688 6757	.037 869 1934	75
	76	13.660 499 6424	361.728 561 2119	.002 764 5038	.073 203 7646	26.479 892 4403	.037 764 5038	76
	77	14.138 617 1299	375.389 060 8543	.002 663 9029	.070 728 2750	26.550 620 7153	.037 663 9029	77
	78	14.633 468 7294	389.527 677 9842	.002 567 2117	.068 336 4976	26.618 957 2128	.037 567 2117	78
	79	15.145 640 1350	404.161 146 7136	.002 474 2606	.066 025 6015	26.684 982 8143	.037 474 2606	79
	80	15.675 737 5397	419.306 786 8486	.002 384 8887	.063 792 8517	26.748 775 6660	.037 384 8887	80
	81	16.224 388 3536	434.982 524 3883	.002 298 9429	.061 635 6055	26.810 411 2715	.037 298 9429	81
	82	16.792 241 9460	451.206 912 7419	.002 216 2781	.059 551 3097	26.869 962 5812	.037 216 2781	82
	83	17.379 970 4141	467.999 154 6878	.002 136 7560	.057 537 4973	26.927 500 0784	.037 136 7560	83
	84	17.988 269 3786	485.379 125 1019	.002 060 2452	.055 591 7848	26.983 091 8632	.037 060 2452	84
	85	18.617 858 8068	503.367 394 4805	.001 986 6205	.053 711 8694	27.036 803 7326	.036 986 6205	85
	86	19.269 483 8651	521.985 253 2873	.001 915 7629	.051 895 5260	27.088 699 2585	.036 915 7629	86
	87	19.943 915 8003	541.254 737 1524	.001 847 5589	.050 140 6048	27.138 839 8633	.036 847 5589	87
	88	20.641 952 8533	561.198 652 9527	.001 781 9002	.048 445 0288	27.187 284 8921	.036 781 9002	88
	89	21.364 421 2032	581.840 605 8060	.001 718 6838	.046 806 7911	27.234 091 6832	.036 718 6838	89
	90	22.112 175 9453	603.205 027 0092	.001 657 8111	.045 223 9527	27.279 315 6359	.036 657 8111	90
	91	22.886 102 1034	625.317 202 9546	.001 599 1884	.043 694 6403	27.323 010 2762	.036 599 1884	91
	92	23.687 115 6770	648.203 306 0580	.001 542 7259	.042 217 0438	27.365 227 3200	.036 542 7259	92
	93	24.516 164 7257	671.890 420 7350	.001 488 3379	.040 789 4143	27.406 016 7343	.036 488 3379	93
	94	25.374 230 4911	696.406 585 4607	.001 435 9428	.039 410 0621	27.445 426 7965	.036 435 9428	94
	95	26.262 328 5583	721.780 815 9519	.001 385 4621	.038 077 3547	27.483 504 1512	.036 385 4621	95
	96	27.181 510 0579	748.043 144 5102	.001 336 8213	.036 789 7147	27.520 293 8659	.036 336 8213	96
	97	28.132 862 9099	775.224 654 5680	.001 289 9487	.035 545 6181	27.555 839 4839	.036 289 9487	97
	98	29.117 513 1117	803.357 517 4779	.001 244 7758	.034 343 5923	27.590 183 0763	.036 244 7758	98
	99	30.136 626 0706	832.475 030 5896	.001 201 2372	.033 182 2148	27.623 365 2911	.036 201 2372	99
	100	31.191 407 9831	862.611 656 6603	.001 159 2702	.032 060 1109	27.655 425 4020	.036 159 2702	100

		XIV COMPOUND AMOUNT	XV AMOUNT OF ANNUITY	XVI SINKING FUND	XVII PRESENT VALUE	XVIII PRESENT VALUE OF ANNUITY	XIX AMORTIZATION	
RATE 4%	PERIODS	AMOUNT OF 1 How $1 left at compound interest will grow.	AMOUNT OF 1 PER PERIOD How $1 deposited periodically will grow.	SINKING FUND Periodic deposit that will grow to $1 at future date.	PRESENT WORTH OF 1 What $1 due in the future is worth today.	PRESENT WORTH OF 1 PER PERIOD What $1 payable periodically is worth today.	PARTIAL PAYMENT Annuity worth $1 today. Periodic payment necessary to pay off a loan of $1.	PERIODS
	1	1.040 000 0000	1.000 000 0000	1.000 000 0000	.961 538 4615	.961 538 4615	1.040 000 0000	1
	2	1.081 600 0000	2.040 000 0000	.490 196 0784	.924 556 2130	1.886 094 6746	.530 196 0784	2
	3	1.124 864 0000	3.121 600 0000	.320 348 5392	.888 996 3587	2.775 091 0332	.360 348 5392	3
	4	1.169 858 5600	4.246 464 0000	.235 490 0454	.854 804 1910	3.629 895 2243	.275 490 0454	4
	5	1.216 652 9024	5.416 322 5600	.184 627 1135	.821 927 1068	4.451 822 3310	.224 627 1135	5
	6	1.265 319 0185	6.632 975 4624	.150 761 9025	.790 314 5257	5.242 136 8567	.190 761 9025	6
	7	1.315 931 7792	7.898 294 4809	.126 609 6120	.759 917 8132	6.002 054 6699	.166 609 6120	7
	8	1.368 569 0504	9.214 226 2601	.108 527 8320	.730 690 2050	6.732 744 8750	.148 527 8320	8
	9	1.423 311 8124	10.582 795 3105	.094 492 9927	.702 586 7356	7.435 331 6105	.134 492 9927	9
	10	1.480 244 2849	12.006 107 1230	.083 290 9443	.675 564 1688	8.110 895 7794	.123 290 9443	10
	11	1.539 454 0563	13.486 351 4079	.074 149 0393	.649 580 9316	8.760 476 7110	.114 149 0393	11
	12	1.601 032 2186	15.025 805 4642	.066 552 1727	.624 597 0496	9.385 073 7605	.106 552 1727	12
	13	1.665 073 5073	16.626 837 6828	.060 143 7278	.600 574 0861	9.985 647 8466	.100 143 7278	13
	14	1.731 676 4476	18.291 911 1901	.054 668 9731	.577 475 0828	10.563 122 9295	.094 668 9731	14
	15	1.800 943 5055	20.023 587 6377	.049 941 1004	.555 264 5027	11.118 387 4322	.089 941 1004	15
	16	1.872 981 2457	21.824 531 1432	.045 819 9992	.533 908 1757	11.652 295 6079	.085 819 9992	16
	17	1.947 900 4956	23.697 512 3889	.042 198 5221	.513 373 2459	12.165 668 8537	.082 198 5221	17
	18	2.025 816 5154	25.645 412 8845	.038 993 3281	.493 628 1210	12.659 296 9747	.078 993 3281	18
	19	2.106 849 1760	27.671 229 3998	.036 138 6184	.474 642 4240	13.133 939 3988	.076 138 6184	19
	20	2.191 123 1430	29.778 078 5758	.033 581 7503	.456 386 9462	13.590 326 3450	.073 581 7503	20
	21	2.278 768 0688	31.969 201 7189	.031 280 1054	.438 833 6021	14.029 159 9471	.071 280 1054	21
	22	2.369 918 7915	34.247 969 7876	.029 198 8111	.421 955 3867	14.451 115 3337	.069 198 8111	22
	23	2.464 715 5432	36.617 888 5791	.027 309 0568	.405 726 3333	14.856 841 6671	.067 309 0568	23
	24	2.563 304 1649	39.082 604 1223	.025 586 8313	.390 121 4743	15.246 963 1414	.065 586 8313	24
	25	2.665 836 3315	41.645 908 2872	.024 011 9628	.375 116 8023	15.622 079 9437	.064 011 9628	25
	26	2.772 469 7847	44.311 744 6187	.022 567 3805	.360 689 2329	15.982 769 1766	.062 567 3805	26
	27	2.883 368 5761	47.084 214 4034	.021 238 5406	.346 816 5701	16.329 585 7467	.061 238 5406	27
	28	2.998 703 3192	49.967 582 9796	.020 012 9752	.333 477 4713	16.663 063 2180	.060 012 9752	28
	29	3.118 651 4519	52.966 286 2987	.018 879 9342	.320 651 4147	16.983 714 6327	.058 879 9342	29
	30	3.243 397 5100	56.084 937 7507	.017 830 0991	.308 318 6680	17.292 033 3007	.057 830 0991	30
	31	3.373 133 4104	59.328 335 2607	.016 855 3524	.296 460 2577	17.588 493 5583	.056 855 3524	31
	32	3.508 058 7468	62.701 468 6711	.015 948 5897	.285 057 9401	17.873 551 4984	.055 948 5897	32
	33	3.648 381 0967	66.209 527 4180	.015 103 5665	.274 094 1731	18.147 645 6715	.055 103 5665	33
	34	3.794 316 3406	69.857 908 5147	.014 314 7715	.263 552 0896	18.411 197 7611	.054 314 7715	34
	35	3.946 088 9942	73.652 224 8553	.013 577 3224	.253 415 4707	18.664 613 2318	.053 577 3224	35
	36	4.103 932 5540	77.598 313 8495	.012 886 8780	.243 668 7219	18.908 281 9537	.052 886 8780	36
	37	4.268 089 8561	81.702 246 4035	.012 239 5655	.234 296 8479	19.142 578 8016	.052 239 5655	37
	38	4.438 813 4504	85.970 336 2596	.011 631 9191	.225 285 4307	19.367 864 2323	.051 631 9191	38
	39	4.616 365 9884	90.409 149 7100	.011 060 8274	.216 620 6064	19.584 484 8388	.051 060 8274	39
	40	4.801 020 6279	95.025 515 6984	.010 523 4893	.208 289 0447	19.792 773 8834	.050 523 4893	40
	41	4.993 061 4531	99.826 536 3264	.010 017 3765	.200 277 9276	19.993 051 8110	.050 017 3765	41
	42	5.192 783 9112	104.819 597 7794	.009 540 2007	.192 574 9303	20.185 626 7413	.049 540 2007	42
	43	5.400 495 2676	110.012 381 6906	.009 089 8859	.185 168 2023	20.370 794 9436	.049 089 8859	43
	44	5.616 515 0783	115.412 876 9582	.008 664 5444	.178 046 3483	20.548 841 2919	.048 664 5444	44
	45	5.841 175 6815	121.029 392 0365	.008 262 4558	.171 198 4118	20.720 039 7038	.048 262 4558	45
	46	6.074 822 7087	126.870 567 7180	.007 882 0488	.164 613 8575	20.884 653 5613	.047 882 0488	46
	47	6.317 815 6171	132.945 390 4267	.007 521 8855	.158 282 5553	21.042 936 1166	.047 521 8855	47
	48	6.570 528 2418	139.263 206 0438	.007 180 6476	.152 194 7647	21.195 130 8814	.047 180 6476	48
	49	6.833 349 3714	145.833 734 2855	.006 857 1240	.146 341 1199	21.341 472 0013	.046 857 1240	49
	50	7.106 683 3463	152.667 083 6570	.006 550 2004	.140 712 6153	21.482 184 6167	.046 550 2004	50
	51	7.390 950 6801	159.773 767 0032	.006 258 8497	.135 300 5917	21.617 485 2083	.046 258 8497	51
	52	7.686 588 7073	167.164 717 6834	.005 982 1236	.130 096 7228	21.747 581 9311	.045 982 1236	52
	53	7.994 052 2556	174.851 306 3907	.005 719 1451	.125 093 0027	21.872 674 9337	.045 719 1451	53
	54	8.313 814 3459	182.845 358 6463	.005 469 1025	.120 281 7333	21.992 956 6671	.045 469 1025	54
	55	8.646 366 9197	191.159 172 9922	.005 231 2426	.115 655 5128	22.108 612 1799	.045 231 2426	55
	56	8.992 221 5965	199.805 539 9119	.005 004 8662	.111 207 2239	22.219 819 4037	.045 004 8662	56
	57	9.351 910 4603	208.797 761 5083	.004 789 3234	.106 930 0229	22.326 749 4267	.044 789 3234	57
	58	9.725 986 8787	218.149 671 9687	.004 584 0087	.102 817 3297	22.429 566 7564	.044 584 0087	58
	59	10.115 026 3539	227.875 658 8474	.004 388 3581	.098 862 8171	22.528 429 5735	.044 388 3581	59
	60	10.519 627 4081	237.990 685 2013	.004 201 8451	.095 060 4010	22.623 489 9745	.044 201 8451	60
	61	10.940 412 5044	248.510 312 6094	.004 023 9779	.091 404 2318	22.714 894 2062	.044 023 9779	61
	62	11.378 029 0045	259.450 725 1137	.003 854 2964	.087 888 6844	22.802 782 8906	.043 854 2964	62
	63	11.833 150 1647	270.828 754 1183	.003 692 3701	.084 508 3504	22.887 291 2410	.043 692 3701	63
	64	12.306 476 1713	282.661 904 2830	.003 537 7955	.081 258 0292	22.968 549 2702	.043 537 7955	64
	65	12.798 735 2182	294.968 380 4544	.003 390 1939	.078 132 7204	23.046 681 9905	.043 390 1939	65
	66	13.310 684 6269	307.767 115 6725	.003 249 2100	.075 127 6157	23.121 809 6063	.043 249 2100	66
	67	13.843 112 0120	321.077 800 2994	.003 114 5099	.072 238 0921	23.194 047 6984	.043 114 5099	67
	68	14.396 836 4925	334.920 912 3114	.002 985 7795	.069 459 7039	23.263 507 4023	.042 985 7795	68
	69	14.972 709 9522	349.317 748 8039	.002 862 7231	.066 788 1768	23.330 295 5791	.042 862 7231	69
	70	15.571 618 3502	364.290 458 7560	.002 745 0623	.064 219 4008	23.394 514 9799	.042 745 0623	70
	71	16.194 483 0843	379.862 077 1063	.002 632 5344	.061 749 4238	23.456 264 4038	.042 632 5344	71
	72	16.842 262 4076	396.056 560 1905	.002 524 8919	.059 374 4460	23.515 638 8498	.042 524 8919	72
	73	17.515 952 9039	412.898 822 5981	.002 421 9008	.057 090 8135	23.572 729 6632	.042 421 9008	73
	74	18.216 591 0201	430.414 775 5021	.002 323 3403	.054 895 0130	23.627 624 6762	.042 323 3403	74
	75	18.945 254 6609	448.631 366 5221	.002 229 0015	.052 783 6663	23.680 408 3425	.042 229 0015	75
	76	19.703 064 8473	467.576 621 1830	.002 138 6869	.050 753 5253	23.731 161 8678	.042 138 6869	76
	77	20.491 187 4412	487.279 686 0303	.002 052 2095	.048 801 4666	23.779 963 3344	.042 052 2095	77
	78	21.310 834 9389	507.770 873 4716	.001 969 3922	.046 924 4871	23.826 887 8215	.041 969 3922	78
	79	22.163 268 3364	529.081 708 4104	.001 890 0672	.045 119 6992	23.872 007 5207	.041 890 0672	79
	80	23.049 799 0699	551.244 976 7468	.001 814 0755	.043 384 3261	23.915 391 8468	.041 814 0755	80
	81	23.971 791 0327	574.294 775 8167	.001 741 2661	.041 715 6982	23.957 107 5450	.041 741 2661	81
	82	24.930 662 6740	598.266 566 8494	.001 671 4957	.040 111 2483	23.997 218 7933	.041 671 4957	82
	83	25.927 889 1809	623.197 229 5233	.001 604 6284	.038 568 5079	24.035 787 3013	.041 604 6284	83
	84	26.965 004 7482	649.125 118 7043	.001 540 5351	.037 085 1038	24.072 872 4050	.041 540 5351	84
	85	28.043 604 9381	676.090 123 4525	.001 479 0928	.035 658 7537	24.108 531 1587	.041 479 0928	85
	86	29.165 349 1356	704.133 728 3906	.001 420 1848	.034 287 2631	24.142 818 4218	.041 420 1848	86
	87	30.331 963 1010	733.299 077 5262	.001 363 7001	.032 968 5222	24.175 786 9441	.041 363 7001	87
	88	31.545 241 6251	763.631 040 6272	.001 309 5329	.031 700 5022	24.207 487 4462	.041 309 5329	88
	89	32.807 051 2901	795.176 282 2523	.001 257 5828	.030 481 2521	24.237 968 6983	.041 257 5828	89
	90	34.119 333 3417	827.983 333 5424	.001 207 7538	.029 308 8962	24.267 277 5945	.041 207 7538	90
	91	35.484 106 6754	862.102 666 8841	.001 159 9547	.028 181 6310	24.295 459 2255	.041 159 9547	91
	92	36.903 470 9424	897.586 773 5595	.001 114 0984	.027 097 7221	24.322 556 9476	.041 114 0984	92
	93	38.379 609 7801	934.490 244 5018	.001 070 1021	.026 055 5020	24.348 612 4496	.041 070 1021	93
	94	39.914 794 1713	972.869 854 2819	.001 027 8867	.025 053 3673	24.373 665 8169	.041 027 8867	94
	95	41.511 385 9381	1012.784 648 4532	.000 987 3767	.024 089 7763	24.397 755 5932	.040 987 3767	95
	96	43.171 841 3757	1054.296 034 3913	.000 948 5002	.023 163 2464	24.420 918 8396	.040 948 5002	96
	97	44.898 715 0307	1097.467 875 7670	.000 911 1884	.022 272 3523	24.443 191 1919	.040 911 1884	97
	98	46.694 663 6319	1142.366 590 7976	.000 875 3757	.021 415 7234	24.464 606 9153	.040 875 3757	98
	99	48.562 450 1772	1189.061 254 4296	.000 840 9996	.020 592 0417	24.485 198 9570	.040 840 9996	99
	100	50.504 948 1843	1237.623 704 6067	.000 808 0000	.019 800 0401	24.504 998 9972	.040 808 0000	100

	XIV COMPOUND AMOUNT	XV AMOUNT OF ANNUITY	XVI SINKING FUND	XVII PRESENT VALUE	XVIII PRESENT VALUE OF ANNUITY	XIX AMORTIZATION	
RATE 4 1/2% PERIODS	AMOUNT OF 1 — How $1 left at compound interest will grow.	AMOUNT OF 1 PER PERIOD — How $1 deposited periodically will grow.	.SINKING FUND — Periodic deposit that will grow to $1 at future date.	PRESENT WORTH OF 1 — What $1 due in the future is worth today.	PRESENT WORTH OF 1 PER PERIOD — What $1 payable periodically is worth today.	PARTIAL PAYMENT — Annuity worth $1 today. Periodic payment necessary to pay off a loan of $1.	PERIODS
1	1.045 000 0000	1.000 000 0000	1.000 000 0000	.956 937 7990	.956 937 7990	1.045 000 0000	1
2	1.092 025 0000	2.045 000 0000	.488 997 5550	.915 729 9512	1.872 667 7503	.533 997 5550	2
3	1.141 166 1250	3.137 025 0000	.318 773 3601	.876 296 6041	2.748 964 3543	.363 773 3601	3
4	1.192 518 6006	4.278 191 1250	.233 743 6479	.838 561 3436	3.587 525 6979	.278 743 6479	4
5	1.246 181 9377	5.470 709 7256	.182 791 6395	.802 451 0465	4.389 976 7444	.227 791 6395	5
6	1.302 260 1248	6.716 891 6633	.148 878 3875	.767 895 7383	5.157 872 4827	.193 878 3875	6
7	1.360 861 8305	8.019 151 7881	.124 701 4680	.734 828 4577	5.892 700 9404	.169 701 4680	7
8	1.422 100 6128	9.380 013 6186	.106 609 6533	.703 185 1270	6.595 886 0674	.151 609 6533	8
9	1.486 095 1404	10.802 114 2314	.092 574 4700	.672 904 4277	7.268 790 4951	.137 574 4700	9
10	1.552 969 4217	12.288 209 3718	.081 378 8217	.643 927 6820	7.912 718 1771	.126 378 8217	10
11	1.622 853 0457	13.841 178 7936	.072 248 1817	.616 198 7388	8.528 916 9159	.117 248 1817	11
12	1.695 881 4328	15.464 031 8393	.064 666 1886	.589 663 8649	9.118 580 7808	.109 666 1886	12
13	1.772 196 0972	17.159 913 2721	.058 275 3528	.564 271 6410	9.682 852 4218	.103 275 3528	13
14	1.851 944 9216	18.932 109 3693	.052 820 3160	.539 972 8622	10.222 825 2840	.097 820 3160	14
15	1.935 282 4431	20.784 054 2909	.048 113 8081	.516 720 4423	10.739 545 7263	.093 113 8081	15
16	2.022 370 1530	22.719 336 7340	.044 015 3694	.494 469 3228	11.234 015 0491	.089 015 3694	16
17	2.113 376 8099	24.741 706 8870	.040 417 5833	.473 176 3854	11.707 191 4346	.085 417 5833	17
18	2.208 478 7664	26.855 083 6970	.037 236 8975	.452 800 3688	12.159 991 8034	.082 236 8975	18
19	2.307 860 3108	29.063 562 4633	.034 407 3443	.433 301 7884	12.593 293 5918	.079 407 3443	19
20	2.411 714 0248	31.371 422 7742	.031 876 1443	.414 642 8597	13.007 936 4515	.076 876 1443	20
21	2.520 241 1560	33.783 136 7990	.029 600 5669	.396 787 4255	13.404 723 8770	.074 600 5669	21
22	2.633 652 0080	36.303 377 9550	.027 545 6461	.379 700 8857	13.784 424 7627	.072 545 6461	22
23	2.752 166 3483	38.937 029 9629	.025 682 4930	.363 350 1298	14.147 774 8925	.070 682 4930	23
24	2.876 013 8340	41.689 196 3113	.023 987 0299	.347 703 4735	14.495 478 3660	.068 987 0299	24
25	3.005 434 4565	44.565 210 1453	.022 439 0280	.332 730 5967	14.828 208 9627	.067 439 0280	25
26	3.140 679 0071	47.570 644 6018	.021 021 3674	.318 402 4849	15.146 611 4476	.066 021 3674	26
27	3.282 009 5624	50.711 323 6089	.019 719 4616	.304 691 3731	15.451 302 8206	.064 719 4616	27
28	3.429 699 9927	53.993 333 1713	.018 520 8051	.291 570 6919	15.742 873 5126	.063 520 8051	28
29	3.584 036 4924	57.423 033 1640	.017 414 6147	.279 015 0162	16.021 888 5288	.062 414 6147	29
30	3.745 318 1345	61.007 069 6564	.016 391 5429	.267 000 0155	16.288 888 5443	.061 391 5429	30
31	3.913 857 4506	64.752 387 7909	.015 443 4459	.255 502 4072	16.544 390 9515	.060 443 4459	31
32	4.089 981 0359	68.666 245 2415	.014 563 1962	.244 499 9112	16.788 890 8627	.059 563 1962	32
33	4.274 030 1825	72.756 226 2774	.013 744 5281	.233 971 2069	17.022 862 0695	.058 744 5281	33
34	4.466 361 5407	77.030 256 4599	.012 981 9119	.223 895 8917	17.246 757 9613	.057 981 9119	34
35	4.667 347 8100	81.496 618 0005	.012 270 4478	.214 254 4419	17.461 012 4031	.057 270 4478	35
36	4.877 378 4615	86.163 965 8106	.011 605 7796	.205 028 1740	17.666 040 5772	.056 605 7796	36
37	5.096 860 4922	91.041 344 2720	.010 984 0206	.196 199 2096	17.862 239 7868	.055 984 0206	37
38	5.326 219 2144	96.138 204 7643	.010 401 6920	.187 750 4398	18.049 990 2266	.055 401 6920	38
39	5.565 899 0790	101.464 423 9787	.009 855 6712	.179 665 4926	18.229 655 7192	.054 855 6712	39
40	5.816 364 5376	107.030 323 0577	.009 343 1466	.171 928 7011	18.401 584 4203	.054 343 1466	40
41	6.078 100 9418	112.846 687 5953	.008 861 5804	.164 525 0728	18.566 109 4931	.053 861 5804	41
42	6.351 615 4842	118.924 788 5371	.008 408 6759	.157 440 2611	18.723 549 7542	.053 408 6759	42
43	6.637 438 1810	125.276 404 0213	.007 982 3492	.150 660 5369	18.874 210 2911	.052 982 3492	43
44	6.936 122 8991	131.913 842 2022	.007 580 7056	.144 172 7626	19.018 383 0536	.052 580 7056	44
45	7.248 248 4296	138.849 965 1013	.007 202 0184	.137 964 3661	19.156 347 4198	.052 202 0184	45
46	7.574 419 6089	146.098 213 5309	.006 844 7107	.132 023 3169	19.288 370 7366	.051 844 7107	46
47	7.915 268 4913	153.672 633 1398	.006 507 3395	.126 338 1023	19.414 708 8389	.051 507 3395	47
48	8.271 455 5734	161.587 901 6311	.006 188 5821	.120 897 7055	19.535 606 5444	.051 188 5821	48
49	8.643 671 0742	169.859 357 2045	.005 887 2235	.115 691 5842	19.651 298 1286	.050 887 2235	49
50	9.032 636 2725	178.503 028 2787	.005 602 1459	.110 709 6500	19.762 007 7785	.050 602 1459	50
51	9.439 104 9048	187.535 664 5512	.005 332 3191	.105 942 2488	19.867 950 0273	.050 332 3191	51
52	9.863 864 6255	196.974 769 4560	.005 076 7923	.101 380 1424	19.969 330 1697	.050 076 7923	52
53	10.307 738 5337	206.838 634 0815	.004 834 6867	.097 014 4903	20.066 344 6600	.049 834 6867	53
54	10.771 586 7677	217.146 372 6152	.004 605 1886	.092 836 8328	20.159 181 4928	.049 605 1886	54
55	11.256 308 1722	227.917 959 3829	.004 387 5437	.088 839 0745	20.248 020 5673	.049 387 5437	55
56	11.762 842 0400	239.174 267 5551	.004 181 0518	.085 013 4684	20.333 034 0357	.049 181 0518	56
57	12.292 169 9318	250.937 109 5951	.003 985 0622	.081 352 6013	20.414 386 6370	.048 985 0622	57
58	12.845 317 5787	263.229 279 5269	.003 798 9695	.077 849 3793	20.492 236 0163	.048 798 9695	58
59	13.423 356 8698	276.074 597 1056	.003 454 2558	.074 497 0137	20.566 733 0299	.048 622 2094	59
60	14.027 407 9289	289.497 953 9753	.003 454 2558	.071 289 0083	20.638 022 0382	.048 454 2558	60
61	14.658 641 2857	303.525 361 9042	.003 294 6176	.068 219 1467	20.706 241 1849	.048 294 6176	61
62	15.318 280 1435	318.184 003 1899	.003 142 8356	.065 281 4801	20.771 522 6650	.048 142 8356	62
63	16.007 602 7500	333.502 283 3335	.002 998 4802	.062 470 3159	20.833 992 9808	.047 998 4802	63
64	16.727 944 8738	349.509 886 0835	.002 861 1494	.059 780 2066	20.893 773 1874	.047 861 1494	64
65	17.480 702 3931	366.237 830 9572	.002 730 4661	.057 205 9393	20.950 979 1267	.047 730 4661	65
66	18.267 334 0008	383.718 533 3503	.002 606 0769	.054 742 5256	21.005 721 6523	.047 606 0769	66
67	19.089 364 0308	401.985 867 3511	.002 487 6496	.052 385 1920	21.058 106 8443	.047 487 6496	67
68	19.948 385 4122	421.075 231 3819	.002 374 8725	.050 129 3703	21.108 236 2147	.047 374 8725	68
69	20.846 062 7557	441.023 616 7941	.002 267 4523	.047 970 6893	21.156 206 9040	.047 267 4523	69
70	21.784 135 5797	461.869 679 5498	.002 165 1129	.045 904 9659	21.202 111 8699	.047 165 1129	70
71	22.764 421 6808	483.653 815 1295	.002 067 5946	.043 928 1970	21.246 040 0668	.047 067 5946	71
72	23.788 820 6565	506.418 236 8104	.001 974 6524	.042 036 5521	21.288 076 6190	.046 974 6524	72
73	24.859 317 5860	530.207 057 4668	.001 886 0556	.040 226 3657	21.328 302 9847	.046 886 0556	73
74	25.977 986 8774	555.066 375 0528	.001 801 5863	.038 494 1298	21.366 797 1145	.046 801 5863	74
75	27.146 996 2869	581.044 361 9302	.001 721 0390	.036 836 4879	21.403 633 6024	.046 721 0390	75
76	28.368 611 1198	608.191 358 2171	.001 644 2194	.035 250 2276	21.438 883 8301	.046 644 2194	76
77	29.645 198 6202	636.559 969 3368	.001 570 9439	.033 732 2753	21.472 616 1053	.046 570 9439	77
78	30.979 232 5581	666.205 167 9570	.001 501 0391	.032 279 6802	21.504 895 7946	.046 501 0391	78
79	32.373 298 0232	697.184 400 5151	.001 434 3408	.030 888 6548	21.535 785 4494	.046 434 3408	79
80	33.830 096 4342	729.557 698 5382	.001 370 6935	.029 559 4783	21.565 344 9276	.046 370 6935	80
81	35.352 450 7738	763.387 794 9725	.001 309 9502	.028 286 5821	21.593 631 5097	.046 309 9502	81
82	36.943 311 0586	798.740 245 7462	.001 251 9715	.027 068 4996	21.620 700 0093	.046 251 9715	82
83	38.605 760 0562	835.683 556 8048	.001 196 6252	.025 902 8704	21.646 602 8797	.046 196 6252	83
84	40.343 019 2587	874.289 316 8610	.001 143 7861	.024 787 4358	21.671 390 3155	.046 143 7861	84
85	42.158 455 1254	914.632 336 1198	.001 093 3355	.023 720 0343	21.695 110 3497	.046 093 3355	85
86	44.055 585 6060	956.790 791 2452	.001 045 1606	.022 698 5974	21.717 808 9471	.046 045 1606	86
87	46.038 086 9583	1000.846 376 8512	.000 999 1543	.021 721 1458	21.739 530 0929	.045 999 1543	87
88	48.109 800 8714	1046.884 463 8095	.000 955 2152	.020 785 7855	21.760 315 8784	.045 955 2152	88
89	50.274 741 9106	1094.994 264 6809	.000 913 2468	.019 890 7038	21.780 206 5822	.045 913 2468	89
90	52.537 105 2966	1145.269 006 5916	.000 873 1573	.019 034 1663	21.799 240 7485	.045 873 1573	90
91	54.901 275 0350	1197.806 111 8882	.000 834 8597	.018 214 5132	21.817 455 2617	.045 834 8597	91
92	57.371 832 4115	1252.707 386 9232	.000 798 2710	.017 430 1562	21.834 885 4179	.045 798 2710	92
93	59.953 564 8701	1310.079 219 3347	.000 763 3126	.016 679 5753	21.851 564 9932	.045 763 3126	93
94	62.651 475 2892	1370.032 784 2048	.000 729 9095	.015 961 3161	21.867 526 3093	.045 729 9095	94
95	65.470 791 6772	1432.684 259 4940	.000 697 9905	.015 273 9867	21.882 800 2960	.045 697 9905	95
96	68.416 977 3027	1498.155 051 1712	.000 667 4877	.014 616 2552	21.897 416 5512	.045 667 4877	96
97	71.495 741 2813	1566.572 028 4739	.000 638 3364	.013 986 8471	21.911 403 3983	.045 638 3364	97
98	74.713 049 6390	1638.067 769 7552	.000 610 4754	.013 384 5427	21.924 787 9409	.045 610 4754	98
99	78.075 136 8727	1712.780 819 3942	.000 583 8459	.012 808 1748	21.937 596 1157	.045 583 8459	99
100	81.588 518 0320	1790.855 956 2670	.000 558 3922	.012 256 6266	21.949 852 7423	.045 558 3922	100

	XIV COMPOUND AMOUNT	XV AMOUNT OF ANNUITY	XVI SINKING FUND	XVII PRESENT VALUE	XVIII PRESENT VALUE OF ANNUITY	XIX AMORTIZATION	
RATE 5% / PERIODS	AMOUNT OF 1	AMOUNT OF 1 PER PERIOD	SINKING FUND	PRESENT WORTH OF 1	PRESENT WORTH OF 1 PER PERIOD	PARTIAL PAYMENT	PERIODS
	How $1 left at compound interest will grow.	How $1 deposited periodically will grow.	Periodic deposit that will grow to $1 at future date.	What $1 due in the future is worth today.	What $1 payable periodically is worth today.	Annuity worth $1 today. Periodic payment necessary to pay off a loan of $1.	
1	1.050 000 0000	1.000 000 0000	1.000 000 0000	.952 380 9524	.952 380 9524	1.050 000 0000	1
2	1.102 500 0000	2.050 000 0000	.487 804 8780	.907 029 4785	1.859 410 4308	.537 804 8780	2
3	1.157 625 0000	3.152 500 0000	.317 208 5646	.863 837 5985	2.723 248 0294	.367 208 5646	3
4	1.215 506 2500	4.310 125 0000	.232 011 8326	.822 702 4748	3.545 950 5042	.282 011 8326	4
5	1.276 281 5625	5.525 631 2500	.180 974 7981	.783 526 1665	4.329 476 6706	.230 974 7981	5
6	1.340 095 6406	6.801 912 8125	.147 017 4681	.746 215 3966	5.075 692 0673	.197 017 4681	6
7	1.407 100 4227	8.142 008 4531	.122 819 8184	.710 681 3301	5.786 373 3974	.172 819 8184	7
8	1.477 455 4438	9.549 108 8758	.104 721 8136	.676 839 3620	6.463 212 7594	.154 721 8136	8
9	1.551 328 2160	11.026 564 3196	.090 690 0800	.644 608 9162	7.107 821 6756	.140 690 0800	9
10	1.628 894 6268	12.577 892 5355	.079 504 5750	.613 913 2535	7.721 734 9292	.129 504 5750	10
11	1.710 339 3581	14.206 787 1623	.070 388 8915	.584 679 2891	8.306 414 2183	.120 388 8915	11
12	1.795 856 3260	15.917 126 5204	.062 825 4100	.556 837 4182	8.863 251 6364	.112 825 4100	12
13	1.885 649 1423	17.712 982 8465	.056 455 7652	.530 321 3506	9.393 572 9871	.106 455 7652	13
14	1.979 931 5994	19.598 631 9888	.051 023 9695	.505 067 9530	9.898 640 9401	.101 023 9695	14
15	2.078 928 1794	21.578 563 5882	.046 342 2876	.481 017 0981	10.379 658 0382	.096 342 2876	15
16	2.182 874 5884	23.657 491 7676	.042 269 9080	.458 111 5220	10.837 769 5602	.092 269 9080	16
17	2.292 018 3178	25.840 366 3560	.038 699 1417	.436 296 6876	11.274 066 2478	.088 699 1417	17
18	2.406 619 2337	28.132 384 6738	.035 546 2223	.415 520 6549	11.689 586 9027	.085 546 2223	18
19	2.526 950 1954	30.539 003 9075	.032 745 0104	.395 733 9570	12.085 320 8597	.082 745 0104	19
20	2.653 297 7051	33.065 954 1029	.030 242 5872	.376 889 4829	12.462 210 3425	.080 242 5872	20
21	2.785 962 5904	35.719 251 8080	.027 996 1071	.358 942 3646	12.821 152 7072	.077 996 1071	21
22	2.925 260 7199	38.505 214 3984	.025 970 5086	.341 849 8711	13.163 002 5783	.075 970 5086	22
23	3.071 523 7559	41.430 475 1184	.024 136 8219	.325 571 3058	13.488 573 8841	.074 136 8219	23
24	3.225 099 9437	44.501 998 8743	.022 470 9008	.310 067 9103	13.798 641 7943	.072 470 9008	24
25	3.386 354 9409	47.727 098 8180	.020 952 4573	.295 302 7717	14.093 944 5660	.070 952 4573	25
26	3.555 672 6879	51.113 453 7589	.019 564 3207	.281 240 7350	14.375 185 3010	.069 564 3207	26
27	3.733 456 3223	54.669 126 4468	.018 291 8599	.267 848 3190	14.643 033 6200	.068 291 8599	27
28	3.920 129 1385	58.402 582 7692	.017 122 5304	.255 093 6371	14.898 127 2571	.067 122 5304	28
29	4.116 135 5954	62.322 711 9076	.016 045 5149	.242 946 3211	15.141 073 5782	.066 045 5149	29
30	4.321 942 3752	66.438 847 5030	.015 051 4351	.231 377 4487	15.372 451 0269	.065 051 4351	30
31	4.538 039 4939	70.760 789 8782	.014 132 1204	.220 359 4749	15.592 810 5018	.064 132 1204	31
32	4.764 941 4686	75.298 829 3721	.013 280 4189	.209 866 1666	15.802 676 6684	.063 280 4189	32
33	5.003 188 5420	80.063 770 8407	.012 490 0437	.199 872 5396	16.002 549 2080	.062 490 0437	33
34	5.253 347 9691	85.066 959 3827	.011 755 4454	.190 354 7996	16.192 904 0076	.061 755 4454	34
35	5.516 015 3676	90.320 307 3518	.011 071 7072	.181 290 2854	16.374 194 2929	.061 071 7072	35
36	5.791 816 1360	95.836 322 7194	.010 434 4571	.172 657 4146	16.546 851 7076	.060 434 4571	36
37	6.081 406 9428	101.628 138 8554	.009 839 7945	.164 435 6330	16.711 287 3405	.059 839 7945	37
38	6.385 477 2899	107.709 545 7982	.009 284 2282	.156 605 3647	16.867 892 7053	.059 284 2282	38
39	6.704 751 1544	114.095 023 0881	.008 764 6242	.149 147 9664	17.017 040 6717	.058 764 6242	39
40	7.039 988 7121	120.799 774 2425	.008 278 1612	.142 045 6823	17.159 086 3540	.058 278 1612	40
41	7.391 988 1477	127.839 762 9546	.007 822 2924	.135 281 6022	17.294 367 9562	.057 822 2924	41
42	7.761 587 5551	135.231 751 1023	.007 394 7131	.128 839 6211	17.423 207 5773	.057 394 7131	42
43	8.149 666 9329	142.993 338 6575	.006 993 3328	.122 704 4011	17.545 911 9784	.056 993 3328	43
44	8.557 150 2795	151.143 005 5903	.006 616 2506	.116 861 3344	17.662 773 3128	.056 616 2506	44
45	8.985 007 7935	159.700 155 8699	.006 261 7347	.111 296 5089	17.774 069 8217	.056 261 7347	45
46	9.434 258 1832	168.685 163 6633	.005 928 2036	.105 996 6752	17.880 066 4968	.055 928 2036	46
47	9.905 971 0923	178.119 421 8465	.005 614 2109	.100 949 2144	17.981 015 7113	.055 614 2109	47
48	10.401 269 6469	188.025 392 9388	.005 318 4306	.096 142 1090	18.077 157 8203	.055 318 4306	48
49	10.921 333 1293	198.426 662 5858	.005 039 6453	.091 563 9133	18.168 721 7336	.055 039 6453	49
50	11.467 399 7858	209.347 995 7151	.004 776 7355	.087 203 7270	18.255 925 4606	.054 776 7355	50
51	12.040 769 7750	220.815 395 5008	.004 528 6697	.083 051 1685	18.338 976 6291	.054 528 6697	51
52	12.642 808 2638	232.856 165 2759	.004 294 4966	.079 096 3510	18.418 072 9801	.054 294 4966	52
53	13.274 948 6770	245.498 973 5397	.004 073 3368	.075 329 8581	18.493 402 8382	.054 073 3368	53
54	13.938 696 1108	258.773 922 2166	.003 864 3770	.071 742 7220	18.565 145 5602	.053 864 3770	54
55	14.635 630 9164	272.712 618 3275	.003 666 8637	.068 326 4019	18.633 471 9621	.053 666 8637	55
56	15.367 412 4622	287.348 249 2439	.003 480 0978	.065 072 7637	18.698 544 7258	.053 480 0978	56
57	16.135 783 0853	302.715 661 7060	.003 303 4300	.061 974 0607	18.760 518 7865	.053 303 4300	57
58	16.942 572 2396	318.851 444 7913	.003 136 2568	.059 022 9149	18.819 541 7014	.053 136 2568	58
59	17.789 700 8515	335.794 017 0309	.002 978 0161	.056 212 2999	18.875 754 0013	.052 978 0161	59
60	18.679 185 8941	353.583 717 8825	.002 828 1845	.053 535 5237	18.929 289 5251	.052 828 1845	60
61	19.613 145 1888	372.262 903 7766	.002 686 2736	.050 986 2131	18.980 275 7382	.052 686 2736	61
62	20.593 802 4483	391.876 048 9654	.002 551 8273	.048 558 2982	19.028 834 0363	.052 551 8273	62
63	21.623 492 5707	412.469 851 4137	.002 424 4196	.046 245 9983	19.075 080 0346	.052 424 4196	63
64	22.704 667 1992	434.093 343 9844	.002 303 6520	.044 043 8079	19.119 123 8425	.052 303 6520	64
65	23.839 900 5592	456.798 011 1836	.002 189 1514	.041 946 4837	19.161 070 3262	.052 189 1514	65
66	25.031 895 5871	480.637 911 7428	.002 080 5683	.039 949 0321	19.201 019 3583	.052 080 5683	66
67	26.283 490 3665	505.669 807 3299	.001 977 5751	.038 046 6972	19.239 066 0555	.051 977 5751	67
68	27.597 664 8848	531.953 297 6964	.001 879 8643	.036 234 9497	19.275 301 0052	.051 879 8643	68
69	28.977 548 1291	559.550 962 5812	.001 787 1473	.034 509 4759	19.309 810 4812	.051 787 1473	69
70	30.426 425 5355	588.528 510 7103	.001 699 1530	.032 866 1676	19.342 676 6487	.051 699 1530	70
71	31.947 746 8123	618.954 936 2458	.001 615 6265	.031 301 1120	19.373 977 7607	.051 615 6265	71
72	33.545 134 1529	650.902 683 0581	.001 536 3280	.029 810 5828	19.403 788 3435	.051 536 3280	72
73	35.222 390 8605	684.447 817 2110	.001 461 0318	.028 391 0313	19.432 179 3748	.051 461 0318	73
74	36.983 510 4036	719.670 208 0715	.001 389 5254	.027 039 0774	19.459 218 4522	.051 389 5254	74
75	38.832 685 9238	756.653 718 4751	.001 321 6085	.025 751 5023	19.484 969 9545	.051 321 6085	75
76	40.774 320 2199	795.486 404 3989	.001 257 0925	.024 525 2403	19.509 495 1947	.051 257 0925	76
77	42.813 036 2309	836.260 724 6188	.001 195 7993	.023 357 3717	19.532 852 5664	.051 195 7993	77
78	44.953 688 0425	879.073 760 8497	.001 137 5610	.022 245 1159	19.555 097 6823	.051 137 5610	78
79	47.201 372 4446	924.027 448 8922	.001 082 2189	.021 185 8247	19.576 283 5069	.051 082 2189	79
80	49.561 441 0668	971.228 821 3368	.001 029 6235	.020 176 9759	19.596 460 4828	.051 029 6235	80
81	52.039 513 1202	1020.790 262 4037	.000 979 6332	.019 216 1675	19.615 676 6503	.050 979 6332	81
82	54.641 488 7762	1072.829 775 5239	.000 932 1143	.018 301 1119	19.633 977 7622	.050 932 1143	82
83	57.373 563 2150	1127.471 264 3001	.000 886 9406	.017 429 6304	19.651 407 3925	.050 886 9406	83
84	60.242 241 3758	1184.844 827 5151	.000 843 9924	.016 599 6480	19.668 007 0405	.050 843 9924	84
85	63.254 353 4445	1245.087 068 8908	.000 803 1567	.015 809 1885	19.683 816 2290	.050 803 1567	85
86	66.417 071 1168	1308.341 422 3354	.000 764 3265	.015 056 3700	19.698 872 5991	.050 764 3265	86
87	69.737 924 6726	1374.758 493 4521	.000 727 4005	.014 339 4000	19.713 211 9992	.050 727 4005	87
88	73.224 820 9062	1444.496 418 1247	.000 692 2828	.013 656 5715	19.726 868 5706	.050 692 2828	88
89	76.886 061 9515	1517.721 239 0310	.000 658 8825	.013 006 2585	19.739 874 8292	.050 658 8825	89
90	80.730 365 0491	1594.607 300 9825	.000 627 1136	.012 386 9129	19.752 261 7421	.050 627 1136	90
91	84.766 883 3016	1675.337 666 0317	.000 596 8946	.011 797 0599	19.764 058 8020	.050 596 8946	91
92	89.005 227 4667	1760.104 549 3332	.000 568 1481	.011 235 2951	19.775 294 0971	.050 568 1481	92
93	93.455 488 8400	1849.109 776 7999	.000 540 8008	.010 700 2811	19.785 994 3782	.050 540 8008	93
94	98.128 263 2820	1942.565 265 6399	.000 514 7832	.010 190 7439	19.796 185 1221	.050 514 7832	94
95	103.034 676 4461	2040.693 528 9219	.000 490 0295	.009 705 4704	19.805 890 5925	.050 490 0295	95
96	108.186 410 2684	2143.728 205 3680	.000 466 4770	.009 243 3051	19.815 133 8976	.050 466 4770	96
97	113.595 730 7818	2251.914 615 6364	.000 444 0666	.008 803 1477	19.823 937 0453	.050 444 0666	97
98	119.275 517 3209	2365.510 346 4182	.000 422 7418	.008 383 9502	19.832 320 9955	.050 422 7418	98
99	125.239 293 1870	2484.785 863 7391	.000 402 4492	.007 984 7145	19.840 305 7100	.050 402 4492	99
100	131.501 257 8463	2610.025 156 9261	.000 383 1381	.007 604 4900	19.847 910 2000	.050 383 1381	100

		XIV COMPOUND AMOUNT	XV AMOUNT OF ANNUITY	XVI SINKING FUND	XVII PRESENT VALUE	XVIII PRESENT VALUE OF ANNUITY	XIX AMORTIZATION	
RATE 6%	P E R I O D S	AMOUNT OF 1 *How $1 left at compound interest will grow.*	AMOUNT OF 1 PER PERIOD *How $1 deposited periodically will grow.*	SINKING FUND *Periodic deposit that will grow to $1 at future date.*	PRESENT WORTH OF 1 *What $1 due in the future is worth today.*	PRESENT WORTH OF 1 PER PERIOD *What $1 payable periodically is worth today.*	PARTIAL PAYMENT *Annuity worth $1 today. Periodic payment necessary to pay off a loan of $1.*	P E R I O D S
	1	1.060 000 0000	1.000 000 0000	1.000 000 0000	.943 396 2264	.943 396 2264	1.060 000 0000	1
	2	1.123 600 0000	2.060 000 0000	.485 436 8932	.889 996 4400	1.833 392 6664	.545 436 8932	2
	3	1.191 016 0000	3.183 600 0000	.314 109 8128	.839 619 2830	2.673 011 9495	.374 109 8128	3
	4	1.262 476 9600	4.374 616 0000	.228 591 4924	.792 093 6632	3.465 105 6127	.288 591 4924	4
	5	1.338 225 5776	5.637 092 9600	.177 396 4004	.747 258 1729	4.212 363 7856	.237 396 4004	5
	6	1.418 519 1123	6.975 318 5376	.143 362 6285	.704 960 5404	4.917 324 3260	.203 362 6285	6
	7	1.503 630 2590	8.393 837 6499	.119 135 0181	.665 057 1136	5.582 381 4396	.179 135 0181	7
	8	1.593 848 0745	9.897 467 9088	.101 035 9426	.627 412 3713	6.209 793 8110	.161 035 9426	8
	9	1.689 478 9590	11.491 315 9834	.087 022 2350	.591 898 4635	6.801 692 2745	.147 022 2350	9
	10	1.790 847 6965	13.180 794 9424	.075 867 9582	.558 394 7769	7.360 087 0514	.135 867 9582	10
	11	1.898 298 5583	14.971 642 6389	.066 792 9381	.526 787 5254	7.886 874 5768	.126 792 9381	11
	12	2.012 196 4718	16.869 941 1973	.059 277 0294	.496 969 3636	8.383 843 9404	.119 277 0294	12
	13	2.132 928 2601	18.882 137 6691	.052 960 1053	.468 839 0222	8.852 682 9626	.112 960 1053	13
	14	2.260 903 9558	21.015 065 9292	.047 584 9090	.442 300 9644	9.294 983 9270	.107 584 9090	14
	15	2.396 558 1931	23.275 969 8850	.042 962 7640	.417 265 0607	9.712 248 9877	.102 962 7640	15
	16	2.540 351 6847	25.672 528 0781	.038 952 1436	.393 646 2837	10.105 895 2715	.098 952 1436	16
	17	2.692 772 7858	28.212 879 7628	.035 444 8042	.371 364 4186	10.477 259 6901	.095 444 8042	17
	18	2.854 339 1529	30.905 652 5485	.032 356 5406	.350 343 7911	10.827 603 4812	.092 356 5406	18
	19	3.025 599 5021	33.759 991 7015	.029 620 8604	.330 513 0105	11.158 116 4917	.089 620 8604	19
	20	3.207 135 4722	36.785 591 2035	.027 184 5570	.311 804 7269	11.469 921 2186	.087 184 5570	20
	21	3.399 563 6005	39.992 726 6758	.025 004 5467	.294 155 4027	11.764 076 6213	.085 004 5467	21
	22	3.603 537 4166	43.392 290 2763	.023 045 5685	.277 505 0969	12.041 581 7182	.083 045 5685	22
	23	3.819 749 6616	46.995 827 6929	.021 278 4847	.261 797 2612	12.303 378 9794	.081 278 4847	23
	24	4.048 934 6413	50.815 577 3545	.019 679 0050	.246 978 5483	12.550 357 5278	.079 679 0050	24
	25	4.291 870 7197	54.864 511 9957	.018 226 7182	.232 998 6305	12.783 356 1583	.078 226 7182	25
	26	4.549 382 9629	59.156 382 7155	.016 904 3467	.219 810 0288	13.003 166 1870	.076 904 3467	26
	27	4.822 345 9407	63.705 765 6784	.015 697 1663	.207 367 9517	13.210 534 1387	.075 697 1663	27
	28	5.111 686 6971	68.528 111 6191	.014 592 5515	.195 630 1431	13.406 164 2818	.074 592 5515	28
	29	5.418 387 8990	73.639 798 3162	.013 579 6135	.184 556 7388	13.590 721 0206	.073 579 6135	29
	30	5.743 491 1729	79.058 186 2152	.012 648 9115	.174 110 1309	13.764 831 1515	.072 648 9115	30
	31	6.088 100 6433	84.801 677 3881	.011 792 2196	.164 254 8405	13.929 085 9920	.071 792 2196	31
	32	6.453 386 6819	90.889 778 0314	.011 002 3374	.154 957 3967	14.084 043 3887	.071 002 3374	32
	33	6.840 589 8828	97.343 164 7133	.010 272 9350	.146 186 2233	14.230 229 6119	.070 272 9350	33
	34	7.251 025 2758	104.183 754 5961	.009 598 4254	.137 911 5314	14.368 141 1433	.069 598 4254	34
	35	7.686 086 7923	111.434 779 8719	.008 973 8590	.130 105 2183	14.498 246 3616	.068 973 8590	35
	36	8.147 251 9999	119.120 866 6642	.008 394 8348	.122 740 7720	14.620 987 1336	.068 394 8348	36
	37	8.636 087 1198	127.268 118 6640	.007 857 4274	.115 793 1811	14.736 780 3147	.067 857 4274	37
	38	9.154 252 3470	135.904 205 7839	.007 358 1240	.109 238 8501	14.846 019 1648	.067 358 1240	38
	39	9.703 507 4879	145.058 458 1309	.006 893 7724	.103 055 5190	14.949 074 6838	.066 893 7724	39
	40	10.285 717 9371	154.761 965 6188	.006 461 5359	.097 222 1877	15.046 296 8715	.066 461 5359	40
	41	10.902 861 0134	165.047 683 5559	.006 058 8551	.091 719 0450	15.138 015 9165	.066 058 8551	41
	42	11.557 032 6742	175.950 544 5692	.005 683 4152	.086 527 4010	15.224 543 3175	.065 683 4152	42
	43	12.250 454 6346	187.507 577 2434	.005 333 1178	.081 629 6235	15.306 172 9410	.065 333 1178	43
	44	12.985 481 9127	199.758 031 8780	.005 006 0565	.077 009 0788	15.383 182 0198	.065 006 0565	44
	45	13.764 610 8274	212.743 513 7907	.004 700 4958	.072 650 0743	15.455 832 0942	.064 700 4958	45
	46	14.590 487 4771	226.508 124 6181	.004 414 8527	.068 537 8060	15.524 369 9002	.064 414 8527	46
	47	15.465 916 7257	241.098 612 0952	.004 147 6805	.064 658 3075	15.589 028 2077	.064 147 6805	47
	48	16.393 871 7293	256.564 528 8209	.003 897 6549	.060 998 4033	15.650 026 6110	.063 897 6549	48
	49	17.377 504 0330	272.958 400 5502	.003 663 5619	.057 545 6635	15.707 572 2746	.063 663 5619	49
	50	18.420 154 2750	290.335 904 5832	.003 444 2864	.054 288 3618	15.761 860 6364	.063 444 2864	50
	51	19.525 363 5315	308.756 058 8582	.003 238 8028	.051 215 4357	15.813 076 0721	.063 238 8028	51
	52	20.696 885 3434	328.281 422 3897	.003 046 1669	.048 316 4488	15.861 392 5208	.063 046 1669	52
	53	21.938 698 4640	348.978 307 7331	.002 865 5076	.045 581 5554	15.906 974 0762	.062 865 5076	53
	54	23.255 020 3718	370.917 006 1970	.002 696 0209	.043 001 4674	15.949 975 5436	.062 696 0209	54
	55	24.650 321 5941	394.172 026 5689	.002 536 9634	.040 567 4221	15.990 542 9657	.062 536 9634	55
	56	26.129 340 8898	418.822 348 1630	.002 387 6472	.038 271 1529	16.028 814 1186	.062 387 6472	56
	57	27.697 101 3432	444.951 689 0528	.002 247 4350	.036 104 8612	16.064 918 9798	.062 247 4350	57
	58	29.358 927 4238	472.648 790 3959	.002 115 7359	.034 061 1898	16.098 980 1696	.062 115 7359	58
	59	31.120 463 0692	502.007 717 8197	.001 992 0012	.032 133 1979	16.131 113 3676	.061 992 0012	59
	60	32.987 690 8533	533.128 180 8889	.001 875 7215	.030 314 3377	16.161 427 7052	.061 875 7215	60
	61	34.966 952 3045	566.115 871 7422	.001 766 4228	.028 598 4318	16.190 026 1370	.061 766 4228	61
	62	37.064 969 4428	601.082 824 0467	.001 663 6642	.026 979 6526	16.217 005 7896	.061 663 6642	62
	63	39.288 867 6094	638.147 793 4895	.001 567 0351	.025 452 5025	16.242 458 2921	.061 567 0351	63
	64	41.646 199 6659	677.436 661 0989	.001 476 1528	.024 011 7948	16.266 470 0869	.061 476 1528	64
	65	44.144 971 6459	719.082 860 7649	.001 390 6603	.022 652 6366	16.289 122 7235	.061 390 6603	65
	66	46.793 669 9446	763.227 832 4107	.001 310 2248	.021 370 4119	16.310 493 1354	.061 310 2248	66
	67	49.601 290 1413	810.021 502 3554	.001 234 5351	.020 160 7659	16.330 653 9013	.061 234 5351	67
	68	52.577 367 5498	859.622 792 4967	.001 163 3009	.019 019 5905	16.349 673 4918	.061 163 3009	68
	69	55.732 009 6028	912.200 160 0465	.001 096 2506	.017 943 0099	16.367 616 5017	.061 096 2506	69
	70	59.075 930 1790	967.932 169 6493	.001 033 1302	.016 927 3678	16.384 543 8695	.061 033 1302	70
	71	62.620 485 9897	1027.008 099 8283	.000 973 7022	.015 969 2149	16.400 513 0844	.060 973 7022	71
	72	66.377 715 1491	1089.628 585 8180	.000 917 7439	.015 065 2971	16.415 578 3816	.060 917 7439	72
	73	70.360 378 0580	1156.006 300 9670	.000 865 0472	.014 212 5444	16.429 790 9260	.060 865 0472	73
	74	74.582 000 7415	1226.366 679 0251	.000 815 4168	.013 408 0608	16.443 198 9868	.060 815 4168	74
	75	79.056 920 7860	1300.948 679 7666	.000 768 6698	.012 649 1140	16.455 848 1007	.060 768 6698	75
	76	83.800 336 0332	1380.005 600 5526	.000 724 6347	.011 933 1264	16.467 781 2271	.060 724 6347	76
	77	88.828 356 1951	1463.805 936 5857	.000 683 1507	.011 257 6664	16.479 038 8935	.060 683 1507	77
	78	94.158 057 5669	1552.634 292 7808	.000 644 0667	.010 620 4400	16.489 659 3335	.060 644 0667	78
	79	99.807 541 0209	1646.792 350 3477	.000 607 2411	.010 019 2830	16.499 678 6165	.060 607 2411	79
	80	105.795 993 4821	1746.599 891 3686	.000 572 5410	.009 452 1538	16.509 130 7703	.060 572 5410	80
	81	112.143 753 0910	1852.395 884 8507	.000 539 8414	.008 917 1262	16.518 047 8965	.060 539 8414	81
	82	118.872 378 2765	1964.539 637 9417	.000 509 0251	.008 412 3832	16.526 460 2797	.060 509 0251	82
	83	126.004 720 9731	2083.412 016 2182	.000 479 9819	.007 936 2106	16.534 396 4903	.060 479 9819	83
	84	133.565 004 2315	2209.416 737 1913	.000 452 6081	.007 486 9911	16.541 883 4814	.060 452 6081	84
	85	141.578 904 4854	2342.981 741 4228	.000 426 8066	.007 063 1992	16.548 946 6806	.060 426 8066	85
	86	150.073 638 7545	2484.560 645 9082	.000 402 4856	.006 663 3954	16.555 610 0760	.060 402 4856	86
	87	159.078 057 0798	2634.634 284 6626	.000 379 5593	.006 286 2221	16.561 896 2981	.060 379 5593	87
	88	168.622 740 5045	2793.712 341 7424	.000 357 9467	.005 930 3982	16.567 826 6963	.060 357 9467	88
	89	178.740 104 9348	2962.335 082 2469	.000 337 5715	.005 594 7153	16.573 421 4116	.060 337 5715	89
	90	189.464 511 2309	3141.075 187 1818	.000 318 3623	.005 278 0333	16.578 699 4450	.060 318 3623	90
	91	200.832 381 9048	3330.539 698 4127	.000 300 2516	.004 979 2767	16.583 678 7217	.060 300 2516	91
	92	212.882 324 8190	3531.372 080 3174	.000 283 1761	.004 697 4308	16.588 376 1525	.060 283 1761	92
	93	225.655 264 3082	3744.254 405 1365	.000 267 0759	.004 431 5385	16.592 807 6910	.060 267 0759	93
	94	239.194 580 1667	3869.909 669 4447	.000 251 8949	.004 180 6967	16.596 988 3878	.060 251 8949	94
	95	253.546 254 9767	4209.104 249 6113	.000 237 5802	.003 944 0535	16.600 932 4413	.060 237 5802	95
	96	268.759 030 2753	4462.650 504 5880	.000 224 0821	.003 720 8052	16.604 653 2465	.060 224 0821	96
	97	284.884 572 0918	4731.409 534 8633	.000 211 3535	.003 510 1936	16.608 163 4401	.060 211 3535	97
	98	301.977 646 4173	5016.294 106 9551	.000 199 3504	.003 311 5034	16.611 474 9435	.060 199 3504	98
	99	320.096 305 2023	5318.271 753 3724	.000 188 0310	.003 124 0598	16.614 599 0033	.060 188 0310	99
	100	339.302 083 5145	5638.368 058 5748	.000 177 3563	.002 947 2262	16.617 546 2295	.060 177 3563	100

	XIV COMPOUND AMOUNT	XV AMOUNT OF ANNUITY	XVI SINKING FUND	XVII PRESENT VALUE	XVIII PRESENT VALUE OF ANNUITY	XIX AMORTIZATION	
RATE 7% PERIODS	AMOUNT OF 1 — How $1 left at compound interest will grow.	AMOUNT OF 1 PER PERIOD — How $1 deposited periodically will grow.	SINKING FUND — Periodic deposit that will grow to $1 at future date.	PRESENT WORTH OF 1 — What $1 due in the future is worth today.	PRESENT WORTH OF 1 PER PERIOD — What $1 payable periodically is worth today.	PARTIAL PAYMENT — Annuity worth $1 today. Periodic payment necessary to pay off a loan of $1.	PERIODS
1	1.070 000 0000	1.000 000 0000	1.000 000 0000	.934 579 4393	.934 579 4393	1.070 000 0000	1
2	1.144 900 0000	2.070 000 0000	.483 091 7874	.873 438 7283	1.808 018 1675	.553 091 7874	2
3	1.225 043 0000	3.214 900 0000	.311 051 6657	.816 297 8769	2.624 316 0444	.381 051 6657	3
4	1.310 796 0100	4.439 943 0000	.225 228 1167	.762 895 2120	3.387 211 2565	.295 228 1167	4
5	1.402 551 7307	5.750 739 0100	.173 890 6944	.712 986 1795	4.100 197 4359	.243 890 6944	5
6	1.500 730 3518	7.153 290 7407	.139 795 7998	.666 342 2238	4.766 539 6598	.209 795 7998	6
7	1.605 781 4765	8.654 021 0925	.115 553 2196	.622 749 7419	5.389 289 4016	.185 553 2196	7
8	1.718 186 1798	10.259 802 5690	.097 467 7625	.582 009 1046	5.971 298 5062	.167 467 7625	8
9	1.838 459 2124	11.977 988 7489	.083 486 4701	.543 933 7426	6.515 232 2488	.153 486 4701	9
10	1.967 151 3573	13.816 447 9613	.072 377 5027	.508 349 2921	7.023 581 5409	.142 377 5027	10
11	2.104 851 9523	15.783 599 3186	.063 356 9048	.475 092 7964	7.498 674 3373	.133 356 9048	11
12	2.252 191 5890	17.888 451 2709	.055 901 9887	.444 011 9592	7.942 686 2966	.125 901 9887	12
13	2.409 845 0002	20.140 642 8598	.049 650 8481	.414 964 4479	8.357 650 7444	.119 650 8481	13
14	2.578 534 1502	22.550 487 8600	.044 344 9386	.387 817 2410	8.745 467 9855	.114 344 9386	14
15	2.759 031 5407	25.129 022 0102	.039 794 6247	.362 446 0196	9.107 914 0051	.109 794 6247	15
16	2.952 163 7486	27.888 053 5509	.035 857 6477	.338 734 5978	9.446 648 6029	.105 857 6477	16
17	3.158 815 2110	30.840 217 2995	.032 425 1931	.316 574 3905	9.763 222 9934	.102 425 1931	17
18	3.379 932 2757	33.999 032 5105	.029 412 6017	.295 863 9163	10.059 086 9097	.099 412 6017	18
19	3.616 527 5350	37.378 964 7862	.026 753 0148	.276 508 3330	10.335 595 2427	.096 753 0148	19
20	3.869 684 4625	40.995 492 3212	.024 392 9257	.258 419 0028	10.594 014 2455	.094 392 9257	20
21	4.140 562 3749	44.865 176 7837	.022 289 0017	.241 513 0867	10.835 527 3323	.092 289 0017	21
22	4.430 401 7411	49.005 739 1586	.020 405 7732	.225 713 1652	11.061 240 4974	.090 405 7732	22
23	4.740 529 8630	53.436 140 8997	.018 713 9263	.210 946 8833	11.272 187 3808	.088 713 9263	23
24	5.072 366 9534	58.176 670 7627	.017 189 0207	.197 146 6199	11.469 334 0007	.087 189 0207	24
25	5.427 432 6401	63.249 037 7160	.015 810 5172	.184 249 1775	11.653 583 1783	.085 810 5172	25
26	5.807 352 9249	68.676 470 3562	.014 561 0279	.172 195 4930	11.825 778 6713	.084 561 0279	26
27	6.213 867 6297	74.483 823 2811	.013 425 7340	.160 930 3673	11.986 709 0386	.083 425 7340	27
28	6.648 838 3638	80.697 690 9108	.012 391 9283	.150 402 2124	12.137 111 2510	.082 391 9283	28
29	7.114 257 0492	87.346 529 2745	.011 448 6518	.140 562 8154	12.277 674 0664	.081 448 6518	29
30	7.612 255 0427	94.460 786 3237	.010 586 4035	.131 367 1172	12.409 041 1835	.080 586 4035	30
31	8.145 112 8956	102.073 041 3664	.009 796 9061	.122 773 0067	12.531 814 1902	.079 796 9061	31
32	8.715 270 7983	110.218 154 2621	.009 072 9155	.114 741 1277	12.646 555 3179	.079 072 9155	32
33	9.325 339 7542	118.933 425 0604	.008 408 0653	.107 234 6988	12.753 790 0168	.078 408 0653	33
34	9.978 113 5370	128.258 764 8146	.007 796 7381	.100 219 3447	12.854 009 3615	.077 796 7381	34
35	10.676 581 4846	138.236 878 3516	.007 233 9596	.093 662 9390	12.947 672 3004	.077 233 9596	35
36	11.423 942 1885	148.913 459 8363	.006 715 3097	.087 535 4570	13.035 207 7574	.076 715 3097	36
37	12.223 618 1417	160.337 402 0248	.006 236 8480	.081 808 8383	13.117 016 5957	.076 236 8480	37
38	13.079 271 4117	172.561 020 1665	.005 795 0515	.076 456 8582	13.193 473 4539	.075 795 0515	38
39	13.994 820 4105	185.640 291 5782	.005 386 7616	.071 455 0077	13.264 928 4616	.075 386 7616	39
40	14.974 457 8392	199.635 111 9887	.005 009 1389	.066 780 3810	13.331 708 8426	.075 009 1389	40
41	16.022 669 8880	214.609 569 8279	.004 659 6245	.062 411 5710	13.394 120 4137	.074 659 6245	41
42	17.144 256 7801	230.632 239 7158	.004 335 9072	.058 328 5711	13.452 448 9847	.074 335 9072	42
43	18.344 354 7547	247.776 496 4959	.004 035 8953	.054 512 6832	13.506 961 6680	.074 035 8953	43
44	19.628 459 5875	266.120 851 2507	.003 757 6913	.050 946 4329	13.557 908 1009	.073 757 6913	44
45	21.002 451 7587	285.749 310 8382	.003 499 5710	.047 613 4887	13.605 521 5896	.073 499 5710	45
46	22.472 623 3818	306.751 762 5969	.003 259 9650	.044 498 5876	13.650 020 1772	.073 259 9650	46
47	24.045 707 0185	329.224 385 9787	.003 037 4421	.041 587 4650	13.691 607 6423	.073 037 4421	47
48	25.728 906 5098	353.270 092 9972	.002 830 6953	.038 866 7898	13.730 474 4320	.072 830 6953	48
49	27.529 929 9655	378.998 999 5070	.002 638 5294	.036 324 1026	13.766 798 5346	.072 638 5294	49
50	29.457 025 0631	406.528 929 4724	.002 459 8495	.033 947 7594	13.800 746 2940	.072 459 8495	50
51	31.519 016 8175	435.985 954 5355	.002 293 6519	.031 726 8780	13.832 473 1720	.072 293 6519	51
52	33.725 347 9947	467.504 971 3530	.002 139 0147	.029 651 2878	13.862 124 4598	.072 139 0147	52
53	36.086 122 3543	501.230 319 3477	.001 995 0908	.027 711 4839	13.889 835 9437	.071 995 0908	53
54	38.612 150 9191	537.316 441 7021	.001 861 1007	.025 898 5831	13.915 734 5269	.071 861 1007	54
55	41.315 001 4835	575.928 592 6212	.001 736 3264	.024 204 2833	13.939 938 8102	.071 736 3264	55
56	44.207 051 5873	617.243 594 1047	.001 620 1059	.022 620 8255	13.962 559 6357	.071 620 1059	56
57	47.301 545 1984	661.450 645 6920	.001 511 8286	.021 140 9584	13.983 700 5941	.071 511 8286	57
58	50.612 653 3623	708.752 190 8905	.001 410 9304	.019 757 9051	14.003 458 4991	.071 410 9304	58
59	54.155 539 0977	759.364 844 2528	.001 316 8900	.018 465 3318	14.021 923 8310	.071 316 8900	59
60	57.946 426 8345	813.520 383 3505	.001 229 2255	.017 257 3195	14.039 181 1504	.071 229 2255	60
61	62.002 676 7130	871.466 810 1850	.001 147 4906	.016 128 3360	14.055 309 4864	.071 147 4906	61
62	66.342 864 0829	933.469 486 8980	.001 071 2723	.015 073 2112	14.070 382 6976	.071 071 2723	62
63	70.986 864 5687	999.812 350 9808	.001 000 1877	.014 087 1132	14.084 469 8108	.071 000 1877	63
64	75.955 945 0885	1070.799 215 5495	.000 933 8819	.013 165 5264	14.097 635 3372	.070 933 8819	64
65	81.272 861 2447	1146.755 160 6379	.000 872 0257	.012 304 2303	14.109 939 5675	.070 872 0257	65
66	86.961 961 5318	1228.028 021 8826	.000 814 3137	.011 499 2806	14.121 438 8481	.070 814 3137	66
67	93.049 298 8390	1314.989 983 4144	.000 760 4621	.010 746 9912	14.132 185 8394	.070 760 4621	67
68	99.562 749 7577	1408.039 282 2534	.000 710 2075	.010 043 9171	14.142 229 7564	.070 710 2075	68
69	106.532 142 2408	1507.602 032 0111	.000 663 3050	.009 386 6384	14.151 616 5948	.070 663 3050	69
70	113.989 392 1976	1614.134 174 2519	.000 619 5272	.008 772 7461	14.160 389 3409	.070 619 5272	70
71	121.968 649 6515	1728.123 566 4495	.000 578 6623	.008 198 8282	14.168 588 1691	.070 578 6623	71
72	130.506 455 1271	1850.092 216 1010	.000 540 5136	.007 662 4562	14.176 250 6253	.070 540 5136	72
73	139.641 906 9860	1980.598 671 2281	.000 504 8978	.007 161 1740	14.183 411 7993	.070 504 8978	73
74	149.416 840 4750	2120.240 578 2140	.000 471 6446	.006 692 6860	14.190 104 4854	.070 471 6446	74
75	159.876 019 3082	2269.657 418 6890	.000 440 5951	.006 254 8468	14.196 359 3321	.070 440 5951	75
76	171.067 340 6598	2429.533 437 9973	.000 411 6017	.005 845 6512	14.202 204 9833	.070 411 6017	76
77	183.042 054 5060	2600.600 778 6571	.000 384 5265	.005 463 2254	14.207 668 2087	.070 384 5265	77
78	195.854 998 3214	2783.642 833 1631	.000 359 2415	.005 105 8181	14.212 774 0268	.070 359 2415	78
79	209.564 848 2039	2979.497 831 4845	.000 335 6270	.004 771 7926	14.217 545 8194	.070 335 6270	79
80	224.234 387 5782	3189.062 679 6884	.000 313 5718	.004 459 6093	14.222 005 4387	.070 313 5718	80
81	239.930 794 7087	3413.297 067 2666	.000 292 9719	.004 167 8685	14.226 173 3072	.070 292 9719	81
82	256.725 950 3383	3653.227 861 9752	.000 273 7305	.003 895 2042	14.230 068 5114	.070 273 7305	82
83	274.696 766 8619	3909.953 812 3135	.000 255 7575	.003 640 3778	14.233 708 8892	.070 255 7575	83
84	293.925 540 5423	4184.650 579 1754	.000 238 9686	.003 403 2222	14.237 111 1114	.070 238 9686	84
85	314.500 328 3802	4478.576 119 7177	.000 223 2853	.003 179 6469	14.240 290 7583	.070 223 2853	85
86	336.515 351 3669	4793.076 448 0980	.000 208 6343	.002 971 6326	14.243 262 3909	.070 208 6343	86
87	360.071 425 9625	5129.591 799 4648	.000 194 9473	.002 777 2268	14.246 039 6177	.070 194 9473	87
88	385.276 425 7799	5489.663 225 4273	.000 182 1605	.002 595 5390	14.248 635 1567	.070 182 1605	88
89	412.245 775 5845	5874.939 651 2073	.000 170 2145	.002 425 7374	14.251 060 8941	.070 170 2145	89
90	441.102 979 8754	6287.185 426 7918	.000 159 0537	.002 267 0443	14.253 327 9384	.070 159 0537	90
91	471.980 188 4667	6728.288 406 6672	.000 148 6262	.002 118 7330	14.255 446 6714	.070 148 6262	91
92	505.018 801 6594	7200.268 595 1339	.000 138 8837	.001 980 1243	14.257 426 7957	.070 138 8837	92
93	540.370 117 7755	7705.287 396 7933	.000 129 7810	.001 850 5835	14.259 277 3792	.070 129 7810	93
94	578.196 026 0198	8245.657 514 5688	.000 121 2760	.001 729 5215	14.261 006 8965	.070 121 2760	94
95	618.669 747 8412	8823.853 540 5886	.000 113 3292	.001 616 3713	14.262 623 2677	.070 113 3292	95
96	661.976 630 1901	9442.523 288 4298	.000 105 9039	.001 510 6273	14.264 133 8951	.070 105 9039	96
97	708.314 994 3034	10104.499 918 6199	.000 098 9658	.001 411 8013	14.265 545 6963	.070 098 9658	97
98	757.897 043 9046	10812.814 912 9233	.000 092 4829	.001 319 4404	14.266 865 1367	.070 092 4829	98
99	810.949 836 9780	11570.711 956 8279	.000 086 4251	.001 233 1219	14.268 098 2586	.070 086 4251	99
100	867.716 325 5664	12381.661 793 8059	.000 080 7646	.001 152 4504	14.269 250 7090	.070 080 7646	100

	XIV COMPOUND AMOUNT	XV AMOUNT OF ANNUITY	XVI SINKING FUND	XVII PRESENT VALUE	XVIII PRESENT VALUE OF ANNUITY	XIX AMORTIZATION	
RATE 8% / PERIODS	AMOUNT OF 1 — How $1 left at compound interest will grow.	AMOUNT OF 1 PER PERIOD — How $1 deposited periodically will grow.	SINKING FUND — Periodic deposit that will grow to $1 at future date.	PRESENT WORTH OF 1 — What $1 due in the future is worth today.	PRESENT WORTH OF 1 PER PERIOD — What $1 payable periodically is worth today.	PARTIAL PAYMENT — Annuity worth $1 today. Periodic payment necessary to pay off a loan of $1.	PERIODS
1	1.080 000 0000	1.000 000 0000	1.000 000 0000	.925 925 9259	.925 925 9259	1.080 000 0000	1
2	1.166 400 0000	2.080 000 0000	.480 769 2308	.857 338 8203	1.783 264 7462	.560 769 2308	2
3	1.259 712 0000	3.246 400 0000	.308 033 5140	.793 832 2410	2.577 096 9872	.388 033 5140	3
4	1.360 488 9600	4.506 112 0000	.221 920 8045	.735 029 8528	3.312 126 8400	.301 920 8045	4
5	1.469 328 0768	5.866 600 9600	.170 456 4546	.680 583 1970	3.992 710 0371	.250 456 4546	5
6	1.586 874 3229	7.335 929 0368	.136 315 3862	.630 169 6269	4.622 879 6640	.216 315 3862	6
7	1.713 824 2688	8.922 803 3597	.112 072 4014	.583 490 3953	5.206 370 0592	.192 072 4014	7
8	1.850 930 2103	10.636 627 6285	.094 014 7606	.540 268 8845	5.746 638 9437	.174 014 7606	8
9	1.999 004 6271	12.487 557 8388	.080 079 7092	.500 248 9671	6.246 887 9109	.160 079 7092	9
10	2.158 924 9973	14.486 562 4659	.069 029 4887	.463 193 4881	6.710 081 3989	.149 029 4887	10
11	2.331 638 9971	16.645 487 4632	.060 076 3421	.428 882 8592	7.138 964 2583	.140 076 3421	11
12	2.518 170 1168	18.977 126 4602	.052 695 0169	.397 113 7586	7.536 078 0169	.132 695 0169	12
13	2.719 623 7262	21.495 296 5771	.046 521 8052	.367 697 9247	7.903 775 9416	.126 521 8052	13
14	2.937 193 6243	24.214 920 3032	.041 296 8528	.340 461 0414	8.244 236 9830	.121 296 8528	14
15	3.172 169 1142	27.152 113 9275	.036 829 5449	.315 241 7050	8.559 478 6879	.116 829 5449	15
16	3.425 942 6433	30.324 283 0417	.032 976 8720	.291 890 4676	8.851 369 1555	.112 976 8720	16
17	3.700 018 0548	33.750 225 6850	.029 629 4315	.270 268 9514	9.121 638 1069	.109 629 4315	17
18	3.996 019 4992	37.450 243 7398	.026 702 0959	.250 249 0291	9.371 887 1360	.106 702 0959	18
19	4.315 701 0591	41.446 263 2390	.024 127 6275	.231 712 0640	9.603 599 2000	.104 127 6275	19
20	4.660 957 1438	45.761 964 2981	.021 852 2088	.214 548 2074	9.818 147 4074	.101 852 2088	20
21	5.033 833 7154	50.422 921 4420	.019 832 2503	.198 655 7476	10.016 803 1550	.099 832 2503	21
22	5.436 540 4126	55.456 755 1573	.018 032 0684	.183 940 5070	10.200 743 6621	.098 032 0684	22
23	5.871 463 6456	60.893 295 5699	.016 422 1692	.170 315 2843	10.371 058 9464	.096 422 1692	23
24	6.341 180 7372	66.764 759 2155	.014 977 9616	.157 699 3373	10.528 758 2837	.094 977 9616	24
25	6.848 475 1962	73.105 939 9527	.013 678 7791	.146 017 9049	10.674 776 1886	.093 678 7791	25
26	7.396 353 2119	79.954 415 1490	.012 507 1267	.135 201 7638	10.809 977 9524	.092 507 1267	26
27	7.988 061 4689	87.350 768 3609	.011 448 0962	.125 186 8183	10.935 164 7707	.091 448 0962	27
28	8.627 106 3864	95.338 829 8297	.010 488 9057	.115 913 7207	11.051 078 4914	.090 488 9057	28
29	9.317 274 8973	103.965 936 2161	.009 618 5350	.107 327 5192	11.158 406 0106	.089 618 5350	29
30	10.062 656 8891	113.283 211 1134	.008 827 4334	.099 377 3325	11.257 783 3431	.088 827 4334	30
31	10.867 669 4402	123.345 868 0025	.008 107 2841	.092 016 0467	11.349 799 3918	.088 107 2841	31
32	11.737 082 9954	134.213 537 4427	.007 450 8132	.085 200 0451	11.434 999 4368	.087 450 8132	32
33	12.676 049 6350	145.950 620 4381	.006 851 6324	.078 888 9306	11.513 888 3674	.086 851 6324	33
34	13.690 133 6059	158.626 670 0732	.006 304 1101	.073 045 3061	11.586 933 6736	.086 304 1101	34
35	14.785 344 2943	172.316 803 6790	.005 803 2646	.067 634 5427	11.654 568 2163	.085 803 2646	35
36	15.968 171 8379	187.102 147 9733	.005 344 6741	.062 624 5766	11.717 192 7928	.085 344 6741	36
37	17.245 625 5849	203.070 319 8112	.004 924 4025	.057 985 7190	11.775 178 5119	.084 924 4025	37
38	18.625 275 6317	220.315 945 3961	.004 538 9361	.053 690 4806	11.828 868 9925	.084 538 9361	38
39	20.115 297 6822	238.941 221 0278	.004 185 1297	.049 713 4080	11.878 582 4004	.084 185 1297	39
40	21.724 521 4968	259.056 518 7100	.003 860 1615	.046 030 9333	11.924 613 3337	.083 860 1615	40
41	23.462 483 2165	280.781 040 2068	.003 561 4940	.042 621 2345	11.967 234 5683	.083 561 4940	41
42	25.339 481 8739	304.243 523 4233	.003 286 8407	.039 464 1061	12.006 698 6743	.083 286 8407	42
43	27.366 640 4238	329.583 005 2972	.003 034 1370	.036 540 8389	12.043 239 5133	.083 034 1370	43
44	29.555 971 6577	356.949 645 7210	.002 801 5156	.033 834 1101	12.077 073 6234	.082 801 5156	44
45	31.920 449 3903	386.505 617 3787	.002 587 2845	.031 327 8797	12.108 401 5032	.082 587 2845	45
46	34.474 085 3415	418.426 066 7690	.002 389 9085	.029 007 2961	12.137 408 7992	.082 389 9085	46
47	37.232 012 1688	452.900 152 1105	.002 207 9922	.026 858 6075	12.164 267 4067	.082 207 9922	47
48	40.210 573 1423	490.132 164 2793	.002 040 2660	.024 869 0810	12.189 136 4877	.082 040 2660	48
49	43.427 418 9937	530.342 737 4217	.001 885 5731	.023 026 9268	12.212 163 4145	.081 885 5731	49
50	46.901 612 5132	573.770 156 4154	.001 742 8582	.021 321 2286	12.233 484 6431	.081 742 8582	50
51	50.653 741 5183	620.671 768 9286	.001 611 1575	.019 741 8783	12.253 226 5214	.081 611 1575	51
52	54.706 040 8354	671.325 510 4429	.001 489 5903	.018 279 5169	12.271 506 0383	.081 489 5903	52
53	59.082 524 1023	726.031 551 2783	.001 377 3506	.016 925 4786	12.288 431 5169	.081 377 3506	53
54	63.809 126 0304	785.114 075 3806	.001 273 7003	.015 671 7395	12.304 103 2564	.081 273 7003	54
55	68.913 856 1129	848.923 201 4111	.001 177 9629	.014 510 8699	12.318 614 1263	.081 177 9629	55
56	74.426 964 6019	917.837 057 5239	.001 089 5180	.013 435 9906	12.332 050 1170	.081 089 5180	56
57	80.381 121 7701	992.264 022 1259	.001 007 7963	.012 440 7320	12.344 490 8490	.081 007 7963	57
58	86.811 611 5117	1072.645 143 8959	.000 932 2748	.011 519 1964	12.356 010 0454	.080 932 2748	58
59	93.756 540 4326	1159.456 755 4076	.000 862 4729	.010 665 9226	12.366 675 9680	.080 862 4729	59
60	101.257 063 6672	1253.213 295 8402	.000 797 9488	.009 875 8542	12.376 551 8222	.080 797 9488	60
61	109.357 628 7606	1354.470 359 5074	.000 738 2960	.009 144 3095	12.385 696 1317	.080 738 2960	61
62	118.106 239 0614	1463.827 988 2680	.000 683 1404	.008 466 9532	12.394 163 0849	.080 683 1404	62
63	127.554 738 1864	1581.934 227 3295	.000 632 1375	.007 839 7715	12.402 002 8564	.080 632 1375	63
64	137.759 117 2413	1709.488 965 5158	.000 584 9701	.007 259 0477	12.409 261 9040	.080 584 9701	64
65	148.779 846 6206	1847.248 082 7521	.000 541 3458	.006 721 3404	12.415 983 2445	.080 541 3458	65
66	160.682 234 3502	1996.027 929 3777	.000 500 9950	.006 223 4634	12.422 206 7079	.080 500 9950	66
67	173.536 813 0982	2156.710 163 7279	.000 463 6692	.005 762 4661	12.427 969 1739	.080 463 6692	67
68	187.419 758 1461	2330.246 976 8261	.000 429 1391	.005 335 6167	12.433 304 7907	.080 429 1391	68
69	202.413 338 7978	2517.666 734 9722	.000 397 1932	.004 940 3859	12.438 245 1766	.080 397 1932	69
70	218.606 405 9016	2720.080 073 7700	.000 367 6362	.004 574 4314	12.442 819 6079	.080 367 6362	70
71	236.094 918 3737	2938.686 479 6716	.000 340 2881	.004 235 5846	12.447 055 1925	.080 340 2881	71
72	254.982 511 8436	3174.781 398 0453	.000 314 9823	.003 921 8376	12.450 977 0301	.080 314 9823	72
73	275.381 112 7911	3429.763 909 8889	.000 291 5653	.003 631 3311	12.454 608 3612	.080 291 5653	73
74	297.411 601 8144	3705.145 022 6800	.000 269 8950	.003 362 3436	12.457 970 7048	.080 269 8950	74
75	321.204 529 9596	4002.556 624 4944	.000 249 8403	.003 113 2811	12.461 083 9860	.080 249 8403	75
76	346.900 892 3563	4323.761 154 4540	.000 231 2801	.002 882 6677	12.463 966 6537	.080 231 2801	76
77	374.652 963 7448	4670.662 046 8103	.000 214 1024	.002 669 1368	12.466 635 7904	.080 214 1024	77
78	404.625 200 8444	5045.315 010 5551	.000 198 2037	.002 471 4229	12.469 107 2134	.080 198 2037	78
79	436.995 216 9120	5449.940 211 3995	.000 183 4883	.002 288 3546	12.471 395 5679	.080 183 4883	79
80	471.954 834 2649	5886.935 428 3115	.000 169 8677	.002 118 8468	12.473 514 4147	.080 169 8677	80
81	509.711 221 0061	6358.890 262 5764	.000 157 2601	.001 961 8952	12.475 476 3099	.080 157 2601	81
82	550.488 118 6866	6868.601 483 5825	.000 145 5900	.001 816 5696	12.477 292 8796	.080 145 5900	82
83	594.527 168 1815	7419.089 602 2691	.000 134 7874	.001 682 0089	12.478 974 8885	.080 134 7874	83
84	642.089 341 6361	8013.616 770 4506	.000 124 7876	.001 557 4157	12.480 532 3042	.080 124 7876	84
85	693.456 488 9669	8655.706 112 0867	.000 115 5307	.001 442 0515	12.481 974 3557	.080 115 5307	85
86	748.933 008 0843	9349.162 601 0536	.000 106 9615	.001 335 2329	12.483 309 5886	.080 106 9615	86
87	808.847 648 7310	10098.095 609 1379	.000 099 0286	.001 236 3268	12.484 545 9154	.080 099 0286	87
88	873.555 460 6295	10906.943 257 8690	.000 091 6847	.001 144 7470	12.485 690 6624	.080 091 6847	88
89	943.439 897 4799	11780.498 718 4985	.000 084 8860	.001 059 9509	12.486 750 6133	.080 084 8860	89
90	1018.915 089 2783	12723.938 615 9783	.000 078 5920	.000 981 4360	12.487 732 0494	.080 078 5920	90
91	1100.428 296 4205	13742.853 705 2566	.000 072 7651	.000 908 7371	12.488 640 7865	.080 072 7651	91
92	1188.462 560 1342	14843.282 001 6771	.000 067 3705	.000 841 4232	12.489 482 2097	.080 067 3705	92
93	1283.539 564 9449	16031.744 561 8113	.000 062 3762	.000 779 0956	12.490 261 3053	.080 062 3762	93
94	1386.222 730 1405	17315.284 126 7562	.000 057 7524	.000 721 3848	12.490 982 6901	.080 057 7524	94
95	1497.120 548 5517	18701.506 856 8967	.000 053 4716	.000 667 9489	12.491 650 6389	.080 053 4716	95
96	1616.890 192 4359	20198.627 405 4485	.000 049 5083	.000 618 4712	12.492 269 1101	.080 049 5083	96
97	1746.241 407 8307	21815.517 597 8843	.000 045 8389	.000 572 6585	12.492 841 7686	.080 045 8389	97
98	1885.940 720 4572	23561.759 005 7151	.000 042 4417	.000 530 2394	12.493 372 0080	.080 042 4417	98
99	2036.815 978 0938	25447.699 726 1723	.000 039 2963	.000 490 9624	12.493 862 9704	.080 039 2963	99
100	2199.761 256 3413	27484.515 704 2661	.000 036 3841	.000 454 5948	12.494 317 5652	.080 036 3841	100

RATE 9% / PERIODS	XIV COMPOUND AMOUNT — AMOUNT OF 1 — How $1 left at compound interest will grow.	XV AMOUNT OF ANNUITY — AMOUNT OF 1 PER PERIOD — How $1 deposited periodically will grow.	XVI SINKING FUND — SINKING FUND — Periodic deposit that will grow to $1 at future date	XVII PRESENT VALUE — PRESENT WORTH OF 1 — What $1 due in the future is worth today.	XVIII PRESENT VALUE OF ANNUITY — PRESENT WORTH OF 1 PER PERIOD — What $1 payable periodically is worth today.	XIX AMORTIZATION — PARTIAL PAYMENT — Annuity worth $1 today. Periodic payment necessary to pay off a loan of $1	PERIODS
1	1.090 000 0000	1.000 000 0000	1.000 000 0000	.917 431 1927	.917 431 1927	1.090 000 0000	1
2	1.188 100 0000	2.090 000 0000	.478 468 8995	.841 679 9933	1.759 111 1859	.568 468 8995	2
3	1.295 029 0000	3.278 100 0000	.305 054 7573	.772 183 4801	2.531 294 6660	.395 054 7573	3
4	1.411 581 6100	4.573 129 0000	.218 668 6621	708 425 2111	3.239 719 8771	.308 668 6621	4
5	1.538 623 9549	5.984 710 6100	.167 092 4570	.649 931 3863	3.889 651 2634	.257 092 4570	5
6	1.677 100 1108	7.523 334 5649	.132 919 7833	.596 267 3265	4.485 918 5902	.222 919 7833	6
7	1.828 039 1208	9.200 434 6757	.108 690 5168	.547 034 2448	5.032 952 8351	.198 690 5168	7
8	1.992 562 6417	11.028 473 7966	.090 674 3778	.501 866 2797	5.534 819 1147	.180 674 3778	8
9	2.171 893 2794	13.021 036 4382	.076 798 8021	.460 427 7795	5.995 246 8943	.166 798 8021	9
10	2.367 363 6746	15.192 929 7177	.065 820 0899	.422 410 8069	6.417 657 7012	.155 820 0899	10
11	2.580 426 4053	17.560 293 3923	.056 946 6567	.387 532 8504	6.805 190 5515	.146 946 6567	11
12	2.812 664 7818	20.140 719 7976	.049 650 6585	.355 534 7251	7.160 725 2766	.139 650 6585	12
13	3.065 804 6121	22.953 384 5794	.043 566 5597	.326 178 6469	7.486 903 9235	.133 566 5597	13
14	3.341 727 0272	26.019 189 1915	.038 433 1730	.299 246 4650	7.786 150 3885	.128 433 1730	14
15	3.642 482 4597	29.360 916 2188	.034 058 8827	.274 538 0413	8.060 688 4299	.124 058 8827	15
16	3.970 305 8811	33.003 398 6784	.030 299 9097	.251 869 7627	8.312 558 1925	.120 299 9097	16
17	4.327 633 4104	36.973 704 5595	.027 046 2485	.231 073 1768	8.543 631 3693	.117 046 2485	17
18	4.717 120 4173	41.301 337 9699	.024 212 2907	.211 993 7402	8.755 625 1094	.114 212 2907	18
19	5.141 661 2548	46.018 458 3871	.021 730 4107	.194 489 6699	8.950 114 7793	.111 730 4107	19
20	5.604 410 7678	51.160 119 6420	.019 546 4750	.178 430 8898	9.128 545 6691	.109 546 4750	20
21	6.108 807 7369	56.764 530 4098	.017 616 6348	.163 698 0640	9.292 243 7331	.107 616 6348	21
22	6.658 600 4332	62.873 338 1466	.015 904 9930	.150 181 7101	9.442 425 4432	.105 904 9930	22
23	7.257 874 4722	69.531 938 5798	.014 381 8800	.137 781 3854	9.580 206 8286	.104 381 8800	23
24	7.911 083 1747	76.789 813 0520	.013 022 5607	.126 404 9408	9.706 611 7694	.103 022 5607	24
25	8.623 080 6604	84.700 896 2267	.011 806 2505	.115 967 8356	9.822 579 6049	.101 806 2505	25
26	9.399 157 9198	93.323 976 8871	.010 715 3599	.106 392 5097	9.928 972 1146	.100 715 3599	26
27	10.245 082 1326	102.723 134 8069	.009 734 9054	.097 607 8070	10.026 579 9217	.099 734 9054	27
28	11.167 139 5246	112.968 216 9396	.008 852 0473	.089 548 4468	10.116 128 3685	.098 852 0473	28
29	12.172 182 0818	124.135 356 4641	.008 055 7226	.082 154 5384	10.198 282 9069	.098 055 7226	29
30	13.267 678 4691	136.307 538 5459	.007 336 3514	.075 371 1501	10.273 654 0430	.097 336 3514	30
31	14.461 769 5314	149.575 217 0150	.006 685 5995	.069 147 8313	10.342 801 8743	.096 685 5995	31
32	15.763 328 7892	164.036 986 5464	.006 096 1861	.063 438 3773	10.406 240 2517	.096 096 1861	32
33	17.182 028 3802	179.800 315 3356	.005 561 7255	.058 200 3462	10.464 440 5979	.095 561 7255	33
34	18.728 410 9344	196.982 343 7158	.005 076 5971	.053 394 8130	10.517 835 4109	.095 076 5971	34
35	20.413 967 9185	215.710 754 6502	.004 635 8375	.048 986 0670	10.566 821 4779	.094 635 8375	35
36	22.251 225 0312	236.124 722 5687	.004 235 0500	.044 941 3459	10.611 762 8237	.094 235 0500	36
37	24.253 835 2840	258.375 947 5999	.003 870 3293	.041 230 5925	10.652 993 4163	.093 870 3293	37
38	26.436 680 4595	282.629 782 8839	.003 538 1975	.037 826 2317	10.690 819 6480	.093 538 1975	38
39	28.815 981 7009	309.066 463 3434	.003 235 5500	.034 702 9648	10.725 522 6128	.093 235 5500	39
40	31.409 420 0540	337.882 445 0443	.002 959 6092	.031 837 5824	10.757 360 1952	.092 959 6092	40
41	34.236 267 8588	369.291 865 0983	.002 707 8853	.029 208 7912	10.786 568 9865	.092 707 8853	41
42	37.317 531 9661	403.528 132 9572	.002 478 1420	.026 797 0562	10.813 366 0426	.092 478 1420	42
43	40.676 109 8431	440.845 664 9233	.002 268 3675	.024 584 4552	10.837 950 4978	.092 268 3675	43
44	44.336 959 7290	481.521 774 7664	.002 076 7493	.022 554 5461	10.860 505 0439	.092 076 7493	44
45	48.327 286 1046	525.858 734 4954	.001 901 6514	.020 692 2441	10.881 197 2880	.091 901 6514	45
46	52.676 741 8540	574.186 020 6000	.001 741 5959	.018 983 7102	10.900 180 9981	.091 741 5959	46
47	57.417 648 6209	626.862 762 4540	.001 595 2455	.017 416 2479	10.917 597 2460	.091 595 2455	47
48	62.585 236 9967	684.280 411 0748	.001 461 3892	.015 978 2090	10.933 575 4550	.091 461 3892	48
49	68.217 908 3264	746.865 648 0716	.001 338 9289	.014 658 9074	10.948 234 3624	.091 338 9289	49
50	74.357 520 0758	815.083 556 3980	.001 226 8681	.013 448 5389	10.961 682 9013	.091 226 8681	50
51	81.049 696 8826	889.441 076 4738	.001 124 3016	.012 338 1091	10.974 021 0104	.091 124 3016	51
52	88.344 169 6021	970.490 773 3565	.001 030 4065	.011 319 3661	10.985 340 3765	.091 030 4065	52
53	96.295 144 8663	1058.834 942 9585	.000 944 4343	.010 384 7396	10.995 725 1160	.090 944 4343	53
54	104.961 707 9042	1155.130 087 8248	.000 865 7034	.009 527 2840	11.005 252 4000	.090 865 7034	54
55	114.408 261 6156	1260.091 795 7290	.000 793 5930	.008 740 6275	11.013 993 0276	.090 793 5930	55
56	124.705 005 1610	1374.500 057 3447	.000 727 5373	.008 018 9243	11.022 011 9519	.090 727 5373	56
57	135.928 455 6255	1499.205 062 5057	.000 667 0202	.007 356 8113	11.029 368 7632	.090 667 0202	57
58	148.162 016 6318	1635.133 518 1312	.000 611 5709	.006 749 3682	11.036 118 1314	.090 611 5709	58
59	161.496 598 1287	1783.295 534 7630	.000 560 7595	.006 192 0809	11.042 310 2123	.090 560 7595	59
60	176.031 291 9602	1944.792 132 8917	.000 514 1938	.005 680 8002	11.047 991 0204	.090 514 1938	60
61	191.874 108 2367	2120.823 424 8519	.000 471 5150	.005 211 7506	11.053 202 7710	.090 471 5150	61
62	209.142 777 9780	2312.697 533 0886	.000 432 3955	.004 781 4226	11.057 984 1936	.090 432 3955	62
63	227.965 627 9960	2521.840 311 0665	.000 396 5358	.004 386 6262	11.062 370 8198	.090 396 5358	63
64	248.482 534 5156	2749.805 939 0625	.000 363 6620	.004 024 4277	11.066 395 2475	.090 363 6620	64
65	270.845 962 6220	2998.288 473 5782	.000 333 5236	.003 692 1355	11.070 087 3831	.090 333 5236	65
66	295.222 099 2580	3269.134 436 2002	.000 305 8914	.003 387 2803	11.073 474 6634	.090 305 8914	66
67	321.792 088 1912	3564.356 535 4582	.000 280 5555	.003 107 5966	11.076 582 2600	.090 280 5555	67
68	350.753 376 1285	3886.148 623 6495	.000 257 3242	.002 851 0061	11.079 433 2660	.090 257 3242	68
69	382.321 179 9800	4236.901 999 7779	.000 236 0215	.002 615 6019	11.082 048 8679	.090 236 0215	69
70	416.730 086 1782	4619.223 179 7579	.000 216 4866	.002 399 6348	11.084 448 5027	.090 216 4866	70
71	454.235 793 9343	5035.953 265 9361	.000 198 5721	.002 201 4998	11.086 650 0025	.090 198 5721	71
72	495.117 015 3883	5490.189 059 8704	.000 182 1431	.002 019 7246	11.088 669 7270	.090 182 1431	72
73	539.677 546 7733	5985.306 075 2587	.000 167 0758	.001 852 9583	11.090 522 6853	.090 167 0758	73
74	588.248 525 9829	6524.983 622 0320	.000 153 2571	.001 699 9618	11.092 222 6471	.090 153 2571	74
75	641.190 893 3213	7113.232 148 0149	.000 140 5831	.001 559 5979	11.093 782 2450	.090 140 5831	75
76	698.898 073 7203	7754.423 041 3362	.000 128 9587	.001 430 8238	11.095 213 0689	.090 128 9587	76
77	761.798 900 3551	8453.321 115 0565	.000 118 2967	.001 312 6824	11.096 525 7512	.090 118 2967	77
78	830.360 801 3870	9215.120 015 4116	.000 108 5173	.001 204 2958	11.097 730 0470	.090 108 5173	78
79	905.093 273 5119	10045.480 816 7986	.000 099 5473	.001 104 8585	11.098 834 9055	.090 099 5473	79
80	986.551 668 1279	10950.574 090 3105	.000 091 3194	.001 013 6317	11.099 848 5372	.090 091 3194	80
81	1075.341 318 2595	11937.125 758 4384	.000 083 7723	.000 929 9373	11.100 778 4745	.090 083 7723	81
82	1172.122 036 9028	13012.467 076 6979	.000 076 8494	.000 853 1535	11.101 631 6280	.090 076 8494	82
83	1277.613 020 2241	14184.589 113 6007	.000 070 4990	.000 782 7096	11.102 414 3376	.090 070 4990	83
84	1392.598 192 0442	15462.202 133 8247	.000 064 6738	.000 718 0822	11.103 132 4198	.090 064 6738	84
85	1517.932 029 3282	16854.800 325 8690	.000 059 3303	.000 658 7910	11.103 791 2108	.090 059 3303	85
86	1654.545 911 9677	18372.732 355 1972	.000 054 4285	.000 604 3954	11.104 395 6063	.090 054 4285	86
87	1803.455 044 0448	20027.278 267 1649	.000 049 9319	.000 554 4912	11.104 950 0975	.090 049 9319	87
88	1965.765 998 0089	21830.733 311 2098	.000 045 8070	.000 508 7075	11.105 458 8050	.090 045 8070	88
89	2142.684 937 8297	23796.499 309 2187	.000 042 0230	.000 466 7042	11.105 925 5092	.090 042 0230	89
90	2335.526 582 2343	25939.184 247 0483	.000 038 5517	.000 428 1690	11.106 353 6782	.090 038 5517	90
91	2545.723 974 6354	28274.710 829 2827	.000 035 3673	.000 392 8156	11.106 746 4937	.090 035 3673	91
92	2774.839 132 3526	30820.434 803 9181	.000 032 4460	.000 360 3813	11.107 106 8750	.090 032 4460	92
93	3024.574 654 2644	33595.273 936 2708	.000 029 7661	.000 330 6250	11.107 437 5000	.090 029 7661	93
94	3296.786 373 1482	36619.848 590 5351	.000 027 3076	.000 303 3257	11.107 740 8257	.090 027 3076	94
95	3593.497 146 7315	39916.634 963 6833	.000 025 0522	.000 278 2804	11.108 019 1060	.090 025 0522	95
96	3916.911 889 9373	43510.132 110 4148	.000 022 9832	.000 255 3032	11.108 274 4093	.090 022 9832	96
97	4269.433 960 0317	47427.044 000 3521	.000 021 0850	.000 234 2231	11.108 508 6324	.090 021 0850	97
98	4653.683 016 4345	51696.477 960 3838	.000 019 3437	.000 214 8836	11.108 723 5159	.090 019 3437	98
99	5072.514 487 9137	56350.160 976 8183	.000 017 7462	.000 197 1409	11.108 920 6568	.090 017 7462	99
100	5529.040 791 8259	61422.675 464 7320	.000 016 2806	.000 180 8632	11.109 101 5200	.090 016 2806	100

TABLE XX: INTEREST FROM DAY OF DEPOSIT[a]

At 5% Compounded Daily (for one quarter)

Quarter	1st Month	2nd Month	3rd Month
1st	January	February	March
2nd	April	May	June
3rd	July	August	September
4th	October	November	December

	1ST MONTH			2ND MONTH			3RD MONTH	
Dep. Date	Factor		Dep. Date	Factor		Dep. Date	Factor	
1	0.0125	7757	1	0.0083	6757	1	0.0041	7507
2	0.0124	3696	2	0.0082	2754	2	0.0040	3562
3	0.0122	9636	3	0.0080	8753	3	0.0038	9619
4	0.0121	5578	4	0.0079	4753	4	0.0037	5678
5	0.0120	1523	5	0.0078	0756	5	0.0036	1739
6	0.0118	7469	6	0.0076	6761	6	0.0034	7802
7	0.0117	3417	7	0.0075	2767	7	0.0033	3866
8	0.0115	9367	8	0.0073	8776	8	0.0031	9933
9	0.0114	5319	9	0.0072	4786	9	0.0030	6002
10	0.0113	1273	10	0.0071	0798	10	0.0029	2072
11	0.0111	7229	11	0.0069	6813	11	0.0027	8145
12	0.0110	3187	12	0.0068	2829	12	0.0026	4219
13	0.0108	9147	13	0.0066	8847	13	0.0025	0295
14	0.0107	5108	14	0.0065	4867	14	0.0023	6374
15	0.0106	1072	15	0.0064	0890	15	0.0022	2454
16	0.0104	7038	16	0.0062	6914	16	0.0020	8536
17	0.0103	3006	17	0.0061	2940	17	0.0019	4620
18	0.0101	8975	18	0.0059	8968	18	0.0018	0706
19	0.0100	4947	19	0.0058	4997	19	0.0016	6794
20	0.0099	0920	20	0.0057	1029	20	0.0015	2884
21	0.0097	6896	21	0.0055	7063	21	0.0013	8976
22	0.0096	2873	22	0.0054	3099	22	0.0012	5069
23	0.0094	8852	23	0.0052	9136	23	0.0011	1165
24	0.0093	4834	24	0.0051	5176	24	0.0009	7263
25	0.0092	0817	25	0.0050	1217	25	0.0008	3362
26	0.0090	6802	26	0.0048	7261	26	0.0006	9464
27	0.0089	2789	27	0.0047	3306	27	0.0005	5567
28	0.0087	8778	28	0.0045	9353	28	0.0004	1672
29	0.0086	4769	29	0.0044	5403	29	0.0002	7780
30	0.0085	0762	30	0.0043	1454	30	0.0001	3889

[a] Tables for interest compounded daily are reprinted here through the courtesy of California Federal Savings and Loan Association.

TABLE XXI: INTEREST TO DATE OF WITHDRAWAL[a]

At 5% Compounded Daily (for one quarter)

	1ST MONTH			2ND MONTH			3RD MONTH	
W/D			*W/D*			*W/D*		
Date	*Factor*		*Date*	*Factor*		*Date*	*Factor*	
1	0.0001	3889	1	0.0043	1454	1	0.0085	0762
2	0.0002	7780	2	0.0044	5403	2	0.0086	4769
3	0.0004	1672	3	0.0045	9353	3	0.0087	8778
4	0.0005	5567	4	0.0047	3306	4	0.0089	2789
5	0.0006	9464	5	0.0048	7261	5	0.0090	6802
6	0.0008	3362	6	0.0050	1217	6	0.0092	0817
7	0.0009	7263	7	0.0051	5176	7	0.0093	4834
8	0.0011	1165	8	0.0052	9136	8	0.0094	8852
9	0.0012	5069	9	0.0054	3099	9	0.0096	2873
10	0.0013	8976	10	0.0055	7063	10	0.0097	6896
11	0.0015	2884	11	0.0057	1029	11	0.0099	0920
12	0.0016	6794	12	0.0058	4997	12	0.0100	4947
13	0.0018	0706	13	0.0059	8968	13	0.0101	8975
14	0.0019	4620	14	0.0061	2940	14	0.0103	3006
15	0.0020	8536	15	0.0062	6914	15	0.0104	7038
16	0.0022	2454	16	0.0064	0890	16	0.0106	1072
17	0.0023	6374	17	0.0065	4867	17	0.0107	5108
18	0.0025	0295	18	0.0066	8847	18	0.0108	9147
19	0.0026	4219	19	0.0068	2829	19	0.0110	3187
20	0.0027	8145	20	0.0069	6813	20	0.0111	7229
21	0.0029	2072	21	0.0071	0798	21	0.0113	1273
22	0.0030	6002	22	0.0072	4786	22	0.0114	5319
23	0.0031	9933	23	0.0073	8776	23	0.0115	9367
24	0.0033	3866	24	0.0075	2767	24	0.0117	3417
25	0.0034	7802	25	0.0076	6761	25	0.0118	7469
26	0.0036	1739	26	0.0078	0756	26	0.0120	1523
27	0.0037	5678	27	0.0079	4753	27	0.0121	5578
28	0.0038	9619	28	0.0080	8753	28	0.0122	9636
29	0.0040	3562	29	0.0082	2754	29	0.0124	3696
30	0.0041	7507	30	0.0083	6757	30	0.0125	7757

[a] Tables for interest compounded daily are reprinted here through the courtesy of California Federal Savings and Loan Association.

TABLE XXII: ANNUAL PERCENTAGE RATE TABLE FOR MONTHLY PAYMENT PLANS

Number of Payments	ANNUAL PERCENTAGE RATE															
	10.00%	10.25%	10.50%	10.75%	11.00%	11.25%	11.50%	11.75%	12.00%	12.25%	12.50%	12.75%	13.00%	13.25%	13.50%	13.75%
	FINANCE CHARGE PER $100 OF AMOUNT FINANCED															
1	0.83	0.85	0.87	0.90	0.92	0.94	0.96	0.98	1.00	1.02	1.04	1.06	1.08	1.10	1.12	1.15
2	1.25	1.28	1.31	1.35	1.38	1.41	1.44	1.47	1.50	1.53	1.57	1.60	1.63	1.66	1.69	1.73
3	1.67	1.71	1.76	1.80	1.84	1.88	1.92	1.96	2.01	2.05	2.09	2.13	2.17	2.22	2.26	2.30
4	2.09	2.14	2.20	2.25	2.30	2.35	2.41	2.46	2.51	2.57	2.62	2.67	2.72	2.78	2.83	2.88
5	2.51	2.58	2.64	2.70	2.77	2.83	2.89	2.96	3.02	3.08	3.15	3.21	3.27	3.34	3.40	3.46
6	2.94	3.01	3.08	3.16	3.23	3.31	3.38	3.45	3.53	3.60	3.68	3.75	3.83	3.90	3.97	4.05
7	3.36	3.45	3.53	3.62	3.70	3.78	3.87	3.95	4.04	4.12	4.21	4.29	4.38	4.47	4.55	4.64
8	3.79	3.88	3.98	4.07	4.17	4.26	4.36	4.46	4.55	4.65	4.74	4.84	4.94	5.03	5.13	5.22
9	4.21	4.32	4.43	4.53	4.64	4.75	4.85	4.96	5.07	5.17	5.28	5.39	5.49	5.60	5.71	5.82
10	4.64	4.76	4.88	4.99	5.11	5.23	5.35	5.46	5.58	5.70	5.82	5.94	6.05	6.17	6.29	6.41
11	5.07	5.20	5.33	5.45	5.58	5.71	5.84	5.97	6.10	6.23	6.36	6.49	6.62	6.75	6.88	7.01
12	5.50	5.64	5.78	5.92	6.06	6.20	6.34	6.48	6.62	6.76	6.90	7.04	7.18	7.32	7.46	7.60
13	5.93	6.08	6.23	6.38	6.53	6.68	6.84	6.99	7.14	7.29	7.44	7.59	7.75	7.90	8.05	8.20
14	6.36	6.52	6.69	6.85	7.01	7.17	7.34	7.50	7.66	7.82	7.99	8.15	8.31	8.48	8.64	8.81
15	6.80	6.97	7.14	7.32	7.49	7.66	7.84	8.01	8.19	8.36	8.53	8.71	8.88	9.06	9.23	9.41
16	7.23	7.41	7.60	7.78	7.97	8.15	8.34	8.53	8.71	8.90	9.08	9.27	9.46	9.64	9.83	10.02
17	7.67	7.86	8.06	8.25	8.45	8.65	8.84	9.04	9.24	9.44	9.63	9.83	10.03	10.23	10.43	10.63
18	8.10	8.31	8.52	8.73	8.93	9.14	9.35	9.56	9.77	9.98	10.19	10.40	10.61	10.82	11.03	11.24
19	8.54	8.76	8.98	9.20	9.42	9.64	9.86	10.08	10.30	10.52	10.74	10.96	11.18	11.41	11.63	11.85
20	8.98	9.21	9.44	9.67	9.90	10.13	10.37	10.60	10.83	11.06	11.30	11.53	11.76	12.00	12.23	12.46
21	9.42	9.66	9.90	10.15	10.39	10.63	10.88	11.12	11.36	11.61	11.85	12.10	12.34	12.59	12.84	13.08
22	9.86	10.12	10.37	10.62	10.88	11.13	11.39	11.64	11.90	12.16	12.41	12.67	12.93	13.19	13.44	13.70
23	10.30	10.57	10.84	11.10	11.37	11.63	11.90	12.17	12.44	12.71	12.97	13.24	13.51	13.78	14.05	14.32
24	10.75	11.02	11.30	11.58	11.86	12.14	12.42	12.70	12.98	13.26	13.54	13.82	14.10	14.38	14.66	14.95
25	11.19	11.48	11.77	12.06	12.35	12.64	12.93	13.22	13.52	13.81	14.10	14.40	14.69	14.98	15.28	15.57
26	11.64	11.94	12.24	12.54	12.85	13.15	13.45	13.75	14.06	14.36	14.67	14.97	15.28	15.59	15.89	16.20
27	12.09	12.40	12.71	13.03	13.34	13.66	13.97	14.29	14.60	14.92	15.24	15.56	15.87	16.19	16.51	16.83
28	12.53	12.86	13.18	13.51	13.84	14.16	14.49	14.82	15.15	15.48	15.81	16.14	16.47	16.80	17.13	17.46
29	12.98	13.32	13.66	14.00	14.33	14.67	15.01	15.35	15.70	16.04	16.38	16.72	17.07	17.41	17.75	18.10
30	13.43	13.78	14.13	14.48	14.83	15.19	15.54	15.89	16.24	16.60	16.95	17.31	17.66	18.02	18.38	18.74
31	13.89	14.25	14.61	14.97	15.33	15.70	16.06	16.43	16.79	17.16	17.53	17.90	18.27	18.63	19.00	19.38
32	14.34	14.71	15.09	15.46	15.84	16.21	16.59	16.97	17.35	17.73	18.11	18.49	18.87	19.25	19.63	20.02
33	14.79	15.18	15.57	15.95	16.34	16.73	17.12	17.51	17.90	18.29	18.65	19.08	19.47	19.87	20.26	20.66
34	15.25	15.65	16.05	16.44	16.85	17.25	17.65	18.05	18.46	18.86	19.27	19.67	20.08	20.49	20.90	21.31
35	15.70	16.11	16.53	16.94	17.35	17.77	18.18	18.60	19.01	19.43	19.85	20.27	20.69	21.11	21.53	21.95
36	16.16	16.58	17.01	17.43	17.86	18.29	18.71	19.14	19.57	20.00	20.43	20.87	21.30	21.73	22.17	22.60
37	16.62	17.06	17.49	17.93	18.37	18.81	19.25	19.69	20.13	20.58	21.02	21.46	21.91	22.36	22.81	23.25
38	17.08	17.53	17.98	18.43	18.88	19.33	19.78	20.24	20.69	21.15	21.61	22.07	22.52	22.99	23.45	23.91
39	17.54	18.00	18.46	18.93	19.39	19.86	20.32	20.79	21.26	21.73	22.20	22.67	23.14	23.61	24.09	24.56
40	18.00	18.48	18.95	19.43	19.90	20.38	20.86	21.34	21.82	22.30	22.79	23.27	23.76	24.25	24.73	25.22
41	18.47	18.95	19.44	19.93	20.42	20.91	21.40	21.89	22.39	22.88	23.38	23.88	24.38	24.88	25.38	25.88
42	18.93	19.43	19.93	20.43	20.93	21.44	21.94	22.45	22.96	23.47	23.98	24.49	25.00	25.51	26.03	26.55
43	19.40	19.91	20.42	20.94	21.45	21.97	22.49	23.01	23.53	24.05	24.57	25.10	25.62	26.15	26.68	27.21
44	19.86	20.39	20.91	21.44	21.97	22.50	23.03	23.57	24.10	24.64	25.17	25.71	26.25	26.79	27.33	27.88
45	20.33	20.87	21.41	21.95	22.49	23.03	23.58	24.12	24.67	25.22	25.77	26.32	26.88	27.43	27.99	28.55
46	20.80	21.35	21.90	22.46	23.01	23.57	24.13	24.69	25.25	25.81	26.37	26.94	27.51	28.08	28.65	29.22
47	21.27	21.83	22.40	22.97	23.53	24.10	24.68	25.25	25.82	26.40	26.98	27.56	28.14	28.72	29.31	29.89
48	21.74	22.32	22.90	23.48	24.06	24.64	25.23	25.81	26.40	26.99	27.58	28.18	28.77	29.37	29.97	30.57
49	22.21	22.80	23.39	23.99	24.58	25.18	25.78	26.38	26.98	27.59	28.19	28.80	29.41	30.02	30.63	31.34
50	22.69	23.29	23.89	24.50	25.11	25.72	26.33	26.95	27.56	28.18	28.80	29.42	30.04	30.67	31.29	31.92
51	23.16	23.78	24.40	25.02	25.64	26.26	26.89	27.52	28.15	28.78	29.41	30.05	30.68	31.32	31.96	32.60
52	23.64	24.27	24.90	25.53	26.17	26.81	27.45	28.09	28.73	29.38	30.02	30.67	31.32	31.98	32.63	33.29
53	24.11	24.76	25.40	26.05	26.70	27.35	28.00	28.66	29.32	29.98	30.64	31.30	31.97	32.63	33.30	33.97
54	24.59	25.25	25.91	26.57	27.23	27.90	28.56	29.23	29.91	30.58	31.25	31.93	32.61	33.29	33.98	34.66
55	25.07	25.74	26.41	27.09	27.77	28.44	29.13	29.81	30.50	31.18	31.87	32.56	33.26	33.95	34.65	35.35
56	25.55	26.23	26.92	27.61	28.30	28.99	29.69	30.39	31.09	31.79	32.49	33.20	33.91	34.62	35.33	36.04
57	26.03	26.73	27.43	28.13	28.84	29.54	30.25	30.97	31.68	32.39	33.11	33.83	34.56	35.28	36.01	36.74
58	26.51	27.23	27.94	28.66	29.37	30.10	30.82	31.55	32.27	33.00	33.74	34.47	35.21	35.95	36.69	37.43
59	27.00	27.72	28.45	29.18	29.91	30.65	31.39	32.13	32.87	33.61	34.36	35.11	35.86	36.62	37.37	38.13
60	27.48	28.22	28.96	29.71	30.45	31.20	31.96	32.71	33.47	34.23	34.99	35.75	36.52	37.29	38.06	38.83

TABLE XXII: ANNUAL PERCENTAGE RATE TABLE FOR MONTHLY PAYMENT PLANS
(CONTINUED)

Number of Payments	ANNUAL PERCENTAGE RATE															
	14.00%	14.25%	14.50%	14.75%	15.00%	15.25%	15.50%	15.75%	16.00%	16.25%	16.50%	16.75%	17.00%	17.25%	17.50%	17.75%
	FINANCE CHARGE PER $100 OF AMOUNT FINANCED															
1	1.17	1.19	1.21	1.23	1.25	1.27	1.29	1.31	1.33	1.35	1.37	1.40	1.42	1.44	1.46	1.48
2	1.75	1.78	1.82	1.85	1.88	1.91	1.94	1.97	2.00	2.04	2.07	2.10	2.13	2.16	2.19	2.22
3	2.34	2.38	2.43	2.47	2.51	2.55	2.59	2.64	2.68	2.72	2.76	2.80	2.85	2.89	2.93	2.97
4	2.93	2.99	3.04	3.09	3.14	3.20	3.25	3.30	3.36	3.41	3.46	3.51	3.57	3.62	3.67	3.73
5	3.53	3.59	3.65	3.72	3.78	3.84	3.91	3.97	4.04	4.10	4.16	4.23	4.29	4.35	4.42	4.48
6	4.12	4.20	4.27	4.35	4.42	4.49	4.57	4.64	4.72	4.79	4.87	4.94	5.02	5.09	5.17	5.24
7	4.72	4.81	4.89	4.98	5.06	5.15	5.23	5.32	5.40	5.49	5.58	5.66	5.75	5.83	5.92	6.00
8	5.32	5.42	5.51	5.61	5.71	5.80	5.90	6.00	6.09	6.19	6.29	6.38	6.48	6.58	6.67	6.77
9	5.92	6.03	6.14	6.25	6.35	6.46	6.57	6.68	6.78	6.89	7.00	7.11	7.22	7.32	7.43	7.54
10	6.53	6.65	6.77	6.88	7.00	7.12	7.24	7.36	7.48	7.60	7.72	7.84	7.96	8.08	8.19	8.31
11	7.14	7.27	7.40	7.53	7.66	7.79	7.92	8.05	8.18	8.31	8.44	8.57	8.70	8.83	8.96	9.09
12	7.74	7.89	8.03	8.17	8.31	8.45	8.59	8.74	8.88	9.02	9.16	9.30	9.45	9.59	9.73	9.87
13	8.36	8.51	8.66	8.81	8.97	9.12	9.27	9.43	9.58	9.73	9.89	10.04	10.20	10.35	10.50	10.66
14	8.97	9.13	9.30	9.46	9.63	9.79	9.96	10.12	10.29	10.45	10.62	10.78	10.95	11.11	11.28	11.45
15	9.59	9.76	9.94	10.11	10.29	10.47	10.64	10.82	11.00	11.17	11.35	11.51	11.71	11.88	12.06	12.24
16	10.20	10.39	10.58	10.77	10.95	11.14	11.33	11.52	11.71	11.90	12.09	12.28	12.46	12.65	12.84	13.03
17	10.82	11.02	11.22	11.42	11.62	11.82	12.02	12.22	12.42	12.62	12.83	13.03	13.23	13.43	13.63	13.83
18	11.45	11.66	11.87	12.08	12.29	12.50	12.72	12.93	13.14	13.35	13.57	13.78	13.99	14.21	14.42	14.64
19	12.07	12.30	12.52	12.74	12.97	13.19	13.41	13.64	13.86	14.09	14.31	14.54	14.76	14.99	15.22	15.44
20	12.70	12.93	13.17	13.41	13.64	13.88	14.11	14.35	14.59	14.82	15.06	15.30	15.54	15.77	16.01	16.25
21	13.33	13.58	13.82	14.07	14.32	14.57	14.82	15.06	15.31	15.56	15.81	16.05	16.31	16.56	16.81	17.07
22	13.96	14.22	14.48	14.74	15.00	15.26	15.52	15.78	16.04	16.30	16.57	16.83	17.09	17.36	17.62	17.88
23	14.59	14.87	15.14	15.41	15.68	15.96	16.23	16.50	16.78	17.05	17.32	17.60	17.88	18.15	18.43	18.70
24	15.23	15.51	15.80	16.08	16.37	16.65	16.94	17.22	17.51	17.80	18.09	18.37	18.65	18.95	19.24	19.53
25	15.87	16.17	16.46	16.76	17.06	17.35	17.65	17.95	18.25	18.55	18.85	19.15	19.45	19.75	20.05	20.36
26	16.51	16.82	17.13	17.44	17.75	18.06	18.37	18.68	18.99	19.30	19.62	19.93	20.24	20.56	20.87	21.19
27	17.15	17.47	17.80	18.12	18.44	18.76	19.09	19.41	19.74	20.06	20.39	20.71	21.04	21.37	21.69	22.02
28	17.80	18.13	18.47	18.80	19.14	19.47	19.81	20.15	20.48	20.82	21.16	21.50	21.84	22.18	22.52	22.86
29	18.45	18.79	19.14	19.49	19.83	20.18	20.53	20.88	21.23	21.58	21.94	22.29	22.64	22.99	23.35	23.70
30	19.10	19.45	19.81	20.17	20.54	20.90	21.26	21.62	21.99	22.35	22.72	23.08	23.45	23.81	24.18	24.55
31	19.75	20.12	20.49	20.87	21.24	21.61	21.99	22.37	22.74	23.12	23.50	23.88	24.26	24.64	25.02	25.40
32	20.40	20.79	21.17	21.56	21.95	22.33	22.72	23.11	23.50	23.89	23.28	24.68	25.07	25.46	25.86	26.25
33	21.06	21.46	21.85	22.25	22.65	23.06	23.46	23.86	24.26	24.67	25.07	25.48	25.88	26.29	26.70	27.11
34	21.72	22.13	22.54	22.95	23.37	23.78	24.19	24.61	25.03	25.44	25.86	26.28	26.70	27.12	27.54	27.97
35	22.38	22.80	23.23	23.65	24.08	24.51	24.94	25.36	25.79	26.23	26.66	27.09	27.52	27.96	28.39	28.83
36	23.04	23.48	23.92	24.35	24.80	25.24	25.68	26.12	26.57	27.01	27.46	27.90	28.35	28.80	29.25	29.70
37	23.70	24.16	24.61	25.06	25.51	25.97	26.42	26.88	27.34	27.80	28.26	28.72	29.18	29.64	30.10	30.57
38	24.37	24.84	25.30	25.77	26.24	26.70	27.17	27.64	28.11	28.59	29.06	29.53	30.01	30.49	30.96	31.44
39	25.04	25.52	26.00	26.48	26.96	27.44	27.92	28.41	28.89	29.38	29.87	30.36	30.85	31.34	31.83	32.32
40	25.71	26.20	26.70	27.19	27.69	28.18	28.68	29.18	29.68	30.18	30.68	31.18	31.68	32.19	32.69	33.20
41	26.39	26.89	27.40	27.91	28.41	28.92	29.44	29.95	30.46	30.97	31.49	32.01	32.52	33.04	33.56	34.08
42	27.06	27.58	28.10	28.62	29.15	29.67	30.19	30.72	31.25	31.78	32.31	32.84	33.37	33.90	34.44	34.97
43	27.74	28.27	28.81	29.34	29.88	30.42	30.96	31.50	32.04	32.58	33.13	33.67	34.22	34.76	35.31	35.86
44	28.42	28.97	29.52	30.07	30.62	31.17	31.72	32.28	32.83	33.39	33.95	34.51	35.07	35.63	36.19	36.76
45	29.11	29.67	30.23	30.79	31.36	31.92	32.49	33.06	33.63	34.20	34.77	35.35	35.92	36.50	37.08	37.66
46	29.79	30.36	30.94	31.52	32.10	32.68	33.26	33.84	34.43	35.01	35.60	36.19	36.78	37.37	37.96	38.56
47	30.48	31.07	31.66	32.25	32.84	33.44	34.03	34.63	35.23	35.83	36.43	37.04	37.64	38.25	38.86	39.46
48	31.17	31.77	32.37	32.98	33.59	34.20	34.81	35.42	36.03	36.65	37.27	37.88	38.50	39.13	39.75	40.37
49	31.86	32.48	33.09	33.71	34.34	34.96	35.59	36.21	36.84	37.47	38.10	38.74	39.37	40.01	40.65	41.29
50	32.55	33.18	33.82	34.45	35.09	35.73	36.37	37.01	37.65	38.30	38.94	39.59	40.24	40.89	41.55	42.20
51	33.25	33.89	34.54	35.19	35.84	36.49	37.15	37.81	38.46	39.12	39.79	40.45	41.11	41.78	42.45	43.12
52	33.95	34.61	35.27	35.93	36.60	37.27	37.94	38.61	39.28	39.96	40.63	41.31	41.99	42.67	43.36	44.04
53	34.65	35.32	36.00	36.68	37.36	38.04	38.72	39.41	40.10	40.79	41.48	42.17	42.87	43.57	44.27	44.97
54	35.35	36.04	36.73	37.42	38.12	38.82	39.52	40.22	40.92	41.63	42.33	43.04	43.75	44.47	45.18	45.90
55	36.05	36.76	37.46	38.17	38.88	39.60	40.31	41.03	41.74	42.47	43.19	43.91	44.64	45.37	46.10	46.83
56	36.76	37.48	38.20	38.92	39.65	40.38	41.11	41.84	42.57	43.31	44.05	44.79	45.53	46.27	47.02	47.77
57	37.47	38.20	38.94	39.68	40.42	41.16	41.91	42.65	53.40	44.15	44.91	45.66	46.42	47.18	47.94	48.71
58	38.18	38.93	39.68	40.43	41.19	41.95	42.71	43.47	44.23	45.00	45.77	46.54	47.32	48.09	48.87	49.65
59	38.89	39.66	40.42	41.19	41.96	42.74	43.51	44.29	45.07	45.85	46.64	47.42	48.41	49.01	49.80	50.60
60	39.61	40.39	41.17	41.95	42.74	43.53	44.32	45.11	45.91	46.71	47.51	48.31	49.12	49.92	50.73	51.55

TABLE XXII: ANNUAL PERCENTAGE RATE TABLE FOR MONTHLY PAYMENT PLANS (CONTINUED)

Number of Payments	18.00%	18.25%	18.50%	18.75%	19.00%	19.25%	19.50%	19.75%	20.00%	20.25%	20.50%	20.75%	21.00%	21.25%	21.50%	21.75%
					FINANCE CHARGE PER $100 OF AMOUNT FINANCED											
1	1.50	1.52	1.54	1.56	1.58	1.60	1.62	1.65	1.67	1.69	1.71	1.73	1.75	1.77	1.79	1.81
2	2.26	2.29	2.32	2.35	2.38	2.41	2.44	2.48	2.51	2.54	2.57	2.60	2.63	2.66	2.70	2.73
3	3.01	3.06	3.10	3.14	3.18	3.23	3.27	3.31	3.35	3.39	3.44	3.48	3.52	3.56	3.60	3.65
4	3.78	3.83	3.88	3.94	3.99	4.04	4.10	4.15	4.20	4.25	4.31	4.36	4.41	4.47	4.52	4.57
5	4.54	4.61	4.67	4.74	4.80	4.86	4.93	4.99	5.06	5.12	5.18	5.25	5.31	5.37	5.44	5.50
6	5.32	5.39	5.46	5.54	5.61	5.69	5.76	5.84	5.91	5.99	6.06	6.14	6.21	6.29	6.36	6.44
7	6.09	6.18	6.26	6.35	6.43	6.52	6.60	6.69	6.78	6.86	6.95	7.04	7.12	7.21	7.29	7.38
8	6.87	6.96	7.06	7.16	7.26	7.35	7.45	7.55	7.64	7.74	7.84	7.94	8.03	8.13	8.23	8.33
9	7.65	7.76	7.87	7.97	8.08	8.19	8.30	8.41	8.52	8.63	8.73	8.84	8.95	9.06	9.17	9.28
10	8.43	8.55	8.67	8.79	8.91	9.03	9.15	9.27	9.39	9.51	9.63	9.75	9.88	10.00	10.12	10.24
11	9.22	9.35	9.49	9.62	9.75	9.88	10.01	10.14	10.28	10.41	10.54	10.67	10.80	10.94	11.07	11.20
12	10.02	10.16	10.30	10.44	10.59	10.73	10.87	11.02	11.16	11.31	11.45	11.59	11.74	11.88	12.02	12.17
13	10.81	10.97	11.12	11.28	11.43	11.59	11.74	11.90	12.05	12.21	12.36	12.52	12.67	12.83	12.99	13.14
14	11.61	11.78	11.95	12.11	12.28	12.45	12.62	12.78	12.95	13.11	13.28	13.45	13.62	13.79	13.95	14.12
15	12.42	12.59	12.77	12.95	13.13	13.31	13.49	13.67	13.85	14.03	14.21	14.39	14.57	14.75	14.93	15.11
16	13.22	13.41	13.60	13.80	13.99	14.18	14.37	14.56	14.75	14.94	15.13	15.33	15.52	15.71	15.90	16.10
17	14.04	14.24	14.44	14.64	14.85	15.05	15.25	15.46	15.66	15.86	16.07	16.27	16.48	16.68	16.89	17.09
18	14.85	15.07	15.28	15.49	15.71	15.93	16.14	16.36	16.57	16.79	17.01	17.22	17.44	17.66	17.88	18.09
19	15.67	15.90	16.12	16.35	16.58	16.81	17.03	17.26	17.49	17.72	17.95	18.18	18.41	18.64	18.87	19.10
20	16.49	16.73	16.97	17.21	17.45	17.69	17.93	18.17	18.41	18.66	18.90	19.14	19.38	19.63	19.87	20.11
21	17.32	17.57	17.82	18.07	18.33	18.58	18.83	19.09	19.34	19.60	19.85	20.11	20.36	20.62	20.87	21.13
22	18.15	18.41	18.68	18.94	19.21	19.47	19.74	20.01	20.27	20.54	20.81	21.08	21.34	21.61	21.88	22.15
23	18.98	19.26	19.54	19.81	20.09	20.37	20.65	20.93	21.21	21.49	21.77	22.05	22.33	22.61	22.90	23.18
24	19.82	20.11	20.40	20.69	20.98	21.27	21.56	21.86	22.15	22.44	22.74	23.03	23.33	23.62	23.92	24.21
25	20.66	20.96	21.27	21.57	21.87	22.18	22.48	22.79	23.10	23.40	23.71	24.02	24.32	24.63	24.94	25.25
26	21.50	21.82	22.14	22.45	22.77	23.09	23.41	23.73	24.04	24.36	24.68	25.01	25.33	25.65	25.97	26.29
27	22.35	22.68	23.01	23.34	23.67	24.00	24.33	24.67	25.00	25.33	25.67	26.00	26.34	26.67	27.01	27.34
28	23.20	23.55	23.89	24.23	24.58	24.92	25.27	25.61	25.96	26.30	26.65	27.00	27.35	27.70	28.05	28.40
29	24.06	24.41	24.77	25.13	25.49	25.84	26.20	26.56	26.92	27.28	27.64	28.00	28.37	28.73	29.09	29.46
30	24.92	25.29	25.66	26.03	26.40	26.77	27.14	27.52	27.89	28.26	28.64	29.01	29.39	29.77	30.14	30.52
31	25.78	26.16	26.55	26.93	27.32	27.70	28.09	28.47	28.86	29.25	29.64	30.03	30.42	30.81	31.20	31.59
32	26.65	27.04	27.44	27.84	28.24	28.64	29.04	29.44	29.84	30.24	30.64	31.05	31.45	31.85	32.26	32.67
33	27.52	27.93	28.34	28.75	29.16	29.57	29.99	30.40	30.82	31.23	31.65	32.07	32.49	32.91	33.33	33.75
34	28.39	28.81	29.24	29.66	30.09	30.52	30.95	31.37	31.80	32.23	32.67	33.10	33.53	33.96	34.40	34.83
35	29.27	29.71	30.14	30.58	31.02	31.47	31.91	32.35	32.79	33.24	33.68	34.13	34.58	35.03	35.47	35.92
36	30.15	30.60	31.05	31.51	31.96	32.42	32.87	33.33	33.79	34.25	34.71	35.17	35.63	36.09	36.56	37.02
37	31.03	31.50	31.97	32.43	32.90	33.37	33.84	34.32	34.79	35.26	35.74	36.21	36.69	37.16	37.64	38.12
38	31.92	32.40	32.88	33.37	33.85	34.33	34.82	35.30	35.79	36.28	36.77	37.26	37.75	38.24	38.73	39.23
39	32.81	33.31	33.80	34.30	34.80	35.30	35.80	36.30	36.80	37.30	27.81	38.31	38.82	39.32	39.83	40.34
40	33.71	34.22	34.73	35.24	35.75	36.26	36.78	37.29	37.81	38.33	38.85	39.37	39.89	40.41	40.93	41.46
41	34.61	35.13	35.66	36.18	36.71	37.24	37.77	38.30	38.83	39.36	39.89	40.43	40.96	41.50	42.04	42.58
42	35.51	36.05	36.59	37.13	37.67	38.21	38.76	39.30	39.85	40.40	40.95	41.50	42.05	42.60	43.15	43.71
43	36.42	36.97	37.52	38.08	38.63	39.19	39.75	40.31	40.87	41.44	42.00	42.57	43.13	43.70	44.27	44.84
44	37.33	37.89	38.46	39.03	39.60	40.18	40.75	41.33	41.90	42.48	43.06	43.64	44.22	44.81	45.39	45.98
45	38.24	38.82	39.41	39.99	40.58	41.17	41.75	42.35	42.94	43.53	44.13	44.72	45.32	45.92	46.52	47.12
46	39.16	39.75	40.35	40.95	41.55	42.16	42.76	43.37	43.98	44.58	45.20	45.81	46.42	47.03	47.65	48.27
47	40.08	40.69	41.30	41.92	42.54	43.15	43.77	44.40	45.02	45.64	46.27	46.90	47.53	48.16	48.79	49.42
48	41.00	41.63	42.26	42.89	43.52	44.15	44.79	45.43	46.07	46.71	47.35	47.99	48.64	49.28	49.93	50.58
49	41.93	42.57	43.22	43.86	44.51	45.16	45.81	46.46	47.12	47.77	48.43	49.09	49.75	50.41	51.08	51.74
50	42.86	43.52	44.18	44.84	45.50	46.17	46.83	47.50	48.17	48.84	49.52	50.19	50.87	51.55	52.23	52.91
51	43.79	44.47	45.14	45.82	46.50	47.18	47.86	48.55	49.23	49.92	50.61	51.30	51.99	52.69	53.38	54.08
52	44.73	45.42	46.11	46.80	47.50	48.20	48.89	49.59	50.30	51.00	51.71	52.41	53.12	53.83	54.55	54.26
53	45.67	46.38	47.08	47.79	48.50	49.22	49.93	50.65	51.37	52.09	52.81	53.53	54.26	54.98	55.71	56.44
54	46.62	47.34	48.06	48.79	49.51	50.24	50.97	51.70	52.44	53.17	53.91	54.65	55.39	56.14	56.88	57.63
55	47.57	48.30	49.04	49.78	50.52	51.27	52.02	52.76	53.52	54.27	55.02	55.78	56.54	57.30	58.06	58.82
56	48.52	49.27	50.03	50.78	51.54	52.30	53.06	53.83	54.60	55.37	56.14	56.91	57.68	58.46	59.24	60.02
57	49.47	50.24	51.01	51.79	52.56	53.34	54.12	54.90	55.68	56.47	57.25	58.04	58.84	59.63	60.43	61.22
58	50.43	51.22	52.00	52.79	53.58	54.38	55.17	55.97	56.77	57.57	58.38	59.18	59.99	60.80	61.62	62.43
59	51.39	52.20	53.00	53.80	54.61	55.42	56.23	57.05	57.87	58.68	59.51	60.33	61.15	61.98	62.81	63.64
60	52.36	53.18	54.00	54.82	55.64	56.47	57.30	58.13	58.96	59.80	60.64	61.48	62.32	63.17	64.01	64.86

TABLE XXII: ANNUAL PERCENTAGE RATE TABLE FOR MONTHLY PAYMENT PLANS (CONTINUED)

ANNUAL PERCENTAGE RATE

FINANCE CHARGE PER $100 OF AMOUNT FINANCED

Number of Payments	22.00%	22.25%	22.50%	22.75%	23.00%	23.25%	23.50%	23.75%	24.00%	24.25%	24.50%	24.75%	25.00%	25.25%	25.50%	25.75%
1	1.83	1.85	1.87	1.90	1.92	1.94	1.96	1.98	2.00	2.02	2.04	2.06	2.08	2.10	2.12	2.15
2	2.76	2.79	2.82	2.85	2.88	2.92	2.95	2.98	3.01	3.04	3.07	3.10	3.14	3.17	3.20	3.23
3	3.69	3.73	3.77	3.82	3.86	3.90	3.94	3.98	4.03	4.07	4.11	4.15	4.20	4.24	4.28	4.32
4	4.62	4.68	4.73	4.78	4.84	4.89	4.94	5.00	5.05	5.10	5.16	5.21	5.26	5.32	5.37	5.42
5	5.57	5.63	5.69	5.76	5.82	5.89	5.95	6.02	6.08	6.14	6.21	6.27	6.34	6.40	6.46	6.53
6	6.61	6.59	6.66	6.74	6.81	6.89	6.96	7.04	7.12	7.19	7.27	7.34	7.42	7.49	7.57	7.64
7	7.47	7.55	7.64	7.73	7.81	7.90	7.99	8.07	8.16	8.24	8.33	8.42	8.51	8.59	8.68	8.77
8	8.42	8.52	8.62	8.72	8.82	8.91	9.01	9.11	9.21	9.31	9.40	9.50	9.60	9.70	9.80	9.90
9	9.39	9.50	9.61	9.72	9.83	9.94	10.04	10.15	10.26	10.37	10.48	10.59	10.70	10.81	10.92	11.03
10	10.36	10.48	10.60	10.72	10.84	10.96	11.08	11.21	11.33	11.45	11.57	11.69	11.81	11.93	12.06	12.18
11	11.33	11.47	11.60	11.73	11.86	12.00	12.13	12.26	12.40	12.53	12.66	12.80	12.93	13.06	13.20	13.33
12	12.31	12.46	12.60	12.75	12.89	13.94	13.18	13.33	13.47	13.62	13.76	13.91	14.05	14.20	14.34	14.49
13	13.30	13.46	13.61	13.77	13.93	14.08	14.24	14.40	14.55	14.71	14.87	15.03	15.18	15.34	15.50	15.66
14	14.29	14.46	14.63	14.80	14.97	15.13	15.30	15.47	15.64	15.81	15.98	16.15	16.32	16.49	16.66	16.83
15	15.29	15.47	15.65	15.83	16.01	16.19	16.37	16.56	16.74	16.92	17.10	17.28	17.47	17.65	17.83	18.02
16	16.29	16.48	16.68	16.87	17.06	17.26	17.45	17.65	17.84	18.03	18.23	18.42	18.62	18.81	19.01	19.21
17	17.30	17.50	17.71	17.92	18.12	18.33	18.53	18.74	18.95	19.16	19.36	19.57	19.78	19.99	20.20	20.40
18	18.31	18.53	18.75	18.97	19.19	19.41	19.62	19.84	20.06	20.28	20.50	20.72	20.95	21.17	21.39	21.61
19	19.33	19.56	19.79	20.02	20.26	20.49	20.72	20.95	21.19	21.42	21.65	21.89	22.12	22.35	22.59	22.82
20	20.35	20.60	20.84	21.09	21.33	21.58	21.82	22.07	22.31	22.56	22.81	23.05	23.30	23.55	23.79	24.04
21	21.38	21.64	21.90	22.16	22.41	22.67	22.93	23.19	23.45	23.71	23.97	24.23	24.49	24.75	25.01	25.27
22	22.42	22.69	22.96	23.23	23.50	23.77	24.04	24.32	24.59	24.86	25.13	25.41	25.68	25.96	26.23	26.50
23	23.46	23.74	24.03	24.31	24.60	24.88	25.17	25.45	25.74	26.02	26.31	26.60	26.88	27.17	27.46	27.75
24	24.51	24.80	25.10	25.40	25.70	25.99	26.29	26.59	26.89	27.19	27.49	27.79	28.09	28.39	28.69	29.00
25	25.56	25.87	26.18	26.49	26.80	27.11	27.43	27.74	28.05	28.36	28.68	28.99	29.31	29.62	29.94	30.25
26	26.62	26.94	27.26	27.59	27.91	28.24	28.56	28.89	29.22	29.55	29.87	30.20	30.53	30.86	31.19	31.52
27	27.68	28.02	28.35	28.69	29.03	29.37	29.71	30.05	30.39	30.73	31.07	31.42	31.76	32.10	32.45	32.79
28	28.75	29.10	29.45	29.80	30.15	30.51	30.86	31.22	31.57	31.93	32.28	32.64	33.00	33.35	33.71	34.07
29	29.82	30.19	30.55	30.92	31.28	31.65	32.02	32.39	32.76	33.13	33.50	33.87	34.24	34.61	34.98	35.36
30	30.90	31.28	31.66	32.04	32.42	32.80	33.18	33.57	33.95	34.33	34.72	35.10	35.49	35.88	36.26	36.65
31	31.98	32.38	32.77	33.17	33.56	33.96	34.35	34.75	35.15	35.55	35.95	36.35	36.75	37.15	37.55	37.95
32	33.07	33.48	33.89	34.30	34.71	35.12	35.53	35.94	36.35	36.77	37.18	37.60	38.01	38.43	38.84	39.26
33	34.17	34.59	35.01	35.44	35.86	36.29	36.71	37.14	37.57	37.99	38.42	38.85	39.28	39.71	40.14	40.58
34	35.27	35.71	36.14	36.58	37.02	37.46	37.90	38.34	38.78	39.23	39.67	40.11	40.56	41.01	41.45	41.90
35	36.37	36.83	37.28	37.73	38.18	38.64	39.09	39.55	40.01	40.47	40.92	41.38	41.84	42.31	42.77	43.23
36	37.49	37.95	38.42	38.89	39.35	39.82	40.29	40.77	41.24	41.71	42.19	42.66	43.14	43.61	44.09	44.57
37	38.60	39.08	39.56	40.05	40.53	41.02	41.50	41.99	42.48	42.96	43.45	43.94	44.43	44.93	45.42	45.91
38	39.72	40.22	40.72	41.21	41.71	42.21	42.71	43.22	43.72	44.22	44.73	45.23	45.74	46.25	46.75	47.26
39	40.85	41.36	41.87	42.39	42.90	43.42	43.93	44.45	44.97	45.49	46.01	46.53	47.05	47.57	48.10	48.62
40	41.98	42.51	43.04	43.56	44.09	44.62	45.16	45.69	46.22	46.76	47.29	47.83	48.37	48.91	49.45	49.99
41	43.12	43.66	44.20	44.75	45.29	45.84	46.39	46.94	47.48	48.04	48.59	49.14	49.69	50.25	50.80	51.36
42	44.26	44.82	45.38	45.94	46.50	47.06	47.62	48.19	48.75	49.32	49.89	50.46	51.03	51.60	52.17	52.74
43	45.41	45.98	46.56	47.13	47.71	48.29	48.87	49.45	50.03	50.61	51.19	51.78	52.36	52.95	53.54	54.13
44	46.56	47.15	47.74	48.33	48.93	49.52	50.11	50.71	51.31	51.91	52.51	53.11	53.71	54.31	54.92	55.52
45	47.72	48.33	48.93	49.54	50.15	50.76	51.37	51.98	52.59	53.21	53.82	54.44	55.06	55.68	56.30	56.92
46	48.89	49.51	50.13	50.75	51.37	52.00	52.63	53.26	53.89	54.52	55.15	55.78	56.42	57.05	57.69	58.33
47	50.06	50.69	51.33	51.97	52.61	53.25	53.89	54.54	55.18	55.83	56.48	57.13	57.78	58.44	59.09	59.75
48	51.23	51.88	52.54	53.19	53.85	54.51	55.16	55.83	56.49	57.15	57.82	58.49	59.15	59.82	60.50	61.17
49	52.41	53.08	53.75	54.42	55.09	55.77	56.44	57.12	57.80	58.48	59.16	59.85	60.53	61.22	61.91	62.60
50	53.59	54.28	54.96	55.65	56.34	57.03	57.73	58.42	59.12	59.81	60.51	61.21	61.92	62.62	63.33	64.03
51	54.78	55.48	56.19	56.89	57.60	58.30	59.01	59.73	60.44	61.15	61.87	62.59	63.31	64.03	64.75	65.47
52	55.98	56.69	57.41	58.13	58.86	59.58	60.31	61.04	61.77	62.50	63.23	63.97	64.70	65.44	66.18	66.92
53	57.18	57.91	58.65	59.38	60.12	60.87	61.61	62.35	63.10	63.85	64.60	65.35	66.11	66.86	67.62	68.38
54	58.38	59.13	59.88	60.64	61.40	62.16	62.92	63.68	64.44	65.21	65.98	66.75	67.52	68.29	69.07	69.84
55	59.59	60.36	61.13	61.90	62.67	63.45	64.23	65.01	65.79	66.57	67.36	68.14	68.93	69.72	70.52	71.31
56	60.80	61.59	62.38	63.17	63.96	64.75	65.54	66.34	67.14	67.94	68.74	69.55	70.36	71.16	71.97	72.79
57	62.02	62.83	63.63	64.44	65.25	66.06	66.87	67.68	68.50	69.32	70.14	70.96	71.78	72.61	73.44	74.27
58	63.25	64.07	64.89	65.71	66.54	67.37	68.20	69.03	69.86	70.70	71.54	72.38	73.22	74.06	74.91	75.76
59	64.48	65.32	66.15	67.00	67.84	68.68	69.53	70.38	71.23	72.09	72.94	73.80	74.66	75.52	76.39	77.25
60	65.71	66.57	67.42	68.28	69.14	70.01	70.87	71.74	72.61	73.48	74.35	75.23	76.11	76.99	77.87	78.76

TABLE XXII: ANNUAL PERCENTAGE RATE TABLE FOR MONTHLY PAYMENT PLANS (CONTINUED)

ANNUAL PERCENTAGE RATE

Number of Payments	26.00%	26.25%	26.50%	26.75%	27.00%	27.25%	27.50%	27.75%	28.00%	28.25%	28.50%	28.75%	29.00%	29.25%	29.50%	29.75%
	FINANCE CHARGE PER $100 OF AMOUNT FINANCED															
1	2.17	2.19	2.21	2.23	2.25	2.27	2.29	2.31	2.33	2.35	2.37	2.40	2.42	2.44	2.46	2.48
2	3.26	3.29	3.32	3.36	3.39	3.42	3.45	3.48	3.51	3.54	3.58	3.61	3.64	3.67	3.70	3.73
3	4.36	4.41	4.45	4.49	4.53	4.58	4.62	4.66	4.70	4.74	4.79	4.83	4.87	4.91	4.96	5.00
4	5.47	5.53	5.58	5.63	5.69	5.74	5.79	5.85	5.90	5.95	6.01	6.06	6.11	6.17	6.22	6.27
5	6.59	6.66	6.72	6.79	6.85	6.91	6.98	7.04	7.11	7.17	7.24	7.30	7.37	7.43	7.49	7.56
6	7.72	7.79	7.87	7.95	8.02	8.10	8.17	8.25	8.32	8.40	8.48	8.55	8.63	8.70	8.78	8.85
7	8.85	8.94	9.03	9.11	9.20	9.29	9.37	9.46	9.55	9.64	9.72	9.81	9.90	9.98	10.07	10.16
8	9.99	10.09	10.19	10.29	10.39	10.49	10.58	10.68	10.78	10.88	10.98	11.08	11.18	11.28	11.38	11.47
9	11.14	11.25	11.36	11.47	11.58	11.69	11.80	11.91	12.03	12.14	12.25	12.36	12.47	12.58	12.69	12.80
10	12.30	12.42	12.54	12.67	12.79	12.91	13.03	13.15	13.28	13.40	13.52	13.64	13.77	13.89	14.01	14.14
11	13.46	13.60	13.73	13.87	14.00	14.13	14.27	14.40	14.54	14.67	14.81	14.94	15.08	15.21	15.35	15.48
12	14.64	14.78	14.93	15.07	15.22	15.37	15.51	15.66	15.81	15.95	16.10	16.25	16.40	16.54	16.69	16.84
13	15.82	15.97	16.13	16.29	16.45	16.61	16.77	16.93	17.09	17.24	17.40	17.56	17.72	17.88	18.04	18.20
14	17.00	17.17	17.35	17.52	17.69	17.86	18.03	18.20	18.37	18.54	18.72	18.89	19.06	19.23	19.41	19.58
15	18.20	18.38	18.57	18.75	18.93	19.12	19.30	19.48	19.67	19.85	20.04	20.22	20.41	20.59	20.78	20.96
16	19.40	19.60	19.79	19.99	20.19	20.38	20.58	20.78	20.97	21.17	21.37	21.57	21.76	21.96	22.16	22.36
17	20.61	20.82	21.03	21.24	21.45	21.66	21.87	22.08	22.29	22.50	22.71	22.92	23.13	23.34	23.55	23.77
18	21.83	22.05	22.27	22.50	22.72	22.94	23.16	23.39	23.61	23.83	24.06	24.28	24.51	24.73	24.96	25.18
19	23.06	23.29	23.53	23.76	24.00	24.23	24.47	24.71	24.94	25.18	25.42	25.65	25.89	26.13	26.37	26.61
20	24.29	24.54	24.79	25.04	25.28	25.53	25.78	26.03	26.28	26.53	26.78	27.04	27.29	27.54	27.79	28.04
21	25.53	25.79	26.05	26.32	26.58	26.84	27.11	27.37	27.63	27.90	28.16	28.43	28.69	28.96	29.22	29.49
22	26.78	27.05	27.33	27.61	27.88	28.16	28.44	28.71	28.99	29.27	29.55	29.82	30.10	30.38	30.66	30.94
23	28.04	28.32	28.61	28.90	29.19	29.48	29.77	30.07	30.36	30.65	30.94	31.23	31.53	31.82	32.11	32.41
24	29.30	29.60	29.90	30.21	30.51	30.82	31.12	31.43	31.73	32.04	32.34	32.65	32.96	33.27	33.57	33.88
25	30.57	30.89	31.20	31.52	31.84	32.16	32.48	32.80	33.12	33.44	33.76	34.08	34.40	34.72	35.04	35.37
26	31.85	32.18	32.51	32.84	33.18	33.51	33.84	34.18	34.51	34.84	35.18	35.51	35.85	36.19	36.52	36.86
27	33.14	33.48	33.83	34.17	34.52	34.87	35.21	35.56	35.91	36.26	36.61	36.96	37.31	37.66	38.01	38.36
28	34.43	34.79	35.15	35.51	35.87	36.23	36.59	36.96	37.32	37.68	38.05	38.41	38.78	39.15	39.51	39.88
29	35.73	36.10	36.48	36.85	37.23	37.61	37.98	38.36	38.74	39.12	39.50	39.88	40.26	40.64	41.02	41.40
30	37.04	37.43	37.82	38.21	38.60	38.99	39.38	39.77	40.17	40.56	40.95	41.35	41.75	42.14	42.54	42.94
31	38.35	38.76	39.16	39.57	39.97	40.38	40.79	41.19	41.60	42.01	42.42	42.83	43.24	43.65	44.06	44.48
32	39.68	40.10	40.52	40.94	41.36	41.78	42.20	42.62	43.05	43.47	43.90	44.32	44.75	45.17	45.60	46.03
33	41.01	41.44	41.88	42.31	42.75	43.19	43.62	44.06	44.50	44.94	45.38	45.82	46.26	46.70	47.15	47.59
34	42.35	42.80	43.25	43.70	44.15	44.60	45.05	45.51	45.96	46.42	46.87	47.33	47.79	48.24	48.70	49.16
35	43.69	44.16	44.62	45.09	45.56	46.02	46.49	46.96	47.43	47.90	48.37	48.85	49.32	49.79	50.27	50.74
36	45.05	45.53	46.01	46.49	46.97	47.45	47.94	48.42	48.91	49.40	49.88	50.37	50.86	51.35	51.84	52.33
37	46.41	46.90	47.40	47.90	48.39	48.89	49.39	49.89	50.40	50.90	51.40	51.91	52.41	52.92	53.42	53.93
38	47.77	48.29	48.80	49.31	49.82	50.34	50.86	51.37	51.89	52.41	52.93	53.45	53.97	54.49	55.02	55.54
39	49.15	49.68	50.20	50.73	51.26	51.79	52.33	52.86	53.39	53.93	54.46	55.00	55.54	56.08	56.62	57.16
40	50.53	51.07	51.62	52.16	52.71	53.26	53.81	54.35	54.90	55.46	56.01	56.56	57.12	57.67	58.23	58.79
41	51.92	52.48	53.04	53.60	54.16	54.73	55.29	55.86	56.42	56.99	57.56	58.13	58.70	59.28	59.85	60.42
42	53.32	53.89	54.47	55.05	55.63	56.21	56.79	57.37	57.95	58.54	59.12	59.71	60.30	60.89	61.48	62.07
43	54.72	55.31	55.90	56.50	57.09	57.69	58.29	58.89	59.49	60.09	60.69	61.30	61.90	62.51	63.11	63.72
44	56.13	56.74	57.35	57.96	58.57	59.19	59.80	60.42	61.03	61.65	62.27	62.89	63.51	64.14	64.76	65.39
45	57.55	58.17	58.80	59.43	60.06	60.69	61.32	61.95	62.59	63.22	63.86	64.50	65.13	65.77	66.42	67.06
46	58.97	59.61	60.26	60.90	61.55	62.20	62.84	63.49	64.15	64.80	65.45	66.11	66.76	67.42	68.08	68.74
47	60.40	61.06	61.72	62.38	63.05	63.71	64.38	65.05	65.71	66.38	67.06	67.73	68.40	69.08	69.75	70.43
48	61.84	62.52	63.20	63.87	64.56	65.24	65.92	66.60	67.29	67.98	68.67	69.36	70.05	70.74	71.44	72.13
49	63.29	63.98	64.68	65.37	66.07	66.77	67.47	68.17	68.87	69.58	70.29	70.99	71.70	72.41	73.13	73.84
50	64.74	65.45	66.16	66.88	67.59	68.31	69.03	69.75	70.47	71.19	71.91	72.64	73.37	74.10	74.83	75.56
51	66.20	66.93	67.66	68.39	69.12	69.86	70.59	71.33	72.07	72.81	73.55	74.29	75.04	75.78	76.53	77.28
52	67.67	68.41	69.16	69.91	70.66	71.41	72.16	72.92	73.67	74.43	75.19	75.95	76.72	77.48	78.25	79.02
53	69.14	69.90	70.67	71.43	72.20	72.97	73.74	74.52	75.29	76.07	76.85	77.62	78.41	79.19	79.97	80.76
54	70.62	71.40	72.18	72.97	73.75	74.54	75.33	76.12	76.91	77.71	78.50	79.30	80.10	80.90	81.71	82.51
55	72.11	72.91	73.71	74.51	75.31	76.12	76.92	77.73	78.55	79.36	80.17	80.99	81.81	82.63	83.45	84.27
56	73.60	74.42	75.24	76.06	76.88	77.70	78.53	79.35	80.18	81.02	81.85	82.68	83.52	84.36	85.20	86.04
57	75.10	75.94	76.77	77.61	78.45	79.29	80.14	80.98	81.83	82.68	83.53	84.39	85.24	86.10	86.96	87.82
58	76.61	77.46	78.32	79.17	80.03	80.89	81.75	82.62	83.48	84.35	85.22	86.10	86.97	87.85	88.72	89.60
59	78.12	78.99	79.87	80.74	81.62	82.50	83.38	84.26	85.15	86.03	86.92	87.81	88.71	89.60	90.50	91.40
60	79.64	80.53	81.42	82.32	83.21	84.11	85.01	85.91	86.81	87.72	88.63	89.54	90.45	91.37	92.28	93.20

TABLE XXII: ANNUAL PERCENTAGE RATE TABLE FOR MONTHLY PAYMENT PLANS
(CONTINUED)

ANNUAL PERCENTAGE RATE

FINANCE CHARGE PER $100 OF AMOUNT FINANCED

Number of Payments	30.00%	30.25%	30.50%	30.75%	31.00%	31.25%	31.50%	31.75%	32.00%	32.25%	32.50%	32.75%	33.00%	33.25%	33.50%	33.75%
1	2.50	2.52	2.54	2.56	2.58	2.60	2.62	2.65	2.67	2.69	2.71	2.73	2.75	2.77	2.79	2.81
2	3.77	3.80	3.83	3.86	3.89	3.92	3.95	3.99	4.02	4.05	4.08	4.11	4.14	4.18	4.21	4.24
3	5.04	5.08	5.13	5.17	5.21	5.25	5.30	5.34	5.38	5.42	5.46	5.51	5.55	5.59	5.63	5.68
4	6.33	6.38	6.43	6.49	6.54	6.59	6.65	6.70	6.75	6.81	6.86	6.91	6.97	7.02	7.08	7.13
5	7.62	7.69	7.75	7.82	7.88	7.95	8.01	8.08	8.14	8.20	8.27	8.33	8.40	8.46	8.53	8.59
6	8.93	9.01	9.08	9.16	9.23	9.31	9.39	9.46	9.54	9.61	9.69	9.77	9.84	9.92	9.99	10.07
7	10.25	10.33	10.42	10.51	10.60	10.68	10.77	10.86	10.95	11.03	11.12	11.21	11.30	11.39	11.47	11.56
8	11.57	11.67	11.77	11.87	11.97	12.07	12.17	12.27	12.37	12.47	12.57	12.67	12.77	12.87	12.97	13.07
9	12.91	13.02	13.13	13.24	13.36	13.47	13.58	13.69	13.80	13.91	14.02	14.14	14.25	14.36	14.47	14.58
10	14.26	14.38	14.50	14.63	14.75	14.87	15.00	15.12	15.24	15.37	15.49	15.62	15.74	15.86	15.99	16.11
11	15.62	15.75	15.89	16.02	16.16	16.29	16.43	16.56	16.70	16.84	16.97	17.11	17.24	17.38	17.52	17.65
12	16.98	17.13	17.28	17.43	17.58	17.72	17.87	18.02	18.17	18.32	18.47	18.61	18.76	18.91	19.06	19.21
13	18.36	18.52	18.68	18.84	19.00	19.16	19.33	19.49	19.65	19.81	19.97	20.13	20.29	20.45	20.62	20.78
14	19.75	19.92	20.10	20.27	20.44	20.62	20.79	20.96	21.14	21.31	21.49	21.66	21.83	22.01	22.18	22.36
15	21.15	21.34	21.52	21.71	21.89	22.08	22.27	22.45	22.64	22.83	23.01	23.20	23.39	23.58	23.76	23.95
16	22.56	22.76	22.96	23.16	23.35	23.55	23.75	23.95	24.15	24.35	24.55	24.75	24.96	25.16	25.36	25.56
17	23.98	24.19	24.40	24.61	24.83	25.04	25.25	25.47	25.68	25.89	26.11	26.32	26.53	26.75	26.96	27.18
18	25.41	25.63	25.86	26.08	26.31	26.54	26.76	26.99	27.22	27.44	27.67	27.90	28.13	28.35	28.58	28.81
19	26.85	27.08	27.32	27.56	27.80	28.04	28.28	28.52	28.76	29.00	29.25	29.49	29.73	29.97	30.21	30.45
20	28.29	28.55	28.80	29.05	29.31	29.56	29.81	30.07	30.32	30.58	30.83	31.09	31.34	31.60	31.86	32.11
21	29.75	30.02	30.29	30.55	30.82	31.09	31.36	31.62	31.89	32.16	32.43	32.70	32.97	33.24	33.51	33.78
22	31.22	31.50	31.78	32.06	32.35	32.63	32.91	33.19	33.48	33.76	34.04	34.33	34.61	34.89	35.18	35.46
23	32.70	33.00	33.29	33.59	33.88	34.18	34.48	34.77	35.07	35.37	35.66	35.96	36.26	36.56	36.86	37.16
24	34.19	34.50	34.81	35.12	35.43	35.74	36.05	36.36	36.67	36.99	37.30	37.61	37.92	38.24	38.55	38.87
25	35.69	36.01	36.34	36.66	36.99	37.31	37.64	37.96	38.29	38.62	38.94	39.27	39.60	39.93	40.26	40.59
26	37.20	37.54	37.88	38.21	38.55	38.89	39.23	39.58	39.92	40.26	40.60	40.94	41.29	41.63	41.97	42.32
27	38.72	39.07	39.42	39.78	40.13	40.49	40.84	41.20	41.56	41.91	42.27	42.63	42.99	43.34	43.70	44.06
28	40.25	40.61	40.98	41.35	41.72	42.09	42.46	42.83	43.20	43.58	43.95	44.32	44.70	45.07	45.45	45.82
29	41.78	42.17	42.55	42.94	43.32	43.71	44.09	44.48	44.87	45.25	45.64	46.03	46.42	46.81	47.20	47.59
30	43.33	43.73	44.13	44.53	44.93	45.33	45.73	46.13	46.54	46.94	47.34	47.75	48.15	48.56	48.96	49.37
31	44.89	45.30	45.72	46.13	46.55	46.97	47.38	47.80	48.22	48.64	49.06	49.48	49.90	50.32	50.74	51.17
32	46.46	46.89	47.32	47.75	48.18	48.61	49.05	49.48	49.91	50.35	50.78	51.22	51.66	52.09	52.53	52.97
33	48.04	48.48	48.93	49.37	49.82	50.27	50.72	51.17	51.62	52.07	52.52	52.97	53.43	53.88	54.33	54.79
34	49.62	50.08	50.55	51.01	51.47	51.94	52.40	52.87	53.33	53.80	54.27	54.74	55.21	55.68	56.15	56.62
35	51.22	51.70	52.17	52.65	53.13	53.61	54.09	54.58	55.06	55.54	56.03	56.51	57.00	57.48	57.97	58.46
36	52.83	53.32	53.81	54.31	54.80	55.30	55.80	56.30	56.80	57.30	57.80	58.30	58.80	59.30	59.81	60.31
37	54.44	54.95	55.46	55.97	56.49	57.00	57.51	58.03	58.54	59.06	59.58	60.10	60.62	61.14	61.66	62.18
38	56.07	56.59	57.12	57.65	58.18	58.71	59.24	59.77	60.30	60.84	61.37	61.90	62.44	62.98	63.52	64.06
39	57.70	58.24	58.79	59.33	59.88	60.42	60.97	61.52	62.07	62.62	63.17	63.72	64.28	64.83	65.39	65.94
40	59.34	59.90	60.47	61.03	61.59	62.15	62.72	63.28	63.85	64.42	64.99	65.56	66.13	66.70	67.27	67.84
41	61.00	61.57	62.15	62.73	63.31	63.89	64.47	65.06	65.64	66.22	66.81	67.40	67.99	68.57	69.16	69.76
42	62.66	63.25	63.85	64.44	65.04	65.64	66.24	66.84	67.44	68.04	68.65	69.25	69.86	70.46	71.07	71.68
43	64.33	64.94	65.56	66.17	66.78	67.40	68.01	68.63	69.25	69.87	70.49	71.11	71.74	72.36	72.99	73.61
44	66.01	66.64	67.27	67.90	68.53	69.17	69.80	70.43	71.07	71.71	72.35	72.99	73.63	74.27	74.91	75.56
45	67.70	68.35	69.00	69.64	70.29	70.94	71.60	72.25	72.90	73.56	74.21	74.87	75.53	76.19	76.85	77.52
46	69.40	70.07	70.73	71.40	72.06	72.73	73.40	74.07	74.74	75.42	76.09	76.77	77.44	78.12	78.80	79.48
47	71.11	71.79	72.47	73.16	73.84	74.53	75.22	75.90	76.60	77.29	77.98	78.67	79.37	80.07	80.76	81.46
48	72.83	73.53	74.23	74.93	75.63	76.34	77.04	77.75	78.46	79.17	79.88	80.59	81.30	82.02	82.74	83.45
49	74.55	75.27	75.99	76.71	77.43	78.15	78.88	79.60	80.33	81.06	81.79	82.52	83.25	83.98	84.72	85.45
50	76.29	77.02	77.76	78.50	79.24	79.98	80.72	81.46	82.21	82.96	83.70	84.45	85.20	85.96	86.71	87.47
51	78.03	78.79	79.54	80.30	81.06	81.81	82.58	83.34	84.10	84.87	85.63	86.40	87.17	87.94	88.71	89.49
52	79.79	80.56	81.33	82.11	82.88	83.66	84.44	85.22	86.00	86.79	87.57	88.36	89.15	89.94	90.73	91.52
53	81.55	82.34	83.13	83.92	84.72	85.51	86.31	87.11	87.91	88.72	89.52	90.33	91.13	91.94	92.75	93.57
54	83.32	84.13	84.94	85.75	86.56	87.38	88.19	89.01	89.83	90.66	91.48	92.30	93.13	93.96	94.79	95.62
55	85.10	85.93	86.75	87.58	88.42	89.25	90.09	90.92	91.76	92.60	93.45	94.29	95.14	95.99	96.83	97.69
56	86.89	87.73	88.58	89.43	90.28	91.13	91.99	92.84	93.70	94.56	95.43	96.29	97.15	98.02	98.89	99.76
57	88.68	89.55	90.41	91.28	92.15	93.02	93.90	94.77	95.65	96.53	97.41	98.30	99.18	100.07	100.96	101.85
58	90.49	91.37	92.26	93.14	94.03	94.92	95.82	96.71	97.61	98.51	99.41	100.31	101.22	102.12	103.03	103.94
59	92.30	93.20	94.11	95.01	95.92	96.83	97.75	98.66	99.58	100.50	101.42	102.34	103.26	104.19	105.12	106.05
60	94.12	95.04	95.97	96.89	97.82	98.75	99.68	100.62	101.56	102.49	103.43	104.38	105.32	106.27	107.21	108.16

Number of Payments	ANNUAL PERCENTAGE RATE															
	34.00%	34.25%	34.50%	34.75%	35.00%	35.25%	35.50%	35.75%	36.00%	36.25%	36.50%	36.75%	37.00%	37.25%	37.50%	37.75%
	FINANCE CHARGE PER $100 OF AMOUNT FINANCED															
1	2.83	2.85	2.87	2.90	2.92	2.94	2.96	2.98	3.00	3.02	3.04	3.06	3.08	3.10	3.12	3.15
2	4.27	4.30	4.33	4.36	4.40	4.43	4.46	4.49	4.52	4.55	4.59	4.62	4.65	4.68	4.71	4.74
3	5.72	5.76	5.80	5.85	5.89	5.93	5.97	6.02	6.06	6.10	6.14	6.19	6.23	6.27	6.31	6.36
4	7.18	7.24	7.29	7.34	7.40	7.45	7.50	7.56	7.61	7.66	7.72	7.77	7.83	7.88	7.93	7.99
5	8.66	8.72	8.79	8.85	8.92	8.98	9.05	9.11	9.18	9.24	9.31	9.37	9.44	9.50	9.57	9.63
6	10.15	10.22	10.30	10.38	10.45	10.53	10.61	10.68	10.76	10.83	10.91	10.99	11.06	11.14	11.22	11.29
7	11.65	11.74	11.83	11.91	12.00	12.09	12.18	12.27	12.35	12.44	12.53	12.62	12.71	12.80	12.88	12.97
8	13.17	13.27	13.36	13.46	13.56	13.66	13.76	13.86	13.97	14.07	14.17	14.27	14.37	14.47	14.57	14.67
9	14.69	14.81	14.92	15.03	15.14	15.25	15.37	15.48	15.59	15.70	15.82	15.93	16.04	16.15	16.27	16.38
10	16.24	16.36	16.48	16.61	16.73	16.86	16.98	17.11	17.23	17.36	17.48	17.60	17.73	17.85	17.98	18.10
11	17.79	17.93	18.06	18.20	18.34	18.47	18.61	18.75	18.89	19.02	19.16	19.30	19.43	19.57	19.71	19.85
12	19.36	19.51	19.66	19.81	19.96	20.11	20.25	20.40	20.55	20.70	20.85	21.00	21.15	21.31	21.46	21.61
13	20.94	21.10	21.26	21.43	21.59	21.75	21.91	22.08	22.24	22.40	22.56	22.73	22.89	23.05	23.22	23.38
14	22.53	22.71	22.88	23.06	23.23	23.41	23.59	23.76	23.94	24.11	24.29	24.47	24.64	24.82	25.00	25.17
15	24.14	24.33	24.52	24.71	24.89	25.08	25.27	25.46	25.65	25.84	26.03	26.22	26.41	26.60	26.79	26.98
16	25.76	25.96	26.16	26.37	26.57	26.77	26.97	27.17	27.38	27.58	27.78	27.99	28.19	28.39	28.60	28.80
17	27.39	27.61	27.82	28.04	28.25	28.47	28.69	28.90	29.12	29.34	29.55	29.77	29.99	30.20	30.42	30.64
18	29.04	29.27	29.50	29.73	29.96	30.19	30.42	30.65	30.88	31.11	31.34	31.57	31.80	32.03	32.26	32.49
19	30.70	30.94	31.18	31.43	31.67	31.91	32.16	32.40	32.65	32.89	33.14	33.38	33.63	33.87	34.12	34.36
20	32.37	32.63	32.88	33.14	33.40	33.66	33.91	34.17	34.43	34.69	34.95	35.21	35.47	35.73	35.99	36.25
21	34.05	34.32	34.60	34.87	35.14	35.41	35.68	35.96	36.23	36.50	36.78	37.05	37.33	37.60	37.88	38.15
22	35.75	36.04	36.32	36.61	36.89	37.18	37.47	37.76	38.04	38.33	38.62	38.91	39.20	39.49	39.78	40.07
23	37.46	37.76	38.06	38.36	38.66	38.96	39.27	39.57	39.87	40.18	40.48	40.78	41.09	41.39	41.70	42.00
24	39.18	39.50	39.81	40.13	40.44	40.76	41.08	41.40	41.71	42.03	42.35	42.67	42.99	43.31	43.63	43.95
25	40.92	41.25	41.58	41.91	42.24	42.57	42.90	43.24	43.57	43.90	44.24	44.57	44.91	45.24	45.58	45.91
26	42.66	43.01	43.36	43.70	44.05	44.40	44.74	45.09	45.44	45.79	46.14	46.49	46.84	47.19	47.54	47.89
27	44.42	44.78	45.15	45.51	45.87	46.23	46.60	46.96	47.32	47.69	48.05	48.42	48.78	49.15	49.52	49.88
28	46.20	46.57	46.95	47.33	47.70	48.08	48.46	48.84	49.22	49.60	49.98	50.36	50.75	51.13	51.51	51.89
29	47.98	48.37	48.77	49.16	49.55	49.95	50.34	50.74	51.13	51.53	51.93	52.32	52.72	53.12	53.52	53.92
30	49.78	50.19	50.60	51.00	51.41	51.82	52.23	52.65	53.06	53.47	53.88	54.30	54.71	55.13	55.54	55.96
31	51.59	52.01	52.44	52.86	53.29	53.71	54.14	54.57	55.00	55.43	55.85	56.28	56.72	57.15	57.58	58.01
32	53.41	53.85	54.29	54.73	55.17	55.62	56.06	56.50	56.95	57.39	57.84	58.29	58.73	59.18	59.63	60.08
33	55.24	55.70	56.16	56.62	57.07	57.53	57.99	58.45	58.92	59.38	59.84	60.30	60.77	61.23	61.70	62.16
34	57.09	57.56	58.04	58.51	58.99	59.46	59.94	60.42	60.89	61.37	61.85	62.33	62.81	63.30	63.78	64.26
35	58.95	59.44	59.93	60.42	60.91	61.40	61.90	62.39	62.89	63.38	63.88	64.38	64.88	65.37	65.87	66.37
36	60.82	61.33	61.83	62.34	62.85	63.36	63.87	64.38	64.89	65.41	65.92	66.43	66.95	67.47	67.98	68.50
37	62.70	63.22	63.75	64.27	64.80	65.33	65.85	66.38	66.91	67.44	67.97	68.51	69.04	69.57	70.11	70.64
38	64.59	65.14	65.68	66.22	66.76	67.31	67.85	68.40	68.95	69.49	70.04	70.59	71.14	71.69	72.25	72.80
39	66.50	67.06	67.62	68.18	68.74	69.30	69.86	70.43	70.99	71.56	72.12	72.69	73.26	73.83	74.40	74.97
40	68.42	68.99	69.57	70.15	70.13	71.31	71.89	72.47	73.05	73.63	74.22	74.80	75.39	75.98	76.56	77.15
41	70.35	70.94	71.53	72.13	72.73	73.32	73.92	74.52	75.12	75.72	76.32	76.93	77.53	78.14	78.74	79.35
42	72.29	72.90	73.51	74.12	74.74	75.35	75.97	76.59	77.20	77.82	78.44	79.07	79.69	80.31	80.94	81.56
43	74.24	74.87	75.50	76.13	76.76	77.40	78.03	78.67	79.30	79.94	80.58	81.22	81.86	82.50	83.14	83.79
44	76.20	76.85	77.50	78.15	78.80	79.45	80.10	80.76	81.41	82.07	82.72	83.38	84.04	84.70	85.36	86.03
45	78.18	78.84	79.51	80.18	80.85	81.52	82.19	82.86	83.53	84.21	84.88	85.56	86.24	86.92	87.60	88.28
46	80.17	80.85	81.53	82.22	82.91	83.60	84.28	84.98	85.67	86.36	87.06	87.75	88.45	89.15	89.85	90.55
47	82.16	82.87	83.57	84.27	84.98	85.69	86.39	87.10	87.81	88.53	89.24	89.95	90.67	91.39	92.11	92.83
48	84.17	84.89	85.61	86.34	87.06	87.79	88.52	89.24	89.97	90.70	91.44	92.17	92.91	93.64	94.38	95.12
49	86.19	86.93	87.67	88.41	89.16	89.90	90.65	91.40	92.14	92.89	93.65	94.40	95.15	95.91	96.67	97.42
50	88.22	88.98	89.74	90.50	91.26	92.03	92.79	93.56	94.33	95.10	95.87	96.64	97.41	98.19	98.96	99.74
51	90.26	91.04	91.82	92.60	93.38	94.16	94.95	95.74	96.52	97.31	98.10	98.89	99.69	100.48	101.28	102.07
52	92.32	93.11	93.91	94.71	95.51	96.31	97.12	97.92	98.73	99.54	100.35	101.16	101.97	102.79	103.60	104.42
53	94.38	95.20	96.01	96.83	97.65	98.47	99.30	100.12	100.95	101.78	102.61	103.44	104.27	105.10	105.94	106.78
54	96.45	97.29	98.13	98.96	99.80	100.64	101.49	102.33	103.18	104.03	104.87	105.73	106.58	107.43	108.29	109.14
55	98.54	99.39	100.25	101.11	101.97	102.83	103.69	104.55	105.42	106.29	107.16	108.03	108.90	109.77	110.65	111.53
56	100.63	101.51	102.38	103.26	104.14	105.02	105.90	106.79	107.67	108.56	109.45	110.34	111.23	112.13	113.02	113.92
57	102.74	103.63	104.53	105.43	106.32	107.22	108.13	109.03	109.94	110.85	111.75	112.67	113.58	114.49	115.41	116.33
58	104.85	105.77	106.68	107.60	108.52	109.44	110.36	111.29	112.21	113.14	114.07	115.00	115.93	116.87	117.81	118.74
59	106.98	107.91	108.85	109.79	110.73	111.67	112.61	113.55	114.50	115.45	116.40	117.35	118.30	119.26	120.22	121.17
60	109.12	110.07	111.02	111.98	112.94	113.90	114.87	115.83	116.80	117.77	118.74	119.71	120.68	121.66	122.64	123.62

TABLE XXIII: METRIC MEASURES WITH U.S. EQUIVALENTS

Length	*Weight*
1 millimeter = 0.039 inch	1 gram[a] = 0.035 ounce
1 centimeter = 0.394 inch	1 kilogram = 2.20 pounds
1 decimeter = 3.94 inches	
1 meter = 39.37 inches	*Liquid Capacity*
= 3.28 feet	
= 1.09 yards	1 liter[a] = 33.8 ounces
1 kilometer = 0.621 mile	= 2.11 pints
	= 1.06 quarts
	= 0.264 gallon

[a] One gram is defined as the weight of 1 cubic centimeter of pure water at 4° Celsius. One liter is defined as the capacity of a cube that is 1 decimeter long on each edge.

TABLE XXIV: U.S. MEASURES WITH METRIC EQUIVALENTS

Length	*Weight*
1 inch = 2.54 centimeters	1 ounce = 28.4 grams
1 foot = 0.305 meter	1 pound = 454 grams
1 yard = 0.914 meter	= 0.454 kilogram
1 mile = 1.61 kilometers	

Liquid Capacity	
1 ounce = 0.030 liter	1 quart = 0.946 liter
1 pint = 0.473 liter	1 gallon = 3.79 liters

Answers to

Problems

SECTION 1, PAGE 14

1. (a) 900   (b) 6,240   (c) 14,800   (d) 32,400
   (e) 285,000   (f) 718,200   (g) 151,632   (h) 24,449,824
   (i) 725,700   (j) 65.1   (k) 25.20   (l) 3.69
   (m) 51.2   (n) 3.33   (o) 16   (p) 243
   (q) 216   (r) 1.0816

3. (a) 15   (b) 6   (c) 70
   (d) 70   (e) 3.9   (f) $-\$55$
   (g) ($250)   (h) $-\$28$ (i) ($674)

5. (a) $\frac{102}{100}$ (b) $\frac{407}{400}$ (c) $\frac{98}{100}$ (d) $\frac{195}{200}$
   (e) $\frac{305}{300}$ (f) $\frac{197}{200}$ (g) 306   (h) 193
   (i) $400+20t$ (j) $540-180r$ (k) $a-abc$

7. (a)   5.1   (b)   7.93   (c) 60.000   (d) 8.8;   3.3
         319.4   14.70   0.404   8.85;   3.26
          26.8   121.34   6.212   8.848; 3.260

9. (a) 116.2; 116   (b) 6.0; 6.0   (c) 24.16; 24.2   (d) 16.2; 16

11. (a) $901.51   (b) $1,801.44   (c) $806.49   (d) $643.88

SECTION 1, PAGE 25

1. $x=15$ **13.** $y=6$ **25.** $n=3$
3. $y=43$ **15.** $x=5$ **27.** $x=\frac{1}{2}$
5. $x=9$ **17.** $v=2$ **29.** $y=18$
7. $t=54$ **19.** $k=\frac{7}{2}$ **31.** $q=45$
9. $c=3$ **21.** $m=\frac{5}{4}$ **33.** $y=14$
11. $x=12$ **23.** $x=\frac{3}{5}$ **35.** $n=32$

SECTION 2, PAGE 29

1. (a) $8n$ (b) $\frac{3}{5}r$ or $\frac{3r}{5}$ (c) $n+5$

   (d) $p-\$15$ (e) $a+b+c$ (f) $x=5y$
   (g) $2(s+t)$ (h) $\$4m$ (i) $j=k+4$

   (j) $d=2.5(y+z)$ (k) $v=\frac{w}{2}-8$ (l) $q=\frac{3r}{4}$

Chapter 2, *Section* 2

3. 58	**15.** $600,000	**27.** Garland 45; White 90
5. $34	**17.** 17	**29.** 700 1st; 840 2nd
7. $54	**19.** $.50	**31.** $240 mortgage; $50
9. 90	**21.** 1,200 sq ft	taxes; $10 insurance
11. 420	**23.** 10	**33.** 15 cowhide; 30 patent
13. 200	**25.** $50	**35.** 40 children; 80 adults

SECTION 3, PAGE 34

1. (a) 3 to 5; 3:5; $\frac{3}{5}$ (b) 1 to 40; 1:40; $\frac{1}{40}$ (c) 3 to 5; 3:5; $\frac{3}{5}$
   (d) 13 to 4; 13:4; $\frac{13}{4}$ or   (e) 22 to 5; 22:5; $\frac{22}{5}$ or

   3.25 to 1; 3.25:1; $\dfrac{3.25}{1}$ 4.4 to 1; 4.4:1; $\dfrac{4.4}{1}$

3. (a) $x = 15$ **11.** $12,000   **19.** 7,200
   (b) $r = 21$
   (c) $b = 20$
   (d) $y = 6$

5. 3 to 40   **13.** $5,000   **21.** $540

7. 18 : 7   **15.** 20   **23.** 120

9. $\dfrac{2.3}{1}$ **17.** 105

SECTION 4, PAGE 38

1. (a) $\frac{1}{3}$ (b) $\frac{2}{11}$ (c) $\frac{26}{111}$
   (d) $\frac{7}{18}$ (e) $\frac{107}{150}$ (f) $\frac{61}{99}$

CHAPTER 3   *Review of Per Cent*

SECTION 1, PAGE 48

1. $\frac{7}{20}$	**13.** $\frac{29}{20}$	**25.** $\frac{3}{800}$
3. $\frac{3}{50}$	**15.** $\frac{29}{2,000}$	**27.** $\frac{2}{9}$
5. $\frac{53}{100}$	**17.** $\frac{1}{500}$	**29.** $\frac{5}{6}$
7. $\frac{53}{200}$	**19.** $\frac{7}{2,500}$	**31.** $\frac{3}{40}$
9. $\frac{83}{2,000}$	**21.** $\frac{9}{8}$	**33.** 73%
11. $\frac{167}{400}$	**23.** $\frac{3}{400}$	**35.** 7%

Chapter 3, Section 1

37. 39.5%

39. 2.8%

41. 235%

43. 174.5%

45. 2.5%

47. 62.5%

49. 0.1%

51. 0.38%

53. 460%

55. 70%

57. $42\frac{6}{7}$% (or 42.9%)

59. $41\frac{2}{3}$% (or 41.7%)

61. 175%

63. $238\frac{6}{13}$% (or 238.5%)

SECTION 2, PAGE 51

1. 15.6

3. 4.5

5. 15.6

7. 0.6

9. 15

11. 0.7

13. $66\frac{2}{3}$% (or 66.7%)

15. 150%

17. 62%

19. $44\frac{4}{9}$% (or 44.4%)

21. 3%

23. 125%

25. 75

27. 150

29. 21

31. 400

33. 20

35. 600

37. 50%

39. $33\frac{1}{3}$% (or 33.3%)

41. 40%

43. 36%

45. $28\frac{4}{7}$% (or 28.6%)

47. 0.5%

SECTION 3, PAGE 55

PART I

1. 3%

3. 18%

5. 5%

7. $62,500

9. 275

11. $22

13. $12,000

15. 25%

17. $12\frac{1}{2}$% (12.5%)

19. 15%

21. 35

23. $50

25. $20

27. $160

29. $400,000

31. $160

PART II

33. 150

35. $60,000

37. $48

39. $40,000

41. 8%

43. 50%

45. 8%

47. $33\frac{1}{3}$% (33.3%)

SECTION 4, PAGE 59

1. $252

3. $52

5. $27

7. $6

9. $21

11. $96

13. $36

15. $40

17. $133

Chapter 3, Section 4

19. $15 **23.** $24 **27.** $17

21. $18 **25.** $54 **29.** $96

CHAPTER 4 *Basic Statistics and Graphs*

SECTION 1, PAGE 73

1. (a) $100; $101.50; no mode (b) 1,250; 1,450; 1,350; and 1,450

3. (a) 2.60 (b) 2.80

5. (a) 86¢ (b) 73¢

7. (a) $240 (b) $202

9. $7,275

11. $35,700

13. 1,580 and 1,640

15. (a) $28 (b) $19 (c) $18

17. (a) 12.4 years (b) 10 years (c) 18 years

SECTION 2, PAGE 79

1. (a) $53\frac{1}{3}$ or 53.3 (b) 55 (c) 60−79

3. (a) $522.92 (b) $510 (c) $450−$499

5. (a) $39\frac{1}{3}$ or 39.3 years (b) 38 years (c) 25−29

7. (a) $43,200 (b) $42,000 (c) $55,000–$64,999

SECTION 3, PAGE 86

1. (a) 84% (b) 2.5% (c) 68%
  (d) 13.5% (e) 2,000 pairs (f) 3,800 pairs

3. (a) 16% (b) 50% (c) 47.5%
  (d) 95% (e) 6,520 (f) 2,560
  (g) 6,720

Chapter 4, Section 3

5. (a) $\sigma = 6$ (c) $\pm 1\sigma$: includes 3 numbers, as expected, between 9 and 21;
$\pm 2\sigma$: includes 5 numbers, as expected, between 3 and 27

7. (a) $\sigma = 4$ (c) $\pm 1\sigma$: 4 of expected 4 numbers between 21 and 29;
$\pm 2\sigma$: 6 of expected 6 numbers between 17 and 33

9. (a) $\sigma = 3$ (c) $\pm 1\sigma$: 4, as expected, between 31 and 37;
$\pm 2\sigma$: 6, as expected, between 28 and 40

11. (a) $\sigma = 2$ (c) $\pm 1\sigma$: 6, when 5 are expected between 50 and 54;
$\pm 2\sigma$: 8, as expected, between 48 and 56

13. (a) $\sigma = 2$ (c) $\pm 1\sigma$: 9, when 7 are expected between 71 and 75;
$\pm 2\sigma$: 9, when 9.5 are expected between 69 and 77;
$\pm 3\sigma$: 10, as expected, between 67 and 79

SECTION 4, PAGE 91

1. (a) $178.10   (b) $145.20   (c) $16.29
(d) Atlanta (187.8)   (e) New York (116)   (f) Dallas (105)
(g) Dallas (94)   (h) Chicago (158.3)   (i) Atlanta (81)

3.

Year	Index
1970	100
1972	95
1974	160
1976	125
1978	135

5.

Year	Index
1971	100
1973	98
1975	126
1977	106
1979	118

CHAPTER 5 *Taxes*

SECTION 1, PAGE 109

1.

		Marked Price	Sales Tax	Total Price		Marked Price	Sales Tax	Total Price
	(a)	x	$ .59	$15.18	(e)	$ 3.00	x	3.12
	(b)	x	2.68	91.93	(f)	19.00	x	19.95
	(c)	x	.00	32.05	(g)	60.00	1.80	x
	(d)	x	.34	17.09	(h)	26.00	.52	x

Chapter 5, Section 1

3. (a) $8.79; $228.29   (b) $10.51; $360.71   **13.** (a) $49.00   (b) $1.96
    (c) $.00; $155.95

5. $.85; $17.80   **15.** (a) $24.75   (b) $.99

7. (a) $18.00   (b) $18.54   **17.** (a) $52.25   (b) $2.09

9. (a) $365   (b) $379.60   **19.** (a) $187.50   (b) $7.50   (c) $15.00

11. (a) $21.00   (b) $.63   **21.** (a) $5.00   (b) $.25   (c) $.50

SECTION 2, PAGE 114

1. (a) 1.4%   (b) $1.38 per C   (c) $13.73 per M

3. (a) 2.138%   (b) $2.14 per C   (c) $21.38 per M

5. (a) Tax: $189   (b) Tax: $231   (c) Tax: $129.60
    (d) Assessed value: (e) Assessed value: (f) Assessed value:
        $8,500 $7,600 $17,600
    (g) Rate: 1.2%   (h) Rate: $1.75 per C   (i) Rate: $13.50 per M

7. $140   **9.** $231   **11.** $10,500   **13.** $27,500

15. 1.5%   **17.** $2.25 per C   **19.** $.50 per M increase

CHAPTER 6   *Insurance*

SECTION 1, PAGE 130

1. (a) $42   (b) 100

	Premium	Refund
3. (a)	$ 55	x
(b)	55	x
(c)	84	$ 16
(d)	150	210

	Insurance Required	Indemnity
5. (a)	$ 8,000	$ 3,000
(b)	27,000	16,000
(c)	20,000	12,000
(d)	81,000	45,000
(e)	56,000	42,000

	Ratio of Coverage	Compensation
7. (a)	3/5	$ 9,000
	2/5	6,000
(b)	1/5	4,000
	1/2	10,000
	3/10	6,000

Chapter 6, Section 1

	Insurance Required	Insurance Carried	Total Indemnity	Compound Ratios	Compound Payments
9. (a)	$120,000	$90,000	$60,000	2/3	$40,000
				1/3	20,000
(b)	56,000	36,000	18,000	5/9	10,000
				4/9	8,000

11. $36

13. (a) $81; $27　　(b) $63; $45

15. (a) $9,000　　(b) $27,000　　(c) $75,000

17. (a) $15,000　　(b) $35,000　　(c) $100,000

19. (a) $2,800　　(b) $22,000　　(c) $48,000

21. (a) $4,500; $3,000　　(b) $12,000; $8,000

23. (a) $7,500; $5,000; $2,500　　(b) $72,000; $48,000; $24,000　　(c) $180,000; $120,000; $60,000

25. (a) $15,000　　(b) $5,000; $10,000

27. (a) $64,000　　(b) $8,000; $32,000; $24,000

SECTION 2, PAGE 144

1. (a) $135.80　　(b) $193.50　　(c) $318.00

3. (a) $53.90　　(b) $162.40　　(c) $173.00

5. $159.50　　**7.** $210　　**9.** $336　　**11.** $393.60

13. (a) $17,500　　(b) $2,000

15. (a) $160　　(b) $0

17. (a) $7,925　　(b) $100

19. (a) $32,750　　(b) $5,050

SECTION 3, PAGE 163

1. (a) $336.40   (b) $995.84   (c) $217.00   (d) $1,414.80

3. (a) 21 years 137 days   (b) $26,705   (c) $12,640   (d) $4,550

5. (a) $55.92; $11.18   (b) $76.10; $7.61

7. (a) 14 years   (b) $200.75   (c) $209.00   (d) $95.00

9. (a) $11,995.00   (b) $4,340.00   (c) $7,655.00
(d) Whole life policy earns nonforfeiture values. Future term will be at a higher rate.

11. (a) $20,716.50   (b) $18,672.00

13. (a) $245.60   (b) $4,912.00

15. (a) $561.20   (b) $6,280   (c) $15,260   (d) 32 years 164 days

17. $2,548

19. (a) $122.46   (b) $6.12

21. (a) $99.00   (b) $4.95   (c) Whole life policy
is less

23. (a) $101.72   (b) $10.17

25. (a) $57.40   (b) Appr. 10 years

27. (a) $133.00   (b) $131.60

29. (a) $13,500   (b) $12,696   (c) Gained $804
(gained $3,500
over face value)

31. (a) $332.50   (b) $27,930.00   (c) $250.50   (d) $21,042.00
(e) Gained $6,888 (lost $22,070 of face value)

CHAPTER 7   *Checkbook and Cash Records*

SECTION 1, PAGE 180

1. $750.95   **3.** $1,285.11   **5.** $886.58

7. (a) Checkbook $1,079.27   (b) $1,058.42   (c) $20.85
Bank balance $1,530.34

Chapter 7, Section 1

9. (a) Checkbook $2,664.10   (b) $2,635.14   (c)$28.96
        Bank balance $2,083.84

SECTION 2, PAGE 186

1. 10¢ short   **3.** 6¢ short

CHAPTER 8   *Wages and Payrolls*

SECTION 2, PAGE 198

1. (a) $105   (b) $2,600   (c) 7%
     (d) $64; $109   (e) 2.5%; $125   (f) $96
     (g) $75; $110   (h) $6,200; $78   (i) $50; $92

3. $826   **9.** $1,400   **17.** $735.20

5. $\frac{3}{4}$%   **11.** $100   **19.** $1,282.50

7. (a) $1,263   **13.** $151   **21.** $6,776.90

     (b) $763   **15.** $591.31

SECTION 3, PAGE 207

1. $881.70   **3.** $691.60   **5.** $473.66

7. (a) $129   (b) $115   (c) $209

9. (a) $184   (b) $181.30   (c) $161.60

11. $978.10

SECTION 4, PAGE 215

1. $97.65   **3.** $99.07   **5.** $704.52

7. $640.79   **9.** $598.10

SECTION 5, PAGE 223

	Total Reg. Wages	Total Over-time	Total Gross Wages	FICA	Inc.Tax	Other	Total Deds.	Total Wages Due
					DEDUCTIONS			
1.	—	—	$740.00	$43.30	$69.20	$ 7.40	$119.90	$620.10
3.	—	—	659.30	38.58	44.60	18.50	101.68	557.62
5.	—	—	849.00	49.67	88.70	84.90	223.27	625.73
7.	—	—	721.00	42.17	36.90	35.50	114.57	606.43
9.	$540.00	$133.50	673.50	39.41	59.10	6.75	105.26	568.24
11.	664.00	99.00	763.00	44.64	79.80	15.26	139.70	623.30

SECTION 6, PAGE 230

1. $\dfrac{\$20}{38}$ $\dfrac{\$10}{3}$ $\dfrac{\$5}{3}$ $\dfrac{\$1}{9}$ $\dfrac{50\cent}{4}$ $\dfrac{25\cent}{2}$ $\dfrac{10\cent}{7}$ $\dfrac{5\cent}{3}$ $\dfrac{1\cent}{15}$ **3.** $817.50

SECTION 7, PAGE 239

Line	Problem 1	Problem 3	Problem 5
10	$5,000	$10,000	$22,000
11	$ 650	$ 1,200	$ 2,500
12	—	—	—
13	$ 650	$ 1,200	$ 2,500
14	($5,000×11.7%) $ 585	($8,000×11.7%) $ 936	($6,000×11.7%) $ 702
15	—	($2,000×5.85%) $ 117	($14,000×5.85%) $ 819
16	$ 585	$ 1,053	$ 1,521
17	—	—	—
18	$ 585	$ 1,053	$ 1,521
19	$1,235	$ 2,253	$ 4,021
20	1,235	2,253	4,021
21	—	—	—

Chapter 8, Section 7

7. $500; $1,300; $4,100

	FICA TAXABLE WAGES			
	1st Qtr.	*2nd Qtr.*	*3rd Qtr.*	*4th Qtr.*
9. (a) A	$ 3,000	$ 3,200	$ 3,500	$ 3,100
B	4,100	3,900	4,100	4,400
C	1,800	2,000	2,500	2,500
D	4,000	4,500	6,000	2,000
(b) Totals	$12,900	$13,600	$16,100	$12,000

Line	Problem **11**	Problem **13**
10	$13,600.00	$15,900.00
13	$ 1,630.00	$ 1,900.00
18	$ 1,591.20	$ 1,404.00
19	$ 3,221.20	$ 3,304.00

		TAXABLE WAGES FOR UNEMPLOYMENT		
	1st Qtr.	*2nd Qtr.*	*3rd Qtr.*	*4th Qtr.*
15. (a) U:	$ 4,000	$200	—	—
V:	3,800	400	—	—
W:	4,200	—	—	—
(b) Totals	$12,000	$600	—	
(c) State:	$192.00	$9.60	—	—
Federal:	—	—	—	$88.20 (for year)
17. (a) A:	$ 3,000	$1,200	—	—
B:	4,100	100	—	—
C:	1,800	2,000	$400	—
D:	4,000	200	—	—
(b) Totals	$12,900	$3,500	$400	—
(c) State:	$270.90	$73.50	$8.40	—
Federal:	—	—	—	$117.60 (for year)

SECTION 1, PAGE 261

The final year of each schedule would read as follows:

		Book Value at End of Year	Annual Depreciation	Accumulated Depreciation
1.	(a)	$700	$300	$1,500
	(b)	700	100	1,500
	(c)	300	300	4,500
	(d)	800	800	5,600

		First Year	Second Year
3.	(a)	$2,400	$ 900
	(b)	3,000	1,200
	(c)	2,400	900
	(d)	1,500	500

5. $2,500 annually

Entries are given for the last year of each schedule:

	Book Value at End of Year	Annual Depreciation	Accumulated Depreciation	
7.	$ 300	$ 60	$ 900	
9. (a)	1,152.48	493.92	3,647.52	(b) $1,152.48
11.	1,000	600	5,500	
13.	400	100	3,600	
15.	640.72	213.57	7,359.28	
17.	455.62	151.88	2,744.38	
19. (a) $2,000	(b) $2,500		(c) $2,500; $500	
21. (a) $2,000	(b) $3,500		(c) $3,250; $1,250	

SECTION 2, PAGE 265

1. (a) $45,000	(b) $ 2,000	**3.** (a) $3,000
15,000	14,000	1,600
18,000	20,000	2,400
9,000	4,000	1,000
3,000		

3. (b) $3,600	**5.** (a) $12,000	(b) $2,800
2,700	24,000	3,500
4,500	6,000	6,300
5,400	12,000	1,400
1,800	30,000	
	36,000	

Chapter 9, Section 2

7. $12,000	**9.** $3,200	**11.** $4,500
18,000	2,400	2,250
37,500	1,200	3,000
60,000	400	1,500
22,500	800	750
	1,600	6,000

CHAPTER 10 *Financial Statement Analysis*

SECTIONS 1 AND 2, PAGE 283

1.

Net sales	$600,000	100.0%
Cost of goods	450,000	75.0
Gross margin	150,000	25.0
Operating expenses	126,000	21.0
Net income	19,000	3.2

3.

Current assets	$120,000	60.0%
Fixed assets	80,000	40.0
Total assets	200,000	100.0
Current liabilities	40,000	20.0
Fixed liabilities	25,000	12.5
Total liabilities	65,000	32.5
Net worth	135,000	67.5
Total liabilities and net worth	200,000	100.0

	X2	X1	Inc./(Dec.)	%	X2 – %	X1 – %
5. Net sales	$ 66,000	$ 60,000	$ 6,000	10.0%	100.0%	100.0%
Goods available for sale	$ 66,000	$ 64,000	$ 2,000	3.1%	100.0%	106.7%
Cost of goods sold	45,000	40,000	5,000	12.5	68.2	66.7
Gross margin	$ 21,000	$ 20,000	$ 1,000	5.0%	31.8%	33.3%
Total expenses	16,500	15,000	1,500	10.0	25.0	25.0
Net income	$ 4,500	$ 5,000	($ 500)	(10.0%)	6.8%	8.3%
7. Current assets	$280,000	$280,000	—	—	70.0%	73.7%
Fixed assets	120,000	100,000	20,000	20.0	30.0	26.3
Total assets	$400,000	$380,000	$20,000	5.3	100.0%	100.0%
Total liabilities	$220,000	$240,000	($20,000)	(8.3%)	55.0%	63.2%
Ardmore equity	180,000	140,000	40,000	28.6	45.0	36.8
Total liabilities and operating expenses	$400,000	$380,000	$20,000	5.3%	100.0%	100.0%

Chapter 10, Sections 1 and 2

9. (a) 3 to 1   (b) 1.25 to 1   (c) 60%
    (d) 40%   (e) 32.5%   (f) 67.5%

11. (a) 3.5 to 1   (b) 1.25 to 1   (c) 11.9%   (d) 1.5 to 1
     (e) 11.1 times   (f) 33 days   (g) 75%   (h) 25%
     (i) 21%   (j) 4%; 3.2%   (k) 70%   (l) 30%
     (m) 55%   (n) 45%

CHAPTER 11   *Distribution of Profit and Loss*

SECTION 1, PAGE 301

1. (a) $.35   (b) $5.20 common   (c) $.50 common
                        $4.00 preferred $18.00 preferred

3. $2.50   **5.** $7.50 common,   **7.** $.40 common,
                            $7.00 preferred $5.00 preferred

9. $.55 common   **11.** $3.00 common,
    $1.80 preferred $16.00 preferred

SECTION 2, PAGE 307

1. (a) $7,500   (b) $ 9,000   (c) $9,000   (d) $3,420
        4,500   15,000   7,000   4,560
        6,000   6,350

3. $4,500   **5.** (a) $3,600   (b) $1,800
                                 4,800   2,400
                                 6,000   3,000
                                 4,800   2,400

7. $9,500   **9.** $7,000   **11.** $12,500
    9,500   9,800   13,500

13. (a) $6,900   (b) $8,100   **15.** (a) $5,000   (b) $8,860
                                                                   8,800

17. (a) $11,920   (b) $7,800   **19.** (a) $5,860   (b) $3,760
         4,560   440   7,420   4,620

SECTION 1, PAGE 321

1. (a) 80%; $12   (b) 85%; $34   (c) 70%; $45   (d) 24%; $50

(e) .6; $33   (f) 4/7; $20   (g) .51; $85   (h) .612; $150

3. (a) $7.68   (b) $7.80   (c) $18   (d) $30

5. $390.75

7. (a) $1.20; .6; 40%   (b) $7; .7; 30%   (c) $6.38; .532; 46.8%   (d) $19.44; .648; 35.2%

9. Young: 32% vs. 31.6%

11. $25   **13.** $5   **15.** $16\frac{2}{3}$%   **17.** 15%; 32%

19. (a) $24; $30   (b) 20%

21. (a) $24; $21.60   (b) 10%

SECTION 2, PAGE 329

1. (a) $310.40   (b) $650   (c) $453.25   (d) $527.65
(e) $403.92   (f) $465.60   (g) $710.50

3. (a) $242.50; $150   (b) $328.30; $335   (c) $600; $576
(d) $400; $365   (e) $380; $200

5. $217.59   **7.** $1,393.71   **9.** $294

11. (a) $784   (b) $396   (c) $1180

13. (a) $750   (b) $750

CHAPTER 13   *Markup*

SECTION 1, PAGE 342

1. (a) $8; $6; $2 profit   (b) $3; $5; $2 loss   (c) $6; $4; $2 profit
(d) $2; $3; $1 loss   (e) $7; $12; $5 loss

Chapter 13, Section 1

3. (a) $27; $9; $33\frac{1}{3}$% (b) $54; $9; $16\frac{2}{3}$% (c) $63; $7; $11\frac{1}{9}$%
(d) $25; $10; $28\frac{4}{7}$% (e) $45; $10; $18\frac{2}{11}$% (f) $28\frac{4}{7}$%; $18; $22\frac{2}{9}$%
(g) 25%; $48; 20%

5. (a) 1.35 (b) $108 (c) $28

7. (a) $33\frac{1}{3}$% (b) 25%

9. (a) 1.4 (b) $5.53; $11.06; $7.63; (c) $28\frac{4}{7}$%
$6.79

11. (a) $2.40 (b) $2.10; 30%

13. (a) 25% (b) 20%

15. (a) $22.50 (b) 20%

SECTION 2, PAGE 348

1. (a) $27; $9; 50% (b) $63; $14; $28\frac{4}{7}$% (c) $39; $13; $33\frac{1}{3}$%
(d) $72; $12; $16\frac{2}{3}$% (e) 30%; $30; $42\frac{6}{7}$%

3. (a) $\frac{9}{5}$ or 1.8 (b) $63 (c) $28

5. (a) $120 (b) $66

7. (a) $\frac{3}{2}$ or 1.5 (b) $7.35; $11.25; (c) 50%
$4.28; $7.50

9. (a) $900 (b) 60% (c) $37\frac{1}{2}$%

11. (a) 25% on selling price (b) 30% on selling price
$(1.33\frac{1}{3}$ vs. 1.25) $(1.42\frac{6}{7}$ vs. 1.40)

13. (a) $\frac{7}{5}$ or 1.4 (b) $35 (c) 40%

15. (a) $15 (b) $\frac{6}{5}$ or 1.2 **17.** $42

SECTION 3, PAGE 355

1. (a) $72; $80 (b) $40; $48 (c) $40; $36; $11\frac{1}{9}$% (d) $80; $64; $6\frac{1}{4}$%
(e) $28; 30%; $40 (f) $36; 40%; $60 (g) $252; $500; $360 (h) $180; $450; $270

3. (a) $35 (b) $40

Chapter 13, Section 3

5. (a) $40   (b) $30   (c) 20%

7. (a) $50   (b) $30   (c) 40%

9. (a) $102   (b) $136   (c) $170

SECTION 4, PAGE 359

1. (a) $40; $60; 96 lb; 63¢ per lb   (b) $400; $520; 23; $22.61   (c) $150; $200; 27 dozen; $7.41 per dozen

3. (a) $80; $100; 18 dozen; 2 dozen; $5.25 per dozen   (b) $18; $24.30; 114 lb; 6 lb; 21¢ per lb

5. (a) $7   (b) 58.3%   (c) 36.8%

7. $2.74 each   **9.** 28¢ per box   **11.** 32¢ per quart

CHAPTER 14 *Markdown and Turnover*

SECTION 1, PAGE 368

1. (a) $22\frac{2}{9}\%$; $28; $27; $1
(d) 25%; $8; $5;($1)
(b) $3; $17; $15; ($2)
(e) $30; 30%; $20; $25
(c) 20%; $15; $15; $65
(f) $15; $3; $12; $7

3. (a) $8; $16; $23; ($7); ($4); 20%
(d) $40; $10; $32; $36; ($6); $6\frac{1}{4}\%$
(b) 40%; $3; $1; ($1); $0; 0%
(c) 26%; $13; $40; ($8); ($3); 7.5%

5. $6.50 profit   **7.** (a) $37\frac{1}{2}\%$ (b) $0

9. (a) $56   (b) ($14.80)   (c) ($6.40); 16%

11. (a) $1.35 per pair   (b) 27¢   (c) 20%

13. (a) $180; $198; $215   (b) Net profit   (c) $17; 9.4%

SECTION 2, PAGE 372

1. $18,000   **3.** $17,300   **5.** 2.8   **7.** 2.75   **9.** 3.52

SECTION 3, PAGE 374

	Weighted Average	FIFO	LIFO
1. (a)	$120	$138	$102
(b)	$286	$305	$266.75

3. (a) $168   (b) $184   (c) $156

5. Gross profit: $148; $164; $136
   %:   37%; 41%; 34%

CHAPTER 15   *Simple Interest*

SECTION 1, PAGE 384

1. (a) $20; $420   (b) $10; $410   (c) $37.80; $667.80
   (d) $31.85; $871.85   (e) $10.80; $550.80

5. 5%   **7.** $\frac{5}{6}$ year or 10 months   **9.** 4.5%

11. $800   **13.** 12.5%

SECTION 2, PAGE 387

1. (a) 256 days   (b) 105 days   (c) 144 days
   (d) 107 days   (e) 125 days   (f) 48 days
   (g) 140 days   (h) 115 days

3. (a) Oct. 13; Oct. 12   (b) Dec. 10; Dec. 7   (c) Nov. 23; Nov. 20

5. (a) Sept. 24; 150 days;   (b) Aug. 17; 210 days;   (c) Aug. 20, 1980; 180 days
      153 days   212 days   182 days
   (d) Apr. 30, 1979;   (e) Feb. 25, 1978;
      90 days; 89 days   120 days; 123 days

SECTION 3, PAGE 389

1. (a) $14.60; $14.40   (b) $43.80; $43.20

3. (a) $9.13   (b) $9.00   (c) $9.28   (d) $9.15

5. (a) $30.40   (b) $15.20   (c) $7.60   (d) $22.80

Chapter 15, Section 3

7. (a) $12   (b) $6   (c) $4   (d) $16

9. (a) $3.20   (b) $9.60   (c) $4.80

11. (a) $3.10   (b) $7.44   (c) $11.16

SECTION 4, PAGE 392

1. $18.50; $1,868.50   **9.** $2; $452   **17.** $13; $793

3. $16; $1216   **11.** $5; $605   **19.** $6.65; $671.38

5. $3.75; $753.75   **13.** $4.05; $364.05   **21.** $2.06; $208.31

7. $11.40; $391.40   **15.** $7.63; $443.63

SECTION 5, PAGE 397

1. (a) $500   (b) George D. Rogers   (c) North Austin State Bank

     (d) July 7   (e) Oct. 5   (f) $500

     (g) 8%   (h) 90 days   (i) $10

     (j) $510

3. (a) 150 days; $20; $620   (b) Oct. 17; $14.64; $494.64   (c) Dec. 23; $2.44; $290.44

     (d) $400; May 6; $414

5. $9.20; $459.20   **11.** 5%   **17.** $420

7. $274.20   **13.** 150 days   **19.** $720

9. $753.60   **15.** 108 days

SECTION 6, PAGE 404

1. (a) $800   (b) $350   **3.** (a) $1,003.96   (b) $799.01

5. (a) $505; $503.32   (b) $205; $203.98

7. $450   **9.** $585.87   **11.** $456.82   **13.** $10,200 in 4 months

CHAPTER 16   *Bank Discount*

SECTION 1, PAGE 417

1. (a) $1,000   (b) Charles N. Oxford   (c) North Carolina National Bank

     (d) March 19   (e) June 17   (f) 8%

Chapter 16, Section 1

   (g) 90 days   (h) $20   (i) $980
   (j) $1,000

3. (a) 90 days; $12; $788   (b) June 9; $20; $620   (c) Nov. 16; $5; $295
   (d) Oct. 17; $6; $444

5. (a) $5.50; $394.50   (b) $5.40; $234.60   (c) $4.90; $835.10

7. (a) June 14; $409.43   (b) Aug. 17; $586   (c) Sept. 4; $227.28
   (d) Sept. 9; $440.80

9. $590   **13.** 8%   **17.** $700; $699.72

11. $\frac{1}{4}$ year or 90 days   **15.** $865.50

SECTION 2, PAGE 423

1. (a) Mar. 26; $720   (b) Dec. 9; $800   (c) Nov. 4; $300
   (d) Aug. 25; $450

3. (a) $382; $396; $14   (b) $879; $896; $17   (c) $1,146; $1,185; $39

5. (a) $510; $504.90; $4.90   (b) $615; $604.75; $4.75

7. $900   **9.** $420

11. (a) $435   (b) $447   (c) $12
   (d) $3

13. (a) $403.97   (b) $3.97   (c) $2.03

15. (a) $1,524.60   (b) $24.60   (c) $15.40

SECTION 3, PAGE 426

1. (a) $358.80; 20 days;   (b) $798.00; 15 days;   (c) $896.00; 20 days;
       $360; $6.12 $800; $14.29 $900; $23.71

3. (a) $1,200   (b) $32.99   **5.** (a) $600   (b) $19.50

SECTION 4, PAGE 429

1. $20; $820   **3.** $20; $460

5. (a) $15; $15   (b) $600; $585   (c) $615; $600

Chapter 16, Section 4

7. $800; $800   **9.** $500; $500

11. (a) $700; $699.37   (b) $700; $699.37   (c) $21; $21.63

13. $357.05   **15.** $426.45

17. (a) $615.11   (b) $15.11   (c) $3.09

19. (a) $707.80   (b) $716.40   (c) $8.60   (d) $3.60

CHAPTER 17   *Multiple Payment Plans*

SECTION 1, PAGE 438

1. (a) $610   (b) $406   (c) $721

3. $1,530   **5.** $1,635

SECTION 2, PAGE 450

1. (a) $3.12   (b) $6.17

3. (a) $12.00 monthly   (b) $3.00 weekly   (c) $12.40 monthly

5. (a) 28.25%   (b) 22.5%   (c) 14.5%   (d) 30.25%

9. $2.33   **11.** $15   **13.** $20.50

15. (a) $54   (b) $21   (c) $554   (d) 11.25%

17. (a) $13.50   (b) 18.25%   **19.** (a) $144   (b) 21.5%

21. (a) $590   (b) $40   (c) 14.5%

23. (a) $1,118.80   (b) $118.80   (c) 20.0%

25. (a) 21.5%   (b) 21.75%   (c) 21.0%

27. (a) $10   (b) $42   (c) 19.75%

29. (a) $54   (b) $109

CHAPTER 18 *Compound Interest*

SECTION 1, PAGE 462

1. (a) 8; 3%   (b) 12; $2\frac{1}{4}$%   (c) 60; $\frac{5}{12}$%   (d) 15; 7%
(e) 72; $\frac{2}{3}$%

3. (a) $629.86; $129.86   (b) $632.66; $132.66

5. (a) $848; $48   (b) $849.09; $49.09

7. (a) $1,030.23; $30.23   (b) $1,030.39; $30.39

9. More interest is earned when interest is compounded more often.

SECTION 2, PAGE 467

1. (a) $629.86; $29.86   (b) $632.66; $132.66

3. (a) $848; $48   (b) $849.09; $49.09

5. (a) $1,030.23; $30.23   (b) $1,030.39; $30.39

7. (a) $847.78; $247.78   (b) $1,206.96; $256.96   (c) $4,921.55; $3,421.55
(d) $4,481.78; $2,081.78   (e) $2,326.55; $1,926.55

9. (a) $141.80; $41.80   (b) $283.61; $83.61   (c) $567.21; $167.21
(d) When principal doubles, interest also doubles.

11. (a) $1,485.95; $485.95   (b) $2,191.12; $1,191.12   (c) $4,660.96; $3,660.96
(d) No

13. (a) $1,425.76; $425.76   (b) $2,032.79; $1,032.79   (c) $4,132.25; $3,132.25
(d) No

15. (a) $1,025.00   (b) $175.00   (c) $1,260.75
(d) $85.75

17. (a) $813.42   (b) $186.58   (c) $1,030.38
(d) $43.80

19. (a) $1,545.34   (b) $454.66   (c) $2,123.36
(d) $168.70

SECTION 3, PAGE 476

1. (a) $.61; $100.61   (b) $25.16; $2,025.16   (c) $6.26; $1,506.26
(d) $3.46; $403.46

3. (a) $7.67; $8.37   (b) $57.97; $62.89   (c) $2.63; $2.92

Chapter 18, Section 3

5. (a) $125.78; $125.00   (b) $31.44; $31.25

7. (a) $39.64; $3,489.64   (b) $56.95; $5,336.95

9. (a) $40.29; $3,040.29   (b) $17.54; $1,017.54

11. (a) $14.95; $1,014.95   (b) $27.71; $2,277.71   (c) $61.70; $4,131.70

SECTION 4, PAGE 481

1. (a) $353.13; $646.87   (b) $1,151.06; $1,648.94   (c) $244.03; $255.97
(d) $727.15; $672.85   (e) $912.77; $1,087.23

3. (a) $2,883.53   (b) $2,116.47

5. (a) $5,930.98   (b) $2,069.02

7. (a) $4,092.96   (b) $5,907.04

9. (a) $6,989.69   (b) $4,300 to $10

11. (a) $1,100   (b) $937.86

CHAPTER 19 *Annuities*

SECTION 1, PAGE 489

1. (a) $10,407.39; $8,400; $2,007.39   (b) $31,456.54; $24,000; $7,456.24   (c) $8,496.77; $5,120; $3,376.77
(d) $13,537.79; $12,000; $1,537.79   (e) $18,405.07; $14,400; $4,005.07

3. (a) $3,399.90   (b) $1,800   (c) $1,599.90

5. (a) $5,016.43   (b) $4,200   (c) $816.43

7. (a) $50,000   (b) $60,030.54   (c) $10,030.54

9. (a) $40,000   (b) $42,781.91   (c) $2,781.91

SECTION 2, PAGE 495

1. (a) $2,198.70; $2,800; $601.30   (b) $3,804.76; $4,800; $995.24   (c) $20,385.49; $30,000; $9,614.51
(d) $17,537.87; $28,800; $11,262.13   (e) $4,239.26; $4,800; $560.74

Chapter 19, Section 2

3. (a) (1) $5,148.96;
    $1,148.96
  (2) $3,132.69;
    $867.31

(b) (1) $23,787.71;
    $8,787.71
  (2) $9,800.22;
    $5,199.78

(c) (1) $3,312.55;
    $432.55
  (2) $2,505.61;
    $374.39

5. (a) $3,287.10

(b) $3,600

(c) $312.90

7. (a) $2,171.15

(b) $2,400

(c) $228.85

9. (a) $14,200

(b) $3,600

(c) $16,400

11. (a) $5,500

(b) $2,400

(c) $4,000

13. (a) $92,000

(b) $51,585.55

15. (a) $87,000

(b) $70,476.85

CHAPTER 20 *Sinking Funds and Amortization*

SECTION 1, PAGE 504

1. (a) $2,558.68; $61,408.32;
    $38,591.68
  (d) $3,869.92; $61,918.72;
    $13,081.28

(b) $3,477.81; $17,389.05;
    $2,610.95
  (e) $2,156.25; $103,500;
    $56,500

(c) $1,525.27; $4,575.81;
    $424.19

3. (a) $411.57

(b) $8,231.40

(c) $1,768.60

5. (a) $7,797.42

(b) $17,620.64

7. (a) $8,988.36

(b) $215,720.64

(c) $184,279.36

	Payment Number	Interest	Payment	Increase	Balance
9. (a)	4	$50.69	$225.23	$275.92	$1,000.02
	Totals	$99.10	$900.92		
(b)	6	$163.31	$753.81	$917.12	$4,999.99
	Totals	$477.13	$4,522.86		

SECTION 2, PAGE 511

1. (a) $3,886.55; $194,327.50;   (b) $379.80; $36,460.80;   (c) $756.48; $9,077.76;
$94,327.50 $6,460.80 $1,077.76
  (d) $583.02; $46,641.60;   (e) $9,775.55; $117.306.60;
$21,641.60 $47,306.60
3. (a) $160.89   (b) $3,514.76

5. (a) $2,339.90   (b) $23,596.00

7. (a) $527.23   (b) $22,723.00   (c) $55,723.00

9. (a) $828.64   (b) $9,662.08   (c) $72,662.08

		Payment Number	Owed	Interest	To Principal
11. (a)	$3,086.69;	4	$2,831.81	$ 254.86	$ 2,831.83
		Totals		$2,346.74	$10,000.02
(b)	$1,476.78;	6	$1,433.77	$ 43.01	$ 1,433.77
		Totals		$ 860.68	$ 8,000.00

SECTION 3, PAGE 514

1. (a) $1,348.85; $348.85   (b) $8,711.07; $3,711.07

3. (a) $741.37; $258.63   (b) $2,869.91; $2,130.09

5. (a) $14.33   (b) $117.89
$859.80 $3,772.48
$140.20 $1,227.52

7. (a) $19.33   (b) $205.39
$1,159.80 $6,572.48
$159.80 $1,572.48

9. (a) $20,156.88   (b) $6,378.62
$16,000 $4,000
$4,156.88 $2,378.62

11. (a) $12,561.10   (b) $2,619.35
$16,000 $4,000
$3,438.90 $1,380.65

13. (a) $3,030.47   (b) $969.53

Chapter 20, Section 3

15. (a) $6,800.61   (b) $800.61

17. (a) $353.83   (b) $661.28

19. (a) $5,328.55   (b) $6,000   (c) $671.45

21. (a) $876.80   (b) $52,608   (c) $47,392

23. (a) $24,351.89   (b) $14,351.89

APPENDIX A *Arithmetic*

SECTION 1 PAGE 525

1. (a) 100   (b) 2,000,000,000   (c) 300,000   (d) 40   (e) 500,000,000

3. (a) Six billion, four hundred eleven million, two hundred ninety-three thousand, eight hundred fifty-seven
  (b) One hundred twenty-three billion, six hundred twenty-five million, eight hundred nineteen thousand, seven hundred forty-three
  (c) Two hundred five million, one hundred thousand, four hundred sixteen
  (d) Fifteen billion, sixty-three million, eight thousand, seven hundred sixty
  (e) Nine billion, three hundred one million, sixty-five
  (f) Six hundred twenty billion, ninety thousand, fifty
  (g) Thirty billion, seven hundred

SECTION 2, PAGE 536

1. (a) $k + l = l + k$

  (b) $45 + 18 \overset{?}{=} 18 + 45$
  $63 = 63$

  (c) $(r + s) + t = r + (s + t)$

  (d) $(9 + 6) + 13 \overset{?}{=} 9 + (6 + 13)$
  $15 + 13 \overset{?}{=} 9 + 19$
  $28 = 28$

  (e) $v \times w = w \times v$

  (f) $12 \times 26 \overset{?}{=} 26 \times 12$
  $312 = 312$

  (g) $(p \times q)r = p(q \times r)$

  (h) $(4 \times 9)3 \overset{?}{=} 4(9 \times 3)$
  $(36)3 \overset{?}{=} 4(27)$
  $108 = 108$

  (i) $x(y + z) = xy + xz$

  (j) $8(2 + 5) \overset{?}{=} 8 \times 2 + 8 \times 5$
  $8(7) \overset{?}{=} 16 \ \ + 40$
  $56 = 56$

3. (a) 20   (b) 23   (c) 25
  (d) 27   (e) 29   (f) 32
  (g) 35   (h) 263   (i) 257

Appendix A, Section 2

5. (a) 25
   (d) 36
   (g) 272

   (b) 23
   (e) 278
   (h) 352

   (c) 37
   (f) 325
   (i) 332

7. (a) 305
   (d) 2,948

   (b) 268
   (e) 30,874

   (c) 2,852
   (f) 82,915

9. (a) 3,560
   (d) 9,520
   (g) 2,660,000
   (j) 7,409,664

   (b) 73,000
   (e) 347,100
   (h) 11,180,000
   (k) 25,155,904

   (c) 58,200
   (f) 15,300,000
   (i) 260,887

11. (a) 478
    (d) 8,006

   (b) 664
   (e) 3,481   R6

   (c) 5,706
   (f) 5,957   R3

13.

Dept.	Mon.	Tue.	Wed.	Thur.	Fri.	Sat.	Dept. Totals
1							2,579.52
2							1,854.28
3							2,050.42
4							1,768.40
5							2,647.66
6							793.84
Daily Totals	2,058.42	1,705.19	1,783.85	1,982.24	2,001.28	2,163.14	11,694,12

15. $ 93.42
     96.45
    174.24
    103.25
     71.25
     49.92
     36.00
     28.14

     $ 61.20
       55.44
       97.60
       93.80
       75.51
     245.88
     272.90
     ———
    Total $1,555.00

SECTION 3, PAGE 554

1. (a) $g + h = h + g$

(b) $\frac{2}{9} + \frac{1}{6} \stackrel{?}{=} \frac{1}{6} + \frac{2}{9}$

$$\frac{4}{18} + \frac{3}{18} \stackrel{?}{=} \frac{3}{18} + \frac{4}{18}$$

$$\frac{7}{18} = \frac{7}{18}$$

(c) $(l + m) + n = l + (m + n)$

Appendix A, Section 3

(d) $(\frac{1}{4}+\frac{5}{6})+\frac{2}{3} \overset{?}{=} \frac{1}{4}+(\frac{5}{6}+\frac{2}{3})$
$(\frac{3}{12}+\frac{10}{12})+\frac{2}{3} \overset{?}{=} \frac{1}{4}+(\frac{5}{6}+\frac{4}{6})$
$\frac{13}{12}+\frac{2}{3} \overset{?}{=} \frac{1}{4}+\frac{9}{6}$
$\frac{13}{12}+\frac{8}{12} \overset{?}{=} \frac{3}{12}+\frac{18}{12}$
$\frac{21}{12}=\frac{21}{12}$
$\frac{7}{4}=\frac{7}{4}$

(e) $h \times k = k \times h$

(f) $3\frac{1}{5}\times 4\frac{3}{8} \overset{?}{=} 4\frac{3}{8}\times 3\frac{1}{5}$
$\frac{16}{5}\times\frac{35}{8} \overset{?}{=} \frac{35}{8}\times\frac{16}{5}$
$\frac{\overset{2}{\cancel{16}}}{\cancel{8}_1}\times\frac{\overset{7}{\cancel{35}}}{\cancel{5}_1} \overset{?}{=} \frac{\overset{7}{\cancel{35}}}{\cancel{8}_1}\times\frac{\overset{2}{\cancel{16}}}{\cancel{5}_1}$
$14 = 14$

(g) $(x\times y)z = x(y\times z)$

(h) $(\frac{5}{7}\times\frac{3}{5})\frac{1}{6} \overset{?}{=} \frac{5}{7}(\frac{3}{5}\times\frac{1}{6})$
$(\frac{\cancel{5}}{7}\times\frac{3}{\cancel{5}})\frac{1}{6} \overset{?}{=} \frac{5}{7}(\frac{\cancel{3}}{5}\times\frac{1}{\cancel{6}_2})$
$(\frac{3}{7})\frac{1}{\cancel{6}_2} \overset{?}{=} \frac{1}{7}(\frac{1}{10})$
$\frac{1}{14}=\frac{1}{14}$

(i) $t(u+v)=tu+tv$

(j) $\frac{1}{3}(\frac{6}{7}+\frac{3}{5}) \overset{?}{=} \frac{1}{3}\cdot\frac{6}{7}+\frac{1}{3}\cdot\frac{3}{5}$
$\frac{1}{3}(\frac{30}{35}+\frac{21}{35}) \overset{?}{=} \frac{1}{\cancel{3}_1}\cdot\frac{\overset{2}{\cancel{6}}}{7}+\frac{1}{\cancel{3}_1}\cdot\frac{\overset{1}{\cancel{3}}}{5}$
$\frac{1}{3}(\frac{51}{35}) \overset{?}{=} \frac{2}{7}+\frac{1}{5}$
$\frac{1}{\cancel{3}}(\frac{\overset{17}{\cancel{51}}}{35}) \overset{?}{=} \frac{10}{35}+\frac{7}{35}$
$\frac{17}{35}=\frac{17}{35}$

3. (a) $\frac{2}{3}$ (b) $\frac{7}{3}$ (c) $\frac{7}{9}$
   (d) $\frac{4}{7}$ (e) $\frac{2}{3}$ (f) $\frac{5}{3}$
   (g) $\frac{3}{4}$ (h) $\frac{6}{5}$ (i) $\frac{9}{11}$
   (j) $\frac{7}{12}$

5. (a) $\frac{5}{16},\frac{3}{8},\frac{7}{12},\frac{2}{3},\frac{3}{4},\frac{5}{6}$ (b) $\frac{3}{10},\frac{1}{3},\frac{2}{5},\frac{5}{12},\frac{7}{15},\frac{5}{6}$

7. (a) $3\frac{1}{2}$ (b) $5\frac{1}{3}$ (c) $4\frac{3}{4}$
   (d) $8\frac{5}{7}$ (e) $5\frac{1}{4}$ (f) $4\frac{5}{9}$
   (g) $8\frac{5}{13}$ (h) $3\frac{5}{6}$ (i) $6\frac{9}{11}$
   (j) $10\frac{2}{3}$ (k) $7\frac{1}{2}$ (l) $14\frac{1}{4}$

9. (a) $\frac{1}{4}$ (b) $\frac{3}{16}$ (c) $\frac{17}{40}$
   (d) $\frac{23}{42}$ (e) $\frac{7}{20}$ (f) $5\frac{5}{24}$
   (g) $6\frac{7}{12}$ (h) $7\frac{4}{21}$ (i) $6\frac{7}{10}$
   (j) $6\frac{15}{28}$ (k) $9\frac{17}{30}$ (l) $21\frac{4}{7}$
   (m) $14\frac{11}{18}$ (n) $21\frac{11}{15}$ (o) $13\frac{19}{28}$

11. (a) $\frac{9}{56}$ (b) $\frac{9}{12}$ (c) 6
   (d) $\frac{7}{9}$

SECTION 4, PAGE 569

1. (a) $v + w = w + v$

   (b) $8.73+9.48 = 9.48+8.73$
       $18.21 = 18.21$

   (c) $(f+g)+h = f+(g+h)$

   (d) $(0.27+0.55)+0.84 = 0.27+(0.55+0.84)$
       $0.82+0.84 = 0.27+1.39$
       $1.66 = 1.66$

Appendix A, Section 4

(e) $s \times t = t \times s$

(f) $0.7 \times 0.8 = 0.8 \times 0.7$
$0.56 = 0.56$

(g) $(p \times q)r = p(q \times r)$

(h) $(0.4 \times 0.7) \times 0.2 = 0.4 \times (0.7 \times 0.2)$
$.28 \times 0.2 = 0.4 \times 0.14$
$0.056 = 0.056$

(i) $k(l + m) = kl + km$

(j) $0.3(0.5 + 0.7) = 0.3 \times 0.5 + 0.3 \times 0.7$
$0.3(1.2) = 0.15 \quad + 0.21$
$0.36 = 0.36$

3. (a) $\frac{1}{10}$
   (b) 2,000
   (c) 30
   (d) $\frac{4}{100}$
   (e) $\frac{5}{1,000}$
   (f) $\frac{6}{100,000}$
   (g) 700
   (h) 8
   (i) $\frac{9}{10,000}$

5. (a) .8
   (b) .75
   (c) .48
   (d) .65
   (e) .675
   (f) .156
   (g) .875
   (h) $.57\frac{1}{7}$ or .571
   (i) $.68\frac{3}{4}$ or .688
   (j) $.58\frac{1}{3}$ or .583
   (k) $.27\frac{7}{9}$ or .278
   (l) $.79\frac{1}{6}$ or .792
   (m) 1.625
   (n) 6.12
   (o) $4.83\frac{1}{3}$ or 4.833
   (p) $6.55\frac{5}{9}$ or 6.556
   (q) $18.36\frac{4}{11}$ or 18.364
   (r) 3.824

7. (a) 15.38
   (b) 247.9
   (c) .36652
   (d) 4.0381
   (e) 711.6
   (f) 4.3
   (g) 104.5
   (h) .06913
   (i) 140
   (j) .007206
   (k) 216,000
   (l) .00822
   (m) 678,000
   (n) .0002
   (o) .00425

9. (a) 165.89
   (b) 2.755
   (c) 16.884
   (d) 291.718
   (e) 28.7956
   (f) 14.879
   (g) 462.275
   (h) 3.679
   (i) 59.4098
   (j) 69.679
   (k) 173.78
   (l) 258.356
   (m) 58.593
   (n) 27.81
   (o) 194.55
   (p) 430.796
   (q) 5.5885

11. (a) 13
    (b) 4.7
    (c) 15.7
    (d) 0.54
    (e) 0.072
    (f) 0.27
    (g) 0.058
    (h) 0.003
    (i) 48
    (j) 16
    (k) 1.25
    (l) 376
    (m) 5.025
    (n) $2.37\frac{32}{39}$ or 2.378
    (o) $34.03\frac{143}{419}$ or 34.033

APPENDIX B *The Metric System*

1. (a) 1000 grams
   (b) 1 decameter
   (c) 1 centiliter
   (d) 0.001 meter
   (e) 0.001 kilometer
   (f) 1 liter
   (g) 1 gram
   (h) 100 centiliters
   (i) 10 decameters
   (j) 1 decagram
   (k) 1 milliliter
   (l) 0.1 kiloliter

Appendix B

3. (a) 150 meters   (b) 1.25 meters   (c) 360 grams
   (d) 2.137 liters   (e) 1.475 kilograms   (f) 1,740 centigrams
   (g) 2.4 decaliters   (h) 50,000 millimeters   (i) 7.5 kilometers
   (j) 0.362 kilogram

5. (a) 3.94 inches   (b) 118.1 inches   (c) 8.80 pounds
   (d) 203 ounces   (e) 21.8 yards   (f) 19.7 inches
   (g) 8.48 quarts   (h) 31.1 miles

7. (a) 20.3 centimeters   (b) 16.1 kilometers   (c) 227 grams
   (d) 5.68 liters   (e) 1360 grams   (f) 0.6 liter
   (g) 1.83 meters   (h) liters

9. (a) 91.4 meters   (b) 109 yards   (c) Swimming; 8.6 meters

11. (a) 178 centimeters   (b) 77.2 kilograms

13. (a) 4,830 kilometers   (b) 40,300 kilometers

15. (a) 3.3 pounds   (b) 14 ounces

Index